Social Welfare Policy

in Canada

Historical Readings

NeW
CANADIAN
READINGS

SERIES EDITOR
J. L. GRANATSTEIN

Titles currently available

Michael D. Behiels, ed., *Quebec Since 1945: Selected Readings*

David J. Bercuson and David Bright, eds., *Canadian Labour History: Selected Readings*, 2nd edition

Carl Berger, ed., *Contemporary Approaches to Canadian History*

Raymond B. Blake and Jeff Keshen, eds., *Social Welfare Policy in Canada: Historical Readings*

Hartwell Bowsfield, ed., *Louis Riel: Selected Readings*

Bettina Bradbury, ed., *Canadian Family History: Selected Readings*

Kenneth S. Coates and William R. Morrison, eds., *Interpreting Canada's North: Selected Readings*

Terry Crowley, ed., *Clio's Craft: A Primer of Historical Methods*

Robin Fisher and Kenneth Coates, eds., *Out of the Background: Readings on Canadian Native History*

Chad Gaffield and Pam Gaffield, eds., *Consuming Canada: Readings in Environmental History*

J.L. Granatstein, ed., *Canadian Foreign Policy: Historical Readings*, revised edition

J.L. Granatstein, ed., *Towards a New World: Readings in the History of Canadian Foreign Policy*

Norman Hillmer, ed., *Partners Nevertheless: Canadian–American Relations in the Twentieth Century*

Michiel Horn, ed., *The Depression in Canada: Responses to Economic Crisis*

B.D. Hunt and R.G. Haycock, eds., *Canada's Defence: Perspectives on Policy in the Twentieth Century*

Tina Loo and Lorna R. McLean, eds., *Historical Perspectives on Law and Society in Canada*

Douglas McCalla, ed., *The Development of Canadian Capitalism: Essays in Business History*

Douglas McCalla and Michael Huberman, eds., *Perspectives on Canadian Economic History*, 2nd edition

R.C. Macleod, ed., *Lawful Authority: Readings on the History of Criminal Justice in Canada*

Marc Milner, ed., *Canadian Military History: Selected Readings*

Morris Mott, ed., *Sports in Canada: Historical Readings*

Fernand Ouellet, *Economy, Class, and Nation in Quebec: Interpretive Essays*, ed. and trans. Jacques A. Barbier

Michael J. Piva, ed., *A History of Ontario: Selected Readings*

John Saywell and George Vegh, eds., *Making the Law: The Courts and the Constitution*

Gilbert A. Stelter, ed., *Cities and Urbanization: Canadian Historical Perspectives*

Veronica Strong-Boag and Anita Clair Fellman, eds., *Rethinking Canada: The Promise of Women's History*, 2nd edition

Gerald Tulchinsky, ed., *Immigration in Canada: Historical Perspectives*

Joseph Wearing, ed., *The Ballot and Its Message: Voting in Canada*

Graeme Wynn, ed., *People, Places, Patterns, Processes: Geographical Perspectives on the Canadian Past*

Social Welfare Policy
in Canada

Historical Readings

Edited by

Raymond B. Blake
Mount Allison University
and
Jeff Keshen
University of Alberta

Copp Clark Ltd.
Toronto

ISBN: 0-7730-5448-0

executive editor: Jeff Miller
editor: Barbara Tessman
proofreader: Camilla Jenkins
design: Susan Hedley, Liz Nyman
cover: Allan Moon
cover photo: Archives of Ontario S13457
typesetting: April Haisell
printing and binding: Metropole Litho Inc.

Canadian Cataloguing in Publication Data

Main entry under title:
Social Welfare policy in Canada: historical readings
Includes bibliographical references.

ISBN 0-7730-5448-0

1. Public welfare – Canada – History – 20th century.
2. Canada – Social policy.   3. Welfare state.
I. Blake, Raymond B. (Raymond Benjamin).   II. Keshen, Jeff, 1962–

HV108.S63   1995   361.6′1′0971   C94-932821-9

Copp Clark Ltd.
2775 Matheson Blvd. East
Mississauga, Ontario
L4W 4P7

Printed and bound in Canada

1 2 3 4 5   5448-0   99 98 97 96 95

FOREWORD

○

The Canadian social safety net is a relatively recent creation. Primitive old age pensions began in the 1920s, unemployment insurance and family allowances during the Second World War, and hospital insurance, medicare, and a variety of assistance programs in the 1950s and 1960s. Very quickly, Canadians came to rely on such programs for support in tough times. Just as important, the social welfare programs put in place by our governments became a crucial component of Canada's national identity, a critical way of differentiating a kinder, more caring Canada from its great neighbour to the south. Medicare, for example, is regularly portrayed in opinion polls as a critical part of Canadian life. Now a rising national debt and regular budget deficits have threatened the social safety net, and for the last decade governments have begun to trim and tax back benefits Canadians took for granted. What is to be done?

This volume, the first to look at the history and development of the nation's social welfare system, does not pretend to prescribe for the future. What it does do is to show clearly how Canadian social programs were debated, how they were created, and how they have evolved to meet changing needs. Professors Raymond Blake and Jeff Keshen have winnowed through the literature to create a guide to our social policies, and their volume will be of great value to students and practitioners in a number of fields.

J.L. Granatstein
General Editor

CONTENTS

o

INTRODUCTION

○

"By 1943 social security was in the air as never before," Leonard Marsh wrote years later in a new introduction for his influential *Report on Social Security for Canada*. As the young research advisor for the federal government's Advisory Committee on Reconstruction, he is often credited with hastily cobbling together the blueprint for Canada's welfare state that was to emerge, piecemeal, in the generation following the Second World War. As we approach the end of the twentieth century, social security is in the air once again, only this time the debate centres on the future of the welfare state in Canada. As governments wrestle with the serious fiscal crisis that hovers like an ominous black cloud over the nation, there is widespread fear that if the social security system is not reformed, it may collapse.[1]

While the welfare state blossomed in Canada after the 1940s, even in earlier colonial times there was some limited assistance for the most destitute. New France had its Bureau des Pauvres, evidence that the poor were a fact of life even in frontier societies. However, the struggling French colony largely allowed the church and its various institutions to care for the poor and destitute.[2] Early administrators adopted two measures to deal with those seeking assistance, measures that have proven remarkably persistent in the delivery of social welfare in Canada. The first was that the poor could move from the towns to farm the land, where, it was felt, any hard-working family could eke out a living. The second was a distinction between the deserving and the undeserving poor. The deserving poor were to be helped to help themselves, while the undeserving were forced to change and cease being a drain on society. After the British conquest of Quebec, the ideology governing the delivery of services to the indigent and the destitute remained largely unaltered.

Such unfortunate individuals also created problems for the British governors and settlers in the rest of British North America.[3] Both Nova Scotia and New Brunswick adopted the English poor law model, which placed responsibility upon the local parishes, townships, or counties. This introduced into Canada the idea that the public was responsible for the care of the destitute. In Prince Edward Island and Newfoundland, the government dispensed meagre aid from the colonial capitals, but both colonies depended heavily upon voluntary charities. When Upper Canada was organized as a colony in 1791, it rejected the English poor law model that had been adopted in Atlantic Canada. Instead, it looked to voluntary charity to provide assistance to those in need. By the early 1820s, it had become clear that this method was insufficient to deal with the social problems caused largely by the influx of immigrants. Consequently, Upper Canada moved toward the institutional mode of care when the colonial treasury provided partial support for the establishment of the Emigrant Temporary Asylum in 1828.

Whatever form charity took in the period before Confederation, its recipients were considered, in most cases, to be personal failures. British North America, a largely rural and agrarian society, maintained a strong belief in individualism and private charity. The assistance rendered either by governments or by private charity was always demeaning and insufficient and was mixed with a fair measure of paternalism. The most common mode of dispensing charity, especially in urban centres, was in the poorhouse, or houses of industry as they were frequently called. Like early prisons, they housed the physically and mentally challenged, the sick, the elderly, orphans, and all other charity cases. Such institutions not only provided basic sustenance but also sought to encourage desirable work habits, foster discipline, and promote morality. The situation for the poor was not much better in rural areas. In New Brunswick, for instance, the poor were sometimes auctioned off. All told, the provinces allocated about 3 percent of their total expenditure to public welfare in 1866.[4]

When the leading politicians from throughout British North America came together in Charlottetown and Quebec City to discuss union in 1864, they did not give much consideration to social welfare. They thought that hospitals, charities, asylums, and other related institutions were of limited interest to the central government and, considering them a local concern, gave responsibility for them to the provinces. Later, when social security issues came to play a more prominent role in Canadian public policy, the division of powers between the provincial and federal governments created serious jurisdictional problems.[5]

In the last third of the nineteenth century, Canada experienced tremendous economic growth. With industrialization came urbanization, and more Canadians became wage earners, dependent upon a steady job and a regular income. Yet, despite the structural changes in the economy, the old myths surrounding public assistance persisted. It was still widely accepted that if a person were poor or unemployed it was not a problem with the economy or society but some moral flaw within the individual. However, a number of Canadians, many for the first time, were concerned about the increasing incidence of poverty, industrial accidents, child labour, prostitution, and other social problems associated with the new economy.[6] These social reformers, particularly women and some male members of the Protestant churches, clearly saw problems with the industrializing society. Their intervention led to the creation of a series of inquiries into public issues.[7] The reformers often called for increased government intervention, especially in the form of increased regulation of the workplace and restrictions on the use of alcohol. Much of their focus was on the municipal and provincial governments, and it was at these levels that the first social security programs were introduced. Following earlier trends in Germany and Britain, Ontario introduced a Workmen's Compensation Act in 1914 that allowed workers a regular cash income while they recovered from injuries sustained on the job, but prevented them from suing their employers in court.[8] Mothers' allowances followed, first in Manitoba in 1916, to assist women who faced difficulty in raising their families without fathers who had gone to the Great War, never to return.[9] Moreover, following the granting of female suffrage in that province in 1916, women's demands took on greater political significance.

The prospects for increased social welfare legislation looked positive as Canada emerged from the First World War. Social work was slowly professionalizing as the religious element that had previously dominated the field was gradually replaced by an "ethos of professional social work practice."[10] Most provincial governments showed a keen interest in welfare measures. Moreover, the federal government assumed much of the responsibility for war pensions and the rehabilitation of veterans.[11] More important, William Lyon Mackenzie King, who had visions of a new social order in *Industry and Humanity: A Study in the Principles Underlying Industrial Reconstruction*, captured the leadership of the Liberal Party on a platform promising old age pensions and health and unemployment insurance. Despite the optimism, only an old age pension scheme was implemented before King lost the 1930 election. Even so, Canada's old age pension, which was cost-shared by the federal and provincial governments and which paid a paltry $20 each month to needy Canadians over seventy who had passed a humiliating means test, was an important, though small, step forward.[12]

The Great Depression proved a watershed in the development of social security in Canada. Still, throughout much of the tumultuous decade, attempts to deal with the destitution caused by a severe economic collapse were patterned after the nineteenth-century model of poor relief, supplemented with a growing dependency on voluntary charity. The federal government maintained throughout that relief was a provincial responsibility, although the sheer volume of Canadians unemployed forced it to become involved. R.B. Bennett, the Conservative prime minister, even admitted to the country that the capitalist system had to be reformed, and he introduced a series of measures, including unemployment insurance, in his "New Deal" to save the system.[13] Canadians doubted the sincerity of his reforms and turfed him from office when the election was held. Even so, the decade ended with many of the old myths governing unemployment and poverty severely shaken, at least for the next generation or two. After the catharsis of the Great Depression, the country finally realized that the economic and social systems had indeed collapsed and that the thousands of destitute Canadians could not be individually accountable for their plight. The period marked an important shift in thinking about both economics and social welfare.[14] No longer did most Canadians believe that all types of social welfare were demeaning.

The Second World War solved the problem of massive unemployment as the country mobilized to fight yet another major conflict. Early on, Canada and many other nations, although clearly intent upon winning the war, showed concern about the postwar period. Memories of the turmoil and uncertainty following the First World War were still fresh in people's minds.[15] So, too, was the prolonged economic crisis of the 1930s. Governments everywhere realized that the transition from war to peace and the period of postwar reconstruction had to prevent a return to the problems of unemployment and want that had characterized the prewar period. These views were reflected in the Atlantic Charter, signed on 14 August

1941, when British Prime Minister Winston Churchill and American President Franklin Roosevelt announced their desire "to bring about the fullest collaboration between all nations in the economic field with the object of securing, for all, improved labour standards, economic adjustment and social security." Over twenty countries from North and South America agreed at a conference held in Chile in 1942 that social security would be one of their prime objectives in the postwar period.

A number of such policies were considered during the war and several important ones adopted, all with the intent of providing the nation with a measure of security. In 1940, the federal government introduced unemployment insurance.[16] As part of its planning for postwar reconstruction, the King government appointed an Advisory Committee on Reconstruction, known as the James Committee after its chair, Dr Cyril James. Leonard Marsh was appointed research director, and his *Report on Social Security for Canada* created considerable debate, following as it did the British report on reconstruction, *Social Insurance and Allied Services*, better known as the Beveridge Report, which promised a social minimum for all citizens. Marsh proposed a "comprehensive and integrated social security system for Canada." In fact, it was a plan for freedom from want for every Canadian from the cradle to the grave. He proposed maternity benefits and children's allowances to cover children until they could earn for themselves. Adults would be able to take advantage of unemployment insurance or assistance, sickness benefits, free medical insurance, and pensions for permanent disability and widows. For the elderly, there were old age pensions and funeral benefits.[17]

Although the federal government ignored much of Marsh's advice about comprehensive, co-ordinated planning, it introduced a universal system of family allowances in July 1945 that paid an allowance, usually to mothers, for all children under the age of seventeen. It followed later that year with a proposal to the provinces for a cost-shared medical and hospital insurance plan, sole federal responsibility for old age pensions for citizens over seventy, a shared pension scheme for those between sixty-five and sixty-nine, and other social security measures. The proposal collapsed when the provinces and Ottawa failed to reach an agreement on revenue sharing, but the 1945 proposals remained a vague blueprint for federal initiatives over the next two decades, which would see major advances in many of these areas. In 1951, Ottawa finally introduced a universal old age pension plan for Canadians over seventy. The same year, it agreed to fund 50 percent of provincial programs designed to assist the blind, and it extended such assistance to the disabled in 1954. In 1956, it enacted the Unemployment Assistance Act to help finance provincial social assistance for the longer-term and seasonally unemployed.

Despite those achievements, progress remained slow in other areas. It was not until after the mid-1960s that many of Canada's social programs were finally instituted. In the area of health insurance, the provinces, particularly Saskatchewan, led by example. In 1947, after Saskatchewan introduced the first hospital insurance plan, the other provinces soon demanded similar programs. The federal government announced in 1957 that it would share with the provinces the cost of hospital insurance and, within four years, all provinces had introduced legislation to have such programs. Saskatchewan was also the first province to adopt a universal, publicly supported medical care insurance plan. In 1966, several years after the successful and popular Saskatchewan initiative, Ottawa passed the Medical Care Act, promising to contribute to provincial plans that met with federal objectives of covering all citizens for a wide range of medical services. It was 1968, however, before all provinces and territories finalized cost-sharing agreements with Ottawa, and by 1971 all had introduced medical care insurance plans.[18]

There were other major social policy achievements, and several came during a period of rapid political upheaval, after John Diefenbaker defeated the reigning Liberals to become the new Conservative prime minister in 1957. To regain power, Lester Pearson and the Liberal Party presented new policy initiatives on social security as well as other issues. In 1963, Diefenbaker was defeated, and the strength of the New Democratic Party in the minority parliament ensured that social security retained a prominent place in Pearson's government. Moreover, the Duplessis regime, which resisted introducing social programs and wrangled with the federal government over shared initiatives, came to an end in Quebec, and that province also embarked upon a series of public policy reforms.

The period saw the introduction of the Canada and Quebec Pension Plans. The CPP/QPP were designed to meet two objectives: first, to improve the standard of living for old age pensioners—nearly half of whom lived in poverty—as most Canadians did not participate in occupational pension plans; and second, to establish a national program that allowed Canadians to remain in a plan even if they changed jobs or moved from one part of the country to another. In 1966, the federal government improved pensions for the elderly when it introduced the guaranteed income supplement, giving everyone drawing an old age pension a minimum income level. Pensioners benefited again when the Canadian government enacted a spouses' allowance in 1975. Another major federal initiative came in 1966, when Ottawa introduced the Canada Assistance Plan, which saw it share the cost for provincial social assistance programs.[19]

Despite continued improvements in social security throughout the 1970s, the decade also saw the welfare state come under threat. Beginning in the mid-1970s and continuing for much of the next two decades, Canada had to deal with various economic problems, including double-digit inflation, a serious economic recession, and a burgeoning debt crisis. Accustomed to a generation of strong economic growth, governments were prompted to examine all areas of expenditure given the slumping economy, high unemployment, and an increase in government deficits. Almost immediately, the rising cost of Canada's welfare state became the centre of attention, followed shortly by a chorus of demands for its reform.

One of the most visible, widely discussed, and expensive social programs was medicare.[20] In 1977, in an effort to control expenditures, Ottawa moved to terminate its cost-shared funding arrangement with the provinces in favour of block funding through the Established Programs Financing Act. This only served to make the provinces more concerned about financing health care and other previously cost-shared programs. To deal with escalating costs in the delivery of health care, some provinces allowed extra billing and hospital user fees. Such practices threatened the principle of universal access of all Canadians to a comprehensive range of medical services. In 1984, Ottawa passed the Canada Health Act, requiring all provinces to eliminate any impediments to universal access within three years or face deductions in federal transfers equivalent to the amount collected in extra charges. The debate on medicare continues as provinces struggle with escalating costs and reduced federal payments.

Despite the increased level of social security, the country was shocked to learn in 1970 that one in four Canadians lived in poverty, including two million who were actually working. The welfare state had obviously failed to provide all Canadians with a decent standard of living. Several provinces responded by introducing measures to supplement the incomes of working-poor families. The Department of National Health and Welfare released a White Paper on Income Security, which called for a guaranteed annual income for families. Despite considerable debate and a lengthy federal–provincial review of the social security system, Ottawa finally dropped its plan for a guaranteed annual income after considerable provincial opposition to the proposal. However, it enacted a new Family Allowances Act in 1974 that virtually tripled payments to an average of $20 per child per month. It also allowed the provinces to vary the payment, but only Alberta and Quebec took advantage of this option. In 1978, the federal government introduced tax credits and refunds, including a child tax credit of $200 per child for families with income below $18 000, to redistribute income. In fact, under the Trudeau Liberals, the government began using the income tax system to distribute welfare benefits.

The decade following saw further inquiries into aspects of the social security system. Canada's unemployment insurance plan has perhaps been the subject of the most intense criticism amid considerable public debate. Unusually high unemployment rates saw the cost of the program escalate sharply, and many Canadians wondered if the mere existence of a generous unemployment scheme contributed to the high rates of unemployment. A royal commission appointed to study the unemployment system proposed a wide array of reforms, including reductions to the weekly rates and a transfer of benefits to job-retraining programs. The Royal Commission on the Economic Union and Development Prospects for Canada, which reported in 1984, called for a sweeping redesign of the social security system. It argued that as the Canadian economy restructured, it was necessary to reform the existing system. It proposed that Ottawa reconsider a comprehensive guaranteed income plan to be financed and administered solely by the federal government. The Conservative government under Brian Mulroney, elected in the same year, agreed that social security reform was necessary, but it had little in the way of a blueprint for the future, although it continued to cut universal income support payments in favour of more selective ones based on financial need. This was the rationale behind ending universality for family allowances in 1993 in favour of a new child tax credit directed toward low-income working families.

The debate over the restructuring and modernization of Canada's social security system may be just beginning. Lloyd Axworthy, the Liberal minister of human resources, has pledged major policy initiatives to reform the welfare state and save it for the next century. In early October 1994, he released an eighty-nine-page discussion paper on social reforms. With the social safety net costing all governments in Canada nearly $130 billion annually, making it the largest single expenditure,[21] there is widespread concern that it is, indeed, costing too much and that it may not be providing Canadians with the best value for their tax dollars. As governments, interest groups, and ordinary Canadians wrestle with the important issue of social policy reforms, this anthology of original and previously published papers is offered to provide Canadians with some guidance to the historical development of social security in this country.

NOTES

1. For a more detailed history of social security in Canada, see Dennis Guest, *The Emergence of Social Security in Canada* (Vancouver, 1985); A.W. Johnson, "Social Policy: The Past as It Conditions the Present" in *The Future of Social Welfare Systems in Canada and the United Kingdom*, ed. Shirley B. Seward (Halifax, 1987); and Allan Moscovitch and Glenn Drover, "Social Expenditures and the Welfare State: The Canadian Experience in Historical Perspective" in *The Benevolent State: The Growth of Welfare in Canada*, ed. Allan Moscovitch and Jim Albert (Toronto, 1987).

2. W.J. Eccles, "Social Welfare Measures and Policies in New France" in *Essays on New France*, ed. W.J. Eccles (Toronto, 1987).

3. See Judith Fingard, "The Relief of the Unemployed in Saint John, Halifax, and St. John's, 1815–1860," *Acadiensis* 5, 1 (Autumn 1975): 32–53; James Whalen, "Social Welfare in New Brunswick, 1784–1900," *Acadiensis* 2, 1 (Autumn 1972): 54–64; and Richard Splane, *Social Welfare in Ontario, 1791–1893* (Toronto, 1965).

4. Moscovitch and Drover, "Social Expenditure and the Welfare State," 16–17.

5. See Leslie A. Pal, "Federalism, Social Policy and the Constitution" in *Canadian Social Welfare Policy: Federal and Provincial Dimensions*, ed. Jacqueline S. Ismael (Montreal, 1985).

6. See R.C. Brown and Ramsay Cook, *Canada, 1896–1921: A Nation Transformed* (Toronto, 1974), and Richard Allen, *The Social Passion: Religion and Social Reform in Canada, 1914–28* (Toronto, 1971).

7. See Herbert Brown Ames, *The City Below the Hill* (Toronto, 1972).

8. R.C.B. Risk, "'This Nuisance of Litigation': The Origins of Workers' Compensation in Ontario" in *Essays in the History of Canadian Law*, vol. 2, ed. David H. Flaherty (Toronto, 1983).

9. Veronica Strong-Boag, "Mothers' Allowances and the Beginnings of Social Security in Canada," *Journal of Canadian Studies* 14, 1 (Spring 1974): 24–34.

10. See John R. Graham, "The Haven, 1878–1930: A Toronto Charity's Transition from a Religious to a Professional Ethos," *Histoire sociale/Social History* 25, 50 (Nov. 1992): 283–306.

11. See Desmond Morton and Glenn Wright, *Winning the Second Battle: Canadians and the Return to Civilian Life, 1915–1930* (Toronto, 1987).

12. See Kenneth Bryden, *Old Age Pensions and Policy-Making in Canada* (Montreal, 1974).

13. See Larry A. Glassford, *Reaction and Reform: The Politics of the Conservative Party Under R.B. Bennett, 1927–1938* (Toronto, 1992).

14. On changes in economic thinking in the period, see Doug Owram, "Economic Thought in the 1930s: The Prelude to Keynesianism," *Canadian Historical Review* 66, 3 (1985).

15. See David Bercuson, *Confrontation at Winnipeg: Labour, Industrial Relations and the General Strike* (Montreal, 1974).

16. See James Struthers, *"No Fault of Their Own": Unemployment and the Canadian Welfare State, 1914–1941* (Toronto, 1983).

17. See Leonard Marsh, *Report on Social Security for Canada 1943* (Toronto, 1975).

18. See Gwendolyn Gray, *Federalism and Health Policy: The Development of Health Systems in Canada and Australia* (Toronto, 1991).

19. See Rand Dyck, "The Canada Assistance Plan: The Ultimate in Cooperative Federalism," *Canadian Public Administration* 19 (Winter 1976).

20. Malcom Taylor, *Health Insurance and Canadian Public Policy: The Seven Decisions That Created the Canadian Health Insurance System* (Montreal, 1978).

21. *Globe and Mail*, 19 Jan. 1994.

section

1

IDEAS OF THE
WELFARE STATE

○

I n general terms, the roots of Canada's social welfare system lie in the rise of urban industrial society. Urbanization and industrialization led to an environment in which worries abounded over surplus labour, class conflict, overcrowding, dirt, crime, disease, and social decay. A wide array of reformers—motivated by conflicting convictions and interests—began to promote the idea of government having responsibility for ensuring a decent standard of living for all citizens.

In fact, by 1900, argues Elisabeth Wallace, the new challenges and problems accompanying the industrial age had ended the attachment by governments to laissez-faire philosophy. In addition to programs to foster economic growth, the state, in an effort to mould an efficient and content population, introduced measures such as free and compulsory education, as well as more equitable rules to regulate workplace relations. The government cast such action as partly derived from utopian aims and influences exerted by reformist movements abroad. But most fundamental, asserts Wallace, was the pragmatic conviction that changes to capitalism were necessary to prevent the social strains associated with modernization from undermining progress.

One should keep in mind that Wallace wrote this article at a time when large-scale intervention by government was still relatively novel, a fact that perhaps explains her tendency to depict early social welfare activity as more far-reaching than it actually was. As well, her characterization of public sector forays as largely devoid of heady idealism or ulterior motives may well be connected to liberal-centrist portrayals of the state popular during the Cold War years.[1]

On the other hand, several more recent studies, perhaps reflecting an environment in which people had become accustomed to higher levels of state support, or in which some cynicism toward authority still reverberated from the radical 1960s, have stressed the meagreness of early government programs. This point, even if not made directly, still becomes evident through the tendency to link most late-nineteenth- and early-twentieth-century social welfare with private organizations and individuals rather than the state. One such account, presented here by Colin Howell, centres upon Nova Scotia doctor Alexander Peter Reid, who sought to apply scientific methodology to social management. Like a slew of other urban-based professionals gaining more attention and respect around the turn of the century, Reid believed that his expertise, if employed by the state, could mould a better, if not a near-idyllic, society. His approach, in mirroring the mores of that time, included not just primitive versions of unemployment insurance and community-based health care, but also what we now see as racist and repressive recommendations premised upon fashionable pseudo-scientific eugenics theory. One can also extrapolate from this paper to suggest that self-interest constituted a concern of some early welfare advocates. After all, Reid benefited personally from the institutional expansion of government to treat social ills. At yet another level, some of his beliefs mirrored aspects of the Progressive ethos then surfacing as a major political force in America, thus calling into question the degree to which Canadians, philosophically speaking, proved more collectivist-minded than their southern neighbours whose society was born out of a revolution supposedly exalting individualism.

From just these two articles it becomes clear that a wide cross section of individuals, groups, and impulses established the roots of Canada's social welfare system. Whether the motivation for a specific policy was beneficence or self-interest, little doubt can remain that the hopes of and initiatives launched by pioneers in this field bequeathed quite a legacy. Not only has the social safety net become part of Canada's political landscape (attracting some support from all major parties), it has become, many would claim, an element of the nation's collective consciousness, constituting one of the ways in which its citizens define themselves as distinct from what is perceived as a more individualistically minded American population.

NOTES

1. See Godfrey Hodgson, *America in Our Time* (New York: Doubleday, 1976), 67–98.

THE ORIGIN OF THE
SOCIAL WELFARE STATE
IN CANADA, 1867–1900 *

ELISABETH WALLACE

○

The welfare state—as a term of abuse or approval, depending on the point of view—is a phrase which has only recently come into common use, although contrasts between the so-called "negative" and "positive" state have been frequently drawn during the past two decades. The idea that the primary function of government is to make a good life possible, is, however, as old as Aristotle, and political theorists in democratic countries have long been agreed that the state exists for the well-being of its citizens, and not vice versa, although their views of what constitutes the welfare of the people have been markedly divergent. The expansion of government activities, which is conveniently summarized under the term "social welfare state," in this country as in others is usually considered a twentieth-century phenomenon. Its origins in Canada, however, may be traced to the first thirty years after Confederation, when the proper function of government was a matter of general concern and wide debate. During this early period public opinion as to what the state ought to do for the social well-being of its citizens developed rapidly, and underwent a marked transformation.

Present-day critics of the British North America Act are given to pointing out that, as a nineteenth-century document drawn up when laissez-faire theories were at their height, it has become increasingly ill-adapted to further social welfare by state action. Yet contemporary historians have shown that in both Great Britain and the United States, during the past century, the

* *Canadian Journal of Economics and Political Science* 16, 3 (Aug. 1950): 383–93. Reprinted with the permission of the author and the Canadian Political Science Association.

classical doctrine of laissez-faire, interpreted as government abstention from interference with individual or group action, was more honoured in theory than in practice.[1] This contention is supported by illustrations of early factory, mines, public health, and education acts in England, and of such American intervention in economic affairs as tariffs and grants to individual industries. There is much evidence that similar developments took place in Canada, which lends support to similar conclusions concerning the mythical nature of laissez-faire.

In this country lip service to the concept was undoubtedly paid over a long period, the peak of enthusiasm for the inactivity of governments probably being reached in the 1860s or 70s; that is to say, about the time of Confederation. Yet the English doctrine, while theoretically upheld in North America, on this continent actually underwent a change in meaning, which even its advocates frequently ignored. Canadian business men, while protesting their devotion to the principles of laissez-faire, have never objected to state intervention in economic matters to benefit industry, and have frequently been clamorous in demanding it. Like the people of other pioneer countries, Canadians early looked to the government to supply the services and capital necessary for the development of natural resources, and state investment in roads and canals was already heavy prior to 1867. The building of the Intercolonial Railroad was part of the agreement written into the British North America Act, while four years later British Columbia exacted the promise of a trans-Canada railway as a condition of joining the Confederation. Sir John A. Macdonald's "National Policy" was inaugurated within the decade, and Canada has since that time remained a high tariff country. State intervention in the development of natural resources, the fostering of industries with protracted periods of infancy, and the supplying of public utilities has been continuous since Confederation.

The kind of action in the economic sphere which social legislation involves has, however, been viewed by Canadians in a very different light. Recognition of the propriety of such intervention has come more slowly, and is still far from unqualified, although its origins may be found surprisingly early. Many of the problems responsible for creating public opinion in favour of social welfare measures were the result of industrialization and the concomitant development of city dwelling, which tended to break down the self-sufficiency of the pioneer family. At the time of Confederation, Canada was largely rural and what would today be described as "social problems" were then viewed as the natural concern of the family, local community, or church, rather than of the state. Consequently when the framers of the British North America Act distributed powers between the Dominion and provinces, with the intention of conferring on the former jurisdiction over "all the great subjects of legislation," the exiguous responsibilities for health and welfare then thought appropriate to governments were considered local and private, and thus properly to come within the provincial sphere. The act did not impose any obligations to provide welfare services upon either the Dominion or the provinces, but simply allocated, with less precision than its framers had hoped to achieve, the various spheres of jurisdiction, any subsequent action being permissive, not mandatory. The cost of public charities, welfare, and education in the four provinces of British North America in 1866 amounted to only 9 percent of total government expenditures, a figure which may be contrasted with the 19 percent allotted for social security payments in the 1950 federal budget, in addition to very large provincial and municipal expenditures for social welfare.

The fathers of Confederation clearly thought they were assigning the provinces the unimportant and inexpensive functions of government, among which education, hospitals, charities, and municipal institutions were then reasonably numbered. They could scarcely have foreseen the way in which time would reverse their expectations, so that the costliness of the responsibilities laid upon the provinces subsequently increased to the point where it was financially impossible to defray them. Within thirty years after Confederation, social and economic conditions had so altered that public opinion was demanding government action on matters held in 1867 to be primarily personal and of no concern to the state.

Widespread support for public provision of social legislation, in the broadest sense of the term, was first shown in the demand for schools. For more than half a century before Confederation, education had been recognized in both the Maritime provinces and Upper Canada as worthy of some public support, but it was not always free. Schools were not established in all parts of the country, and attendance was nowhere compulsory. Prince Edward Island passed a free education act in 1852 and twelve years later Nova Scotia inaugurated free elementary and secondary education in its county academies. In the course of the 1870s primary schooling became free in Ontario, British Columbia, and Manitoba, but within the decade scanty attendance showed that if education were to be universal, it would have to be made not only free but also compulsory. This proposal provoked a violent controversy. Some maintained that the well-being of a democracy required educated citizens, that consequently no children should be allowed to grow up in absolute ignorance, and that the provision of schools should be a first charge upon public funds. Others considered that such a plan struck at the root of parental responsibility and would inevitably bring about the disintegration of family life. Indignant taxpayers asked why they should be forced, against their will, to be their brother's teacher, and attacked the principle of free education as well as that of compulsion on the ground that "it kills the sense of duty in the parent, who is naturally bound to educate, as well as to feed and clothe the children whom he brings into the world, while experience seems to teach that what is gratuitous is less valued, and that attendance is better with a moderate fee. As to compulsion, though it may be practical under the strong governments of Europe, it appears to be impracticable in communities like these."[2] Not until 1891, when truant officers were appointed to enforce the provisions for compulsory attendance, did education really become general in Ontario.

By that time a Canadian legislator who refused to admit the principle of free elementary education was described as a curiosity, and free high schools were becoming common, although complaints were heard that this encouraged pupils, who might have been better employed in manual labour, to think themselves above the station in life to which they were born.[3] By the turn of the century, however, the propriety of free and compulsory schooling was no longer a matter of debate, and the Ontario minister of education was referring with pride to the fact that "a good education is easily within the reach of all, and the door to preferment opens on equal terms to the son of the poor and of the rich."[4] A contemporary commentator noted a change in attitude so sweeping that a boy or girl in the 1890s took as a matter of course educational opportunities that fifty years earlier had not been available even to the children of the most fortunate.[5]

During the 1870s and 80s most of the Canadian universities began to admit women students, although the proposal that they do so at first aroused much criticism. Goldwin Smith considered that pitting young men and women against each other in university examinations was repugnant to sentiment. He had, however, little real hope of stemming the tide of innovation with regard to votes and higher education for women, since already, as he gloomily pointed out, "Woman has made her way to the smoking-room and has mounted the bicycle."[6] Principal Grant of Queen's, on the other hand, as early as 1879 had shown himself well in advance of his day in stating publicly that he knew of no reason "that can be urged against women studying in our recognized colleges that has not been urged from time immemorial against every step in advance taken by the race, against every reform that has ever been made in the realm of thinking or of action."[7]

Interest in the development of public education and of public libraries went naturally together. If it was desirable that the state should provide schooling for children of all classes, a parallel case could be made for offering their parents opportunities for informal education through free access to books. The first public aid for libraries was given in Upper Canada in 1835 through grants to Mechanics' Institutes, which lent books in addition to sponsoring adult education programs.[8] Free public libraries began to be established in the 1880s and by 1900 were fairly common in many of the larger Canadian cities and towns. Half a century later, however, 95 percent of the country's rural population is still unprovided with library services.

At the time of Confederation, Canada was almost entirely agrarian, and was just beginning to be influenced by the Industrial Revolution, whose effects in the United States had for some time been marked. Between 1880 and 1900 the urban population more than doubled, rising from 14 to 37 percent of the whole. Frontier conditions placed a premium upon self-reliance, which was a tenable doctrine when a family or community produced and consumed most of the goods which it needed. Those who for any reason were unable to make their own way were apt to be looked down upon as lazy or weaklings, but were generally kept from starvation by the efforts of relatives, friends, or private charitable or religious organizations. The expanding frontier offered new opportunities for those who found conditions difficult at home. Independence was a matter of pride, and there was small temptation to look to the state for assistance in matters of social welfare, as practically no public provisions were available, save in the Maritime provinces, where a fairly close approximation to the Elizabethan Poor Law, with the accompanying poorhouses and overseers of the poor, had long been established. Where this system was in operation, its attractions were minimal, as may be illustrated by the fact that it was not until 1900 that Nova Scotia added to its Poor Relief Act a clause stating that "The overseers shall not provide for the maintenance of the poor by putting up the same at public auction." The theory that the Lord helps those that help themselves was considered appropriate from both a religious and an economic point of view. The assumption, however, that work was available for everyone who wanted it, and that those who would not work had no claim on society, largely ignored the special needs of such groups as the old, the widowed, the orphaned, and the mentally and physically incapacitated. It also ignored the new phenomenon of unemployment.

Before the turn of the century, Canada had experienced three depressions (then described as recessions of trade), from 1873–1879, 1884–1887, and 1893–1896. By the 1880s, unemployment had ceased to be a novelty, particularly among the immigrants, of whom some one and a half million were brought into the country between 1871 and 1901, although during the same period more than two million people left for the United States. As early as 1881 the idea that no one in Canada who was willing to work need want bread was characterized as an illusion of the past, and support began to develop for the view that the government ought to make some provision for the relief of the poor. The proposal encountered the criticism that this would remove opportunities for the exercise of moral virtues such as parental devotion, filial piety, and Christian benevolence, and might also have the unfortunate result of discouraging private alms-giving.

Contemporary articles, however, began to reveal a growing doubt as to whether the poor were, after all, the chief architects of their own poverty, and showed uneasiness at the idea of building large institutions, named after the most lavish contributors, to house people who needed care, while providing no preventive measures whereby the old, the sick, and the poor could live without begging.[9] Although it was not until the twentieth century that the phrase "social security" was invented, and emphasis placed upon the need for prevention as more important than cure in attacking social problems, the germ of the idea may be found well before 1900.

Arguments in favour of providing some public assistance received practical reinforcement from the inconvenience of having the jails filled with men out of work and elderly infirm people without homes, who, seeking food and shelter, flocked to the prisons, where they shared cells with those awaiting trial or already convicted of offences. Among the culprits sentenced in 1880 to six months in an Ontario reformatory, after having first served fourteen days in the common jail, was a small girl convicted of the crime of stealing a gooseberry from a garden. Not until 1894 was one of the first children's courts on the continent established in Toronto.

The trade union movement and factory legislation developed concurrently, the former doing a good deal to stimulate the latter. By the early 1870s both the Conservative and Liberal parties thought it worth while to compete for the favour of industrial workers, who were beginning to make known their desire for social legislation. Sir John A. Macdonald, in passing the Trade Union Act of 1872, which freed unions from liability to be charged with conspiracy for acting in restraint of trade, posed as the protector of labour. The claim evidently rankled, for Edward Blake subsequently maintained that the Liberals were, after all, the truest and most natural friends of labour, and that the Liberal government in power from 1874 to 1878 had "paid more attention to the well-being, the social status and the interests of the workingmen than any administration which preceded or followed it."[10] There is, however, no real evidence to indicate that during this period social legislation was a serious concern of either of the parties, and it was the difficulties encountered in trying to secure measures such as minimum wages and the limitation of hours of work that led the unions to think of the desirability of taking direct political action. A few labour representatives began to be elected to municipal and provincial legislatures before the turn of the century, and in 1900 the first Independent Labor member was returned to the Dominion parliament.

The trade unions were the chief promoters of the movement for a nine-hour day, which by 1872 was occasioning considerable discussion. Its supporters claimed that legal limitation of the hours of work would help to relieve unemployment as well as to give working men more leisure. Opponents of the idea countered that the ten-hour day then considered normal was an advantage to the working classes, who otherwise would probably fail to make proper use of their free time. By 1886, however, there were advocates of the view that a working day of eight hours or less would eventually be the rule in practically every trade. Productive capacity had been so increased by the introduction of new machinery that men were being thrown out of work for lack of adequate markets for the goods they could produce, and acute economic depression provided an argument that a shorter working day would help to redistribute labour and production more evenly.[11]

The principle of minimum wages similarly came up for discussion, a controversy occurring in 1889 in the Toronto City Council over the suggestion of an alderman that no labourers employed on municipal contracts should be paid less than 15 cents an hour. Critics of the proposal argued that anyone receiving so exorbitant a wage would spend most of it in drink. *Saturday Night*, however, supported the alderman's proposal, remarking that it was "really a pity that our social organization seems to have nothing in it but competition among those who are strong enough to compete and the poorhouse for those who have fallen in the fight."[12]

Industries were developing quickly, fostered by the protective tariff and expansion in the west. The factory system, with its accompanying problems, which in older countries grew up gradually, Canada acquired within a few years. Public concern about this development was evidenced by the introduction in the federal parliament between 1880 and 1886 of seven Dominion factory bills.[13] Despite considerable public support, none of these passed, some being withdrawn owing to representations made by employers, and others being attacked as ultra vires the jurisdiction of the federal government. The Royal Commission on the Relations of Labour and Capital, reporting in 1889, described the employment of six-year-old children for a nine- or ten-hour day in factories, and strongly advocated Dominion regulation, maintaining that if there were doubt whether such action lay within the competence of the federal parliament, some way should be found of removing that doubt.[14] While in point of fact the Dominion was never given jurisdiction in this sphere, the agitation undoubtedly stimulated the development of factory, mines, and employers' liability acts in the various provinces.

The churches in Canada prior to the turn of the century gave little evidence of interest in helping to shape an earthly paradise through such mundane means as social legislation, their interest in current problems being largely confined to the issues of temperance and whether street-cars should or should not run on Sundays. The Methodist Church showed some concern for early factory legislation, but opposed the movement for an eight-hour day on the ground that the workers were not apt to make a wise use of their leisure time. Religious articles of the 1870s and 80s for the most part condemned socialism, attacked strikes, and advocated cheap skilled labour as necessary to the well-being of society. Church papers openly stated their lack of faith in the endeavour to abolish poverty by acts of parliament. Accepting as axiomatic the statement that the poor we have with us always, they were inclined to deplore any encroachment by government upon the sphere of charity, still regarded at that time in many parts of English- as well as of French-speaking Canada as the proper province of the church. "There is no agency," declared the *Christian Guardian*, "which can so effectively mitigate the sufferings of poverty as organized and rightly directed Christian benevolence."[15] A changing point of view was reflected in a statement issued a few years later by the Methodist Church at its General Conference in 1894: "We consider it not only a privilege, but also a duty of all Christians . . . to watch the social movements of the day and to make all proper efforts to secure the most satisfactory economic conditions through appropriate legislation." In general, however, the Canadian churches during this period made little direct contribution to the cause of social reform, being more interested in the sins of individuals than those of society. The Methodists were distinguished by their advocacy of free public education, and the indirect effect of the emphasis laid by religious bodies on the right of groups to freedom of association and expression was significant. Yet theological intolerance, where it existed, did not make for liberalism in social outlook any more than for abstract philosophical speculation.

Practical concern for social legislation was paralleled, however, in most circles, by widespread interest in the underlying social and political theories implicit in the extension of government functions. In discussions of such matters the emphasis gradually shifted from individual rights and liberties to a stress on the well-being of the group and the wider interests of the community as a whole. Questions such as the meaning and relationship of socialism and individualism and democracy, commonly thought of as mid-twentieth century problems, were burning issues in the Canada of the 1890s.

Canadian interest in these matters can be traced in part to influences outside the country, such as Bismarck's social insurance program in Germany, the activities of the Fabian Society in England, and the social legislation of the Liberal government that took office in New Zealand in 1891. Contemporary Canadian comment on social insurance schemes ranged from horror to an ironic appreciation of Bismarck's political astuteness. Among the most apprehensive was Professor Mavor of the University of Toronto, who held that all pension schemes were a method of subsidizing low wages, and objected to social insurance on the ground that malingering was likely to be so prevalent as to make the system unworkable.[16] He was asked by the Ontario government to make a study of the workmen's compensation plan established sixteen years earlier in Germany, and to consider the advisability of similar action being taken by the province. His report, presented in 1900, noted that employers' liability measures had recently been enacted by almost every country in Europe, but deplored the tendency toward bureaucratic management particularly noticeable in Germany. He admitted the force of the argument that in an under-populated country like Canada there were cogent practical reasons for encouraging immigrants by social legislation, in order to make the country a desirable place for people to live. Nevertheless he considered that compulsory insurance against industrial accidents imposed a tax on management and capital which might discourage the development of industry in Ontario, where many manufacturing concerns already operated upon a very narrow margin. He accordingly advised the province to delay taking action in the matter until Britain and Germany had had more experience with their respective schemes. Although state ownership and administration seemed to him to breed autocracy, he yet maintained that accident insurance was not socialistic, because it neither interfered with the wages system nor with the private ownership of the means of production. The promoters of social legislation in Germany, he pointed out, "while opposed to laissez-faire and all that that implies," yet "had no thought of abolishing the system of wage labour and private capitalism; but had in their minds chiefly a new State which should not be merely a policeman, but which should have as its primary business the positive welfare of the people."[17]

Canadian interest in European social legislation was further stimulated by the steady influx to the country of British immigrants. The suggestion made in 1897 by Joseph Chamberlain, then secretary of state for the colonies, that the United Kingdom might introduce old age pensions, provoked comment in Canada, where a government annuity scheme, with all contributions paid by the beneficiary, was considered the most suitable policy for a new country, as being likely to encourage habits of thrift among the working-classes.[18] Articles in the Canadian press noted that the European idea of inaugurating semi-socialist measures as a counter-irritant to socialism was not working out too well on the continent, where they appeared powerless to halt the spread of the radicalism against which they were directed. A writer in the *Canadian Monthly* lamented the fact that by encouraging state socialism Bismarck had created a Frankenstein monster which threatened his master's destruction. A parallel illustration to the unhappy experience of Germany might, he feared, be found in Canada.[19]

Canadians showed little sympathy with the German tendency to personify and idealize the state, being inclined rather to stress that it had no existence apart from the members of the community and to urge the stimulation of individual energy and of native invention. Confusion of thought would be avoided, they held, by conceiving the state as simply the citizens in their organized capacity, and not as an entity with rights and duties of its own, much less a soul. At the same time there was apparent a growing disinclination to limit the sphere of government to its traditional functions of national defence, maintenance of public order, and protection of the rights of property. It began to be urged that paternalism on occasion became the state, as in the case of children employed in factories, who could not take care of themselves, or of public health regulations, whose enforcement was required for the well-being of the community.[20] It was fitting, people were coming to believe, that the government should intervene to prevent men and women from dying of hunger in the street, whether or not their destitution were their own fault.

By 1892 journalists were arguing that proposals for the extension of government activities should be considered empirically, on their own merits, since "Wisely or unwisely, rightly or wrongly, nothing is much more certain than that the old policy of *laissez-faire*, which left the whole question to be settled by the law of demand and supply, that is, between the purse of the capitalist and the necessities of the labourer, is doomed."[21] Debate was vigorous as to whether laws regulating minimum wages, working conditions in factories, public health, and compulsory education were or were not properly to be described as socialistic. One school of thought claimed that none of these measures was as autocratic as the Ontario legislation governing Sabbath observance. Professor Shortt of Queen's maintained that "the taking over by the state of certain economic functions and services is no more a practical application of socialism than the relishing of a moderate meal is a practical illustration of gluttony."[22] Others saw liberty as consisting in the least government feasible, with the widest scope left for private initiative and "the largest possible exemption for all of us from legalized fads," and inveighed against theories endeavouring to prove that people could grow rich without work and happy by government action.[23]

So unlikely a radical as the attorney general of Nova Scotia, however, the Hon. J.W. Longley, defined socialism as

> the right of the whole people or body politic to regulate certain things in the interests of the whole state [and added that] in order to make things fair and just to all, certain individual rights must give way, be abridged, or swept away. Surely there is nothing to be alarmed at in this. It means nothing more than organized government. The first Statute ever passed by a Legislature was essentially socialistic, for it was a recognition of the right of the majority to make regulations for the benefit of the mass, and that, too, at the expense of individual rights and desires. ... Let us forever give over all fear of either Socialism or socialistic ideas. They are at the bottom of all legislation. ... Both Socialism and Individualism are consistent with true liberalism.[24]

Such a view did not go unchallenged, but it was illustrative of an attitude already widespread by 1900.

Toward the end of the century, the relations between the rich and the poor were described as the great question of the age, a modern note being introduced by the attribution of growing dissatisfaction with social and economic conditions to "designing agitators," as well as to misguided philanthropists who believed that radical wrongs in the existing social system demanded radical reforms.[25] On the other hand, numerous articles referred to public education, the protective tariff, and to municipal gas, telephone and street-railway companies, as well as the post-office, as all distinctly collectivist, public undertakings for the public good. A marked socialistic tendency in everything except the getting and spending of money was noted by *Saturday Night* in 1890, in an article commenting on the change from private giving to organized charity.[26] Four years later, a journalist declared that it could "safely be asserted that socialism in a mild form—the form called democracy—has taken deep root in Canada. Assuming this as proved, and knowing that socialism is a movement essentially characteristic of this century, growing stronger as the century advances, it must be admitted that the movement is likely to become more radical."[27]

The origins of the modern twentieth-century interest in state action to combat problems of unemployment, old age, and poverty, and to provide labour legislation, are thus all to be found within a few years of Confederation. By the end of the nineteenth century, Canadians looked to the government to provide education and libraries, as well as art galleries, parks, and playgrounds. This attitude was a natural enough concomitant, not only of the growth of cities, but of increasing state activity in economic and industrial enterprises, whose benefits to the ordinary person were certainly no more obvious than was the provision of free schools or publicly subsidized hospitals. At no time since 1867 were laissez-faire theories consistently practised or government intervention in economic and social matters considered inappropriate. It can be argued that belief in the social welfare state was already well-developed by 1896, when the *Queen's Quarterly* published an article contending that "Almost the whole machinery of government is socialistic in . . . a limited sense. . . . The only question is one of expediency or degree. . . . The cry of alarm with which socialism is met in some quarters is . . . that of men who begin to see the walls which surround and protect them giving way before the steady advance of fuller knowledge and wider responsibility."[28]

NOTES

1. Cf. J. Bartlet Brebner, "Laissez Faire and State Intervention in Nineteenth Century Britain," *Journal of Economic History,* supplement 8 (1948): 59–73, and Carter Goodrich, "Public Spirit and American Improvements" *Proceedings of the American Philosophical Society* 92, 4 (1948): 305–9.

2. *The Bystander* 3 (1883): 215. Cf. also Ernest Heaton, "Ontario's Weakness," *Canadian Magazine* 8 (1886–87): 265.

3. *The Week*, 25 July 1890 and 10 April 1891.

4. Hon. R. Harcourt, "Canada's Destiny" (speech delivered at the centenary celebrations, Toronto, 17 Sept. 1892) in J. Robert Long, *Canadian Politics, with Speeches by the Leaders of Reform and Progress in Canadian Politics and Government* (St Catharines, 1903), 120.

5. John Reade, "Half a Century's Progress," *Canadian Magazine* 16 (1900–1): 270.

6. From an article entitled "Women's Place in the State" (University of Toronto Library, n.d., n.p.), 524. His views on the subject were elaborated in another article, "Conservatism and Female Suffrage," *National Review* 60 (Feb. 1888): 737.

7. Inaugural lecture of the ninth session of the Montreal Ladies' Educational Association, published in the *Canadian Monthly* 3 (July–Dec. 1879): 516–17.

8. Edwin A. Hardy, *The Public Library* (Toronto, 1912), 26–40.

9. Norman Patterson, "Canadian People: A Criticism," *Canadian Magazine* 13 (1898): 135.

10. Hon. Edward Blake, *Speeches in the Dominion Election Campaign of 1887* (Toronto, 1887), 330–48, 356–68, 371–75.

11. *Toronto Morning News*, 18 Feb. and 3 May 1886.

12. 2 Feb. 1889.

13. Discussed by Dr Eugene Forsey in his "Note on the Dominion Factory Bills of the Eighteen-Eighties," *Canadian Journal of Economics and Political Science* 13, 4 (Nov. 1947): 580–85.

14. Royal Commission on the Relations of Labour and Capital in Canada, *Report* (Ottawa, 1889), 10, 36–37, 79, 89.

15. 18 Jan. 1888. Cf. also the *Christian Guardian*, 2 April 1879 and 29 June 1887.

16. James Mavor, "The Relation of Economic Study to Private and Public Charity," *Annals of the American Academy of Political and Social Sciences* 4 (1893): 55.

17. James Mavor, *Report on Workmen's Compensation for Industries*, printed by order of the Legislative Assembly of Ontario (Toronto, 1900), 29, 42, 45–47.

18. Andrew T. Drummond, "Some Workingmen's Problems," *Queen's Quarterly* 5 (July 1897): 67.

19. Carroll Ryan, "Political Morality," *Canadian Monthly* 3 (July–Dec. 1879): 407.

20. *The Bystander* 3 (1883): 284, and *The Week*, 24 April 1884, 2 Sept. 1893, and 8 March 1895.

21. *The Week*, 12 Aug. 1892, 15 Dec. 1887, and 17 Nov. 1893.

22. Adam Shortt, "Recent Phases of Socialism," *Queen's Quarterly* 5 (July 1897): 18. He upheld the same view in an earlier article in the *Queen's Quarterly* 3 (July 1895): 22.

23. Arnold Haultain, "Complaining of Our Tools," *Canadian Magazine* 9 (1897): 189. Cf. also W.D. LeSueur, "State Education and 'Isms,'" *Canadian Magazine* 2 (1893): 6–7.

24. Hon. J.W. Longley, "Socialism—Its Truths and Errors," *Canadian Magazine* 6 (1895–96): 297–301.

25. *Saturday Night*, 22 Feb. 1890, and *The Week*, 30 Jan. 1891.

26. *Saturday Night*, 21 June 1890.

27. John A. Cooper, "Canadian Democracy and Socialism," *Canadian Magazine* 3 (1894): 334–36.

28. John Hay, "Socialistic Schemes," *Queen's Quarterly* 3 (April 1896): 293–94.

MEDICAL SCIENCE AND SOCIAL CRITICISM: ALEXANDER PETER REID AND THE IDEOLOGICAL ORIGINS OF THE WELFARE STATE IN CANADA *

COLIN D. HOWELL

o

The development of the modern welfare state, and more particularly the introduction of state-supported health insurance, is often seen in relation to the divergent intentions of competing interest groups. Such has been true of most treatments of the coming of medicare to Canada, where the competing and often shifting attitudes of organized labour, health reformers, politicians, medical organizations of various types, and civil-service bureaucrats are dissected in order to explain the timing of medicare's introduction.[1] What is often missed in this approach is the relationship between state involvement in health matters, the emergence and rising authority of the scientific professions, and the involvement of those professions in movements for social and economic reform. In this sense the roots of state medicine can be found in the nineteenth century, particularly in the liberal reform impulse commonly referred to as progressivism.

An amalgam of various elements, progressivism involved a faith in a scientifically rationalized and efficient capitalist system that would be able to overcome the abuses and social dislocations of too-rapid industrialization.[2] Professionals of various kinds took a leading role in the turn-of-the-century reform movement, asserting their expertise in the management of social problems and calling for a reorganization of society in accordance with new notions of scientific orthodoxy.[3] Faith in scientific management

---

* From David C. Naylor, ed., *Canadian Health Care and the State: A Century of Evolution* (Montreal: McGill-Queen's University Press, 1992), 16–37. Reprinted with the permission of the publisher.

and professional expertise permeated the reform of politics, municipal government, criminal justice, labour relations, and industrial production,[4] and extended to the field of medicine and public health as well.[5] Furthermore, as Howard Segal has argued in his *Technological Utopianism in American Culture*, the progressive belief in science and social engineering stimulated a vision of a utopian society that would promote efficiency and social co-operation, place technical expertise above partisan political authority, and eschew wasteful individualism. [6]

This paper investigates the relationship between professionalization, progressive reform, and state intervention in the late nineteenth-century Maritimes by examining the career of medical doctor and progressive social critic Alexander Peter Reid. An asylum and hospital superintendent, public-health advocate, and a leading figure in the professionalization of medicine in the Maritimes, Reid pursued a career that sheds light on the relationship between medical professionalization, the veneration of scientific knowledge, and the promotion of sanitary, social, and moral reform. It should be noted at the outset that no claims are made here that Reid was typical of the rank and file of the medical profession; he was instead a member of that profession's own elite, many of whom were, like him, proponents of progressive social reform. At the same time Reid's commitment to a new and somewhat utopian social order—which could be achieved, he believed, through social planning and expert management—lent credibility to the idea of greater state involvement in matters involving the nation's mental, moral, and physical well-being.

Modern urban and industrial capitalism came to the Maritimes in the last third of the nineteenth century, fuelled by railroad and mineral development and the protectionist policies of the Canadian state.[7] As was true elsewhere, rapid industrialization and urbanization focussed public attention on a wide range of social issues, from the living conditions of the poor to crime, prostitution, alcoholism, disease, child labour, women's rights, mental hygiene, and public sanitation. Doctors soon found themselves offering advice upon the sanitary condition of factories, schools, and tenements, the need for pure water, milk, and unadulterated food, the value of playgrounds and other recreational facilities, and the need for city sewers and refuse collection. Hitching a faith in science to a progressive concern for social improvement, many doctors began to envisage a hygienic utopia administered by a cadre of professional experts and appropriately trained agents of the state. What were needed, argued the progressive politician Dr J.B. Black of Windsor, Nova Scotia, were federal and provincial departments of health fully equipped with inspectors, sanitary engineers, bacteriologists, and chemists, assisted by city, town, and county boards of health with their own appropriately salaried officers. "When governments, national, provincial, and municipal, properly undertake the prevention of preventable disease," Black wrote, "then shall preventable diseases disappear from the civilized world."[8]

As the late nineteenth-century medical profession became more interested in questions of public health and sanitation, doctors gradually came to realize that their own social utility extended beyond the treatment of disease into a consideration of the various maladies of the body politic. Concerned that the rapid advance of civilization was contributing to the increase of nervous disorders, sexual debility, and moral degeneracy, doctors in the Maritimes—like their counterparts elsewhere—served up a coherent interpretation of social deviance and what had to be done to eradicate it.[9] In the process, the hygienic utopia of the late nineteenth-century medical profession took on the character of a moral utopia as well, extending beyond the public-health movement to a broader interest in social and moral regeneration. Applying what they considered appropriate scientific remedies to social dislocation, doctors like Reid hoped to rid society of the "degenerative" influences of crime, insanity, gender conflict, and class antagonism and to replace competitive individualism with a blend of social co-operation and technical expertise.[10] Implicit in this progressive reform vision was a critique of traditional institutions such as the church, the family, and the old-line political parties, which were seen to have failed to address the abuses of the modern industrial order. The involvement of medical doctors in the progressive movement thus contributed to the medicalization of concerns that hitherto had been the province of the family, the church, the institutions of criminal justice, and the patronage-based party system, and represents an early first step in the direction of the modern therapeutic and capitalist welfare state.[11]

Alexander Peter Reid was one of the most articulate and prolific exponents of this vision of progressive reform and social regeneration in the late Victorian Maritimes. A committed scientist whose career spanned the half-century between Confederation and the First World War, Reid was convinced that the application of scientific and therapeutic principles to the social body would liberate mankind from the irrationality of modern urban and industrial society and fulfil hopes for a prosperous and disease-free future. Jettisoning the doctrines of survival of the fittest, competitive individualism, and retributive justice in favour of the corporate and therapeutic ideology of the welfare state, Reid remained a life-long proponent of the practical utility and applicability of science to daily life. Like other technological utopians, of course, he overestimated the extent to which modern science and technology could address the problems that science and technology had helped to create. Instead he shared the fanciful vision of Benjamin Ward Richardson, who in a memorable address to the Health Section of the British Social Science Association in 1875 fashioned the mythical "Hygiea," a disease-free urban utopia supervised by a hierarchy of medical officers, registrars, sanitary inspectors, chemists, and scavenging personnel.[12]

Reid's belief in the practical value of science and the importance of professional expertise in solving social problems stemmed from an early education that rejected the notion of "knowledge for its own sake." Born in London, Ontario, on 22 October 1836, Reid attended a private school in London until the age of twelve, when his father, a Scottish artisan who had emigrated to Upper Canada during the 1820s, took him out of school, complaining that he was not learning enough of practical benefit. Upon leaving school Alexander worked alongside his father as a cooper's assistant and pursued his education on his own. Picking out the subjects to be proficient in—Latin, algebra, geometry, and Greek—the young Alexander spent his unoccupied time in the morning and evening preparing for a useful career. In 1845 he enrolled in the Faculty of Medicine at McGill University, graduating four years later with the faculty's *materia medica* prize for his thesis on strychnia.

After graduation Reid spent a year of further study in Britain, returning to Canada in 1859 to practise medicine in Exeter and Clanboye near London, Ontario. Apparently, however, a rural practice in a frontier environment provided an insufficient challenge to Reid's scientific inquisitiveness and restless curiosity, and in the following year he closed his practice and began a journey across the continent and back. Travelling first to the Red River Settlement in the North-Western Territory, he dabbled in natural science, collecting information on skunks and the migration patterns of birds that formed the basis of a number of papers presented subsequently to the Nova Scotia Institute of Science. In 1861 he left the prairies for the Pacific coast, following it south to California. Although the American Civil War had already begun, Reid continued his travels, arriving in New York City sometime in 1862, where he undertook studies that led to another degree in medicine. In 1864 he journeyed to Halifax, and for the next fifty years he was a leading actor in the professionalization of medicine and psychiatry and a tireless advocate of closer ties between the state and the medical profession in public-health and social-reform matters.[13]

Reid arrived in Halifax in the midst of a movement to upgrade the professional and scientific status of the region's doctors. During the 1850s and 1860s the medical elite of Halifax was engaged in a program of professional self-improvement and reform that included the development of a provincial medical society (1854) and—with state assistance—the establishment of the Nova Scotia Hospital for the Insane (1859), the opening of the City and Provincial Hospital (1867), and the refinement of existing medical legislation. Within a few years of arriving in the city, Reid had become a prominent figure in the Halifax medical fraternity. He was a founding member of the Scientific Branch of the Halifax Medical Society in 1867, gained notoriety as the first proponent of the germ theory in Nova Scotia, and was founder and president of the Clinical Society of Halifax, established in 1869. His other pursuits included efforts to legalize dissection (resulting in the Anatomy Act of 1868), assistance in drafting the legislation of 1872 that gave the medical profession the right to self-regulation, and participation in the founding of the Dalhousie Medical Faculty in 1868 (subsequently the Halifax Medical College). Reid was the first dean of the faculty and later president of the Halifax Medical College, and held successively the chairs of physiology, practice of medicine, hygiene, and medical jurisprudence.[14]

Reid's continuing interest in the application of scientific knowledge to the management of society led him in 1878 to apply for and accept the position of superintendent at the Nova Scotia Hospital, usually referred to as the Mount Hope Asylum. Already exhibiting many of the assumptions of the late nineteenth-century progressive, including faith in progressive education and an antipathy to sectarian animosities, Reid referred in his letter of application to his long-term interest in the "progress of education," his opposition to unfortunate and unscientific religious sectarianism, and his attraction to the asylum as a laboratory for social reform. Asylum administration was a particularly significant vocation, he observed, because no other area within medicine offered a wider field for human observation or greater promise for developing scientific principles upon which a new social order could be established. Indeed, Reid's work at the hospital over the next decade and a half provided him with the opportunity to develop therapeutic principles that could be applied both to the treatment of the insane in Nova Scotia and more generally to the reshaping of Canadian industrial capitalism.[15]

In appointing Reid as superintendent, the province revealed its own interest in having the asylum run in a more efficient, businesslike, and scientific manner. Reid's predecessor at the hospital, Dr James R. DeWolfe, had been removed from his position after a commission of inquiry in 1878 raised questions about the treatment of patients under his care. DeWolfe also came under fire for providing liberally for his family, who lived with him on the hospital grounds.[16] Ironically, DeWolfe had at one time been a reformer in his own right. A graduate of Edinburgh Medical School, an institution widely noted for its humanitarian attitudes and its reliance upon moral treatment as an alternative to more Draconian forms of incarceration, DeWolfe regularly impressed upon his staff the virtues of non-restraint of the insane and the therapeutic value of work, religious instruction, and recreation. Other than this articulation of general principles, however, DeWolfe tended to let the institution run itself. His subordinates were not encouraged to bring specific concerns about the operation of the hospital before him, and his medical assistant, Dr Fraser, was once reported not to have conferred with DeWolfe for over four years. In the end the report of the commission occasioned a complete dismissal of all senior staff at the asylum, and led in turn to Reid's appointment as superintendent.[17]

Reid's approach to the treatment of the insane was very much in line with that of other North American asylum superintendents, who regarded hereditary predisposition and physical imperfections in the brain as the major causes of insanity. Concerned that moral treatment had no scientific basis and that asylum superintendents without a scientific therapeutic orientation were essentially indistinguishable from prison wardens, many late-nineteenth-century alienists sought a plausible scientific rationale for treatment that would both legitimize the profession and help to cure the insane. In search of a scientific explanation for insanity, therefore, Reid adhered to the prevalent somatic theory, which suggested that derangement originated in lesions of the brain or spinal cord. Like many of his contemporaries he attributed mental illness to physical disorders "of the higher ganglia of the nervous system . . . most frequently in their minute structure," the capillary vessels.[18] Just as the germ theory suggested the specificity of disease and hence of therapeutics, Reid believed that medical science would eventually be able to predict a particular lesion with a given case of insanity. Once that was done, the mental hospital would be in a position to establish effective therapy and liberate society from the burden of insanity. The institutionalization of the insane and the advancement of science would have served a social purpose: the cured would return to the workaday world normal and well adjusted.[19]

Unfortunately, the relationship between physical disorders and mental derangement could not be demonstrated scientifically. No matter how much asylum superintendents like Reid sought a somatic rationale for therapy, asylum care remained custodial. Somatic theory did little more than legitimize existing managerial techniques.[20] The therapeutic limitations of somaticism, moreover, help to explain Reid's continuing reliance on moral treatment during the 1880s, despite his growing discomfort with its seemingly unscientific basis. In his first annual report for the year 1878, Reid had outlined the kind of therapy generally provided at Mount Hope. Treatment included manual labour (including work in the garden or on the hospital farm, ditch digging, plastering, painting, and cleaning) and exercise and recreation (including walking, music, and dancing). Although religious instruction was usually a major component of moral treatment, Reid made no mention of it. Instead, he emphasized the need to acquire funds to improve the library, decorate the walls, and furnish improvements.[21] There is little indication that Reid's approach to treatment at Mount Hope changed over the next decade.

Reid did not rely totally on moral treatment of the insane, however. Like many of his contemporaries elsewhere in North America, he also advocated mild forms of restraint, which, he believed, would protect the insane from self-injury and ensured a more placid asylum community. Where James DeWolfe had relied upon solitary confinement and sedation to control potentially violent patients, Reid employed restraining devices such as the "muff," a canvas or leather muff secured to the hands, armless jackets and dresses, crib beds, and strong canvas bedcovers, calling restraint a necessary activity that "the higher faculties must exercise over the baser ones inherent in our common humanity." Mild restraint also served as an alternative to physical force, which, "if used with sufficient energy to keep a patient overpowered ... [the patient] suffers in many ways, of which broken ribs are not infrequent forms." It also rendered unnecessary both the use of sedatives, "which deaden or weaken rather than strengthen or benefit the debilitated nervous system," and solitary confinement, in which the abnormal imagination might conjure up fearful phantasms and frightful delusions.[22] In Reid's mind the role of the superintendent was to protect the insane from their own self-destructive tendencies with a minimum amount of physical coercion.

The notion that the weakest members of society had to be protected from themselves and prevented from undermining social cohesion was a recurring theme not only in Reid's therapeutic approach to insanity but in his larger social vision. To Reid insanity and mental weakness implied biological degeneracy, which, if left untreated and unmanaged, would retard social progress and the advance of civilization. Furthermore, in order to treat the insane and to ensure social improvement, it was essential to recognize the importance of heredity in human behaviour. In Reid's view the prime factor in cases of insanity was hereditary predisposition,[23] which posed particular problems for a province experiencing the initial incursions of modern industrial capitalism, as Nova Scotia was during the 1880s. Among other things, the demographic shift from countryside to town and city strained existing family units, reduced the respect for traditional forms of work, threatened the dignity of labour, altered gender relations, and set class against class. As Reid and like-minded progressives saw it, the great classes, held in organic harmony for centuries, were now being pulled asunder by the coming of industrial capitalism. What is more, the massive exodus from the Maritimes of those who could not be absorbed into the new industrial economy contributed to further social instability. Reid believed that this outmigration, which began in the 1870s and took on significant proportions in the years before the First World War, siphoned off those with the strongest nervous systems and thus exerted a degenerative influence on the province as a whole. Mental weakness, he argued, had been introduced into Nova Scotia from the "old countries" by the parent stock. Furthermore, because those with weak nervous systems lacked the drive "that impels the 'pushing class' . . . [to] go to foreign or distant parts to better their condition," they would stay in the province and continue to pass on their mental weakness to their offspring. Nova Scotia's insane population was thus bound to increase. Asylums would be forced to extend accommodation for the insane in an increasing ratio "until society solves the problem of how to prevent its natural increase."[24]

Reid's hereditarian ideas led him gradually to lose faith in the asylum's curative potential. As these institutions became filled with chronic patients, occupying spaces designed to accommodate those more amenable to treatment, effective treatment suffered. Overcrowding of this sort, of course, was a difficulty common to all asylums. In London, Ontario, Dr Richard Maurice Bucke, an acquaintance of Reid's, treated recent and chronic cases in separate buildings, as did a number of institutions in Britain and the United States.[25] Reid advocated the introduction of this widely touted "cottage system" to Nova Scotia and called in turn for an elaborate system of county asylums that would receive chronic patients and allow the provincial asylum to concentrate on those cases where the chances of successful treatment were higher. Unfortunately for Reid, the Nova Scotia government was then facing a severe fiscal crisis and could not act on his suggestions. County asylums were not developed in the province until the late 1880s.[26]

Reid's disillusionment with the therapeutic limitations of the asylum led him ultimately to propose a broader plan for dealing with the country's "unfit," "degenerate," "weak," and "impecunious" population. Although this plan included many objectionable suggestions, it none the less embodied a progressive faith in scientific management and social engineering. Reid argued for an alliance between the state and the scientific professions to regulate excessive competition in the marketplace and to provide the "respectable" poor with appropriate protection from exploitation and disease. A reformed social order, Reid believed, should include a system of marriage control or eugenics to stem social degeneracy, a greater involvement of the state in public-health matters, and a revamping of the existing capitalist system to eradicate destructive class conflict. Reid's blueprint for this new social system appeared in various medical periodicals, in a number of papers read to the Nova Scotia Institute of Natural Science, and in the publications arising out of his later career in public-health administration.

Reid's late-nineteenth-century efforts to extend medical authority beyond concerns of health and disease and into non-medical matters such as marriage control or economic regulation helped to rationalize what Robert Nye has called "the intrusive medicalization of the twentieth century welfare state."[27] As Nye has pointed out, medical advice in the late nineteenth century was growing in public esteem: progressive politicians, administrators, and jurists—themselves imbibing a faith in scientific expertise—increasingly turned to doctors to prescribe remedies for social ills. In explaining and offering remedies for alcoholism, prostitution, juvenile delinquency, and venereal disease, moreover, doctors like Reid often turned to contemporary degeneration theory and the idea of hereditary transmission for their inspiration. Finding examples of social and moral degeneration wherever he looked, Reid suggested that sanitary practice, expert management of the economy, and a program of scientific breeding or eugenics would stem the decline.

One of the more comprehensive statements of Reid's progressive utopianism can be found in "Stirpiculture or the Ascent of Man," a paper read before the Nova Scotia Institute of Natural Science in January 1890 and published the following year in pamphlet form for wider public distribution. Addressing the many influences that could alter what he called the "culture of the race," Reid pointed out that horticulturists and stock-breeders routinely applied Darwin's evolutionary principles to the improvement of the stock, and suggested a series of "laws" that should be followed to ensure the "ascent of man." These included the prevention of hereditary transmission of defective characteristics; the sanctity of the marriage bond and its home associations; a correct appreciation of the dignity of labour; moral training with fixed or positive religious ideas; a general and practical education; and definite instruction in sanitary laws. The first of these—the prevention of the hereditary transmission of congenital defects—was directed at what Reid called the "irresponsibles," which included the insane, the idiotic, and the criminal; the remainder were for the great bulk of humanity, those "moulded by . . . association and learning."[28]

Reid's hygienic utopia involved isolating and eventually eradicating "deviance" through selective breeding and sterilization. Reliance on marriage control and eugenics, he believed, would reduce the incidence of crime, and allow for a more efficient distribution of the state's resources. In addition, it would protect children from being born with the sins of their parents inflicted upon them.[29]

In his support for marriage control and eugenics, Reid was taking a position that had widespread support among medical men in the Maritimes and elsewhere. For example, when Reid left the Nova Scotia Hospital in 1894 to assume the position of superintendent of the Victoria General Hospital in Halifax, a successor as asylum superintendent, William Hattie, quickly revealed himself to be a staunch advocate of "scientific" marriage. In addition to arguing for legal restrictions upon "the marriage of the unfit," Hattie cautioned parents to take a rational rather than a sentimental approach to their children's marriages. Arguing that debilitating conditions such as tuberculosis or arthritis in parents tended to result in a lack of vigour in the nervous organization of their children, Hattie called for "the sacrifice of self as opposed to the sacrifice of offspring." In most cases, Hattie believed, moral suasion would suffice to prevent "promiscuous" or unsafe marriage. In the case of the feeble-minded, however, Hattie called for the legal prevention of their right to marry.[30] Dr A.B. Atherton of Fredericton was even more outspoken than Hattie. In his presidential address to the Maritime Medical Association in August 1907 Atherton expressed a widespread turn-of-the-century concern about the declining purity of the race and called for legislation to prevent the marriage of "those who are defective in physical and mental or perhaps even moral qualities." Society, Atherton argued, has a right and a responsibility to prevent diseased or defective individuals from transmitting defective characteristics "to a rising generation." In Atherton's opinion the insane, the feeble-minded, the diseased, and the chronic criminal "should be required to submit to sterilization."[31]

Marriage control and eugenics had a particular attraction to public-health advocates and asylum superintendents in the Maritimes, most of whom called for preventive measures both to protect against disease and degeneracy and to ensure physical and mental hygiene. Dr G.E. Coulthard, secretary to the New Brunswick Board of Health, for example, deplored the lack of attention given to the fight against tuberculosis and called for the prohibition of consumptives from travelling on buses, coaches, and railways. At the same time, he was convinced that TB sufferers passed on a damaged constitution to their offspring, and called for restrictions on their right to marry. If law-makers could prohibit drinking, he argued, surely they "could say authoritatively that these persons should not marry."[32] Other public-health officials and asylum superintendents in the Maritimes, such as George L. Sinclair, William Bayard, James T. Steeves, James A. Steeves, George Hetherington, Edward S. Blanchard, J.V. Anglin, and V.L. Goodwin, held similar views. Anglin stressed the need for the state and the churches to refuse marriage licences or to perform marriages "except in cases where there is reasonable prospect of healthy issue proceeding from such a marriage." James T. Steeves noted the need to prevent "neurotic subjects from . . . extending the volume of degeneracy down the path of human existence."[33] Similarly, Charlottetown's Dr Edward Blanchard, superintendent of the Prince Edward Island Hospital for the Insane, warned that insanity would increase as the struggle for living became more competitive and that the costs of sustaining the insane in institutions would eventually become prohibitive. Blanchard's solution was the complete asexualization of all who showed signs of mental and moral weakness.[34]

When pressed, advocates of the eugenicist solution defended their position as an expression of modern scientific principles, a necessary prerequisite to the new hygienic utopia. In supporting their case, moreover, they could draw upon the work of criminal anthropologists such as Cesare Lombroso, Enrico Ferri, Havelock Ellis, and Henry Maudsley, all of whom regarded crime as a symptom of degeneracy both in the individual and in society. The most influential of these quasi-scientific treatises was Lombroso's *Criminal Man* (1876), which defined crime as a function of the partly pathological and partly atavistic personality. Lombroso described the criminal as an atavistic being who revealed in his or her anti-social behaviour the ferocious instincts of primitive man and the inferior animals. Lombroso's theory also undertook to explain the apparent "stigmata of degeneration," the enormous jaws, large ears, drooping eyelids, and asymmetrical facial features that signified a criminal personality.[35] At the same time Lombroso suggested the possibility of scientific intervention to halt social decline and to encourage social regeneration. Indeed, despite its reactionary characteristics, Lombroso's new "science" of criminal anthropology proposed to reform an antiquated, unscientific, and retributive criminal justice system and replace it with a therapeutic and scientifically grounded legal system in which the expertise of the medical profession was essential.[36] Dr O.J. McCulley of Saint John, who shared Reid's progressive views and was an outspoken advocate of therapeutic justice, drew heavily upon Lombroso's writings. The criminal, wrote McCulley, "is morally infirm and we should treat him in the same spirit as we treat the physically infirm. . . . This must be done in no spirit of vindictiveness, with no mawkish sentimentality, but with scientific methods." These methods would be directed at transforming the criminal from an anti-social into a social being, and failing that preventing the propagation of the criminal's kind, through either sterilization or capital punishment.[37]

Like many progressives who feared social degeneracy, Reid also remained convinced of the possibility of social regeneration. In particular he believed that the state and the educational system could encourage moral improvement by inculcating Christian principles, instructing in the duties of citizenship, protecting society from disease through regular instruction in sanitary laws, and developing a state-supported system of public-health administration. Predictably, Reid took a leading role in the development of Nova Scotia's public health apparatus, assuming the position of secretary to the Provincial Board of Health in 1893. As the most active proponent of a progressive public-health system in the province, he continually encouraged his colleagues to enter the political arena in order to secure "a thorough, systematic, well-trained, and well-paid sanitary department"[38] and demanded greater involvement at all levels of government, from the province to the county to the municipality. What was needed, he argued, was for doctors to emulate the legal profession, where judges not only sat in high courts but in "every corner." Largely because of Reid's campaign, the provincial government abolished the Provincial Board of Health in 1903, replacing it with a Health Department under the provincial secretary and with a salaried executive officer known as the provincial health officer. Reid was the first to serve as health officer for the province, and continued in that position for another decade.[39]

Like many other progressive reformers in Canada and the United States, Reid's interest in the sanitary movement was coloured by deeply held nativist bias. Just as he had attributed the source of much mental weakness to people from the "old countries," Reid was convinced that immigration infected Canada with disease and class antagonism. In this he shared the sentiments of many of his colleagues, who believed that immigrants were usually from the "lower orders" and not only carried with them inherited or epidemic diseases but a "degraded moral nature derived from inherited tendency and criminal surroundings."[40] Canada, he believed, not only needed protection against insanity but against the degenerative impact of unrestricted immigration. In a paper in the *Maritime Medical News* for September 1899 entitled "Sanitary Progress," Reid drew upon a biblical analogy in order to demonstrate how prophylactic principles could result in the "uplifting of society." The mission of Moses, the law-giver, Reid argued, was to elevate his followers to a higher level, to turn an "ignorant, diseased, immoral, irreligious and effeminate" race of slaves whose highest ambitions were "the fleshpots of Egypt" into a liberated people. To achieve this objective a plan in "harmony with . . . present knowledge" was applied. The Israelites were quarantined in the desert; the diseased were placed outside the camp and were prohibited communication with the healthy. Moses, Reid wrote, "took forty years to accomplish a journey easily made in forty hours, and this was the secret of his success." Because every individual who left Egypt, even Moses himself, died before the entry into the promised land, the new race was composed of individuals sprung from the best of the old stock brought up under the best sanitary surroundings, trained and educated, and made to conform to very strict sanitary regulations.[41] The point of this allegory is clear: Reid considered scientific expertise, immigration restriction, and an effective public-health apparatus essential to the process of social regeneration.

The final component of Reid's progressive reform vision involved the reconstruction of the existing capitalist system in accordance with the principles of scientific management, state regulation, efficient production, and co-operative enterprise. Reid was particularly critical of an excessively competitive marketplace, which created a great gulf between wealth and poverty and led to destructive class conflict. At the same time he found business organization to be unscientific, irrational, and biased towards the powerful. In Nova Scotia, for example, the province's underdeveloped business class not only lacked technical and theoretical knowledge but, in competing with more industrialized areas, was rendered ineffective by its insufficient access to capital. Reid thus forecast limited industrial growth for the Maritime provinces in the future and argued for the exploitation of the natural advantages that the region had in its primary-resource sector. In a speech to the Dairymen's Association of Nova Scotia in 1890, for example, he outlined the problems confronting an inefficient regional dairy industry as it faced competition from large oleo-margarine producers elsewhere in the country, and suggested the development of production and marketing co-operatives. "Experience has dissipated a fond delusion I had in the efficiency of joint stock companies," Reid wrote. "The capital is apt to be limited and as well uselessly dissipated by want of skill in the directorate board, or the promoters—technical ability is too apt to be measured by the number of friends the applicant may have on the board of directors."

Instead, Reid favoured the co-operative ownership of the dairy industry by the producers themselves. These co-operatives could be established through the introduction of a toll system, in which a farmer would give a percentage of raw material to the state in return for the capital required to produce and market dairy products.[42]

Some years earlier Reid had applied a similar analysis to the fishing industry, emphasizing the importance of state support and scientific practice in developing the resource. Fishermen who followed the practical man's "rule of thumb" in catching, curing, and selling fish, Reid argued, failed to appreciate the very important economic potential of increased scientific knowledge of the life cycle, feeding habits, and food chain of marine species. To improve the understanding of market conditions and to stimulate scientific research, Reid called for an academy of science—either state-operated or privately endowed—which would increase scientific understanding and "eliminate the theory of chance and the so-called bad years from the list of probabilities." In addition he advocated more emphasis on natural science in the school curriculum, called for greater state assistance in promoting an equivalent to agricultural co-operatives for the fishing industry, and proposed a marine aquarium that, in educating youth about the animals that contributed to the region's prosperity, would establish a foundation of "provincial greatness."[43]

In general Reid saw a future in which a benevolent state and a cadre of professional experts would put science before profit, thus replacing competitive individualism with expert management. The result would be economic prosperity, social justice, and class peace. This was the theme of Reid's *Poverty Superseded: A New Political Economy for Canada* (1891), which, in calling for a reorganization of the capitalist marketplace, laid down a rationale for the modern Canadian welfare state. Drawing heavily from both Henry George's analysis of the antagonistic character of progress in *Progress and Poverty* and the scientific utopianism of Edward Bellamy's *Looking Backward*, Reid began his study of existing political economy with a critique of competitive individualism and the emerging credit system. The inevitable result of the free market, he suggested, was inequality, for even if the economic race were adjusted to the point of equality, some would soon come to dominate it. Most individuals were skilled producers when operating under the guidance of skilled administrators, he believed, but few had the mental ability to command and direct economic affairs. As a small number of effective managers succeeded, therefore, their success encouraged others to enter into competition, which in turn led to diminishing profits and the failure of many businesses.

The difficulties faced by the weak in the competitive marketplace, Reid argued, led naturally to the emergence of the credit system, which he saw as a major social and economic evil. To Reid, credit led to indulgence in unnecessary luxuries and encouraged the less judicious to live beyond their means. In the long run this would increase the difficulty of the debtor as it enhanced the power of the creditor. Taken together, competitive individualism and the credit system meant wealth for the few and poverty for the many. *Poverty Superseded* tried to address this dichotomy by having the state assume the care of the weak. Reid wrote:

> Since the Government, local or general, must assume the care of the impecunious or incapable, it should have the right to direct to some extent the way the earnings of the community are disposed of, and this leads to the principle underlying Communism, a principle not so much questioned as the methods designed to carry it out. This is very well worked out by Bellamy in his *Looking Backward*, and also to a certain extent by Henry George in his *Progress and Poverty*. General Booth deals with this problem but his plan is rather adapted to relieve present want, immorality and crime than a method which would eliminate them.

In addition to abolishing laws providing for the collection of debts—which he believed would destroy the credit system—Reid suggested that the state be given the right to collect a percentage of the income of every wage-earner, male or female, which then would be placed to his or her credit at interest, dispensed by the state if the person needed relief. But if a person was required to set aside a percentage of his earnings, he asked, did it not follow that he or she should be assured a continuous means of earning? In Reid's view the state should be held responsible for ensuring full employment, and this could be achieved through the introduction of public works programs funded in part by the revenues collected from wage-earners. In this way, he argued, "the whole country ... would become a mutual benefit society."[44]

While arguing for a society run on co-operative principles rather than upon the doctrine of competitive individualism, Reid was none the less careful to point out that state regulation should not threaten the principle of private ownership of the means of production. In Reid's view the state should operate merely as a medium of regulation, transferring wealth to those who needed assistance. It was not desirable, Reid argued, that it interfere with or attempt to control the trade or business of the country in any way. In the case of industrial stagnation, however, the state could act as a reservoir into which surplus products would flow and from which they would then flow out again when a demand arose. At the same time, government should be given the power to curtail production when the supply of particular commodities far exceeded demand, and be empowered to direct labour into some other channel. In this way the state would "relieve the misery which *strikes, lockouts,* or *clogged markets* impose on the wage earner."[45]

Reid's desire to have the state actively engaged in protecting the economic interests of the weak also led him to call for a government-sponsored system of general life insurance. This was by no means an original notion: Charles Tupper, for example, had once supported the idea but chose not to act upon it owing to the opposition of private insurance companies. Reid argued, however, that the good of society was of greater importance than the selfish interests of private capital. "The management of a country," he wrote, "cannot be run solely in the interest of these financial corporations." At present, Reid pointed out, it was only the well-off who patronized these companies, and they should be encouraged to continue to do so. It was the poorer classes who needed state protection. A government scheme, therefore, should insure applicants only to a necessary minimum level, thereby allowing for the continuing profitability of private companies.[46]

In calling for the remodelling of Canadian capitalism along progressive lines, Reid was convinced that he was transcending the class interests of capital, replacing competitive individualism with a more scientific, responsible, and benevolent social order. "So far society has depended upon the ability of the individual to manage the increasing mass of labour and as might have been expected the individual works chiefly for his personal gain," wrote Reid, "and wielding those powerful engines—capital and combination—the ideal state of society . . . has been obliterated." The concentration of economic power in the hands of a few, moreover, carried with it the heavy price of enduring class conflict and interrupted production. Strikes paralysed society, and the capitalists reacted with violence to suppress workers. This kind of disorder, Reid concluded, would continue until "society as represented by Government, undertakes—I would say is forced to undertake—the regulation of industry."[47] It would be more than a decade, however, before the kind of progressive view of labour–management relations that Reid subscribed to would gain political currency in Canada. Even then the commitment to a tripartite resolution of labour disputes—one that involved the participation of the state, the business class, and labour and was enshrined in legislation like the Industrial Disputes and Investigations Act of 1907—served the interests of capitalists more than it did those of working people.[48]

Although many of Reid's ideas—particularly his eugenicist notions— were never acted upon, his call for the reform of Canadian society along progressive lines reveals a growing belief in the need for a scientific solution to the problems besetting late nineteenth-century capitalist society.[49] In calling for the rehabilitation of the capitalist system, for an increased state involvement in public-health matters, and an increasing respect for the social value of professional expertise, Reid shared many of the assumptions of those turn-of-the-century progressive reformers who were discarding Spenserian notions of "survival of the fittest" in favour of the doctrine of social responsibility and moral regeneration. Reid's veneration of science, his faith in the wisdom of the medical profession, and his commitment to the medicalization of social problems that had long been the responsibility of other institutions, moreover, helped to shape his vision of a future hygienic utopia, free of poverty, crime, disease, and class antagonism.

Reid's progressive vision, which included a commitment to what Christopher Lasch has called the modern "therapeutic state,"[50] grew out of his work in medicine, the asylum, and the field of public health. His faith in medical science and its practical application led him to advocate an enhanced role for the professional expert in the articulation of social policy. His experience as an asylum superintendent was also important here, reinforcing his concerns about biological and social degeneracy and confirming his belief that the diseased society, like the diseased mind and body, needed the therapeutic intervention of the scientific practitioner. To Reid the eradication of mental disorder through selective breeding and eugenics was a scientific and even humanitarian policy, and like efficient public-health initiatives promised a hygienic and prosperous future. Reid's work and writings, like those of many reformers in the Maritimes and elsewhere, moreover, helped to shape the emerging progressive reform impulse and contributed to the emergence of that new managerial class of benevolent experts that attached itself to the developing welfare state. Unfortunately, Reid's faith in science "practically applied" led not to utopia but instead to the new form of expert management—often hostile to traditions of self-help and more radical forms of social criticism—that has accompanied the coming of welfare-state capitalism in the twentieth century.

NOTES

1. See, for example, C. David Naylor, *Private Practice, Public Payment: Canadian Medicine and the Politics of Health Insurance 1911–1966* (Montreal: McGill-Queen's University Press, 1986), and Malcolm G. Taylor, *Health Insurance and Canadian Public Policy: The Seven Decisions That Created the Canadian Health Insurance System* (Montreal: McGill Queen's University Press, 1978).

2. Samuel P. Hays, *The Response to Industrialization: 1885–1914* (Chicago: University of Chicago Press, 1957); Robert Wiebe, *Businessmen and Reform* (Cambridge: Harvard University Press, 1962); Samuel Haber, *Efficiency and Uplift: Scientific Management in the Progressive Era* (Chicago: University of Chicago Press, 1964); James Weinstein, *The Corporate Ideal in the Liberal State* (Boston: Beacon Press, 1968). For Canada, see Robert Craig Brown and Ramsay Cook, *Canada 1896–1921* (Toronto: McClelland & Stewart, 1974).

3. Burton J. Bledstein, *The Culture of Professionalism: The Middle Class and the Development of Higher Education in America* (New York: W.W. Norton, 1976), and Thomas Haskell, *The Emergence of Professional Social Science* (Urbana: University of Illinois Press, 1977).

4. Samuel P. Hays, "The Politics of Reform in Municipal Government in the Progressive Era," *Pacific Northwest Quarterly* 55 (1964): 157–69; Stanley Schultz and Clay McShane, "To Engineer the Metropolis: Sewers, Sanitation, and City Planning in Late Nineteenth Century America," *Journal of American History* 65 (1978): 389–411; Reginald Whitaker, "The Liberal Corporatist Ideas of Mackenzie King," *Labour/Le Travailleur* 2 (1977): 137–69; Alfred Chandler, *The Visible Hand: The Managerial Revolution in American Business* (Cambridge: Harvard University Press, 1977); H.V. Nelles, *The Politics of Development* (Toronto: Macmillan, 1974).

5. George Rosen, "The Efficiency Criterion in Medical Care, 1900–1920," *Bulletin of the History of Medicine* 50 (1976): 28–44; Barbara Gutmann Rosenkrantz, *Public Health and the State: Changing Views in Massachusetts, 1842–1936* (Cambridge: Harvard University Press, 1972); Heather MacDougall, "The Genesis of Public Health Reform in Toronto, 1869–1890," *Urban History Review* 10, 3 (1982); and "Public Health and the 'Sanitary Idea' in Toronto, 1866–1890" in *Essays in the History of Canadian Medicine*, ed. Wendy Mitchinson and Janice Dickin McGinniss (Toronto: McClelland & Stewart, 1986), 62–87;

Colin Howell, "Reform and the Monopolistic Impulse: The Professionalization of Medicine in the Maritimes," *Acadiensis* 11, 1 (Autumn 1981): 3–22.

6. Howard Segal, *Technological Utopianism in American Culture* (Chicago: University of Chicago Press 1985).

7. T.W. Acheson, "The National Policy and the Industrialization of the Maritimes," *Acadiensis* 1, 2 (Spring 1978): 3–28.

8. J.B. Black, MD, MP, "Race Suicide with Suggestions of Some Remedies," *Maritime Medical News* 19, 7 (July 1907): 248–49.

9. Robert A. Nye, *Crime, Madness, and Politics in Modern France: The Medical Concept of National Decline* (Princeton, NJ: Princeton University Press, 1984). On the idea of degeneracy see Ruth Friedlander, "Benedict-Augustin Morel and the Development of the Theory of Degenerescence" (PhD diss., University of California, 1983); Richard Walker, "What Became of the Degenerate? A Brief History of a Concept," *Journal of the History of Medicine and Allied Sciences* 11, 4 (1956): 422–29.

10. There is no comprehensive treatment of the idea of degeneracy in Canada. Samuel E.D. Shortt, *Victorian Lunacy: Richard Bucke and the Practice of Late Nineteenth Century Psychiatry* (Cambridge: Cambridge University Press, 1986), 99–103, provides a brief summary of the concept.

11. On the origins of the welfare state in Canada, see Allen Moscovitch and Jim Albert, eds., *The Benevolent State: The Growth of Welfare in Canada* (Toronto: Garland, 1987).

12. J.H. Cassidy, "Hygiea: A Mid-Victorian Dream of a City of Health," *Journal of the History of Medicine and Allied Sciences* 17, 2 (April 1962): 217–18.

13. Public Archives of Nova Scotia (hereafter PANS), Vertical File, "Alexander Reid"; Henry Morgan,

Canadian Men and Women of the Time (Toronto, 1898), 850.

14. Colin D. Howell, "Elite Doctors and the Development of Scientific Medicine: The Halifax Medical Establishment and 19th Century Professionalism" in *Health, Disease, and Medicine: Essays in Canadian History*, ed. Charles G. Roland (Toronto, 1984), 105–22.

15. Alexander Reid to Hon. P.C. Hill, Provincial Secretary, 29 Dec. 1877, PANS, Nova Scotia Hospital Records, RG 25A, vol. 16.

16. *Acadian Recorder*, 6 April, 15 May 1878.

17. Ibid., 11 April 1878.

18. 22nd Annual Report, Medical Superintendent, Nova Scotia Hospital, *Journals and Proceedings of the House of Assembly of the Province of Nova Scotia* (hereafter *JHA*) 1880, app. 3, p. 5.

19. Ibid., 6–10.

20. L.S. Jacyna, "Somatic Theories of Mind and the Interests of Medicine in Britain, 1850–1879," *Medical History* 26, 3 (1982): 233–58.

21. 21st Annual Report, Medical Superintendent, Nova Scotia Hospital, *JHA* 1879, app. 3, pp. 4–6.

22. 22nd Annual Report, Medical Superintendent, Nova Scotia Hospital, ibid., 1880, app. 3, pp. 7–10.

23. 25th Annual Report, Medical Superintendent, Nova Scotia Hospital, ibid., 1883, p. 7.

24. Ibid.; Alan A. Brookes, "Out-Migration from the Maritime Provinces, 1860–1900: Some Preliminary Considerations," *Acadiensis* 5, 2 (Spring 1976): 26–55.

25. Cheryl Krasnick, "'In Charge of the Loons': A Portrait of the London, Ontario, Asylum for the Insane in the Nineteenth Century," *Ontario History* 74, 3 (1982): 143.

26. The fiscal crisis is dealt with in Colin D. Howell, "W.S. Fielding and the Repeal Elections of 1886 and 1887 in

Nova Scotia," *Acadiensis* 8, 2 (Spring 1979): 28–46.

27. Nye, *Crime, Madness, and Politics*.

28. Alexander P. Reid, *Stirpiculture and the Ascent of Man* (Halifax: T.C. Allen, 1890), 4.

29. Ibid., 6. The history of the eugenics movement is touched upon in a number of sources. See in particular Mark Haller, *Eugenics: Hereditarian Attitudes in American Thought* (New Brunswick, NJ: Rutgers University Press, 1963); Donald Pickens, *Eugenics and the Progressives* (Nashville: Vanderbilt University Press, 1968); Kenneth Ludmerer, *Genetics and American Society: A Historical Appraisal* (Baltimore: Johns Hopkins University Press, 1972); Angus McLaren and Arlene Tigar McLaren, *The Bedroom and the State* (Toronto: McClelland & Stewart, 1986); Charles Rosenberg, "The Bitter Fruit: Heredity, Disease, and Social Thought in 19th Century America," *Perspectives in American History* (Cambridge: Harvard University Press, 1974), 8: 189–235.

30. W.H. Hattie, "The Prevention of Insanity," *Maritime Medical News* 16, 2 (Feb. 1904): 41–48.

31. A.B. Atherton, "Presidential Address to the Maritime Medical Association," *Maritime Medical News* 19, 8 (July 1907): 247–54. Atherton even added cured tuberculosis patients to the list of those who should be prevented from siring children. "Even if cured," he asked, "why should they be allowed to bring children into the world who will inherit a . . . pronounced tendency to the same disease?"

32. 8th Annual Report of the Provincial Board of Health, New Brunswick, *JHA* 1895.

33. Report of the Medical Superintendent of the Provincial Hospital, ibid., 1914.

34. Ibid., 1893.

35. Gina Lombroso Ferrero, ed., with an introduction by Cesare Lombroso, *Criminal Man According to the Classification of Cesare Lombroso* (New York, 1911). See also Henry Maudsley, *The Physiology and Pathology of Mind* (London: Macmillan, 1867).

36. See, e.g., Enrico Ferri, *Criminal Sociology* (New York, 1897).

37. O.J. McCulley, "The Doctor and the Criminal," Presidential Address to the Saint John Medical Society, *Maritime Medical News* 17 (Feb. 1905): 41–53. McCulley's address, which received the unqualified endorsement of the Saint John Medical Society, included a long disquisition on the physical indications of degeneracy and the hereditary predisposition to crime.

38. A.P. Reid, "The Relations of the Profession to Society," *Maritime Medical News* 1, 5 (July 1889): 102–3.

39. "The Nova Scotia Public Health Association," *Maritime Medical News* 19, 4 (April 1907): 128; "The Public Health Act of Nova Scotia," ibid., 18, 6 (July 1906): 216–20.

40. Dr Edward Farrell, "President's Address before the Annual Meeting of the Maritime Medical Association," *Maritime Medical News* 7, 8 (1895): 162–63.

41. Alexander Reid, "Sanitary Progress," *Maritime Medical News* 2, 9 (Sept. 1899): 301–8.

42. A.P. Reid, "The Dairy of the Future— or—Theory and Practise Combined," paper read before the Dairyman's Association, Halifax, 18 May 1889 (Halifax: T.C. Allen, 1890).

43. A.P. Reid, "Natural History of the Fisheries," *Proceedings and Transactions of the Nova Scotia Institute of Science, Halifax, Nova Scotia* 4, 2 (1875–76): 131–36.

44. A.P. Reid, *Poverty Superseded: A New Political Economy for Canada* (Halifax: T.C. Allen, 1891), 7.

45. Ibid., 10.

46. Ibid., 11.

47. Ibid., 15.

48. For a discussion of the impact of the IDIA on labour–management relations, see Ian McKay, "Strikes in the

Maritimes, 1901–1914," *Acadiensis* 13, 1 (Autumn 1983): 40–43.

49. For a discussion of the growth of a scientific progressivism and its relationship to an earlier ethical and Christian progressivism, see David B. Danborn, *'The World of Hope': Progressivism and the Struggle for Ethical Public Life* (Philadelphia: Temple University Press, 1987), and Ramsay Cook, *The Regenerators: Social Criticism in Late Victorian Canada* (Toronto: University of Toronto Press, 1985).

50. Christopher Lasch, *The Culture of Narcissism: Life in an Age of Diminishing Expectations* (New York: W.W. Norton, 1978).

2

PATTERNS OF EARLY
STATE INTERVENTION

○

P rior to World War II, government welfare was distributed both grudgingly and haphazardly. Admittedly, provincial and federal politicians were constrained by limited revenue, but they usually subscribed to the ethos that "big government" would bring unmanageable debt, damage business prospects, and, in the realm of social welfare, create a dependent and unproductive population.

Among the most severely affected by this parsimony was Canada's Native population. As the article by Vanast shows, even those spared by geographic isolation from overt pressure to assimilate confronted government officials so eager to minimize costs and so inured to paternalistic notions about the ability of welfare to corrupt this "child" race, that the results nearly engendered genocide. But this treatment, while reprehensible and intensified by prejudice, was, in general terms, not unique in the very limited realm of early social welfare. Indeed, as Desmond Morton makes clear, not even Canada's returned heroes from the Great War were immune from the miserly conduct of government, despite Ottawa's very public promises to help them reintegrate. While the measures introduced established important precedents in areas such as health care, so far as veterans themselves were concerned, most of the war disabled had good reason to feel resentment over a package obviously conceived with an eye toward cost control and supposedly preventing their enfeeblement. Meanwhile, when it came to Canada's elderly, for whom there was supposedly greater respect in bygone days, the prevailing view among legislators was that their care should be a family and not state responsibility. Not until 1927 did Ottawa implement a shared-cost old age pension scheme with the provinces. During its first quarter-century of operation, this plan provided a paltry sum to those over seventy who could show a certain level of destitution—a stinginess that, as James Snell writes, was actually exceeded in the semi-autonomous Dominion of Newfoundland and became one of the reasons why its people opted for confederation with Canada in 1949.

Some scholars, noting the antipathy of governments toward welfare during this time, approached many of the initiatives rather cynically, claiming that they derived from an agenda having little to do with beneficence. Robert Babcock, besides examining the issue about whether the Canadian approach in this field diverged much from the American experience, covers the considerable academic debate revolving around the introduction of workers' compensation legislation in several states and provinces. Support, he notes, came from organized labour and reform elements desiring to alleviate the repercussions of a rising industrial accident rate; but also, in some jurisdictions, businessmen led the charge to avoid the possibility of hefty court settlements should a worker's injury be attributed to their negligence. Mixed motivations, writes Veronica Strong-Boag, also lay behind the support for mothers' allowances. Prompted by casualties from the Great War, five provinces, between 1916 and 1920, introduced legislation to assist widowed mothers. By 1937, the program had spread nationwide and usually added to the list of recipients women married to the insane, the seriously ill, or the imprisoned, and in some areas, those who had been deserted by their husbands. While the legislation helped many avoid the placement of their children in foster homes or with adoption agencies, it also, insists Strong-Boag, was used as a control mechanism to strengthen traditional standards of propriety, including the notion of women having their proper sphere. Funds were commonly denied to the divorced or to those who gave birth out of wedlock. All recipients were subject to visits from government employees whose job was to ensure that the women behaved as appropriate guardians—a practice that continued until the allowances ceased when the child reached school-leaving age. Such actions buttressed the belief that a woman's worth primarily related to her role as caregiver.

The idea that welfare should reinforce the traditional social and moral fabric was also, asserts Rebecca Coulter, evident with the initial policies governing juvenile delinquents, a group who, in the early-twentieth-century city, had become a major source of concern. Focussing her attention upon the Alberta experience, she finds, in addition to an idealistic "child-saving" ethos among numerous reformers, a desire by the state to impose strict controls over wayward youth so they not become a social threat. Nonetheless this was to be done in a way that would minimize costs and not see the government displace the family unit, something which, it was contended, would bring social disintegration.

While the general rise of urban industrial society and the social dislocations caused by the Great War moved more Canadians toward acceptance of state intervention and welfare, this process was undoubtedly intensified by the Great Depression of 1929–1939. As chronicled by several scholars,[1] the slow and niggardly response of politicians to alleviate suffering gave rise to a number of third parties and charismatic figures both at the national and provincial level, preaching various panaceas usually through large-scale economic intervention. In Quebec, for instance, the Union Nationale overwhelmed the Taschereau Liberals because, as B.L. Vigod writes, the latter, while willing to experiment economically to some degree, still proved trapped by old theories and suspicions. By 1938, the King government, in responding to public pressure, began practising deficit financing—a process that, during the Second World War, blossomed into full-fledged Keynesian-type planning—not to mention implementing the universality principle with some social welfare.

Like the articles in this section, the papers in the final three sections exhibit much disagreement over the goals and effects of later and more comprehensive policies. Were they grounded in idealism, and did they prove meaningful to the masses, or did they constitute a minimal response to mollify citizens into accepting a socio-economic system still fundamentally geared for the benefit of the few?

NOTES

1. See John Herd Thompson and Allen Seager, *Canada, 1922–1939: Decades of Discord* (Toronto: McClelland & Stewart, 1985), and H. Blair Neatby, *The Politics of Chaos* (Toronto: Copp Clark Pitman, 1982).

"HASTENING THE DAY OF EXTINCTION": CANADA, QUEBEC, AND THE MEDICAL CARE OF UNGAVA'S INUIT, 1867–1967[*]

WALTER J. VANAST

o

Dr B.H. Hamilton, government physician to Canada's James Bay Cree Indians, was at a loss. In the summer of 1930, on the southwest shore of the Ungava Peninsula, he encountered destitute families over whose care he had no jurisdiction. Many were ill, poorly dressed, and undernourished. Disregarding criticism he might well receive from his Ottawa superiors, he provided medical help and distributed clothing and food. At Great Whale River (Kuujjuaraapik), he cared at length for fourteen-year-old Isaac Mikpighak. Jagged ends of bone protruded through an open wound on the boy's arm. To ensure recovery, Hamilton brought his patient south to his own Moose Factory residence. From a humanitarian point of view, the doctor's trip north was clearly satisfactory: he had accomplished a great deal. His care of Mikpighak, however, precipitated an administrative nightmare that affected the health of Ungava's coastal inhabitants for decades.

In setting Mikpighak's fractured arm, Hamilton had stepped outside his assigned responsibilities. The destitute coastal residents he had looked after were not Indians; they were Inuit. Barely surviving on Ungava's treeless shores, they hunted increasingly rare land and marine mammals. Long before Hamilton's visit, reports of high death rates and widespread disease had reached the South. Yet neither Canada nor the Province of Quebec to which—by federal fiat—their terrain had belonged since 1912, would assume responsibility for their care. Why that situation came about, what it led to, and how it was resolved is the subject of this article.

---

[*] From *Études Inuit Studies* 15 (1991): 55–84. Reprinted with the permission of the journal.

Of necessity, much of the material presented here refers to hunger, malnutrition, sickness, physical suffering, and premature death. Thus, by nature of the subject, the discussion at once takes on a note of pathos. As a result, some readers may anticipate a foregone conclusion: that governments failed to intervene because of a deliberate policy designed to effect the disappearance of Ungava's Inuit. That this was not the case will become more than evident. This article, in other words, is not an attempt to write northern colonial history in the style Gérard Duhaime described as *lecture machiavélique* or *analyse manichéiste*.[1]

Much as one would like to escape that and other pejorative labels, there are times when historical documents make it difficult not to portray a tawdry picture. Put another way, even when one tries very hard to avoid the "Century of Shame" approach, the North occasionally presents us with stories that remain highly unflattering to many of its southern participants. The evolution of European medical services in Ungava is a case in point.[2]

Although Ungava provides an exquisitely documented case study of the politics of health care provision to a North American indigenous society, medical historians have largely ignored such "internal colony" or "Fourth World" settings.[3] Several recent works, however, point to a new interest in postcontact conditions among Canada's original northern peoples. T. Kue Young's 1988 study of the relationship between subarctic cultural change and health conditions provides a welcome initiative. Anne Keenleyside has examined the effects of whaling on Inuit health.[4] I have reviewed the role of northern Oblate hospitals[5] and explored European attitudes to traditional Inuit healing methods.[6] In collaboration with myself,[7] the National Film Board of Canada has just released a documentary study of tuberculosis among the Coppermine Inuit in the late 1920s.[8] Clearly, public and scholarly interest in the medical history of the North is increasing.

"SQUALID, STARVED, MISERABLE NATIVES": EARLY MEDICAL CONDITIONS AMONG UNGAVA'S INUIT

Like most of the mainland of what is now Canada, Ungava was once part of Rupert's Land, a vast domain consisting of all territory draining into Hudson Bay and adjacent waters.[9] From 1670 on, through rights acquired by Charter from the British Crown, the Hudson's Bay Company exercised a trade monopoly in the region. Post managers had absolute rule over Inuit and Indians. In practice, little of that changed in 1870 when Britain awarded Rupert's Land to the three-year-old (and still tiny) Canadian nation.

When Britain created Canada in 1867, it assigned Indian affairs to federal administration. The enabling legislation (the British North America Act) did not mention Inuit: not a single one lived in the southerly terrain that then constituted the new country. Later, as the young nation acquired its northern possessions (Rupert's Land and the North West Territories in the 1870s, the Arctic Archipelago in 1880), no one thought to correct the omission. Thus, no formal mechanism came into being that would shield

Canada's Inuit from the ill effects of European invasion. That a need for such protection existed even then is abundantly clear from the eyewitness reports from the Ungava region.

Already, fur traders had changed the lifestyle of Ungava's Inuit immensely. Tea, tobacco, and flour had become staples. Rather than hunt only what a traditional family had always required, Inuit now trapped and killed to establish credit at outsiders' stores. Seal, walrus, and caribou declined in numbers. Once disturbed, the fragile ecology of Ungava's desperately poor terrain failed its human population. Malnutrition lowered resistance to illness, while contact with whites exposed Inuit to diseases they had never known and to which they were highly susceptible. Often, infection slew hunters in the full vigour of life. As early as 1872, Father Charles Arnaud, a Roman Catholic missionary, noted six impoverished widows at the Fort Chimo (Kuujjuaq) trading post near southwestern Ungava Bay. Some were sick and greatly debilitated; others were about to become so through the "twin ravages" of hunger and despair, both clearly visible on their faces.[10]

Tuberculosis, contemporary medical opinion notwithstanding, lost none of its virulence once unleashed in the Far North.[11] On Dead Man's Island in Hudson Bay, members of Canada's 1884 arctic expedition saw the dread word "consumption" carved into wooden headboards on the graves of young New England whalers.[12] But the expedition leader, a man with degrees in both medicine and geology, did not determine if the disease affected Inuit. On Ungava's northern shore, he and his fellow officers encountered a sick woman on what turned out to be her deathbed. No one deigned to examine her: all feared she might have lice. Just a few years later, in the same location, a visiting Catholic priest remarked how few Native families he encountered.[13] Because of disease, they were disappearing with "frightening speed." He accomplished little beyond "the baptism of a few dying infants."

Reverend E.J. Peck, Anglican missionary in the Great Whale River (Kuujjuaraapik) area in the 1880s, had more success in finding candidates for conversion. The high prevalence of tuberculosis helped his evangelizing efforts: ill Inuit seemed eager to avow their acceptance of Christian faith. But high mortality kept the nucleus of professed church members to a minimum. In rapid succession Peck lost his first three Native catechists to consumption. Many of the friends he had made were soon "cut down."[14] The resourceful minister tried to see events in the best possible Christian light, but there is little doubt of his discouragement. His seeming victories for God did not diminish the magnitude of the medical disaster he was witnessing.

Peck did more than hand out bibles and platitudes. Decent food and the ministrations of a doctor, he recognized, might well assist divine intervention. He shared what limited provisions he could. When little Joseph Ryjack (who had lost his mother to disease but a short time earlier) developed symptoms of tuberculosis, Peck took him five hundred miles south from Great Whale River to the only doctor in the region. At Moose Factory, a major trading depot, the Hudson's Bay Company staff doctor ministered to the boy's needs. Rapid consumption, nevertheless, soon led to Joseph's death.[15] In that he received medical care, he was most certainly an exception. Ungava had no resident doctor until 1967, eighty years later.

Canada, preoccupied with development of its southern terrain, treated its Arctic with almost willful neglect. Only threats to its northern sovereignty, particularly from the United States, stimulated interest.[16] First discovery of land, the nation learned to its consternation, did not ensure possession. Indeed, by international law, ownership lapsed in the absence of active occupation. Canada's answer was to send not doctors and nurses (as Denmark had done in Greenland) or teachers (as was the American approach in Alaska), but policemen. Establishment of northern police posts—adjacent to points of entry used by foreign ships—served to show the flag near remote terrain whose Canadian ownership might well be questioned. In 1905, when Ottawa appointed a commissioner for the North West Territories, it chose a senior officer of the North West Mounted Police. He took no action to safeguard Native well-being, despite receiving detailed reports of widespread illness. Nor, between 1905 and 1921, did he venture from Ottawa to witness the Inuit's rapidly changing lifestyle and shrinking numbers.[17] In particular, he learned nothing of the profound needs on the Ungava peninsula.

Remote from medical care, unaware of the value of quarantine measures, Ungava's Inuit continued to succumb to acute infectious diseases.[18] Lack of health care for the region astounded visiting geologists and naturalists, many of them Americans. C.K. and A.T. Leith, travelling near Great Whale River in 1911, wondered how the Hudson's Bay Company could have so much control, yet provide so little medical assistance. Tuberculosis was prevalent, but "entirely ignored." The only recognition that such illness existed on the part of Company men was the euphemistic comment that "so and so has a sore chest and cannot do as much as he used to." There was not a single doctor on all of Hudson Bay. Post managers tried to help severe cases of illness with a small stock of patent medicines and advice from outdated popular medical guides—Great Whale River's had been printed in Britain in 1787.[19]

Insinuation of Christian religious tenets into long-held spiritual concepts, combined with the stress of hunger and disease, led to violence and mental illness. One Native, the Leiths reported, killed seven women and children before he himself succumbed to hunger. Another, near Richmond Gulf (Umiujaq), murdered thirteen Inuit. At Great Whale River, a deranged man uttered "terrible threats" that made the community live in fear. Given the circumstances, there seemed "no alternative but to shoot persons of this kind, as one would a mad dog."[20]

In 1912, Ottawa allowed Quebec to extend its northern border to the salt waters of Hudson Bay and Hudson Strait. The Ungava Peninsula, soon known as "Nouveau-Québec," provided the province with territory several times as large as that within its 1867 borders.[21] Law enforcement, health care, and relief provision for the region now came under provincial, rather than federal legislation, as provided by the British North America Act. But

Quebec showed little interest in fulfilling these obligations; it instituted no northern medical or welfare services of its own. Federal officials, meanwhile, continued their policy of denying medical or welfare services to Inuit populations.

Canada felt no obligation to supply medical aid to any of its widely scattered Inuit communities, whether in Quebec or in the North West Territories. Indians, having signed away their lands, had a right to federal health care as part of the treaty bargain.[22] Inuit, however, had never been enticed into such agreements. Ottawa had not sought extinction of their rights as long as immigrants and entrepreneurs had no need for their terrain or its natural resources. In law, as a consequence, the Inuit were ordinary citizens—no different from Canadians of European stock. No legislation, federal or provincial, compelled governments to provide free health care to any citizen.

For humanitarian reasons, despite their "ordinary citizen" status, the federal Department of Indian Affairs occasionally supplied Inuit with food and clothing. It allowed its field officers to care for Inuit encountered at the edges of their administrative domains. It also filled requests for medications and relief supplies from missionaries or traders in remote arctic locations, including Ungava. In time, it came to consider itself as having a loose responsibility for Inuit care.[23] Indian Affairs agents, however, rarely travelled beyond the treeline. As a result, the needs of Ungava's Inuit went largely unheeded.

Visitors to Quebec's northern regions, giving wide vent to their criticism in published works, continued to express their amazement at the neglect. Entrepreneurs W. Tees Curran and H.A. Calkins (whose 1916 account of their northern travels reached a large American readership) underlined the desperate need for a hospital on the east coast of Hudson Bay. The health situation, they felt, demanded periodic medical attention, at short intervals, for the entire population. Widespread illness required "the advantages of doctor, nurse and comfortable quarters."[24]

Captain Henry Toke Munn, an independent American trader, commented on the state of Ungava Inuit in 1923, when he visited the Port Burwell HBC post on Hudson Strait.[25] He had never seen such "squalid, starved, miserable natives." The region's population had declined so greatly, it was becoming difficult to maintain a profitable trading station. If only Inuit could get back to their "normal life," their traditional existence, they might do better. But of that, he concluded, there was little chance. Southern culture had made an irreversible impact.[26]

In 1927, Major L.T. Burwash, a former military officer employed by Ottawa, found Ungava's Inuit to be worse off than any other eastern arctic community.[27] Virtually all the caribou had disappeared. Neither seals nor foxes (then in demand by fur companies) were as plentiful as elsewhere in the North. Inuit health left "plenty of room for improvement." Childhood deaths were abnormally high. Clearly, the patchwork system of care provided through Indian Affairs had proved most inadequate. But Burwash had merely witnessed the beginning of what would be one of Ungava's darkest trials. Quebec's Inuit were soon to enter a period of even greater neglect on the part of southern society. Ironically, that decline in care was linked to improvements in Inuit health services in other parts of the country.

Promise of riches—hope of extracting vast mineral resources—provided one of the major stimuli to Canadian interest in the North. In 1921 already, after an oil discovery along the Mackenzie River, Ottawa had assigned northern administrative duties to the North West Territories and Yukon Branch (NWTYB) of the Department of the Interior. The newly created office controlled mineral exploration permits and collected duties from commercial enterprises. It had no responsibilities, however, for Native well-being. Not until 1928, when officials anticipated an explosion of mining activity on the arctic coast, did Canada give a thought to provision of medical care for its Inuit.[28]

Recovery of arctic mineral deposits, Canada hoped, would allow it to join the great industrial nations. Medical protection of white pioneers in that endeavour was essential. Care for Inuit came in the context of industrial need: without their labour and assistance in the forbidding cold, construction of mines would be difficult. In great haste, Ottawa sent doctors to regions most visited by white men or close to areas where entrepreneurs would soon send their crews. "Development of the Nation is at Stake" proclaimed government announcements of health services for the Arctic's original inhabitants. Rather than have Indian Affairs develop its own chain of high arctic medical stations, Canada transferred all responsibility for "Eskimo Affairs" to NWTYB. But Ungava's Inuit benefited not a whit from this surge in northern medical activity.

DEFRAYING EXPENSES:
THE LEGAL RIGHT NOT TO CARE

Until 1928, Indian Affairs' stop-gap provision of food, clothing, and medicines for Ungava had created few problems. Ottawa officials tolerated the arrangement as long as Parliament voted them sufficient funds to continue the limited system of Inuit relief. All that changed abruptly. Indian Affairs, no longer responsible for Inuit matters, stopped sending drugs and supplies beyond the treeline. NWTYB officials, greatly worried about their budget, balked at the cost of looking after what they considered provincial citizens. Quebec, meanwhile, thought itself free of any responsibility. Inuit, it insisted, were just another tribe of Indians. Since the British North America Act assigned Indian affairs to federal administration, the province felt absolved from provision of care.

Initially, Canada and Quebec reached a compromise. The province would pay "relief" costs; Ottawa would administer distribution of clothing and food, pay invoices, and present the total bill to Quebec on an annual basis. For a short time, the arrangement worked. In 1931, however, just after Doctor Hamilton visited Great Whale River and cared for Isaac Mikpighak, the accord collapsed. The Great Depression—and the policy of "retrenchment" in government spending it evoked—precipitated confrontation. Quebec delayed payment of the annual Ungava bill submitted by Ottawa.

Anticipating complete cessation of reimbursement from the province, Ottawa officials refused to pay suppliers.

Mikpighak's bad luck, as it turned out, had not ended with his broken arm. Not very long after he came to live with his medical benefactor in Moose Factory, the house burned down, resulting in the loss of all of his clothes. Hamilton bought him "a pair of breeches" and sent the trader's bill to NWTYB. Then, suddenly, the doctor died. Mikpighak now had to live with an officer of the Royal Canadian Mounted Police, who thought a charge of $1.00 a day for board more than reasonable, given the cost of food in the North.

On 14 March 1931, rather than make interim payments, Ottawa forwarded invoices for Mikpighak's breeches and lodging directly to Quebec. Canada had no desire, said an accompanying letter, "to continue, beyond the fiscal year, the practice of defraying expenses incurred on behalf of destitute and needy Eskimo resident in the Province of Quebec."[29] Provincial politicians were outraged. They held, it seems, a deep grudge over northern lands lost to the Dominion of Newfoundland and Labrador through a 1927 decision of Britain's Privy Council. In addition, Canada had sold off portions of Indian reservations in southern Quebec and retained the proceeds. "We have claims," said the province's telegraphed answer, "against the Federal Government for an amount above three hundred thousand dollars re surrendered Indian Reserves. Suggest entering amount re Eskimos against this account subject always to settlement of the sum due and to discussion of the liability of the Eskimo claim."[30] Mikpighak's breeches had precipitated Quebec's high dudgeon. A legal battle over payment of Ungava's medical and welfare needs had begun.

For seven years, while the conflict dragged its way through the nation's Supreme Court, Canada did as little as it possibly could for Ungava's Inuit. Federal provision of care would have strengthened Quebec's case. The province, meanwhile, maintained its refusal to supply medical services or food relief. Thus, federal and provincial administrations remained paralysed by the dispute at the very time when Ungava's Inuit most needed their assistance.

By 1935, Ottawa officials admitted privately to abundant "reason for concern." From numerous sources, they had received "evidences of destitution and sickness among adults and infants." No doctor had visited Ungava Bay for almost a decade. The only medical visit on record, in 1926, was that of a Hudson's Bay Company ship's physician, making the most fleeting of visits while the crew hurriedly unloaded cargo. Investigation by a doctor with public health training was long overdue.[31]

Changes in the fur trade, meanwhile, worsened Ungava's economic situation. As southern demand for fur plummeted in the 1930s, Inuit earned less and less credit at traders' stores. For some time, competition between companies had served to make traders sympathetic to Inuit demands for food and ammunition. By providing hunters with extensive credit, store managers hoped to acquire their furs at the end of the season. Some traders charged the federal government for destitute rations for needy Inuit families, but left the recipients with the distinct impression that this obliged them to bring in their furs at the end of the hunting season.[32] Despite such tactics, a drop in fox prices on the international fur market made it difficult for smaller companies to make a profit. Many closed their posts. When competition disappeared, so did much of the helpfulness.

Managers of Ungava's Hudson's Bay Company stores (the only ones that survived) suddenly became wary of dispensing on credit. Visiting government agents, particularly NWTYB's Major D.L. McKeand—the man in charge of the Eastern Arctic Patrol, the annual summer visit to coastal settlements by Ottawa officials—impressed on them the need to lower relief costs.[33] No longer would Ottawa accept the bill for supplies issued to needy Inuit at the beginning of the hunting season.[34] Suddenly, neither credit nor welfare arrangements allowed a hunter to recover from a difficult year. Many elderly Ungava Bay Inuit still remember being unable to acquire ammunition or food essential to a winter's travels on the land.[35]

In 1939, Quebec won its case against Ottawa: the Supreme Court ruled that Inuit were indeed Indians. Ottawa, not Quebec, was responsible for Inuit welfare.[36] But the judgment provided little benefit to Ungava's starving people. Ottawa hoped, as soon as World War II ended, to appeal the ruling to Britain's Privy Council, which then still held ultimate say in Canadian legal matters. In the meantime overzealous federal bureaucrats actually *reduced* food and ammunition "relief" supplies to needy Inuit by almost 90 percent from levels they had reached in the late 1920s.[37]

Adverse circumstances reinforced one another. Termination of "relief" handouts made for inadequate ammunition and food when on the hunt. Ungava Bay elder Noah Angnatok remembers an elderly man, inadequately equipped with bullets, being mauled by a polar bear.[38] Sick Inuit, barely able to stand because of hunger, pursued scarce wildlife. Such conditions also meant less fur brought into trading posts. Increasingly, the Hudson's Bay Company closed its smaller stations. This had another unfortunate effect: the *Nascopie*, the Company's summer supply vessel, no longer made its annual stop in the community. Since Major McKeand and his staff always travelled on that ship, federal eyes no longer witnessed conditions at communities with the worst economic situation.[39] Soon, Ottawa began to hear of "distressing cases of physical and mental disorders."[40]

Catholic priests, Oblates of Mary Immaculate (a missionary order dedicated to work among the poor and destitute), documented a rapid deterioration in Inuit health during the war years. Having established themselves in tiny Hudson Strait settlements in the late 1930s, they maintained their vigil despite meagre conversions. Desperately, they coped with hunger, frequent deaths, and widespread tuberculosis. "If in the neighborhood of Wakeham Bay [Kangiqsujuaq] no Eskimo has died from hunger during recent years," Father A. Steinmann advised Ottawa, "it is because we have watched over them."[41] Unfortunately, he had been unable to provide for other settlements. He had heard of deaths from starvation in Payne Bay (Kangirsuk) and nearby communities. "Since the Eskimos are citizens of Canadian territory," he admonished, "the government should be willing to pay some attention."[42]

HBC trader P. Dalrymple begged his superiors to bring Ungava's health crisis to Ottawa's attention. Inuit, he pleaded, "come under the heading of Government Wards."[43] Some form of medical care ought to be provided if only to show visitors to the region (by which he meant Americans at the Fort Chimo World War II airbase) that Ungava's Inuit were not the "Forgotten People."[44] HBC employees could not possibly fulfill the role of doctor. "While we do all we can," Dalrymple explained, "both our knowledge and our time is very limited." It was all very well to have medical instructions relayed to a remote outpost by radio, but such stop-gap measures were never as good as "personal supervision by a competent medical person."

MAJOR McKEAND: "A VERY STUPID MAN"

Major McKeand took disturbing information about Inuit health care (such as that supplied by Dalrymple) as a personal insult. He was a pompous figure, much given to retelling stories of his military career, his childhood proximity to Queen Victoria's carriage, and his adult meeting with King George. Dressed in his army regalia, he presided over the government party as it landed at northern trading posts, where he delivered a formal speech to the Inuit about the government's good intentions. Many whites who worked with him still discuss him with disdain. In interviews I conducted in 1992, several former northerners asked me to turn off the recorder and then called him "a very stupid man."[45]

Visitors to the North, McKeand liked to point out, had no long experience (as he claimed to have) with the ways of the Inuit. Conditions at Wakeham Bay (Kangiqsujuaq), he agreed, were the very worst in the Arctic. But, it was unfair to see all of the government's northern policies denigrated on that basis. Much of his response occurred on an *ad hominem* basis. Father Steinman lacked credibility: he was not a naturalized Canadian. Perhaps, once he got his citizenship, he would "learn the responsibilities" that came with that privilege.[46] One of those duties, apparently, was not to comment on lack of health care for Ungava. In a similar vein, in response to criticism from a visiting physician, McKeand noted the man

> had no previous experience with Eskimo nor had he any knowledge of their language, customs, habits, etc., before 1943. Consequently, he was compelled to accept the information and advice supplied by white residents some of which would give their own ideas of Eskimo welfare and, therefore, the value of the report from an administrative standpoint is practically negligible.[47]

When biologist Tom Manning noted the absence of government medical activity on Hudson Strait and documented the horrid state of Inuit in the area, McKeand brushed his report aside. Manning, he fumed, had "never been a team player" and had never learned to respect authority.[48] Such personal accusations, however, formed but a minor part of federal officials' handling of the Ungava situation. McKeand directed his most contemptuous broadsides at the Province of Quebec.

Quebec, the major liked to point out, had neglected its Inuit and was unlikely ever to take an interest in their welfare. It had failed to initiate "any kind of administrative policy." It had not provided medical attention, educational facilities, or relief services. It did not enforce game laws to protect the Inuit's livelihood. Yet it profited from furs traded by Native hunters, collecting a $1.50 tax, 50 percent higher than that in other parts of the country, on every white fox. In 1943 alone, by McKeand's calculations, this had generated $18 000 in provincial revenue—$12 000 more than what it had cost Ottawa to provide medicines and relief to Ungava's Inuit that very year. Clearly, he observed with sarcasm, they were no "burden" to their provincial masters.[49]

Quebec, according to McKeand, had won its legal challenge over the Indian status of Ungava's Inuit, but the court decision had not removed provincial jurisdiction over health care. Even if Inuit were Indians, that fact alone did not guarantee them medical services. They had not, he reminded his superiors, signed treaties; they had not exchanged land for protective measures and care. Hospitals and doctors, it followed, remained a provincial responsibility. Canada would not provide more than a "limited amount of relief."[50]

Among themselves, NWTYB officials readily conceded Ungava's severe medical needs, but pleaded impotence to effect change. Federal activities, they admitted, had been hopelessly inadequate. The Inuit's condition was "deplorable"; these people were "the worst off of any natives for whom the Dominion has accepted responsibility." Surely they deserved "a chance to survive." The need for a hospital had been "a burning question" for more than fifteen years. Unfortunately, Ottawa had no medical jurisdiction on provincial terrain.[51]

Dr George Hooper, physician with the 1944 Eastern Arctic Patrol, saw his intense medical concerns negated by Ottawa's insistence that Quebec held sole responsibility for Inuit health care.[52] His brief examinations of a few Ungava families more than convinced him of the need for a hospital. His request for such an institution, however, got nowhere. "From what I understand," he wrote in his final report, "hospitals placed in the Province of Quebec may open up an administrative and political problem that must be considered." Hooper's expert opinion fell, of legal and political southern necessity, on deaf ears. Had it not been for World War II, and the invasion of Canada's North by American military personnel and other "outsiders," Ungava's unhappy health care situation might have remained unknown to southern Canadians much longer.

"TO SAVE THESE INTERESTING TRIBES": THE INFLUENCE OF OUTSIDE CRITICS

Ungava lay directly on the northern military route to Europe. American airplanes flew across Nouveau-Québec to bases on Greenland, Iceland, and the British Isles. The United States, in need of a supply base and meteorologic station, built an enormous camp at Fort Chimo (Kuujjuaq), stretching for several miles along the river estuary. By 1944, it was equipped to handle, if necessary, seven hundred soldiers and up to a thousand planes a month.[53] Often, medical officers provided care to needy Inuit in the region. Others handed out food to an obviously starving population. Many Ungava Bay Inuit attribute the survival of their people to the Americans' intervention.[54] Canadian physicians, too, travelled through on military planes. Some, "very critical of the condition of the Eskimos in Northern Quebec," made Ottawa aware of their concerns.[55] They called for immediate medical inspection of the region. Archibald Fleming, Anglican Bishop of the Arctic, joined the chorus, offering to build and operate a hospital at Fort Chimo.[56] The need for such an institution, others confirmed, had long been evident and should no longer be denied. Still, Canada took little effective action.

In 1946, Dr George Gowie, crew physician on the M.V. McLean (a Marine Department vessel that serviced northern navigation buoys) delivered a damning report on the state of eastern arctic Inuit. He was particularly appalled by conditions in communities on the Quebec side of Hudson Strait. In all the history of Canada, he wrote, "no race had been so neglected and misused and exploited." If the "ultimate destruction" of the Inuit was the aim of the nation's northern policy, it was certainly having the desired effect. Within a few years, within a few generations at most, the "problem of the Esquimo" would be "forever settled." A race of truly great and unparalleled Native civilization would soon be extinguished. "Is that desirable?" he asked. "If so, let us continue as heretofore and do all in our power to hasten that day of extinction." The federal government's provision of medical care seemed designed to bring about such an outcome: it lacked planning, purpose, and concentrated effort. If Canadians wanted the Inuit to survive and to multiply, they should "lay extensive plans and get down to the serious business of righting the wrongs we have allowed to creep in and to eradicate the infectious diseases that our coming has brought to a happy and contented people."[57]

Ottawa, it appeared initially, had no intention of paying heed to Gowie's findings. Instead, Canada regaled southern citizens with glowing reports of northern medical accomplishments. Newspapers across the country dutifully reproduced self-congratulatory federal press releases. "Relevé Médical du Gouvernement en Pays Esquimau," proclaimed the thick headline of Ottawa's Le Droit on 7 November 1946. That same day, in English, the Calgary Herald told the identical story. In the largest health survey undertaken to date, fifteen hundred Inuit had been examined. A picture of a typically charming northern baby and his beaming mother, Soudlo, illustrated how Inuit were learning to feed their children "scientifically." "Soudlo," crowded the Regina Leader-Post, "proud of her thriving child, is an enthusiastic booster for the white man's way." A uniformed nurse at her side, representing all that was good about southern medicine, confirmed the extent of Ottawa's helpful endeavours in a remote and forbidding land. Other photographs showed happy Natives receiving glasses, having their teeth fixed, and being examined by a doctor. In the Far North, captions emphasized, there was "little organic disorder, no throat infection or venereal disease." All was well, it seemed, in the romantic land of the midnight sun. One newspaper, however, was having none of it. Quebec City's *Le Soleil* had already printed a very different version of the state of the Inuit health.

For once, Ottawa had been caught out. Its northern ships, sailing each summer for briefly open arctic waters, had their base in the harbour of Quebec City. When the M.V. *Nascopie*, (which served Hudson's Bay Company posts and carried the staff of the Eastern Arctic Patrol) or the M.V. *McLean* (which serviced northern navigation aids) returned to the South, debarking officials often met representatives of Quebec's francophone newspapers. What they revealed about northern medical conditions was vastly different from Ottawa's propaganda. Thus, in the fall of 1946, shortly after the *McLean* returned to its winter dock, Quebec editors became aware of the essence of Dr Gowie's findings.

After each of Ottawa's summer expeditions to the North, *Le Soleil* told its large readership, government propagandists distributed well-chosen photographs to the nation's newspapers. Illustrations showed "vigorous types"; accompanying legends led one "to believe that the Eskimo are pleased with their fate." There was, however, an entirely different side to the story. The government did not publish reports of missionaries and doctors "who ask for a more humane treatment for these big children of nature." Within a century, unless Canada went to their help, the Eskimo would be extinct: they would die of hunger and tuberculosis. Ottawa was well aware of these facts, but did not dare make them public. The federal administration knew "the true situation of the Eskimo." Matters were rapidly deteriorating and had reached an alarming state. "Why," demanded the article, "aren't the necessary measures taken to save these interesting tribes? It is a duty which the Federal Government cannot set aside." Other newspapers picked up the story.[58]

Revelations of medical neglect in its western Arctic had already embarrassed the nation.[59] Federal expenditures on northern health, nevertheless, had continued to decline—despite a four-fold increase in NWTYB's overall budget between 1944 and 1946.[60] Now, with an even worse situation in the eastern Arctic out in the open, Canada could no longer hide behind a legalese defence of its Ungava policies. At the United Nations, its spokesmen were clamouring for aid to underdeveloped nations. To save face, it would have to institute medical services for Quebec's Inuit, regardless of the potential for political conflict with the province.[61]

"FREEDOM AND WHITE BREAD": MALNUTRITION AND DISEASE IN THE POSTWAR YEARS

Nowhere in Canada did the state of Native people seem more cruelly ironic than in northern Ungava. Fort Chimo's enormous airbase, built from nothing in a few short months at enormous cost, lay largely abandoned in the postwar years. Canada, in order to impress on its southern voters that it had not lost its North to the United States, would soon purchase the disintegrating physical plant for six million dollars, $600 000 for the refrigeration unit alone.[62] Runways, exposed to Ungava's harsh winds, created a vast plain of eroding, shifting sands. Numerous buildings, losing their footing, tilted toward a landscape whose delicate balance had been irretrievably damaged for miles on end by bulldozers and heavy vehicle traffic. A skeleton crew maintained a hotel for transient dignitaries. Inside, plush leather chairs imparted the ambience of an Oxford senior common room or a London club. A large refrigerator supplied beer, while the kitchen served the best of meals in enormous quantities. In 1946, roast chicken, several different vegetables, and canned fruits were common fare. Yet, in the Native community nearby, a family of eleven starved to death that very year. At Payne Bay (Kangirsuk), too, three Inuit succumbed to lack of food. The white airbase manager blamed it all on the Inuit's inability "to conserve things properly." He lamented their working habits, comparing them unfavourably with Natives from other regions.[63]

Nicholas Polunin, a well-travelled arctic botanist and a visitor at the hotel, bemoaned the Inuit's loss of their "wonderful adaptation to a unique way of life." Having adjusted to white ways of doing things—particularly after many of them had earned regular wages at the airbase—they had lost the ability to hunt seal or even make boots. No wonder, he concluded, these nomads continued to starve to death. Despite the massive expenditure that Fort Chimo's military installations had entailed, the Inuit's fate had changed little in the fifteen years since he had first come across their emaciated corpses on nearby Akpatok Island.[64]

Inuit hunger, neither Polunin nor the base manager realized, had little to do with lack of hunting skills. Lassitude, rather than being a sign of local racial inferiority, resulted from malnutrition. Government destitute rations, as some outsiders pointed out, contributed to vitamin deficiencies. In 1946, food handouts consisted of white flour, sugar, and tea, in amounts "barely enough to keep the poor alive." Ungava's Inuit, biologist Tom Manning's wife noted, had "freedom and white bread," but lacked food essential to good health.[65]

Inuit children, a Queen's University study confirmed, were underweight, some almost emaciated. All ages showed findings suggestive of riboflavin and ascorbic acid deficiency. Those conclusions, moreover, were based on examinations at Southampton Island where, compared to the south side of Hudson Strait, Inuit lived "in a land of plenty." Ungava's Inuit were far worse off than the Southampton Islanders. The Strait people, according to Mrs Manning, caught few fish, an occasional seal, and a rare walrus. So exhausted were their hunting grounds, they clung to white settlements in order to at least get their rations. They had reached the stage where "they felt unsafe away from the posts." Their stamina and initiative were gone.[66] The first federal nurse installed in Ungava (in 1948) confirmed these grim impressions. At Port Harrison (Inukjuak), she noted the slim appearance of Inuit children. With extra food obtained from Ottawa, she provided a single daily meal. Twenty-eight youngsters participated; almost immediately, a marked increase in their weight became evident.[67]

Despite such accounts, Ottawa showed great concern about "handouts." Free food and hunting supplies, it feared, would "pauperize" Ungava's Inuit. Hunters who shot and trapped fewer animals than expected by white traders received special attention on the part of Ottawa's remote authorities. Bureaucrats labelled them "inefficient." An inefficient able-bodied hunter, said their directives, "should seldom be granted relief assistance as this would inevitably encourage a continuation of his indolence."[68]

Officials, like Chimo's airbase manager, failed to consider that "indolence" might well be a reflection of decreased physical powers due to disease and lack of food. Ungava wildlife was scarce and a successful hunt required extraordinary effort.[69] Even the households of renowned Inuit marksmen often lacked food. A hunter's illness, consequently, further jeopardized the marginal well-being of his wife and children. Still, federal bureaucrats feared the danger of "handing out assistance indiscriminately." Their instructions, they reminded officials in the field, had "never been intended to place all widows on relief as a matter of routine, but evidently this has occurred in some instances." They planned to devote "special attention" to stop the practice.[70] Postwar separation of federal administrative duties (welfare by one department; health care by another) prevented a more co-ordinated response.

In the meantime, malnutrition fostered ideal conditions for the spread of tuberculosis. Between 1946 and 1951, Ungava's death rate from that disease was enormous: fifty times higher than its present toll.[71] Only very slowly, however, was Ottawa able to shed its medical inertia. The intensive case-finding and isolation programs of an organized anti-tuberculosis campaign did not become effective until well into the 1950s.

ELIMINATING TUBERCULOSIS: THE ACTIVE FEDERAL HEALTH CARE PERIOD

Once again, increased northern medical activity had a link to southern enterprise in the region. Americans, in force, had returned to Canada's North, building radar stations to provide their country with early warning of across-the-pole Russian bomber attacks. Construction companies needed Native labour. Far too often, said Percy Moore, director of Canada's northern health services, tuberculosis constituted a "barrier to the acceptability of the Eskimo for employment in non-native settlements."[72] Infected Inuit would be a threat to the health of transient whites. Rapidly, he expanded Ungava's medical services.

That same year, Moore sent a husband and wife team into the Ungava Bay region. Mrs Ross, the government hoped, would "make herself responsible for health matters in and near Fort Chimo." Mr Ross would spend much of his time travelling along the coasts of Hudson Strait and Ungava Bay with a portable X-ray machine. By this means, Ottawa meant to make a start on the eradication of tuberculosis in Ungava. The M.V. *C.D. Howe*, a hospital ship, would complement this service during its annual summer voyages by dispatching helicopters far inland in search of patients.

Numerous infected Inuit were evacuated to southern sanatoria. Clearly, Canada was making an intensive therapeutic effort.

By 1968, in addition to Port Harrison (Inukjuak) and Fort Chimo (Kuujjuaq), nurses served Sugluk (Salluit), Wakeham Bay (Kangiqsujuak), Great Whale River (Kuujjuaraapik), and Povungnituk; lay dispensers provided for seven other locations. Ottawa had accomplished a great deal.[73] By then, twelve Ottawa-funded schools and thirty-six teachers served Ungava's population of 3000 Inuit.[74] The ratio of federal employees to Inuit had become impressive. There was irony, however, in Quebec's reaction to the mounting white anglophone presence.

Parallel with the late 1950s increase of federal outsiders in Ungava, Quebec's desire to assume active governmental control over the peninsula mounted. By 1964, the province no longer saw a problem in providing its Inuit with "services on exactly the same basis and under the same financial arrangement as other provincial citizens."[75] Within a decade of that pronouncement, Quebec programs had replaced Ottawa's Inuit health initiatives. How the change in attitude and the takeover came about, I have dealt with elsewhere.[76] One of the most remarkable features of that transition period was the presence of both federal and provincial medical agencies, providing duplicate services and actively courting Inuit allegiance.

Not long after it assumed responsibility for the medical care of its Inuit, Quebec announced the James Bay Hydro-Electric Power Project, a massive undertaking to tap the energy of Ungava's rivers. One of the streams whose thundering waters would be changed forever was Rivière de La Baleine, Great Whale River. Its course, as it reached Hudson Bay, took it directly by the Inuit settlement where Isaac Mikpighak had broken his arm forty years earlier.

CONCLUSION

There was no conspiracy to keep Ungava's Inuit unfed and unhealthy. Yet the outcome was not much different than if there had been one. Events in Ungava unfolded because a remarkable (but accidental) conjunction of geographic, political, philanthropic, economic, and administrative factors kept access to southern help blocked in the first half of this century.

Inuit lived too far north to be included in the terrain that composed the Canadian nation in 1867. Thus the country's founding documents contained no reference to them as a separate people. That lack of legal standing created the conditions under which later governments could deny responsibility for Inuit care.

Ungava lay too far south to play a role in the international arctic sovereignty disputes of the first third of this century: no foreign nation eyed its terrain or adjacent waterways. Hence Canada saw no reason to demonstrate its legitimate possession of Ungava by making a show of providing health and welfare services, a tactic it employed elsewhere in the Arctic.

Climate dictated the entry of difficult federal–provincial relations into decisions about northern health care delivery. The line delimiting arctic weather conditions (and hence the treeline) moves increasingly downward in its west-to-east sweep across the Canadian land mass. When, in the first two decades of this century, Canada created new provinces and allowed old ones to expand northward to salt water, only Quebec (being the most easterly of the newly enlarged jurisdictions) acquired arctic-type, treeless terrain and Inuit citizens. All of Canada's other Inuit lived in the federally administered North West Territories.

Having ceded Ungava to Quebec, Ottawa felt it had no obligation to the peninsula's Inuit, whom it considered to be "ordinary" provincial citizens. But the province insisted that Inuit were Indians and still subject to federal Canadian guardianship. As happened with the bill over Mikpighak's care, disagreements over northern medical care took on the larger historical burden of ill-will and suspicion between the francophone province and the mainly anglophone federal administration. Escalation of conflict and aggressive confrontation (in the courts) served to stake out jealously guarded boundaries of financial and legal responsibility.

No outside mechanisms provided backup when governmental neglect took its price: humanitarian agencies largely ignored Quebec's subarctic. Elsewhere in Canada's North, European missions often played an active role in health care provision. Indeed, hospital services were greatest in areas where Christian churches had become strong advocates for Native needs.[77] In Ungava, however, no church-operated medical institutions alleviated Inuit suffering.

Ungava's horrid weather, dangerous shores, and meagre wildlife made a missionary's life particularly miserable. Its Inuit population, frequently assaulted by epidemics, failed to rise above two thousand souls throughout the first four decades of this century. Small settlements, stretched out over vast distances, offered little hope of gaining a large congregation. Under such trying conditions, few men of God were willing to battle for long for a few souls when their European funding agencies wanted to hear of large numbers of converts. By the 1920s, most Protestant organizations had decided their funds were better spent on the "teeming masses" of China than on Canada's scattered native bands.[78] Moravians and Anglicans abandoned or minimized their Ungava missions.

When Catholic priests moved into Hudson Strait settlements in the late 1930s, much of their energy went into coping with Inuit hunger and tuberculosis. Their humanitarian role remained local and palliative. Despite impassioned pleas to Ottawa, their tiny missions (converts were few because the Inuit continued to adhere to the Anglican religion) lacked the clout to make advocacy effective.

The Great Depression sapped federal finances; after 1929, cost-cutting politicians stripped the bureaucracy of many workers. A skeleton Ottawa staff, so small there was little room for more than one opinion, ran the entire gamut of arctic services. These few officials knew that continued employment hinged on staying within a severely limited budget, maintaining the status quo, and avoiding disclosures of embarrassing situations. In that setting, a buffoon like Major McKeand could flourish: as he travelled north each summer in uniformed first-class splendour, the Arctic became his personal empire. While privately admitting to problems, he could brook no outside criticism. He and his superiors rejected witnesses' descriptions of the poor condition of Ungava's people. Indeed Ottawa maintained a carefully managed policy of releasing flattering news items about Inuit health to southern newspapers. The coming of World War II, with government and press attention focused on matters overseas, allowed that state of affairs to continue well into the mid 1940s.

Ungava's postcontact situation—almost complete absence of outside medical assistance in the first half of this century—represents a "worst case" scenario. The events precipitated by Dr Hamilton's treatment of Mikpighak's broken arm demonstrate what happened to an isolated indigenous community when governments lacked motives for providing help and humanitarian agencies were busy elsewhere.

NOTES

1. Gérard Duhaime, "La sédentarisation au Nouveau-Québec Inuit," Études Inuit Studies 7, 2 (1983): 25–52.

2. Another example is the fraud involved in the northern medical career of Dr Leslie Livingstone. See Walter J. Vanast, "'The First Eskimo Tumor': Fraud, Incompetence, and Medical Malpractice in the Arctic Career of Dr Leslie Livingstone" (paper presented to the History of Medicine section of the Royal College of Physicians and Surgeons of Canada annual meeting, Ottawa, 11 Sept. 1992).

3. Located in marginal geographic regions, subordinate politically and economically to an immigrant population, internal colonies consist of an area's original inhabitants; often, their resources have been exploited without consultation. Nelson H. Graburn, "1, 2, 3, 4 . . . Anthropology and the Fourth World," Culture 1, 1 (1981): 66–70. See Canadian issues related to the North in Gurston Dacks, A Choice of Futures: Politics in the Canadian North (Toronto: Methuen, 1981); to Native perspectives in George Manuel and Michael Posluns, The Fourth World: An Indian Reality (New York: Free Press, 1974); and to Ungava inter-ethnic relations in Duhaime "La sédentarisation au Nouveau-Québec Inuit." For exam- ples of non-historian health studies see Corinne Hodgson, "The Social and Political Implications of Tuberculosis Among Native Canadians," Canadian Review of Sociology and Anthropology 19, 4 (1982): 503–11; Jody F. Decker, "'We Should Never Again Be the Same People': The Diffusion and Cumulative Impact of Acute Infectious Diseases Affecting the Natives of the Northern Plains of the Western Interior of Canada" (PhD diss., York University, 1989); John D. O'Neil, "The Politics of Health in the Fourth World: A Northern Canadian Example," Human Organization 45, 2 (1986): 119–28; and Charles W. Hobart, "The Impact of Resource Development on the Health of Native People in the North West Territories," Canadian Journal of Native Studies 4, 2 (1984): 257–78. For "internal" and hagiographic northern medical histories see Dudley Copland, Livingstone of the Arctic (n.p.: Canadian Century Publishers, 1978; first published 1967); C. Graham Cumming,"Health of the Original Canadians, 1867–1967," Medical Services Journal of Canada 23, 2 (1967): 115–66, and "Northern Health Services," Canadian Medical Association Journal 100 (1969): 526–31; B.H. Brett, "A Synopsis of Northern Medical History," Canadian Medical Association Journal 100 (1969): 521–26;

and J.D. Martin, "Health Care in Northern Canada: An Historical Perspective" in *Proceedings of the Fifth International Symposium on Circumpolar Health*, ed. J.P. Hansen and B. Harvald (Copenhagen: Nordic Council for Arctic Medicine Report, Series 33, 1981), 80–87, and "History of Medicine in the North West Territories," *Annals of the Royal College of Physicians and Surgeons* 22, 5 (1989): 315–20. For British Empire medicine see K. David Arnold, *Imperial Medicine and Indigenous Societies* (Manchester: Manchester University Press, 1988), and Roy McLeod and Milton Lewis, eds., *Disease, Medicine, and Empire: Perspectives on Western Medicine and the Experience of European Expansion* (London: Routledge, 1988).

4. Anne Keenleyside, "Euro-American Whaling in the Canadian Arctic: Its Effects on Eskimo Health," *Arctic Anthropology* 27, 1 (1990): 1–19.

5. Walter J. Vanast, "Compassion, Competition, and Conviction: Bishop Gabriel Breynat and the Oblate Medical Institutions in the Western Canadian Subarctic, 1912–1945" (MA thesis, University of Wisconsin, Madison, 1992), and "Compassion, Cost, and Competition: Factors in the Evolution of Oblate Health Care Services Provision in the Canadian North," *Western Oblate Studies* 2, Occasional Paper no. 1 (Centre for the Study of North American Religion, Mellon Press, 1992).

6. Walter J. Vanast, "'Ignorant of Any Rational Method': European Assessments of Indigenous Healing Practices in the North American Arctic," *Canadian Bulletin of the History of Medicine* 9 (1992): 57–69.

7. Walter J. Vanast, "The Death of Jennie Kanayuk: Tuberculosis, Religious Competition, and Cultural Conflict in the Canadian Arctic," *Études Inuit Studies* 15, 1 (1992): 75–104.

8. National Film Board of Canada, *Coppermine: Consequences of Contact with the Outside* (1992).

9. For details of Rupert's Land's cultural and political history see Richard C. Davis, *Rupert's Land: A Cultural Tapestry* (Waterloo: Wilfrid Laurier University Press, 1988).

10. Charles Arnaud, *Journal des voyages de Charles Arnaud 1872–1873*, transcr. Huguette Tremblay (Montreal: Les Presses de l'Université du Québec, 1977), 29.

11. Nicolas Senn, a prominent midwest American surgeon, praised the North's tuberculosis-healing properties; he strongly supported efforts to send tuberculous patients into the high Arctic during the summer months. Senn, *In the Heart of the Arctics* (Chicago: W.B. Conkey, 1907). Until the 1940s, some federal administrators in Ottawa continued to believe that tuberculosis could not take hold in the North. Walter J. Vanast, "The Sunshine Therapy Concept and Its Effects on Tuberculosis Management in the Canadian Arctic" (paper presented to the Canadian Society for the History of Medicine, Quebec, May 1989). The treatment advocated in the South, after all, was sunshine and fresh air—and of this arctic residents were thought to get plenty .

12. Charles E. Tuttle, *Our North Land* (Toronto: C. Blackett Robinson, 1885), 60–61.

13. Archives des Pères Oblats, Montreal, Father Zacharie Lacasse to Father Célestin Augier, 9 May 1888.

14. Peck provided cryptic details of their departures. Neppingerok's last act was to "read the Word of God." Charlotte Ooyaraluk died calmly and joyfully, realizing—in Peck's interpretation of events—that "to depart and be with Christ is far better than the weary pilgrimage and warfare of this world." Another patient turned to his relatives just before expiring, telling them not to weep as he was going to live with Jesus. Disease wore Akaputsak down to a shadow before "the Lord called his ransomed one to 'Come Home.'" Henry Oochunguk, a mighty hunter and a man of much

force of character and intelligence, was refused in his request that another Native strangle him to end his suffering. Instead, he left this world cheered and solaced by "the comforting, sustaining presence of Jesus." Thomas Fleming passed away to be, his missionary trusted, "for ever with the Lord." Arthur Lewis, *The Life and Work of the Reverend E.J. Peck Among the Eskimos* (London: Hodder and Stoughton, 1905): 103–7, 113–14, 120–22, 132–33, 140–41, 146–47, 181, 193, 198.

15. Ibid., 144.

16. For details of Canada's early policies toward its Arctic see Kenneth Coates, *Canada's Colonies: A History of the Yukon and Northwest Territories* (Toronto: Lorimer, 1985); J.L. Granatstein, "A Fit of Absence of Mind: Canada's National Interest in the North to 1968" in *The Arctic in Question*, ed. E.J. Dosman (Toronto: Oxford University Press, 1976); Morris Zaslow, *The Opening of the Canadian North, 1870–1914* (Toronto: McClelland & Stewart, 1971); Richard J. Diubaldo, "The North in Canadian History: An Outline" *Fram* 1, 1 (1984): 187–96; Robert Page, *Northern Development: The Canadian Dilemma* (Toronto: McClelland & Stewart, 1984), esp. ch. 1; L.E. Chamberlin, "Home and Frontier," *Queen's Quarterly* 89, 2 (1982): 325–37; J.W. Grant, *Moon of Wintertime: Missionaries and the Indians of Canada in Encounter Since 1534* (Toronto: University of Toronto Press, 1988); and William R. Morrison, *Showing the Flag: The Mounted Police and Canadian Sovereignty in the North, 1894–1925* (Vancouver: University of British Columbia Press, 1985), and "Eagle over the Arctic: Americans in the Canadian North, 1867–1985)," *Canadian Review of American Studies* (Spring 1987): 61–75.

17. Diamond Jenness, *Eskimo Administration*, vol. 2, *Canada* (Montreal: Arctic Institute of North America, 1964).

18. In 1902 at Great Whale River, measles took a frightening toll. In 1908, epidemic illness killed over 100 Inuit in the region. Three years later, grippe and pneumonia took the lives of 30 Natives at one trading post alone. C.K. Leith and A.T. Leith, *A Summer and Winter on Hudson Bay* (Madison, WI: n.p., 1912). Ungava's Inuit numbered less than 2000 at the time.

19. Ibid.

20. Ibid., 165–66.

21. For details of the transfer, see Robert Rumilly, *Histoire de la province de Québec*, vol. 17 (Montreal, n.d), 22, 24, 29, 39, 90–92, 97, 116, 188 and 189, and Clifford D. Hastings, "The Canadian State and the North: The Creation of Nouveau-Québec, 1870–1912" in *Conflict in Development in Nouveau-Québec*, ed. Ludger Muller-Wille, McGill Subarctic Research paper no. 37 (Montreal: Centre for Northern Studies and Research, McGill University, 1983). For discussion and copies of documents relating to Aboriginal rights in Quebec since the time of the English conquest, including the 1912 Quebec Boundaries Extension Act, see Indians of Quebec Association, "Aboriginal Rights," vol. 1, ch. 2 (1973).

22. Canada signed eleven Indian treaties between 1871 and 1921. For medical promises, see René Fumoleau, *As Long as This Land Shall Last: A History of Treaty 8 and Treaty 11, 1870–1939* (Toronto: McClelland & Stewart, 1973), 30–39, and R. Davis and Mark Zannis, *The Genocide Machine in Canada: The Pacification of the North* (Montreal: Black Rose, 1973), ch. 12.

23. In 1924, the relationship became briefly entrenched in legislation. For administration details, see Jenness, *Eskimo Administration*, 32, 44–48, and chs. 5 and 7.

24. W. Tees Curran and H.A. Calkins, *In Canada's Wonderful Northland* (New York: G. P. Putnam, 1917), 121.

25. In 1912, when Canada gave Ungava to the Province of Quebec, it retained all islands off the Ungava coast, keeping them under the jurisdiction of the North West Territories

Council. Culturally, however, the Killineq islanders remained part of the Inuit community that lived just a few miles away on Ungava's shores.

26. Capt. Henry Toke Munn, *Prairie Trails and Arctic Byways* (London: Hurst and Blackett, 1932), 274–81.

27. Jenness, *Eskimo Administration*, 39.

28. Walter J. Vanast, "'Dead Eskimos Trap No Foxes': The Relationship Between Arctic Medical Services and Northern Resource Extraction" (unpublished paper, 1992).

29. National Archives of Canada (hereafter NAC), RG85, file 6955, R.A. Gibson to C. Lanctôt, 2 July 1931.

30. Ibid., C. Lanctôt to T.G. Murphy, 21 March 1932.

31. Avataq Cultural Institute, RG85, vol. 72, file 102-1, pt 10, R.A. Gibson to R.E. Wodehouse, 10 April 1935.

32. NAC, RG85, file 8276, T.H. Manning, Extract from preliminary report concerning Eastern Arctic, 1943.

33. For a recent overview of Eastern Arctic Patrol history, see C.S. McKinnon, "Canada's Eastern Arctic Patrol, 1922–68," *Polar Record* 27, 161 (1991): 93–101.

34. At Wakeham Bay, for example, prior to the closure of the Hudson's Bay store in 1940, the trader annually dispensed government relief supplies costing between $1000 and $1500 (NAC, RG85 file 8276, D.L. McKeand to R.A. Gibson, 7 June 1944). By 1942–43 "relief costs" had dropped to a mere $3000 total for *all* of Ungava's Inuit (around 1950 souls). "It is understood that no relief will be issued where a trading company has no competition" (ibid., Director, Lands Parks and Forests Branch to Deputy Minister of Dept of Interior, 11 Nov. 1943). "The reduction in relief costs as well as other improvements in native welfare can be attributed directly to the prestige of the government party (not one or two representatives but a group) on the regular supply ship" (ibid., McKeand to Gibson, 26 Jan. 1944).

35. Walter J. Vanast, "Where Was the White Man Then? Ungava Elders' Account of the Hunger Years, 1935–50" (paper presented to the Canadian Society for the History of Medicine, Victoria, June 1990). Transcriptions of these January 1990 Kangiqsualujjuaq interviews are on deposit at Avataq in Montreal.

36. Richard J. Diubaldo, "The Absurd Little Mouse: When Eskimos Became Indians," *Revue d'Études Canadiennes* 16, 2 (1981).

37. NAC, RG85, file 8276, D.L. McKeand to R.A. Gibson, 26 Jan. 1944.

38. Noah Angnatok, interview with the author at Kangiqsualujjuaq, Jan. 1990. Recordings and transcriptions on file at Avataq, Montreal.

39. Avataq, NAC, RG85, file 252-253, pt 1, D.L. McKeand to R.A. Gibson, 6 Aug. 1942.

40. NAC, RG85, file 8276, D.L. McKeand to R.A. Gibson, 25 Feb. 1944.

41. Ibid., André Steinmann, OMI, to R.A. Gibson, Dept. 1943.

42. For an overview of Father Steinmann's Ungava health-care-related activities, see his autobiography, *La petite barbe* (Montreal: Éditions de l'Homme, 1976).

43. NAC, RG 85, file 8276, P. Dalrymple to Ungava District Manager, 24 Jan. 1944.

44. During a flu epidemic among the Inuit in January 1944, Dalrymple obtained much assistance from the Americans at the nearby Fort Chimo air base, or, as he called them "the medical people up the street."

45. For a devastating depiction of McKeand's bombastic personality see R.C. Cockburn, ed., "Prentice G. Downe's Eastern Arctic Journal, 1936," *Arctic* 36, 3 (1983): 232–50.

46. NAC, RG85, file 8276, D.L. McKeand to R.A. Gibson, 16 Dec. 1943.

47. Ibid., 8 June 1944.

48. Ibid., 16 Dec. 1943.

49. Ibid., 11 Nov. 1943, 10 Jan. 1944, 25 Feb. 1944.

50. Ibid., D.L. McKeand to R.A. Gibson, 25 Feb. 1944; ibid., R.A. Gibson to C.P. Edwards, 14 June 1944.

51. Ibid., D.L. McKeand to R.A. Gibson, 11 Nov. 1943, 12 April 1944; ibid., R.A. Gibson to D.L. McKeand, 3 April 1944.

52. Ibid., G. Hooper, Eastern Arctic Patrol medical report.

53. Shelagh D. Grant, *Sovereignty or Security? Government Policy in the Canadian North, 1936–1950* (Vancouver: University of British Columbia Press, 1988), 136.

54. The other side of this medical coin is far more frequent occurrence of viral epidemics through contact of Inuit with soldiers recently arrived from the South. Thus, the overall effect of the American presence on Inuit illness and mortality may even have been negative. This may have contributed to the sudden increase in voices calling for federal services in the Hudson Strait and Ungava Bay region.

55. NAC, RG85, file 8276, R.A. Gibson to D.L. McKeand, 3 April 1944.

56. Ibid., A.L. Fleming to R.A. Gibson, 15 Jan. 1944.

57. Ibid., Ship's medical report for the M.V. *McLean*.

58. *Le Droit* (Ottawa), 28 Oct. 1946. English translation in ibid.

59. G.J. Wherrett, "Survey of Health Conditions and Medical and Hospital Services in the North West Territories," *Canadian Journal of Economics and Political Science* 11 (1945): 51–60.

60. Grant, *Sovereignty or Security*, 142.

61. For embarrassing questions raised by American military men in the eastern Arctic about this time, see statement "Condition of Eskimo at Southampton Island and U.S. Criticism," attached to NAC RG85, file 8276, T.H. Manning to Hon. Brooke Claxton, Minister of National Health and Welfare, 15 Sept. 1946.

62. Granatstein, "A Fit of Absence of Mind," 21.

63. Nicholas Polunin, *Arctic Unfolding* (London: Hutchison & Co., 1949).

64. Ibid., and Polunin, *The Isle of Auks* (London: Edward Arnold, 1932).

65. Tom Manning, *A Summer on Hudson's Bay* (London: Hodder & Stoughton, 1949).

66. Ibid.

67. Avataq, NAC, RG85, vol. 1127, file 201-1-8, pt 2, Eastern Arctic Patrol Report for Port Harrison, 24 Aug. 1948.

68. NAC, RG85, file 253-1, pt 2, S.J. Bailey to Mr Wright, 23 Nov. 1948.

69. Vanast, "Where Was the White Man Then?"

70. Avataq, NAC, EG 85, file 253-1, pt 2, R.A. Gibson to R.H. Chesshire, 7 Feb. 1949.

71. Robert Choinière, Marco Levasseur, and Norbert Robitaille, "La Mortalité des Inuit de Nouveau-Québec de 1944 à 1983: Evolution selon l'âge et la cause du décès," *Recherches Amérindiennes au Québec* 18, 1 (1983): 29–37.

72. NAC, RG85, file 540-543, pt 2, P.E. Moore to B.G. Sivertz, 7 June 1957.

73. Between 1945 and 1970 Ungava Inuit infant mortality declined from 330 to 136 per thousand. Louise Normandeau and Jacques Legaré, "La mortalité infantile des Inuit du Nouveau-Québec," *Canadian Review of Sociology and Anthropology* 16, 3 (1979): 260–74. These rates were, respectively, 4.5 and 4.0 times as high as those for Quebec as a whole. The improvement was greatest in areas with access to nursing stations, as in Ungava Bay, and least in areas without, as in some portions of the Hudson Bay coast. The most significant change was in the number of delivery-related deaths.

74. Avataq, NAC, RG85, 1958, A-1000-8, pt 4, R.G. Helbecque, memo, 16 Sept. 1964; Avataq ref. 628.19, R. Jocelyn, memo, 26 July 1968 (original in NAC).

75. Avataq, NAC, RG85, vol. 1928, file 1006-8, pt 9, p. 2, Jean Lesage to Lester B. Pearson, 7 Dec. 1964.

76. Walter J. Vanast, "'Taking Care of the Dog': René Lévesque and Quebec's Takeover of Federal Inuit Health Services in the Ungava Peninsula" (paper presented to the Royal College of Physicians and Surgeons of Canada, annual meetng, Quebec, Sept. 1991).

77. Between 1912 and 1942, for example, Catholic Bishop Gabriel Breynat pushed Ottawa hard for medical services for his Mackenzie River flock. His determination resulted in an impressive chain of western Arctic hospitals. Vanast, "The Death of Jennie Kanayuk" and "'Dead Eskimos Trap No Foxes.'"

78. For an overview of Canadian missions to Indians see Grant, *Moon of Wintertime*. It does not include missions to the Far North. D.B. Marsh, "History of the Anglican Church in Northern Quebec and Ungava" in *Le Nouveau-Québec: Contribution à l'étude de l'occupation humaine*, ed. Jean Malaurie and Jacques Rousseau (Paris: Mouton, 1964), and Gaston Carrière, OMI, "L'Oeuvre des Oblats de Marie-Immaculée dans le Nord Canadien oriental" in ibid., provide "internal" histories of, respectively, Anglican and Oblate activities in Ungava.

"NOBLEST AND BEST": RETRAINING CANADA'S WAR DISABLED, 1915–1923 ◇

DESMOND MORTON

○

For most Canadians, the loss of 60 661 men and women was the most palpable cost of their participation in the First World War but there was another, even greater price to be paid. By 1 September 1920, 69 583 veterans, maimed in mind and body, had qualified for disability pensions for their service and more would join them. By 1929, Canada's annual pension bill stood at $34 441 621. After the interest payments on the public debt, it was the largest item in the national accounts.[1]

Canadians had recognized the necessary burden of caring for their war-disabled, and Sir Wilfrid Laurier, adding the eloquence few compatriots could match, had pledged "the noblest and best" of the nation in solving their problems.[2] Like other belligerents, Canada set out to ease the disabled's burden and her own by making them self-supporting. She did so amidst great disadvantages. Unlike France, Belgium, Germany, or even Britain, Canada had no mature system of vocational education and almost no experience of re-training handicapped adults. A royal commission, reporting in 1913, had confirmed the primitive state of industrial education in Canada.[3] Ontario's pioneering Workmen's Compensation Act was primarily concerned with insurance, not rehabilitation.[4] Across Canada, crippling illness or disease remained a family catastrophe mitigated, if at all, by a patchwork of philanthropy. A conscientious employer might re-hire an

◇ *Journal of Canadian Studies* 16, 3 and 4 (Fall–Winter 1981): 75–85. Reprinted with the permission of the journal. Research for this article was assisted by a grant from Labour Canada. Inspiration, guidance, and a rich store of knowledge were provided by Glenn T. Wright, Public Archives of Canada.

injured worker as a caretaker or night watchman. The blind were widely regarded as helpless human beings.

Wounded veterans surely deserved more of their country but Canadian visitors to London had regularly been shocked at the sight of maimed ex-soldiers eking out their pensions by begging.[5] Canadians had also been disdainful of the successful lobbying efforts of the Grand Army of the Republic in persuading Congress to steadily greater generosity to survivors of the American Civil War.[6] Yet Canada's relative immunity from war left most Canadians unaware of the limitations of their own military pension arrangements. Hurriedly formalized in the wake of the Northwest Campaign of 1885, militia pension regulations had not altered in principle since the War of 1812. A lieutenant colonel who lost an arm could count on a year's pay and a pension of $1200 a year. A private, totally disabled and in need of constant care, was pensioned at 45–60 cents a day without even the promise of medical treatment.[7] If the maximum rate for a private—or his widow—had risen to $264 by 1914, the government had nonetheless spoken eloquently of the value it placed on the life of the country's humblest defenders.

The First World War transformed the historic status of the wounded veteran as a tragic but forgettable detritus of conflict. Huge citizen armies could no longer be recruited from the least influential members of society. A society which suddenly assumed full responsibility for a solder's welfare, including his family, could not easily relinquish it. Many recruits, certified fully fit, suffered from tuberculosis and other hidden disabilities.[8] Improvements in medical science and the stability of battle fronts meant that, for the first time, the great majority of wounded would survive their ordeal.[9]

Like most of the consequences of Canada's blithe entry into war in August 1914, the impact of the disabled was unforeseen. In due course, the disabled would transform the role of the government. Canadians would experience government-run health and hospital care, vocational training, job placement, and life insurance. A government of businessmen would establish its own monopoly in prosthesis manufacture. Adjusting pensions and retraining pay to family size would become a precedent for family allowances. The problem of elderly "burnt-out" veterans became an argument for old age pensions. Programs developed for blind and tubercular veterans would eventually be shared with their civilian counterparts. At the same time, the rush to return to "normal" conditions, to limit spending and to eliminate programs that seemed too ambitious or costly for postwar Canada, meant that more promises were made to the disabled than the government or people would keep.

That promises were possible and even partially fulfilled was due to an unlikely agency, the Military Hospitals Commission. Like much else in Canada's war effort, it was an improvised response. If anyone had asked Sir Sam Hughes or his officials in 1914 how the wounded and sick would have been treated, their answer would have been based on the experience of militia camps or the 1885 campaign. They would be cared for in the few military hospitals or in Britain, discharged and, on the advice of a hurriedly convened medical board, recommended for pension. Certainly no special arrangements were made for the trickle of medical rejects from the mobilization camp at Valcartier nor for the larger flood of victims of illness and accident who returned from the CEF's muddy camp on Salisbury Plain. By December 1914, when the Princess Patricia's Canadian Light Infantry entered the line, the Germans began contributing to the flow of Canadians no longer fit for service. With splendid military obtuseness, Canadian staff officers assembled drafts of sick, wounded, and unwanted discipline problems and shipped them steerage class to Canada. At Quebec or Halifax they were stripped of their uniforms, provided with a cheap suit of clothes and sent home to waiting friends and relatives.[10]

Treating wounded heroes like criminals was only one of many follies in Sir Sam Hughes's Militia Department and the minister's own solution to the problem, a tented hospital at Valcartier, backed by a sprinkling of convalescent homes across the county, did not inspire confidence.[11] Using the discreet claim that Hughes was too busy dispatching soldiers to look after their return, Sir Robert Borden adopted a familiar precedent: what was beyond the government's competence, voluntarism would manage. The support of soldiers' families was assigned, as it had been during the South African War, to a revived Canadian Patriotic Fund. Scandals in Militia Department contracts led to a War Purchasing Commission. Furious citizens protesting the treatment of returning soldiers led Sir Robert Borden to create a Military Hospitals Commission, armed with full powers to provide the treatment and care of sick and wounded Canadians invalided from the front.[12]

Launched by order-in-council on 30 June 1915, the MHC's chairman, James A. Lougheed, was Conservative leader in the Senate and an eminent Calgary lawyer and real estate speculator. Commission members, serving for a nominal ten dollars a day, included an array of politicians, businessmen, and regional worthies, from Sir Henry Pellatt and Sir Rodolphe Forget to a single doctor, F.J. Shepherd.[13] Lougheed had no intention of bothering his fellow commissioners and grumbled as their numbers grew. Instead, he seems to have placed his faith in his energetic secretary, Ernest Scammell, formerly an official with the Canadian Peace Centenary Association.

Lougheed and Scammell faced no easy task. Convalescent homes and hospitals had to be found and staffed without knowing how many Canadian invalids would return to fill them or when. Since most of the Commission's work invaded provincial jurisdiction, Scammell had to work with and sometimes create a variety of local committees. Doctors and nurses had to be selected amidst minefields of political patronage and professional jealousies. The wealthy philanthropists who had bombarded the Militia Department with offers of unused summer homes had to be treated with sublime tact since Lougheed sensibly concluded that a scattering of small hospitals would be costly and inefficient.

By October, 1915, Lougheed and Scammell could report the securing of eleven convalescent homes with 530 beds. They were looking for sources for artificial limbs and eyes. In due course they concluded that taking over a single private factory would guarantee standardization and quality. True to their faith in voluntarism, they launched a Disablement Fund with an initial contribution of $100 000 from James Carruthers, a Montreal millionaire. By diverting money collected by everyone from provincial governments to school children for the purchase of machine guns into the Disablement Fund, Lougheed argued, the full cost of rehabilitating the disabled might well be met from private charity.[14]

At his most hopeful, Lougheed may even have imagined that Carruthers' initiative might have provided supplements to Canada's obviously inadequate pensions. Certainly something had to be done before rising indignation hurt recruiting. The government's answer, a year after it created the MHC, was a Board of Pension Commissioners with three members appointed for ten-year terms and ostentatiously above politics.[15] Immediately, maximum pensions were raised from $264 to $384 for widows, $480 for totally disabled privates and more for those of higher rank. By 1917, at $600, Canadians could claim that their pension was the highest of any belligerent, although wartime inflation sadly outpaced its growth.[16]

The new pension regulations of June 1916 added considerable sophistication to a deceptively simple process and a thriving bureaucracy soon spread from Ottawa into seventeen regional offices. Disability would soon be refined in twenty categories by percentages, rather than six. Unlike the veterans of 1885 or of the Fenian Raids, who had at least retained their tiny pensions undisturbed, disabled pensioners would be recalled and their pensions readjusted to their current state of disability. Following strong advice from the French, pensions would be based solely on disability. Yet what was the basis of disability? The men of the CEF ranged from highly trained professionals to illiterate labourers. Was the loss of a leg an equal catastrophe for a carpenter and an accountant? The new Board established its rationale and stuck by it:

> The Soldier brings to the service of his country the healthy mind and body of a man in the class of untrained labourer. If he shows ability he will gain high rank. If he shows none, he will remain a private. . . . The earning power of a man in the class of untrained labourer will be sufficient to provide decent comfort for himself and his family, that is to say a little more than enough for subsistence.[17]

Such a conclusion doubtless struck the Board as logical and democratic; it was also unquestionably economical, and it averted almost impossible judgments about past or prospective earnings. It also provided a basis for the program that now engrossed Scammell and the Military Hospitals Commission—achieving rehabilitiation through re-training.

Such an idea was virtually without Canadian precedent. If it had a spark it was in a letter from Miss Ina Matthews, a Sydney teacher, to her MP, E.M. Macdonald. Forwarded under Macdonald's signature, the proposal for comprehensive vocational training for veterans was passed for comment to F.H. Sexton, Nova Scotia's director of technical education. His enthusiasm captured Scammell and Carruthers' gift seemed to ease the financial problems. By October 1915, following overseas visits by Commission members, the accumulation of data from French and Belgian experience and the preparation of a report by Scammell, the prime minister was persuaded to summon provincial premiers to Ottawa to explore the entire problem of rehabilitating disabled veterans.[18]

The conference, on 18 October, was all that Lougheed and Scammell could have wished. The provincial representatives listened respectfully to Scammell's array of suggestions, ranging from land settlement schemes to free tuition at technical colleges, cheerfully accepted Ottawa's obligation to pay for such programs, and agreed to help the MHC by organizing provincial committees to find work for veterans. The basic division of responsibility for the period of the war and reconstruction had been settled.[19]

Under Lougheed and Scammell, the MHC could be depended on to resist both extravagance and paternalism. If Canada's responsibility to her disabled solders "can not be considered as being extinguished by the award of a pension from public funds," it was because it was just as important to the nation as it was to the veteran to make him productive.[20] Free vocational training was not a reward for valour but a businesslike investment. "There must be minimum of sentiment," Scammell sternly insisted, "and a maximum of sound, hard business sense concerning the future of the returned solider of civil life."[21]

Business sense was not a complete guide to innovation. Even overseas experience could be confusing. Most Canadians, including Scammell, looked to the French as the most advanced of the allies in rehabilitation as they were in recuperative surgery. French experience suggested the value of military discipline and strict routine in getting the disabled to help themselves. Employment agencies, specially designed for the disabled, only helped to identify their clients as "damaged goods," subject to low wages. French employers were suspected of exploiting disabled trainees rather than instructing them.[22]

Common to both sides of the Atlantic was a concern about the apathy of the disabled and their apparent reluctance to help themselves. Warnings abounded that wartime gratitude would wither rapidly with the return of peace. Such tough-minded advice was a staple in re-training propaganda. Not even the guarantee that pensions would be unaffected by new skills or earnings solved the problem. "Disabled men who receive money alone and are not assured of an occupation," warned a Canadian medical officer in the *Canadian Medical Association Journal*, "almost always deteriorate and lose their social position."[23] On the other hand, the low educational and occupational attainments of many CEF members made it realistic to believe that, with training, even the disabled might improve themselves. "Very few have started in an occupation which suited their capacities," explained F.H. Sexton, "and proceeded thence in continually acquired promotion."[24] Was it utopian to believe, with D.C. McMurtrie, that "it would be cause for national pride if, in the future, such men could date their economic success from the amputation of their limb, lost in their country's service"?[25]

Realizing such dreams began in earnest only in January 1916, when Lougheed appointed a fellow Calgarian, Thomas B. Kidner, as vocational secretary of the Commission. Kidner, the director of technical education in Calgary, had devoted his spare time to advising returned soldiers. His first task was to help organize the provincial employment committees which the premiers had promised but which only Ontario, through its Soldiers Aid Commission, had yet delivered. By the spring of 1916, the first training courses began at the MHC's scattered hospitals and homes. Inevitably they were tailored to limited facilities, equipment, and instructors: general education, English for foreign-born soldiers, mechanical drawing, woodworking, and, with warmer weather, gardening and poultry-raising. Since soldiers were discharged before any course was complete, an order-in-council in June authorized a training allowance of 60 cents a day in addition to the pension, with more for men with a wife and children. The principle of pay and allowance during training had been established.[26]

Much else was unsatisfactory. Kidner's limited program was more recreational than vocational. Courses were interrupted by hospital and military routine. Medical staff could be suspicious or scornful. Classes included serious trainees and others interested in a few hours of occupational therapy. Long months of convalescence bred apathy and even despair among the more seriously disabled and the somewhat academic approach imposed by both Kidner and the circumstances was ill-designed to appeal to men with few warm memories of school. A further stage in the program was reached when Samuel Armstrong, an Ontario civil servant, became MHC director in December 1916. As well as expanding the Commission's own hospital facilities, Armstrong visited universities to add their training resources to the Commission's program. In Saskatchewan, only the university possessed any vocational facilities.[27]

A more substantial change came in the summer of 1917. In its first report, in May 1917, the MHC justified its decision not to use apprenticeship by fear of employer exploitation. That drew an angry response from the Toronto Joint Committee on Technical Organizations. Deploying the familiar arguments for on-the-job training as opposed to school-based courses, the committee blasted Kidner's program. A school-based training system allowed him to offer only thirty-nine occupations, and more than half his 638 students were in one of four trades. A quarter of the disabled had enrolled in clerical or commercial courses and more potential chauffeurs were learning motor mechanics than could ever be employed. Armstrong dutifully met the committee and one of its key members, Walter Segsworth, an American-trained mining engineer, became the MHC's new director of vocational training.[28]

While Kidner continued on the sidelines, Segsworth soon transformed the vocational program. For the first time, training was sharply separated from therapy. Patients in hospitals and convalescent homes were encouraged and soon required to engage in "ward occupations" if they were still bed-ridden. As instructors, the MHC created a corps of ward aides, young women recruited for the purpose, trained in crafts and hospital routine at the University of Toronto's Hart House, and deployed in military hospitals at a wage of $60–75 a month. When sufficiently fit, the invalided soldiers moved to "curative workshops" where they could practise woodworking, motor mechanics, shoemaking, or whatever occupations were available. The purpose, Segsworth insisted to those who complained about grown men doing embroidery or "carpenters" graduating before they were competent, was that hospital training was solely useful for strengthening muscles, occupying morale, and reviving a sense of purpose.[29]

Vocational training was a very different matter. For a start, it was limited to those veterans who could show that they were too disabled to return to their former occupation. Choosing a new one might be the man's own business but he was powerfully guided by a Disabled Soldiers Training Board, composed of a vocational officer and a representative of local business or industry. Under an appearance of freedom, the direction was clear: a trainee should pick a related trade or occupation. A disabled house carpenter could become a cabinet-maker, a typographer could easily adapt to monotype or linotype equipment and even an illiterate miner could learn to operate a concentrating table. By studying mechanical drawing and shop arithmetic, a crippled machinist might become a superintendent. One area from which MHC propaganda consistently warned off applicants was clerical work or "mere paper-scratching." The idealized veteran, "Private Pat" and his French counterpart, "Poil-aux-Pattes," duly expressed their horror at being cooped in an office for the rest of their lives.[30]

To find potential occupations for the disabled, Segsworth turned to G.A. Boate, a Canadian who had helped American ship-building firms find workers. Instead of adding to the flood of government questionnaires, Boate recruited interviewers, trained them and sent them out on an industrial survey to find jobs that handicapped men could do. Helped by the acute wartime manpower shortage, Boate's interviewers reported more than two hundred industries ready to try disabled workers.[31]

Although Segsworth championed apprenticeship and emphasized its significance in his program, most students received their training in existing schools, colleges, and universities or in schools especially established by his branch. For instructors, he turned to returned men themselves. By the end of 1917, 37 percent were veterans and the proportion grew to 73 percent by the end of 1918.[32] Most courses were intended to be six to eight months. Since men had to know "how" not "why," and since they were preparing students for the rigours of the workplace, Segsworth ran them year-round, for six to seven hours a day. The arrangement saved money and, Segsworth insisted, satisfied those trainees who were impatient to become self-supporting. The hard pace was also a useful rebuttal to those who claimed that the courses attracted the work-shy.[33]

Students placed in industry were supervised by inspectors. A trainee "received sound advice as to his future line of conduct, and emphasis is laid that he is there for the purpose of applying himself diligently to the learning of his new trade."[34] Weekly visits by the inspector were meant to prevent exploitation and to assess progress. Throughout training, the student earned pay and allowances as high as $110 a month for a couple with three children, an income calculated, like his pension, to give "decent comfort" but often significantly more than he would be offered by employers, once trained.

Although Scammell and Segsworth stoutly protested their devotion to business principles and their opposition to "paternalism" in any form, it was hard to avoid. High absenteeism among trainees persuaded Segsworth to employ social service workers to alleviate the family problems that distracted students from their courses. Social workers reported that they settled quarrels, taught mothers hygiene and financial management, and converted whole families to the benefits of vocational training. Because disabled students suffered frequent relapses, Segsworth finally won them free medical treatment during their courses—all in the name of saving the public's investment in their re-training.[35]

Each category of disability presented special vocational challenges. Men with head or abdominal wounds tended to look sufficiently plump and healthy that instructors and employers refused to believe their acute physical problems. Amputees, compelled to languish for months before stumps shrank sufficiently to be fitted with prostheses, suffered more than their share of institutional debility. Wooden legs, manufactured in the MHC's own factory, could allow a leg amputee to walk and even to perform hard agricultural labour but there was no satisfactory arm. After frustrating struggles with straps, pulleys and hooks, most arm amputees tended to get what use they could from their stump. Fortunately, leg amputees outnumbered arm amputees 2659 to 1143.[36]

Canada's war blind suffered from small numbers, organizational jealousy, and sentimentality. Visitors lavished praise on St Dunstan's Hostel in London's Regent's Park. Established for blinded soldiers by Sir Arthur Pearson, a blind British publisher, it emphasized vocational skills, recreation, and an impressive degree of self-reliance. Canadian charities devoted to the blind were indignant to find Canadians training at St Dunstan's and insisted, successfully, on their share. Segsworth, for one, was outraged. "The afflicted and helpless ailments of blindness as a disability were being paraded as a stimulus to public philanthropy."[37] By the summer of 1918, he had established his own special section for the blind, with a well-known blinded Canadian veteran of the South African War, Colonel Lorne Mulloy, in charge and Captain E.A. Baker, a St Dunstan's graduate, as manager. Not only did Canadians go back to St Dunstan's but its philosophy was established in Canada at Pearson Hall and, later, at the Canadian National Institute for the Blind.[38]

Although St Dunstan's helped push the Canadian war blind past the grim tradition of handicrafts and broom-making, not every hope was fulfilled. Claims that poultry-raising, piano-tuning, and stenography could be successful careers proved true in only a few cases. Massage proved more satisfactory and D.J. McDougall, a blinded PPCLI veteran, placed second out of 320 candidates in his British qualifying exams. He began his career at the University of Toronto instructing massage and physiotherapy at Hart House but he ended it, more comfortably, as a professor of history. Few of the 171 Canadian war blind did as well.[39]

Amputees and the blind fitted most Canadians' stereotype of the war disabled; the largest single category did not. No disease had so caught the imagination or aroused the fears of prewar Canadians as had tuberculosis. Combatting the "white plague" had become a reforming crusade. "Phthisiophobia" sent neighbourhoods into panic at the fear of contagion. However, primitive diagnostic techniques were ineffective in barring tubercular recruits from the CEF and highly inaccurate in discerning them from other respiratory cases once in uniform. By the end of the war, 8571 of the 590 572 members of the Canadian army had been diagnosed as tubercular, twice the rate for the comparable civilian age group.[40]

Tuberculosis was the single most serious health problem to affect the MHC; in turn, as Katherine McCuaig has indicated, military involvement in treating the disease transformed attitudes and approaches to the disease. By 1917, the Commission had taken over fourteen sanatoria, expanding and transforming them from "glorified summer camps to hospital-like institutions."[41] Though the government might well suspect that most of its tubercular soldiers had brought the disease with them, it accepted full financial responsibility for their treatment and pensions.

Yet, for Segsworth's re-training program, tubercular soldiers presented special problems. During the war years, an older faith in cure through fresh air and exercise was supplanted by a new belief in rest. Sanatorium superintendents found the young men confined to them rebelled at enforced idleness and caused acute disciplinary problems.[42] "Ward occupations" and "curative workshops" helped but it was no longer possible to suggest that framing and outdoor work would provide suitable future careers. On the contrary, specialists insisted, no occupations would be more fatal. Perhaps it was enough to discover that three-quarters of the cases recovered sufficiently to resume their old work.[43]

Some categories were scarcely considered for re-training. Although so-called "incurables," collected at Euclid Hall in Toronto, were taught typewriting and basket-weaving, the mentally ill were simply consigned, at federal expense, to provincial asylums. "Shell-shock" cases, hospitalized at Cobourg, were subjected, by the MHC's own testimony, to "every imaginable treatment" from warm baths to shock therapy. Playing golf allegedly restored one bank accountant to his stool.[44]

Despite the frustrations and fresh problems, Segsworth's task was in many ways easier than Kidner's simply because the Military Hospitals Commission continued to expand dramatically. By the end of 1917, it had more than 11 000 patients in a hundred institutions, with 3000 in training courses and 869 learning new trades. There was now a critical mass of manpower to justify a necessarily elaborate structure of courses, surveys, assessment, and placement.

The Commission was also sufficiently significant to attract a counter-attack from the department it had supplanted more than two years before. Whatever pride Lougheed and his staff might take in their achievements, the painful anomaly of civilians managing a military responsibility rankled with the Militia Department and the Canadian Army Medical Corps. A long and sometimes bitter bureaucratic struggle began in the fall of 1916, persisted through 1917 and finally ended in a military victory on 21 February 1918, with the transfer of fifty-one of the MHC's hospitals and 12 369 of its beds to the Army Medical Corps. The MHC (re-named at army insistence the Invalided Soldiers' Commission) retained only twenty-seven institutions, 5575 beds and responsibility for incurables, the insane, tuberculars, and anyone else the Militia Department could cheerfully discharge from further service.[45]

For Lougheed and his staff, it was no defeat. By prior arrangement, the Alberta senator emerged as minister of soldiers' civil re-establishment, a responsibility which could only grow as the Militia Department would surely dwindle. Armstrong, Scammell, and most of the MHC staff joined him. So did the substantive functions of the old Commission. After a few months of shadowy existence through the publicity the new department felt compelled to issue, giving details about its achievements and plans, the ISC simply ceased to exist.[46]

So far as the re-training program was concerned, the change made no difference. Segsworth's limited vocational activities within the military hospitals comfortably survived the transition. Beyond them, the divide between military and civil life had become all the clearer. The vague military organization the MHC had felt compelled to maintain for the sake of discipline and routine, the Military Hospitals Commission Command, was finally superfluous. Segsworth, like Kidner before him, had come to the conclusion that "militarization" almost ranked as a disability in itself:

> When a civilian entered the army everything was done to make him a small unit in a large organization. He was taught to obey rather than to think; he was for the most part relieved of the care of his dependents; clothing, food and a place to sleep were provided for him. If he was guilty of a misdemeanour he was punished, but he was not deprived of the necessities of life, whereas in civil life he would have been discharged. Thus the whole system, for the time being, tended to reduce the action of his own will and relieve him of all sense of responsibility.[47]

When the war ended on 11 November 1918, Canada could finally prepare to welcome the 350 000 victims of that militarization process who were still in uniform. Policies and experiences matured during the war years would be put to the test in a few hectic years of re-establishment. Organizations like the Great War Veterans' Association, formed in 1917 and led for the most part by men who had returned disabled from the war, would be transformed by the influx of able-bodied veterans. Egalitarian pressures would level Canadian pensions up to the rates accorded the lowest commissioned rank, ending more than a century of gross rank discrimination and, at least with married and family allowances, giving Canadians the highest pensions in the world. A long and ultimately futile struggle for a substantial re-establishment bonus would divert and divide the veterans during the critical postwar years, as they struggled to realize the vague benefits promised by wartime politicians.[48]

Re-training, however, was not one of the benefits extended to returning able-bodied soldiers or even to those of the 70 000 disabled who could return to their old occupations. The wartime rules persisted, breached only by a single exception: soldiers who had left school to enlist under-age were allowed to share in the bounty of paid occupational training. "It should be remembered," Segsworth explained, "that these boys for the main part enlisted as privates and their association with older men in the army has developed the worst features of their character, although, when they enlisted, a number of them were potentially the best men in the country."[49]

By the end of 1919, the DSCR's vocational training department had approved 27 602 courses, 7495 of them for the under-aged. Although the Great War Veterans' Association pressed half-heartedly for training to be extended to the able-bodied, its criticisms of the quality of instruction and the length of courses were probably more to the point. It is unlikely that existing training facilities could have absorbed much more than Segsworth's organization sent them. Despite his emphasis on apprenticeship and training on the job, less than a fifth of the men in training in January 1919 were in industrial establishments, 465 of them across Canada. The great majority were in the Department's fifty-three schools or in sixty-six co-operating institutions. The range was still impressive. At the University of Toronto, fifty-five veterans studied motor mechanics while in nearby Central Technical School, thirteen learned motion picture operating while three learned how to make show cards. At Charlottetown, M. Ross taught two would-be tailors and in Montreal, a Dr Watson instructed five potential dental mechanics. In Manitoba, where the university somehow failed to cooperate, the DSCR attempted to duplicate its resources, provoking at least one demonstration by disgruntled students.[50]

As disabled soldiers recovered or were discharged as invalids into the care of the Department of Soldiers' Civil Re-establishment, the numbers in the re-training program rose to a peak of 26 022 in February 1920, and rapidly fell to only 4714 at the end of the year. By then, Segsworth himself had returned to his interrupted career as a mining consultant and, under the pressure of postwar retrenchment, his elaborate organization had begun to disintegrate. Training centres closed, the Department's Information and Service Branch was wound up and with it the after-care organization Segsworth had designed to check on the effectiveness of both re-training and placement. At least for historians and policy analysts, that was a serious misfortune. The last available figures, for mid-1919, were impressive— 67.94 percent employed as trained, 22.26 percent employed otherwise, and only 5.74 percent unemployed. A year later, figures for Toronto alone showed 69.13 percent employed as trained and 11.13 percent unemployed. In a period of dislocation and recession, re-training appeared to have passed an early test.[51]

Segsworth himself would probably have agreed that the real test of re-training belonged in a longer term. How many of the 59 521 veterans who had received training by the end of 1920 reached the goal of economic independence?[52] How many, beyond the DSCR's carefully selected success stories, actually improved their position because of an unexpected opportunity for vocational training? Such questions now seem virtually impossible to answer. Some hint may be found in the continuing pressure for a more generous interpretation of pension regulations culminating in the Ralston Commission of 1922–1924. If re-training had been designed to alleviate pension agitation by impoverished veterans and their political allies, it signally failed. Thousands of pages of testimony confirmed that veterans, not unreasonably, now looked to the government and not to themselves or their families for more generous relief from their disabilities.[53]

Among the prophets of the postwar, few can have surpassed the optimism of Major J.L. Todd. "During reorganization after the war," he assured members of the American Academy of Political and Social Science, "it will be unbelievably easy to achieve social ideals which before the war seemed impracticable and impossible of attainment." Wartime examples, he believed, would inspire peacetime reforms. "The fact that former sailors, soldiers and their families are protected against the risks of death, accident and ill-health will inevitably lead towards the extension of social, health and life insurance to all citizens."[54] Todd's optimism was only premature, not wrong. The comprehensive responsibility Canada accepted for its soldiers and particularly for its disabled would be eroded and sometimes abandoned but its influence would be felt immediately when plans were made for reconstruction after a second world war. The need to relate income to family, understood by the army and absorbed by the MHC and the DSCR, would re-emerge as the long struggle for family allowances in Canada. The plight of older and often over-age veterans, worn out by their service and yet not technically disabled, would be a reminder of civilians too old and debilitated to support themselves and yet beyond the consideration accorded "returned men."[55]

For the civilian disabled, there would be a slow sharing of benefits devised for soldiers under the pressure of war, most conspicuously for the blind and for victims of tuberculosis, less obviously or immediately for those who might now seek work because an employer had discovered an unexpected role for the handicapped. Yet it remained a mild, cautious change because Canada, unlike more battered belligerents like France or Germany, resisted pressures to compel employers to hire quotas of disabled or even reserve public contracts to those who voluntarily played their part.[56]

Re-training the war disabled embodied only a little of the noblest or the best in Canada. It was a shrewd and often imaginative business venture, aimed at making most of the disabled self-sufficient and, in consequence, to alleviate the long-term burden of pensions on the Canadian taxpayer. As an investment of $27 million, most of it in training pay and allowances that might otherwise have been payable in pensions, it probably achieved its purpose. As a source of lessons and warnings, it can probably continue to serve still other purposes.

NOTES

1. *Report of the Department of Soldiers' Civil Re-establishment*, 1921; Canada, House of Commons, *Debates*, 15 March 1920, 408–9; *Canadian Annual Review*, 1920, 459; ibid., 1929–30, 46. Death and changes in disability steadily altered totals of disability pensioners.

2. Sydney *Post*, 6 Nov. 1917, cited by D. Owen Carrigan, *Canadian Party Platforms, 1867–1968* (Toronto, 1968), 73.

3. *Royal Commission on Industrial Training and Technical Education*, Canada, Sessional Papers, 1912,

1913. See Robert England, *Discharged* (Toronto, 1944), 31.

4. Michael Piva, "The Workmen's Compensation Movement in Ontario," *Ontario History* 67, 1 (March 1975).

5. For example, A.F. Messervey to Sir Robert Borden, 17 March 1915, Public Archives of Canada (hereafter PAC), Borden Papers, OC 323 (1) (a) 36548.

6. For example, Maj. F.J. Munn to O.C., MHC Command, 8 March 1917, PAC Kemp Papers, vol. 105. The United States government attempted to prevent a repetition of the process by establishing a War Risk Insurance for their soldiers, partly funded by premiums deducted from a soldier's pay, offering $30.00 a month for the totally disabled. Formation of the influential American Legion helped defeat such ingenuity. On Canadian envy, see Sir George Foster to Borden, 26 Aug. 1919, Borden Papers, OC 323, 138748.

7. *Militia General Orders*, 14 July 1885. On the War of 1812, see C.G. Roland, "War Amputations in Upper Canada," *Archivaria* 10, 2 (Summer 1980). On the pensions, see *Report of the Department of Militia and Defence*, 1886, xii–xv; *Public Accounts*, 1913, Canada, Sessional Papers, no. 1, 1914, O-151-2.

8. By October 1916, 18 percent of Canadians reaching England were obviously unfit for service anywhere, 13 percent might become so. See Maj. W.F. Kemp to Adjutant General, CEF, 31 Oct. 1916, PAC, RG9, III, vol. 90, 10-12-15. See also RG24, vol. 1144, HQ 54-21-51-9.

9. Sir Andrew Macphail, *Official History of the Canadian Forces in the Great War, 1914–1919: The Medical Services* (Ottawa, 1925). In the CEF, 35 128 were reported as killed in action, 12 048 died of wounds, and 154 361 survived wounds.

10. See Borden Papers, OC 323 (1) (a) 36631-58 for examples of experiences and complaints.

11. Sir Sam Hughes to Borden, 1 May 1915, ibid., 36579.

12. Mrs Minden Cole of the Soldiers' Wives League, Montreal Branch, proposed that the Canadian Patriotic Fund assume responsibility for returning soldiers. Herbert Ames, chairman of the fund, and Sir Thomas White, Hon. Treasurer and also Minister of Finance, politely declined, though they agreed to form a relief committee "until the Government makes some provision to care for them." No such committee was needed.

13. On Lougheed, see PAC Daly Papers, MG27 III, F 9, vol. 2; on MHC, *Canadian Annual Review*, 1915, 263; PC 2412, 15 Oct. 1915, Borden Papers, OC 323 (1) (a) 36769.

14. *Canadian Annual Review*, 1915, 263. The commission illustrated the claim of R.C. Brown and Ramsay Cook, *Canada 1896–1921: A Nation Transformed* (Toronto, 1974), 223, as "accustom[ing] the public, both recipient and donor, to think in terms of government responsibility for social services."

15. On the Board of Pension Commissioners, see PC 1334, 3 June 1916.

16. *Canadian Annual Review*, 1917, 534. The American maximum was $360; the British, $351. Veterans before the 1917 committee still complained that the pensions were inadequate.

17. The rationale is presented most clearly in the Royal Commission on Pensions and Reconstruction (hereafter Ralston Commission), *Second Interim Report*, 1923, 43. See also Herbert Marler, Canada, House of Commons, *Debates*, 26 June 1922, 3291.

18. Walter L. Segsworth, *Retraining Canada's Disabled Soldiers* (Ottawa, 1920), 10; *The Provision of Employment for Members of the Canadian Expeditionary Force on their Return to Canada*, Canada, Sessional Papers 35a, 1916. In his memoirs, *Reminiscences, Political and Personal* (Toronto, n.d.), Macdonald makes no reference

to his contribution nor that of Miss Matthews.)

19. *Canadian Annual Review*, 1915.

20. *Provision of Employment*, 5.

21. Ibid., 7. See T.B. Kidner, "Vocational Work of the Invalided Soldiers Commission of Canada," *Annals of the American Association of Political and Social Science* 80 (Nov. 1918): 145.

22. Maj. J.L. Todd, "The French System of Return to Civil Life of Crippled and Discharged Soldiers," *American Journal of Care for Cripples* 5, 1 (1917): 5–45; Major, CAMC, "Returned Soldiers and the Medical Profession," *Canadian Medical Association Journal* (April 1917): 8. See also E.M. von Eberts, "Functional Re-education and Vocational Training of Soldiers Disabled in War," ibid. (March 1917).

23. Todd, "French System," 6. On warnings, see Major, CAMC, "Returned Soldiers," 6. See also Lt. Col. J.S. Dennis, "Provision for Crippled Soldiers by the Military Hospitals Commission of Canada," *American Journal of Care for Cripples* 5, 1 (1917): 177.

24. Sexton to Scammell, 29 Jan. 1917, RG38, vol. 204.

25. D.C. McMurtrie, "Reconstructing the War Cripple in Alberta," *American Journal of Care for Cripples* 5, 2 (1917): 232. See also McMurtrie, *The Disabled Soldier* (New York, 1919).

26. Segsworth, *Retraining*, 11–12; P.C. 1742, 29 June 1916. For subsequent rates, see P.C. 1366, 22 June 1918; *Canadian Annual Review*, 1919, 596. By 1919, though a single man received $60 a month, a married man with five children could earn $137. See Ralston Commission, *Final Report*, Canada, Sessional Papers, 203a, 1925, 23.

27. Segsworth, *Retraining Canada's Disabled Soldiers*, 12. Armstrong was Assistant Provincial Secretary in Ontario. His presence may explain why the MHC acquired the Guelph Reformatory (bars and iron doors removed) as one of its institutions.

Armstrong had overseen its construction and development as Ontario's main provincial prison. His role in developing the Whitby hospital may also explain its temporary acquisition by the MHC.

28. Ibid., 12–14.

29. Ibid., 24; *Department of Soldiers Civil Re-Establishment* (booklet published for the Canadian National Exhibition, 1919, and now in the Scammell Collection), 11–12; *The Soldiers' Return: How the Canadian Soldier is being Refitted for Industry* (Ottawa, 1919), 17, 31. Both booklets, bound by Scammell, were kindly made available to me by Mr Glenn Wright of Ottawa.

30. "The 'Boarding' is a sympathetic, practical and thorough process in which the disabled soldier is an active participant" *Canada's Work for Wounded Soldiers: A Private View* (Ottawa, 1918, Scammell Collection). See Segsworth, *Retraining Canada's Disabled Soldiers*, 8, 123–24, 164; *The Soldier's Return: A Little Chat with Private Pat* and *Le Soldat revient: une causerie avec Poil-aux-Pattes* (Ottawa, 1917, Scammell Collection).

31. Segsworth, *Retraining Canada's Disabled Soldiers*, 100–5.

32. Ibid., 68–69; on veteran-instructors, 14. Several of the leaders of the Great War Veterans' Association and other organizations, including C.G. MacNeil and Harry Flynn, were among this group.

33. Ibid., 74–75; *Canada's Work for Wounded Soldiers*.

34. *Department of Soldiers' Civil Re-establishment*, 22.

35. Segsworth, *Retraining Canada's Disabled Soldiers*, 16–17. Barbara Wilson has noted one illustration of both exploitation and paternalism when, with the approval of the Department of Militia and Defence and the encouragement of the Great War Veterans' Association, 6 wounded veterans were sent to New York ostensibly for patriotic exhibit at the 1st New York International

Exposition, in fact to work for a private showman, James F. Kerr. When Kerr failed to pay the men, they returned to Montreal after a month. Eventually an embarrassed Militia Department reimbursed the 6 angry veterans.

36. On amputees, see Robert England, *Twenty Million Veterans* (Toronto, 1950), 46–47; Von Eberts, "Functional Re-education," 7; *The Soldiers' Return*, 18–20; Ralston Commission, *Final Report*, 51.

37. On St Dunstan's, see J.S. McLennan and Maj. R.T. MacKeen, *Report on the Inter-Allied Conference on the After-Care of Disabled Men*, London, 20–25 May 1918 (Ottawa, 1919), 30–33.

38. On Baker, see M.W. Campbell, *No Compromise: The Story of Colonel Baker and the CNIB* (Toronto, 1955); *The Soldiers' Return*, 24–25.

39. On the blinded, see Ralston Commission, *Final Report*, 46–47; Segsworth, *Retraining Canada's Disabled Soldiers*, 135; DSCR, *Report*, 1919, 45–47.

40. *The Soldiers' Return*, 30; Board of Tuberculosis Consultants, *Summary of Report* (Ottawa, 1921), 4–6; Memorandum relative to Re-establishment, Borden Papers, vol. 247, pt II, 138788; Ralston Commission, *Final Report*, 58. There were 4962 pensions for tuberculosis or 11.4 percent, averaging 70 percent disability, representing the tubercular share of the pension burden.

41. See Katherine McCuaig, "From Social Reform to Social Service: The Changing Role of Volunteers—The Anti-Tuberculosis Campaign, 1900–1930," *Canadian Historical Review* 61, 4 (Dec. 1980): 486; *The Soldiers' Return*, 27.

42. Ibid., 29; Board of Tuberculosis Sanitorium Consultants, *The Care and Employment of Tuberculous Ex-Servicemen . . .* (Ottawa, 1921), 41–43, urging sheltered employment and subsidy; see also Ralston Commission, *Final Report*, 48–74 on tubercular veterans' problems.

43. McCuaig, "Anti-Tuberculosis Campaign," 486; Tuberculosis Consultants, *Report*, 17–18; Sanatorium Consultants, *Care and Employment*, 6, 9–10.

44. *The Soldiers' Return*, 27; Ralston Commission, *Final Report*, 76–77.

45. PC 432–4, 21 Feb. 1918; Macphail, *Medical Services*, 317–20; *Canadian Annual Review*, 1916, 381; ibid., 1917, 577; Kemp Papers, vols. 105–7 and particularly Mewburn to Borden, 19 Feb. 1918, ibid., vol. 107.

46. On the department, see Scammell, *Canadian Annual Review*, 1923, 905–6; *Back to Mufti*, I, 1 (Feb. 1919); DSCR, *Report*, 1919, 5; Canada, House of Commons, *Debates*, 5 July 1919, 4676–81.

47. Segsworth, *Retraining Canada's Disabled Soldiers*, 64. For similar views, see Kidner, "Invalided Soldiers' Commission," 142–45; J.L. Todd, "The Meaning of Rehabilitation," *Annals of the American Academy of Political and Social Science* 80 (Nov. 1918): 6. For illustrations of "civilianization," see McMurtrie, "Alberta," 234.

48. On postwar problems of able-bodied veterans see Desmond Morton and Glenn Wright, "Soldiers from the Wars Returning . . ." (unpublished paper delivered at the Western Studies Conference, Banff, Jan. 1981).

49. Director of Vocational Training memorandum, 25 March 1919, RG38, vol. 210. McLennan and MacKeen had urged retraining of able-bodied veterans returning with rusty skills to a world where "the foot rule standard of 1915" had become "that of the micrometer gauge of 1917." See McLennan and MacKeen, *Inter-Allied Conference*, 20.

50. Segsworth, *Retraining Canada's Disabled Soldiers*, 78. On criticisms, see, for example, *The Veteran* 2, 10 (Sept. 1919): 16–18; England, *Twenty Million Veterans*, 44.

51. Department of Soldiers' Civil Re-Establishment, 32.

52. Ibid., 29–32; Segsworth, *Retraining Canada's Disabled Soldiers*, 164–69.

53. Ralston Commission, *Final Report*, 24; refusing a second chance at classification and training: "It must, in the opinion of the Commission, be frankly recognized that the fact that the vocational training student was able to depend on pay and allowances for a substantial period of his transition from military to civil life was in very many cases almost as genuine a benefit as the instruction actually received. It gave him the opportunity to look around and get his bearings, and at the same time had in it none of the elements of a gratuity or bonus since he was pledging his time and energy in exchange."

54. Todd, "Rehabilitation," 2, 5.

55. Ralston Commission, *Final Report*, 43–45; England, *Discharged*, 29–30 on "burnt-out veterans."

56. Ralston Commission, *Final Report*, 35.

THE NEWFOUNDLAND
OLD AGE PENSION
PROGRAM, 1911–1949 ◊

JAMES G. SNELL

○

In 1911 Newfoundland established the first state-operated old age pension scheme in Canada, more than two decades before such a program was adopted in any of the Maritime provinces. As an early program, the Newfoundland scheme bore a number of unique and distinctive features, which are suggestive both of the island's political and social culture and of the perceptions of the elderly at the time. Though old age pension programs elsewhere clearly affected the character and timing of the island scheme, the Newfoundland government's approach to dealing with the needy elderly was different from both the Canadian and the United Kingdom programs. The Newfoundland scheme was based on very limited funds, was available only to those aged seventy-five or more and, most strikingly, only to men. Throughout its forty-year history the Newfoundland old age pension program remained the most blatantly gendered scheme for the needy elderly in the western world. The island old age pension program was also distinct in the kind of bureaucratic support it received and in the parallel programs of state aid available to those excluded from the more generous pensions program. In reflecting on the history of this pioneer pension plan, it also becomes clear that the special features of the program were profoundly shaped by the level and character of state formation in twentieth-century Newfoundland.

◊ *Acadiensis* 23, 1 (Autumn 1993): 86–109. Reprinted with the permission of the journal. The research for this article was carried out through the support of a grant from the Social Sciences and Humanities Research Council of Canada. The author would like to thank Laurel Doucette for generously sharing her knowledge of the Memorial University Folklore and Language Archives, Jeff Walker for patiently instructing me in the "art" of graphing, and Peter Neary, James Overton, Ian Radforth, and the anonymous readers of *Acadiensis* for their comments on earlier drafts of this article.

The timing of the program's adoption was approximately contemporaneous with the United Kingdom's 1908 introduction of a means-tested program for those aged seventy or more and with the 1908 Canadian adoption of a very different program to assist the aged, the government annuities plan.[1] In 1906 parliamentary discussion of non-contributory, state-funded old age pensions occurred in both Westminster and Ottawa, arguably the two jurisdictions with the most influence on the ideas circulating in Newfoundland. It is no surprise that the Newfoundland government found it appropriate that similar discussions would occur on the island. New beliefs about the elderly, new ideas about the appropriate role of the state, and concerns about poverty amongst the elderly, particularly in the outports, shaped the Newfoundland government's response.[2]

A proposal for a Newfoundland scheme was first made in the legislature in March 1906. A.B. Morine, then leader of the Opposition, suggested that men aged sixty-five and older should be paid a pension of $40 annually, rising to $50 at age seventy and $60 at age seventy-five, a scale presumably reflecting aging men's declining access to income-producing work. The program would not be needs-tested, but it was expected that the well-to-do would not exercise their right to a pension. The result was that the House of Assembly adopted a motion approving some such pension scheme as a means "to improve the condition of the aged poor, and for providing for those who are helpless and infirm." Though age was an important criterion for qualification, poverty and infirmity were more fundamental, old age being simply perceived as a characteristic common to the poor and the infirm. Old age was increasingly regarded as a "social problem" requiring co-ordinated state response. The existing limited programs providing relief to the dependent of any age and the provincial Poor Asylum in St John's were no longer seen as adequate responses to the needs of the elderly, who were now singled out for particular attention and support.[3] Existing mechanisms of informal support— community and family, reinforced through parents' maintenance legislation— needed to be supplemented with new state programs.

The 1906 resolution called for the appointment of a royal commission to investigate old age pensions and was supported by all political elements in the House.[4] By late 1907 the commission was appointed,[5] and it soon met to request the collection of data related to the subject. Having completed these preliminary steps, however, the commission never proceeded further with its mandate; no report was ever written.[6]

Nevertheless, the issue remained before the public as the leading elements in a confused political scene searched for potent issues. Political expediency added the final element to the underlying concerns and attitudes prompting state response. Old age pensions quickly became something of a political football, as both major parties vied for public credit in their commitment to the idea. The government pledged its support in the 1908 Speech from the Throne and attacked Edward Morris's promises of reduced taxation as undermining the prospects of establishing any pension scheme for the poor and elderly.[7] The political turmoil of 1908 and 1909 provides at least a partial explanation as to the failure of the royal commission. General elections were held in both 1908 and 1909, and the then prime minister, Sir Robert Bond, terminated the proceedings of the commission once the 1908 election was called. Old age pensions played a significant role in the campaign platforms and debates. When Bond's government failed to mention old age pensions in the governor's speech closing the session, the People's Party of Edward Morris saw its opportunity to make a pension scheme a central part of its platform.[8] Bond's Liberal Party questioned Newfoundland's financial ability to sustain such a scheme, particularly without raising taxes as Morris had promised. Nevertheless, Sir Robert Bond's party declared itself in support of an old age pension program "for the weak and worn-out fishermen and working men, yes, and old women, old people who have no friends to help or give them assistance," though taxation would have to be raised to sustain the scheme.[9] The two parties continued to outbid each other regarding the value and extent of the scheme, promising to put ever larger public sums into the program.[10]

The Morris government, once elected, proceeded cautiously with its proposal. Though legislative action was promised in 1909, it was not until 1911 that a bill was introduced. The government proposed to offer an old age pension of $50 annually, paid quarterly, to those aged seventy-five or more who were in needy circumstances. The most striking characteristic of the new scheme was that only men could qualify for such a pension. This was in spite of the government's own evidence regarding the plight of elderly women. The number and proportion of the total elderly were growing steadily (see Figures 1 and 2). In 1901 those aged seventy or more totalled 5433; by 1951 the comparable figure was 14 419. But amongst the "old old," as gerontologists call them—those aged seventy-five or more— the numbers of women at least equalled those of men. Women in this cohort made up a slightly higher proportion of the female population than was true for men (see Figure 2)—1.34 percent in 1901 and 2.27 by 1951 (compared with 1.28 and 2.09, respectively, for men).[11] What is more, a far higher proportion of older women were already in necessitous circumstances and in receipt of state aid. According to figures collected for the royal commission on old age pensions in 1908, 844 men aged 65 or more had received $14 242.20 in aid, while 2147 women of the same age group had received $34 385.96.[12] Comparing these figures with the 1911 census, just less than 9 percent of older men had received support while the same had been true for more than 23 percent of older women. The women had, however, received slightly less support on a per capita basis—$16.02, compared with $16.88 for men.

In spite of this clear evidence of older women's needs and regardless of the British precedent giving old age pensions to women and men both, only men would be directly aided by the proposed Newfoundland scheme. What was more, in the debate on the plan the government felt under no obligation to explain, much less defend, this sexual discrimination. The Opposition attacked several features of the legislation, but no mention was made of this discrimination against women, although the needs of both elderly men and women were discussed. The limitation to men was, according to the prime minister, a first step, implying that the scheme would eventually be expanded to include older women as well. In the meantime, it was pointed out, older women would benefit indirectly through the pension received by a husband or brother.[13] The economic power of men would be sustained even among the elderly.

As eventually enacted, Newfoundland's initial old age pension program had one further feature setting it off from more recent such schemes. Not everyone meeting the scheme's sexual and financial criteria gained a pension. Rather than being open to all who qualified, the government controlled costs by establishing a fixed limit to the total funds available for expenditure.[14] In the first year funds for four hundred pensions were voted. These funds were distributed to the various districts in proportion to their total population (rather than to their share of the elderly population or of the poor population). No matter how many elderly men were in poverty, only four hundred would receive a pension. Since the elderly were not evenly distributed across the country but the pensions were, inevitably the criteria for acceptance would be harsher in some districts than in others. In some districts long waiting lists occurred, while in others there were vacancies for which there were no applicants.[15] It was also virtually inevitable

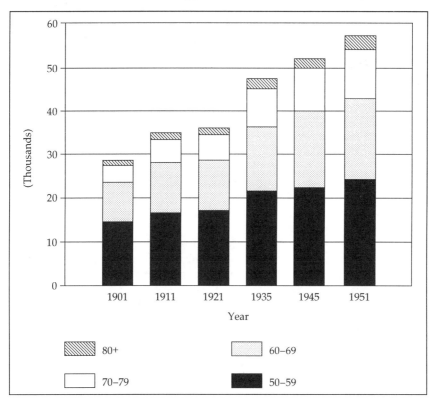

FIGURE 1 *ELDERLY POPULATION, NEWFOUNDLAND, 1901–1951*

Source: *Census of Newfoundland, 1901* (St John's, 1903), 1: 444–47; *Census of Newfoundland, 1911* (St John's, 1914), 1: 492–95; *Census of Newfoundland, 1921* (St John's, 1923), 1: 498–501; *Census of Newfoundland and Labrador, 1945* (St John's, 1949), table 7; Canada, *Census of 1951* (Ottawa, 1953), 1: table 19.

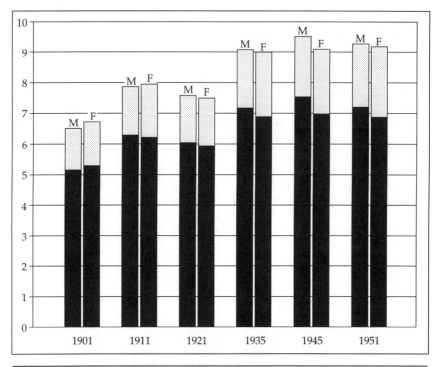

F I G U R E   2   *ELDERLY POPULATION BY SEX,*
NEWFOUNDLAND, 1901–1951

Source: *Census of Newfoundland, 1901* (St John's, 1903), 1: 444–47; *Census of Newfoundland, 1911* (St John's, 1914), 1: 492–95; *Census of Newfoundland, 1921* (St John's, 1923), 1: 498–501; *Census of Newfoundland and Labrador, 1935* (St John's, 1937), table 32; *Census of Newfoundland and Labrador, 1945* (St John's, 1949), table 7; Canada, *Census of 1951* (Ottawa, 1953), 1: table 19.

that the awarding of a pension became somewhat discretionary. So discretionary did it become that officials began to waive the seventy-five-year age limit. The prime minister himself commented in 1925: "It is a fact that this pension is being apportioned pro rata to the districts and that men who are not seventy years of age have got it on the recommendation of the district members because they were worn out before the allotted time. I think that it is a matter of record that the pension has been given to men of seventy."[16] Such discretionary processes cleared the way for patronage-influenced distribution of the pension.

Judging from the one extant case in the pre-Commission of Government period, the award was based on a variety of factors. Patronage was clearly of central importance, reflecting the traditional pattern of local political processes; also influential were the timing of the application and the competitive influence of local worthies. In 1922 the government received an appeal against a recently awarded pension for a vacancy on the list for the Bonavista Peninsula. A local clergyman complained that a justice of the peace had falsified the winner's birth date so as to make him eligible for the pension; the cleric's preferred candidate was allegedly qualified, and both applications had been received on the same day. Enough evidence of possible fraud was uncovered that a full investigation of the award was launched by the government, once influential politicians had been persuaded to interest themselves in the case. The clergyman who launched the complaint suggested that such fraud was far from uncommon and was partially policed within the local community on an informal basis:

> It seems to me that there is a great deal wrong going on with regard to this Old Age Pension and a number of people get help who are not entitled to it by their age. I myself have stopped more than one case. About the same time that I sent the above case on, I had sent on the name of a worthy man for Whitbourne, fortunately he has the Pension now. But at the same time actually there was a man appointed and had the "help" for some 6 months. Apparently his age was no more than 69. . . . He died a few months ago.[17]

Such discretionary processes were fundamental to the pension process in Newfoundland. Without denying their centrality, the fact that some form of misrepresentation was often necessary for influential persons to gain pensions for their candidates suggests that there were also authoritative community criteria which had to be met for the candidate to attain an old age pension.[18]

More than a decade later much the same process remained in place. In 1934, five days after a local pensioner had died, a provincial magistrate on Bonavista Bay wrote the pension bureaucracy with the support of a local cleric, recommending a local seventy-six-year-old man whose pension application had been on file since he had celebrated his seventy-fifth birthday sixteen months earlier. Not only did the man deserve the pension, but the region had a claim to its share of state aid: "He have his application filled this long time, and as this is the second pensioner to die in this Vicinity without an appointment being made, we consider it right and proper that [he] . . . is the right person to receive it."[19] Community interests were involved in the direct support of individual elderly, and they were equally concerned with claims to a fair share of the distribution of state funds.

The 1911 legislation established an old age pension program that was fundamentally shaped by the character of state formation in Newfoundland. As was typical of programs elsewhere, the onus was on applicants to prove both their need for support and their residency of twenty years in Newfoundland prior to receipt of the pension, for example. But the limited impact of new views about the state on the character or extent of the state machinery meant that the bureaucratic support for the program and demands on prospective pensioners were quite limited. Unlike the later Canadian scheme, there was no legislative provision calling for repayment of the pension from the pensioner's estate, where possible. Nor was there any possibility of payment of a partial pension to those in slightly less needy circumstances.[20] In practice, the bureaucratic structure to operate the scheme was inadequate to handle any but the simplest of eligibility criteria and operating provisions. One clerk in the Department of

Finance and Customs was assigned responsibility for administering the program.[21] Deserving recipients were nominated in each district by a clergyman, the local relief officer or magistrate, or some other government official whenever a vacancy on the district list occurred. Nominations to the list went to the local member of the House of Assembly, who, duly exercising his powers of patronage, made the final recommendation. In this, as with so much else, the local member acted as a vital channel for individuals to their government and reduced any pressures for development of a more sophisticated bureaucracy.

The program differed from several other processes through which members of the House of Assembly exercised their influence. Though their influence over the selection of recipients was considerable, pensions were distributed geographically in proportion to the general population, rather than to the political affiliation of the member. Here was one program for which a member of the Opposition was able to exercise a level of influence comparable to that of a government member.[22] This may help to explain the bipartisan support for the program over the following decades. There is no evidence that any officially articulated eligibility criteria, apart from the approved ones of age and sex (and marital status for women). The amount of property owned by most elderly men was small and of limited value; most were no longer able to perform income-earning work on much of a scale and were ready to stop work as soon as a pension was available, if not earlier.[23] Once approved, the pensioner remained on the list until death. Investigations of applicants were very limited (usually restricted to questions of residency and age), and for the early years there is no evidence of any provision for investigating pensioners' continuing eligibility. It may well be that the program again relied on informal community checks to the extent that this was a concern. Certainly a number of the program's features relied on extra-state processes for maintaining the program.

In the years following its initiation, the pension program scheme slowly expanded. In 1912 the government planned to provide for adding a further four hundred pensioners to the program. The rhetoric of the Speech from the Throne suggests the sort of political appeal intended by the Morris government: the expansion of the program "will be hailed with satisfaction by the toil-worn fishermen of this Colony, who are now at last assured of some provision in their old age, and who can see for themselves that an honest, earnest effort has been made to cope with this matter after it had been played with by others [the Bond government] for so many years."[24] This sort of rhetoric was spurred by the rise of the Fishermen's Protective Union as a political force, which from its inception in 1909 argued for a generous state pension program. Its 1912 Bonavista platform specifically pointed to a more generous pension scheme (beginning at age seventy at $50 and rising eventually to $100 annually, prodding the Morris government to continue its commitment to the plan. The 1913 Speech from the Throne promised to lower the minimum age to seventy, though no such change was made.[25] On the other hand, governments repeatedly committed further funds to the program in the following years.

With the departure of Morris from politics and the decline of the Fishermen's Protective Union, the pension program was removed from the arena of partisan politics until the late 1940s, though political debate certainly recurred from time to time. By 1926–1927 the legislature voted $117 000 annually to the fund, while leaving the maximum pension unaltered. The result was that up to 2340 full pensions could now be awarded across the country. In most years, however, not all the funds were expended, because a few districts could not fill all their vacancies. In 1926–1927, for example, $114 425 was spent.[26] According to the 1921 census, there were only 2019 men on the island aged seventy-five or more, though the number rose significantly in the following years. Nevertheless, it is clear that there were sufficient funds for almost every old man in Newfoundland.

By the mid-1920s the weaknesses of the old age pension scheme were generating public criticism. Concerted opposition centred particularly on the failure to provide pensions for elderly women. Yet even here the attacks accepted the dependent position of such women, seeking only to protect them within the context of their continuing dependency. Considerable popular criticism of the fate of the widows of pensioners led to a February 1925 public meeting at the Society of United Fishermen Hall in Bonavista. A petition was drawn up and signed by 138 men, demanding that henceforth the widows of pensioners be eligible to continue to receive an old age pension.[27] Up to this date elderly couples had received the pension through the husband, establishing their dependency on state support, only to have the support terminated with the husband's death.[28]

At the same time that adult women gained the franchise in Newfoundland in 1925, the legislature acted to protect dependent, elderly widows. Provided that they were at least sixty-five years of age when widowed and remained unmarried, widows of pensioners were eligible to continue to receive the pension. The bill originally stipulated an age of seventy, but because of the flexibility regarding men's ages, it was felt desirable to lower the widow's minimum age. Sympathy for the plight of older women was considerable—"the age should be sixty-five or even sixty, as at that age a woman is helpless and not able to do anything for herself," commented one legislator—but always within the context of their marital status. Just as marriage and their breadwinner husbands supported and protected them through the adult life course, the state would accept the dead husbands' responsibilities. Commentators, at least publicly, gave no thought to including unmarried older women within the program.[29] The fundamental importance of marital status was further emphasized when members of the legislature insisted that the bill be amended to end the pension as soon as a widow remarried.[30] The state was given the role of surrogate husband for widows more than that of a protector of elderly women.

Throughout the debates on the pension legislation in 1911, 1925, and 1926, the lack of opposition to the role of the state in funding old age pensions is striking. While criticisms were made regarding who was included or excluded or how much money was being allocated, no one questioned whether this was the sort of program in which the state should involve itself. One member spoke for many in 1926 when he commented: "I hope the time will come when old people will not have to be 75 before they are pensioned, and that as time goes on it will be brought down to 65 or 70. I believe that as men get older it is the duty of the State to look after those who are not able to look after themselves." The minister of justice responded in kind: "where anyone, man or woman, having reached an advanced age, I do not say necessarily seventy-five, but where they have become dependent on charity, that it is the duty of the State to come forward to their support."[31] These assumptions about the state were central to the development of old age pensions in all western societies, though their immediate impact on state formation obviously varied.

In much of Canada, parents' maintenance statutes had been passed and these were used as regulatory devices to force adult children, where possible, to support their parents.[32] Only as a last resort were elderly Canadians expected to resort to state pensions. In Newfoundland, despite the long-standing existence of such legislation, there is no evidence that the state enforced the legal obligation to support elderly, destitute parents until the changing economic and political circumstances of the 1930s. Nevertheless, the low level of pension support for old men and the limited eligibility of old women suggest just how strongly the culture of old age remained tied to family and community culture. The elderly remained largely dependent on private means; beyond their own assets, support came from family and neighbours. State pensions were intended merely to supplement this private support and certainly not to undermine it.

Newfoundland was susceptible to many of the ideas becoming popular in Canada and across the western world regarding old age, and some local pressure began to be exerted in the 1930s to reduce the pension rolls by forcing greater reliance on families. In 1930, for example, the Royal Commission on Health and Public Charities argued that many relatives "would probably be willing to assist if the duty to do so were specifically brought to their attention." Such pressure, it was recommended, should be brought to bear through "a watchdog of the Treasury" who, using "tactful, persistent and very firm" techniques, should elicit support from individual relatives. Similarly, the royal commission recommended that the state enact legislation to recover from pensioners' estates monies paid out in individual pensions. Indeed, as Newfoundland entered the 1930s and as various Canadian provinces began adopting the federal old age pension legislation,[33] the Newfoundland scheme came under greater pressure to adopt approaches which were coming to be thought of as universal. If the royal commission were to have its way, the Newfoundland program would become more generous in its level of support and in its age and gender conditions, but stricter in determining eligibility and in recovering costs.[34]

The result of these pressures was the passage of the 1931 Health and Public Welfare Act, bringing within one administrative body the wide range of welfare and charitable policies. The efficiency that this centralized bureaucracy was expected to bring would help to eliminate duplicate processes of individual support and thus spread the meagre benefits to as many people as possible.[35] The legislation created a central ministry designed to bring a new bureaucratic order to the confusion of Newfoundland health and welfare processes. It also emphasized particular philosophies with which the legislators sought to imbue those processes. The most striking was the legislative stress on the supportive responsibilities of the family. Despite the fact that parents' maintenance legislation was already on the statute books (though little used), an entire section of the 1931 Health and Public Welfare Act was devoted to maintenance of family members—parents, wives, and children. The statute confirmed the power of dependent parents, or state officials on their behalf, to use the courts in order to force support from adult children who had the necessary means; failure to obey any consequent court order could result in imprisonment. But like most such statutes elsewhere, the legislation had no teeth and was largely ignored.[36] There remained no systematic consideration of adult children's income or capacity to support needy parents; any use of parents' maintenance legislation, either directly against the children or indirectly through the parents, was on an ad hoc basis. Nevertheless, the new legislation emphasized some of the impact of Newfoundland's exposure to external currents and approaches. The timing of the creation of the new ministry makes it clear that the impact of these attitudes predated the establishment of the Commission of Government, which subsequently facilitated further developments along the same lines.

These new cost-conscious attitudes regarding efficiency and discrimination among the "needy" and "unneedy" poor were reflected among local officials as well. Relief officers for the north shore (Cape St John to Musgrave Harbour), for example, judged in 1934 that 20 percent of the current pensioners had sufficient means to make the old age pension unnecessary for them; cancellation of these pensions would allow the funds to be shifted to those in real need.[37] Local officials were encouraged in such attitudes by missives from St John's. A 1936 pronouncement to all relief officers, for example, called for stricter enforcement of welfare regulations and for absolute refusal to aid families capable of being self-supporting: "The general attitude seems to be that the wage earner can be as wasteful and extravagant as he pleases without having to pay what would normally be the penalty of want and privation for his dependencies and himself. The idea is becoming firmly fixed that the state will save them from the consequences of their sins of omission and commission in such connections—that under no circumstances will the State permit them to starve."[38] This point of view was echoed by one relieving officer at the top of the northern peninsula:

> The idea still persists that these allowances are a matter of right and are due and payable at the age of 75, or because of widowhood alone. Upon investigation a number of cases have been found to possess means of support which rendered Governmental support unnecessary. However, practically all those who have been recommended for continuance on Permanent Poor Relief are in the worst imaginable circumstances. The condition of these people impresses on one the utter inadequacy of the present allowance to provide even a fraction of the maintenance of a destitute beneficiary. . . . It

has also been observed that Old Age Pensioners whose wives are still living and who are entirely dependent on the Old Age Pension for support are finding it impossible to provide enough of the bare necessities of life. During normal times this condition would not be considered quite so serious, as some help would be forthcoming from neighbours, friends, etc. But today, in many of these places, with practically a majority of the population on Relief the plight of these people is to say the least really desperate.[39]

This mixture of toughness and genuine sympathy for the plight of the elderly poor characterized the pension system throughout the 1930s.

The old age pension program was part of a spectrum of welfare measures available to the needy in Newfoundland. Those persons too young to qualify for an old age pension could receive direct relief if the local relieving officer had the funds available and judged the support to be needed. Older women (and occasionally men under age seventy-five) could receive funds through this means or through the funds voted annually for widows, orphans, and the infirm, for which there were no statutory or regulatory parameters.[40] The government paid boarding allowances to private individuals who agreed to take in a dependent person; this was particularly common for single men who typically lacked domestic skills. Institutional care at the Poor Asylum in St John's (recently renamed the Home for Aged and Infirm) was available for a very small number of chronically ill or "unmanageable" persons. Aid in kind as well was available for the needy: coal or clothing (or even building material to repair inhabitable accommodations) from public sources, clothing and footwear from private charities. The economic difficulties of the 1930s placed great strain on these sources of aid, however, and many of the private charities ceased activity.

Government officials sought to cope with the increased demand on the weaker public purse in the 1930s by tightening regulations and investigations of applicants. One "loophole" that was closed was the payment of pensions to Newfoundlanders living abroad. Elderly parents often paid extended visits to adult children or other relatives living in Canada or the United States, and their pensions had continued to be paid; late in 1931 this was stopped.[41] Attacking the indiscriminate grants of the past, the government ordered investigators to check on the circumstances of individual cases, altering the money awarded or even terminating the grant depending on needs. Burial expenses of pensioners were no longer paid, except on direct application. In 1934 new instructions to relief officials emphasized the importance of applying a needs-test to pension applicants. In 1936 new regulations recognized the different conditions outside St John's: early in 1936 residents of St John's with at least $450 capital or $26 monthly income were declared ineligible for the old age pension, while for those outside St John's the limits were $250 capital or $10 monthly. Through this regulation, old age pensions were no longer made available as they had been in such earlier cases as where income already exceeded $300 annually, or where a war pension of $20 a month was already being received, or where a small business was owned.[42] For the first time the needs test had been quantified for the Newfoundland pension plan, allowing for greater standardization in the treatment of the country's elderly.

Following on the creation of the Department of Public Health and Welfare in 1931, the Commission of Government brought a new bureaucratic mentality to the pension program. The articulation of needs-test standards was just part of a broader process that brought the local pensions closer to the processes employed in public pensions programs elsewhere. Investigators began to check pensioners' circumstances regularly, annually where possible; recognizing the cost and difficulty of reaching many in outports, an annual self-reporting process was developed, similar to that already in place in Canada, though there is no hint of any direct Canadian influence. This annual update was not regularly carried out until approximately 1945. Officials became more insistent on proper procedures being followed and full information being provided by applicants, and new questions were added to the application section designed to apply the needs-test. Regular audits of the program now prevented, or at least inhibited, much of the earlier informal leniency in individual cases. But the sophistication of that bureaucracy remained quite limited. All of the cheques (up to 12 000 annually), for example, were typed individually and signed by hand, necessitating preparation up to two months in advance of issue. New equipment was only slowly added to permit a more efficient administration.[43] Yet it is striking that even the enhanced bureaucratic mentality of the Commission of Government failed to end the scheme's gendered character or to alter the simplistic geographical formula for the distribution of pensions that was so unresponsive to real need.

The records of the Commission of Government permit a more definite picture of how the old age pension program worked.[44] In 1936, for example, there were funds for 3000 pensions;[45] in two quarters of that year, 2986 and 2888 pensions were actually paid.[46] The vacancies in the pension list were concentrated in St John's East and St John's West, where approximately half of the possible pensions had not been awarded; the Grand Falls, Burin, Harbour Main, and St Barbe districts also had a number of vacancies. On the other hand, the earlier practice of transferring an applicant informally to a district that had vacancies had now been regularized. Sixteen districts contained a total of 265 old age pensions in excess of their allotment. Individual districts were now allowed to "overdraw" on their allotment up to the national funding limit.[47] The number of elderly seeking the pension was still so considerable in some districts that "most pensioners are over the age of 75 before they receive payment," reported one official. While the earlier leniency toward some of the younger elderly in need had ceased, the Newfoundland program was certainly less harsh and much less bureaucratic than the Canadian program. In Newfoundland the payment was made at the start of the quarter and no provision was in place to try to recoup funds paid for the period after a pensioner's death.[48] Additional relief in kind was not prohibited, and parents' maintenance laws were not rigorously used as an obstacle to pensions.

Pressure for stricter investigation of applicants' eligibility and for more rigorous enforcement of a needs test continued to mount in the 1930s and

1940s. The result was a considerable conflict, both bureaucratic and familial. Officials in the office of the Comptroller and Auditor General clashed with those in Public Health and Welfare over the priority given to efficiency and financial exigencies compared with the social, financial, and familial circumstances of individual elderly. In 1944, for example, a lengthy and sometimes heated exchange occurred over these issues. The auditor general's officers particularly pushed welfare investigators to examine the capacity of adult children to assist their parents. Here, as in various Canadian provinces, parents hesitated to approach their children for financial help, and adult children tried to help their parents in ways that would supplement state aid, rather than replace it, allowing the elderly to maximize their income and support from all sources. The secretary for justice, when consulted by both government departments, and the commissioner for finance both advised that the parents' maintenance legislation was so difficult and impracticable to enforce that it did not bar state aid in the form of either the widows' allowance or the old age pension.[49] The auditor general also unsuccessfully challenged the legality of welfare officers providing additional aid to persons already receiving the pension.[50]

The different responsibilities of the two departments produced quite different priorities. The result was a vigorous clash over particular cases. In one case the commissioner for public health and welfare defended the grant of an old age pension, but agreed to cancel it. In two other cases he insisted on the correctness of the original award. One old fisherman on the Burin Peninsula had two children; his son was a sea captain, and a married daughter lived in New York, neither of whom had been investigated as to their capacity to support their father, according to the auditor general. Yet the commissioner refused to alter this award: "It was never before questioned that an old worn out fisherman, even though he had one son who was working as a Captain for some months of the year should be granted the Old Age Pension. The Legislature intended that the allowance should be given to such cases. That was why the Old Age Pension Vote was instituted, and I question the right of any Auditor to combat my judgement in cases such as this."[51] With such bureaucratic conflict over the relative roles of the state and the family and with such limited official support for enforcement of parents' maintenance legislation, it is not surprising that local officials were also ambivalent. While a few local investigators clearly wanted to push adult children, particularly unmarried sons, to provide greater support,[52] most officials took it for granted that the adult children had their own more immediate family obligations and were already doing what they could to assist elderly parents.[53]

By 1942 the pension program had been in place for more than thirty years, but the amount of pensions payable had remained the same, disregarding the rising cost of living. This situation was brought home to Newfoundlanders in the changing economic circumstances occasioned by the Second World War and the proliferation of American and Canadian military bases on the island. The Commission of Government authorized various increases in welfare payments in 1941 and 1942, including a raise in the old age pension to $60 annually. In the fall of 1943 payment levels rose again to $72 for a single pensioner and $120 for a married pensioner.[54] For the first time, marital status affected the amount of the pension, previously an elderly pensioned couple being expected "to live as cheaply as one." It is clear that the economic circumstances of the elderly were particularly harsh. By 1943 there were many fewer vacancies on the pension roll than in 1936, and all but three districts had applicants simply waiting approval for their pensions to start; this is partially explained by the reduction in the number of pensions funded, which was down to 2800. Welfare officials found it necessary to supplement the pension "in many cases . . . because of the couples' inability to exist on the smaller amount." The commissioner for public health and welfare originally planned to ask for an increase to $100 for a married pensioner, but when one of his Commission colleagues encouraged him to seek $144, the commissioner asked for $120 since "two people living together can live somewhat cheaper than one." Such a pension "would be fair and somewhat generous for this country," he successfully argued.[55] Yet the maintenance of gender and geographical restrictions undermine any claims to the overall "fairness" of the program.

Despite these increases in payment levels, the Newfoundland old age pension program remained very inefficient as a scheme to raise the income of the needy elderly. The payments were insufficient and always had been. Older women continued to be excluded, except through their husbands; when widowed, these women did not automatically continue to receive the pension; reapplication was necessary and resulted in several months' delay before payments recommenced; if widowed before age sixty-five, women were ineligible;[56] unmarried older women or widows whose husbands had never been pensioners were completely barred. The age limit had never been lowered, thereby excluding a majority of those elderly no longer able to support themselves adequately. The process by which the pension list was established was very ineffective in addressing real need. By the mid-1940s there continued to be a significant number of vacancies and undistributed pensions. On average for the four quarters of 1944, for example, 2620 pensions were actually being paid, 103 applications awaited approval each quarter, and there were 77 vacancies.[57] Without disputing the fact that significant support was reaching some elderly, the administration of the program was simplistic, and its design remained inadequate. In 1946 the number of possible pensions expanded to 3000 and the actual number rose to more than 2800 that year and more than 2900 in 1947, but the administrative process still left a surprising number of undistributed old age pensions.[58] In the first quarter of 1947, 1071 couples, 1011 single men, and 808 widows received an old age pension.[59] It may be that details of the program were inadequately known among potential recipients.[60]

This was the situation in the late 1940s when the prospect of a different, much more generous old age pension program was held out to Newfoundlanders during the debate over joining Confederation. In May 1947 the Canadian pension rose to a maximum monthly payment of $30, and then rose again in May 1949 to $40.[61] This was means-tested using much more explicit criteria than those in place in Newfoundland, but it was available to anyone, male or female, who was at least seventy years of age.

The Canadian pension would thus be accessible to an enormously larger proportion of the Newfoundland elderly by age and by sex; what was more, a single pensioner would receive, by 1949, $480 annually, rather than $72, and a married couple both of whom were pensioners would receive $960, rather than $120.[62] Such potential benefits from the Canadian program thus offered to improve the financial circumstances of Newfoundland elderly (and their families and local communities) very significantly.

As Newfoundlanders considered their constitutional options in 1947–1949, the practical benefits of Confederation with Canada were best exemplified by the hard cash that programs such as family allowances and old age pensions would put into circulation in an often cash-starved local economy. Pro-Confederate literature emphasized such Canadian programs, and many Newfoundlanders found the prospects of these benefits very attractive. It was not merely the elderly themselves who could see immediate advantages in the Canadian old age pension. Their families, on whom the needy elderly remained considerably dependent, would benefit through the much reduced pressure for financial support and through shared resources.[63] It is difficult to measure just what role such prospects played in the referendum voting by individual Newfoundlanders. There is no doubt, however, that Joey Smallwood sought to make the most effective use of these programs in the 27 May 1949 provincial election and 3 June federal election that followed union with Canada on 31 March. In the fight to confirm his premiership he wanted to drive home to individual voters the cash benefits of these various payments to Newfoundlanders. Smallwood had nine weeks after union to get some practical examples of these programs into the hands of the voters, and that is just what he set out to do in the case of old age pensions.

On 25 April 1949 a small number of Ottawa bureaucrats flew into St John's to help Newfoundland officials set up the changing program. The correspondence back to Ottawa over the next month offers an interesting window on Canadian reactions to the newest province and on the state of the existing old age pension machinery. The Canadians were strikingly patronizing in their perceptions. The chief Canadian official, E.R. Swettenham of the Department of Finance, reported that conditions were "rather primitive" when he first arrived, and in the following days he saw nothing to change his mind. Three days later he met a local bank manager "who expressed the view [that] this province is fifty years behind any other in the Dominion. We agreed with this view. One has to spend but a few days here to become disgusted with the lack of systematic control. . . . Files relating to provincial relief assistance are mixed with old age pensions cases. Dead files are mixed in with the cases in issue. . . . Many cases are in pay for which no application has yet been placed in the filing jacket relating to the claim for pension."[64] These perceptions simply confirmed existing Canadian stereotypes about Newfoundland backwardness.

Newfoundland officials, pushed by the Smallwood government, were anxious to see the Canadian pension program in operation as quickly as possible. Unfortunately, there was a delay in printing the appropriate application forms. Though existing pensioners would automatically be transferred to the Canadian program, there were thousands of men aged seventy to seventy-four and women aged seventy or more who were eligible to apply for the first time. All needed to fill out the appropriate forms, to establish their financial circumstances, and to provide proof of age, all to the satisfaction of the Ottawa officials, whose government paid 75 percent of the pension costs.[65] Beyond the physical problem of getting the application forms into the hands of the elderly, there was a very real problem regarding proof of age. Ottawa officials had found from past experience that simple affidavits from applicants were quite inadequate, individuals being quite willing to swear false evidence in the face of the prospect of receiving considerable advantages. Instead, more impersonal forms of proof were required. This was a serious problem in Newfoundland in particular because the government birth registration process had been quite relaxed.[66]

The federal officials' letters to Ottawa provide a running account of the provincial government's anxiety to get some substantial proof of the benefits of Confederation into the hands of the electorate as soon as possible. On 25 April the provincial minister, H.L. Pottle, announced that he wanted to advise the elderly by radio to apply by letter, without waiting for the government form, so as to establish eligibility by 1 May. According to Swettenham, the following day further pressure to allow this was exerted:

> While engaged in drafting forms this morning with Mr. Farquhar and the Minister, the Premier called the latter on the phone and explained to him in no uncertain language and quite loudly that Mr. Pottle was to broadcast a message tonight to prospective pensioners telling them to send a telegram to the Old Age Pensions Board before the end of the month and that receipt of such a telegram before May 1 and pursuant to the completion later of an application for pension by the applicant, the pension, if granted, would commence as from May 1. Although seated several feet away from the 'phone I heard such expressions as "cut the red tape" and "cheques must be in the hands of pensioners before May."

The federal bureaucrats were aghast at this cavalier treatment of their procedures and expressed "amazement" that the federal minister (Paul Martin) had, in direct telephone conversation with Smallwood, agreed to go along with this plan. No forms had yet been drafted (much less printed), no provincial board had yet been appointed, there was no machinery for imprinting the monthly cheques, and there was no office equipment for the as-yet-non-existent office staff.[67] Fortunately, the need for such informal application procedures was obviated when the federal government agreed that formal applications received during May 1949 would be treated as though they had been received prior to 1 May, thus making the applicants eligible to receive an old age pension for May. The new forms were soon available for distribution through local post offices.

Nevertheless, the flow of letters and applications on outdated forms was considerable, as eligible Newfoundlanders demonstrated their undoubted willingness to take advantage of their new constitutional position. A small number of veterans studying at Memorial College were hired and trained as temporary investigators for the flood of new applicants; if these were insufficient in number, the plan was to hire local school teachers. On 5 May Swettenham wrote that the "corridor leading to the Registrar General's office was crowded all day with applicants for birth certificates and the hall leading to the rooms set aside for the old age pension staff were [sic] lined with aged persons bringing their completed forms for pension." Without extensive assistance from seconded federal officers, Ottawa officials in St John's feared that the outdated procedures could not be remodelled in time to prevent "a colossal mess" in handling old age pension applications. "The primitive methods in effect here are amazing," commented Swettenham. "How some departments operate is difficult to understand."[68] Agreement on adopting new procedures was complicated not only by the conflicting attitudes and different cultures of local and Ottawa officials, but also by the absence of the minister of public health and welfare, who was on the campaign trail.[69]

By the end of the second week in May the provincial board had finally been appointed and a few investigators were already busy examining applicants' circumstances. At least six inspectors, authorized to take oaths, were investigating cases in the St John's area. Within a week this had been expanded to ten in the St John's area and a further four for Bell Island; investigators for the outports simply could not be selected and trained prior to the provincial election. Office staff were finally hired and on the job, organizing the office in the way the federal visitors wished. The Ottawa officials were concerned to articulate detailed standards to test need, to set monetary values for various forms of support already in the hands of the elderly, and to check for various forms of fraud. Federal officials were also worried that strict auditing procedures might not be adopted, and were pleased to learn that the provincial auditor general had come to Newfoundland from the prestigious British civil service just a few years earlier. "Although the machinery is running like a car of 1914 vintage, it is operating," wrote Swettenham on the eve of the provincial election.[70]

As the date of the provincial election drew closer, pressure to issue cheques increased. "I received a request to go through the approved cases and give priority to the cases in a particular area," wrote Swettenham—who refused to comply on the bureaucratic ground that this "would disrupt the procedure we had planned and all cases will be dealt with in numerical order as filed."[71] In case the cheques arrived too late to influence voters, the premier sent out a letter to at least some of the pension applicants personally promising them an old age pension cheque for at least $30 a month for the rest of their life.[72] By 24 May Swettenham could report that all of the previous Newfoundland pensioners had been mailed their April cheque—most would have received a $30 cheque for one month, in contrast to the $18 cheque for three months received in the past January.[73] With this Smallwood and his political cohorts had to be content; when a means test necessitated investigation of each application, the bureaucratic pension process could not be made to work any faster.

Although the old age pension cheques were probably not in the hands of the elderly soon enough to please the provincial and federal Liberal parties fully, it was not long before such substantial evidence of the benefits of Confederation was becoming apparent. By mid-June there were about fifty temporary investigators working in the districts outside St John's.[74] The provincial board soon realized that for a large number of new cases it would be several months before investigations could be completed, all information collected and regular pension cheques authorized. In the meantime, the elderly would be without state aid, although eventually individual payments would be made retroactive to 1 May. The provincial board's solution was to issue relief payments equal to the value of prospective pension cheques, using provincial funds; when the pension was eventually authorized, the provincial funds could be recouped from Ottawa.[75] In this way the financial problems of the elderly could be addressed and the political advantages cemented.

By the end of the first year a substantial endeavour to place larger sums of financial support into the hands of the needy elderly had been largely successful. Smallwood and his colleagues had the political result that they wanted, though the extent of popular satisfaction with Confederation is not directly measurable. A sizeable bureaucracy had been created provincially, offering useful patronage opportunities to the provincial government.[76] By early 1950 there were sixteen persons employed at the St John's board office, and eighty-five investigators worked for the program on a part-time basis; before the end of 1950, twenty-five permanent welfare officers replaced the part-time investigators. In the first year of the Canadian program, \$2 229 446 in cheques reached the hands of the needy elderly in Newfoundland; that sum would be much larger thereafter once most of the eligible elderly were on the pension list for the full year.[77] Individual cheques initiating the pension for new pensioners could be very large; retroactive payments over several months often resulted in cheques from \$65 to as high as \$150, surely the largest sums ever handled privately by many of the recipients.[78] By the end of the first year in the Canadian program Newfoundland had much the highest proportion of its elderly receiving the old age pension compared with the other provinces.[79] Whatever the local and individual impact of this massive expansion of government and of state aid, its contrast with the earlier Newfoundland program is striking. The differences could not have escaped the notice of individual Newfoundlanders, although the conclusions that they drew await further investigation.

Two elements of the Newfoundland response to old age pensions in the first half of the twentieth century provoke particular response. The first is the character of state formation in Newfoundland during this time. Some of the cultural elements common to state formation elsewhere are apparent in this account of the Newfoundland pension program. The assumptions that the dependent elderly now required more active support and that the state was the proper source of that support were familiar across the western world at this time. That the old age pension program itself should be needs-based and non-contributory was also common. Not so common, however, was the relatively slow change in the Newfoundland state's capacity to administer such a program. Elsewhere state bureaucracies had adapted to the changing views of the state's responsibilities so that officials developed the tools and techniques associated with state formation. But in Newfoundland the bureaucracy tended to grow or adapt to the new environment rather less than elsewhere. In the old age pension program there was a continuing reliance on the local community and elites, which delayed the concentration of power among the bureaucrats themselves. The bureaucracy itself tended to grow at a different pace from the changing cultural perceptions associated with the role of the state. Most surprisingly, this continued to be true, though less so, even when the Commission of Government took over the reins of power. While we might well want to be sceptical about the patronizing comments of Canadian bureaucrats in the spring of 1949, the evidence regarding the Newfoundland program across a forty-year period nevertheless suggests that state formation in Newfoundland had its own quite distinctive history, and that this history clearly shaped the character of that program.

The second intriguing element in the history of the island old age pension program was gender. It is not surprising that gender was a factor or that the program was initially limited to men, for the early German old age pension scheme had some of the same restrictions.[80] What stands out is that the gendered character of the program was subjected to so little legislative debate or challenge across the period[81] and that it changed so little. Elderly women were fundamentally and massively disadvantaged through a state program that accepted, legitimated, and entrenched their dependency on husband, on family, and on community. Denied direct support from the state as an entitlement, elderly women were forced to turn as supplicants to other sources of support. That this was so acceptable for so long a period is very suggestive of the role of gender in the local culture. It also suggests that Confederation in 1949 challenged the local culture in some very fundamental ways that beg investigation.

NOTES

1. On the United Kingdom's pension scheme see Pat Thane, *Foundations of the Welfare State* (London, 1982), 81–84, 142–43, 196–200, 245; Pat Thane, ed., *The Origins of British Social Policy* (London, 1978), 84–106. On the government annuities scheme and the old age pension in Canada, see Dennis Guest, *The Emergence of Social Security in Canada* (Vancouver, 1980), 34–36; Kenneth Bryden, *Old Age Pensions and Policy-Making in Canada* (Montreal, 1974).

2. See, for example, W. Andrew Achenbaum, *Old Age in The New Land: The American Experience since 1790* (New York, 1978); Howard Chudacoff, *How Old Are You? Age Consciousness in American Culture* (Princeton, 1989); Thomas R. Cole, "The Prophecy of Senescence: G. Stanley Hall and the Reconstruction of Old Age in America," *Gerontologist* 24, 4 (Aug. 1984): 360–66; Janet Roebuck, "When Does Old Age Begin?: The Evolution of the English Definition," *Journal of Social History* 12, 3 (Spring 1979): 416–29; Philip Corrigan and Derek Sayer, *The Great Arch: English State Formation as Cultural Revolution* (Oxford, 1985); Allan Greer and Ian Radforth, eds., *Colonial Leviathan: State Formation in Mid-Nineteenth-Century Canada* (Toronto, 1992). There is no evidence

regarding the role of capital in the impetus for old age pensions or for state formation generally.

3. I discuss the St John's Poor Asylum extensively in a forthcoming study of the Canadian elderly, 1900–51.

4. The resolutions and the debate are reprinted in the St John's *Evening Telegram*, 23, 27, 28, 29, 30 March 1906.

5. The members of the royal commission were James S. Pitts (minister without portfolio and member of the Legislative Council), R.H. O'Dwyer (commissioner of public charities), John Harvey, Edgar R. Bowring, W.B. Grieve, and E.M. Jackman (minister of finance and customs and member of the House of Assembly).

6. Newfoundland, *Proceedings of the House of Assembly, 1911*, 458–60, 468.

7. Newfoundland, *Journal of the House of Assembly, 1908*, 5, 65–66.

8. Sidney J.R. Noel, *Politics in Newfoundland* (Toronto, 1971), 52, 56, 58. Morris's connection with the indigent elderly was longstanding, since his father had been keeper of the St John's Poor Asylum, the sole institutional response to the needy elderly in nineteenth-century Newfoundland; ibid., 32.

9. Newfoundland, *Proceedings of the House of Assembly, 1911*, 461, 467–71.

10. See, for example, ibid., 499–500.

11. *Census of Newfoundland, 1901* (St John's, 1903), 1: 444–47; *Census of Newfoundland, 1911* (St John's, 1914), 1: 492–95; *Census of Newfoundland, 1921* (St John's, 1923), 1: 498–501; *Census of Newfoundland and Labrador, 1935* (St John's, 1937), table 32; *Census of Newfoundland and Labrador, 1945* (St John's, 1949), table 7; Canada, *Census of 1951* (Ottawa, 1953), 1: table 19.

12. Newfoundland, *Proceedings of the House of Assembly, 1911*, 460, where the data are reprinted on a district-by-district basis.

13. Newfoundland, *Proceedings of the House of Assembly, 1911*, 481–82.

14. In 1911 the Morris government found itself with a sizeable surplus in its budget and allocated almost half of that surplus ($200 000) to form the basis of an old age pension fund invested in colonial debentures. To the $8000 interest from these funds was added $12 000 from current revenue to provide $50 pensions for four hundred elderly. The plan was to invest more funds each year from expected surpluses. See Patrick T. McGrath, *Newfoundland in 1911* (London, 1911), 250.

15. Newfoundland, *Proceedings of the House of Assembly, 1926*, 978–79.

16. Newfoundland, *Proceedings of the House of Assembly, 1925*, 811. See also, ibid., *1926*, 979–80.

17. Rev. C. Jeffery to Sir W. Horwood, Whitbourne, Nfld., 8 Nov. 1922, Horwood to Jeffery, [St John's], 29 Nov. 1922, G. Bursell to Horwood, [St John's], 28 Nov. 1929, Governor's Miscellaneous and Local Correspondence, GN1/3/A, 820/1922, Public Archives of Newfoundland and Labrador (hereafter PANL).

18. See, for example, survey card 3, ms 79-018, Memorial University of Newfoundland Folklore and Language Archives (hereafter MUNFLA).

19. L. Squires to Board of Pensioners, Eastport, 18 Aug. 1934, Old Age Pension Records, GN37/1, box 1, file 1352, PANL.

20. Newfoundland (1911), 1 George V, c. 29. A comparison with the Canadian scheme can be gained from Bryden, *Old Age Pensions*.

21. *A Year Book and Almanac of Newfoundland: 1913* (St John's, 1913), 190; ibid., *1922*, 208; ibid., *1928*, 185. It is unclear why the program was managed by the Department of Finance rather than the colonial secretary's department, which usually handled matters relating to health and welfare.

22. Noel, *Politics in Newfoundland*, 20–21.

23. Ms 79-484/p. 5, MUNFLA.

24. Newfoundland, *Proceedings of the House of Assembly, 1912*, 13.

25. Noel, *Politics in Newfoundland*, 99–100;
Ian D.H. McDonald, *"To Each His
Own": William Coaker and the Fisher-
men's Protective Union in Newfoundland
Politics, 1908–1925* (St John's, 1987),
21–44; William F. Coaker, ed., *The
History of the Fishermen's Protective
Union of Newfoundland* (St John's, 1920),
11, 25, 40, 120; Stuart R. Godfrey,
*Human Rights and Social Policy in
Newfoundland, 1832–1982* (St John's,
1985), 37–38.

26. Newfoundland, *Journal of the House
of Assembly, 1927*, appendix, 123;
ibid., *1928*, appendix, 261.

27. Petition [Feb. 1925], J.W. Lawrence
to the Premier, 23 Feb. 1925, Colonial
Secretary's Special Files, GN2/5, file
418v, PANL.

28. There was a widows' and orphans'
allowance throughout these years,
but in the case of the widows'
allowance—popularly known as the
widow's mite—it was not age specific and was not as generous or as
secure as an old age pension. The
allowance was also considered to be
welfare, whereas the pension could
be accepted as a matter of "right."

29. The aggregate data in the Newfoundland censuses do not permit
retrieval of information regarding
marital status by age, so that information is missing regarding the
number of unmarried older women.

30. Newfoundland (1925), 15 George V,
c. 31; Newfoundland, *Proceedings of
the House of Assembly, 1925*, 811–13.
A further amendment in 1926 (16
George V, c. 27) applied the legislation retroactively.

31. Newfoundland, *Proceedings of the
House of Assembly, 1926*, 978, 980.

32. James Struthers, "Regulating the
Elderly: Old Age Pensions and the
Formation of a Pension Bureaucracy
in Ontario, 1929–1945" *Journal of the
Canadian Historical Association* 3
(1992): 245; James G. Snell, "Filial
Responsibility Laws in Canada: An
Historical Study," *Canadian Journal
on Aging* 9 (1990): 268–77.

33. The federal legislation was passed in
1927 and adopted by the various

provinces over the following decade:
British Columbia 1927, Saskatchewan
1928, Manitoba 1928, Alberta 1929,
Ontario 1929, Prince Edward Island
1933, Nova Scotia 1934, New
Brunswick 1936, and Quebec 1936.
Both New Brunswick (1929–30) and
Nova Scotia (1928–30) had royal
commissions on the subject, and their
activities and reports may have stim-
ulated further spread of attitudes
and ideas in the region. On the New
Brunswick royal commission, see
RS24, RS642, 1930 RE/2, Provincial
Archives of New Brunswick. On the
Nova Scotia royal commission, see
Journals of the House of Assembly, 1930,
2, appendix 29.

34. Newfoundland, *First Interim Report
of the Royal Commission on Health and
Public Charities, June 1930* (St John's,
1930), 167–68, 202, 204–6; *Proceedings
of the Legislative Council, 1931*, 41.
Building on these attitudes, the secretary for public health and welfare
in 1934 called for the passage and
enforcement of parents' maintenance
legislation, unaware that such a
measure was already in the statute
books; see H.M. Mosdell to J.C.
Puddester, 18 June 1934, Department
of Public Health and Welfare
Records, GN38/S6-6-1, file 6, PANL.

35. Newfoundland, *Proceedings of the
House of Assembly, 1931*, 295.

36. Newfoundland (1931), 22 George V,
c. 12, ss. 571–74; Snell, "Filial
Responsibility Laws." Ontario, for
example, established a similar
department of public welfare in
1930.

37. Hussey & Howe to Puddester, 5
Aug. 1934, GN38/S6-1-1, file 2,
PANL.

38. Department of Public Welfare &
Health and War Pensions to "All
Relief Officials," 4 April 1936,
GN38/S6-6-1, file 7, PANL.

39. Inspector Barron's Report from
Flower's Cove Section, Sept. 1936,
GN38/S6-6-1, file 7, PANL. See also
W.R. Bishop to H.M. Mosdell,
Flower's Cove, 9 Feb. 1938, GN38/S6-
6-4, file 1, PANL.

40. The widows' allowance varied with the circumstances of the recipient, ranging annually from $20 to $60, with $40 being standard until the mid-1940s, when it was raised to $60 for most.

41. The chair of the Nova Scotia old age pension commission complained in 1942 about the number of older Newfoundlanders who moved to Nova Scotia to live permanently with their adult children, thus qualifying for the Canadian old age pension: "We have had a very considerable number of people from Newfoundland and other parts of the British Empire who come here only after their earning period was ended. Many widows and men up in years, living in Newfoundland, came to Nova Scotia to live with a son or daughter in Cape Breton, and when the twenty year [residency] period is up, they qualify for pension, (some after sixteen years of residence, having perhaps visited for a short time in Nova Scotia years before)." See E.H. Blois to J.R. Forest, 9 Dec. 1942, Records of the Department of National Health and Welfare, RG29, vol. 33, 208-5-2, pt 3, National Archives of Canada (hereafter NAC).

42. J.C. Puddester to Secretary for Commission of Government, 7 April 1936; Memo to all relieving officers and relief inspectors, St John's, 27 Feb. 1939; S6-1-1, file 47, Mosdell to Puddester, 4 March 1936; file 2, Comptroller and Auditor General to Puddester, 13 Dec. 1935; Mosdell to Puddester, 2 Jan. 1936, GN38/S6-1-3, file 36, PHW.8-'36, PANL. At the end of the Second World War, the maximum allowable assets were raised to $400 or $20 monthly income outside St John's and $600 or $40 respectively in St John's; see Debates of the Newfoundland National Convention, 31 March 1947, 898–99. However, an examination of extant pension case files (see note 44) suggests that these income barriers were not rigidly adhered to.

43. Comptroller and Auditor General to Puddester, 13 Dec. 1935; Mosdell to Puddester, St John's, 2 Jan. 1936; GN38/S6-1-1, file 2, PANL.

44. The PANL holds a collection of files (GN37/1) consisting of the state welfare records of some of those applying for an old age pension from April 1949 to the end of 1951, comprising the period in which Newfoundlanders became eligible for a Canadian means-tested old age pension to the point at which those pensions became universally available to all those aged seventy or more. If the individual applied for a Canadian pension in the 1949–51 period, the file contains records of various forms of state support both before and after the 1949–51 period. The examination of the applied character of the Newfoundland program is based on a subjective analysis of these files.

45. It is unclear when the number of pensions was expanded to 3000—probably in the early 1930s, and certainly by 1933—but by 1937 the number was being reduced again to 2800. See "Report of the Committee on Public Health and Welfare" to the National Convention, 1947, 22.

46. According to the Annual Report of the Commission of Government for the Year 1936 (London, 1937), there were 2998 old age pensioners in 1936. Approximately half of the total elderly were directly receiving an old age pension, but the distribution between old men and old women would have been quite unbalanced—just how unbalanced is impossible to estimate with any claim to accuracy. There were 2918 men and 2910 women aged seventy-five or more and a further 9631 women aged sixty-five to seventy-four in Newfoundland in 1935. Among the women, only those who were widows of pensioners would have been eligible for their own pension, and aggregate census figures do not permit any estimates of local eligibility; about two-thirds would have been widows, if local demographic trends followed Canadian patterns.

47. Mosdell to Puddester, 4 March 1936, enclosure 7 April 1936, GN38/S6-1-1, file 47, PANL.

48. Comptroller and Auditor General to Puddester, 13 Dec. 1935, GN38/S6-1-1, file 2, PANL. One old man on the southwest coast recalled later: "My poor father, I will always remember, was 82 years old when he got his first old age pension cheque and he wouldn't have got it then if Mr. S ... hadn't died": see ms 79-633/p. 21, MUNFLA.

49. G.P. Bradney to Puddester, 15 Jan. 1944; 20 Jan. 1944; Puddester, Memo, St John's, 17 Jan. 1944; file 36, Secretary for Justice to Bradney, 12 Feb. 1944; Commissioner for Finance to Puddester, 21 Feb. 1944, GN38/S6-1-3, file 4, PANL.

50. Bradney to Puddester, 10 June 1944, GN38/S6-1-3, file 4, PANL.

51. Bradney to Puddester, 15 Jan. 1944; 20 Jan. 1944; Puddester, Memo, St John's, 17 Jan. 1944, GN38/S6-1-3, file 4, PANL. See also Bradney to Secretary for Justice, 21 Jan. 1944, Department of Justice Records, GN13/2/A, box 117, file 2, PANL.

52. See, for example, files 1963, 2388, GN37/1, box 2, PANL.

53. There were, however, occasional examples of officials putting considerable pressure on adult children to contribute more fully to their parents' support. In one case a seventy-seven-year-old man had been dependent on state support for seven years in 1945 when the welfare department challenged his two married sons to accept their filial responsibility; the officials contacted the sons' employer to ascertain their wages, wrote threatening to take legal action, and did indeed begin legal action before the sons signed a support agreement. See file 9351, GN37/1, box 7, PANL.

54. Puddester to Commission of Government, 4 May 1942, GN38/S6-1-8, file 12, PHW.10-'42, and Puddester to Commission of Government, 3 Dec. 1942, GN38/S6-1-3, file 36, PHW.27-'42, PANL; Puddester to Commissioner for Finance, 31 Oct. 1942; Commissioner for Finance to Puddester, 19 Nov.

1942; Newfoundland (1942), c. 21. The original proposal in the fall of 1942 had been for a $75 pension, but it was bureaucratically desirable to use a number easily divisible by four, to facilitate quarterly payments. Officials tried to insist that husbands share the pension with their wives, threatening at times to pay the additional $48 directly to a wife living separately; see file 638. GN37/1, box 1, PANL.

55. Puddester to Commission of Government, 19 July 1943, GN38/S6-1-2, file 15, PHW.40-'43, PANL. Puddester to Commission of Government, 25 Sept. 1943, enclosure, PHW 40(a)-'43, PANL; Newfoundland (1943), c. 40.

56. *Debates of the Newfoundland National Convention*, 1 April 1947, 920–21.

57. Old Age Pension statistics for January, April, July, and October quarters 1944, GN38/S6-1-8, file 12, PANL.

58. Old Age Pension statistics for 1946 and 1947, GN38/S6-1-8, file 12, PANL.

59. "Report of the Committee on Public Health and Welfare" to the National Convention, 1947, 22.

60. *Debates of the Newfoundland National Convention*, 1 April 1947, 918–19.

61. The individual provinces had the power to control the timing of the implementation of these increases. Nova Scotia delayed implementation of the 1947 increase until August of that year, and Newfoundland, probably because of the extensive bureaucratic confusion existing at the time and the considerable delay in processing initial applications, postponed implementation of the 1949 increase until April 1950. See Bryden, *Old Age Pensions*, 96.

62. A confidential report in 1947 to the Canadian cabinet committee on Newfoundland calculated that Newfoundland, with a higher proportion of elderly in its population, spent $0.77 per capita on old age pensions, while Canada spent $1.46.

See RG29, vol. 131, 208-5-0, pt 1, p. 95, NAC.

63. William J. Browne, *Eighty-four Years a Newfoundlander*, vol. 1, *1897–1949* (St John's, 1981), 299, 339, 340–41, 346; Frederick W. Rowe, *The Smallwood Era* (Toronto, 1985), 97; Peter Neary, *Newfoundland in the North Atlantic World, 1929–1949* (Kingston, 1988), 355. Local reports suggest that the old age pensions attracted a good deal of pro-Confederate support, but that this dissipated over time in some areas; see file Englee, Ranger C. Matthews to Chief Ranger, Englee, 13 Dec. 1947; file Harbour Breton, Ranger D.A. Crowther to Chief Ranger, Harbour Breton, 15 Jan. 1948, GN38/S2-5-2, PANL.

64. E.R. Swettenham to J.R. MacFarlane, 25, 28 April 1949, RG29, vol. 131, 208-5-0, pt 2, NAC. The descriptions of local accommodations and social amenities are very amusing; see, for example, Swettenham to MacFarlane, 25 April, 2, 5 May 1949.

65. Each province had its own legislation and regulations, all of which dovetailed with the pre-eminent federal legislation and regulations; Ottawa paid 75 percent of the old age pensions, while each province paid 25 percent and the costs of all local administration.

66. Because of this sort of difficulty Newfoundland retained its own parallel old age pension program after joining Confederation to pay a slightly lower pension ($25 monthly) to those who could not establish their eligibility to the satisfaction of federal officials; see, for example, box 4, file 3961, GN37/1, PANL.

67. Swettenham to MacFarlane, 26 April 1949, RG29, vol. 131, 208-5-0, pt 2, NAC.

68. Swettenham to MacFarlane, 5 May 1949, RG29, vol. 131, 208-5-0, pt 2, NAC.

69. Swettenham to MacFarlane, 11, 16, 24 May 1949, RG29, vol. 131, 208-5-0, pt 2, NAC.

70. Ibid.

71. Swettenham to MacFarlane, 11 May 1949, RG29, vol. 131, 208-5-0, pt 2, NAC.

72. Browne, *Eighty-four Years*, 1: 340. One pensioner from Bonne Bay commented in 1950: "Anyway last year election time I had a confederate paper saying we get 30 in may and 40 in June and would get 40 the rest of our life i was a confederate": see box 2, file 1807, GN37/1, PANL.

73. Swettenham to MacFarlane, 24 May 1949, RG29, vol. 131, 208-5-0, pt 2, NAC.

74. R.R. Roberts to Swettenham, 22 June 1949, RG29, vol. 131, 208-5-0, pt 2, NAC.

75. MacFarlane to G.F. Davidson, 18 Jan. 1950, RG29, vol. 131, 208-5-0, pt 2, NAC. The federal officials argued that this process was illegal, in that old age pension funds could be paid only to the pensioner (and not to the provincial government to repay it for provincial outlays); see MacFarlane to Davidson, 18 Jan. 1950; H.L. Pottle to Davidson, 17 Feb. 1950, RG29, vol. 131, 208-5-0, pt 2, NAC.

76. Browne, *Eighty-four Years*, 341.

77. Memo "Investigation," vol. 131, 208-5-0, pt 2, Pottle to Davidson, 21 April 1950, RG29, vol. 1940, R249/101, NAC.

78. The benefits extended beyond the elderly and their immediate family; the local economy could reap considerable general gains, as could individuals dealing directly with the elderly. Those boarding the elderly, for example, raised their charges to take advantage of their boarders' higher income. See, for example, PANL, file 13056, GN37/1, box 9.

79. By March 1950, 77.4 percent of the Newfoundland elderly received the pension, 82.6 percent by March 1951, and 86.4 percent by December 1951, after which the program became universal for those aged seventy or over. At the latter date the participation rate in the other Atlantic provinces was 71.6 percent in New Brunswick (the second highest rate in the country), 59.3 in Nova Scotia (third highest), and 50.6 in Prince

Edward Island (fifth highest). The national average was less than 50 percent of the elderly. See Canada, Department of National Health and Welfare, *Report on the Administration of Old Age Pensions and Pensions for Blind Persons in Canada, 1949–50* (Ottawa, 1950), 12–13; *Report on . . . Old Age Pensions . . . 1950–51* (Ottawa, 1951), 10–11; *Report on . . . Old Age Pensions . . . 1951–52* (Ottawa, 1952), 10–11.

80. On some of the ways in which gender shaped the Canadian old age pension program, see James G. Snell, "The Gendered Construction of Elderly Marriage, 1900–1950," *Canadian Journal on Aging* (Dec. 1993).

81. It may well be that there was public debate about this, but if so, it was not recognized in the state sources used as a basis for this study.

BLOOD ON THE FACTORY FLOOR: THE WORKERS' COMPENSATION MOVEMENT IN CANADA AND THE UNITED STATES *

ROBERT H. BABCOCK

o

INTRODUCTION

During the late nineteenth and early twentieth centuries, a movement to reduce the socio-economic impact of workplace injuries through a non-litigious method of compensating victims or their dependents gained momentum. Originating in Europe and New Zealand during the late nineteenth century, the movement quickly swept across the United States and Canada between 1890 and 1920 in campaigns waged at both the state, or provincial, and federal levels. While organized labour and powerful business interests exerted a preponderant influence on the content of the statutes in each of the nearly sixty state or provincial jurisdictions, myriad intervening variables provoked somewhat different outcomes. To a significant extent, those states or provinces that had pioneered in workers' compensation legislation provided models that shaped later debates in the remaining political arenas. Robert Asher concludes that "workmen's compensation was the most widespread and palpable legislation bringing tangible benefits to workers to be enacted by the American states before World War I."[1]

After examining the problem of industrial accidents in North America at the turn of the century, this paper summarizes the existing literature explaining the origins of workers' compensation legislation in several

---

* This paper has not been previously published. It is used here with the permission of the author. This essay is derived from a paper, "The Hartz-Lipset Thesis Reconsidered: The Problem of Industrial Accidents in the United States and Canada," originally presented by the author at the Biennial Conference of the Association for Canadian Studies in the United States, New Orleans, Nov. 1993.

American states and Canadian provinces. To this survey the author adds findings from his own investigation of the reform movement in the state of Maine and the province of New Brunswick. There is a widely held assumption among social scientists that Canadians rely more heavily than Americans upon collectivist solutions to social problems.[2] But the history of the origins of workers' compensation laws belies that assertion, because in this case statist mechanisms surfaced on *both* sides of the 49th parallel. Indeed, the evidence presented here suggests that pioneering laws, rather than values derived from a more collectivist political culture, exerted greater influence on Canadian legislation in this field.

THE SCOPE OF THE INDUSTRIAL ACCIDENTS PROBLEM

During the age of iron and steam, the factory became an increasingly dangerous workplace. Exploding boilers, rapidly spinning shafts, exposed gears and cogs, unprotected saw blades and planing knives, clouds of dust, overcrowding, poor sanitation, and the absence of fire escapes all magnified the dangers. Piece work intensified the labour process and thereby increased the risk of injury. On the American side, defining the scope of this problem remains complicated by the absence of a central source of national data on industrial accidents. Much of the information on the frequency of mishaps is buried in the reports of state bureaus of industrial statistics; only a small portion has been correlated. One turn-of-the-century student who examined the problem reported that, between 1899 and 1908, 19 469 coal miners were killed and 5316 injured in mines located in twenty-two states that produced 98 percent of American coal.[3] In nearly the same period (1900–1907), 23 895 employees of American railways lost their lives, and 335 946 were injured.[4] He also estimated that one-half of 126 567 deaths reported in the U.S. Census between 1900 and 1906 resulted from accidents to males in American factories.[5] Not only the workers themselves suffered: between 1899 and 1908 the 11 328 coal miners killed at work in Illinois and Pennsylvania left 6183 widows and 14 444 children.[6] Nationwide, it was estimated that more than 10 000 widows and 25 000 children could be "charged to the account of American coal production" during this decade.[7] A recent student of the compensation reform movement concludes that the United States suffered the highest accident rates of any leading industrial power before World War I.[8]

In Canada, the task of finding national industrial accident data is somewhat easier. Ottawa set up a Department of Labour in 1900, which, among other tasks, accumulated information on workplace mishaps. Each month the department's *Labour Gazette* reported accident data; each year it summarized fatal and non-fatal accidents according to a variety of industries or trades. Table 1 presents the data for 1904. Assuming the population of Canada to be about one-tenth that of the United States in 1904, the chart suggests that, proportionately, death and injury rates may not have been as great north of the border as those in the United States reported by

T A B L E   1   *INDUSTRIAL ACCIDENTS IN CANADA DURING 1904*

	Non-Fatal Accidents	Fatal Accidents
Lumbering	59	119
Mining	106	117
Building trades	43	139
Metal trades	73	492
Woodworking trades	12	154
Printing trades	–	10
Clothing trades	3	20
Textile trades	4	25
Food, tobacco preparation	6	55
Leather trades	2	4
Railway service	273	360
General transport	104	169
Miscellaneous trades	43	191
Unskilled labour	30	121

Source: *Labour Gazette* 5 (Jan. 1905), 742–73 (totals include agriculture and fishing).

Campbell. Then again, the pace of industrial capitalist development in Canada lagged behind that of its neighbour. No doubt many accidents that had taken place in remote locations on the staples-driven frontier were never reported. In any case, the fact that Ottawa took pains to collect this data suggests that many Canadians considered the industrial carnage to be a significant socio-economic problem.

Until the turn of the century, victims of industrial accidents and their families could only seek legal remedies if they believed they were not at fault and if they possessed sufficient resources (most did not) to employ counsel and pay court fees. Even if they could afford a lawyer, common law precedents in both Canada and the United States stacked the deck in favour of the rights of employers. First of all, the assumption-of-risk doctrine held that victims of industrial accidents had already accepted "the natural and ordinary risks and perils" of a job when they had begun work, and normally they could not hold the employer responsible. In theory, judges expected workers to reject conditions they considered to be dangerous by quitting and seeking "safer" work; in reality, too many workers chased too few jobs for anyone to be that choosy. Secondly, in order for judges to find employers liable for unsafe conditions, the injured worker was required to prove that the employer himself, and not just his foreman or manager, had contributed to the "extraordinary" danger. A bold worker might make this charge, but it was easy for the boss to deny responsibility and difficult for the worker to prove it. Thirdly, according to the courts' fellow-servant rule, employers could not be held accountable if the injured worker or another employee had been partially responsible for the mishap.[9] Judges implied that the victim could sue his shopmate, but from the injured's viewpoint it made no sense to bring costly legal action against an impoverished co-worker. As a result of these well-entrenched common law doctrines, then, the vast majority of injured workers and their families found themselves dependent upon an employer's sympathy, their family resources, or public charity rather than on courts of law. Only an estimated 15 percent of injured workers actually obtained damages through lawsuits, and lawyers often claimed a big chunk in fees. To protect themselves, workers in a few larger shops organized into mutual benefit societies for insurance purposes, and some skilled craftsmen ultimately earned enough to afford insurance policies purchased from trade unions or fraternal orders. But for the vast majority of turn-of-the-century Canadian and American workers, blood-stained factory floors seemed tilted in favour of employers. Over the next two decades, the balance between labour, capital, and the state gradually shifted in both Canada and the United States and, as a result, the tilt and the colour of North American factory floors began to change.

Three nations initially addressed the problem of industrial accidents. In 1871 Germany placed more liability for accidents upon employers, and fourteen years later required them to provide accident insurance.[10] An English employers' liability statute of 1880 put some limits on common law judgments by abolishing the fellow-servant rule; then a compensation law enacted in 1897 allowed workers to choose between seeking a legal remedy or accepting a fixed schedule of payments based upon the severity of the injury. Finally, in 1906, England adopted a comprehensive no-fault compensation system paying benefits to injured workers or their kin.[11] New Zealand, the third pioneering society, adopted a wide range of industrial reforms, including no-fault accident compensation, during the last decade of the nineteenth century. An influential group of North American reformers, including Henry Demarest Lloyd and Richard T. Ely in the United States and W. Frank Hatheway in Canada, closely followed events in these countries. Lloyd returned from a visit determined to "New Zealandize" America, concluding that "the state could and should create a just social and economic order."[12] Soon workers' compensation became a continental movement in which German, English, and New Zealand laws were heralded as models.

THE MOVEMENT FOR WORKERS' COMPENSATION LEGISLATION IN THE UNITED STATES

Only a few scholars have investigated the origins of workers' compensation legislation in a handful of states or provinces, and consequently much of what is known in others comes from barebones surveys by contemporary Washington and Ottawa bureaucrats. In the United States, the earliest legislation appeared at the turn of the century. First, employers' liability laws redefined portions of the common law precedents and often placed limits on juried awards, but they did not abandon the legal principle of fault-finding. As a result, lawsuits remained the only compensatory remedy. Later, workers' compensation bills adopted a no-fault stance, considering accidents to be an unavoidable cost of doing business, and established a benefit schedule for workplace victims. Now businessmen could estimate the costs of accidents by covering their liability through insurance policies whose annual premiums were passed on to the consumer.

By 1907, twenty-seven states or provinces had adopted employers' liability laws; most of them modified the fellow-servant doctrine while a few limited the other two court tests (assumption of risk and contributory negligence) as well.[13] In 1902, Maryland enacted the first North American law to provide benefits without suit or proof of negligence, but only two years later a court ruled it unconstitutional.[14] In 1908 Congress drew attention to the problem when it granted certain government employees the right to compensation for injuries sustained at work. A year later, Montana became the first state to enact a compulsory law requiring contributions from both employers and workers, but once again a court threw it out. The Massachusetts bill of 1907 escaped this fate only by allowing employers to elect to participate.[15] Canadian legislatures enacted compensation laws during the same era. British Columbia set up a compensation plan in 1902; Alberta followed in 1908, Quebec in 1909, and Manitoba in 1910. Most were initially employers' liability statutes that mirrored British legislation. Soon on both sides of the border the movement for no-fault compensation accelerated, governments acted, judges yielded, and by 1920 forty-three states and seven provinces (plus the Yukon) had joined the reform bandwagon.[16]

Because outcomes of the various provincial and state battles for workers' compensation laws differed, it is necessary to examine these movements separately (and to some extent chronologically) before hazarding any generalizations. Nearly thirty years ago, Roy Lubove and James Weinstein presented two distinct but overlapping interpretations of the origins of workers' compensation in the United States. Lubove traced the movement to popular indignation over high industrial accidents and to studies challenging the conventional wisdom that 95 percent of accidents were a result of worker carelessness. For instance, evidence from the Pittsburgh Survey, a social science study completed in the early twentieth century, revealed that only 21 percent of factory mishaps could be attributed to this factor. Employers welcomed the no-fault principle, Lubove argued, for two reasons: first, they found existing employers' liability laws to be too slow, wasteful, and unfair, and secondly, they believed that compensation "would substitute a fixed, but limited charge for a variable, potentially ruinous one."[17] In short, compensation became a form of cost control. Lubove concludes that business imperatives rather than a desire for equity "proved more influential in shaping the workmen's compensation system."[18]

Starting from a somewhat different perspective on the Progressive era, James Weinstein shares many of Lubove's conclusions about the importance of business interests in establishing no-fault workers' compensation. Big businessmen wanted to stabilize their position and undercut efforts by workers to engage in independent political action. Organized labour, fearing state intervention, initially opposed workers' compensation but reversed its position after 1908 when the National Civic Federation (NCF), an alliance of big businessmen and labour leaders, "threw its whole weight into the fight for compensation legislation."[19] The NCF circulated a model bill, based on German and English laws, to state legislatures. By early 1909, several states had appointed commissions to look into workers' compensation acts; the big battle took place in New York State, Weinstein says, where businessmen conceded a higher benefits package in return for funding payments through private rather than state insurance.[20]

To date Robert Asher offers the most extensive, systematic study of the workers' compensation movement in the United States through a comparison of the origins of these laws in New York, Wisconsin, Minnesota, Massachusetts, and Ohio. He concludes that the business community reflected a diversity of views on the no-fault approach and failed to dominate the legislative process as much as Lubove and Weinstein had argued. The middle class supported the movement in order to relieve class tensions; labour ultimately endorsed it because more workers gained than those who might hope to win juried cash awards.[21] But the interaction of these interest groups, as we will see below, differed in the six states examined here: Massachusetts, Wisconsin, Minnesota, Washington, New York, and Maine.

In Massachusetts, Asher finds, workers' compensation came about as a result of a business–labour consensus. A "moderate" employers' liability law adopted in 1887 proved ineffectual because of congested court dockets and high lawyers' fees. Employers worried about rising insurance costs. Organized labour, initially opposed to no-fault compensation, finally endorsed it. A voluntary law was adopted in 1908 but covered only 20 percent of the industrial force in the state. Soon large employers demanded a more stringent act. The legislature debated three different bills initially barring casualty companies from writing compensation insurance, but the insurance industry's lobbyists won amendments scuttling this provision. Finally a bill covering 80 percent of the state's industrial workforce became law in 1910. Asher concludes that Weinstein overstated the role of the big business and failed to note the "negative effects [of] cost-conscious conservative employers" on the reform movement. The Massachusetts law, he says, was "truly a compromise measure, . . . supported by labor and either endorsed or tolerated by employers" because of their dissatisfaction with earlier liability laws.[22]

In Wisconsin, Asher finds, Progressive Republicans endorsed workers' compensation legislation for a quite different reason: they wanted to detach the working-class vote from that state's prominent, ethnically rooted social democratic movement. Organized labour worked with businessmen on bills to replace the antiquated liability system with a no-fault law. While they fought over the details, Wisconsin's 1911 compensation act also reflected compromises between these two interests. Workers could elect common law defences rather than scheduled compensation benefits; private casualty companies rather than a state insurance fund would continue to underwrite employer's liability.[23]

In Minnesota, a radical political movement, the Non-Partisan League, provoked an ideological conflict over state insurance of workers' compensation. Some private insurance companies backed such laws because they were believed to promise the industry higher premiums and more predictable losses, while others opposed them because they feared the competition from monopoly state insurance. Organized labour sided with the League but was unable to overcome opposition in the upper house of the Minnesota legislature. Ultimately, postwar hostility toward government intervention and fear of radicalism eroded the League's support and killed state insurance. Among other factors, Asher concludes, "an extensive network of private [insurance] organizations was already functioning in the compensation field" in Minnesota, and legislators decided these could be regulated rather than replaced.[24]

The workers' compensation movement in the state of Washington was the product of a consensus among labour leaders and businessmen in one industry—lumber. In fact, Washington State lawmakers, not Canadian provincial legislators, set up the first North American government-run insurance fund. By 1910, 65 percent of the state's wage earners worked in the lumber industry, and west coast lumbermen were "anxious to rid themselves of personal injury litigation." Higher accident rates, falling prices, a growing number of lawsuits, and escalating insurance rates forced lumber entrepreneurs to stabilize costs. "There was no denying the mutual desire of labor and lumbermen," Joseph Tripp concludes, "to escape the morass of litigation." Despite opposition from many lawyers, urban businessmen, and other so-called "progressives," the Washington legislature enacted a workers' compensation law in 1911 that established a state accident fund administered by an independent commission. Ultimately, seven more states and most, if not all, Canadian provinces followed Washington's example.[25]

While acknowledging the contributions of social progressives to the movement for workers' compensation laws, Weinstein, Asher, and Tripp maintain that big business played a major role in several American states in order to establish control over labour costs. Later, organized labour, initially sceptical of government intervention into labour–capital relations, joined the campaign. Robert Wesser identifies all three groups in the New York State reform effort, but he argues that labour played a more important role in this state than business did. A state commission established in 1909 systematically collected information on German and English laws before conducting public hearings. Its report incorporated many suggestions from organized labour, lauded the British plan, and urged elimination of the assumption-of-risk rule and relaxation of the other two common law doctrines. Nevertheless, two-thirds of the state's businessmen remained opposed to the commission-sponsored legislation, mostly because workers could still choose between fixed compensation and a lawsuit. State courts declared the law unconstitutional in 1911. Over the next two years, organized labour in New York State, capitalizing on rivalry between Democrats and Republicans, as well as on the latter's split between factions favouring either William Howard Taft or Theodore Roosevelt, took control of the movement for workers' compensation. In 1913, the New York State legislature enacted a law providing for compulsory compensation with benefits administered by a state commission. Employers could choose a variety of ways to insure themselves. Wesser concludes that the New York workers' compensation law was a "significant triumph" for organized labour rather than for big business.[26]

At the turn of the century, the relatively small labour movement in rural Maine, as in many other states, actively promoted an employers' liability bill. But the dominant Republican Party, a stalwart defender of property rights, steadfastly ignored these requests until their grip on the political situation began to weaken. When the state's biggest business, the pulp and paper industry, demonstrated an interest in stabilizing the costs of industrial accidents, Republicans enacted an employers' liability law in 1909. The measure modified common law assumptions, put limits on the size of awards, but excluded farm workers, domestic servants, and those engaged in the lumber industry. If workers accepted benefits under the law, they were barred from filing lawsuits.[27]

In 1910, the national Progressive political whirlwind swept through Maine, and a year later the Democrats, aided by a strong labour vote, won control of both houses and the governorship for the first time in decades. Three laws were promptly enacted on behalf of the state's workers. The first upgraded a bureau of labour statistics into a full department in the governor's cabinet whose head was given power to collect accident data and to order employers to promote workplace safety. The second law required factory supervisors to report all deaths or serious injuries within ten days. Under the provisions of this law, 814 accidents were tallied from mid-1911 to mid-1912, thirty-one of them fatal. The third measure required Maine's employers to pay weekly wages. At the same time, the legislature rejected a bill to require safeguards on machinery or to exempt injured workers from proving that they had been exercising "due care" at the time of their accident. As a result, courts still found workers liable for seven-eighths of all accidents, and the injured received less than 40 percent of juried awards.[28]

During the next four years (1910–1914) the reform tide ebbed and flowed within the ranks of Democrats, Republicans, and Progressives. Gradually, elements of all three parties—big business among traditional Republicans, organized labour in the Democratic Party, and social reformers in the Progressive fold—converged behind a call for no-fault workers' compensation legislation. By 1914, all three parties had nailed this plank to their party platforms, and a bill was introduced in the legislature. Yet powerful Maine lumbermen, unlike their counterparts in Washington State, remained strongly opposed to compensation legislation, probably because the industry in the Pine Tree State still consisted of small units that subcontracted much of their work and engaged mostly seasonal, part-time employees. Since woods workers laboured by themselves, employers said, businessmen should not be held responsible for their injuries. Ultimately the bill was scuttled through a complicated parliamentary manoeuvre.[29]

When the Democratic Party captured both the governorship and the lower house of the state legislature in 1914–1915, prospects for a workers' compensation bill measurably improved, and a no-fault law went into effect on 1 January 1916. It covered just 73 percent of the state's labour force, excluding farm labour, domestic service, loggers, part-time workers, and small shops with less than six employees. Covered workers gave up their right to sue, and employers lost common law protections if they refused to participate. Court appeals were limited only to questions of law. No state-administered fund was specified; businessmen could insure themselves or buy liability insurance from private companies. The Maine compensation statute fixed dollar limits for both partial and full disabilities. A three-person board administered benefits, originally fixed at 50 percent of wages and later raised to 60 percent.[30]

Despite the law's obvious shortcomings, some Maine labour leaders justifiably called it "without doubt the most important piece of legislation ever passed in Maine in favor of industrial employees." Others lamented the compromises and pressed for amendments at the next session. In 1919, the law was rewritten to reduce the waiting period, raise benefits, expand the state governing board to four members, and allow its chair to take legal dispositions. Having received endorsements from both parties and the governor, the revised statute sailed into law. One Maine labour leader concluded that the 1919 version of workers' compensation was "one of the best there is in the United States."[31]

In Maine as in the other states, large and small businessmen, organized labour, and a shifting political context affected the drive for workers' compensation legislation. Gains by the state Democratic Party and a split in Republican ranks after 1910 created a political opening for the reform movement. Divisions in the business community between small woods contractors and giant pulp and paper companies initially blocked legislation in 1913, but two years later organized labour tilted the balance in favour of a compensation law that was subsequently refined and adjusted for wartime inflationary conditions. Thanks to the influence of big business and its servants, the casualty companies, a state insurance fund was never considered.

THE MOVEM1ENT FOR WORKERS' COMPENSATION IN CANADA

The origins of workers' compensation laws in Canada are less well-known, and thus far scholars have examined the movements only in Quebec, Ontario, and New Brunswick. In the course of surveying the condition of Montreal workers at the turn of the century, Terry Copp briefly reviewed the industrial accidents problem. He noted that Quebec's inspectors described the factory floor as "a real battlefield with its dead and wounded." Between 1890 and 1907, inspectors looked into 4608 accidents in which 263 workers were killed, yet only one in three mishaps had been reported as required by law. The casualties left the province's charitable institutions "hard-pressed." Aware of growing concern in Europe and North America about this problem, in 1907 a Quebec government-appointed commission recommended enactment of a provincial compensation law. While both the province's employers and organized labour supported the measure, most of the initiative for the Quebec workers' compensation law of 1909 came from neither business nor labour but from a successful lobbying campaign by Louis Guyon, Quebec's factory inspector. Although not, as Copp claims, the first such act in North America, the

Quebec law did establish a schedule of payments and death benefits. Courts administered it until an independent board was set up in the early 1930s.[32]

The workers' compensation movement in Ontario was particularly influential because the outcome regulated Canada's largest and most industrialized province and served as a model for less industrialized provinces. In 1886, Ontario adopted an employers' liability law based on the 1880 British statute; at first "justice was irregular and sporadic,"[33] although workers won more verdicts after 1900.[34] Labour, not big business, initiated the movement for reform, and workers' compensation became their "central issue." Responding to a rising tide of working-class political consciousness, in 1910 a Conservative government appointed the province's chief justice, William Meredith, to head a commission of inquiry. At the hearings, the Canadian Manufacturers Association (CMA) endorsed the principle of no-fault compensation; like so many of their American counterparts, Ontario businessmen complained about expensive liability insurance, ambulance-chasing lawyers, and the need to regularize and reduce costs. Yet when the commission finally presented a bill, the CMA condemned it because they thought the benefits were too high and they wanted employees to contribute to insurance costs.[35]

Ultimately the Ontario compensation law of 1914 represented a compromise between business and labour. Businessmen obtained a simpler measure covering all workers. The law divided employers into groups according to relative risks and assessed their payrolls proportionately. They also called for state insurance like their counterparts in some American jurisdictions such as Washington State because they believed it would be less expensive. A provincial workers' compensation board levied payroll assessments and administered the benefits. Rather than abolishing all common law rights of recovery, the Ontario law suspended them if the worker accepted compensation under the new law. Like most North American acts, the Ontario law excluded those working in agriculture and domestic service; unlike American legislation, it covered the victims of many industrial diseases. Organized labour subsequently agitated for additional benefits such as the cost of medical treatment.[36]

Why did Ontario set up a provincial compensation board and a state-controlled insurance fund? Not primarily as a result of an inherent bias in favour of state action, it would appear. First of all, the insurance industry "made surprisingly little effort" during and after the hearings to avoid this result. Their lawyers appeared late in the sessions and "neither their participation nor their briefs were impressive or forceful defences of insurance."[37] Secondly, the head of the inquiry, Chief Justice Meredith, was determined to block judicial administration of benefits. Thus Ontario's compensation legislation came about because the CMA had openly endorsed the principle, labour had shown "strong and widespread support," and "most important[ly]," because of Meredith's influence.[38]

The reform movement in New Brunswick, as in Maine, reflected motley internal and external influences. Initially a small group of middle-class Saint John progressives led by W. Frank Hatheway, a tea merchant, joined with leaders of the powerful local longshoremen's union in the spring of

1901 to study the "labour question." Discussion soon turned to the need for
employers' liability laws. After the group had examined the English statute,
it asked the provincial government to enact a similar measure.[39] Rather than
run an unnecessary political risk, the reigning Liberals postponed action
until they had won an election. Then they enacted a modest bill that somewhat modified common law doctrine but required workers to continue to
press claims through lawsuits. Subsequently, the Grits also approved a factory law in 1905, which provided for the inspection of workplace conditions. Neither went far enough to satisfy the province's workers,
particularly the most politically conscious segment in Saint John, and the
Tories, Hatheway among them, swept into provincial office in 1908.[40]

From his position in the assembly, Hatheway promptly orchestrated a
movement to enact a tighter liability law. The new measure, endorsed by
Saint John longshoremen and millmen, set aside the fellow-servant rule,
made employers liable for accidents caused by unsafe machines, and established a benefit schedule. Nevertheless, workers still faced the costs, delays,
and dilemmas of proving their injuries in a court of law. Businessmen still
lacked a financial incentive to introduce safety measure.[41] "When I suggest
that some dangerous parts of machinery should be covered," the factory
inspector complained, "I am told it is not necessary, because it has been in
that condition some five, ten or fifteen years, and no one has been
injured."[42] With the gradual dissipation of the provincial labour movement
after 1907, the movement to enact a comprehensive, no-fault compensation
law ground to a halt.

By 1916, three factors had impelled the government of New Brunswick
to change its stance. As an election approached, the Tories found themselves in political trouble and prepared to shore up their position. Secondly,
the rate of industrial accidents showed no signs of diminishing; there were
seventy-four in 1916, eight of them fatal. Thirdly and perhaps most importantly, in 1915 Nova Scotia had enacted an up-to-date, no-fault law.
Assured of support from the Tory premier, a revitalized New Brunswick
Federation of Labour immediately launched an all-out effort to get a law
modelled on both the Nova Scotia and Ontario statutes. When the Tories
subsequently dragged their feet, going only so far as to appoint a commission to conduct another study, they lost labour's confidence as well as the
ensuing election.[43]

Although the Liberals were returned to power, the report commissioned by their Tory predecessors set the stage for New Brunswick's abandonment of the old common law doctrines regarding fault. The report
identified three types of laws: (1) employers' liability acts similar to those
that had been adopted in 1903 and 1908; (2) a system whereby employers'
submitted payrolls to a government agency that grouped the industries
according to risk and levied varying assessments in order to carry the liability; and (3) a state insurance fund.[44] Ontario had been the first province to
implement the second type, in 1915, followed by British Columbia and
Nova Scotia. In 1918, the new Liberal government of W.E. Foster in New
Brunswick followed their example. Citing Ontario's experience as well as
provisions of the Nova Scotia act, it abolished the fellow-servant rule. Then

contributory negligence was taken out of the hands of judges and juries and given to an impartial board that would take this factor into account when assessing damages. A government-appointed workers' compensation board (whose labour member had been active in the fight for the law), rather than the provincial treasurer, received funds collected from employers. The board also took over the courts' power to make awards. The new act covered millmen but excluded farm labour, domestic servants, miners, fishermen, city employees, clerks, part-time workers, and—notably—loggers, a particularly contentious omission in this heavily forested province. In 1920, the Liberals, perhaps worried about the impact of a local United Farmers' movement on their political standing, upgraded the workers' compensation statute, adopting a schedule for industrial diseases, increasing benefits, and extending coverage to workers in the lumber industry.[45]

In retrospect, several factors shaped both the timing and content of New Brunswick's response to the problem of industrial accidents. Most importantly, a rising political consciousness among workers, particularly in Saint John, goaded politicians into responding to an accelerating social problem. Secondly, at different periods both middle-class progressives and working-class leaders played key roles in articulating solutions borrowed from path-breaking laws already enacted in the British Empire rather than from American models. Thirdly, because neither the Grits nor the Tories securely controlled the levers of power during this period, both parties vied for the attention of working-class voters more than they had been accustomed to doing. Fourthly, unlike the situation in Ontario, representatives of the insurance industry testified in Fredericton on behalf of their interests, and the final bill contained a provision authorizing the provincial cabinet to sanction private insurance for any employer who petitioned for it.[46] Hence New Brunswick actually established a competitive (state-controlled or private) fund like those in nine American states.

CONCLUSION

While business, organized labour, and reform-minded individuals or groups played significant parts in all these jurisdictions, outcomes differed from place to place depending upon such variables as the specific political contexts, the relative influence exerted by the contending interest groups on the political process, and the model laws most appealing to the interested parties. The trend in both countries was toward the establishment of no-fault, government-run workers' compensation commissions rather than the perpetuation of fault-finding by the courts. Several states and provinces appointed commissions to conduct investigations, hold hearings, and draft model bills for legislators to consider. In all of these jurisdictions, either the advocacy or at least the acquiescence of some important sectors of the business community was vital to the ultimate success of the movement. Similarly, organized labour played a crucial role in both nations, although it appears to have been a more important factor in Ontario, New Brunswick, New York, and Maine than in some other jurisdictions. The significant role of progressive-minded leaders crops up time and time again in the origins of workers' compensation, whether it was Louis Guyon in Quebec, Chief Justice Meredith in Ontario, Frank Hatheway in New Brunswick, Judge Wainwright in New York, or Carroll Wright in Massachusetts.

A comparison of provisions in American and Canadian accident compensation laws in 1920 suggests the controlling influence of historical contingencies rather than underlying national values in explaining the differences.[47] For instance, the "remarkably uniformity" in Canadian laws noted by Hookstadt resulted from the overriding influence of two models—the British statutes and Ontario's pioneering compensation law—rather than from an underlying "statist" disposition. In 1920 all the Canadian compensation statutes were compulsory for employers while a majority (thirty-one) of American laws remained elective. But this difference most likely reflected the impact of court decisions in states like Massachusetts, which had forced lawmakers to insert elective provisions that usually denied common law protections to those employers who opted out. Canadian jurists, traditionally less interventionist in the political process and probably more closely attuned to legal developments in the United Kingdom, simply did not throw out compulsory accident compensation legislation after 1900 like their American counterparts. Finally, we should note that the workers' compensation laws in fourteen American states were no less compulsory in 1920 than the statutes in Canadian provinces.

As for the issue of state vs. private casualty insurance, it would appear once again that statist values did not divide at the 49th parallel. By 1920 in Canada, five of the seven jurisdictions with accident compensation laws had erected state insurance funds, whereas in the United States seventeen of the forty-five states had either exclusive or competitive state funds, and twenty-eight states relied solely upon private casualty or mutual insurance firms. These facts hardly support the notion of a rigidly statist or anti-statist bias in either Canada or the United States.

But there was one underlying difference between the approaches of the two nations in dealing with this problem between 1890 and 1920 that deserves mention. Canadian laws assumed liability on the part of the province; that is, injured workers received payments regardless of whether or not employers had contributed their premiums to a province-run compensation fund. Defaulting employers could be sued by the provincial workers' compensation board. No American states assumed such liability, and as a result injured workers lost compensation benefits when the employer or insurance carrier fell into insolvency. In short, whereas Canadian provinces assumed ultimate responsibility for the welfare of the injured, American states did not.

NOTES

1. Robert Asher, *Dissertation Abstracts International* 1971, 2587-A.

2. For a recent statement of this view see S.M. Lipset, *Continental Divide: The Values and Interpretations of the United States and Canada* (Toronto: C.D. Howe Institute, 1989).

3. Gilbert Lewis Campbell, *Industrial Accidents and Their Compensation* (Boston, 1911), 10.

4. Ibid., 15.

5. Ibid., 5.

6. Ibid., 22.

7. Ibid.

8. Robert Asher, "Industrial Safety and Labor Relations in the United States, 1865–1917" in *Life and Labor: Dimensions of American Working-Class History*, ed. C. Stephenson and R. Asher (Albany, 1986), 116.

9. For common law precedents see J.R. Commons and J.B. Andrews, *Principles of Labor Legislation* (New York, 1967 reprint), 227–31.

10. Ibid., 232.

11. Durand Halsey Van Doren, *Workmen's Compensation and Insurance* (New York, 1918), 33–34, 45.

12. Peter J. Coleman, "New Zealand Liberalism and the Origins of the American Welfare State," *Journal of American History* 69 (Sept. 1982): 372–91.

13. James Weinstein, "Big Business and the Origins of Workmen's Compensation," *Labor History* 8 (1967): 159.

14. Commons and Andrews, *Principles of Labor Legislation*, 236.

15. Ibid., 236–37.

16. Ibid., 256; Roy Lubove, "Workmen's Compensation and the Prerogatives of Voluntarism," *Labor History* 8 (1967): 262–63.

17. Lubove, "Workmen's Compensation," 259–62.

18. Ibid., 268.

19. Weinstein, "Big Business and Origins of Workmen's Compensation," 162.

20. Ibid., 167–70, 174.

21. Asher, "Workmen's Compensation in the US, 1880–1935," *Dissertation Abstracts International*, 1971, 2587-A.

22. Robert Asher, "Business and Workers' Welfare in the Progressive Era: Workmen's Compensation Reform in Massachusetts, 1880–1911," *Business History Review* 43 (1969): 452–75.

23. Robert Asher, "The 1911 Wisconsin Workmen's Compensation Law: A Study in Conservative Labor Reform," *Wisconsin Magazine of History* 57 (1973): 123–40.

24. Robert Asher, "Radicalism and Reform: State Insurance of Workmen's Compensation in Minnesota, 1910–1933," *Labor History* 14, 1 (Winter 1973): 19–41.

25. Joseph F. Tripp, "An Instance of Labor and Business Cooperation: Workmen's Compensation in Washington State (1911)," *Labor History* 17 (Fall 1976): 530–50.

26. Robert Wesser, "Conflict and Compromise: The Workmen's Compensation Movement in New York, 1890s–1913," *Labor History* 12, 3 (Summer 1971): 345–72.

27. *Maine Register*, 1900, 162; 1902–3, 158; 1905–6, 160; 1907–8, 160; *Maine Legislative Graveyard*, 1907, RG1, box 928, folder 5; box 956; *Maine Legislative Record*, 1909, 65, 67, 186, 268, 300, 750, 814, 838, 974; *Acts and Resolves*, 1909, 30; Maine Department of Labor and Industry, *Report*, 1911–12, 248–51; 1913, 151–52; *10th Annual Report of Maine State AFL*, 1913, 25.

28. *Maine Register*, 1911–12, 160; 1920, 221–22; *Original Papers of the Maine Legislature*, 1911; *10th Annual Convention of the Maine AFL*, 1913, 27.

29. *Maine Register*, 1913–14, 160; 1915–16, 160; 1920, 221–22; Legislative Committee, *10th Annual Convention of Maine AFL*, 1913, 2 ff., 37–41; *Maine Legislative Graveyard*, 1913, box 1000, folders 2, 3, 4; *Maine Legislative Record*, 1913, 8, 256, 258, 278, 321, 1142; Maine Department of Labor and Industry, *Report*, 1913–14, 252.

30. *Maine Legislative Record*, 1915, 1103–6; *Workmen's Compensation Act of the State of Maine, Effective January 1, 1916* (Waterville, 1917); *Third Biennial Report of the Department of Labor and Industry*, 1915–16, 9.

31. Maine State AFL, *Proceedings*, 1917, 19–20; 1918, 33; 1919, 37, 71; *Maine Legislative Record*, 1917, 624–25, 636, 819–20, 1036–40; 1919, 1085, 1087–88, 1203; Maine Department of Labor and Industry, *Report*, 1917–18, 9–18.

32. Terry Copp, *The Anatomy of Poverty: The Condition of the Working Class in Montreal, 1897–1929* (Toronto, 1974), 106–25.

33. Michael J. Piva, "The Workmen's Compensation Movement in Ontario," *Ontario History* 67 (1975): 43.

34. R.C.B. Risk, "'This Nuisance of Litigation': The Origins of Workers' Compensation in Ontario" in *Essays in the History of Canadian Law*, vol. 2, ed. David H. Flaherty (Toronto, 1983), 432.

35. Piva, "The Workmen's Compensation Movement," 39–56.

36. Ibid.

37. Risk, "'This Nuisance of Litigation,'" 465.

38. Ibid., 472.

39. Saint John *Daily Sun*, 24 April, 11 Sept., 9 Oct. 1901; Saint John *Daily News*, 13 Nov. 1901; card, *The Fabian League* in H.H. Stuart Collection, box 1, no. 14 "Labor," Harriet Irving Library, University of New Brunswick (hereafter UNB), Fredericton; letters W.F. Hatheway to Premier L.J. Tweedie, 15, 23 Jan., 14 Feb. 1902, in Legislative Council Records, Provincial Archives of New Brunswick (henceforth PANB), Fredericton.

40. "Our New Brunswick Policy Is . . . " campaign flyer used in 1903 election, W.F. Hatheway Papers, Harriet Irving Library, UNB; *Canadian Annual Review*, 1903, 169–71, 1904, 330, 1905, 332, 338; 1906, 395–406; 1907, 623–28; 1908, 388, 390, 397; New Brunswick *Synoptic Report*, 30 April 1903, 135; 6 May 1903, 182–84; Trades and Labor Congress, *Proceedings*, 1903, 22; *Labour Gazette* 5 (June 1905): 1364–66; Saint John *Sun*, 31 Jan., 1 Feb. 1908.

41. New Brunswick, *Journals of the House of Assembly, 1909*, Supplementary Appendix, Factory Inspector's Report 1908–9, 142–49; *Eastern Labor News*, 24 Dec. 1910.

42. New Brunswick, *Journals of the House of Assembly, 1911*, Supplementary Appendix, Report of the Factory Inspector, 28.

43. *Canadian Annual Review*, 1916, 631, 638; 1917, 695, 697; Trades and Labor Congress, *Proceedings*, 1915, 32–33; 1916, Report of the NBFL, 76–77; NB *Synoptic Report*, 1916, 172.

44. NB Journals, 1917, Supplementary Appendix, *Report of the Commission Appointed into the Working of the Ontario and Nova Scotia Workmen's Compensation Act*; 8 George V (1917), c. 30.

45. *Canadian Annual Review*, 1918, 661; 1919, 707; 1920, 696, 704, 714; NB *Synoptic Report*, 1918, 33–34, 250, 260, 277–79; 1919, 234, 245–52; 8 George V (1918), c. 37; 9 George V (1919), c. 7; 10 George V (1920), c. 12.

46. NB *Synoptic Report*, 1917, 71; 8 George V (1918), c. 37, s. 53.

47. Carl Hookstadt, *Comparison of Workmen's Compensation Laws of the United States and Canada up to January 1, 1920*, U.S. Dept. of Labor, Bureau of Labor Statistics No. 275 (Washington: GPO, 1920), 131–40.

"WAGES FOR HOUSEWORK": MOTHERS' ALLOWANCES AND THE BEGINNINGS OF SOCIAL SECURITY IN CANADA ◇

VERONICA STRONG-BOAG

○

When poverty was "re-discovered" in the 1960s and 1970s, sole support mothers were easily recognized as its prime victims. The Royal Commission on the Status of Women in 1970 identified these citizens as among the most disadvantaged in the country.[1] For all the indignation that such announcements provoked, the poverty of female-headed families was not new. The experience of such mothers and children traditionally has been precarious and marginal. Indeed their plight, more than that of any other group, has called forth numerous efforts at remedy throughout Canada's history. One of the most notable occurred in the early decades of this century, when social critics and feminists employed the predicament of mother-led families to initiate Canada's first experiments with formal income support programs.

The enabling legislation, variously referred to as mothers' pensions and, more often, mothers' allowances, represented a critical stage in the history of child welfare in this country. Its emphasis on the reconstruction of the nuclear family as the unequalled environment for optimal child development entailed a significant break with much of previous practice. In the past, institutions such as orphanages, refuges, and industrial schools were designed to compensate for the shortcomings of inadequate, usually poor, families. Increasingly, however, more advanced social thinkers and those in

◇ *Journal of Canadian Studies* 14, 1 (Spring 1979): 24–34. Reprinted with the permission of the journal. The author would like to thank Jennifer Stoddart for her comments on an earlier draft of this article.

the new profession of social work condemned such large aggregations of children as injurious to youth and harmful in the long run to the community. The mother, not the matron, was the best employee the state could hope for.

THE CAMPAIGN FOR MOTHERS' ALLOWANCES

By the First Great War thoughtful Canadians were informed as never before about the threat that family instability, juvenile delinquency, and impoverished maternity posed to national survival. Men and women such as Nellie McClung, Stephen Leacock, James Shaver Woodsworth, Elizabeth Smith Shortt, and J.J. Kelso came to agree that the state should actively encourage and protect a better type of motherhood and family life. In concert with other political and economic reforms such intervention would enforce the moral, physical, and material standards that the middle class held dear.

The assault on laissez-faire liberalism emerged from two distinctly different ideological perspectives. The guiding principles of liberal suffragists like Nellie McClung were egalitarian and practical. They emphasized not female weakness, but the community's failure to give full rein to women's maternal qualities. The potential for nurture was women's particular strength. The state's recognition of the value of childbearing would demonstrate society's commitment to the set of more humane values that women as a sex more clearly espoused.[2]

Leacock, the anti-feminist McGill professor, on the other hand, found supporters among "red tory" conservatives when he insisted that

> social policy should proceed from the fundamental truth that women are and must be dependent. If they cannot be looked after by an individual . . . they must be looked after by the State. To expect a woman, for example, if left by the death of her husband with young children without support, to maintain herself by her own efforts, is the most absurd mockery of freedom ever devised.[3]

According to this view, women warranted special attention so that the preservation of the race (not to mention sexual differences) would be guaranteed.

Naturally not all conservatives sought state intervention. Many, certainly the majority of the clerically influenced right wing in Quebec, resisted such a solution as modernist and secularist. In their minds voluntary philanthropy retained its traditional favour.[4] Nevertheless, in English Canada, the West in particular, mothers' allowances supplied a cause that brought together a broad spectrum of articulate, middle-class Canadians.

Their agreement about the value of state assistance underlay a concerted campaign to introduce mothers' allowances legislation in every province in the first decades of the century. Such a campaign found sympathetic audiences because, then as now, mothers and children were judged more often the victims than the authors of misfortune. Accounts of their suffering could be counted on to open purse strings and hearts. This made it almost inevitable that mother-headed families would become the first clients of the new state-run public welfare apparatus which emerged in the twentieth century. With them "the nineteenth-century tradition against public home relief"[5] began to come unstuck.

Anxiety about the family has existed throughout Canada's history but the experience of the 1914–1918 war added credence to those voices that criticized the shortage of adequate child care services. Losses on the battlefield could most logically be made up by renewed efforts to reduce infant mortality. Improved care for mothers and their children would also ensure a generation physically and morally fit to inherit the "brave new world" for which Canada's soldiers had fought.[6] When wartime crises made every manpower question a matter of urgency, the significance of the maternal role, long stressed by feminists, won new recognition.

Such views were given specific focus after the ministrations of the Canadian Patriotic Fund throughout the war had accustomed citizens to the support and supervision of large numbers of fatherless families.[7] Whereas in the past institutions had been expected to succour the human victims of families struck by disaster, Fund workers rejected this solution.[8] Above all their goal was the maintenance of the home life, enriched if possible, of Canada's fighting men. It seems very probable that the good results that the CPF demonstrated in improved school attendance, better housekeeping, lessened mortality, and increased family stability helped further other efforts to shore up the nuclear family as the best guarantor of social order.

"Family case work," which became the leitmotif of social work in the 1920s and 1930s, sought "to reinforce and strengthen the endangered family, by drawing in the community's resources, not only in material relief, but in character and spiritual strength as well."[9] Mothers' allowances would ensure that those families, particularly among the lower classes, that were increasingly designated by case studies as deviant and distressed, could be both brought into line and sustained by efficient professionals, as an essential step in modernizing the whole process of relief assistance in the Dominion. The 1914 resolution of the Social Services Council of Canada in favour of mothers' allowances helped make possible the careers in family management that pioneer social workers like Charlotte Whitton would begin to build.[10] Through them the state entered into inadequate homes as the active agent of middle-class values.

Pushed by such forces mothers' allowances legislation came thick and fast between 1916 and 1920. The five provinces west of Quebec, beginning with Manitoba in 1916, Saskatchewan in 1917, Alberta in 1919, and British Columbia and Ontario in 1920, led their eastern counterparts in this area as they did too in woman suffrage. In response to numerous appeals, two more provinces offered allowances before the Second World War—Nova Scotia beginning in 1930 and Quebec from 1937. New Brunswick had an act on the books from 1930 but no funds were distributed until 1944.

As so often in the history of public welfare, the first efforts originated with public-spirited volunteers. In Manitoba, the campaign to inaugurate mothers' allowances began in 1910 when the Mother's Association of Winnipeg paid a woman using their day nursery to "stay at home and look after her children."[11] Although this subsidy ceased after one year when the woman remarried, the initiative was influential. The Associated Charities of Manitoba's capital soon joined the Association in its experiment with income supplements for needy mothers. By the fall of 1915, however, the Association's responsibilities outstripped its resources and it called for the province to step in. By this time, too, the newly established Social Workers' Club of the same city had instituted a study of mothers' allowances, or pensions, in the United States and a survey of 124 widows known to the Associated Charities. Its favourable report, calling for "State Salaries for Mothers," was subsequently circulated to every member of the local legislature. In November, the Convention of Manitoba Municipalities endorsed this proposal. The new Liberal government of Premier Norris, elected on a reform ticket with feminist support, repaid "debts" in the spring of 1916 with the passage of the Mothers' Allowances Act.

Within a short time events proceeded very similarly in British Columbia, Alberta, Saskatchewan, and Ontario. In B.C., for example, the cause was taken up between 1911 and 1914 by women's groups including the WCTU, the IODE, the National Council of Women, the Woman's Branch of the Maccabees, the Dominion Order of King's Daughters, the Woman's New Era League, the University Women's Club, and the Equal Franchise Association. As elsewhere, the onset of the war at first diverted attention and then ushered in a new wave of support. Bending before the progressive tide, the new reform-minded Liberal administration of Premier Oliver passed the necessary legislation in April 1920.

Nova Scotia, Quebec, and New Brunswick all received studies favourable to the assistance program some years before they acted.[12] Their delay reflected the greater weight of progressive sentiment in the more western provinces and the more sophisticated welfare tradition which had already grown up by 1914.[13]

The testimony of witnesses before the Ontario inquiry into the value of allowances recalled the precise concerns that motivated the measure's supporters in every province. Ministers, social workers, feminists, patriotic fund workers, and doctors were unanimous in condemning the infant mortality and juvenile delinquency that so often shipwrecked mother-led families. They insisted, too, on the community's responsibility to hapless women who, through no fault of their own, were denied minimum security and dignity. Many drew on their own experience to mount a sustained attack on custodial institutions such as orphanages which they proclaimed completely inadequate substitutes for domestic supervision and affection. A few witnesses even broached the difficult topic of widowers with children. This potentially revolutionary topic was, however, allowed to die because of the inability to conceive of a father being paid to stay home and the fear of outraging public morality should a female non-relative be employed as housekeeper.[14] The final report neatly summed up the consensus of the public hearings:

Sorrow and disappointment in the break-up of families, the insufficiency of institutional life, the stigma later attached to the institutional child, the overcrowding of our institutions, all these were advanced as arguments by many speakers. The family remains the unit of society and nothing compensates the child for the lack of a mother's care.... And with homes intact and mothers at home to take care of their children, there would be less of juvenile waywardness and crime.[15]

Such views were commonplace among the legislation's supporters everywhere in the Dominion.

Although great promise was held out for the new laws, there was also the time-honoured anxiety lest public assistance encourage the growth of a pauper or dependent class. As Alberta's Superintendent of Neglected and Dependent Children warned,

It is understood that great care will have to be exercised in working out such legislation. Mothers who are the most worthy will, in all probability, be the most timid and backward about making application to such a fund, while those who have the least to recommend them will be the most persistent in presenting their claims.[16]

The undeserving poor, or "welfare bums" as they came to be called, were as much a concern at the onset of Canada's social security experiment as they are today.

MOTHERS' ALLOWANCES LEGISLATION

Not surprisingly, provinces differed in the methods of separating the deserving and the undeserving. Eligibility, for instance, always included needy widows with two or more children, but not in every case the wives of the insane, the ill, or the imprisoned. Unmarried mothers and divorcees also regularly faced discrimination, with B.C. the most "liberal" in its allocations. Applicants with only one child were nowhere a priority, but some administrations enrolled the most desperate cases. In addition, children's eligibility ended at school-leaving age, although rules were stretched occasionally for very bright students. Whatever the number of dependants, fairly rigorous means and residence tests attempted to screen out all but the most needy.

In all jurisdictions the mother was to be a "fit and proper" person to exercise authority. Biological parenthood did not bring automatic inclusion, as the Ontario Commission indicated:

The mother is regarded as an applicant for employment as a guardian of future citizens of the State, and if she does not measure up to the State's standards for such guardians, other arrangements must be sought in the best interests of the children and to prevent increase in the number of dependents of this nature.[17]

Such reservations supplied the basis for extending the acts to cover suitable foster mothers who might offer a better upbringing than institutions, the only other alternative. Such wider interpretations of the allowances' principle occurred after the initial passage of the legislation. Nevertheless, concern persisted lest the addition of new classes increase costs or even encourage paternal irresponsibility.

Once she qualified, a woman received funds that varied a good deal, depending where she lived. On a scale of generosity, provinces could generally be ranked from first to last, Manitoba, Alberta, B.C., Ontario, Quebec, Nova Scotia, and Saskatchewan. In 1929, for instance, a Manitoban family with a mother and three offspring, one between twelve and fifteen years of age, one between seven and eleven, and one between one and six, would receive $74.00 a month. In contrast, the maximum allowance for a Saskatchewan family of any size would be $30.00. These sums were, in most instances, to be supplemented by the earnings of beneficiaries, both mothers and children. A portion of such income was deducted from the allowance. This latter requirement endeavoured to prevent the creation of a "class that would tend to relax personal effort and lean on public benevolence."[18]

Of course such fears had to be balanced against the best interests of the family concerned. It was after all essential that employment did not negate the good intentions of the legislation itself. In this regard the attitude of the Ontario Mothers' Allowances Commission was typical. Right from the onset it made an effort "to obtain part time instead of full time employment for the mother in order that she may arrange to spend more time in the home or to arrange for her to earn without leaving the home, as by keeping roomers, dressmaking or doing laundry work in the home."[19] As Charlotte Whitton pointed out, such arrangements were also intended to provide the basis for full-time occupations later on:

> Altogether, employment gives her [the recipient] a different outlook on life by putting her in touch with the outside world. It also prepares her to be self-supporting when she can no longer benefit under this act. If the mothers' allowances administration does not gradually prepare her to stand on her own feet, it fails in one of its objectives.[20]

Whatever the anticipated advantages of such employment, one deleterious side effect included the maintenance of a pool of vulnerable, cheap, and part-time labour. In this way women's marginal status within the paid labour force was yet again confirmed.

The interpretation and enforcement of these regulations, which soon grew to cover thousands of families, required extensive personnel. In the beginning there was a concerted effort to co-ordinate a large number of volunteers with a small core of paid professionals. In Ontario, for example, ninety-six local boards of concerned citizens were appointed to visit applicants in their districts. In Manitoba the original act compelled municipalities to appoint investigation committees. Only in Saskatchewan, and the latecomers Nova Scotia and Quebec, was there no formal inclusion of volunteers at the onset. Over time the tendency was to depend more and more heavily on the professionals whose responsibility was more clearcut and standards more codified. Charlotte Whitton, in the Report of the Manitoba Royal Commission to Inquire into the Administration of the Child Welfare Division of the Department of Health and Public Welfare (1928), offered one influential argument for the need for trained personnel:

> The fact that such a large percentage of the families who had been dependent before coming on Mothers' Allowances still required assistance after cancellation, is significant in that it is another evidence of the necessity of employing trained social workers to deal with problem cases were [sic] chronic dependence is caused by such uncontrollable factors as mental deficiency, or innate degeneracy. Such problems, if the definite goal of rehabilitation of the family is to be attained, require the grim determination of a strong personality coupled with the utmost skill and training. On the other hand, skill and experience are equally required to "weed out" those families where such factors are so persistent and hopeless that it is a waste of human effort and public funds, to seek the establishment of social stability and independency.[21]

Although not all could meet Whitton's rigorous standards, there is little doubt that mothers' allowances investigators endeavoured to set a model of industry and independence for their clients. To supplement their own example they instituted, inasmuch as they could since they were generally understaffed and overworked, a program of home supervision. This included checking on school attendance, child hygiene, mental health, work histories, household budgets, and home maintenance. Such efforts were frequently augmented by other middle-class professionals. Manitoba, for instance, appointed a "visiting housekeeper" to instruct mothers, arguing that "when the contract of employment between the mothers and the Province is signed, and the mother in receipt of her salary that the Province should satisfy itself that the services rendered for the salary are accomplishing what was intended...."[22]

There is little doubt that some mothers found such supervision irksome and patronizing.[23] As an Ontario investigator indicated, however, others viewed it in a more favourable light:

> Several mothers have spoken to me of the relief to their minds of having someone to visit with whom they could talk over their problems. Sometimes it is a wayward boy or girl, or it may be financial worries, or health needs. I have often had a woman say to me "do call again soon. I feel so much better since talking this over with you. This is one way in which I miss my husband so much."[24]

In view of the desperate situation of so many sole-support mothers, supervision was a price they might well willingly pay for new security. Certainly the prior experience of so many of them with local charities would have been little better. Nevertheless, for all its undeniable advantages, such supervision constituted an extension, through the state apparatus, of the middle class's ability to control the behaviour and development of working-class Canadians.

Although, as the regulations suggested, a real effort was made to keep costs at a minimum, mothers' allowances soon proved a heavy expenditure for the provinces. Unlike shared cost programs such as the Employment Service of Canada established in 1918 and the Old Age Pensions scheme created in 1927, which saw Ottawa assume a major role, allowances included no federal involvement whatsoever.[25] Except for Saskatchewan, the first wave of provinces to subsidize needy mothers shared costs with local municipalities. In time, administrative and financial difficulties brought increased centralization. The result left provincial governments with sole responsibility for costs (see Tables 1 and 2). The increasing expense could be borne so long as revenues remained buoyant. When incomes slid, as they did particularly in the 1930s, assistance for mother-led families became a part of the crisis in provincial budgeting that formed the background to the Rowell-Sirois Commission and the Marsh Report on Reconstruction.

TABLE 1 AMOUNTS EXPENDED ON MOTHERS' ALLOWANCES (or their equivalent) 1916-17 TO 1938-39 (to the nearest dollar)*

	Man.	Sask.	Alta.	B.C.	Ont.	N.S.	Quebec
1916–17							
1917–18							
1918–19							
1919–20		36 955					
1920–21	437 237	103 210			774 667		
1921–22	329 259	158 300			1 382 138		
1922–23	426 148	194 480			1 612 701		
1923–24	406 020	219 480	257 412		1 715 155		
1924–25	295 527	252 775	283 439		1 790 680		
1925–26	415 206	301 280	314 298		1 886 095		
1926–27	413 924	322 066	340 000		2 017 614		
1927–28	470 445	355 610		612 645	2 205 877		
1928–29	543 507	521 880	355 000		2 324 388		
1929–30		467 575	396 755	759 698	2 478 205		
1930–31		544 250	466 536	816 272	2 582 221	333 346	
1931–32		483 618	479 607	842 977	2 698 789	348 172	
1932–33		403 915	439 139	779 640	2 806 239	358 158	
1933–34		407 993	439 983	621 502	3 030 415	356 074	
1934–35		440 580	462 393	589 622		413 997	
1935–36	444 874	474 120	507 502	616 555	3 946 816	363 981	
1936–37	445 550	484 068	613 564	682 588	4 851 642	400 066	
1937–38	433 384	495 988		748 272	4 851 641	426 448	
1938–39	427 782	498 048	620 299	790 101	5 000 041	424 615	2 064 733

* This information is culled from a variety of sources, which accounts for its incompleteness.

TABLE 2 NUMBER OF MOTHERS OR FOSTER MOTHERS ON ALLOWANCES 1916–17 TO 1938–39

	Man.	Sask.	Alta.	B.C.	Ont.	N.S.	Quebec
1916–17	129 (June '17)						
1917–18	175						
1918–19	362	148					
1919–20	479	232		636	189		
1920–21		519			2 660		
1921–22	575	725	619	771	3 559		
1922–23	604	754		785	3 870		
1923–24	670	902	594	847	4 058		
1924–25				943	4 185		
1925–26				986	4 798		
1926–27				1 100	5 540		
1927–28				1 233	5 139		
1928–29				1 370	5 357		
1929–30		1 426		1 468	5 623		
1930–31		1 633		1 568	5 998	1 030	
1931–32		1 691		1 437	6 228	1 101	
1932–33	1 074	1 766	1 724	1 514	6 523	1 158	
1933–34	1 092	1 771		1 436	7 065	1 168	
1934–35	1 110	1 906		1 410	7 517	1 239	
1935–36	1 141	2 068		1 485	10 413◊	1 229	
1936–37	1 053	2 120	2 317	1 567	11 420	1 260	
1937–38	1 079	2 174	2 304	1 691	11 903	1 295	
1938–39	1 055			1 751	12 218	1 291	5 176

◊ This dramatic increase reflects the addition of needy mothers with one school-age child to the allowances' lists.

THE RECIPIENTS

Inspired by social work's fascination with data collection and case studies, provinces were intent on pinpointing the sources of dependency. The result was a great wealth of statistical information, some of which has survived. This offers an unusual opportunity to examine the nature and circumstances of those citizens for whom poverty otherwise dictated obscurity. What follows is a first step in that investigation.

The Report of the New Brunswick Child Welfare Survey in 1929 set out the conditions that had inspired earlier legislation in other provinces. Investigators uncovered large numbers of "widowed mothers and their children, who are struggling against almost overwhelming odds of economic need and continuous pressure on their reserves of health, strength and morality."[26] The author, the ubiquitous Whitton, reminded the tardy Maritimers that low wages and seasonal employment made it impossible for many men to provide for their families in case of emergency. Nor were most women able, on the paltry salaries they commanded, to support their children. Family breakdown, child prostitution, baby farming, child beating, and worse were the all too common outcome of the state's indifference. Whitton's damning reminder to New Brunswick's institutions for children was similarly familiar:

> Every orphanage must face the fact that the consensus of opinion in all modern social work is that the best institution in the world is no substitute for the family home, that institutional care is only wise when custodial care is necessary or when extremely specialized equipment for treatment is needed. . . . Every normal child in an institution represents a failure of the community.[27]

New Brunswick, operating as it did with Poor Law institutions, was exceptionally backward in its welfare services. Nevertheless. the dreadful conditions Whitton described could be duplicated to some extent at least in every jurisdiction. The case of one Ontario family, for instance, demonstrated the personal tragedy that had so often overtaken applicants for government aid.

> The files show the record of another family, in a rural district, where the mother of three small boys, when her husband died, was unsuccessful in her efforts to keep them with her. She was obliged to sell her furniture and place the children with neighbours to whom she paid a small amount for their board in order that she might not lose her claim upon them. She took a post in the city as a domestic and regularly paid her children's board. She later made another unsuccessful attempt to re-establish her home and returned in despair to domestic service, boarding her children as before.[28]

As this individual history indicated, families were extremely vulnerable to the loss, for any reason, of the male breadwinner. The precarious income of labourers, small farmers, miners, clerks, and small businessmen in particular often provided barely enough when they were alive. Disaster almost inevitably cast their families on charity of some sort.[29] In particular, illness, especially tuberculosis with its resulting disability and death, was identified as a major cause of dependency.[30] The inadequate health services and low vitality of so many poorer families was poignantly illustrated by the large proportion of fathers who fell victim to the great flu epidemic of 1918–1919. Manitoba, for example, ascribed 117 or 28.08 percent of its client families in that period directly to this malady.[31]

Provincial investigators sought explanation for dependency not only in illness but also in ethnicity. Findings varied a good deal from one jurisdiction to another. British Columbia, for instance, regularly recorded a majority of British-born (including Irish). The year 1930 was typical, when 54.22 percent, 29.84 percent, 7.63 percent, and 8.3 percent of all female applicants were born in the British Isles, Canada, the United States, and all other places respectively. In contrast, Ontario, an older province, registered 63.48 percent, 27.41 percent, and 9.10 percent respectively Canadian-born, British-born, and those born in all other nations including the United States in

1929–1930.[32] As might be expected, the prairie provinces, which had recently welcomed large numbers of newcomers, enrolled substantially greater percentages of eastern and southern European origin, while long-settled Nova Scotia counted more Canadian-born. Unfortunately such ratios cannot tell us how ethnicity affected the reception of applications. One suspects, however, that cultural considerations weighed in the social worker–client relationship. Further investigation is needed before we will understand that influence.

Before coming on to mothers' allowances, women used every possible means of keeping themselves afloat. They turned regularly to other forms of public assistance, to relatives and adult children, to employment, to boarders, and to savings and insurance for additional funds. Every province acknowledged what sacrifices mothers made to keep their families intact. Ontario's report on 3870 applicants in 1922–1923, for instance, revealed 2140 or 55.29 percent to be engaged in some type of employment: 924 charring, 450 taking roomers, 249 knitting or sewing, 182 in factory work, 135 in farm work, fruit picking and the like, 102 clerking, 26 nursing, 7 in professions, and 65 in business.[33] Desperation could sometimes produce highly unorthodox solutions. Such was the case with an Ontario woman who supported five children and a husband with terminal cancer. By "fishing, shooting and trapping and acting as a guide in summer to hunters" she was able to provide her family with food and a "two-roomed shack."[34]

The impact of a regular source of additional income on such families could be tremendous. The custodians of public welfare were unanimous in observing that "with the haunting fear of dire want removed ... many mothers have been able to carry on cheerfully and courageously, and by their own efforts produce home surroundings which are a credit to themselves."[35] For some at least the generally predictable provincial grants must have been a more certain source of comfort than wages which economic disaster or a husband's whim could withhold.[36] The impact of receiving money that was demonstrably her own, for her own allocation, albeit under some supervision, can only be imagined for a woman who until that time might be largely or entirely dependent on individual males. Did the grants produce, as feminists hoped, an enhanced appreciation of the dignity and value of motherhood? Government observers appeared to think they did, but a great deal more research needs to be done before we will know for sure.

Although the legislation was of immense significance to poorer women, the early shift in nomenclature from pensions to allowances reflected the quickly emerging focus on "the needs of bereaved and dependent children rather than ... [on] the needs of women who happen to be mothers of these children."[37] The singling out of children ensured that the women's predicament, with all the shortcomings it underlined in marriage law and economic opportunity, went largely ignored. The fact that "the primary object of this legislation is the conservation of home life"[38] meant in effect that once again women were considered deserving of recognition only inasmuch as they were mothers. In an ironic fulfillment of the feminists' maternalist ideology, the most important reform legislation passed after the woman suffrage campaign in English Canada subsumed the cause of women under that of children.

The affirmation of the parental home which mothers' allowances aimed for was intended to create a milieu in which healthier, happier, and more "adjusted" young people would be produced. State assistance would, it was hoped, reduce juvenile delinquency since "Children who carry the key while their mothers work all day are not long in getting beyond their mothers' control."[39] Proper guidance was further ensured through contact in some localities with a "Kiwanis Daddy" who was expected to help keep the child on the straight and narrow.[40] Unfortunately the data is insufficient at present to establish the success of such efforts, although the investigators themselves remained optimistic.

Mothers' allowances also helped, together with "fostering out," which gained momentum during the post-war period, check the numbers of institutionalized children. Fewer admissions to orphanages and other residences were designed to reduce public outlay and benefit the children.[41] Mothers were also enabled to rescue offspring they had been forced to abandon in a variety of settings. The reunion could be crucial. One Ontario recipient, for example, saw her son who, along with his brother, had attended school intermittently during her absence and who had been "termed dull and stupid" improve so much "that he passed his last exam with honours and his teacher considers him a clever boy."[42]

Reports from every provincial agency proudly enumerated the improved health and hygiene of these client families. School and public health nurses as well as local doctors and hospitals were alerted so that illness and disability found earlier treatment than otherwise would have been the case. Benefits could begin very early, as was the case when "Mothers with young infants . . . [were] enabled to nurse their children instead of the artificial feeding to which they would otherwise have had to resort were they forced into full time employment."[43] Instruction on hygiene and nutrition together with encouragement to move to more salubrious surroundings were part of the same campaign to upgrade health standards.

Among the most notable advantages for children were enhanced opportunities for education. The fact that "the average worker's child cannot afford to stay out of the factory after it reaches the age of ten or twelve years"[44] had shocked numerous observers for some years before the appearance of allowances. The introduction of factory acts barring child labour and compulsory schooling up to certain ages still proved ineffectual when family need was great. As a result every jurisdiction sought to use income supplements to keep young people in school at least until the official school-leaving age.

The outcome of all this attention was to be "desirable citizens and social assets to the community," in other words "the development of wholesome, healthy citizenship."[45] Children from assisted homes would help compensate for the losses of war and affirm Canada as the "Land of the Fair Deal." It was an integral part of the wave of legislation that began with Ontario's

Act for Dependent and Neglected Children in 1893 and climaxed with the creation of the federal Division of Child Welfare in 1919. Like those initiatives, mothers' allowances promised both a better life for young Canadians and a more orderly community for those who feared social unrest.

The shift to the mother as the paid representative of the state and away from custodial institutions reflected disappointment with earlier solutions and the emergence of social work with its professional commitment to the maintenance of family ties. These factors operated in concert with conservative forces which feared the rising tide of modern morality and feminists who had tied their suffrage campaign irrevocably to the celebration of the maternal ideal. The result, over the short term at least, undeniably benefitted poorer women and children who otherwise would have found survival still more difficult. Over the longer term, however, one wonders how the shortcomings of Canada's present social security system are related to the direction taken some fifty and more years ago. Wages for housework or state salaries for women, for instance, were inextricably connected to a narrow vision of human potential, as the self-congratulatory comment of one Mothers' Allowances' Commission makes abundantly clear: "The number of beneficiaries who have remarried is gratifying; this return to the normal home where the man is the wage-earner and the mother the home-maker constitutes the best solution of the problem of the support and care of these dependent children."[46]

The fact that the state chose to recognize female citizens most particularly in their capacity as mothers reflected how far women were from full equality. Today's welfare mothers are, at least in part, the direct casualties of a society's failure to distinguish between the cause of women and that of children. To transfer from dependence upon one man to reliance upon a male-dominated state is not liberation, as Stephen Leacock knew well, but merely the familiar dependence in a new form.

NOTES

1. Canada, Royal Commission on the Status of Women, *Report* (Ottawa, 1970), 319–25. See also Doris E. Guyatt, *The One Parent Family in Canada* (Ottawa, 1971) for a useful review of the situation of mother-led families in Canada.

2. See N.L. McClung, "What Will They Do With It?" *Maclean's*, July 1916, 36–38, for her support for mothers' pensions, and her *In Times Like These* (Toronto, 1972) for a more extended discussion of women's superior qualities.

3. S. Leacock, *The Social Criticism of Stephen Leacock*, ed. and intro. A. Bowker (Toronto, 1973), 60.

4. For a useful analysis of the complexity of conservative/clerical opinion in Quebec on the question of the state's role in welfare see B.L. Vigod, "Ideology and Institutions in Quebec: The Public Charities Controversy 1921–1926," *Histoire sociale/Social History* 11, 21 (May 1978): 167–82.

5. W.I. Trattner, *From Poor Law to Welfare State: A History of Social Welfare in America* (New York, 1974), 190.

6. See Suzann Buckley, "Ladies or Midwives? Efforts to Reduce Infant and Maternal Mortality" in *A Not Unreasonable Claim: Women and*

Reform in Canada 1880–1920, ed. Linda Kealey (Toronto, 1979), and V.J. Strong-Boag, *The Parliament of Women* (Ottawa, 1976), 311. See also Provincial Archives of Ontario (henceforth PAO), Papers of the Department of Labour (henceforth DL), General Subject Files 2, file "Mothers' Allowances 1919," "Mothers' Pension Allowance. Hamilton Inquiry, Feb. 20, 1919," the testimony of Mrs P.D. Crerar.

7. See R.C. Brown and R. Cook, *Canada 1896–1921: A Nation Transformed* (Toronto, 1974), 222–23 and Strong-Boag, *Parliament of Women*, 323–24.

8. Regarding the older tradition see D.J. Rothman, *The Discovery of the Asylum* (Boston, 1971). For an insightful discussion of the shift see Trattner, *From Poor Law to Welfare State*, ch. 6, "Child Welfare." Unfortunately, no Canadian study yet explores this transformation. Nevertheless a comparable pattern can be discerned in M.K. Strong, *Public Welfare Administration in Canada* (Chicago, 1930) and R. Splane, *Social Welfare in Ontario, 1791–1893* (Toronto, 1965).

9. McGill University, School of Social Work, Greater Victoria Survey Committee, *Problems in Family Welfare, Relief and Child Development*, c. 1931, p. 5. For similar views see McGill, School of Social Work, Fredericton Community Survey, *Interim Report*, 1930; Canadian Council on Child and Family Welfare, *Social Welfare Conditions in the City of Saskatoon (with especial reference to families in distress)*, 1930; Canadian Welfare Council, *Report of Field Survey in Greater Ottawa, Gloucester, Nepean, Eastview*, June–Sept. 1935; and Canadian Welfare Council, *The Welfare Services of the City of Galt*, 1938–39.

10. Charlotte Whitton is clearly one of the critical figures in the history of Canadian social work. After completing degrees at Queen's in 1918 she became assistant secretary of the Social Service Council of Canada and joint editor of *Social Welfare*. From 1925 to 1942 she was executive director of the Canadian Welfare Council.

11. Manitoba, Mothers' Allowances Commission, *Report* 1916–17, 1.

12. See Nova Scotia, Royal Commission on Mothers' Allowances, 1921; [Charlotte Whitton], *Memorandum on Child and Family Welfare in the Province of Quebec (exclusive of any references to the fields of Public Health or Child Hygiene)*, March 1931, and Whitton, *Report of the New Brunswick Child Welfare Survey*, 1929. For a useful discussion of developments in Quebec in particular see Dorothy Aitkin, "The Role of the Montreal Council of Social Agencies in the Establishment of Public Assistance" (MA thesis, University of Chicago, 1950).

13. See R. Allen, *The Social Passion* (Toronto, 1971), passim, and Mary Jennison, "Study of the Canadian Settlement Movement" (typescript, School of Social Work, University of Toronto, 1974).

14. PAO, DL, General Subject Files 2, file "Mothers' Allowances 1919," "Mothers' Pension Allowance. Hamilton Inquiry, Feb. 20, 1919," testimony by Mr Axford, pp. 57–58. See also the sympathy of the first chair of the Ontario Mothers' Allowances Commission, Peter Bryce, for this proposal, "Mothers' Allowances," *Social Welfare* 1, 6 (1 March 1919): 131–32.

15. Ibid., W.A. Riddell, "Report on Mothers' Allowances," 9.

16. Alberta, Superintendent of Neglected Children, *Annual Report*, 1917, 8.

17. Ontario, Mothers' Allowances Commission, *Annual Report*, 1920–21, 27.

18. British Columbia, Mothers' Pension Act, *Annual Report*, 30 Sept. 1920, 2.

19. Ontario, Mothers' Allowances Commission, *Annual Report*, 1920–21, 21.

20. Manitoba, Royal Commission to Inquire into the Administration of the Child Welfare Division of the Department of Health and Public Welfare, *Report*, 1928, 45.

21. Ibid., 93.

22. Manitoba, Mothers' Allowances Commission, *Annual Report*, 1916–17, 4–5.

23. See for instance the case of Mrs "A" cited in the Manitoba Royal Commission to Inquire into the Administration of the Child Welfare Division . . . , *Report*, 86.

24. Ontario, Mothers' Allowances Commission, *Annual Report*, 1924–25, 11.

25. For a critical appraisal of the Employment Service of Canada see James Struthers, "Prelude to Depression: The Federal Government and Unemployment, 1918–29," *Canadian Historical Review* 58, 3 (Sept. 1977): 277–93.

26. Charlotte Whitton, *Report of the New Brunswick Child Welfare Survey*, 1929, 193.

27. Ibid., 191–92.

28. Ontario, Mothers' Allowances Commission, *Annual Report*, 1921–22, 25.

29. Reports from every province document the majority of husbands as employed in such occupations.

30. For an early appraisal of this serious problem see Geo. D. Forter, "Canada and the Tuberculosis Problem," *The Survey* 28 (15 June 1912): 444–45. See also the efforts of the NCWC to deal with the malady, Strong-Boag, *Parliament of Women*, 266, 311–12, 372.

31. For an important study of the flu see J.P. Dickin McGinnis, "The Impact of Epidemic Influenza: Canada 1918–19," *Canadian Historical Association Historical Papers* (1971): 21–40.

32. British Columbia, Mothers' Pensions Act, *Annual Report*, 1930, 7; Ontario, Mothers' Allowances Commission, *Annual Report*, 1929–30, 14.

33. Ontario, Mothers' Allowances Commission, *Annual Report*, 1922–23, 13.

34. Ontario, Mothers' Allowances Commission, *Annual Report*, 1924–25, 12.

35. British Columbia, Mothers' Pensions Act, *Annual Report*, 1929, 1.

36. This had also been discovered by CPF investigators. One report, for instance, commented: "During the first two years of the war at least, a very large proportion of soldiers' dependents were in receipt of more money than they had been accustomed to receive from their husbands while the latter were in civilian life," P.H. Morris, ed., *The Canadian Patriotic Fund: A Record of Its Activities from 1914–1919* (n.p., 1919), 42.

37. W.C. Kierstead, "Mothers Allowances in Canada," *Canadian Congress Journal* 4, 7 (July 1925): 27. See also F.J. Bruno and L. Towley, *Trends in Social Work 1874–1956* (New York, 1957), 177.

38. Alberta, Superintendent of Neglected Children, *Annual Report*, 1918, 8.

39. PAO, DL, General Subject Files 2, file "Mothers' Allowances 1919," W.A. Riddell, "Report on Mothers' Allowances," 9.

40. See Ontario Mothers' Allowances Commission, *Annual Report*, 1921–22, 10.

41. See the goals set out by Rose Henderson, "Pensions for Mothers," Social Service Congress, *Report of Addresses and Proceedings* (Ottawa, 1914), 110.

42. Ontario, Mothers' Allowances Commission, *Annual Report*, 1921–22, 25.

43. Ontario, Mothers' Allowances Commission, *Annual Report*, 1920–21, 20.

44. Henderson, "Pensions for Mothers," 109–10.

45. Quebec, Royal Commission on Social Insurance, [Charlotte Whitton], *Memorandum on Child and Family Welfare in the Province of Quebec . . .* , p. 8.

46. Ontario, Mothers' Allowances Commission, *Annual Report*, 1920–21, 29.

"NOT TO PUNISH BUT TO REFORM": JUVENILE DELINQUENCY AND THE CHILDREN'S PROTECTION ACT IN ALBERTA, 1909–1929◇

REBECCA COULTER

○

In 1920 sixteen-year-old Albert B. was sent to Canada by his father presumably to seek his fortune, but the twenty-five dollars the boy had in his pocket when he left England did not last long in his new homeland. Albert was arrested in a rural area of Alberta, charged with vagrancy, convicted and sentenced to four months of hard labour at the Fort Saskatchewan Gaol. His case would likely have passed unnoticed except for the fact that a police magistrate sympathetic to the child saving movement angrily wrote to the Attorney General's Department to complain about the harsh sentence handed down.

> It is to me an almost incredible story. A boy of only sixteen, about six thousand miles from home, without work and needing to eat— could he be blamed if he stole something, or are there not some other people in the world more responsible for the theft than he would be?[1]

The letter went on to suggest that Albert should have received a suspended sentence, been found work on some farm and "helped to do the right thing, as probably, with a full stomach, he would not have any temptation to steal."[2]

◇ *Studies in Childhood History: A Canadian Perspective* (Calgary: Detselig, 1992), 167–84. Reprinted with the permission of the publisher. The author wishes to acknowledge the support of the Social Sciences and Humanities Research Council of Canada and the Alberta Heritage Scholarship Fund.

In defence of the original sentence and the magistrate who imposed it, Superintendent Bryan of the Alberta Provincial Police informed the deputy attorney general that Albert had actually stolen a car and when apprehended had given "a lot of evasive and contradictory statements as to his movements." In addition, argued Bryan, the man's conviction would "probably have the effect of stopping other cases of a like nature."[3]

It is not clear whether Police Magistrate Primrose's intervention on Albert's behalf resulted in a suspended sentence[4] but this anonymous youth's life, revealed in some fragmentary correspondence, serves to illustrate the conflicting views of childhood and juvenile delinquency prevalent in the early part of this century. Was Albert a boy or a man?[5] Was the environment responsible for delinquent behaviour or must individuals be held responsible for deviant acts? Should the courts be concerned with reforming or with punishing delinquents? Answers to satisfy all parties were never found (indeed, have yet to be found), but in Alberta, at least, the social reform position which argued for a prolonged, protected childhood, for the paramountcy of environmental influences as a determinant in child life and for the need to reform juvenile delinquents predominated between 1909 and 1929. That is not to say that the practice of juvenile justice always reflected the social reform position nor even that the child savers were always consistent in their explanations or actions. Conflicting interpretations and practices existed and over the course of twenty years Alberta's child welfare officials, like those elsewhere, became more and more enamoured of efficiency and "scientific" and "professional" social work. Nonetheless, on the whole it is safe to say that the sentiment and ideas of social reform continued to inform practice in a major way throughout the period.

Of the many social problems facing the new province of Alberta, juvenile delinquency was among the first to be tackled. In 1908 the Legislative Assembly of the province passed the Industrial Schools Act in order to make provisions for the treatment of juvenile delinquents. This act empowered the attorney general to appoint a superintendent of industrial schools. He chose R.B. Chadwick for the position and immediately instructed the new appointee to investigate and bring in recommendations about the best way to deal with delinquent and neglected children in the province. In preparing his report, Chadwick toured the North American continent and investigated forty-five industrial schools, visited fifty-five juvenile courts, and looked at various other institutions.[6]

In the end, he recommended that the Province of Alberta enter into an agreement with the Province of Manitoba in order that delinquent boys needing industrial school training could be admitted to the school at Portage la Prairie. He felt that the costs involved in building a modern cottage system[7] in Alberta would be prohibitive and, since Manitoba was willing to accept boys from Alberta, this arrangement ought to be pursued. In addition he recommended a broad system of child welfare laws for Alberta. Both his recommendations were accepted, the latter one being incorporated into law as An Act for the Protection of Neglected and Dependent Children (1909), and more commonly referred to as the Children's Protection Act.

With its passage, the act became the first major piece of welfare legislation in the province.[8]

Although the Alberta act was modelled very closely on its counterpart in Ontario, it was understood, according to its initiator, R.B. Chadwick, "that amendments would be made from time to time in order that the Act would become workable under conditions as found in the Province of Alberta."[9] Chadwick also noted that Alberta's act was regarded as the "broadest" on the continent. This was because Alberta's act defined "neglected child" in a way which was "sufficiently broad to meet almost any condition or contingency which may arise in reference to the question of what constitutes a neglected child."[10] According to the act,

> "Neglected child" shall mean a child who is found begging, receiving alms, thieving in a public place, sleeping at night in the open air, wandering about at late hours, associating or dwelling with a thief, drunkard or vagrant, or a child who by reason of the neglect, drunkeness or vice of its parents, is growing up without salutary parental control and education, or in circumstances exposing such child to an idle and dissolute life; or who is found in a house of ill-fame, or known to associate with or to be in the company of a reputed prostitute; or who is a habitual vagrant; or an orphan and destitute; or deserted by its parents; or whose only parent is undergoing imprisonment for crime; or why by reason of ill-treatment, continual personal injury or grave misconduct or habitual intemperance of its parents or either of them is in peril of loss of life, health or morality; or in respect to whom its parents or only parent have or has been convicted of an offence against this Act, or under *The Criminal Code*; or whose home by reason of neglect, cruelty or depravity, is an unfit place for such child, and "neglected children" shall mean two or more of such children.[11]

The normative nature of this definition allowed officials of the Department and Children's Aid Societies to intervene in nearly any situation they wished, an advantage they felt was particularly appropriate when it came to protecting children. The act was further strengthened in this regard in later years by the addition of two clauses so that the definition of a neglected child also included one "who is incorrigible or cannot be controlled by its parents; or who is employed anywhere between the hours of ten o'clock p.m. of one day and six o'clock a.m. of the following day. . . ."[12] Additionally, the act was extended by changing the definition of "child" from "a boy or girl actually or apparently under sixteen years of age" (1909), to seventeen in 1910 and eighteen in 1916. Furthermore, Chadwick noted, "The problems of dependent and delinquent children are so closely interwoven that they have been made as one as far as circumstances will permit, in the Province of Alberta."[13] Thus both dependent and delinquent children were considered to fall under the more inclusive term "neglected."

As well as defining the clientele, the act provided for the establishment of an administrative framework. To encourage, direct and supervise the work of the Children's Aid Societies[14] and to act in place of these societies where none existed, the lieutenant governor in council was entitled to appoint a superintendent of neglected children. Every city or town with a population over 10 000 (changed to 5000 in 1916) was instructed to provide a home or shelter where children could be temporarily housed prior to placement in a foster home. The children placed in a shelter were to be supervised and managed by the Children's Aid Society, if it had been established, or, by the superintendent, if it had not. Municipalities were held responsible for the maintenance of children although they or the Children's Aid Societies could apply for a court order to force parents to contribute to a child's upkeep.

The act went on to outline the procedure to be followed in apprehending children and placing them in foster homes. The municipal police, the Royal North West Mounted Police, officers of a Children's Aid Society (authorized by a district judge) or the superintendent could apprehend a child without a warrant. If a judge[15] found the child to be neglected within the meaning of the act, the child was transferred to the care of the Children's Aid Society or the superintendent of neglected children, either of which then became the legal guardian of the child and responsible for its placement in a suitable foster home. Foster homes and shelters were both subject to inspection by the superintendent or his designate.

In this way the Children's Protection Act managed to legally define provincial, municipal, parental, and voluntary activity in the field of child welfare. While various amendments were made throughout the years, mainly to expand the administrative machinery, the basic intent of the act remained the same. Wide-ranging powers were necessary to deal adequately with child welfare problems argued Canadian social reformers. Alberta's legislators apparently agreed and so do many historians.[16]

To put into practice the provisions of the Children's Protection Act, the attorney general promoted R.B. Chadwick to the position of superintendent of neglected children. In appointing Chadwick, the attorney general ensured that Alberta would enter into the mainstream of current child welfare thought and practice. Chadwick, a native of Ontario, had come to Edmonton in 1906 to serve as general secretary to the Young Men's Christian Association. He had had previous experience in boys' work both in New York and Toronto[17] and throughout his tenure as superintendent of neglected children retained and enlarged his contacts with social reformers throughout North America, Europe, and Australia. By 1913 he was vice president of the American Prison Association and assistant secretary of the Canadian Conference of Charity and Corrections[18] and in 1914 he sat on the national council of the Canadian Welfare League[19] along with such notables as J.S. Woodsworth. The network of contacts Chadwick established was maintained by his successors, who continued to attend conferences in both Canada and the United States, often presenting papers while there. Additionally, Alberta hosted visiting reformers. For example, in 1909, J.J. Kelso, the well-known superintendent of neglected children in Ontario, visited Alberta.[20] In 1918, the annual meeting of the Canadian Conference of Public Welfare was held in Edmonton[21] and in 1922, C.C. Carstens, director of the Child Welfare League of America, spoke to the annual conference of the Department of Neglected Children.[22]

Chadwick was frank in acknowledging his indebtedness to the work of social reformers elsewhere. As has been already noted, the Children's Protection Act nearly replicated Ontario's, and in the early annual reports Chadwick notes the contributions of the United States, Australia, Germany, France, Scotland, Great Britain, Norway, Sweden, and Austria. It is not surprising, then, that Alberta, as a member of the transnational and international network[23] should develop policies and procedures for dealing with child neglect and juvenile delinquency very much like those in operation elsewhere in Canada, and especially in Ontario where, Rutherford claims, a small group of central Canadians were mainly responsible for articulating the theories and tactics of the national social reform movement.[24] But if central Canadians selected one idea from here and one idea from there to construct a child welfare system that they *knew* was superior, as Sutherland[25] suggests, then Albertans, at least, exhibited that same smug attitude toward Ontario's system. Ontario's system was good but Alberta's was better.[26]

How did the last, best West deal with the problem of juvenile delinquency? By 1912 Alberta had a functioning system of juvenile courts. Thus children charged with juvenile delinquency would appear before a commissioner of the Juvenile Court. These commissioners most often had no legal training but had been appointed to the position because of their interest in child saving. Often they were ministers like Bishop H. Allen Gray or Rev. Michael Murphy, local businessmen in small communities or women like Alice Jamieson or Annie Langford. The approach used by these commissioners was closely modelled on the court procedures adopted by the famous Judge Ben Lindsay of Denver, Colorado,[27] a man who was frequently quoted with approval by the superintendents of neglected children.

Juvenile courts were held separately from the proceedings of adult courts in keeping with the child savers' views that children must be protected from any contact with adult vices. Hearings were conducted informally without juries and commonly without benefit of counsel. It was understood that the presiding commissioner would, in the manner of a kind, concerned adult, inquire into the events surrounding the charge and determine what should be done with the child. A.M. McDonald, the man who became superintendent of neglected children after Chadwick's death in 1915, likened the juvenile court procedures to medical ones when he quoted, with obvious approbation, an analogy made by Judge James Hodge Rocks of Richmond. When a child is physically ill, he goes to a doctor who examines the youngster, diagnoses the ailment and prescribes the remedy. Similarly, the juvenile judge should minister to the "morally ill" delinquent in the "moral clinic," the court.[28]

In the matter of delinquency, three remedies were open. The child could be placed on probation, made a ward of the Department of Neglected Children, or lastly a boy could be sent to the Industrial School at Portage la Prairie or a girl to one of the provincial social service homes.

In keeping with the social reformers' emphasis on the efficacy of family life, the preferred course of action was probation. Thus the child would be left in his natural home but would be supervised by a probation officer who, in the cities, was usually the agent of the Children's Aid Society. The probation officer was expected to oversee the probationer's pursuits, friends, and amusements.[29] This concept of probation was designed to meet Section 31 of the Dominion Delinquents Act, which stated in part "that as far as practicable every juvenile delinquent shall be treated, not as a criminal, but as a misdirected, misguided child, and one needing aid, encouragement, help and assistance."[30]

If probation proved to be unworkable or unsatisfactory, the child could be made a ward of the Neglected Children's Department and would then be "placed out" in the hopes that a suitable home would turn the child into the right paths of behaviour. Placement in an institution was seen as the last resort to be employed only in cases of the "more hardened type of child" who needed "the rigid system of discipline offered in an Industrial Training School."[31] The "hardened" child was one "who is in the habit of defying authority, an habitual thief, an incorrigible or a child who does not respond to the milder treatment of probation or to the influences which are thrown around him by the Department of Neglected Children. . . ."[32]

While a few juvenile court commissioners seemed bent on sentencing children who appeared before them in a way which would set an example for others, deterrence and retribution were not supposed to be considered as motives when bringing down a judgment.

> The old attitude of "an eye for an eye, and a tooth for a tooth" is frequently met with in those going through the channels of the Juvenile Court, but for this attitude there is substituted, as far as possible, the idea that preventive and educative reformation are the ends sought, and as far as possible records and terminology eliminate the idea of criminality.[33]

This issue of punishment versus reformation was the source of some friction between the Department and the Alberta Provincial Police. Superintendent McDonald wrote to the deputy attorney general on 5 September 1918 with a request that the relationship between the APP and the Department of Neglected Children be clarified.[34] McDonald accused the police of dealing with juveniles without consulting the Department and further complained of the tendency of members of the APP, acting as commissioners, to sentence children to the Portage la Prairie Industrial School unnecessarily.

While part of McDonald's concern no doubt arose from financial considerations,[35] it is, nonetheless, true that the child savers' conviction that unsatisfactory home conditions generally caused delinquency gave them an attitude toward youthful offenders that was more sympathetic than that of most police officers. Child savers often described delinquents as "more sinned against than sinning" and for this reason much of the work of the Department of Neglected Children and the Children's Aid Societies tended to blur the distinction between dependent and delinquent children as

Chadwick had originally intended it should. The police, on the other hand, were more inclined to draw a line between delinquent and neglected children. The constables' manual used by the Alberta Provincial Police was unequivocal: "A delinquent child is one which breaks the law and therefore is liable to punishment; a neglected child is one which has been neglected or abandoned, and therefore to be cared for and pitied, not punished."[36] Police officers were reminded, however, that neither class of children was to be allowed to mix with other criminals.

Susan Houston[37] has argued that the tendency of child savers to treat both types of children—the dependent and the delinquent—as one indicates that the real motivation for child welfare work was social control. She claims that by seeing dependent children as potentially or actually delinquent, the child savers were able to justify their interference in the lives of poor children and their families in terms of "the common good." There is no doubt some justification to this argument, especially for nineteenth-century Ontario, but it does ignore the two-edged nature of the child savers' position. If failing to distinguish between dependent and delinquent children resulted in harsher treatment for the former, it might also be argued that it resulted in a more humane treatment for the latter. Given the reality of institutional life in the early twentieth century, it seems likely that young delinquents and their families would be quite happy to trade incarceration for home supervision.

In any event, while probation theoretically meant that a probation officer could supervise both the delinquent and his parents, the simple fact was that financial considerations prevented it. Both provincial and municipal governments were extraordinarily parsimonious and even with the assistance of volunteers, the Department of Neglected Children was never able to come close to thoroughly supervising the cities, never mind the rural areas.[38] Lack of funds also meant that child welfare officials had practical as well as ideological reasons for trying to keep delinquent and neglected children in the parental home. Department officials claimed they tried to avoid apprehending children because "The home of the child is the natural place of protection and the parents are its natural guardian."[39] They might have added that it was cheaper to let families feed, clothe, and house their young than to have children's shelters or reformatories take on the responsibility.

This is not to imply, however, that those involved in child welfare work were duplicitous characters propounding the benefits of home life as a cover-up for monetary concerns. The financial imperative was not of their making but they had to live within its constraints. Thus, for example, the third superintendent of neglected children, K.C. McLeod, opposed staff cuts in his department by arguing that it was important to have an officer of the department present at all juvenile cases because otherwise

> many Magistrates become incensed against boys and wish to send them at once to the Reformatory, without the chance of probation. Our Officer there, accepting charge of the boy on probation, can . . . save him from being sent to Portage, and the Province from the expense of at least $2000.00.[40]

Similarly the most compelling argument made against raising the age of children coming under the Dominion Delinquents Act was the financial one. If the age were raised by two years from sixteen to eighteen, a significant increase in the number of children coming into care would be experienced and the Department had neither the facilities nor the staff to cope. Indeed, throughout the 1920s the Department of Neglected Children was constantly under pressure to reduce spendings and decrease staff.[41]

While child and family welfare work, like other reform measures, can be shown to have an important role to play in legitimizing capitalist society, it is clear that in Alberta the mediating influence of social service work was to be restricted by more immediate pecuniary concerns. It was simply impossible, given the available resources, for social reformers to effect a wholesale supervision of the lives of the children of the working class, much less their parents as well. The impact of their work was to be felt not so much in what they actually did but in how they contributed to what Sutherland has called the "twentieth century consensus" but others have called the ideological hegemony of capitalism.[42]

The approach to the causes of juvenile delinquency is a case in point. Because of the emphasis on environmental factors as the primary cause of delinquency, it became easy to blame poor families for crime. Child savers used the following model of the three stages of child development to explain the centrality of an appropriate family life. The first eight years of life, said Chadwick, were distinguished by an absolute dependency on adults and the child simply reflected the home. If the home were good, then *ipso facto*, the child would be good. Conversely, bad homes made bad children. The second period of childhood occurred between the ages of nine and thirteen. It was at this stage, Chadwick felt, that the child was learning habits and morals by imitation. Thus it was important that wholesome adult models be available to the child. The third stage of childhood was from the age of thirteen to the age of seventeen and this period, warned the superintendent, was fraught with danger. Chadwick quotes freely from the works of G. Stanley Hall to show that adolescence is filled with emotional upset, that this is the impulsive age. In explaining adolescence Chadwick said,

> During this period the child is up against the most serious time of its life. Rapid physical and mental growth, lack of knowledge of how to conduct itself under new conditions and circumstances, the ambitions and desires of men and women with the experience of children to carry them through this trying time, are but a few of the many trials to which the child is subjected.[43]

Furthermore, while the religious impulse was considered to be strong at this age so was the tendency towards criminal behaviour. If firm and loving parents failed to correct misbehaviour, the child would become a criminal for life.

Since most juvenile delinquents in Alberta were twelve years of age and older[44] and since a large proportion of them came from working class homes, homes often beset by unemployment, the loss of one parent, or very marginal incomes,[45] it was easy to create an explanation for delinquency based on the psychopathology of both adolescents and working class families. While some delinquent activity was put down to "the desire for fun" or "mischief-making," much more was blamed on the failure of parents to provide the proper home life. This was especially true in the case of the delinquent girl who, "as a rule, comes from a home where immorality and vice are more or less common and in the majority of cases she is compelled to house herself in crowded and unsanitary quarters with others of her kind. As a general rule these girls are stubborn and untractable."[46]

Thus both the families and the girls were to blame. Chadwick was also critical of parents who sent their girls out to work and of these working girls themselves because they sought some pleasure in life by attending dances, parties, and dinners. Chadwick seemed particularly distressed with young girls who eschewed domestic service for jobs elsewhere. He was critical of girls who "prefer to work as waitresses in cheap restaurants, or even in the capacity of dishwasher, in order that they may have their evenings free, that they may be able to enter and leave their rooms at their own discretion, bring in their own companions, and entertain whom they will."[47] In instances such as these, Chadwick seemed more concerned with the degree of independence of the young women rather than with anything else. Did he favour domestic service because employers in this situation could be seen as surrogate parents for the girl who had been allowed or encouraged to leave her own home and was not yet under the protection of a husband? Certainly, girls were seen as in special need of protection because they became women and women became mothers. As the "Angels of the Home" they then were responsible for the proper rearing of the next generation of children. In other words, the future of the country lay in the hands of mothers so it was important that they themselves be brought up correctly.

The reformers were also concerned about the sexual activity of girls because girls could lose "all that was valuable in their lives" before they realized "the sacredness of preserving the purity of their bodies and of their minds."[48] Reformers recognized the double standard of sexual morality existing in society but simply acceded to it.

> A boy who makes a mistake is welcomed back into society, and there is rarely any difficulty in finding a good private home for him. A girl who has gone wrong has lost so much that it would be difficult to regain her place in society, even if society were as ready to welcome her as her erring brother. The fact is that she is not so welcomed.[49]

Chadwick had noted in 1911 that one of the reasons girls received harsher treatment in the matter of "sex crimes" was the fact that the consequences of their behaviour were so glaringly obvious[50] and, indeed, throughout the years illegitimate children became a growing concern for the Department of Neglected Children.

Among working class families, the immigrant family, especially, was subjected to close scrutiny. Despite the fact that the majority of the immigrants in Alberta were English-speaking, the Department defined "immigrant children" as those who could not speak English. Consequently,

Superintendent Chadwick felt able to claim that immigrant children, "lacking knowledge of the language, . . . readily fall into mistakes, violate the laws and commit many misdemeanours. . . . "[51] That they could not speak English was thus considered an essential part of the explanation for their delinquent behaviour.

On the other hand, once these same children learned English they were a threat of another sort. When they could speak English and their parents could not, these children were suspected of devising "schemes under the eyes of the parents" who were too ignorant to realize what was going on.[52] Additionally the children were seen as able to "indulge in many habits and actions which are incomprehensible to their parents"[53] because the parents did not understand the ways of the city. Thus, whether the immigrant children knew English or not, they were viewed as more prone to delinquent behaviour. An additional problem with the children of the foreign born as opposed to the Canadian born was alleged to be their precociousness in sex matters and their tendency to "succumb more readily to immorality."[54] Furthermore, their parents were often seen as forcing the children out of the home to work—the girls in unskilled restaurant and hotel jobs and the boys in street trades, both of which endeavours it was said led rapidly to the criminal life.

On some occasions the reformers recognized that the average immigrant had come to Canada to better his life and that immigrants had contributed to the opening of the West. However, the faster they could be brought to a "high grade" of Canadian citizenship, the better it would be. Chadwick felt so strongly about the necessity of absorbing immigrants into the Canadian way of life, that he was able to cite this story seemingly unaware of how it contradicted his other notions about the respect owed by children to their parents and the importance of human dignity in general.

> There has been a tendency for the Canadian-bred child to look down upon the child of the foreign-born as not so fortunate as he, owing to the fact that he has not been born a Canadian. This all has a good effect in bringing the child of foreign-born parents to be a good Canadian. The sentiment is best expressed in the attitude of a small boy who, after having been punished by his father, said he did not object to being punished when he needed it but he hated to be thrashed by a dirty foreigner.[55]

An uncritical analysis of the delinquency statistics of the Department tends to support its assertion that the delinquency rate was higher among immigrant children than among others. With the exception of the years 1910 and 1911, when 15.57 percent of the population had its origin in non-English speaking lands and 15.58 percent of the delinquents had a similar origin, children of the "foreign-born" were over-represented in the delinquency statistics.[56] Several explanations can be postulated. More immigrant children may have been committing acts considered delinquent because in the troubled economic times after 1912 their families were the ones likely to suffer first from unemployment. On the other hand, the "self-fulfilling prophecy" may have been at work. The child savers and police assumed immigrant children were inclined to be delinquent and therefore may have spent more time looking for delinquents in the immigrant neighbourhoods and thus found more. There may have been a tendency, exacerbated by prejudice, to deal more firmly with immigrant children than with other children so that immigrant children would be placed on probation while English-speaking children would be let off with a warning. This state of affairs has been noted in the historical context by Gillis and Platt and in the modern one by, among others, William Ryan.[57] Unfortunately the evidence for the Alberta situation does not allow for a firm conclusion on this matter at this time. What we can note, however, is the fact that by the end of World War I, the superintendent of neglected children was less inclined to single out the children of the "foreign-born" for special mention when he was discussing juvenile delinquency.[58]

What forms did juvenile delinquency take in Alberta between 1909 and 1929? According to the statistics included in the annual reports, most cases of delinquency seem to have related to theft for boys and sexual offences for girls. From the evidence available, it can be postulated that, while some of these delinquencies were "childish pranks" and "mischief making," many of them resulted from adolescents trying to meet the necessities of life. A large number of the recorded thefts, for example, were of articles of clothing such as sweaters, boots, and socks. This was particularly true in the winter. The testimony of girls charged with sexual offences shows that they had often lost their jobs, had been unable to find a job, or had felt forced into a sexual relationship in order to keep a job.

J.E. Robbins points out that between 1911 and 1931 wage earners, on the whole, were gaining financially, with the exception of the young and the old. He notes a continuous gap of about two years between the school-leaving age and the attainment of economic independence. Robbins further claims that the loss of independence was especially severe among the boys, whose relative earning capacity dropped by 35 percent from 1911 to 1931.[59]

With this increasing dependency, the strain on poor families must have been noticeable. While hourly wage rates were increasing, so was the cost of living. Moreover, much of the work was seasonal in nature. In 1921, for example, in Calgary, labourers worked an average of only 40.87 weeks in the year.[60] Children in families such as these would need to go out to work as early as possible in order to support themselves or add to the family income. Yet the young were experiencing increasing difficulty in finding jobs. Thus it is not unreasonable to expect that, when work was unavailable, they and their families would have to survive as best they could.

Louis Chevalier has argued in his book *Labouring Classes and Dangerous Classes* that the city houses a segment of the population that lives in the twilight zone between crime and unskilled labour, working when work is available but turning to crime when it is necessary for survival. Stephen Humphries, in looking specifically at juvenile delinquency, convincingly argues that much juvenile crime was "social crime."[61] By this he means that a great part of youthful stealing was done in order to supplement family economies. Pilfering, from the corner store or raiding a vegetable garden, for example, brought in additional food. Shoplifting or stealing from a clothesline added clothing to the family wardrobe. Other forms of illegal activity also helped a family get by as the case of an Edmonton boy shows. He was eventually caught shoplifting but he had begun his life of "crime" by sweeping up the wheat left in railroad box cars. This he would sell for a little money and it was only after this route to additional income was closed that he turned to stealing from stores. In summarizing this case in his 1932 thesis on juvenile delinquency, Hermin Lewis King observed "As the family was large and the father's income small, it appeared to me as though the boy was to some extent forced to 'sweep up the grain,' and this led to his subsequent antisocial acts."[62] Here is an example of how the family was held responsible for a son's delinquency. He was "forced" into illegal activity by his parents. No blame is attached to the economic system that allowed unemployment and poverty.

Of course not all delinquent behaviour was directed toward the noble cause of family survival. Young males of all classes stole cars in which to go "joy riding" and at least one adult wondered if boys were contributing to their own delinquency by acquiring "French safes."[63] Rather trivial cases also appear in the records. For example, a local school board charged a young lad with throwing a stone through a school window. The boy was acquitted, the school board appealed to the attorney general, an inspector was sent out to investigate and, after a volume of paperwork, a settlement was finally reached.[64] Childhood scraps seem to have sometimes ended in court too. A young lad, L., in Peace River called one of his peers a "son-of-a-bitch," a bit of a brouhaha ensued, and the boys ended up in juvenile court. A police report summarized the results of the case.

> His Worship in reviewing the evidence stated that the accused had received a great deal of provocation, and that to the majority of people the words used by L. _____ meant "Fight." The parents of the two boys were present in Court, and his Worship lectured them rather severely on their attitude in the latter, stating they should exercise more control over their children.[65]

The accused boy was given a suspended sentence pending good behaviour.

This last case indicates an interesting trend in community attitudes toward youthful behaviour. As the formal structure of a juvenile justice system took hold in Alberta more and more adults seemed to be turning to this formal state mechanism to control the pranks and indiscretions of children. For example, Hallowe'en tricksters who over-turned outhouses, rolled away garbage barrels, or hid front gates could easily find themselves facing police questioning and possibly a juvenile court hearing.[66] Adult attitudes in the 1920s, especially, began to harden when middle class youths appeared to increasingly involve themselves in a variety of delinquent acts. Delinquents from well-to-do families were a puzzle. Their family life—so very much like that of the child savers themselves—could obviously not be blamed. These young criminals were, of course, tainted by their adolescence but firm and loving parents were supposed to be able to control the raging emotions of this life stage. Part of the blame fell on "the gang" but working class youths had gangs too. Thus, more and more, juvenile delinquents of the "better class" who, it was felt, committed crimes for "thrills," found a hardened attitude awaiting them. This particular type of juvenile offender, blessed with the fortunes of life, was clearly a perverse, intractable individual—a "bad seed."

Newspapers of the 1920s reflect a growing concern on the part of adults for the "wayward youth" of the land. Fears about the loose and immoral behaviour of the young grew and cigarette smoking, drinking, dancing, and movies all had to accept their share of blame for delinquent behaviour.[67] With the arrival of the Depression and a corresponding increase in crime rates, "respectable" citizens, primarily out of fear for their property, demanded harsh treatment for young "hoodlums." One prominent Edmonton financier, commenting on a rash of crime, demanded the return of the lash and said, "Most of these would-be bandits are probably boys in their 'teens who dread the lash and it would soon end these hold-ups."[68] Despite some public outcry, however, child savers were able to hold to the notion of reformation rather than punishment[69] although they, too, continued to be exasperated with incorrigible youths.

Between 1909 and 1929, large numbers of Albertans also worked in ways designed to prevent delinquency. While the Children's Aid Societies and the Department of Neglected Children "rescued" children from the more desperate circumstances, most churches and many men's and women's service clubs and organizations involved themselves in boy and girl work. Much of this work was designed to provide healthy recreational activities for young people under the supervision of trustworthy adults. The Young Men's and Young Women's Christian Associations and community leagues afforded opportunities to participate in a wide range of athletic pursuits including swimming, gymnastics, and basketball. Service clubs such as the Rotary International and church-related groups like the Canadian Girls in Training provided summer camping experiences. Through these forms of recreation it was hoped that young people would use their time profitably and would, through the example and training of adult leaders, behave "decently," eschewing the diversions of the street and alley which, it was thought, ultimately led to delinquency. It must be noted, as well, that many prominent social reformers devoted themselves to improving social services in general so as to lend support to families that were the victims of poverty. The struggle for Mothers' Allowances is one case in point.

Throughout the twenty years from 1909 to 1929, juvenile delinquency continued to trouble child welfare workers. Despite the child savers' best efforts in both prevention and treatment, young people persisted in breaking the law. In 1927 a note of pessimism, born of frustration, was heard at the Social Service Conference held in Edmonton. Perhaps the boys and girls of 1927 were inferior to those of twenty years ago. Not so, responded Brother Rogatian. Parents must simply learn to adjust to current conditions and be prepared to guide and control rather than drive and coerce the young. Other speakers reiterated the old faith. The time-worn clichés, "Give the kid a chance" and "More sinned against than sinning" were rolled out and delegates were sent on their way to promulgate and practise the precepts of child welfare much as they had been established in Chadwick's day.[70] Indeed, despite developments that have occurred since 1929, it is clear that the fundamental philosophy of child life and child care enunciated early in this century by the child savers has left an indelible mark on current thought and practices. This is especially true with respect to the view that a family home is the natural and proper place in which to rear children and that with the proper environmental influences young offenders can be reformed.

NOTES

1. P.G.H. Primrose to A.G. Browning, 2 Dec. 1920, Department of Neglected Children, file 6-C-5, box 124, acc. no. 75.126, Provincial Archives of Alberta (hereafter PAA).

2. Ibid.

3. Supt. Bryan to A.G. Browning, 8 Dec. 1920, Department of Neglected Children, file 6-C-5, box 124, acc. no. 75.126, PAA.

4. Primrose also demanded that his colleague who had imposed the sentence be struck from the rolls. A decision on this was avoided because the sentencing magistrate died four days after Primrose wrote his complaint.

5. In the strictly legal sense, at sixteen Albert was no longer a juvenile delinquent but an adult criminal.

6. Alberta, Department of Neglected Children, *Annual Report*, 1912, 7 (hereafter *AR*).

7. A cottage system generally involved the construction of one main building with kitchen, laundry, schoolrooms, and other facilities along with several small "cottages" in which the boys would live in a setting thought to be more like a real home situation.

8. For a discussion of the early history of welfare legislation in Alberta see David Edgar Lysne, "Welfare in Alberta, 1905–1936" (MA thesis, University of Alberta, 1966).

9. *AR*, 1912, 8. Discussions of Ontario's act can be found in Neil Sutherland, *Children in English-Canadian Society: Framing the Twentieth Century Consensus* (Toronto: University of Toronto Press, 1976), and in Andrew Jones and Leonard Rutman, *In the Children's Aid: J.J. Kelso and Child Welfare in Ontario* (Toronto: University of Toronto Press, 1981).

10. *AR*, 1911, 12.

11. Alberta, An Act for the Protection of Neglected and Dependent Children, 1909, 9 Edward VII, c. 12, *Statutes of Alberta*, 206–7.

12. Alberta, An Act for the Protection of Neglected and Dependent Children, 1922, 12 George V, c. 217, *Statutes of Alberta* 3: 2674 (s. 2, s.s.h.).

13. *AR*, 1909, 9.

14. A Children's Aid Society was a society approved by the lieutenant governor in council and having as one of its objects the protection of children and the care and control of neglected children.

15. Because of the wide powers assigned a "judge" in the Children's Protection Act, it is worth noting that, according to section 2(e), "'Judge' shall mean a judge or a retired judge of the Supreme Court or of the District Court, or a police magistrate, or a justice of the peace appointed as a commissioner for the trial of juvenile offenders, or two justices."

16. For example, see the sympathetic view of Canadian child savers and their work in Sutherland, *Children in English-Canadian Society*; Jones and

Rutman, *In the Children's Aid*; and H.C. Klassen, "In Search of Neglected and Delinquent Children: The Calgary Children's Aid Society, 1901–1920" in *Town and City: Aspects of Western Canadian Urban Development*, ed. Alan F.J. Artibise (Regina: Canadian Plains Research Center, 1981), 375–91.

17. C.W. Parker, ed., *Who's Who and Why* (Vancouver: International Press, 1913).

18. *Men and Makers of Edmonton, Alberta* (n.p., 1913?).

19. J.S. Woodsworth to H.M. Tory, 26 June 1914, Henry Marshall Tory Papers, University of Alberta Archives.

20. Reported in *Calgary Daily Herald*, 15 Jan. 1909.

21. Department of Neglected Children Files, box 123, acc. no. 75. 126, PAA.

22. *AR*, 1922, 16.

23. For a discussion of these networks see Sutherland, *Children in English-Canadian Society*; Paul Rutherford, ed., *Saving the Canadian City: The First Phase 1880–1920* (Toronto: University of Toronto Press, 1974); Tamara Hareven, "An Ambiguous Alliance: Some Aspects of American Influence on Canadian Social Welfare," *Histoire sociale/Social History* 3 (April 1969): 82–98.

24. Rutherford, *Saving the Canadian City*, xiii.

25. Sutherland, *Children in English-Canadian Society*, 236–37.

26. See, for example, *AR*, 1912, 8.

27. The work of Judge Ben Lindsay and the American juvenile justice system in general has been the subject of much study. See, for example, Joseph Hawes, *Children in Urban Society: Juvenile Delinquency in Nineteenth Century America* (New York: Oxford University Press, 1971); Robert M. Mennel, *Thorns and Thistles: Juvenile Delinquents in the United States, 1925–1940* (Hanover, NH: University Press of New England, 1973); Anthony M. Platt, *The Child Savers: The Invention of*

Delinquency (Chicago: University of Chicago Press, 1969); Stephen Schlossman, *Love and the American Delinquent: The Theory and Practice of "Progressive" Juvenile Justice, 1825–1920* (Chicago: University of Chicago Press, 1977).

28. *AR*, 1919, 28.

29. *AR*, 1914, 13.

30. Ibid., 12.

31. *AR*, 1911, 18.

32. Ibid.

33. *AR*, 1914, 12.

34. A.M. McDonald to A.G. Browning, 5 Sept. 1918, Department of Neglected Children, file 6-C-5, box 123, acc. no. 75.125, PAA.

35. It was far more expensive to keep a boy in the Industrial School than it was to put him on probation or place him in a foster home, and the records of the Department of Neglected Children make frequent reference to this cost consideration. The figure most often mentioned was $2000 for a two-year term.

36. "The Constables' Manual," Alberta Provincial Police Files, file 1302, box 81, acc. no. 66.166, PAA.

37. Susan Houston, "Victorian Origins of Juvenile Delinquency: A Canadian Experience," *History of Education Quarterly* 12 (Fall 1972): 254–80.

38. Rebecca Coulter, "Alberta's Department of Neglected Children, 1909–1929: A Case Study in Child Saving" (MEd thesis, University of Alberta, 1977), 68.

39. *AR*, 1912, 13.

40. K.C. McLeod to A.G. Browning, 12 May 1923, Department of Neglected Children Files, file 6-C-5, box 123, acc. no. 75.126, PAA.

41. See continuing correspondence in Department of Neglected Children Files, box 123, acc. no. 75.126, PAA.

42. Sutherland, *Children in English-Canadian Society*. For a brief summary of arguments about the concept of hegemony and its application to

schooling and crime see Peter Seixas, "From Juvenile Asylum to Treatment Center: Changes in a New York Institute of Children 1905–1930" (MA thesis, University of British Columbia, 1981), ch. 2.

43. *AR*, 1911, 8.

44. See statistics in *AR*, 1909–29.

45. See Hermin Lewis King, "A Study of 400 Juvenile Delinquent Recidivists Convicted in the Province of Alberta During the Years 1920–30" (MA thesis, University of Alberta, 1932).

46. *AR*, 1911, 26–27.

47. *AR*, 1913, 25.

48. *AR*, 1918, 38.

49. *AR*, 1916, 14.

50. *AR*, 1911, 26.

51. *AR*, 1913, 17.

52. *AR*, 1912, 19.

53. Ibid.

54. *AR*, 1913, 19.

55. *AR*, 1914, 26.

56. In making these calculations it was assumed that immigrants from the United States and Great Britain could speak English.

57. John Gillis, *Youth and History: Tradition and Change in European Age Relations 1770–Present* (New York: Academic Press, 1974); Platt, *The Child Savers*; William Ryan, *Blaming the Victim* (New York: Vintage Books, 1976).

58. In 1914 the term "foreign born" was replaced with the expression "Canadians To Be."

59. Canada, Dominion Bureau of Statistics (hereafter DBS), "Dependency of Youth," by J.E. Robbins, *Seventh Census of Canada, 1931: Monographs*, vol. 13 (Ottawa: King's Printer, 1942), 377–439.

60. Canada, DBS, *Sixth Census of Canada, 1921*, vol. 111 (Ottawa: King's Printer, 1927), xvii.

61. Louis Chevalier, *Labouring Classes and Dangerous Classes*, trans. Frank Jellinek (London: Routledge and Kegan Paul, 1973); Stephen Humphries, "Steal to Survive: The Social Crime of Working Class Children 1890–1940," *Oral History Journal* 9 (Spring 1981): 24–33.

62. King, "A Study of 400 . . . ," 38.

63. F.B. Rolfross to J.E. Brownlee, 13 June 1922, Department of Neglected Children Files, file 6-C-5, box 123, acc. no. 75.126, PAA.

64. "Earl F. Case," Department of Neglected Children Files, file 6-C-5, box 124, acc. no. 75.126, PAA.

65. APP Report, 21 Jan. 1922, Department of Neglected Children, file 6-C-5, box 124, acc. no. 75.126, PAA.

66. See, for example, "Damage Done Hallowe'en Night," City Police Department Special Report, 28 Nov. 1930, Commissioner's Files, Police—Crime 1926–1966, box 195, acc. no. 73-52, City of Edmonton Archives (hereafter CEA).

67. See, for example, "Report of Gerald V. Pelton to the Government of Alberta on Enquiries Instituted in Colorado, California, Oregon, Washington, and British Columbia, into Some of the Causes and Cures for Juveniles Delinquency Among Boys," Premier's Papers, file 235, acc. no. 69.289, PAA.

68. "Citizens Demand Swift Action . . . ," 6 Nov. 1930, "Edmonton Crime" File, Newspaper Clippings Collection, box 17, acc. no. A77/18, CEA.

69. See, for example, M. Gutteridge to City Commissioners, 22 Nov. 1927, RG11, class 3, file 1, CEA and T.S. Magee to City Commissioners, 16 Nov. 1935, "Children's Shelter," uncatalogued City Commissioners' Papers, CEA.

70. "Social Service Conference Held in Edmonton," *Western Catholic*, 17 Feb. 1927, 6.

THE QUEBEC GOVERNMENT AND SOCIAL LEGISLATION DURING THE 1930s: A STUDY IN POLITICAL SELF-DESTRUCTION*

B.L. VIGOD

o

According to Pierre Elliott Trudeau's highly influential essay, French-Canadian social thinkers of the interwar period were so obsessed with "national" considerations that they ignored (among other things) Quebec's desperate need for progressive social legislation.[1] It is probably true that during the 1920s, few laymen or clergy cared to challenge the excessively conservative or negative interpretation that the Quebec church and allied nationalist ideologues gave to Catholic social doctrine. But this was manifestly not the case during the Depression, especially following publication of the papal encyclical *Quadragesimo Anno* in 1931. A modernization of *Rerum Novarum* (1891), this document unequivocally declared the state responsible for protecting the economically weak members of an industrial society. No longer, observed Father Joseph-Papin Archambault, need Quebec clergy fear that in demanding various social reforms they would be "meddling in politics."[2]

Combined with evidence furnished by the Depression itself that the existing system was inadequate, *Quadragesimo* inspired immediate results. A provincial Royal Commission on Social Insurance, appointed by the Taschereau government in 1930, went far beyond its original limited mandate. Under the chairmanship of Edouard Montpetit, the commission spent more than two years formulating dozens of recommendations: regulatory laws, a fundamental change in existing legislation governing state support

* From *Journal of Canadian Studies* 14, 1 (1979): 59–69. Reprinted with the permission of the journal.

for private charitable institutions, and, most significantly, such direct payment schemes as needy mothers' and family allowances, old age pensions,
and subsidized health insurance.[3] Meanwhile, the Jesuit-sponsored Semaine
Sociale of 1932 devoted itself to the "social question," and in the spring of
1933 Father Archambault invited several priests to design a *Programme de
Restauration Sociale*, which he then published under the auspices of his Ecole
Sociale Populaire. The *Programme* does indeed contain many of the traditional and "corporatist" prescriptions maligned by Trudeau. But it also calls
upon the state "d'assurer, par une meilleur repartition des richesses, le
relèvement des classes populaires" (Article 1), to protect workers against
deprivation due to accident, sickness, old age, and unemployment, to insure
farmers against their occupational hazards such as fire, animal disease, crop
failure, and seizure of property (Article 8), to require salaries sufficient to
support average sized families, to supplement the income of large families
(Article 9), and to subsidize medical and hospital care for the poor (Article
11).[4] In other words, a varied program of income security.

The foundation of the Co-operative Commonwealth Federation and the
circulation of its Regina Manifesto persuaded Archambault that a further,
more comprehensive statement was necessary to combat the influence of
socialism in French Canada. Philosophically the goal was to distinguish
between the abuses of capitalism, which the church recognized and
deplored, and the inherent evil of property, which it denied. More importantly, however, Archambault wanted to demonstrate that the capitalist system could be satisfactorily reformed on the basis of Catholic doctrine.[5] He
therefore organized a committee of expert laymen to produce and elaborate
upon a second *Programme de Restauration Sociale (PRS)* containing specific
legislative proposals. Trudeau acknowledged only the first *Programme*,
stressing its conservative motivation and rhetoric. There is no mention at all
of the second document, even the excellent commentary on proposed social
legislation written by Alfred Charpentier, the Catholic Union leader.
Modelled upon but often surpassing Montpetit's recommendations, the second *PRS* demanded a contributory social insurance scheme financed by the
individual, his employer, and the government, temporary but immediate
application of the Federal Old Age Pension law in Quebec pending creation
of a purely provincial system, a needy mothers' allowance, salaries sufficient to support average families, an experimental family allowance system,
a law requiring companies to pay wages before dividends, a minimum
wage for day-labour, slum clearance, and various labour laws improving
the bargaining strength of unions.[6] Even before they were published, several of these proposals were carried to the leadership convention of the
provincial Conservative Party in Sherbrooke and became its official policy.[7]
In June of 1934, the Action Libérale Nationale adopted the *Programme* virtually intact as the manifesto for its rebellion against Taschereau Liberalism.
In other words, French Canada's "social thinkers" did formulate progressive and realistic proposals, and thrust them into the political arena.[8]

But the Taschereau government reacted as if it were completely oblivious to these proposals. Although such behaviour corresponds precisely to

the regime's reactionary historical reputation, it still demands some explanation. After all, politicians and parties as successful as Taschereau and the Liberals had been since 1900 must have developed some instinct for political survival. And on other issues, Taschereau did reveal this instinct as the 1935 provincial election approached. In 1934, his Forest Resources Protection Act belatedly but effectively gave Cabinet discretionary power over newsprint manufacturers who were slaughtering Quebec's pulpwood resources and, in the process, mercilessly exploiting forest and mill workers. At the same legislative session, his government acceded to a longstanding labour request by enacting the Collective Agreements Extension Act. Later that year it responded to growing pressure for a major new colonization initiative, even though Liberals had always suspected the agrarian ideology underlying Quebec's colonization movement. In 1935 came a package of legislation effectively regulating the hydro-electric industry—laws whose inherent virtue continues to be ignored because, like R.B. Bennett's New Deal legislation, they seemed to constitute a deathbed repentence.[9] Taschereau even enacted certain recommendations of the Montpetit Commission, advancing child protection, public health, and other regulations and freeing the Quebec Public Charities Bureau from severe financial and legislative constraints. (Previously, the Bureau could only subsidize institutional care and receive funds only from specially designated sources. Now it was authorized to support charitable work performed "ex mures"— poor relief—and given access to general provincial revenues.) Only when it came to proposals for permanent income security did Taschereau's political acumen desert him entirely. It was one thing to say no, provincial revenues cannot even support emergency relief, hence statutory payments to individuals are unthinkable at the moment. But to reject the proposals in principle and for all time, and to denigrate the advocates as well, was pure folly. Nor was he the least bit subtle about it. Pensions and family allowances were "remèdes pernicieux qui compromettront l'avenir." The "bourgeois" proponents invited "social revolution" by encouraging the masses to expect "everything" from the government.[10]

Certainly it would be an exaggeration to claim that this performance alone brought down the forty-year-old Liberal regime in Quebec. Despite the leader's remarkable personal health, the government could not avoid looking old. Taschereau was sixty-eight in 1935, had been in cabinet for twenty-eight years, and maintained the same inner circle formed at the onset of his premiership fifteen years previously. Quebec had been suffering more than any other region of Canada from the Depression and nowhere in the country was provincial government policy so closely linked with economic conditions in the public mind. Since the Taschereau government technically survived the 1935 election moreover, the immediate cause of its demise was the spectacular Public Accounts scandal of 1936. Still, Taschereau's apparent indifference to human suffering probably contributed more than any other single factor to the 1934 revolt of young Liberals,[11] to the loss of that public respect and confidence which had long compensated for his lack of genuine popularity with the electorate, and to his unfavourable historical image. With only a minimum of literary licence, therefore, an analysis of Taschereau's violent resistance to the idea of income security could be described as a study in political self-destruction.

To a considerable extent, Taschereau and his colleagues were imprisoned by political memories of the early 1920s, when several moderate and sensible pieces of social legislation had provoked violent controversies. The worst of these followed passage of the Public Charities Act, a measure designed to rescue private (i.e. religious) and municipal charitable institutions from severe postwar financial distress. Taschereau sincerely contended that by increasing and regularizing provincial support for hospitals, orphanages, crèches, and night shelters, his government was upholding traditional values and institutional arrangements concerning charity. But almost immediately ultramontane journalists and theologians accused him of "secularizing" charity, of attacking the internal discipline of the church, and of aiding an anti-clerical conspiracy against the church's social influence. Before long ecclesiastical authorities began tacitly endorsing this charge, and Taschereau's political opponents could not resist exploiting the evident tension between church and state. Although the government adamantly refused to surrender and only grudgingly opened a path of dignified retreat for the hierarchy, clerical agitation had an obvious impact. Taschereau, forced repeatedly to proclaim his religious fidelity, would not tamper any further with the sectarian organization and control of charitable activity.[12]

In the prosperity and optimism of the later 1920s, Taschereau found that such abstention enjoyed broad social and political consensus. Quebec's rejection of the federal Old Age Pensions Act offers an excellent illustration. Taschereau and Jacob Nicol, the provincial treasurer, raised three basic objections to this legislation: it questioned the moral and social importance of individual responsibility, it implied higher taxation, and it invaded the constitutional jurisdiction of the provinces.[13] Their position did not correspond merely to the self-interests of industrialists and financiers. Virtually no one considered individual reliance upon the state desirable, for besides eroding the virtues of work and thrift, it weakened the sense of family and community obligation. Only a few trade union spokesmen, and they most vaguely, perceived that these values were based upon essentially rural or pre-industrial concepts of poverty and charity and could not remedy the economic weakness and insecurity of an urban proletariat. The bias against taxation was probably even more pervasive. For reasons dating back to the nineteenth century, "taxeur" was a most feared political epithet; provincial "budgets" became little more than annual propaganda exercises designed to show declining indebtedness.[14] Naturally Taschereau's defence of provincial rights elicited general support as a matter of principle. But old age pensions also demonstrated the practical danger of federal interference: legislation unsuited to Quebec's unique social situation. If implemented, the scheme would burden Quebec taxpayers with administrative costs previously shouldered by religious organizations.[15] Comparing his overwhelming victory in the 1927 provincial election to the losses suffered in 1923, Taschereau was tempted to conclude that there was no political advantage in social initiatives.

The appointment of the Montpetit Commission did not signal any real departure either from this political assumption or from Taschereau's own philosophy. Rather, it came in response to pressure from organized labour, the one significant source of support for old age pensions in Quebec. Acknowledging the force of the constitutional objection, labour spokesmen began pressing provincial authorities to incorporate old age security within Quebec's system of workmen's compensation, which had been under review for some years anyway. They argued that since few workers earned enough to accumulate savings, poverty in retirement or during periods of unemployment was just as much an occupational hazard as injury or illness during working years. Realizing that individual employers alone could not afford such extensive "compensation," labour proposed that they contribute to a provincial fund managed and subsidized by the government.[16] Taschereau and Labour Minister Antonin Galipeault preferred a private fund and hedged on the question of state support. But they finally conceded that a provincial social insurance scheme to which workers also contributed would not violate the doctrine of self-reliance.[17] Montpetit was instructed to design a plan for Quebec based on the contributory principle and on a thorough study of existing social insurance systems in Catholic Europe. To some extent the government was undoubtedly stalling, but delay was not the only motive for such an elaborate inquiry. By citing examples of Catholic states in Europe, and also by including one of Quebec's most conservative ecclesiastics, Mgr Courchesne, on the commission, Taschereau was taking out a little "insurance" of his own—against a recurrence of the Public Charities fiasco. No one would be able to complain that Protestant or secular influences underlay the eventual legislation. (Canon F.G. Scott was appointed to the commission as a representative of the religious minority and one labour spokesman was English, but the advice of McGill social scientist Leonard Marsh was sought informally and with the utmost discretion.[18])

Even as the full force of the Depression descended upon Quebec, Taschereau continued to proclaim and honour the same social and political formulae. To emphasize the private and religious quality of charity, he urged the wealthy to "adopt" one or more destitute families by channelling regular payments through church agencies, and he set a generous personal example.[19] For the sake of individual dignity and morale, he strongly preferred subsidized colonization and public works to direct relief.[20] During the 1931 provincial election he vaguely committed himself to Montpetit's recommendations on social insurance ("leur rapport nous éclairera sur la route à suivre pour regler ces questions") but otherwise tried to dampen expectations of the state. "Il faut éviter les promesses imprudents et irréalisables. . . . La population saine, religieuse et respecteuse des lois, ne demande que ce qui est juste et raisonable. . . . L'équilibre dans nos finances—c'est la première condition d'une bonne administration. . . ."[21] When deficit budgeting could no longer be avoided, Taschereau made clear his regret and quaintly described the increased provincial debt as an obligation imposed by the present crisis on future generations.[22] While accepting federal grants for unemployment relief, Taschereau was as vigilant a defender of provincial rights as ever. At an interprovincial conference in

January 1933, he rejected the idea of federal unemployment insurance (and made no commitment toward a provincial scheme).[23]

The months following that conference were the period when Taschereau should have sensed a changing climate of opinion within Quebec. The seventh and final report of the Montpetit Commission, recommending contributory, state-subsidized social insurance was drawing praise not only in labour circles but also within the church and Catholic Action movements and among members of the Liberal Party itself. True to form, Mgr Courchesne dissented from this and other proposals for permanent state intervention, but his conservatism was not shared throughout the hierarchy. Even before Father Archambault's first *Programme de Restauration Sociale* appeared in May, Archbishop Cardinal Villeneuve proclaimed in Taschereau's presence that the state must elaborate and implement a social policy based on papal teaching.[24] Villeneuve was fresh from contact with the European Catholic thinkers who had inspired *Quadragesimo*, but there were also practical domestic reasons why he was prepared to concede a greater role to the state than his predecessors. With no provincial or municipal apparatus existing when the Depression began, the St Vincent de Paul societies in Quebec's major cities had agreed to administer unemployment relief. Before long people began holding them responsible for delays and material insufficiencies that they were powerless to correct. In fact, as the visible relief agencies, they became general targets of discontent and frustration. In Montreal the laymen and clergy who led these societies concluded that their original mission, organizing charity at the parish level, could be permanently damaged by the loss of prestige. In 1933 they finally withdrew, forcing Montreal to set up its own relief administration.[25] The lesson could hardly escape higher religious authorities: the church ran a grave risk discharging functions beyond its own institutional and financial resources. Within Liberal ranks, social legislation was a major subject of discussion at meetings of restless young Montrealers organized by Paul Gouin. Gouin personally would soon join Archambault's lay committee, becoming an unsigned co-author of the second *Programme*. Federal Liberals had long urged Taschereau to participate in their old age pensions scheme; now in Opposition, they were particularly afraid that Taschereau's rigidity would cost the party its control of the provincial government as well.[26] For the most part their opinion was loyally and discretely conveyed to the premier but Edouard Lacroix, the MP for Beauce, loudly insisted that Taschereau had promised old age security, farm credit, and minimum wage legislation in exchange for his support in the 1931 election.[27]

Why did Taschereau miss or ignore all these signals? Ironically one reason was the extent of Taschereau's personal efforts to combat the effects of the Depression. As premier he negotiated the annual relief agreements with Ottawa. As his own municipal affairs minister, he dealt directly with the growing list of bankrupt municipalities whose financial affairs had to be taken over by the Quebec Municipal Commission.[28] He was even provincial treasurer for a year, conscious almost daily of declining revenues and soaring relief costs. By 1933 he was well on the road to personal direction of the pulp and paper industry, angrily reminding mill owners in company towns of their moral and social obligation,[29] trying to reorganize the bankrupt Price Brothers Company, and seeking the co-operation of manufacturers, American newspaper publishers, and the Ontario government in controlling ruinous competition.[30] In this time of financial crisis, he considered it all the more important to attend the meetings of boards of major financial institutions that had offered him directorships. For "relaxation," he continued to shoulder the office of attorney general. While outside observers marvelled at Taschereau's stamina, his private secretary noticed the strain and expressed relief when Taschereau found time for a vacation.[31]

In Taschereau's mind these efforts amply demonstrated that he was neither oblivious nor indifferent to poverty. No reasonable person would question his dedication or his competence to deal with the situation. On the contrary, it was the proponents of social security legislation who lived in a dream world if they believed that the province could afford such measures. The government and the still solvent municipalities were contracting heavy debts just to meet the cost of relief, and also making tax and other financial concessions to keep industries from closing. In these circumstances even the consideration of permanent schemes for the future was unwise, for it could diminish lenders' confidence in Quebec's fiscal responsibility.[32] The preoccupation with daily problems also discouraged Taschereau from seriously reconsidering the application of his social philosophy. Perhaps no amount of reflection could alter fundamental beliefs this late in his life. It is difficult to imagine him abandoning fiscal orthodoxy, for example, even if Keynesian theory had been quicker to penetrate Canadian economic thought. Decades of conditioning, reinforced by weekly personal contact with Montreal financiers, would have prevented that. But he could have realized that individual self-reliance and private institutional charity could not deal adequately with the mass economic vulnerability characteristic of industrial society. He had often made pragmatic adjustments before and in fact used to lecture ultramontanes on the dangers of rigid adherence to traditional formulae: this could discredit the very principles one sought to uphold.[33] Yet now it was the Church, both internationally and to some degree within Quebec, which saw that continued respect for law, authority, and property required the state to ensure greater social justice. And it was Taschereau who contemptuously dismissed proposals for reform as concessions to "une mauvaise mentalité."

Taschereau's heavy workload was not the sole reason, however, for his failure to take seriously what certain clergy were now saying about social legislation. He also suspected the motives of any clergy who, by criticizing or embarrassing the Liberal Party, threatened the harmony between church and state. The all-too-brief reign of Archbishop Rouleau at Quebec (1926–1931) proved to Taschereau that fruitful co-operation was possible between ecclesiastical authorities and a Liberal government. (Rouleau had severely curtailed the public warfare between priests of his archdiocese and Cabinet ministers, and given no encouragement to other critics of the regime. For its part, the government had abstained from new initiatives challenging the institutional prerogatives of the church. Rather, provincial authorities had sought and received clerical support in their rural public health campaign, defended the interests of *caisses populaires* in which many clergy were involved, and placated clerical opinion by opposing female suffrage.) Such co-operation was all the more important now that social stability was being threatened by an economic crisis. The role and responsibility of the church was to be a bulwark against the revolutionary ideologies that other societies had mistakenly embraced. Said Taschereau,

> Nous traverons des jours très sombres et on se demande parfois si toute civilisation ne chancelle pas. Elle est née avec le Christ, il y a dix-neuf siècles, elle a vécu sous son égide depuis, n'est-ce pas alors dans sa doctrine et ses enseignements qu'il faut chercher et trouver les facteurs de survivance?
>
> .... C'est le code de morale chrétienne qui enseigne l'obéissance à l'autorité, le respect des lois et de la propriété, la sainteté de foyer, la souveraineté du père de famille dans son petit royaume, l'assurance que la mort n'est pas un terme mais un commencement.[34]

In contrast, it was the height of irresponsible folly for priests to encourage or sanction rhetoric that destroyed people's respect for authority. When the Montreal Jesuits made their auditorium available for a rally of the militant Jeune Canada movement, Taschereau was furious. "Si on permet à ceux qui seront la classe dirigeante de demain, de prêcher ainsi la revolte, sous la haute protection d'un ordre respecté comme les Jésuites, je ne sais trop combien tout cela finira." Statements at the rally in question, Taschereau noted, were more subversive than those frequently uttered by Communists and others against whom the government had waged war "à la demande des plus hautes autorités religieuses." Finally, "ceux qui leur ont donné l'abri ... ne doivent pas oublier qu'ils seront les premiers appelés à disparaître en cas de révolution." He emphatically rejected the advice of the Jesuit Father Dugré who asked, "Serait-il sage de vouloir étouffer toutes les voix, qui combattent ce mal [gross inequality of wealth] chez nous? C'est déjà calmer la mauvaise humeur que de lui permettre de s'exprimer." Even Mgr Gauthier, administrator of the Archdiocese of Montreal, admitted on this occasion "qu'il ne faut pas souffler sur le feu."[35]

For Taschereau there was only one possible explanation for such perverse behaviour. His ancient enemies, the clerical nationalists, could not resist the opportunity to renew their attacks on his family name, his party and most importantly the philosophy for which his government stood. It would not be the first time that these reactionaries had disguised their fundamental rejection of the industrial age as a crusade for social and economic reform. This had been his interpretation of the prewar *nationaliste* challenge to Lomer Gouin, and of virtually every subsequent criticism of the industrial system as it evolved in Quebec. Taschereau even considered the liberal–ultramontane conflicts of his youth to be battles in the same war. In those days intellectual freedom rather than material advancement had been the central issue, but the rival static and dynamic prescriptions for French-Canadian *survivance* were already well defined. He was unshakably confident that he represented the forces of progress, and his opponents those of isolation and stagnation.[36] Having nothing but contempt for the messenger, Taschereau would not judge the message on its own merits.

Admittedly, this gross *ad hominem* attack was so convenient for Taschereau that one might suspect it was just a cynical diversion. But in all fairness, he could not fail to be influenced by the identity and behaviour of many of the clergy involved. In the Quebec City area, the priests who most loudly condemned social injustice were E.V. Lavergne and Pierre Gravel. Lavergne made no effort to disguise the views he shared with his cousin Armand, a long time nationalist politician as well as Taschereau's self-appointed personal nemesis.[37] Gravel had been nursing a personal grudge since 1924, when Taschereau had him ousted from his teaching post at the Petit Séminaire de Québec for slandering Liberals in front of his students.[38] Quebec also had the daily *L'Action Catholique*, whose editors were mostly laymen but which for years had been spouting its retrograde, paranoid, and racist message in the name of the archdiocese.[39] Clerical militants in Montreal had less of a personal axe to grind with Taschereau, and the premier did not consider them Castors in quite the literal sense of being preoccupied with religious prerogatives. He did feel the Montreal Jesuits were biased against his party,[40] but what really frightened him were the newer church-sponsored lay organizations and movements. Jeune Canada's guiding spirit was Abbé Lionel Groulx, who had been preaching racial conflict since the early 1920s. Taschereau was therefore not surprised at this group's xenophobic nationalism and antisemitism, which drowned out its calls for "reform."[41] Groulx had also revived *Action Française*, his nationalist monthly of the 1920s. Now called *Action Nationale* it abandoned all pretence of progressive ideology and heaped praise on the right-wing Catholic dictators of Europe.[42] Then there was Oblate Father Henri Roy's Jeunesse Ouvrière Catholique, the mushrooming organization founded to immunize working-class youth against communist and socialist viruses. If that simply meant reinforcing respect for traditional rights and authority Taschereau had no objection. But the "Jocistes" proved to be as bigoted, exclusivist, and antidemocratic as any of the older "Catholic Action" associations.[43] Rooted in local St Jean Baptiste societies and parish organizations, and tacitly endorsed by higher religious authorities, was the *achat chez nous* movement. Nominally, and perhaps originally, it called upon French Canadians to defend their own small entrepreneurs by boycotting large "foreign" concerns. But its central message quickly became a vicious and unrestrained antisemitism, which placed its sponsors very close to Adrien Arcand's National Social Christian (Nazi) Party.[44]

Taschereau reacted in much the same way to the second *Programme de Restauration Sociale*. That is, he suspected the motives of the authors and ignored or lost sight of its constructive proposals amidst the predominantly negative character of the document. And again, there was just enough truth in his analysis to permit this kind of self-deception. The signatories were all affiliated with nationalist or Catholic Action movements, and several had been active Conservative partisans.[45] Père Archambault himself anticipated the problem of credibility in urging Liberals like Paul Gouin to endorse the

Programme: "Ce serait une grosse déception pour nous si votre nom n'y apparaissant pas. Il aurait moins d'effet sur l'opinion."[46] As far as the content of the PRS was concerned, the presence of traditional formulae (especially colonization) and rhetoric (moral judgments of "large" capital, emphasis on "social" solidarity) alone would no doubt have raised Taschereau's suspicions. "Large" was a code word for "foreign," "social" really meant "national," and colonization connoted the old notion that industrialization per se was destructive of French-Canadian nationality. But at least two sections of the *Programme* were undisguised political assaults on the Taschereau government: Hamel's on "Trusts et Finances" and Wilfrid Guerin's on "Réformes Politiques." Thus, while Charpentier's proposals for social and labour legislation were not accusatory, they remained part of a document whose premises Taschereau could never accept.

The most crucial (and for Taschereau's reputation, tragic) *ad hominems* were those he directed against young Liberal proponents of social legislation. Again it is conceivable that no genuine self-deception occurred, but the fatal ingredients—half truths—were unquestionably present. Personal relations between Taschereau and Paul Gouin had been strained almost since the death of the latter's father, Sir Lomer, in 1929. At root, apparently, were Taschereau's refusal to make Gouin curator or assistant curator of the Quebec Museum and Gouin's refusal to do anything more "worthy" than write poetry and support foolish crusades.[47] It was not so much that Taschereau interpreted Gouin's Action Libérale rebellion as an act of vengeance, although such an accusation surfaced during the bitter election fight of 1935. Rather, Taschereau assumed that Gouin's colleagues shared their leader's expectations of obtaining a soft job through family or political influence, and attributed their espousal of social welfare to the same mentality.[48]

Any hope that Taschereau would objectively consider Action Libérale proposals evaporated between April and July of 1934, as Gouin began constructing an independent political organization. Taschereau had always considered party loyalty an important matter of principle, and some Actionnistes evidently agreed with his definition of legitimate dissent: like advanced Liberals of his own generation, they should urge their ideas but accept the wisdom of experienced leaders until their day to govern arrived.[49] Taschereau's attitude was reinforced by the adherence of various nationalists to Gouin's new party, signified by the name "Action Libérale Nationale" and by an official platform nearly identical to the second *Programme de Restauration Sociale*. Making common cause with the Hamel, Groulx, and Archambault crowd was a "curious" way to "reliberalize the Liberal Party."[50] In fact, long before the ALN concluded its 1935 electoral alliance with the Duplessis Conservatives, Taschereau was chiding Gouin for "marching" with Tory reactionaries. Either the rebels were incredibly naive, or else personal ambition meant more to them than liberal reform.[51]

Were there no Taschereau loyalists able and willing to argue the case for social welfare legislation? It was as part of an "armed truce" with Ottawa Liberals in 1935 that he grudgingly promised to introduce old age pensions. Prior to that, however, it appears that genuine liberal reformers whom Taschereau respected said little or even reinforced his obstinacy. Olivar Asselin was profoundly disturbed by the quality of French-Canadian nationalism in the 1930s and denounced the *PRS* as "une machine de guerre dressée par les Jésuites contre le parti libérale."[52] Jean-Charles Harvey, the anticlerical journalist who did battle with Taschereau's nationalist critics in the pages of *Le Soleil*, was exceedingly frank and revealing in his unpublished memoirs.

> Mr. Taschereau was a most remarkable man and his council of ministers formed an excellent team; but so much could not be said about an army of parasites which swarmed around the Parliament buildings.
>
> For many reasons I remained faithful to this party. In addition to my inability to find elsewhere the friendship and protection [against clerical censorship] of a Prime Minister, the Opposition factions inspired me with grave doubts. They included in their fold every extreme-right Laurentian, supernationalists, fascists, anglophobes, isolationists, separatists and clericals.[53]

Among prestigious active politicians, Ernest Lapointe and T.D. Bouchard were both rumoured sympathetic to Action Libérale proposals. In fact, while Lapointe made it clear he would not help Gouin split the Liberal Party, Bouchard was long considered a possible leader for the rebels.[54] But Lapointe could argue for social legislation only on "tactical" grounds, and this ran counter to Taschereau's definition of statesmanship.[55] Bouchard was evidently satisfied to convert Taschereau on the hydro-electric question, and joined the Cabinet to do battle with the forces of reaction. The crucial silence, however, was probably that of Provincial Secretary Athanase David. David had inspired numerous progressive social and educational initiatives during the early 1920s and was a very close personal friend of Social Insurance Commissioner Montpetit. Unfortunately, personal problems overcame him in the 1930s and he lost the considerable influence he had previously enjoyed with Taschereau.[56]

While the foregoing may help to explain Taschereau's performance on the question of social assistance, it does not constitute a valid excuse. Ultimately he was in charge, and his own concept of political responsibility certainly would have included greater flexibility in the face of changing circumstances and greater objectivity in judging new proposals. However much Gouin's revolt stiffened his resistance in mid-1934, there would likely have been no internal Liberal rebellion if Taschereau had acknowledged the real source of pressure for welfare measures: grim social reality. Nevertheless, this sad tale of political self-destruction may hold more than biographical significance. That the fear of reactionary clerical nationalism could so impair Taschereau's judgment and yet also ensure him the loyalty of genuinely reform-minded Liberals, raises some important questions about the period.[57] Were there actually two distinct strains of French-Canadian nationalist thought during the early 1930s, one admittedly impractical and reactionary but the other (Gouin's) positive and progressive? Or, with a few exceptions, did the real "left wing" remain in the Liberal Party waiting for Taschereau's retirement and proving themselves during the Godbout administration?[58] Did Duplessis really subvert a progressive social movement through devious political manoeuvering or did he harness forces that were reactionary all along? Such revisions of conventional wisdom would certainly make the character and longevity of the Duplessis regime more comprehensible. After all, while some disappointed individuals abandoned him, Duplessis did not have to go searching for new allies within French-Canadian society. The likes of Cardinal Villeneuve and Curé Lavergne, who practised blatant partisanship in 1935[59] in the name of "social justice" and an end to the "abuses of capitalism," fell silent on these issues with Duplessis in office. Serious reformers could hardly have been satisfied with the modest social measures (small allowances for needy mothers, blind persons, and similar unfortunates) introduced between 1936 and 1939, so one suspects that their real priority was to guard the church's ideological and institutional hegemony. In Duplessis' first term they and other clerical nationalists were evidently reassured by his cynical exploitation of French-Canadian fears and prejudices. After World War II, when liberal modernizing forces could not all be dismissed as alien, Duplessis put the power and the more buoyant revenues of the state at the service of a blind and perverse resistance.[60]

Looking again at Trudeau's essay, one must still conclude that he was technically in error: the social thought of French Canada did not completely ignore the daily material needs of Quebec's working class. But in losing sight of the nationalists' practical and constructive proposals, he perhaps followed Taschereau, Bouchard, and company in conveying a more fundamental and important reality.

NOTES

1. Pierre Elliott Trudeau, "La Province de Québec au Moment de la Grève" in *La Grève de l'Amiante* (Montreal, 1956).

2. "Avant Propos," *École Sociale Populaire* 232–33 (mai–juin 1933).

3. The Montpetit recommendations are conveniently summarized in Serge Mongeau, *Evolution de l'Assistance au Québec* (Montreal, 1967), 60–62.

4. L. Chagnon, "Directives Sociales Catholiques," *École Sociale Populaire* 232–33 (mai–juin 1933).

5. "Introduction au Programme de Restauration Sociale No. 2," *École Sociale Populaire* 239–40 (déc. 1933–janv. 1934).

6. "La Question Ouvriére" in ibid. The second *PRS* was a collective effort, but Charpentier contributed this section to "Le Programme de Restauration Sociale Expliqué et Commenté," to which *ESP* 239–40 was devoted.

7. Some had in fact appeared in the 1931 election platform. Jean-Louis Roy, *Les Programmes Electoraux du Québec* (Montreal, 1971), 2: 246–49.

8. Trudeau was not alone in missing this point. Antonin Dupont, "Louis-Alexandre Taschereau et la Législation Sociale au Québec 1920–1936," *Revue d'Histoire de l'Amérique Française* (déc. 1972), inexplicably fails to consider either the Montpetit Commission or the *PRS*.

9. The hydro-electric legislation followed intense negotiation between Taschereau and T.D. Bouchard, a leading critic of the industry. Bouchard then became minister of municipal affairs, industry and commerce, with responsibility for implementing many of the new provisions.

10. *Le Devoir*, 13 janv. 1933; below, note 35.

11. Patricia G. Dirks, "The Origins of the Union Nationale" (PhD diss., University of Toronto, 1974), 226.

12. B.L. Vigod, "Ideology and Institutions in Quebec: The Public Charities Controversy 1921–1926," *Histoire sociale/Social History* (May 1978).

13. Public Archives of Canada (hereafter PAC), Ernest Lapointe Papers, "Minutes of Dominion–Provincial Conference [1927]," 4 Nov. 1927; *Canadian Annual Review*, 1928–29, 386.

14. Stewart Bates, *Financial History of Canadian Governments* (Ottawa, 1939), 146ff; André Bernard, "Parliamentary Control of Finances in Quebec" (PhD diss., McGill University, 1965), 147–91.

15. Only extreme anticlericals dared point out that the church did receive compensation for these services in the form of property tax exemptions.

16. Roger Chartier, "La Réparation des Accidents du Travail et la Commission du Salaire Minimum des Femmes (1925–1931)," *Relations industrielles/Industrial Relations* (janv. 1963).

17. Confédération des Travailleurs Catholiques du Canada, *Procès Verbal*, 1929, 15, 40.

18. "Quebec Has Plans for Insurance," *Saturday Night*, 24 Dec. 1932.

19. Montreal Gazette, 16 Oct., 23 Nov. 1931; Robert Rumilly, *La Plus Riche Aumône: Histoire de la Société Saint-Vincent-de-Paul au Canada* (Montreal, 1946), 159.

20. Robert Rumilly, *Histoire de la Province de Québec* (hereafter *HPQ*) 33: 74, 177–80, 219.

21. Roy, *Les Programmes Electoraux*, 2: 242, 244.

22. Montreal *Star*, 30 Aug., 1933; *Action Catholique*, 18 sept., 1933.

23. *HPQ*, 33: 135.

24. *Action Catholique*, 28 avril, 1933.

25. *HPQ*, 33: 69, 150–51, 176, 207.

26. PAC, Raoul Dandurand Papers, Dandurand to Taschereau, 19 sept. 1927, 17 janv. 1929; PAC, Escott Reid Papers, Interview with C.G. Power.

27. Lacroix's claim is rapidly becoming a historical "fact" through repetition, but his own testimony remains the only evidence and contemporaries acknowledged that he bore more personal grievances against Taschereau. Conrad Black, *Duplessis* (Toronto, 1977), 702, note 30; Jean Provencher, "Joseph-Ernest Grégoire, Quatre Années de Vie Politique" (MA thesis, Université Laval, 1969), 98.

28. Montreal apparently remained outside the aegis of the commission only for political reasons. *HPQ*, 33: 42, and 34: 22–23, 34.

29. E.g., Archives Nationales du Québec, Fonds L.-A. Taschereau, Taschereau to Alexander Smith (Abitibi Power and Paper), 1 April 1931.

30. The best published account is in Vincent W. Bladen, *An Introduction to Political Economy* (Toronto, 1941), 157ff.

31. Montreal *Gazette*, 11 Jan. 1935; *Le Devoir*, 2 nov. 1935; *Maclean's*, 1 Feb. 1934 and 15 Jan. 1936; PAC, C.A. Fitzpatrick Papers, R.A. Benoît to Fitzpatrick, 26 June 1933.

32. *HPQ*, 33: 143, 208, and 34: 80–91, indicating reasons for Taschereau's sensitivity.

33. Fonds Taschereau, *Discours* 24 déc. 1925; L.-A. Taschereau, *Une Réplique au Chef de l'Opposition* (Quebec, 1927), 11.

34. *Action Catholique*, 28 avril 1933 (the same occasion as Cardinal Villeneuve's declaration, cited earlier).

35. Fonds Taschereau, Taschereau to Père Henri Roy, 17 nov.; to Mgr Gauthier,

19 nov.; to Alexandre Dugré, 24 nov.; Dugré to Taschereau, 23 nov. 1933. *Le Devoir*, 14 nov. 1933.

36. I have elaborated on this theme in "Alexandre Taschereau and the Negro King Hypothesis," *Journal of Canadian Studies* 13, 2 (Summer 1978): 6–8.

37. Once a collaborator at *Action Catholique*, Lavergne had become curé of Notre Dame de Grâce in 1924. Immediately following Cardinal Rouleau's death, he launched an unrestrained vendetta against Taschereau both from the pulpit and through his parish weekly, *La Bonne Nouvelle*. Taschereau complained early in 1932 (Fonds Taschereau, Taschereau to Mgr E.K. Laflamme, 27 janv.), but Villeneuve proved unable or unwilling to control the priest's activities.

38. Archives du Séminaire de Québec, "Journal du Séminaire," 11: 238–40.

39. Richard Jones, *L'Idéologie de l'Action Catholique 1917–1939* (Quebec, 1974), passim.

40. Fonds Taschereau, Taschereau to Alexandre Dugré, 24 nov. 1933.

41. Lita-Rose Betcherman, *The Swastika and the Maple Leaf* (Toronto, 1975), 34–35; Denis Monière, *Le Développement des Idéologies au Québec* (Montreal, 1977), 283. Abbé Groulx recalled the hostility toward Jeune Canada exhibited by Jean-Charles Harvey, a journalist very close to Taschereau. *Mes Mémoires* (Montreal, 1972), 3: 256.

42. In the early 1920s, the concern of *Action Française* with language rights and the ambivalence of its call for French-Canadian economic independence made it possible for Edouard Montpetit, Henry Laureys, Beaudry Leman, and others in the "progressive" tradition of Etienne Parent and Errol Bouchette to contribute. No such names appear in the 1930s, when its philosophy was most starkly revealed in Anatole Vanier, "Les Juifs au Canada," *Action Nationale* (hereafter *AN*), sept. 1933, and Jacques Brassier (a Groulx

pseudonym), "Pour qu'on vive," *AN*, janv., nov. 1934.

43. The emphasis is clear even in Rumilly's sympathetic description, *HPQ* 34: 99, 210–11. Roy was also among those responsible for the notorious Jeune Canada rally.

44. Betcherman, *The Swastika and the Maple Leaf*, 23; Michael Oliver, "The Social and Political Ideas of French Canadian Nationalists, 1920–1949" (PhD diss., McGill University, 1956), 293–94. Taschereau had always seemed well disposed toward Jews, possibly because even in his youth they had been vilified by clerical nationalists. For his denunciations of French-Canadian antisemitism during the 1930s, see Montreal *Gazette*, 31 Oct. and 3 Nov. 1930; *Le Soleil*, 19 fév. 1932.

45. Besides his nationalistic crusade against the "electricity trust," Philippe Hamel was known for his active support of Conservative candidates in 1931. Albert Rioux's Union Catholique des Cultivateurs had been a consistent critic and active political opponent of the government since its formation in 1924. Charpentier's Catholic labour followers were generally more discreet, but still less sympathetic to Taschereau than the Quebec Trades and Labour Council. Lawyer René Chaloult, economist Esdras Minville, journalist Arthur Laurendeau, credit union leader Wilfrid Guérin and Archambault (as "Pierre Homier") were all directors and writers for *Action Nationale*. V.-E. Beaupré had been president of both the St Jean Baptiste Society and the Association Catholique de la Jeunesse Canadienne in Montreal. Dr J.B. Prince "s'occupa d'oeuvres et fut l'un des protagonistes de la presse catholique," according to Lionel Groulx, *Mes Mémoires* (Montreal, 1970), 1: 276.

46. PAC, Paul Gouin Papers, Archambault to Gouin, 28 sept. 1933.

47. Gouin Papers, Gouin to L.A. Richard, 30 mai 1930; to Honoré Mercier, 10 sept. 1930; to Taschereau, 5 déc. 1931;

Taschereau to Gouin, 8 août and 9 déc. 1931. Fonds Taschereau, Gouin to Taschereau 13 and 19 juil. 1931. *Le Soleil*, 22 oct. 1934. Gouin agreed to chair a province-wide Colonization Committee organized by Ernest Laforce, and defendant J.J. Harpell (a Hamel-like crusader against the insurance industry) in a libel suit initiated by Sun Life President T.B. Macauley.

48. *Maclean's*, 15 Jan. 1936, interview by Erland Echland. Taschereau was reportedly quite angry that some who did have government jobs (including Gérald Coote, his own nephew) were flirting with the rebels. Gouin Papers, Seraphin Vachon to Gouin, 20 juil. 1934.

49. *La Presse*, 22 sept. 1934; *L'Evènement*, 9 sept. 1935. Dirks, "Origins of the Union Nationale," 239–40, mentions those who left the Action Libérale when it formally decided on independent political action.

50. *La Presse*, 22 sept. 1934.

51. When Gouin did unite with Duplessis on 7 November, he naturally reinforced Taschereau's cynicism still further. It was not literally true that "le contrat . . . ne parle nullement des principes politiques mais se contente d'une distribution d'honneurs et de place," but no one in Quebec political circles seriously believed that Duplessis was a social reformer, or that Gouin would be a match for him within the alliance. Sincere Liberals now "doivent perdre toutes leurs illusions" about Gouin, *Le Devoir*, 8 nov. 1935.

52. Cited in *HPQ*, 33: 214. Asselin's distaste for Camilien Houde first brought him to Taschereau's defence in 1930, but the former nationaliste had little regard for Duplessis either. Bibliothèque Municipale de Montréal, Collection Olivar Asselin, Asselin to Antoine Giguère, 2 déc. 1930; Marcel A. Gagnon, *La Vie Orageuse d'Olivar Asselin* (Montreal, 1962), 2: 277.

53. Bibliothèque de l'Université de Sherbrooke, Fonds Jean-Charles Harvey, "Memoirs" (ms), ch. 3, p. 1.

54. Fonds Taschereau, vol. 35, "Notes Confidentielles," 24 janv. 1935; *HPQ*, 33: 38, 48–49, 62; Gouin Papers, Gouin to Edouard Lacroix, 16 mars 1935; Gouin to Philippe Hamel, 27 mars 1935.

55. *CAR*, 1921, 641. Fonds Taschereau, *Discours* 1930 "Elites and Democracy"; N. Ward, ed., *A Party Politician: The Memoirs of Chubby Power* (Toronto, 1966), 322. For tactical reasons, Lapointe also urged Taschereau to scuttle R.B. Bennett's relief efforts (Fonds Taschereau, Lapointe to Taschereau, 2 oct. 1934) and like other federal Liberals withheld support for Bennett's "New Deal" social reforms.

56. Only Colonization Minister Irenée Vautrin, who joined the Cabinet in mid-1934, apparently tried to compensate. E.g., Fonds Taschereau, Vautrin to Taschereau, 27 déc. 1934. Referring to his earlier initiatives, David later recalled how Taschereau had "témoiné d'un sens parfait politique et . . . acquiescé à ces propositions qui semblaient peu politiques à certains autres." Ibid., David to Taschereau, 6 oct. 1939.

57. Rumilly (*HPQ*, 33: 212–13) perceived that veteran Liberals suspected the motives of their critics, but understood it only in terms of Conservative partisanship, not clerical reaction.

58. Dirks, "Origins of the Union Nationale," 236–38, 456–57, strongly suggests that the influence of genuine radicals like Jean Martineau was short-lived or perhaps never preponderant at all. Oscar Drouin returned from the Union Nationale to serve in the Godbout administration alongside men he had bitterly denounced.

59. Liberals had long suspected Villeneuve himself of partisanship since he refused to control Curé Lavergne or *Action Catholique*. After a rather stiff correspondence with Taschereau early in 1935, he evidently promised support to the Quebec City ALN, and issued statements on political morality obviously directed against the party in power. During

the election campaign he managed to be absent from the country, allowing Lavergne, Gravel, and other priests to campaign openly for the opposition. He then responded ambiguously and half-heartedly to Liberal complaints. Some Liberals felt that widespread clerical intervention in the election rose from a fear that Taschereau would soon hand the reins of power to Bouchard, a notorious anticlerical. *HPQ*, 33: 100; Fonds Taschereau, Taschereau to Villeneuve, 23 janv., 26 déc. 1935; 9, 15 janv. 1936;

Villeneuve to Taschereau, 25 janv., 28 déc. 1935; 7, 10, 24 janv. 1936; Hector Perrier to Taschereau, 9 fév. 1936; two anonymous letters to Taschereau, 4 déc. 1935; Gouin Papers, Hamel to Gouin, 26 mai 1935; Gouin to Hamel, 31 mai 1935; *Le Devoir*, 2 août 1935.

60. Although Duplessis' recent biographers would not describe the resistance as blind and perverse, Rumilly and Black both furnish abundant factual evidence on this point.

WORLD WAR II:
THE CRITICAL YEARS

T he World War II period witnessed a revolution with respect to the federal government's role in managing economic affairs as well as its willingness to address social welfare matters. Assuming a clear lead over the provinces, Ottawa implemented, among other measures, unemployment insurance, universal family allowances, and an assistance package for veterans far exceeding that offered in 1918. Moreover, it accepted in principle the 1945 White Paper on Income and Employment, committing it to Keynesian-type planning in order to prevent another depression.

A number of factors account for this metamorphosis. Far more mechanized than the Great War, the 1939–1945 conflict required unparalleled economic mobilization and state supervision, trends that, significantly, numerous citizens came to prefer over the hands-off approach, since the planned economy had brought full employment with minimal inflation (due to wage and price controls). Moreover, to underwrite the costs of war, the central government sought, and, after heated debate with several provinces, put into effect the recommendation of the 1940 Rowell–Sirois Commission that it assume control over income and corporate tax fields as well as succession duties in exchange for an annual payment to the provinces. Doug Owram notes that, to run the new interventionist state, a number of professional economists were recruited who, even before the general rise and dissemination of Keynesian theory, had espoused the belief that more government intervention was essential in order to make capitalism function more effectively. Also stressing the crucial role played by the new mandarin class, albeit with a far more idealistic slant, was Allen Irving, whose analysis centres upon Harry Cassidy and Leonard Marsh, two generally acknowledged architects of modern Canadian welfare policy who were guided by Fabian and social democratic philosophy. However, Irving admits that high-principled convictions did not necessarily guide the politicians who chose what suggestions to act upon as well as their scope.

The belief that welfare was implemented for reasons other than social justice is strongly argued by Alvin Finkel. In the context of the World War II period, Finkel writes that the principal aim of welfare was to undercut support, especially among a more powerful labour movement, for left-wing groups whose policies threatened to bring real income distribution. Indeed, Finkel goes so far as to cast Ottawa's policies as a product of collusion with leading capitalists who realized that measures like unemployment insurance would not only help co-opt the potentially rebellious but also stabilize the economy by maintaining some spending during hard times. While admitting that the goal of undercutting CCF support loomed large in Prime Minister King's mind, Raymond Blake also argues that the Liberal leader possessed a sincere ideological commitment to social security and saw an opportunity to act upon that conviction given international trends toward welfare and the promise by Ottawa to maintain full employment after the war.

Whether wartime welfare was passed to reform, improve, or save capitalism remains unsettled. What is indisputable, however, is that during these years, a more activist administration emerged in Ottawa. Having secured new sources of revenue and the experts to organize economic affairs, and urged on by bona fide challenges from the left, the federal government tossed aside its timidity with economic intervention to adopt a Keynesian model and, in some areas of social welfare, replaced the means tests with the principle of universality. Quickly citizens became accustomed to this new role and level of service, and, soon enough, began demanding more. The result was an evolution toward the modern welfare state that, in ultimately extending to so many areas, forced federal and provincial administrations—both for financial and jurisdictional reasons—to co-ordinate their activities as never before.

ECONOMIC THOUGHT IN THE 1930s: THE PRELUDE TO KEYNESIANISM

DOUG OWRAM

○

Economics in Canada came of age in the 1930s. A discipline that had only recently become an established part of the university curriculum in Canada began, under the stimulus of the worst depression in Canadian history, to challenge traditional descriptions of the way in which the economy worked. As it did so it increasingly undermined the theories on which those descriptions were based and began in a serious fashion to search for a new approach to economics. By the time that English economist John Maynard Keynes published his famous *General Theory of Employment, Interest and Money* in 1936, Canadian economists were more than ready to abandon an obsolete view of the economic universe in favour of a structure that offered greater hope for comprehension of the world around them.

A change in theory was accompanied and its impact accelerated by a changing role for professional economists. To an unprecedented degree the Depression caused the public to look to economists for advice on public policy. This change was the result of a conjuncture of circumstances including the relatively improved state of economics departments in Canadian universities in the years after World War I, theoretical developments at the national and international levels, and, most importantly, the quest for a solution to the worst economic crisis in Canadian history. Together these factors catapulted the "dismal science" into a prominent role in Canadian governmental planning and reform. Thus, for example, in 1930 the

◇ *Canadian Historical Review* 66, 3 (1985): 344–77. Reprinted with permission of the author and University of Toronto Press. The author wishes to thank K. Gupta of the Department of Economics of the University of Alberta for his comments on an earlier draft of this paper.

Canadian civil service had only one civil servant with graduate training in economics, O.D. Skelton, and he was in External Affairs rather than in an economic position. A decade later when Skelton died he had been followed by experts like W.C. Clark, R.B. Bryce, W.A. Mackintosh, his own son Alex Skelton, and numerous others.[1] World War II would see the proliferation continue unabated as economists flowed from academic positions or graduate schools into increasingly central positions in the public service. For the first time in Canadian history the economist could claim to have played an important role in defining the agenda for change.

○

Economics in Canada on the eve of the Depression was little more than a generation old and was just reaching a degree of institutional maturity. Until the last years of the nineteenth century "political economy," if taught at all, was considered a general enough discipline to be handled by whatever philosopher or divine might have some free time. Then, responding to the growing concerns of the public about industrialism and its implications for society, universities began to move towards the establishment of political economy as a full-fledged discipline. The appointment of William Ashley to the staff of the University of Toronto in 1888 marked the arrival of economics as a discipline at Canada's largest English-speaking institution. At Queen's University Adam Shortt's appointment to the John A. Macdonald Chair of Political Economy in 1891, when coupled with James Mavor's appointment in the same year at Toronto, has often been taken to mark the real beginning of academic study of economics in Canada. In Montreal the next years would see the appointment of Stephen Leacock at McGill, while French-speaking universities followed with posts for Edouard Montpetit and Henry Laureys. These small beginnings were followed in the years after 1900 by the steady growth of academic study in Canada. By the later 1920s most major universities had created departments of political economy of some sort and even minor colleges felt compelled to make at least an effort to acquaint their students with a discipline which claimed to be able to unravel some of the complexities of modern society. Through the 1920s economics continued to increase in popularity in Canada. Departments of social science, variously described, sprang up across the country so that, by the end of the decade, only the smaller universities continued to employ some harried individual teaching everything from economics to philosophy as their only involvement in the new discipline.[2]

It is difficult to provide a picture of those who practised the profession that is both detailed and exact. The rapid evolution of the academic community of economists as well as the fuzziness between the boundaries of the social sciences makes such precision impossible. Even so, a rough delineation of those who taught Canadian economics at the beginning of the 1930s reveals certain distinct characteristics. The first is age. As of 1930 half of the Canadian academic community was under the age of thirty-five.[3] Canadian economists generally reflected this youthful tendency. Of course there were the senior figures like O.D. Skelton and W.W. Swanson of the University of Saskatchewan, both over fifty when the Depression struck. More typical, however, were those like W.C. Clark of Queen's, Harold Innis of Toronto, or W.B. Hurd of Brandon College, all between thirty-five and forty. The teaching and writing of Canadian economics in these years was thus increasingly shaped by a generation that had grown up amidst the rapid industrialization and urbanization of the Laurier years. New problems and new values springing from the tremendous changes of the early twentieth century separated them from those who had gone before.

Above all, what separated them from earlier generations was the experience of World War I. For this age group the war was a direct experience and a good many had served overseas. Even for those who had not, however, the war marked a watershed which separated their youth from their adulthood and which forever altered their perceptions of the world. In this sense as well they were irrevocably committed to the realities, problems, and solutions of the twentieth century. They had grown up in similar times, had shared a similar historical experience, and thus shared certain perspectives on the economic crisis of the 1930s.

The second common characteristic was education. Of the approximately forty-five economists teaching in Canadian universities in 1929–1930, the majority held doctorates, though there was still a considerable minority with lesser degrees. It was not just the common degrees that linked the profession but the common sources of these degrees. Until 1936, when G. Britnell of the University of Saskatchewan completed his doctorate at Toronto, all Canadian academics with degrees in economics had obtained them abroad. In particular three universities, Chicago, Harvard, and Oxford, account for more than 60 percent of the "most advanced degrees" held by Canadian academic economists in the period 1929–1935. If we add to the list such prominent civil servant economists as O.D. Skelton (Chicago), D.A. Skelton (Oxford), and S.A. Cudmore (Oxford) the concentration becomes even more pronounced.[4]

A third unifying factor is less precise and perhaps less universal but deserves comment nevertheless. Many economists came from families with a similar class and occupational background. In particular, most came from a middle-class background in which educational or literary attainments had been important. The classroom and the pulpit, accordingly, provided the parents of many academics with a livelihood. University of Saskatchewan economist Peter McQueen's father was a Presbyterian minister while Toronto professor A.F.W. Plumptre's father was an Anglican canon. From the families of teachers came individuals like O.D. Skelton, whose father was a school superintendent, and B.S. Kierstead, who joined his father on the faculty of the University of New Brunswick. These are only examples, of course, and there are exceptions, but a pattern does seem to exist where the intellectual community of one generation provided a central role in shaping the next. The shift from humanistic and religious to social scientific studies may reveal something about the changing nature of the Canadian perspective on intellectual requirements.

Age, class, and education provided the prerequisites for a sense of community among Canadian economists. Institutional links helped bring that community into being. The central institution for the economics community was the Canadian Political Science Association. Initially established in 1913 under the guidance of Adam Shortt and O.D. Skelton, the CPSA lapsed into inactivity during World War I. On the eve of the Depression it was revived, largely through the efforts of University of Alberta economist and grain commissioner, D.A. MacGibbon.[5] This time the body flourished in spite of, or perhaps because of, the Depression. By the time it met in Toronto in 1932 it had become a well-known institution of some importance to Canadian economists. Through its links to the Canadian Institute of International Affairs, the Canadian Historical Association, and the Canadian clubs it was also coming to play an important role within the wider world of Canadian thought.[6] The association and its annual meetings were supplemented by the growth of scholarly journals. In 1928 the University of Toronto political economy department fostered the annual *Contributions to Canadian Economics*, and in 1935 C.A. Curtis of Queen's and Vincent Bladen and Harold Innis of the University of Toronto were instrumental in establishing the quarterly *Canadian Journal of Economics and Political Science*.[7] These new outlets for scholarly publication encouraged a sense of professional distinctiveness while the editorial board provided one more meeting place for Canadian economists.

The series of educational, personal, and institutional ties that had developed by the early 1930s meant that the great majority of the small community of Canadian academic economists and economist civil servants were familiar with the interests and work of their colleagues and, in an increasing number of cases, also knew each other personally. There were of course, exceptions. Individual professors remained isolated from the professional community. This was especially the problem in smaller colleges where heavy teaching loads and limited opportunities for research allowed little intellectual involvement in the discipline outside of the classroom. Even given such realities, however, the ties were such that it is possible by the Depression to talk of economists as a distinguishable group of professionals with certain common interests and views. In other words, the establishment of economics as a discipline in Canada in the first third of the twentieth century had been paralleled by the establishment of economists as a professional community.

By the later 1920s as well a pattern of economic scholarship in Canada had been established. This pattern was neatly revealed in a 1929 piece by Harold Innis when he complained that economics "must be brought level with history and political science." Furthermore, he argued that "Canadian economic history is in a sense at the root of the problem. Its elaboration will strengthen the anchorage of economics which is so essential to a rapidly growing young country such as Canada."[8] Given the relatively established state of economics within the social sciences, these comments appear somewhat overly critical. They are nevertheless revealing, for in his emphasis on the relationship with political science and history and in his own emphasis on the importance of economic history Innis correctly noted the prevailing tendency of Canadian economics on the eve of the Great Depression.

The importance Innis assigned to economic history was widespread within the profession. The orientation toward history within Canadian economic writing was deeply rooted. Adam Shortt had seen history as the key to economics while W.J. Ashley, the first political economist at the University of Toronto, had also been appointed as a professor of constitutional history.[9] As the discipline developed the tradition remained intact. In the years after World War I many of the best known publications of Canadian economists were in the field of economic history. Innis followed his 1922 publication on the Canadian Pacific Railway a decade later with the monumental *Fur Trade in Canada*. Skelton had written more historical than economic monographs by the time he joined External Affairs. Biographies of Laurier and Galt, historical studies of railway construction in Canada, and his 1914 *General Economic History of Canada* testified to his orientation. Indeed, when Queen's University set out to find a replacement for Skelton as head of the department, they passed over one able economic historian, W.A. Mackintosh, in favour of another, Herbert Heaton.[10] So powerful was the trend to economic history in these years that a whole generation of economists gained reputations as being among Canada's top historians. For a younger generation of historians proper like Donald Creighton and A.R.M. Lower, inspiration came not from the constitutional orientation of their own profession but from the economic studies of men like Innis and Shortt.[11]

There was a second major concern of Canadian economic writing in the postwar years—the agrarian sector and, in particular, western agriculture. The importance of the wheat boom in the years before 1914, the longstanding belief in the necessity of western development, and the great political upheavals originating in the West after World I all provide explanations for this focus.[12] In total, these factors led to the belief that the western experience in Canada was both unique and important to the national future. In the frontier experience of the West there existed problems that mirrored the difficulties of new societies while in the experiments with co-operative ownership, government regulation, and populist politics lay the possible future of democracy. Economic writings on the frontier regions of Canada were as popular as writings on its history. The tradition was especially strong at Queen's, where Clifford Clark wrote on the country elevator, Humfrey Michell on agricultural credit, and W.A. Mackintosh on the problems of the Prairie provinces.[13] By the Depression the interest in the West led to major publications from other institutions. Thus MacGibbon was publishing work on prairie settlement and, in 1932, *The Canadian Grain Trade*, while P.C. Armstrong undertook a major work entitled, simply, *Wheat*.[14] The Depression saw a major undertaking with the Canadian Frontier of Settlement series under the general editorship of Mackintosh.[15] In an increasingly urban society Canadian economists still viewed the agricultural sector as central to understanding Canadian economic development.

Of course, other sectors received attention. Transportation was a much studied topic and primary resources other than agriculture interested economists.[16] These studies, however, simply reinforce the conclusion that Canadian economic writing had distinct biases in these years. That writing was infused with historicism and focussed on specific events and institutions rather than work with abstraction or theory. It revealed, in other words, strong ties to the historical school of nineteenth-century German economic thought or, perhaps more directly, to the North American offshoot, the "institutional school" of turn-of-the-century United States.[17]

The dominance of this approach was furthered by the state of economic theory at the beginning of the Depression. As early as the decade before World War I, economic theory had become relatively fixed. This does not mean that there were not economists looking for new approaches to problems. The work of Veblen in the United States or Schumpeter in Austria and the States provided interesting theoretical challenges. Nevertheless, classical economic theory, modified by the marginal utility theorists of the late nineteenth century, had become so strongly entrenched in economic thought that the most promising direction for the economist who wished to con-tribute something to his discipline did not seem to be a restatement or modification of hypothetical arguments on the way in which the economy worked. Only through high-quality studies of specific problems in actual real-world circumstances would a means be found to test theory. Theory became less relevant in the short term than empirical testing. Macro-economic theory was pushed into the background as micro-economic analysis predominated. The argument of dominion statistician R.H. Coats in 1931 that "the need for economic and social research lies wholly on the inductive side" would not have been disputed by many of his economic colleagues.[18]

This outlook affected not only the specialized monographs but the whole approach to the discipline. Robert Lekachman's study of John Maynard Keynes underlined the contributions of his subject to economics by comparing two general textbooks written in the United States, Garver and Hansen's 1937 edition of *Principles of Economics* and Paul Samuelson's 1964 edition of *Economics*. Not only the details and conclusions had changed, he noted, but the whole organization of the subject.[19] The same test applied to Canada leads, not surprisingly, to the same result. Thus, for example, MacGibbon's popular *Introduction to Economics*, first published in 1924 and republished in 1931 and 1935, taught economics by setting the principles of the discipline firmly within historical and institutional frameworks. Such subjects as production, credit, and consumption were described not as a set of economic laws but in terms of specific Canadian events. Whole chapters were devoted to descriptions of Canadian labour unions, primary industries, manufacturing, transportation, and other similar matters. In the 1924 edition the business cycle was not even mentioned and nor were the concepts of elasticity of demand, national income, recession, or depression. There was discussion of the Canadian merchant marine, trade with New Zealand, and the Hudson Bay route.[20] As one reviewer commented, "it seems clear that one criterion of a good general textbook will be that it contains the least possible economic theory as such." Ironically, MacGibbon was criticized as being too theoretical.[21] The gap between this work and that of Samuelson or any other standard postwar textbook on economics is as marked in Canada as in the United States. As Lekachman commented, "in a generation economists have learned to concentrate on different problems, redefine the scope of their principles, reinterpret public policy, and transform their nomenclature."[22]

In the years after World War I and culminating in the depression years, a series of challenges confronted the intellectual traditions of the discipline. First, and perhaps most important, the rising importance of the social sciences and the secularization and professionalization of social work in the 1920s altered conceptions of the causes of social ills. Before 1914 a jumble of "causes" had been assigned in searching for the root of social problems. These could vary from personal failure, such as laziness, self-indulgence, or immorality, to environmental factors such as poor living conditions, lack of education, "demon rum," or other forces, but in most cases the sources of the problem tended to be immediate. Moreover, the basic economic problems of poverty or unemployment tended to be viewed as an effect rather than a cause or, at best, as an intermediate cause stemming from a previous source.[23]

Tendencies within the progressive movement and the growing influence of social scientific thought, however, began to alter these analyses. The decline in the power of religion had decreased expectations about the possibilities of ethical reformism, while the growing sense of the complex interdependence of modern society led observers to assign increasingly remote causes in the assessment of any problem. From the individual, social workers and social gospellers moved the perspective outward to physical environment and family living conditions. Urban reformers looked to neighbourhood and city. By the time of World War I, causation had shifted to the basic industrial trends which had determined the flight from the farm, the rise of the city and, therefore, the urban environment in which so many social problems arose. Finally, by the 1920s, the key to that environment, to the demographic shifts that had taken place, and to many of the other social forces present were centred increasingly on man's search for economic security. As social worker Charlotte Whitton argued, social workers had to accept the fact that the problems they face "are economic rather than moral in their origins."[24] "Poverty," as another social worker commented, "must be viewed as an economic ill."[25] Between the prewar and postwar societies a revolution occurred that attached increased importance to economic factors. Not surprisingly, the Depression reinforced this trend. Here was demonstrable evidence that remote economic events could shape the lives of thousands of men and women whose past environment, habits, and outlook had none of the classical symptoms of social problem groups. By the 1930s few within the intellectual community and fewer still within the social sciences would have argued with the notion that the "sources of unemployment may generally be found in causes wholly independent of the workmen involved and over which they have no control."[26] The belief developed that economics determined other environmental and personal conditions and that those economic factors were largely beyond the control of the individual. As this perception of social conditions grew, those who could claim some expertise in the mysteries of economic causation rose in prestige accordingly.

Together these factors thrust the economist to the forefront for the first time in Canadian history. With the Depression the opportunity existed for these academics to assume a new role in Canadian life and acquire new personal and professional prestige. As Innis commented, "Periods of prosperity may be characterized by the most intensive work in economics but periods of depression have been characterized by attempts at application."[27]

Sudden prominence brought not only opportunity but problems. No longer could the academic economist toil away quietly at his historically oriented work with little or no thought to the more immediate problems facing the country. As economics acquired new importance, those who practised it suddenly found their pronouncements being widely discussed in the papers and among the wider public. Economists were newly sought after, in the cynical words of one of them, to play the role of "Medicine Man" and "to cause the buffalo of peace and plenty to appear."[28] Public and political expectations were all too often unrealistic given the state of the profession and the complexity of the problems it faced. As Saskatchewan economist George Britnell commented to Innis, "there are times when I get really frightened at the things which lawyers and politicians think economists should be able to do by turning a handle and mixing a few statistics in a hat."[29] Whatever the anxiety, there was general agreement among economists that they had an important role to play in solving the crucial problems facing the nation. Even Innis argued that "Political parties must draw to an increasing extent on the economic intelligence at hand."[30] Given this dependence, the real question was whether the theoretical and empirical base of Canadian economics was adequate for the task ahead.

o

It is impossible to deal with the evolution of economics theory in the Great Depression without first considering the place of Cambridge economist John Maynard Keynes. His importance to this and succeeding generations of economists cannot be disputed, for his 1936 publication, the *General Theory of Employment, Interest and Money,* was a major force in reshaping Canadian economic thinking as it was elsewhere. There is, however, somewhat of a myth surrounding the impact of Keynesian theory and this myth leads to two dangerous simplifications. First, some later Keynesians have seen the *General Theory* as not merely good economic theory but as permanent economic law. Keynes seems all too often to have been seen as having cut the gordian knot of business cycle theory and to have ushered in a new era in which severe economic dislocations were unthinkable.[31] Such writings, more popular twenty years ago than they are today, overstate the case. Economists have not resolved their debates on basic principles and are unlikely to do so within the foreseeable future, if ever. In the general context of economic theory, therefore, Keynes must be accorded a prominent place without being deified.

There is also a danger in portraying Keynesian theory as bursting upon the mid-Depression as a revelation out of nowhere. The emphasis accorded the "Keynesian revolution" in much literature tends to leave the casual reader with an image of two distinctly defined eras in economic thought. The first begins with Adam Smith's *Wealth of Nations*, published in 1776, and stretches barely perturbed by the work of Malthus, Ricardo, Marshall, and others throughout the nineteenth century and into the twentieth. The second comes into being when economists read the *General Theory*, see the light, and convince politicians of the error of their ways. This is a deliberate overstatement of course but it is employed to emphasize the problems contained in the concept of a "Keynesian revolution" occurring sometime in the years after 1936. Instead, the influence of Keynesian writing on Canadian economic thought must be assessed with two facts in mind. First, Keynes did not become important only in 1936. From at least 1919 with the publication of *The Economic Consequences of the Peace* he was an economist of international repute. Later publications such as *Essays in Persuasion* (1931) and the two-volume *Treatise on Money* (1930) enhanced an already significant stature within the profession. Not only professional economists in Canada but those "amateurs" with an interest in economics, such as J.W. Dafoe, felt it important to try and wade through Keynes's works.[32] Thus the economics profession in Canada was aware of Keynes's evolving ideas on theory. Those ideas, it is true, were not fully developed until the mid-1930s but those in Canada who followed economics were fully aware of the line of Keynes's thought and modifications he was making to traditional economic theory. Second, long before 1936 there were doubts about the relevance of classical economic theory to modern conditions. The problem, as MacGibbon pointed out, was that the world of the classical economist rested on philosophical and sociological assumptions which seemed increasingly dubious as the twentieth century wore on.[33] Bit by bit Canadian economists began to discover rot within the edifice of classical economic theory. By the time of the Depression much of the basis on which nineteenth-century economic thought had rested was, if not discredited, under serious challenge. Only some reasonably acceptable alternative theory was necessary to convince the bulk of Canadian economists that the structure was not worth saving.[34]

The basic problem with classical economics was its strong assumption of the essential stability of the economic world. When the great Cambridge economist Alfred Marshall opened his 1890 work, *Principles of Economics*, with the comment that the "general theory of the equilibrium of demand and supply is a Fundamental Idea running through the frames of all the various parts of the central problem of Distribution and Exchange," he was stating both an economic principle and an assumption about social organization as well as making a statement of personal experience. Late Victorian Europe, as viewed from the Cambridge backs, gave the impression that stability was indeed the natural order of things.[35] For Marshall and for those many who followed his writings, equilibrium was not only one aspect of economics but a central notion that carried with it subordinate notions of social stability and a self-correcting price system.

Though the variables could be bewildering, the process by which the price system achieved equilibrium was relatively straightforward. As economists like a young W.C. Clark argued, in a recession manufacturers would cut production and wages to rid themselves of excess inventories and reduce production costs. At the same time investment in manufacturing would decrease and money would, like labour, become a cheaper commodity. At some point, however, inventories would be run down and the costs of production lowered sufficiently to encourage an increase in production. Demand would also increase because of the lower costs for the goods. The need for workmen would thus increase until unemployment eased and wages rose. The increase in demand would also make new investment worth while and cause interest rates to recover. Demand and supply would have been achieved, under conditions of full production and employment. Eventually, of course, excessive demand could push up the cost of wages and money to the point where prices of the product would increase, excessive new capacity come on stream, and the downturn begin. Through it all, however, was the assumption that the business cycle was self-correcting in its effects and that its natural tendency was to move toward full production and employment—that magic point where demand met supply.[36]

Closely related was a theory of money that also reflected the stability of the nineteenth century and emphasized the self-correcting systems within the marketplace. The "quantity theory of money" as it had evolved under the guidance of the Cambridge theorists argued two basic points. The first was that any change in the quantity of money in circulation had a direct effect, *ceteris paribus*, in the price level. The expansion of the money supply was thus, in most cases, inflationary, and a more or less constant money supply seen as characteristic of a sound economy. Second, money affected the achievement of equilibrium in that the demand for investment would increase demand for this relatively fixed good, thus forcing an increase in interest rates. In accordance with the normal laws of supply and demand, the demand for money would thus decrease and the pressure for investment would be eased. Conversely, in recessionary times the demand for money would be low and interest rates would adjust downwards, making investment more attractive.[37]

Demand and supply functions thus worked in both the monetary and manufacturing worlds to adjust the economy toward full employment and production. Disruptions could and would occur but the emphasis in much of the writing of the Marshall school was that politicians must resist the temptation to interfere in the economy when such disruptions occurred. They would only make matters worse. This does not mean that Marshall, or those Canadians who accepted his principles, opposed all government activism. What they did fear, however, was a return to medieval principles of guilds, legal monopolies, and excessive regulations designed to destroy the price system's natural workings. "Nearly all the founders of modern economics were men of gentle and sympathetic temper," Marshall reminded his readers. They insisted that the government allow the economic system to work unhindered because excessive interference would have hurt rather than helped the people most vulnerable to economic downturn.[38]

In placing Canadian economic writing to the 1920s within this classical-marginalist tradition, two qualifications must be made. The first is that there was always a distinction in Canadian economic writing between the workings of the marketplace and the necessities of ameliorative action. Few, if any, Canadian economists took their defence of classical economic theory to the point where they translated it into a social philosophy. The idealist tradition in Canada was simply too strong and from the beginning of the century men like Shortt and Mavor had been involved in reform movements which accepted increased government involvement in social matters.[39] Mackenzie King, another economist and idealist, had been active in drawing the Laurier government into some involvement, however modest, in the protection of many groups affected by rising industrialism.[40] The Canadian academic community thus never saw the extreme defences of laissez faire typified by such U.S. economists as Amasa Walker and Laurence Laughlin.[41] Instead, Canadian economic thought sought to preserve the integrity of the price system while recognizing a role for modern government in ameliorating the negative side-effects of modern industrial capitalism.[42]

In the years around World War I, as the Christian idealist impulse began to weaken, this ameliorative tendency began to become integrated into basic economic theory. The emphasis on equilibrium was joined by a concern for the fluctuations between the points of equilibrium. Periods of disequilibrium began to seem as prevalent as those of relative equilibrium. The first Canadian "industrial" recessions in 1907, 1912–1913, and 1919–1920 revealed the vulnerability of the Canadian economy to economic downturns. Economists in turn became less sanguine about allowing the automatic forces within the marketplace to make the necessary corrections. As early as 1909, Skelton urged the government to plan its spending in such a way as to act as a "flywheel" in the business cycle. By planning public works ahead of time but postponing them in good times while accelerating them in bad, the government could ease inflationary pressures at the top end of the cycle and increase employment at the bottom.[43] The idea was restated by the Ontario Commission on Unemployment 1913, and became increasingly common thereafter.[44]

The marketplace was thus an insufficient means of regulating economic activities for two reasons. First, Canadian economists had from the beginning thought that amelioration of individual hardship was a necessary and desirable role for the government. The basic price system should not be disturbed, however, through excessive interference. Thus even though classical theory of the business cycle was accepted, there was a readiness to provide assistance for those caught by the normal fluctuations of the economy. Second, by the 1930s there was at least discussion of the possibility of reacting to the cycle in another way. The use of public works on a massive scale could both assist workers by providing additional employment and also "prime the pump" by moving public funds into the marketplace. Though it was a long way from these limited concepts of involvement in the marketplace to the later self-confident assertions that the business cycle was controllable, these ideas were no longer pure classical economics.

The results of these changes were somewhat paradoxical. The basis of Canadian economic writing remained classical in outlook, yet in several specific instances that classical theory was being ignored in the face of modern problems. This paradox was explained by the argument that the classical theories propounded by people like Marshall were correct and made complete sense, but only for Marshall's world. That world, unfortunately, had ended with World War I. Marshall's theories of equilibrium depended on a world in which international trading relationships were stable and unhindered by artificial barriers; specifically, his thesis required stable prices domestically and stable exchange rates internationally. Given the actual situation of late nineteenth-century Europe such assumptions were not unreasonable, especially from the vantage point of the British empire. The gold standard was intact, buttressed by the strength of the British pound and the belief in free trade. Such stability in key areas allowed the market forces to work their way through the system in a relatively smooth fashion, thus balancing supply and demand at the point of equilibrium. Between 1914 and 1919, however, the economic order had been seriously disrupted. Monetary relationships were destabilized by the costs of fighting the war, the abandonment of the gold standard by many nations, and the rising creditor status of the United States. The attempts to restore that standard in the postwar years had only made matters worse because key currencies like the pound sterling were valued incorrectly. Also, drawing from Keynes, Canadian economists criticized the peace conference of 1919 and the hefty reparations forced upon Germany. They were unrealistic and only added to the imbalances that were already so chronic in the modern world.[45]

Most of these arguments are unexceptionable today both as history and as economic theory. The implication of such writings in the 1920s and 1930s, however, was that theories which applied to the stable pre-1914 period were of doubtful applicability in an era that experienced depression, hyperinflation, speculative boom, and crash, all within the space of ten years. This was not a world that mirrored Marshall's state of equilibrium or exhibited the smooth workings of Adam Smith's invisible hand. Faced with new and volatile circumstances, Canadian economic writing shifted from an emphasis on stability to a concern with the problems of change and dislocation. The authority of Marshall was increasingly challenged by the ideas of Veblen, Schumpeter, and Keynes. In formal terms classical economic theory remained intact. The belief still held that the natural point of equilibrium was at full employment and production. So many destabilizing forces had come into play, however, that the point of equilibrium seemed more a utopian ideal than the normal state of things.

○

It was thus with a qualified adherence to the traditional tenets of classical economics that Canadian economists turned their attention to the Depression when it hit in 1929–1930. Various specific factors were assigned the blame for the downturn. Imbalances in Canadian trade, excessive reliance on foreign markets, a lack of protection for domestic production, the collapse of the wheat market, the end of an era of expansion, and other themes appeared and reappeared in popular journals, scholarly articles, and learned monographs as central to the coming of the Great Depression.[46] Traditional ideas also died hard and there was a great deal of moralizing on the part of economists to the effect that Canadians and others in the Western world had simply gotten too greedy. The search for material success in the postwar world had allowed the promoter to undertake an "orgy of speculative development."[47] Banking expert and University of Toronto professor Gilbert Jackson charged in 1933 that the "root cause of the depression lies in no fault of this economic mechanism by which we live, but in ourselves." The Depression merely proved to him that economics was "an exemplification of the moral law." Man had gotten too greedy and now was paying the price.[48]

While all of these factors were, to one degree or another, relevant in assessing the coming of the Depression, none of them went beyond problems in the Canadian economy to what Innis termed "the Canadian problem."[49] It was one thing to point to specific, and usually obvious, vulnerabilities in the Canadian economy. It was quite another to arrive at a complete enough understanding of the business cycle to comprehend why, in this instance, that cycle was so severe. Even to arrive at such an understanding was part of the process, for government and public looked to economists not merely to find what had gone wrong but to find remedies. Identifying the problem accurately therefore was the important first step in finding a solution.

A 1932 editorial in the *Canadian Banker*, likely penned by W.A. Mackintosh, thought it had discovered certain patterns in the various assessments of the Depression. There was, it concluded, a "monetary school" and a "disequilibrium school" on the causes of the collapse. The monetary school looked back to the Great War and emphasized the shortage of gold and its misallocation. The disequilibrium school also looked back to the war but argued that massive upheavals in production and technology had left "the world with greatly expanded productive equipment in food and raw materials producing countries especially." Normally, adjustment would have occurred in the postwar period. In democracies, however, public pressures had led government to seek popularity by means of price regulations and other schemes designed to thwart the necessary market changes. The readjustment was thus not allowed to run its course and the pressures within the system continued to build. Thus "the severity of the present depression is not to be regarded as primarily cyclical but rather as the result of the necessity of working through these accumulated maladjustments suddenly."[50]

Though it is impossible to separate completely the monetary and disequilibrium factors brought about by the war, the hypothesis of the *Canadian Banker* is correct insofar as it states the existence of two schools of thought in the Depression. The monetary school began with two strong beliefs within the Canadian economic community. The first was that the gold standard was the best means of ensuring stable international price relations. In spite of the occasional bimetallist such as Humfrey Michell of McMaster, the great majority of Canadian economists remained convinced of the wisdom of this traditional economic system.[51] The second belief was that the gold standard was in a shambles. When the United Kingdom abandoned gold in 1931 it aggravated an already chaotic situation and marked the end of attempts to patch up the monetary system on the basis of pre-1914 standards. If the gold standard was no longer possible then what was needed, economists agreed, was an orderly readjustment of international monetary relationships. What was actually occurring was, as Clifford Clark noted, of an "every-country-for-itself, devil take the hindmost character."[52]

A variation of this monetary theory argued that the world faced a "price crisis, the result of a prolonged and apparently not yet completed rise in the scarcity and value of the monetary unit."[53] Drawing on the quantity theory of money, this hypothesis argued that World War I and other events had forced an increase in nominal prices, thus leaving the quantity of money available for the carrying on of normal transactions insufficient. Inevitably, money supplies had to increase or prices fall. Since the world had clung to the gold standard without allowing for sufficient revaluation of the price of gold, the 1920s had seen a serious disequilibrium develop as too little money chased too many purchases at an ever increasing rate.[54] With the speculative frenzy on the stock exchanges in New York and elsewhere the shortage of funds became even more acute and before long there "was not enough money left in the ordinary channels of business to conduct the trade of the world and the trade of the world broke down."[55]

As this and other theories held by the monetary school recognized, the self-righting mechanisms of classical theory were, at best, going to take effect only in the long run. The continued instability of the international monetary structure, the increase in currency restrictions and barriers to international trade all meant that the situation was being subjected to new shocks on an almost weekly basis. Only a combination of co-operation on foreign exchange rates, the place of gold in future monetary arrangements, and domestic efforts to achieve a stable price level would resolve the basic problems underlying the collapse of 1929–1930. There was, however, no indication that the necessary co-operation was developing or even that economists, bankers, business, and government could agree as to what direction prices should be heading.

The other school of thought, termed by the *Canadian Banker* the disequilibrium school, had at its basis the traditional arguments of classical theory. To put it most simply, various forces had thrown the economy out of equilibrium. The Depression was but another trough in the ongoing business cycle similar to those of 1873, 1893, 1907, and 1912–1913. Each economist had his own theories as to why this trough should be more severe than earlier ones though the most popular theory centred on the dislocations of World War I. Harold Innis, for example, saw the war as marking a fundamental watershed in the nature of industrial production. The first stage of the industrial revolution had been developed on the basis of coal and iron and areas with abundant supplies of these materials became economically powerful. World War I had caused a shift away from these materials, however, and the old "paleotechnic" capitalist economy began to yield to the "neotechnic" world of internal combustion engines, hydro-electric power, and other sources of power. Paleotechnic areas sank into an increasingly depressed state while investment flowed to new areas. The result was severe structural dislocation as the world economies sought to adjust to this new stage of capitalism. "Neotechnic industrialism superimposed on paleotechnic industrialism involved changes of great implication to modern society and brought strains of great severity."[57] Until the transition was made the economic disequilibrium would remain. It was but a short step from the idea of modern society as undergoing basic technological shifts to the conclusion that the Depression marked not the evolution of capitalism but its most severe crisis to date. In many writings, and not just among Marxists, there was a suspicion that capitalism itself was one gigantic business cycle, containing within it many smaller ones. That cycle had begun its rise in the eighteenth century, peaked in the nineteenth, and exhibited increasing signs of instability in the twentieth. Finally, in 1929 it began the collapse. When the cycle began again it would be under a different socio-economic system.

There were, many economists felt, elements within the capitalist system that foreshadowed impending collapse. Most importantly, it appeared as if the efficiency of production had run ahead of the efficiency of consumption. There were too many goods and too few markets for those goods. In 1932, for example, W.B. Hurd of Brandon College argued that the "greatly enhanced efficiency of large scale production is perhaps the strongest argument for the prevailing competitive system; yet the widespread adoption of capitalistic technique has created a series of business problems of unprecedented magnitude."[57] Writing three years later Stephen Leacock made essentially the same argument. Adam Smith's classical economic theories were a failure, Leacock concluded, because they failed to comprehend the problems of long-term overproduction.[58] Even R.B. Bennett picked up on the theme in the opening New Deal speech in 1935. Only a redistribution of wealth would allow the preservation of the capitalist system. "It has become increasingly clear to thoughtful minds in all industrial countries that what is needed for the restoration of industrial equilibrium is practically a change in our social system."[59] The "invisible hand" seemed no longer to function and only a basic restructuring of the economy seemed able to remove the basic flaws of modern capitalism.

Such views raise the question of what had happened to those classical self-correcting forces which were supposed to lift economies out of recession? Specifically, classical theory argued that if overproduction were a problem, falling sales and rising inventories would lead businessmen to close down production and workers, faced with rising unemployment, to accept lower wages. The combination of fewer goods being put on the market and being produced at less cost would eventually remove the glut. According to Hurd, however, this pattern was not quite so automatic in modern times. Large-scale industrial enterprises had high fixed costs in plant and machinery. These fixed costs encouraged the continuation of production even after a glut had developed for a particular product. Industries were under continual pressure to keep plant and machinery functioning. If things continued to worsen, of course, the company would reduce production but as soon as the upturn began the pressure to utilize idle machinery would increase and production would resume long before the economy had fully disposed of the glut. Pressure would then be brought to bear upon governments to preserve domestic markets for domestic industry, thus encouraging a series of barriers to trade in the form of restrictions or prohibitive tariffs. The results could be seen simply by looking at the modern world. "The effect of increased competition, coupled with the practical closing of foreign markets, on industrial centres with economies and population structures geared up to productive capacity much beyond requirements has verged on the catastrophic."[60] Innis, in a variant on this theme, argued that expanding economies had encouraged firms and nations to assume high levels of debt. Those debts represented fixed costs which prevented the price system from making the necessary adjustments to restore equilibrium.[61]

Though the theories of Hurd and others were open to criticism on points, the important matter to note is that the Depression led many economists to chip yet more away from the already crumbling edifice of classical economics. Most importantly, the belief that equilibrium existed at the point of full employment and production had been thrown into serious doubt before the publication by Keynes of the *General Theory*. For both monetary and disequilibrium theorists the frictional problems in the way of reaching equilibrium were seen as so great that stability at full employment and production was at best an illusory goal. For the more pessimistic, who saw in the Depression a crisis of capitalism, the problems with classical theory were even more fundamental. Classical economics had developed to explain capitalism and capitalism was now on the verge of collapse. Given these criticisms and doubts, is it any wonder that when Keynes published his *General Theory* in 1936 and provided the theoretical justification for laying to rest the concept of equilibrium at full employment, he was well received?

○

From an analysis of the problem it was necessary to move toward solutions. Many solutions of varying sophistication and relevance were suggested, but it is probably best to categorize the major writings of academic economic thought in the decade in terms of the monetary and disequilibrium schools already mentioned.

On the monetary side, economists were able to come up with a clear proposal for change. Moreover, they set out to have that proposal implemented by the federal government. What they wanted and eventually got was a central bank for Canada. Yet the campaign for the bank, though successful, must be viewed as a modest first step in the minds of the economics community. They campaigned hard for it not because they saw it as a panacea for depression but because it was the one feasible step that could be taken domestically on monetary matters.

The rapid development of support for the central bank has to be set against two historical backdrops. The first is the decline in prices that occurred during the period 1929–1933. Declining prices, though they helped those with savings, severely aggravated the problems of groups like farmers who were faced with large fixed debts and declining income. Second, there was a strong tradition in North America of responding to this predicament, especially within the agrarian sector, with demands for deliberate inflation of prices. Some of the most powerful waves of rural protest had gained their momentum from the cry for currency reform. Stretching from the Greenback and free silver movements of nineteenth-century United States through the Non-Partisan and Progressive movements of Canada, "easy money" had been a frequent cry on the frontier. In the 1930s the theme was revived most persistently in the writings of Major C.H. Douglas, the Social Crediter whose teachings were appearing with ever increasing regularity among the splintered ranks of farm parties in the Canadian West.

Though a recurring theme in Canadian and American history, the idea of easy money had never been acceptable in traditional business and academic circles. For the economists the ideal was price stability because, as has been pointed out, it removed one more source of disequilibrium. For the banker and businessman not only was sound money thought good for the economy but there was a strong ethical belief that a contract between the debtor and creditor was violated, at least morally, when the value of money changed dramatically. The gold standard, because it restrained expansion in money supplies, provided the desirable stability.

Yet as has been indicated, by the early 1930s there was no clear choice between a stable gold system and some other less favoured approach to the monetary structure of the nation. The former was in a state of collapse. Economists had to find some means of achieving the monetary stability that had been so routine before the war.[62] The international situation was so complex and chaotic that few held out much hope that it would be resolved in the near future. Domestically, however, improvement seemed possible with the formation of a Canadian central bank to oversee matters of currency, credit, and foreign exchange rates. It was thus not economic theory that had altered but the circumstances. A stable price level and a sound monetary structure remained the goal of the economic profession. What had altered was the belief that such stability could be achieved only if the government became directly involved in monetary matters.

As with so many other changes in Canadian economic activities, this one must be traced not only from the Depression but from World War I. For until 1914 the Canadian government had, as one writer has put it, seen "the preservation of the established external value of the dollar" as "the sole monetary objective of the government."[63] Banks, though restricted in terms of procedures for note issue, necessary reserves, and other matters, were generally expected to handle most other monetary and exchange functions. Generally the system did not work badly and early suggestions for change were scorned as dangerous. "In this pre-1914 period," as one historian has noted, "bankers and government officials enjoyed an easy and confident support."[64] Moreover, with the economic profession in Canada just beginning to develop, it was the banking profession that had the reputation as the real experts of the economy among government officials.[65] Individuals like Edmund Walker of the Bank of Commerce were widely respected within the intellectual community and the government for his advice. Indeed, when the government of Sir Robert Borden appointed "near banker" Thomas White as minister of finance it received high praise from those interested in sound planning and reform.[66] Thus the banking community played a central role as the arbiter of economic wisdom and financial planning in the years before 1914, just as the economic community would in the period after 1930.

Ironically, it was under the administration of White that changes began to occur. The necessities of war forced the government to alter previously acceptable arrangements and to pass the 1914 Finance Act. This act, which tied bank deposits either to gold or to dominion notes, eased pressures on the gold standard by effectively suspending it. It was touted as a war measure but remained in place when peace returned. The result was a contradiction in dominion monetary structures. The system no longer operated automatically because it was not based purely on gold, yet government had neither the power nor the expertise to manage the monetary system of the nation.[67] Over the next few years various amendments only patched up a rather cumbersome and inefficient structure of monetary management.[68]

By the 1930s positions on the existing situation had hardened. On the one side were the great majority of commercial bankers who felt that whatever the shortcomings of the Finance Act, it at least left the basic decisions on monetary and credit matters to those best qualified to make those decisions— themselves. Moreover, any central bank was likely to be structured in such a way as to compete with them or at the very least, remove their long-standing privilege of note issue. Most important of all was the fear that a government-controlled central bank would, whatever the intentions of the government of the day, eventually become a pawn in political moves to inflate the currency and thereby undermine the soundness of the currency. It was a formidable lobby, especially given the strong reputation of Canadian banks in government circles, a reputation enhanced by their success in surviving the economic collapse.

Opposing the bankers were the majority of Canadian economists. Their basic criticism of monetary policy in the dominion was, in the words of Toronto professor A.F.W. Plumptre, that "it did not exist."[69] A group of Queen's economists termed the Finance Act, which was supposed to provide a framework for that monetary policy, a "dangerous piece of legislation" on two grounds: first, because it required no reserve for notes issued under its provisions and, second, because it was under the control of the Department of Finance, a politically controlled body which could manipulate the bank for political purposes.[70] For Canadian economists the management of credit in Canada was too important to be left in the hands of commercial banks even if, as most economists accepted, they were generally competent in their operations. "The world in which we live . . . is a very different one from that of pre-war days and it is doubtful if we could recover the environment in which our pre-war monetary legislation operated."[71]

In theoretical terms, Canadian economists saw a central bank as a potentially important agent of government economic policy. The function of a central bank is to determine the quantity of credit that will be made available by the commercial banks to the business public, noted the Queen's Department of Economics, but that function could operate in numerous ways.[72] The issue of notes, reserve requirements, open market operations, and other activities could make the bank a major force in the determination of price levels and interest rates within the country. Moreover, the bank could operate so as to stabilize foreign exchange rates and thus affect Canada's international trading relationships. It was, all in all, a very powerful tool to aid in the control of business cycles. As C.W. Hewetson of the University of Alberta commented, "in the light of our present knowledge of economic matters it would appear that the greatest hope of bringing trade fluctuations under some measure of control lies in the artificial regulation of bank credit with a view to greater stability of the general price level."[73] The drive for the bank among Canadian economists thus indicated a growing belief that, given the right tools, business cycles could indeed be manipulated. Macro-economic management, so long submerged by the rhetoric of self-correction and inevitability, was beginning to surface in Canadian economic writing.

Canadian economists thus stood pitted against the bankers in the debate over a central bank.[74] It is an interesting indication of the growing power of the new discipline that the economists found themselves with as much access to key figures in the political world as did the leaders of the banking community. Thus, for example, the Queen's economists, proponents of a strong bank, found various ways in which to steer discussion in the right direction. Initially, of course, they had access to O.D. Skelton, who was himself sympathetic to a central bank and who had the ear of both Prime Minister Bennett and other leading politicians. Further, Queen's political scientist and Liberal party advisor Norman Rogers introduced his colleague C.A. Curtis to Mackenzie King as an expert on banking. Before long Curtis delivered a memorandum on central banking to the leader of the opposition that King used to good effect in the House of Commons. It was, he said, "an excellent memo, most helpful."[75] Most important, however, was the 1932 appointment of Clark to the deputy ministership of finance. As with so many of his Queen's colleagues, he was committed to the formation of a central bank. As the man charged under the Finance Act of 1923 with responsibility for its regulations, he was in the perfect position to argue that the act was deficient.[76] Over the next two years he did everything he could to ensure that the government adopted the view of the Queen's economists.

By 1933 the economists had gained the upper hand over the bankers. The Liberal party had come out in favour of the principle of a central bank while Bennett's Conservatives, noting the drift of public opinion in the country, appointed a royal commission to investigate the matter. At the annual Canadian Political Science Association meeting that year Clark found a great deal of sympathy for a bank and, as it was up to him to find a secretary for the royal commission, he naturally looked among his supportive colleagues. The man he chose was A.F.W. Plumptre of Toronto. As Plumptre had been involved with Curtis and others in Massey's study groups on central banking, his pro-bank views were well known. The commission was thus given a gentle prod in the right direction by the placement of a pro-bank economist in a key position.[77]

The Royal Commission on Banking, or Macmillan Commission, saw the next stage played out in the debate between the old and new elites of economic experts. The great majority of bankers remained opposed to a central bank and argued that the existing system, while far from perfect, had proven its worth over the years. The tone was set on the first day of hearings when the president of the Canadian Bankers Association concluded that the system "had provided Canada with a financial structure which is at the same time extremely strong, and singularly flexible; with a structure well adapted to the needs of the country. . . ."[78] As the hearings moved across the country, banker after banker pointed with some pride to the accomplishments of their companies and, in explicit fashion, challenged the need for a central bank.

On the other side the great majority of economists called the formation of a central bank a necessity. Most enthusiastic were the Queen's economists, Mackintosh, Curtis, and F.A. Knox, who urged wide latitude for the central bank in its activities and significant powers over commercial banks. Others were slightly more cautious but there was widespread support for the principle from men like Hurd of Brandon College, Elliot and Hewetson of Alberta, and Carrothers, Topping, and Drummond of British Columbia.[79] There were opponents, of course, but in a way the reasons for opposition help prove that the preponderance of economic thought in Canada favoured a central bank. First, of seventeen economists who appeared before the commission, only four opposed the bank. Second, two of these opponents. Edouard Montpetit and M. Gregoire of Laval, seemed to be as concerned with centralized government control and its impact on Quebec as they were the economic functions of the bank. Their monetary views were thus affected by their desire to preserve provincial autonomy.[80] The other two opponents were men with somewhat unorthodox views. Michell of McMaster was about the only bi-metallist among academic economists in Canada and it was his view that bi-metallism rather than a central bank would resolve any monetary problems. Even Swanson of Saskatchewan, an extremely conservative individual who looked to aesthetic solutions to the Depression, admitted that changes were needed.[81]

In the end, the preponderance of economists won out over the preponderance of bankers. The Macmillan Commission's analysis of the problem and limitations of the Finance Act and its operation in Canada paralleled in all essentials the viewpoint of the majority of economists testifying before it. The act, the commission concluded, "did not provide Canada with the organization needed to undertake the task which the maintenance of the restored gold standard implied."[82] Only a central bank could provide the necessary objectivity, expertise, and facilities to provide the sort of credit management that was needed in modern circumstances. The decision was a close one, however. Two of the five commissioners, Sir Thomas White and Beaudry Leman, dissented from the report, believing that a central bank would hinder rather than facilitate monetary objectives on Canada.[83] Given such a narrow victory of the principle of a central bank, the role of the professional economics community, both within and without the commission, may well have been decisive.

In 1934 the Conservative government established the Bank of Canada and, though there was considerable controversy to come over the relationship of the bank to the government and other matters, the important battle had been won. The economics profession had demonstrated the degree of influence it had in Ottawa. Clifford Clark then sought to consolidate that influence by ensuring that the bank become an agency of economic planning run by economists. What was needed in the way of a governor, he told Bennett, was not a banker but an economist. "The major problem of central banking is not one of routine administration but rather of economic interpretation and monetary principles."[84]

An economist was not appointed. Instead the government brought in Graham Towers, assistant general manager of the Royal Bank and one of the few commercial bankers who had not been opposed to a central bank. Though not an academic economist, Towers was a man regarded with some respect within political and economic circles as an innovative banker.[85] He also had credentials in economics, having studied under Leacock at McGill and being one of the few bankers in Canada to belong to the Canadian Political Science Association. Finally, he was thirty-seven at the time of his appointment and he possessed characteristics similar to the group of economists with whom he would have to work.[86] Towers' appointment did not mean that the economics profession was without influence on the Bank of Canada. On the contrary, the bank provided a whole new area of recruitment for bright, well-trained intellectuals. Here, as in so many cases, the personnel were drawn from a specific social-intellectual class with common acquaintances and similar university backgrounds. At the centre of this group in the bank was Alex Skelton, Rhodes scholar and son of O.D. Skelton, who was hired to head up the bank's research department. The brilliant and somewhat erratic Skelton would attempt over the next few years to ensure that the bank was imbued with reformist zeal. In future years the brightest and best students of the Canadian economics profession found their way into the bank. Men like John Deutsch and Louis Rasminsky both ensured that the influence gained in the thirties would remain intact in the war and postwar worlds.

For all the potential of the bank, however, the economics community recognized that this institution would not, in itself, provide sufficient control over the economy to make a real difference in the Depression. Caution, it was sensed from the beginning, was more likely to be the tendency of the bank than a full-fledged assault on the monetary problems of the nation. "In the present state of the science of economics and the art of central banking there has been achieved no great exactness in the control of price levels through central bank operations. The direction in which the control operates is well understood, but the degrees to which it operates are not to be predicted accurately."[87] Thus, even those who most strongly advocated the creation of the bank did not expect too much from the institution. It was just as well. Towers and his senior staff were carefully orthodox in their monetary policy and cautious enough not to push the bank into new ventures too quickly. Even with the arrival of the *General Theory*, the governor of the bank remained concerned lest enthusiasm for monetary reform lead to debasement of the currency. As Towers warned, "inflation was a form of taxation" and one that hit fixed incomes the most.[88] It was thus to be some time before the bank moved into the full range of monetary operations.[89] Other measures were patently necessary if the nation were to take full advantage of the possibilities of economic control of the economy.

o

One obvious alternative possibility for resolving the problems posed by the Depression was to tackle the issue on the assumption that disequilibrium was the basic factor in determining the nature of the crisis. Perhaps steps could be taken to remove some of the forces creating or continuing that disequilibrium and thus allow the business cycle to move toward full employment and production. The most obvious tool to deal with disequilibrium in current circumstances was the concept of pump priming—the injection of funds into a slack economy in order to create jobs for workers and business for employers. This was a far from radical proposal for, as has been mentioned, the concept of the government as a "flywheel" had been around from before World War I. Later proposals had become relatively sophisticated, arguing for what would later be known as a shelf of public works, planned and ready to go should economic circumstances warrant. As early as 1930 Keynes, testifying before the British Macmillan Commission, had advocated massive government works as a response to the downturn.[90] Moreover, the use of public works to combat the Depression was an issue of some immediate importance. The Conservative government passed a series of public works measures, first becoming involved directly and then providing a series of grants to the provinces. Thus both as a practical policy and as a theoretical tool of contra-cyclical economic management, Canadian economists were well aware of the use of government funds to encourage recovery.

Yet the reaction of the Canadian economists toward such schemes reveals the conservative side of the profession. If anything, economists were even cooler than politicians toward such large-scale expenditures in the name of recovery. They recognized that if the pubic works expenditures were to be meaningful they would have to be on a large scale. Thus, for example, the $50 million proposed by Bennett in 1934 was criticized by Gilbert Jackson and others as insufficient to prime the pump. "We must spend on a large enough scale."[91] At the same time, economists were as convinced as the most cautious backbencher that government spending was dangerously out of control. World War I, they argued, had pushed the total Canadian debt load to a dangerously high level. In addition, the creation of the Canadian National Railway system and other modern acquisitions had aggravated the situation. Then, with the Depression and the decline in government revenues, the debts, which remained fixed, became a millstone on the Canadian economy.[92] Thus, although deficit financing was an accepted economic principle, as was the use of public works for recovery, Canadian economists doubted whether they were desirable in Canada at the present time. "The increasing proportion of national incomes which is now being diverted by governments, together with the increasing burden of debt charges," warned economist D.C. MacGregor in 1934, "raises the question of whether or not public finance is approaching the limits of its effectiveness and soundness within a capitalistic economy."[93] Jackson, after criticizing Bennett's public works expenditures as too small to have an effect, argued not for greater expenditure but for the "ruthless balancing of all budgets, governmental and municipal."[94] R.H. Coats asked with concern of the various unemployment insurance schemes being promoted how they "could possibly avoid bankruptcy."[95]

The orthodox economic viewpoint was best revealed in the actions of Clifford Clark in his first years as deputy minister of finance. Clark was well aware of the possibilities of deficit financing, having trained under Skelton, but as with the majority of economists was cautious about its use in Canada. For him wartime debts and problems brought on by German reparation and currency instability lay at the bottom of the Depression. Frivolous or excessive government expenditure would only aggravate a problem that was already extremely serious. Fiscal conservatism continued to be the style of the Department of Finance even after it came under the control of its first professional economist.[96]

If it was not possible to spend one's way out of the Depression, then the question was whether some structural or institutional reforms might be possible to improve the situation. This view was strongly favoured by non-economists among Canadian intellectuals and co-incided with the view that the Depression represented either the end of capitalism or at the very least a crisis in its development. Not surprisingly, the social democratic League for Social Reconstruction argued that the Depression was linked to the evolution of capitalism. Years of growth and innovation as new technologies developed and new lands opened had now been replaced by depression in the era of "monopoly capitalism." Serious maldistribution of wealth and problems of overproduction would continue to plague the present system. Only a basic reform of institutions and the development of "socialized monopoly" would remedy the basic problems of the Canadian economy. "Planlessness, rigidities and above all the restriction of markets enforced by pursuit of profit produces a situation in which consumption chronically lags behind capacity to produce."[97]

Even those who rejected socialism often accepted the critique of capitalism and the argument that basic structural changes were necessary T.W.L.

MacDermot and Francis Hankin, both Liberals and friends of Brooke Claxton, F.R. Scott, and other Montreal reformers, wrote *Recovery by Control* in 1933. Drawing its inspiration from the Roosevelt New Deal, its basic premise was that the only way to overcome the blind forces of "economic anarchy" was to curb capitalist excesses in the name of social security and stability. Uncontrolled private ownership would have to yield to public interests. Pointing to the Post Office, CBC, Ontario Hydro, and other publicly controlled operations, they argued that the basic principles in operation in these bodies should be widely extended. The reason was essentially economic. In spite of Adam Smith, they concluded, the reconciliation of self-interest among millions of individuals was essentially impossible. The invisible hand was a myth. Thus the world was forced to operate in ruthless competition, which created maldistribution of wealth and gave "rise to the violent fluctuations in the purchasing power of consumer. That it is which bedevils economic security."[98]

The failure of business to prevent the Depression, and the seeming inability of the self-righting mechanisms of classic economics to work, all prompted this argument that structural change and ongoing government involvement in the economy were necessary. Many economists were coming to the same conclusion. On the National Employment Commission, appointed by Mackenzie King on his return to power, it was the one professional economist, W.A. Mackintosh, who argued strongly for a system of unemployment insurance.[99] In the Department of Finance, Clark was throughout the decade a strong advocate of improved housing programs in order to assist potential homeowners and a construction industry in a state of near collapse. At the same time, economics was still a relatively conservative discipline. This mix of conservatism and reform was revealed in 1934 when the Canadian Institute of International Affairs held a study group on the Canadian economy in Montreal. Included was a cross-section of Canadian economists with such well-known individuals as Innis, Vincent Bladen, Plumptre, Robert McQueen, Britnell, and H.R. Kemp. Also present were non-economist intellectuals such as Norman Rogers, Frank Underhill, and a young Manitoba historian, J.W. Pickersgill. Various solutions were debated, with lively disagreements as to whether Underhill's defence of "radical political and economic reconstruction" made sense. In the end, though the group refused to accept Underhill's more radical proposals, there was a strong feeling that social and structural reforms were necessary if recovery was to take place. The marketplace could not be left to work the disequilibrium out of the economy. Instead, a new view was developing. Disequilibrium must be managed through direct and ongoing intervention. The conference decided in favour of a national planning council "with the implication of a considerable degree of social and economic planning."[100]

The commitment to the principle of planning as well as to the various specific measures revealed a profession that had by the mid-1930s both a theoretical perspective and a policy-making influence that would help shape the nature of the so-called Keynesian revolution in Canada. In terms of theory, Canadian economists had, before the publication of the *General*

Theory, despaired of classical views of the economic recovery process. As a result they were ready to accept plausible new theories and were especially receptive to theories that echoed their own conviction that a greater degree of government intervention was a necessary part of economic policy in the modern era. Keynes, for all his complexities and for all the debates he would bring forth, thus faced an audience in Canada that was amenable to change.

From the practical point of view, economists were in a relatively good position to influence the course of public policy in the years after Keynes's *General Theory*. It was true that economists lamented then, as they lament now, the failure of politicians to take their proffered advice. Yet within the new Bank of Canada, the Department of Finance, and the political parties themselves modern economic thought and those who practised it were much more influential than they had been even a decade before. The very fact that young Keynesians like R.B. Bryce could enter the department in 1938 and, within a year, have sufficient influence to be involved in drafting a federal budget with definite Keynesian overtones reveals something of the way in which modern economic thought was operating near the centre of power.[101] By World War II, Keynesian thought was beginning to play a role in the ongoing transformation of the state in Canada but the groundwork for that transformation had been well begun by the time the *General Theory* reached the classrooms and cities of North America.

NOTES

1. The best study of the changing nature of the civil service is J.L. Granatstein, *The Ottawa Men: The Civil Service Mandarins, 1935–1957* (Toronto, 1982).

2. See Robin Harris, *A History of Higher Education in Canada 1663–1960* (Toronto, 1976); S.E.D. Shortt, *The Search for an Ideal: Six Intellectuals in an Age of Transition* (Toronto, 1976); Ian Drummond, *Political Economy at Toronto: A History of the Department 1888–1982* (Toronto, 1983).

3. *Census of Canada*, 1931, vol. 1, table 83

4. These statistics are drawn from two sources: *Yearbook of the Universities of the Empire*, 1929–35 and obituaries in the *Canadian Journal of Economics and Political Science* (hereafter *CJEPS*) between 1935 and 1967.

5. Canadian Political Science Association (hereafter CPSA), *Annual Report*, vol. 1 (1930), 1.

6. Public Archives of Canada (hereafter PAC), MG28, Papers of the Canadian Political Science Association, vol. 1, S.A. Cudmore to C.A. Curtis, 20 May 1932, talks about efforts to form links with other bodies. F.A. Knox to Cudmore has a membership list. See also the Canadian Institute of International Affairs meeting of 1934 on the economy with participation by economists such as Gilbert Jackson. A.F.W. Plumptre, D.C. MacGregor, H.A. Innis, and others. H.A. Innis and A.F.W. Plumptre, *The Canadian Economy and Its Problems* (Toronto, 1934), appendices IV and V.

7. Vincent Bladen, "A Journal is Born," *CJEPS* 26, 1 (Feb. 1960).

8. H.A. Innis, "The Teaching of Economic History in Canada," *Contributions to Canadian Economics* 2 (1929): 58.

9. Drummond, *Political Economy*, 21.

10. Queen's University Archives, W.A. Mackintosh Papers, Mackintosh to

Skelton, 1 June 1925; Mackintosh to Principal Taylor, 30 June 1925. Skelton was furious about the failure of the principal to appoint Mackintosh, commenting that "after wrecking the English Department it has been felt it would be invidious not to wreck the Economic Department also." Skelton to Mackintosh, 9 June 1925.

11. C. Berger, *The Writing of Canadian History* (Toronto, 1976), ch. 5.

12. See also Barry Ferguson, "The New Political Economy and Canadian Liberal Democratic Thought: Queen's University 1900–1925" (PhD diss., York University, 1982), ch. 8. He argues that the interest in the West was part of a long-standing tradition at Queen's and an attempt to discover the roots of modern democracy.

13. W.C. Clark, "The Country Elevator in the Canadian West," *Queen's Quarterly* 24, 1 (July 1916); W.A. Mackintosh, "The Canadian Wheat Pools," *Queen's University Bulletin of the Department of History and Political Science* 51 (Nov. 1925); and *Agricultural Co-operation in Western Canada* (Toronto, 1924); H. Michell, "Profit Sharing and Producers' Co-operation in Canada," *Queen's University Bulletin of the Departments of History and Political and Economic Science* 26 (Jan. 1918).

14. D.A. MacGibbon, "Economic Factor Affecting the Settlement of the Prairie Provinces," *Pioneer Settlement* (1932); P.C. Armstrong, *Wheat* (Toronto, 1930).

15. Ferguson, "The New Political Economy," 329.

16. Perhaps the best known of these studies was Harold Innis, *A History of the Canadian Pacific Railway* (London, 1923), but see also as examples James Mavor, *Niagara in Politics: A Critical Account of the Ontario Hydro-Electric Commission* (New York, 1925); W.T. Jackman, *The Economics of Transportation* (Toronto, 1926); Eugene Forsey, "Economic and Social Aspects of the Nova Scotia Coal Industry," *McGill University Economic Studies* 5. Good bibliographies of publications in these years may be obtained in the volumes of the *Canadian Historical Review*, beginning in 1922, and the University of Toronto publication *Contributions to Canadian Economics*, running from 1928 to 1933.

17. Eric Roll, *A History of Economic Thought* (London, 1973), 303–11.

18. PAC, J.W. Dafoe Papers, M75, Coats to Dafoe, 7 March 1932.

19. Robert Lekachman, *The Age of Keynes* (New York, 1966), 78–81.

20. D.A. MacGibbon, *An Introduction to Economics for Canadian Readers* (Toronto, 1924). The 1935 edition showed the impact of the Depression and included a section on the business cycle. It is also relevant to apply the comments on Carver and Hansen to Canada as that work was a standard textbook in Canadian universities. See Drummond, *Political Economy*. E.J. Hanson, *The Department of Economics of the University of Alberta: A History* (Edmonton, 1983), 15, indicates that no Canadian textbooks were used at the University of Alberta in sample years during the 1920s.

21. A.F.W. Plumptre and A.E. Gilroy, "Review of Economics Texts," *Contributions to Canadian Economics* 7 (1934): 124.

22. Lekachman, *The Age of Keynes*, 81.

23. See on this theme Thomas Haskell, *The Emergence of Professional Social Science: The American Social Science Association and the Crisis of Authority* (Urbana, IL, 1977).

24. PAC, Charlotte Whitton Papers, vol. 19, "Dependency and Organized Relief Work."

25. Grace Towers, "Is Poverty an Economic Ill," *Social Welfare* 9, 7 (April 1927).

26. F.W. Learmouth, "Social Effects of Unemployment," *Social Welfare* 4, 5 (1 Feb. 1922).

27. H.A. Innis, "The Penetrative Power of the Price System," *CJEPS* 4, 3 (Aug. 1938): 318.

28. W.W. Swanson, *Depression and the Way Out* (Toronto, 1931), 141.

29. University of Toronto Archives, H.A. Innis Papers, vol. 1. G. Britnell to Innis, 27 Sept. 1937.

30. H. Innis, "Government Ownership and the Canadian Scene" in *Canadian Problems as Seen by Twenty Outstanding Men of Canada* (Toronto, 1933), 73.

31. For good examples see Michael Stewart, *Keynes and After* (London, 1972), and Lekachman, *The Age of Keynes*.

32. Dafoe Papers, M76, Dafoe to Harry Sifton, 11 Jan. 1934.

33. See D.A. MacGibbon, "Economics and the Social Order," *CJEPS* 2, 1 (Feb. 1936).

34. In this sense what was occurring in Canada fit Thomas Kuhn's paradigm on changes in scientific theory. See his *The Structure of Scientific Revolutions* (Chicago, 1970). See also Don Patinkin, *Anticipations of the General Theory* (Chicago, 1982).

35. Alfred Marshall, *Principles of Economics*, 8th ed. (London, 1930), viii.

36. W.C. Clark, "Business Cycles and the Depression of 1920–1," Queen's University *Bulletin of the Departments of History and Political and Economic Science* 40 (Aug. 1921). The classic description of the business cycle written in the interwar period comes in Wesley Mitchell, *Business Cycles: The Problem and Its Setting* (New York, 1927).

37. Alfred Marshall, *Money, Credit and Commerce* (London, 1923), book 4.

38. Ibid., 47.

39. Shortt, *The Search for an Ideal*, ch. 8; A.B. McKillop, *A Disciplined Intelligence* (Montreal, 1979), 216–28.

40. On King's idealism see Paul Craven, *"An Impartial Umpire": Industrial Relations and the Canadian State 1900–1911* (Toronto, 1980), chs. 2–3.

41. Sidney Fine, *Laissez Faire and the General Welfare State* (Ann Arbor, 1956), 48–49. The closest example in Canada would be the elder James Mavor, but his idealism always moderated his laissez faire.

42. See, for example, S.J. Maclean, "Social Amelioration and University Settlement," *Canadian Magazine* 8, 6 (April 1897); Adam Shortt, "Current Events," *Queen's Quarterly* 7, 3 (Jan. 1904); James Mavor, "The Relation of Economic Study to Public and Private Charity," *Annals of the American Academy of Political and Social Science* 4 (1893–94).

43. O.D. Skelton, "Current Events," *Queen's Quarterly* 16, 4 (April 1909).

44. See, for example, Bryce Stewart, "The Problem of Unemployment," *Social Welfare* 3, 8 (March 1921); J.B. Alexander, "Business Depressions," *Canadian Bankers* 34, 4 (July 1927).

45. E.S. Bates, *Planned Nationalism: Canada's Effort* (Toronto, 1935): W.C. Clark, "Current Events," *Queen's Quarterly* 38, 4 (Autumn 1931); Gilbert Jackson, "The World in Which the Central Bank Will Work" in *The Canadian Economy and Its Problems*, ed. Innis and Plumptre (Toronto, 1934); Bank of Nova Scotia, *Monthly Review* (March 1934).

46. J.A. Aikin, *Economic Power for Canada* (Toronto, 1930), 32–39; W.W. Swanson, *Depression and the Way Out* (Toronto, 1931), 3–8, 14.

47. Bates, *Planned Nationalism*, 87.

48. Gilbert Jackson, *An Economist's Confession of Faith* (Toronto, 1935), 29, 33–34.

49. Harold Innis, "Economics for Demos," *University of Toronto Quarterly* 3, 3 (Nov. 1933): 392.

50. "Central Banking and Business Recovery," *Canadian Banker* 38, 4 (July 1931).

51. H. Michell, "Monetary Reconstruction," *CJEPS* 8, 3 (Aug. 1942).

52. W.C. Clark, "The Flight from the Gold Standard," *Queen's Quarterly* 38, 4 (Autumn 1931): 762. See also Queen's University Archives, Norman Rogers Papers, box 1, Steven Cartwright to Rogers, 19 Jan. 1933, attached memorandum.

53. B.K. Sandwell, "The Plague of the Amateur Economists," *Canadian Banker* 39, 3 (April 1932): 340.

54. In terms of the quantity theory of money developed by American Irving Fisher in the years before the Depression, M (money) × V (Velocity with which money changes hands) = P (prices) × T (level of transactions). Since P increased, either T had to decrease proportionately or M and/or V increase proportionately. The implication is that in the 1920s V increased but that in the longer term the quantity of money was insufficient and the velocity of transactions unstable. In 1929 both P and T began to decline.

55. Jackson, *Economist's Confession of Faith*, 34.

56. H.A. Innis, "The Penetrative Power of the Price System," *CJEPS* 4, 3 (Aug. 1938). See also his introduction to Innis and Plumptre, *The Canadian Economy and Its Problems.*

57. W.B. Hurd, "The Dilemma of Mass Production," *Canadian Banker* 39, 2 (Jan. 1932): 193.

58. Stephen Leacock, "What is Left of Adam Smith," *CJEPS* 1, 1 (Feb. 1935).

59. Conservative Party, *The Premier Speaks to the People* (Ottawa, 1935). A copy is available in PAC, Ian Mackenzie Papers, MG27, vol. 42.

60. Hurd, "The Dilemma of Mass Production," 197.

61. Innis, "The Penetrative Powers of the Price System."

62. For a good expression of the orthodox position see Bank of Canada Archives, Graham Towers Papers, Memorandum no. 17, June 1936.

63. R.C. MacIvor, *Canadian Monetary, Banking and Fiscal Development* (Toronto, 1958), 101.

64. Linda Grayson, "The Formation of the Bank of Canada" (PhD diss., University of Toronto, 1974), 7.

65. Ibid., 10.

66. R.C. Brown, *Robert Laird Borden: A Biography* (Toronto, 1977), 1: 200, notes that White was the choice of the Toronto group headed by Sifton, Edmund Walker, and Willison. See also John English, *The Decline of Politics* (Toronto, 1977), 52.

67. MacIvor, *Monetary, Banking and Fiscal Development*, 102–3.

68. Statutes of Canada, Finance Act of 1914, c. 3.

69. A.F.W. Plumptre, "Canadian Monetary Policy" in *The Canadian Economy and Its Problems*, 165.

70. Queen's University Department of Political Science and Economics, "The Proposal for a Central Bank," *Queen's Quarterly* 40, 3 (Aug. 1933): 434.

71. Ibid., 439.

72. Ibid., 425.

73. Royal Commission on Banking and Currency (Macmillan Commission), *Proceedings*, 3: 1053.

74. There were, of course, exceptions, with some bankers in favour of a central bank and some economists against it.

75. PAC, MG26, J13, Mackenzie King Diaries, 30 Sept. 1932; King Papers, J4, vol. 52, file 303, contains the report by Curtis to the Liberal Party, which recommended a central bank. See also C.A. Curtis, "Credit Control in Canada," *Proceedings of the Canadian Political Science Association* (1930), as one of many published pieces by Curtis supporting a central bank.

76. Clark supported a central bank as far back as the early 1920s when he did some work for W.C. Good on the idea. See Grayson, "The Formation of the Bank of Canada," 53.

77. On Clark's influence on the appointment of Plumptre see ibid., 145. My thanks to R.B. Bryce who notes that the mood of the CPSA was, by this time, overwhelmingly in favour of the bank. Bryce, in turn, was told by Clark. On the Liberal study groups see Rogers Papers, box 1, Steven Cartwright to Rogers, 7 Oct. 1932, 19 Jan. 1933. Plumptre was less than neutral even after he took the position, writing an anonymous article for the *Financial Post* challenging the testimony of the bankers. See article by "Economist" in the *Financial Post* of 16 Dec. 1933. A marginal note by Clark in PAC, Department of Finance Records, RG19, vol. 3974, identifies the author as Plumptre.

78. Macmillan Commission, *Proceedings*, 1: 101, testimony of J.A. Macleod.

79. For a breakdown of commission testimony see A.F.W. Plumptre, "The Evidence Presented to the Canadian Macmillan Commission," *CJEPS* 2, 1 (Feb. 1936).

80. Macmillan Commission, *Proceedings*, 3: 2554–75. Ironically, Montpetit was later recommended for the position of deputy governor of the bank. See PAC, R.B. Bennett Papers, M962, J.A. Barrette to Bennett, 3 Dec. 1934.

81. Macmillan Commission, *Proceedings*, 3: 1357–95.

82. *Report of the Royal Commission on Banking and Currency* (Ottawa, 1933), 59.

83. Ibid., 85–89, 95–97.

84. Bennett Papers, vol. 95, Clark to Bennett, 27 Jan. 1934.

85. Ian Drummond, *The Floating Pound and Sterling Area 1931–1939* (Cambridge, 1981), 60.

86. Granatstein, *The Ottawa Men*, 52–53.

87. Queen's University Department of Political and Economic Science, "The Proposal for a Central Bank," 426.

88. Towers Papers, Memorandum no. 17, June 1936.

89. Thomas Courchene, "The Interaction Between Economic Theory and Bank of Canada Policy" in *Economic Policy Advising in Canada*, ed. David C. Smith (Montreal, 1981). See, however, Towers Papers, Memorandum no. 177, re "letter from Alvin Hansen to Stuart Garson," 31 Aug. 1938. There are indications that the bank was a little more activist than Courchene argues.

90. Lekachman, *The Age of Keynes*, 69–76.

91. Jackson, *An Economist's Confession of Faith*, 46–47.

92. B.K. Sandwell, "One Good Thing About Private Ownership," *Canadian Banker* 39, 1 (Oct. 1931).

93. D.C. MacGregor, "Outline of the Position of Public Finance" in *The Canadian Economy and Its Problems*, 3.

94. Jackson, *Economist's Confession of Faith*, 51.

95. James Struthers, *No Fault of Their Own: Unemployment and the Canadian Welfare State* (Toronto, 1983), 232.

96. See W.C. Clark, "What's Wrong with Us," *Institute Bulletin, Journal of the Professional Institute of the Public Service* 10 (Dec. 1931). A copy is available in PAC, Department of Finance Records, vol. 3993.

97. The League for Social Reconstruction, *Social Planning for Canada* (Toronto, 1935), 125, 195.

98. Francis Hankin and T.W.L. MacDermot, *Recovery by Control: A Diagnosis of the Relations Between Government and Business in Canada* (Toronto, 1933), 272.

99. Struthers, *No Fault of Their Own*, 141–84, has the best description of the activities of this committee.

100. K.W. Taylor, "A Summary" in *The Canadian Economy and Its Problems*, 195. See appendix 3 for the participants in the conference.

101. See Department of Finance Records, vol. 3444, Monteith Douglas to Bryce, 14 Sept. 1939; Bryce to Walter Salant, 12 Oct. 1939.

CANADIAN FABIANS: THE
WORK AND THOUGHT OF
HARRY CASSIDY AND
LEONARD MARSH, 1930–1945◇

ALLAN IRVING

o

During the Depression and war years, 1930–1945, Canada became a welfare state. Before 1930, the individual had been regarded as being almost totally responsible for his own well-being; after 1945, the state was seen as having an increasing obligation to provide a minimum standard of welfare for the population. Canadian historian Michael Bliss has observed that, although the change to a welfare state in Canada was a development of great importance, "very little has been written about the nature of this transition, the conceptions underlying it, the social, economic, and political environment in which it took place, or the men involved."[1] This article seeks to redress in part the scarcity of writing about the individuals involved by examining aspects of the work and thought, during those years 1930–1945, of two of the most energetic exponents of welfare reform: Harry Cassidy and Leonard Marsh.

In the 1930s, Cassidy and Marsh conducted or were involved in a number of pioneering social surveys. The range of subjects scrutinized in these surveys—unemployment, housing, labour conditions, health—indicates that the two men were "fully employed, indeed over-employed, in the desperate struggle to develop the specialized understanding of Canadian society and its problems that would be essential to the development of modern social welfare legislation."[2] Their work and thought during this decade culminated in 1943 with the publication of Cassidy's *Social Security and Reconstruction in Canada* and of Marsh's *Report on Social Security for*

◇ *Canadian Journal of Social Work Education/Revue canadienne d'éducation en service social* 7, 1 (1981): 7–28. Reprinted with permission.

Canada, both of which analysed the inadequate response to current social requirements and recommended the establishment in Canada of a comprehensive system of social security.

Both Harry Cassidy and Leonard Marsh were members of the League for Social Reconstruction, which came into existence in the dreary Depression winter of 1932 and which, as is generally acknowledged, modelled itself on the English Fabian Society.[3] The review of Cassidy and Marsh undertaken here traces the Fabian strain in their work, in order to determine just how significant Fabian ideas were for their particular conception of social welfare as social reform. Throughout, a thematic approach is adopted, and no attempt is made to describe or analyse in detail their various works. The conclusion is reached that they were both representative Canadian Fabians, and the implications of this perspective for social welfare are discussed briefly.

Harry Cassidy (1900–1951) completed his undergraduate education at the University of British Columbia and received his PhD in economics from the Robert Brookings Graduate School of Economics and Government, Washington, DC, in 1926. In 1929, after three years as an assistant professor of economics at the University of North Carolina and Rutgers University, he came to the Department of Social Science (which, in 1941, became the School of Social Work) at the University of Toronto, where his creative work in the social welfare field began. He remained there as an assistant professor until 1934, when, enticed by the reform-oriented Liberal government that had been elected the previous year, he went to British Columbia as director of social welfare. From 1939 to 1944, he was a professor and then dean of the School of Social Welfare at the University of California, and from 1945 until his early death in 1951, he was director of the School of Social Work at the University of Toronto. Cassidy was involved in a great many other activities during his career; for example, he served as director of training for the United Nations Relief and Rehabilitation Administration (UNRRA), 1944–1945, and as technical advisor on social security to the Canadian Department of National Health and Welfare in 1947. There was an insistent, driving energy and a sense of urgency: shortly after his death, a close friend commented that "Harry was never a consolidator—he was a creator, a builder. An inner compulsion drove him on and on."[4]

Leonard Marsh (1906–1982) received his undergraduate education in England at the University of London and a PhD in Economics from McGill in 1940.[5] From 1931 to 1941, he was director of social research for the pioneering program of Research in the Social Sciences at McGill, which a grant from the Rockefeller Foundation had made possible. From 1941 to 1944, he was research advisor for the federal government's Advisory Committee on Post-War Reconstruction, which resulted in the publication of the *Report on Social Security for Canada*, and from 1944 to 1946, he was first a welfare advisor and then a senior information officer for UNRRA. From 1947 to 1964, he was director of research at the School of Social Work, University of British Columbia, and from then until his retirement in 1972 he was professor of educational sociology in the university's Faculty of Education. Like Cassidy, Marsh was constantly and intensely involved in a variety of activities: he served on occasion as an advisor to the Dominion Bureau of Statistics and acted in an advisory capacity during an important meeting of the Canadian Federation of Mayors which made a major presentation to the federal government on the Canadian unemployment and relief situation.

Both Cassidy and Marsh were empiricists rather than idealists, with a strong pragmatic bent toward factual inquiry. They had a remarkable ability to impose order on data that would have been unmanageable by all but the most disciplined social investigator. They both admired the great British social scientist, William Beveridge, the last of the prominent Edwardian social reformers, and they profited from a careful reading of his book, *Unemployment: A Problem of Industry*, in which Beveridge had been among the first to point out that "distress through want of employment is not a temporary but a chronic evil."[6] During the Thirties, Cassidy and Marsh were practically the only two academics in Canada doing major work in the field of social welfare. They always kept informed on each other's work, which from time to time they reviewed in the pages of the *Canadian Forum* and the *Canadian Journal of Economics and Political Science*.

Before considering their work in more detail, a summary review of Fabianism and of the League for Social Reconstruction is helpful.

Of all the societies for social reform that emerged in Britain during the 1870s and 1880s, the Fabian Society, which advocated a mild democratic socialism, became the most prominent.[7] This undoubtedly could be attributed largely to the fact that it numbered among its members Bernard Shaw, Sidney and Beatrice Webb, and Graham Wallas. Established in 1884, the Society first became well known with the publication in 1889 of the celebrated *Fabian Essays*, which helped to focus what was becoming a general concern over continuing and degrading poverty, unemployment, and social unrest. The Society produced a steady stream of tracts, designed to help the layman better understand questions of public policy. The title of its very first tract, "Why Are the Many Poor," indicated the Society's predominant concern with poverty. Its general aims were to work for "the abolition of poverty, through legislation and administration; [for] the communal control of production and social life, and [for] the conversion of the British public and of the British governing class [to socialism] . . . by a barrage of facts and 'informed' propaganda."[8]

The Fabians viewed the development from capitalism to socialism as a gradual but inevitable process, an outlook summed up in Sidney Webb's phrase, "the inevitability of gradualness." Since change was seen as evolutionary, a continuity with the past would be preserved, and the tradition from which the Fabians drew their intellectual inspiration was the liberal thought of Jeremy Bentham and John Stuart Mill. In the words of Max Beer, "Webb stands on the shoulders of J.S. Mill. He is the direct mental descendant of the last great Utilitarian. He has taken up the work of socialism where Mill left it—namely, half-way between individualism and social reform, and has carried it a good distance further."[9]

The Fabians felt that the utilitarian ideal of the "greatest happiness of the greatest number" could be preserved and extended throughout society and through socialism. Canadian historian Frank Underhill recognized the liberal nature of Fabian socialism when he remarked that "English socialism has always emphasized that it is only another method of seeking the same ends which the individualistic generation that preceded it had in view. Its end is the emancipation of individuality, the free development of personality."[10] The Fabians invariably extolled the parliamentary system that would guarantee individual liberty in the new collectivist age. Socialism from their perspective was a direct result of the development of democracy: "The main stream which has borne European society towards Socialism during the past 100 years is the irresistible progress of democracy."[11] In general, their outlook was empirical and pragmatic rather than utopian. They were non-doctrinaire, tolerant of other points of view, and they directed their appeal to all groups in society. The Fabians were of the opinion that a permanent reconciliation among classes could be achieved through the state becoming an instrument for general social betterment.

In the Fabian philosophy, social reconstruction could best be brought about by an efficient and well-organized bureaucracy of experts who would be in a position to direct and manage the kind of social engineering needed to achieve the "greatest happiness of the greatest number." The state would become a central instrument of social policy and would secure, through social welfare legislation, a national minimum of well-being that would abolish substantially the worst forms of poverty. The 1909 *Minority Report of the Poor Law Commission*, written by the Webbs as a Fabian blueprint for the welfare state, found its way *mutatis mutandis* over thirty years later into the 1942 Beveridge *Report on Social Insurance and Allied Services*.

The Fabians maintained that an impressive and accurate foundation of fact was necessary to persuade others by rational argument of the need for reform and progressive welfare policies. This foundation of fact would be established primarily through social research and through extensive social surveys. Beatrice Webb had had a first-rate training in the social survey method, having taken part in Charles Booth's monumental survey, *Life and Labour of the People in London*, carried out between 1886 and 1903 and published in seventeen volumes.[12] The data from the surveys could then be used to educate the public: the seriousness of particular social problems could be demonstrated empirically, and specific remedies for reform legislation could be put forward. This appeal to research and education, or "measurement and publicity" as the Webbs called it, became a major tenet of the Fabian approach.

Research and education would also be the means to achieve another Fabian goal: permeation. The Fabians believed that there was no clear demarcation between socialists and non-socialists, and that even those who were in the latter category could often become influential allies in the crusade for reform, once they had been exposed to the thoroughly persuasive case that could be made through careful research. It was the Fabians' belief that the civil service and the political parties could be "permeated" and gently encouraged to support and enact civilizing reforms. Members of the Fabian Society were thoroughly convinced that permeation was the best possible method for social change, since it would only be a matter of time before their rational and humane suggestions, buttressed by columns of facts, were seen to be desirable by even the most intransigent opponent. One clear example of permeation at work is to be found in the social security legislation passed by the British Liberal government after it returned to power in 1906. Fabian ideas had had an impact; old age pensions, unemployment and health insurance all represented a triumph for the strategy of permeation.

It is an interesting light on Canadian history to see how far Cassidy and Marsh, during the critical 1930s and 1940s, exemplified so many of these Fabian characteristics.

In the fall of 1931, a group of socially conscious individuals, many of them academics, met regularly at Harry Cassidy's house in Toronto to discuss the need for research into glaring social problems, notably unemployment, that were being rendered worse by the continuing Depression. Later that year, Frank Underhill commented that "the time is ripe for a Canadian Fabian society to organize itself, define its aims and start campaigning."[13] Early in 1932, the League for Social Reconstruction was established by a group of socialist intellectuals in Montreal and Toronto that included F.R. Scott, Frank Underhill, Eugene Forsey, Graham Spry, King Gordon, Harry Cassidy and J.F. Parkinson; Leonard Marsh joined a short while later. Like its English counterpart, the League envisaged its primary purpose as having two components: carrying out social research, and suggesting proposals for reform.

The League very quickly became known as the "CCF Brain Trust," and, although it never formally affiliated itself with the party, it maintained a close relationship with the CCF until it ceased to function in 1942. Members of the League—primarily Frank Underhill, but also others—including Harry Cassidy—wrote the original drafts of the Regina Manifesto of 1933.[14]

Although the League was formed primarily in response to the degradation of the Depression, it also "represented a transference, as well as an intense politicization, of some of the main themes of the twenties, especially the enmity towards the blotched and wasteful standards of the business civilization."[15] Its manifesto made clear the intentions of the organization:

> The League for Social Reconstruction is an association of men and women who are working for the establishment in Canada of a social order in which the basic principle regulating production, distribution and service will be the common good rather than private profit.
> The present capitalist system has shown itself unjust and inhuman, economically wasteful, and a standing threat to peace and democratic government. . . . Despite our abundant natural resources the mass of the people have not been freed from poverty and insecurity. Unregulated competitive production condemns them to alternate periods of feverish prosperity, in which the main benefits go to speculators and profiteers, and to catastrophic depression, in which the common man's normal state of insecurity

and hardship is accentuated. . . . We therefore look to the establishment in Canada of a new social order which will substitute a
planned and socialized economy for the existing chaotic individualism and which, by achieving an approximate economic equality
among all men in place of the present glaring inequalities, will
eliminate the domination of one class by another.[16]

The League's manifesto called for the creation of a National Planning
Commission, a concept long advocated by Fabians. The League put great
trust in governmental planning, social engineering, and the rational reconstruction of society. They viewed as essential a system of continuous planning that would involve three stages: a technique of survey; the formulation
of an overall, co-ordinated program; and the execution and administration
of the program. The members of the League felt that such planning was
necessary if democracy was to be preserved: "In an age when rapid technological changes are daily shifting the whole material basis of our civilization, our political democracy must trust itself more and more to technical
experts and must develop a leadership which is experimental in temper and
capable of quick decisions."[17]

Although the League's aim was a radical reconstruction of society, its
favoured methods reflected the democratic approach to socialism. Change
would come about through parliamentary reforms; the methods of Marx
were to be avoided. Many of the reform measures supported by the League
can be seen in the social service state of today: "social legislation to secure
to the worker adequate income and leisure, freedom of association, insurance against illness, accident, old age, and unemployment . . . publicly organized health, hospital and medical services."[18] It is important to note there
was no suggestion that social workers would no longer be required:
"Schools of social work would not be closed in a socialized Canada; they
would be accorded adequate state support instead of being left dependent
on inadequate and uncertain private funds, and their facilities extended to
enable them to supply their needed quota to the social service personnel
that the new state will require."[19]

Thus, the major impact of the League, accompanied by the policies
advocated by the CCF, was the birth of the Canadian welfare state.[20] In the
1940s the Canadian Liberal Party, in the footsteps of the British Liberal
Party thirty years earlier, adopted many of the welfare reforms advocated
by the League and by the CCF. The fact that these reforms (at first unemployment insurance and later family allowances) were implemented by
parties in power to avoid the threat from socialism and to maintain the
essentials of the capitalist social system was acceptable from a Fabian point
of view; the process was part of the gradual evolution from capitalism to
socialism that modernity required.

One of the decisions that the League for Social Reconstruction made in
its first year was to undertake the writing and publication of a book "that
would bring together in a single volume important bits of individual
research and spell out in some detail a plan of social and political action

based on the LSR Manifesto."[21] Cassidy, who was head of the League's Research Committee, assumed editorial responsibility for the book. In line with their Fabian approach, Cassidy and the other members of the Research Committee noted: "The Members of the Committee recognize frankly that the general approach of the book may not be acceptable to a number of very competent people who would, nevertheless, be willing to assist in the preparation of particular sections. It is hoped, therefore, that such people, even if they cannot subscribe fully to the frank socialist approach of the book, will be willing to render assistance and criticism on particular topics about which they are informed."[22] A series of contributions, large and small, were sent to the LSR on this basis.

After Cassidy went to British Columbia in 1934, Leonard Marsh took on the editorial duties, and the book, *Social Planning for Canada*, was finally published in 1935. In 1938, Marsh and F.R. Scott produced an abridged version called *Democracy Needs Socialism*. Cassidy wrote two chapters for *Social Planning for Canada*: "A Code for Labour" and "Health and Welfare Services." His recommendations included a national labour code, wage regulation, a system of family allowances, unemployment and health insurance, and the extension of public social services. It is interesting to note that Cassidy's name was not listed among the authors of the book; by the time the book was published in 1935, he was a top civil servant in the Liberal government of British Columbia, and it would have been politically unwise for his name to appear in a book that rejected capitalist society and openly favoured socialism.

Not surprisingly, as members of an organization with a Fabian cast, Cassidy and Marsh exhibited many recognizable Fabian characteristics. They were vitally concerned about poverty and the ill effects of unemployment. As Marsh wrote in the Social Security Report of 1943, "Provision for unemployment, both economically and socially, is the first and greatest need in a security programme designed for the modern industrial economy."[23] "Social welfare" was social reform being brought about through democratic parliamentary means, the enactment of specific welfare legislation. Both "permeated" Liberal governments—Cassidy in British Columbia and Marsh nationally—and assisted at various points in drawing up legislative proposals. They both urged greater governmental efficiency in administering social welfare programs, and they were certainly not adverse to having experts plan for general betterment through techniques of social engineering.

Both Cassidy and Marsh rejected any form of Marxism: Cassidy once told the poet, Earle Birney, "that it was unnecessary to read Marx"; Marsh saw a concern with Marxist complexities as only interfering with the "empirical analysis of Canadian social structure" that was a necessary prelude to any democratic reform.[24] Cassidy and Marsh, as did others in the League, saw not only research in itself, but the use of research in educating the public on the need for reform, as being of paramount importance. The League's manifesto spelled this out specifically: "The League will work for the realization of its ideal by organizing groups to study and report on particular problems, and by issuing to the public in the form of pamphlets, articles, lectures, etc., the most accurate information obtainable about the nation's affairs in order to create an informed public opinion."[25]

During the 1930s and 1940s, no two members did more to lay a foundation of fact and to educate the public on the need for reform than Cassidy and Marsh, and their indebtedness to the democratic convictions of Fabianism is unmistakable.

In the spring of 1931, when the university term was over, Cassidy made a number of inquiries about social research projects in which he might become involved. He wrote to the dominion statistician to ask whether any of the departments in Ottawa would "be interested in an investigation into the unemployment relief activities of the past year." As well, he contacted J.S. Woodsworth and suggested that his knowledge of research methods might be helpful for the Ginger Group which was preparing background memoranda on topics of social concern.[26] That summer, Cassidy became involved with the Unemployment Research Committee of Ontario, a group of citizens who had become convinced of the necessity for investigating and collecting data on unemployment. The committee felt that those who were interested in remedying this affliction had "been hampered by the absence of reliable information both as to the amount of unemployment and the success attending the many and varied experiments in its social treatment."[27] The plan that the committee devised was:

1. To obtain the services of a competent, trained social investigator who would make a fact-finding survey of unemployment relief in a typical group of Ontario cities.
2. To make an appraisal of the social results flowing from the relief programme.
3. To publish a statement of findings and interpretations.[28]

This was ideally suited to Cassidy's predilections and, becoming director of the survey, he assumed the responsibility for planning and conducting the project. He relentlessly and vigorously set to work without remuneration, and the following year, *Unemployment and Relief in Ontario 1929–1932: A Survey and Report* was published, thereby becoming the first book on unemployment relief in Canada.

In a review of the book, Leonard Marsh commented that "in no subject has active interest in the extension and improvement of social provision been stimulated more than that of unemployment. But we cannot get far without facts. There can be nothing but praise, therefore, for Professor Cassidy in having undertaken and carried through in so short a time ... a comprehensive survey of unemployment relief since 1929 covering in greater or less detail a representative group of nineteen Ontario towns."[29] As well as providing an account of the personal tragedy of unemployment, the book, written in clear and unadorned prose, surveyed in historical perspective relief policies at all levels of government. It is an indispensable chronicle of the Depression years in Canada. Among the many recommendations which were intended to guide those who had responsibility for social policy were the following:

Public responsibility for relief and for dealing with the unemployment problem in general must be continued and extended. . . .
The Dominion and the Province . . . must continue to assist [the
municipalities] . . . on an even more generous scale than in the past
and the two larger units of government must take the lead in the
development of permanent policies. . . .
[The services] of professionally trained social case workers . . .
should be made available along with material assistance. . . .
The administration of public relief must be of a high order of competence, and it calls for revision and improvement in methods and
machinery. . . .
It is of fundamental importance that more effort be made to collect
and compile statistical information upon unemployment and relief.
Unless this is done, it is impossible to see those trends and developments clearly which point the way towards desirable changes of
policy. This is work which must be done by the Dominion or the
provincial government, or both. . . .
In Canada and in [the provinces] it is essential that forward planning of a preventive as well as ameliorative nature should be
undertaken by governments . . . [T]he important thing is the
assumption of leadership by the Dominion or the Province, or
both.[30]

The proposals, particularly those for more competent administration and
government planning, had definite Fabian reverberations.

In the book, Cassidy briefly mentioned unemployment insurance as a
possible ameliorative measure for unemployment. This measure was to
become a chief interest of his over the next few years, and he wrote several
articles urging its implementation.[31] In 1933, he strongly advocated unemployment insurance to a Conservative summer school at Newmarket,
Ontario, when he spoke on the subject, "An Unemployment Policy: Some
Proposals." He argued that, unless measures such as unemployed insurance
were adopted, "it is very likely that radicalism will continue to grow and
that it will overwhelm the defenders of the existing order. . . . Surely, then,
it is necessary for Conservatives who are true to their basic convictions to
urge upon the state a positive policy of caring for the unemployed and of
stabilizing government that will destroy the main grievances upon which
radicalism thrives and that will check the assault upon capitalist institutions."[32] He repeated the message to a group of Liberals at the first Liberal
summer conference later that year.[33]

Here was permeation and persuasion at its best. Cassidy's exhortations
would have had considerable appeal to his listeners that summer, since
there was a very real fear during the Depression, on the part of those who
supported the status quo, that a rising tide of working-class militancy
would sooner or later sweep away the old order. The Winnipeg General
Strike of 1919 was not yet just a memory, and "Dominion Day" in 1935 saw
relief-camp protestors, provoked by the RCMP, shed blood in a riot in
Regina.[34]

As positive measures to allay the discontent and smouldering resentments which were now thriving on unemployment, Cassidy recommended three things: "a generous and humane system of relief, a scheme of unemployment insurance, and a programme of employment stabilizations, all . . . on national lines under the leadership and the direction of the Dominion Government."[35] The relief system could be improved vastly, he proposed, by putting in place a skilled administration that would be supported by "professional social workers, whose special efforts would be directed towards preserving and restoring the morale of relief recipients."[36] Unemployment insurance would provide benefits "as a right" to the person who became legitimately unemployed, and would do away at least partially with the degrading and stigmatizing "means test." Overall, what was needed, Cassidy suggested, was "a thinking, planning agency . . . at the centre of things," and he recommended the establishment of a Dominion Board of Employment Stabilization, "assisted by an Advisory Council and an expert staff. . . . The expert staff would consist of economists, engineers, statisticians and others with thorough technical training for their work."[37] Unemployment was the supreme social evil for Cassidy, and he always stressed that social workers could play an important role in making the public aware of its implications: "Social workers . . . can do nothing more effective in the cause of conquering unemployment than to . . . hammer home on every possible occasion what unemployment means in human terms."[38]

Cassidy continued to participate in surveys and studies while he was teaching at the University of Toronto. With F.R. Scott, he undertook an investigation of labour conditions in the men's clothing industry under the joint sponsorship of the Amalgamated Clothing Workers of America, a trade union, and the Canadian Association of Garment Manufacturers, an employers' association. The study was undertaken, Cassidy and Scott wrote, "to indicate what are, in our opinion, appropriate measures of reform."[39] The evidence they gathered was presented in 1934 before the Parliamentary Committee on Price Spreads and Mass Buying, chaired by the tempestuous H.H. Stevens, minister of trade and commerce in the government of R.B. Bennett. The study described a situation in which "both manufacturers and workers had suffered in recent years . . . from cut-throat competition, disorganized marketing and general instability," and the workers from "unemployment, underemployment and the revival of the sweatshop in its most obnoxious forms."[40]

Another study that Cassidy became involved in at the same time was prompted by Dr H.A. Bruce, the lieutenant governor of Ontario, who urged that a program of community action for slum clearance and better housing be undertaken during Toronto's centennial year, 1934. Taking up his suggestion, the Toronto Board of Control appointed a committee, with Cassidy as secretary, to investigate housing conditions in Toronto. In the fall of 1934, the committee published a comprehensive report, which Cassidy had had a major hand in writing. The report concluded:

> There are thousands of families living in houses which are insanitary, verminous and grossly overcrowded. . . . Bad houses are not

only a menace: they are active agents of destruction. The Committee is satisfied from its investigations and enquiries that they destroy happiness, health and life. They destroy morality and family ties. They destroy the basis of society itself by their destruction of self-respect and their promotion of delinquency and crime.[41]

As had Cassidy's studies on unemployment and labour conditions, the housing report recommended greatly increased government intervention to bring about reforms, the need for which had been scientifically documented.

When Cassidy went to British Columbia in 1934 as director of social welfare, he entered the civil service of an enlightened Liberal government that had been elected in the fall of 1933. The Liberals had campaigned on a reform program, with the slogan, "Work and Wages," and one of their pledges had been to set up a system of state health insurance. Initially, Premier T. Dufferin Pattullo supported and encouraged the establishment of a progressive system of state social services, intimating that what was needed in contemporary society was a "socialized capitalism."[42] This outlook was close to Cassidy's own. In his new position, Cassidy was instrumental in preparing the health insurance legislation and was responsible for planning its implementation.[43] However, difficulties soon arose as massive and sustained protests were launched by the medical profession. In the spring of 1938 the plan was shelved and the commission set up to administer it disbanded. Even Cassidy's customary sanguine disposition disappeared when the health insurance plan was sabotaged. He was certainly prepared to work for reform within a Liberal government—this was true to the idea of permeation—but he was not prepared to accept cowardly withdrawal under pressure from interest groups such as the medical profession. The next year, he left to take up the position at the School of Social Work at the University of California. Cassidy's indignation was still at a high pitch several years later, when he mercilessly castigated his former employer: "Caught between the cross-fire of the doctors' heavy artillery and the rifles of the common people, a pusillanimous and divided government has sheltered for more than five years in a funkhole behind a moribund commission and dead letter act, lacking the courage either to go forward or to retreat. Thus did British Columbia ingloriously lose the distinction of being the first legislative jurisdiction in North America to put state health insurance into effect."[44]

In 1943, Cassidy published *Social Security and Reconstruction in Canada*, which outlined his ideas on a comprehensive social security scheme. The book indicated his continuing adherence to certain Fabian principles:

> Unless heroic efforts are made to build up efficient administrative machinery throughout the country there is small chance of a great national programme of social security in Canada realizing its objectives. . . . Here [in the book] the emphasis will be upon the problem of social security as a technical question. . . . The business of the social services represents a new type of social engineering. . . . There is great need . . . for the rapid completion of certain studies that will contribute to the construction of a master plan of social security.[45]

Cassidy concluded his book by citing the Webbs' view that the most severe impediment to a comprehensive plan of restorative and preventative social security was not the inability to raise funds for the services required or the disinclination to spend them, but the "lack of machinery."[46] In 1945 Cassidy published a sequel to *Social Security and Reconstruction in Canada* entitled *Public Health and Welfare Reorganization* which repeated similar themes, although the analysis was now focussed on questions of reorganizing and developing provincial and local health and welfare services in order to fit them into a comprehensive national plan of social security.

Throughout his work in this fifteen-year period, even when he was in the United States, Cassidy relentlessly championed the creation and reconstruction of Canada's health and welfare services. His approach was essentially a Fabian one: stressing the necessity for laying a foundation of fact; permeating the civil service and political gatherings to work and argue for reform; emphasizing the need for welfare reform and a national plan of social security that called for the state to create an efficient administration under central planning, with social engineering and expert guidance being the means for achieving a more comprehensive society.

Leonard Marsh, as director of McGill University's social research program between 1931 and 1941, conducted a number of pioneering social surveys that were instrumental in providing data on which reform could be based. Under the McGill program, thirty-two studies on various aspects of employment and unemployment were planned, to be carried out by members of different social science departments. Marsh suggested that unemployment should be treated by social scientists "as a subject for research rather than a subject for protest . . . [for] if the problems of employment are to be properly planned for they must be brought . . . on to an objective plane."[47] He pointed out that adopting a scientific approach to social problems did not necessarily mean that one would be unsympathetic to the plight of those studied; in his view, the factual survey provided "the best foundation for the construction . . . [and] the advocacy of improvements and reforms."[48] Marsh was fundamentally in favour of planning in social and economic affairs, and he stated that methods that had been tremendously successful in the natural sciences could be re-fashioned for an all-out assault on social problems: "The task of social engineering demands the same scientific attitude and the same systematic appeal to facts."[49] Marsh saw that great value could be derived from encouraging social research in universities, and he was excited by the possibility that research into social problems would attract young people who would be prepared to bring the approach and attitudes of the scientist "into alliance with their enthusiasm for social improvement and reform."[50] Social research as a necessary prelude to reform was the topic he chose in addressing the Fifth Canadian Conference on Social Work in 1937. A number of remarks on that occasion suggest a Fabian orientation:

> [The researcher] must have an interest . . . in promoting "the greater happiness of the greater number". . . . [R]esearch of a dozen different kinds is needed as an *instrument of policy*. . . . [T]he vital depen-

dence of an active and enlightened policy upon research is surely clear . . . [R]esearch is necessary to spread and improve *education and publicity* on social welfare matters. Social workers will be among the first to agree that the general public is not sufficiently informed on the extent, the wider causes and the social repercussions of many of our chief social ills. . . . [I]n the long run social research and progressive government grow together. . . . [We need social workers and others trained in social research to deal with] our needs of social engineering today and tomorrow.[51]

In 1938, Marsh, in conjunction with two medical doctors, published *Health and Unemployment*, the seventh book in the McGill Social Research Series. Perhaps the first book in Canada to take a thorough look at the socio-economic aspects of medicine, *Health and Unemployment* was particularly important since the problems of sickness, medical care, and nutrition were as yet unmeasured on a national basis. Although most of the data for the book were gathered through surveys conducted in Montreal, *Health and Unemployment* included commentary on the national scene by examining the provisions of medical care in eastern and western Canada. Before the Depression was considerably advanced, the cost of medical care had not been considered important enough to be covered by unemployment relief. During the early 1930s, the federal government did not include medical costs in any of the provincial grants-in-aid provided for in successive Relief Acts. As a result, those who were unemployed and without adequate financial resources had to depend on the charity of the medical profession for needed medical attention. Marsh and his colleagues concluded that there was a direct relationship "between the employment status of individuals, families or communities, and the prevalence and duration of illness," and that "if medical care is a contingency left to each individual to secure as best he can, it becomes a function of the distribution of wealth."[52] In recommending a national program of health insurance, the authors cautioned that it would be very important to mediate between the business interests of doctors and the responsibility of the state for ensuring adequate medical care for its citizens. One outstanding feature of the study was that it showed that a productive relationship between the social sciences and the medical profession could be effected in the course of working for the amelioration of adverse social conditions. The doctor alone would have difficulty interpreting the social and economic data, and the social scientist would be considerably hindered by his lack of medical knowledge.

Canadians In and Out of Work: A Survey of Economic Classes and Their Relation to the Labour Market appeared in 1940 and was described recently as "the most comprehensive study of employment and the Canadian social structure before John Porter's *The Vertical Mosaic*."[53] It is a long and detailed study, with many charts and tables, and was intended "to weave all the contemporary statistics which [were] available into a factual picture of the Canadian working force, employed and unemployed; and to furnish a basic social perspective."[54] According to Marsh, this probing of "the socio-economic strata of the nation" was necessary to assess a country's social problems and to arrive at proposals for a national welfare policy.[55] He acknowledged that measurement was "only the first step towards practical policies, but a very necessary one."[56] The study assembled important information that formerly had been widely scattered. Marsh presented data on the size of twelve occupational groups which ranged in a hierarchy from unskilled and manual to managerial and proprietary. Each group belonged to one of the main social classes: the working, farming, middle, and well-to-do. He outlined and analysed the unemployment picture for each group: unemployment was concentrated acutely in the unskilled and industrial wage-earner classes.

Marsh concluded in *Canadians In and Out of Work* that the structure of Canadian government needed a substantial reorganization in order to deal adequately with unemployment. As did Cassidy, Marsh felt that strong dominion leadership was crucial if the inequalities in local and provincial welfare administration were to be overcome: "Everything hinges on Dominion leadership."[57] Anticipating the recommendations that he was to make in his *Report on Social Security in Canada* three years later, Marsh urged that a progressive and direct approach to the problem of unequal distribution of income should be the establishment of a system of social insurance. Legislation of this kind would begin to deal not only with the hazards of unemployment, but also with risks such as sickness, old age, and disability. This would need to be coupled with progressive income-tax legislation. Marsh also argued that an extensive program of public works would be required if full economic recovery was to be achieved. Such a program would include projects of benefit to the nation as a whole: conservation of natural resources, housing, electric power development, and rural reconstruction. Marsh's fundamental point was that, whether they spent funds on capital works projects or on direct welfare measures, governments would need to put vast amounts of money into circulation if employment stabilization were to become a lasting reality. There were marked Keynesian echoes in these economic proposals.

To those who might suggest that his social welfare as social reform proposals did not go far enough, Marsh had the perfect Fabian answer:

> To liberalize the class structure is not to abolish it altogether. The practical answer, however, must surely be that long before the classless society as an ideal is to be discussed today, the furtherance of even a partial democracy must be valued against its competing and harshly vocal alternatives. . . . To recognize class differences or to denounce socially created inequalities is not to espouse a doctrinaire theory of class conflict. Social classes are the data, not the dynamite, of an alert democracy. They do not lead inevitably to the prognosis of a revolutionary crisis between "the capitalist class" and the exploited proletariat; they do not necessarily show that the economic trends of capitalist society must ultimately force everyone to adopt the ideology of one or the other of these opposing forces.[58]

For Marsh, data properly used could lead, in a progressive evolutionary approach, to the removal of the more glaring inequalities and resentments between classes. The desirable way to effect these changes would be through social legislation; only a democratic government using parliamentary methods could abolish through "peaceful and constructive methods" the tensions and frictions of unequal opportunity, thereby achieving "a lasting federation of classes."[59]

Marsh's *Report on Social Security for Canada* (1943) has been called "the most important single document in the history of the development of the welfare state in Canada."[60] When Marsh's report was released in March of 1943 it was widely assumed (and is often still assumed) that it was a sort of Canadian version of the Beveridge Report. Although aided in its acceptance by the wide publicity given the British Beveridge Report in late 1942, *Social Security for Canada*'s historical roots are to be found elsewhere: in Marsh's work at McGill in the 1930s; in meetings Marsh had with key social workers from Montreal, Toronto, and Ottawa during the report's preparation; and in consultations between Marsh and one of the leading international experts on social insurance from the International Labour Office (ILO), who was in Montreal during the war.[61]

The report advocated a comprehensive social insurance program to be complemented by social assistance and by children's allowances. Social insurance, for both Cassidy and Marsh, was the cornerstone of any social security system: "The genius of social insurance is that it enlists the direct support of the classes most likely to benefit, and enlists equally the participation and controlling influence of the state."[62] Provision would be made for both employment risks and for what he called universal risks—sickness, disability, and old age. Unemployment insurance was to be integrated completely with a comprehensive keyed-in training program which would include occupational guidance, regional mobility, and industrial co-operation; as well, a remodelled Employment Service was to be introduced. The report also further developed Marsh's recommendation in *Canadians In and Out of Work* for an extensive public works program, proposing a billion-dollar program for the first year following the war.

The outcome of Marsh's social security program would be "to lay the foundation of a social minimum," a notion that harked back to the Webbs' conception of a "minimum standard of civilized life."[63] Children's allowances were important to Marsh for two different reasons: as a fundamental part of the "social minimum" which would, of course, vary for families of different sizes; and as the "key to consistency" of the entire approach, by freeing unemployment insurance (and other similar special provisions) from the necessity of separate benefits for single and married people and those with or without children. The civil-service economists who advised the government after Marsh had left in 1944 recommended children's allowances because they would "raise the level of purchasing power"—piecemeal "keynesianism."[64]

Marsh once commented that the historical process by which the state comes to deal with social problems develops in two stages: the first, which is often a protracted one, involves research and the presentation of facts to the population, arousing in the public a desire for reform; the second encompasses the working out of details in the application of specific reform measures and the solving of practical problems of administration.[65] Marsh and Cassidy assisted the historical process in both respects.

This paper has argued that Fabian ideas were tremendously influential in guiding Harry Cassidy's and Leonard Marsh's thinking about social welfare reform during the period 1930–1945. In conclusion, it is important to ask, what are the implications of the Fabian position for social welfare policy? Fabianism conceives of the state as having a major role in guiding economic and social development. When, in the 1930s, Cassidy and Marsh and the other social democrats in the League for Social Reconstruction assigned to the state a major social purpose, they "were elaborating the fundamental tenet of their philosophy that parliament and the rule of law could be made the instrument of all classes and not simply that of the ruling elites. Their belief was that education, research, and the introduction of modern technology lead to better government, more planning, and a set of administrators more in tune with the needs of the people."[66]

During the 1940s, the federal Liberal party adopted a "statist" approach to social welfare and began to establish the machinery for making the Canadian state an instrument of social policy. While the motivations of the Mackenzie King government in doing this undoubtedly were complex, at least three are significant: the government was moved by genuine humanitarian concerns; it was pressed at this time by the CCF and perceived the latter as a threat to its continuing in power; and it realized that a "statist" approach to social policy and social welfare could be used to give the appearance of reform while maintaining the essential capitalist configuration.[67]

As noted earlier in this paper, a case has been made that the major influence of the League for Social Reconstruction, acting through the CCF, was on the development of the Canadian welfare state.[68] Since Harry Cassidy and Leonard Marsh were the two most notable members of the League who articulated the need for social welfare as social reform from 1930 to 1945, one could argue that they had, if not a direct, then certainly an indirect, effect on the development of the Canadian welfare state; there appears to be little question that both contributed substantially to the general stock of ideas about social welfare reform.

Because they were Fabians and, therefore, tolerant and non-doctrinaire in their approach to social reform and social change, non-socialist parties— the Liberals in British Columbia and the Liberals federally—had no particular philosophical difficulty in employing Cassidy and Marsh and in seeking their advice on welfare matters as in Marsh's *Report on Social Security for Canada*. As Fabians, they would not have been greatly disturbed by the fact that non-socialist governments eventually implemented many of the proposals they had advised, for, within the pragmatic Fabian approach, reforms should be implemented immediately as the need for them becomes apparent. Gradual but inevitable change was the crucial determinant for Fabians, and the change to a welfare state, although still within a capitalist

context, was, for them, momentous progress in the movement from capitalism to socialism. Many small reforms would lead eventually to a transformation of society.

One could criticize Fabianism or "statism" for over-emphasizing the
role of the state in social development and for downplaying workers' control, class conflict, and participatory democracy; however, the alternative
would be a "non-statist" approach to the governance of Canadian society,
an idea entirely new to the historical development of Canada and requiring
a radical departure from all tradition. Fabians would be most reluctant to
countenance such a departure.[69]

On the Fabian stained-glass window at Beatrice Webb House, above the
figures of Shaw and Webb building a new world, were the words,
"Remould It Nearer to the Heart's Desire." During the period of 1930–1945,
Harry Cassidy and Leonard Marsh were unflagging in their efforts to
remould Canadian society through social welfare perceived as social
reform. That society needs remoulding today detracts not at all from their
considerable achievement.

NOTES

1. Michael Bliss, preface to Leonard
Marsh, *Report on Social Security for
Canada* (Toronto, 1975), ix. The
Marsh report was first published in
1943.

2. Ibid., x.

3. A history of the League for Social
Reconstruction is to be found in
Michiel Horn, "The League for
Social Reconstruction: Socialism and
Nationalism in Canada 1931–1945"
(PhD diss., University of Toronto,
1969). See also Horn, "The League
for Social Reconstruction and the
Development of a Canadian Socialism,
1932–1936," *Journal of Canadian
Studies* 7, 4 (Nov. 1972): 3–17.

4. Allon Peebles, "Harry Morris
Cassidy, 1900–1951," *Canadian
Welfare* 27, 6 (Dec. 1951): 5.

5. For a brief but excellent account of
Marsh's life and work see Michiel
Horn, "Leonard Marsh and the
Coming of a Welfare State in
Canada," *Histoire sociale/Social
History* 9, 17 (May 1976): 197–204.

6. William Beveridge, *Unemployment: A
Problem of Industry* (London, 1909;
1930), 70.

7. The literature on Fabianism is exten-
sive, and the present writer bene-
fited from reading the following:
Max Beer, "The Fabian Society" in *A
History of British Socialism*, intro. R.H.
Tawney (London, 1919), 2: 274–97;
Margaret Cole, *The Story of Fabian
Socialism* (Palo Alto, CA, 1961);
G.D.H. Cole, "Fabianism," *Encyclo-
paedia of the Social Sciences* (New
York, 1931), 6: 46–49; G.D.H. Cole,
Fabian Socialism (London, 1943);
Edward R. Pease, *The History of the
Fabian Society*, 2nd ed. (London,
1925); G.B. Shaw, ed., *Fabian Essays*
(London, 1889). A significant Canadian
assessment is Frank H. Underhill,
"Fabians and Fabianism," *Canadian
Forum* 25 (March 1946): 227–80, and
26 (April 1946): 8–12.

8. Cole, *Story of Fabian Socialism*, xii.

9. Max Beer, "Fabian Society," 281.

10. Frank H. Underhill, "Bentham and
Benthamism," *Queen's Quarterly* 39
(Nov. 1932): 666.

11. G.B. Shaw, *Fabian Essays*, 31.

12. It is interesting to note that Marsh
was the assistant secretary of the
new "Survey of London Life and

Labour," a re-cast of the Charles Booth survey, conducted in the late 1920s under William Beveridge's direction. In a letter to the present writer (20 Feb. 1980), Marsh observed that "this was my 'baptism' in field work on housing, rents, family income, [and] social problems generally in the poorer districts of London." Marsh's contributions are acknowledged in four of the twelve subject-chapters in the first volume, *New Survey of London Life and Labour*, vol. 1, *Forty Years of Change* (London, 1930). One of these chapters was on unemployment in London (and Britain) from 1890 to 1920.

13. F.H. Underhill, "O Canada," *Canadian Forum* 12 (Dec. 1931): 93.

14. See Michiel Horn, "Frank Underhill's Early Drafts of the Regina Manifesto 1933," *Canadian Historical Review* 54, 4 (Dec. 1973): 393–418.

15. Carl Berger, *The Writing of Canadian History* (Toronto, 1976), 68. For background information on the Depression itself, see Victor Hoar, ed., *The Great Depression: Essays and Memoirs from Canada and the United States* (Vancouver, 1969); Michiel Horn, ed., *The Dirty Thirties: Canadians in the Great Depression* (Toronto, 1972); H. Blair Neatby, *The Politics of Chaos: Canada in the Thirties* (Toronto, 1972); A.E. Safarian, *The Canadian Economy in the Great Depression* (Toronto, 1970).

16. Research Committee of the League for Social Reconstruction, *Social Planning for Canada* (Toronto, 1975), ix–x. The book was first published in 1935. The 1975 edition contains an introduction by F.R. Scott, Leonard Marsh, Graham Spry, J. King Gordon, Eugene Forsey, and J.S. Parkinson.

17. Ibid., 495.

18. Ibid., x–xi.

19. Ibid., 404.

20. Horn notes in a summary statement at the beginning of his thesis that "the League's major impact on Canadian society took place through the CCF. At least in its reformist proposals, which the LSR saw, perhaps

mistakenly, as initial steps in the creation of a socialist Canada, it seems to have had a significant influence on the evolution of the Canadian 'welfare state' since 1944."

21. *Social Planning for Canada*, xv.

22. Ibid.

23. Leonard Marsh, *Report on Social Security for Canada*, 7.

24. Horn, "League for Social Reconstruction: Socialism and Nationalism," 267, 269–70.

25. *Social Planning for Canada*, xi.

26. University of Toronto Archives, H.M. Cassidy Papers, box 61, Cassidy to R.H. Coates, 13 April 1931; box 61, Cassidy to J.S. Woodsworth, 2 May 1931.

27. H.M. Cassidy, *Unemployment and Relief in Ontario 1929–1932: A Survey and Report* (Toronto, 1932), 7.

28. Ibid.

29. L.C. Marsh, "Public Works and Relief," review of *Unemployment and Relief in Ontario 1929–1932* by H.M. Cassidy, *Canadian Forum* 13 (Feb. 1933): 188.

30. Cassidy, *Unemployment and Relief*, 279–90.

31. See H.M. Cassidy, "Unemployment Insurance for Canada," *Queen's Quarterly* 38 (Spring 1931): 306–34; "The Case for Unemployment Insurance," *Canadian Forum* 11 (May 1931): 290–92; "Is Unemployment Relief Enough?" *Canadian Forum* 14 (Jan. 1934): 131–33.

32. H.M. Cassidy, "An Unemployment Policy—Some Proposals" in *Canadian Problems* (Toronto, 1933), 55–56.

33. H.M. Cassidy, "The Relief and Prevention of Unemployment," in *The Liberal Way* (Toronto, 1933), 83–90.

34. A full account of the Winnipeg Strike is to be found in Kenneth McNaught, *A Prophet in Politics: A Biography of J.S. Woodsworth* (Toronto, 1959), ch. 8. See also D.C. Masters, *The Winnipeg General Strike* (Toronto, 1950), and

Norman Penner, ed., *Winnipeg 1919: The Strikers' Own History of the Winnipeg General Strike* (Toronto, 1973). For an account of the Regina riot, see Ronald Liversedge, *Recollections of the On to Ottawa Trek* (Toronto, 1973), ch. 5.

35. H.M. Cassidy in *Canadian Problems*, 59.

36. Ibid., 61.

37. Ibid., 64–66.

38. H.M. Cassidy, review of *Case Studies of Unemployment* by the Unemployment Committee of the National Federation of Settlements, *Social Welfare* 14, 1 (Oct. 1931): 14.

39. F.R. Scott and H.M. Cassidy, *Labour Conditions in the Men's Clothing Industry: A Report* (Toronto, 1935), vi.

40. Ibid.

41. *Report of the Lieutenant-Governor's Committee on Housing Conditions in Toronto* (n.p., 1934), 115. For a review of this report, see L.C. Marsh, review of *Report of the Lieutenant-Governor's Committee on Housing Conditions in Toronto, Canadian Journal of Economics and Political Science* 1, 1 (Feb. 1935): 119–22.

42. For an account of this era of British Columbia politics, see Margaret Ormsby, "T. Dufferin Pattullo and the Little New Deal," *Canadian Historical Review* 43, 4 (Dec. 1962): 277–97.

43. For accounts of the health insurance plan, see H.F. Angus, "Health Insurance in British Columbia," *Canadian Forum* 17 (April 1937): 12–14; H.M. Cassidy, "The British Columbia Plan of Health Insurance," *Proceedings of the 62nd National Conference of Social Work* (Montreal, 1935), 544–56.

44. H.M. Cassidy, *Social Security and Reconstruction in Canada* (Toronto, 1943), 23.

45. Ibid., viii, 18, 89, 190.

46. Ibid., 194.

47. Leonard C. Marsh, *Employment Research: An Introduction to the McGill Programme of Research in the Social Sciences* (Toronto, 1935), x.

48. Ibid.

49. Ibid.

50. Ibid., xi.

51. L.C. Marsh, "Research in Social Welfare," *Proceedings of Fifth Canadian Conference on Social Work* (Ottawa, 1937), 39–41.

52. Leonard C. Marsh in collaboration with A. Grant Fleming and C.F. Blackler, *Health and Unemployment: Some Studies of Their Relationships*, McGill Social Research Series, no. 7 (1938), 3, 216. Contributions for this compilation were made by eight or more persons and welfare agencies who organized studies during the year preceding the publication.

53. Bliss, preface to *Report on Social Security for Canada*, x.

54. Leonard C. Marsh, *Canadians In and Out of Work: A Survey of Economic Classes and Their Relation to the Labour Market*, McGill Social Research Series, no. 9 (1940), xvii.

55. Ibid.

56. Ibid., 341.

57. Ibid., 427.

58. Ibid., 447.

59. Ibid., 451.

60. Bliss, preface to *Report on Social Security for Canada*, ix.

61. The Geneva-based ILO had found temporary domicile at McGill University during the war. Information on the origins of the Marsh report was given to the present writer by Dr Marsh (letter, 20 Feb. 1980). See also Leonard Marsh, Introduction to *Report on Social Security for Canada*, xx.

62. Marsh, *Report on Social Security for Canada*, 14.

63. Ibid., 30.

64. Marsh to present writer, 20 Feb. 1980.

65. L.C. Marsh, review of *Report of the Lieutenant-Governor's Committee on Housing Conditions in Toronto*, 119.

66. Daniel Drache, "Rediscovering Canadian Political Economy, " *Journal of Canadian Studies* 11, 3 (Aug. 1976): 10.

67. For an account of the King government's move to the implementation of family allowances, see J.L. Granatstein, *Canada's War: The Politics of the Mackenzie King Government, 1939–1945* (Toronto, 1975), ch. 7. For an interesting empirical analysis of the influence of left-wing politics on the policies of mainstream parties, see William Chandler, "Canadian Socialism and Policy Impact: Contagion from the Left?" *Canadian Journal of Political Science* 10, 4 (Dec. 1977): 755–80.

68. See note 20.

69. The pioneering work on the "statist" tradition in Canada is J.A. Corry, *The Growth of Government Activities since Confederation: A Report Prepared for the Royal Commission on Dominion–Provincial Relations* (Ottawa, 1939). See also H.G.J. Aitken, "Defensive Expansionism: The State and Economic Growth in Canada" in *Approaches to Canadian Economic History*, ed. W.T. Easterbrook and M.H. Watkins (Toronto, 1967), 183–221; A. Brady, "The State and Economic Life in Canada," *University of Toronto Quarterly* 2, 4 (July 1933): 423–41.

ORIGINS OF THE WELFARE
STATE IN CANADA[◊]

ALVIN FINKEL

o

Social democrats have argued that the movement since the 1930s toward
greater state provision of social security for citizens is evidence that capitalism can be controlled and that the political power of the bourgeoisie can be
reduced without fundamental changes occurring in the structure of ownership and control of industry. The CCF-NDP threat; the influence of middle-
class professionals; the bleeding hearts of depression and wartime
politicians; and the collective national spirit that characterized the war and
postwar reconstruction period: all are invoked to explain the expansion of
the state's role in providing social security. The major survivors of the
League for Social Reconstruction, founded during the Depression as the
intellectual brain trust of the nascent CCF, recalled forty years later:

> What is difficult for us to grasp today is that the social planning
> which was prescribed by the LSR in the thirties was a major heresy
> for those in government and in the business community. Govern-
> ment had its role and business had its role and the two roles had to
> be kept separate. Government's "interference" in business was
> restricted to the enactment and enforcement of safety and health
> standards in factories and mines, subsistence minimum wages, and
> regulations for the adjudication of industrial disputes—at best a
> guardian and umpire role. But for the government to intervene in
> the self-regulating economic system for the purpose of setting social
> goals that might inhibit the full play of the profit motive was
> regarded as a cardinal sin. To suggest further that government

◊ From Leo Panitch, ed., *The Canadian State: Political Economy and Political Power*
(Toronto: University of Toronto Press, 1977), 344–70. © University of Toronto Press
Incorporated, 1977. Reprinted with the permission of the publisher.

should plan the nation's economic life in the interests of the good of the majority of its people was to challenge the foundations of the faith.[1]

The problem with the LSR analysis is that it totally ignores the class nature of the state. It is assumed that where government planning exists and where a number of welfare programs exist—although Canada's welfare state is generally conceded to be incomplete—that the direction of economic planning is "in the interests of the majority of the people." What is to be argued here, however, is that the "welfare state," while it places a floor on the standard of living of working people, was not constituted, even in its incomplete Canadian form, to reduce the economic and political power of the business leaders.[2] Indeed, the opposite is the case. It was devised by governments that wished to preserve the power of the ruling class but saw that power threatened by working-class militancy directed against an economic system that seemed unable to provide jobs or security. The upsurge of radicalism in the working class first in the Great Depression and then during the war forced an important section of the bourgeoisie to rethink its strategies with regard to the role of the state. The Canadian state had financed much of the infrastructure for Canadian industry and had intervened, when necessary, to defeat working-class attempts to improve wages and living standards through the formation of unions and the waging of strikes. Now, however, the provision of police and railroads alone could not create sufficient economic stability to fend off the working-class attack. The result was a rethinking among many businessmen of the proper relations between the state, industry, and the people.

In the first place, however, it is important to question whether the term "welfare state" does not conceal more about Canada than it reveals. It is true of course that welfare programs place a floor on income and to that extent the winning of such programs has been a victory for the Canadian working class. Nevertheless, the Economic Council of Canada reported in 1972 that at least 27 percent of Canadians must be said to be living in poverty if poverty were defined as "an insufficient access to certain goods, services, and conditions of life which are available to everyone else and have come to be accepted as basic to a decent, minimum standard of living."[3] A study prepared for the council indicated that governments, while establishing programs that transferred wealth to the lowest income group, used methods of taxation that involved "extreme regressivity . . . at the lower end of the income scale and the lack of any significant progressivity over the remainder of the income range."[4] Statistics Canada data indicate that negligible redistribution of wealth has occurred in Canada since 1950 (see Table 1). Moreover human "welfare" is not an easily quantifiable economic proposition. Ecological destruction, the destruction of health in many factory and mine jobs, and the psychological problems created for people who do seemingly mindless work over which they have no control are less quantifiable but no less important measures of human welfare.

What is to be examined here are the origins of the "welfare state" in Canada. The period studied covers the years 1930 through to 1945, that is, from the onset of the Great Depression to the end of the war that terminated

TABLE 1 *AFTER-TAX INCOME DISTRIBUTION BY QUINTILE, 1951 AND 1972*

	1951 (%)	1972 (%)
Top 20 percent	41.1	39.1
2nd 20 percent	22.4	23.7
3rd 20 percent	17.4	18.3
4th 20 percent	12.9	12.9
5th 20 percent	6.1	5.9

Source: *Income Distribution by Size in Canada, Selected Years: Distribution of Family Incomes in Canada* (Ottawa, 1972).

the depression. It was during this period that the dictates of political economy created the debate on the "welfare state" and finally the establishment of certain policies that provided the framework of the Canadian "welfare state." Of course, there were further programs added after 1945 that are not dealt with here. Nor are all the programs introduced by 1945 examined in detail. But the motivations behind welfarist policies as a whole are suggested by the debate on the particular policies discussed here. In short, by focussing on a few policies at a particular period, an attempt is made to reconstruct the motivations of the Canadian state in introducing welfarist policies. In particular, the question of the class nature of Canadian government is examined against the background of policies that certain critics, as above noted, thought to be of necessity directed against the bourgeoisie and in favour of the working class.

○

Social legislation in Canada before the Great Depression was minimal. The working class had not long been the majority group in the country and the agricultural class, over-represented in voting by rurally weighted electoral boundaries both at the federal and provincial levels, had little understanding of urban society and largely supported the capitalist class in its resistance to social legislation. The trade union movement, while it pressed for legislative changes, was weak and politically unimportant. Before the First World War the only victories it could claim were the winning of free public education and a number of public health services—though, in the case of Montreal and probably other cities, even these victories had not really been won by 1914. The public education debate, it might be noted, centred in part on the need for a partially literate work force for industry.[5]

Additional social legislation came slowly. Workmen's compensation had been introduced by all provinces except Prince Edward Island by 1920. An American study of the introduction of compensation indicates that this measure was desired by large corporate interests as a means of fending off the more radical employer-liability type of legislation which made employers legally responsible for employees injured at work. A state-wide program would remove the onus on individual businessmen and thus remove the need for shorter working hours and costly safety measures. A recent study of the origins of workmen's compensation in Ontario suggests that

Canadian employers thought along the same lines. While the Canadian Manufacturers' Association and its provincial branches often opposed specific features of proposed compensation legislation, they did not sway from their support of the principle itself. Before the introduction of workmen's compensation in Ontario in 1915, many employers taken to court by employees under the province's employer-liability legislation had been found negligent and therefore liable by juries sympathetic to the injured employees. Jury awards to injured employees for compensation by the employers were common enough and generous enough that many companies found themselves unable to find insurance companies that would provide them with insurance against liability.[6]

The high rate of unemployment before the First World War and the expected return to high unemployment at the war's end prompted the Ontario government to name a Royal Commission on Unemployment in 1916. The commission discussed and rejected the idea of a government-run unemployment insurance scheme, though it urged the province to aid financially company and trade union private programs for unemployment benefits.[7] The end of the war did bring some social legislation in the form of federal pensions for war widows and legislation in most provinces for mothers' allowances. Throughout the 1920s, however, the Trades and Labour Congress pressed unsuccessfully for universal old age pensions, unemployment insurance, sickness insurance, and disability insurance. And the only program passed by the federal government was a pension scheme for the needy poor. The scheme, which provided only $20 a month and was available only from age seventy, was a concession won by the small Labour group in the House of Commons, under the leadership of J.S. Woodsworth, for support of King's precarious minority Liberal government of 1925.[8]

Few would have thought that the Conservative government of R.B. Bennett, elected in 1930 on a campaign of high tariffs for Canadian manufacturers and primary producers, would have been interested in introducing new programs for social security. Bennett was one of Canada's leading capitalists and had important holdings in almost all sectors of the economy. He had been a partner with Lord Beaverbrook in the financial manoeuvrings that had created such concerns as the monopolistic Canada Cement Company; he was the majority shareholder in the Eddy Match monopoly and in the E.B. Eddy Newsprint Company and had some say in Eddy policies even as prime minister; he had been western solicitor for the Canadian Pacific Railway; he was the second largest individual shareholder in the Royal Bank; he had been president of the Turner Valley operations of Imperial Oil as well as Imperial's chief lawyer, and held thousands of shares in metal-mining companies; he was a past vice-president of Alberta Pacific Grain Elevators and a past director of such oligopolies as Imperial Tobacco and Canada Packers; at his death in 1947 he was worth $40 million.[9] Truly, here was a man who might claim to represent the big bourgeoisie as a whole and use the power of the state to achieve compromises among its different—though partly interlocked—sectors. Bennett's Cabinet included many other men who had ties with big corporations, and the government's appointment of top civil servants and members of royal commissions reflected a belief that success in private business was a chief qualification for government service.[10] The tenor of Bennett's government might be thought to be best encapsulated by his oft-quoted statement that the "iron heel of repression" was to be applied to those who rebelled against the existing order. Trade union organizing attempts were suppressed with state aid, Communists were imprisoned, militants of foreign birth were deported, and unemployed young men were put in remote camps where they received no wages and were fired upon when they tried to come to Ottawa to seek redress.[11] Yet it was this clearly anti-labour government that introduced unemployment insurance, a federal manpower agency, government mortgage-lending, and a variety of marketing boards. It also promised in 1935, if re-elected, to introduce a universal pension program and health insurance. Why? A.E. Grauer, writing for the Royal Commission on Dominion–Provincial Relations in 1939, summed up the type of philosophy that began to make certain social reforms acceptable to conservatives not only in Canada but in many industrialized nations:

> Since the Great War, the Great Depression has been the chief stimulus to labour legislation and social insurance. The note sounded has not been so much the ideal of social justice as political and economic financial expediency. For instance, the shorter working week was favoured in unexpected quarters not because it would give the workers more leisure and possibilities for a fuller life but because it would spread work; and the current singling out of unemployment insurance for governmental attention in many countries is dictated by the appalling costs of direct relief and the hope that unemployment insurance benefits will give some protection to public treasuries in future depressions and will, by sustaining purchasing power, tend to mitigate these depressions.[12]

Social insurance, then, from this particular Depression point of view, was intended to stabilize destabilized economies and not necessarily to redistribute wealth. That later studies should indicate that wealth had not been redistributed would only validate the view of conservatives who believed certain social reforms, if carried out in a certain way, would reinforce rather than disturb the status quo.

Sir Charles Gordon, president of Canada's then-leading bank, the Bank of Montreal, and president of Dominion Textiles, the country's leading textiles firm, was one conservative who argued that unemployment and old age insurance programs were necessary to stabilize the economy. Accepting that structural unemployment was inevitable, Gordon told the Bank of Montreal annual meeting that an organized national system of social security was cheaper and more efficient than the haphazard municipal systems of relief that were in effect during the Depression. The British experience was cited as proof that a country could weather better an economic recession if it collected funds in boom times to be released to the unemployed when the economy faltered.[13]

Gordon, who was second only to Sir Herbert Holt in assets over which he had trusteeship, was especially concerned that unemployment insurance be introduced. Reflecting the views of the bankers, Gordon wrote Bennett in January 1934 to urge unemployment insurance as an alternative to direct relief. The result of direct relief was that many municipalities and even provinces were in so much debt that they were "threatening to strangle their general credit to the point where it would be difficult if not impossible to carry through refunding operations for any maturing issues, letting alone the finding of money for any new capital undertaking."

The need to prevent future recourse to extensive direct relief convinced Gordon of "the urgent desirability of invoking some system of unemployment insurance." The British Parliament's recently reorganized unemployment insurance scheme was presented as a model, especially since it covered four-fifths of all working people. Concluded Gordon: "May I suggest to you that *for our general self-preservation* some such arrangement will have to be worked out in Canada and that if it can be done soon so much the better."[14]

The Bank of Nova Scotia's executives cautioned against expectations that unemployment insurance would completely obviate the necessity for direct relief. But they endorsed the principle as going at least part way in decreasing the burden of relief on national and local budgets. Like many advocates of insurance, the bank advised that a workable insurance scheme must be tied to a better-developed and nationally co-ordinated system of unemployment bureaus such as existed in Great Britain. Only in this way could unemployment insurance become a scheme for re-employing the unemployed rather than a fund for "malingerers."[15]

The municipalities' supposed profligacy with relief was not the result of control of the lower levels of government by benevolent individuals glad to open up the public purse to those experiencing hard times. Rather it was the result of well-organized and generally Communist-led campaigns of the unemployed workers in the major municipalities. Supported by trade unionists, the massed unemployed presented the spectre of a revolt of the workers to the frightened pillars of communities in charge of municipal councils. The councils were forced to grant more relief, often at the price of defaulting on the cities' debts. As a result, both the municipal leaders and their banker-creditors looked to the federal government to provide programs that would calm the militancy of the unemployed and preserve the credit of the municipalities.[16]

Unemployment insurance was seen as the first plank of a program of social security that would take care of those out of work and reduce the number of people seeking jobs. A.O. Dawson, 1934–1935 president of the Canadian Chamber of Commerce, president of Canadian Cottons, and director of many firms, was, like his fellow textile executive, Sir Charles Gordon, interested in copying the British example for social security programs. Speaking on employer–employee relations to the Canadian Chamber of Commerce in September 1934, Dawson urged the government to establish a fund for sickness, unemployment, and old age. It would be financed through a compulsory contribution of 5 percent of every employee's wages with contributions of an equivalent amount also to be made by the employers and the government. A reasonable pension for workers retiring at the age of sixty-five would be one of the benefits from this program, argued Dawson, who was concerned that technological changes would prevent the employment of all available hands even after the Depression was over. (Canadian Cottons had endured a bitter strike in 1929 in its Hamilton plant where lay-offs accompanied the introduction of assembly-line techniques.[17]) Insurance programs would reduce the total labour force by retiring its oldest members and giving sustenance to younger workers laid off while they sought new jobs. The result would be that individual employers would not need to fear the consequences of labour-saving machinery and of speed-up techniques meant to reduce total labour requirements; responsibility for the unemployed and the aged would be socialized. Like Dawson, *Pulp and Paper of Canada*, the organ of the newsprint industry in Canada, saw a comprehensive insurance scheme as necessary to control working-class discontent. Pensions would be useful because they would vacate jobs for younger workers. The journal observed that keeping young people idle between the leaving of school and the time of finding a job "breeds shiftlessness, discontent and ultimately disorder."[18] Just as the militancy of the unemployed had forced increases in relief payments, it also forced a debate among businessmen on the question of social insurance as a means of preventing recurrences of such militancy during times of unemployment, whether caused by cyclical or by structural factors.

Bennett largely shared the sentiments of people like Gordon and Dawson and the pulp and paper executives. Promising a universal old age pension scheme in the 1935 election as an extension of the social security program that had been begun earlier that year with the introduction of unemployment insurance, Bennett vowed to reduce the age of retirement to sixty. "Labour-saving machinery, elimination of duplication and growing concentration of business make it impossible to ever supply again work for all the people," commented Bennett. On the other hand, these advances meant increased production and, if the state had some role in the distribution of the benefits of this increase in national income, more and more people could legitimately be removed from the labour force and provided for by the state.[19] Bennett, like Dawson, believed that unemployment insurance would head off the militancy that resulted from cyclical unemployment and that might also result from structural unemployment as it had in the case of Canadian Cottons.

"Iron-Heel" Bennett also recognized that repression alone might not be sufficient to preserve the existing system against the threat of socialism. As he wrote a New Brunswick publisher, "Tim Buck has today a very strong position in the province of Ontario and he openly demands the abolition of the capitalist system. A good deal of pruning is sometimes necessary to save a tree and it would be well for us in Canada to remember that there is considerable pruning to be done if we are to preserve the fabric of the capitalist system."[20]

Unemployment insurance was introduced as part of a "reform" package in the parliamentary session of 1935, a package generally referred to as the "Bennett New Deal." The New Deal legislation, presented on the eve of a general election, was designed to reinvigorate a discredited Conservative government through a program of construction, social insurance, government mortgage-lending, and producers' marketing boards, which it was hoped would pacify demands of workers and farmers and restore investors' confidence. Unemployment insurance was introduced with a promise that health and old age insurance would follow; a national minimum wage and maximum hours law was passed; the public works program was expanded and the government entered the second mortgage-lending field in order to spur home construction; a producers' marketing boards program introduced the previous year was also expanded.[21]

Workers and farmers were not impressed by the apparent death-bed conversion of the Bennett government. But it has been wrongly argued that the general reaction of the business community was negative. It is true that CPR president Edward Beatty and the Montreal *Gazette*, among others, were, as the *Gazette* put it, "shocked and startled."[22] But the response of the manufacturing and financial sectors which traditionally supported the Conservative Party was generally one of positive support. The Conservatives, unable in the two years before the New Deal to collect corporate contributions, appeared to have been revived.[23] While the New Deal may not have been the major reason for this resurgence in party finances, it did not seem to hinder Tory fund-raising.

A veritable "who's-who" of Canadian manufacturing and finance wrote to Bennett to pledge their support for the New Deal effort. Included were such luminaries of Canadian business as: A.O. Dawson, president of the Canadian Chamber of Commerce and president of Canadian Cottons; H.B. Henwood, president of the Bank of Toronto; C.H. Carlisle, president of Goodyear Tire and later also of the Dominion Bank of Canada; Colonel the Hon. H. Cockshutt, president of Cockshutt Plough; Thomas Bradshaw, president of North American Life; J.D. Johnson, president of Canada Cement; Ward Pitfield, president of Ward Pitfield Investments; W.W. Butler, president of Canadian Car and Foundry; J.W. McConnell, president of St Lawrence Sugar Refining and the *Montreal Star*; C.J. Ballantyne, president of Sherwin-Williams Paints; James McGroary, chairman of George Weston Bread; Arthur Purvis, president of CIL and Dupont; and F.N. Southam, president of Southam Publications.[24] Conspicuous by its absence was support from industrialists in the primary sectors.

There were business opponents of the New Deal. It is difficult to divorce business views on social welfare from their views on other subjects. For example, the leading department store officials, having been roasted before the Stevens Royal Commission on Price Spreads, had no good words for any Tory policies even though Stevens had been forced to resign both from the chairmanship of the commission and from the Cabinet. The department stores, as importers, were also opposed to the super-protective tariffs that were fundamental to the manufacturers' support of the Conservative Party. Nevertheless, Sir Joseph Flavelle, chairman of the Canadian Bank of Commerce and former president of Simpson's as well as Canada Packers, had been a life-long Conservative. It is difficult to determine whether his denunciation by Stevens or his generally reactionary views or both caused him to turn against that party and support the King Liberals in

1935. Similarly, CPR president Edward Beatty, another Liberal convert, was also a thorough-going reactionary who might have switched allegiances even had the New Deal not been introduced. Beatty had attempted for five years to convince his friend Bennett, former chief western solicitor for the railroad, to hand over the publicly owned Canadian National Railways to the CPR. While Bennett introduced the policy of non-competition between the two railway systems, it was politically impossible for him to bequeath the CN to the CP. Beatty, obsessed with the idea of gobbling the CN, felt betrayed.[25]

The existence of these opponents of reform is hardly surprising. Bennett, after all, was himself a newcomer to the idea that these reforms were necessary to stabilize and legitimize the existing political and economic arrangements. The onset of an election no doubt played an important role in persuading Bennett to act. But one must remember that Bennett, as the head of the capitalist state, could not afford to wait until every capitalist was convinced that change was necessary. "To save the fabric of the capitalist system" was his aim and while certain individual capitalists and even capitalist sectors as a whole might disagree with his solutions, sufficient overall support and encouragement existed in the ruling class to allow him to act. Nor had Bennett completely rejected the "iron-heel" approach to class conflict. The repression of the on-to-Ottawa trek of relief camp inmates, after all, occurred after the New Deal session of Parliament. But Bennett had realized that the stick alone, while it could play some role in intimidating the working class, had proved an insufficient instrument for mediating class conflict in favour of the bourgeoisie. The carrot was also necessary.

Bennett lacked neither traditional Conservative business support nor newspaper support for his New Deal: the defeat of his government was less the rejection of the New Deal than of a government that had waited five years to act upon problems already obvious when it took power. Bennett had not launched the "legislative assault on the corporate elite" which Richard Wilbur attributed to him and he was defeated not by the corporate elite but by the working people and farmers.[26]

Insurance and other programs, while meant to counter the communist threat, were not meant to redistribute wealth. Bennett made this clear in the debates on unemployment insurance in the House of Commons. In one debate, A.A. Heaps and the small Labour caucus argued for a non-contributory plan financed by a steeply graded income tax. A communist campaign among organizations of the unemployed, trade union locals, and labour councils called for a similar plan. Bennett attacked such a plan and said that "insurance involves premiums and premiums should be paid by the joint action alike of the insurer and the insured themselves and with the assistance of the state."[27] Insurance programs then were seen as a kind of forced savings by workers for times of unemployment, old age, or infirmity rather than as a means of increasing the relative overall income for workers. As the *Financial Times*, speaking for St James Street, commented on 5 August 1932, workers did not have the foresight that corporations had, to build reserves "against distress in the event of future unemployment." Indeed, whatever redistribution might take place as a result of the contributions of the employers and the state was to be taken away by increasing the income tax collected from working people.

In 1930 only 3 or 4 percent of working-age Canadians earned the $3000 per annum above which income tax was paid. Bennett believed these men were treated unfairly since they also paid taxes on dividends, and the money from which dividends was received was, in turn, subject to corporation tax.[28] Bennett reduced the personal tax exemption to $2000 and though inflation in the war and post-war period devalued the dollar time and again, governments did not raise the exemption. Workers who before the 1930s paid no direct taxes were faced then with both income taxes and insurance premiums to be deducted from their wages. Income that the worker once received to dispose of as he saw fit has been deducted from workers' wages for specific state "welfare" programs. Such deductions from wages—as opposed to the stiff taxes on profits and salaries called for by the left—provided the state with an income for social programs without necessitating a redistribution of wealth. While the left wanted to rob Peter to pay Paul, the state saw fit to rob Paul to pay Paul. The worker would simply have his wages rationalized so that a large portion went, through taxes and premiums, to pay for services that he previously had to set aside money for on his own.[29]

The Mackenzie King Liberals, resurrected in 1935, were rooted in this period mainly in the primary industries—metal-mining companies, the Winnipeg Grain Exchange, the lumber industry—and supported by importers and exporters, in general. The export sector, while interested in achieving class harmony, thought the Bennett programs exacted too high a price. While the banks and the largely domestic-oriented manufacturing industries saw these programs as leading to a greater stability in the domestic market, the export-oriented sectors feared their result would be higher costs of operation.[30] The compromise that was worked out over time by the Liberals involved the granting of exemptions from various taxes to the exporters, particularly the mines, as compensation for the burden of insurance programs. Low taxes for these exporters has meant higher taxes on income for working Canadians.

The control of the export sectors and particularly the mines over the provincial governments in whose spheres they largely operated was a constant complaint of Mackenzie King.[31] Ontario and Quebec, in particular, resisted King's attempts to reintroduce a federal unemployment insurance scheme after the Bennett scheme was judged unconstitutional by the Judicial Committee of the Privy Council in 1937.[32] King, leading a federal party that traditionally emphasized provincial rights and which depended for much of its finances upon the same "provincial" interest groups that dominated the junior governments,[33] was wary about reintroducing the Bennett schemes and rejected the requests of what he told his diary were "Tory" big business interests who sought to impose expensive self-interested legislation without regard to the provisions of the constitution. For the most part, King, at this point, quite opposite to Bennett, still rejected the idea that manufacturing was decisive in the Canadian economy or that the purchasing power of the urban workers was the crucial factor in the home market. In a revealing diary entry on 8 November 1937, King tells of his tariff discussions with

American secretary of state Cordell Hull and indicates a hewers-of-wood, drawers-of-water conception of the Canadian economy:

> I spoke of the home market argument, pointing out that the home market in Canada was the purchasing power in the hands of our agriculturists for manufacturers while the home market in the United States was the purchasing power in the hands of the manufacturers and those employed in industries for the purpose of agricultural products. This, the result of Canada being an exporter chiefly in natural products; the United States an exporter wholly of manufactured products.

The overall conversion of the "national" business community to social insurance measures was indicated by the hostile reaction to the ruling of the Judicial Committee in 1937 that federal unemployment insurance was unconstitutional. The Ontario Associated Boards of Trade and Chambers of Commerce, representing all the boards in the province, congratulated King on his efforts to join with the provinces in securing an amendment to the British North America Act to permit unemployment insurance and labour agencies under federal authority.[34] In December 1937 *Canadian Business*, house organ of the Canadian Chamber of Commerce, attacked the "constitutional fetish" of the three provinces—Quebec, Ontario, and New Brunswick—that were opposing federal insurance, largely, in the case of the first two provinces, at the behest of the mining companies.

The Royal Commission on Dominion–Provincial Relations, which was not empowered to deal with the merits of social insurance, nevertheless heard calls for such legislation from such groups as the Retail Merchants' Association, the Ontario Association of Real Estate Boards, and the Canadian Manufacturers' Association. The merchants argued for contributory unemployment insurance as a means of increasing purchasing power when recessions struck. The real estate men added that unemployment insurance was a proper substitute for relief which was paid by municipal property taxation; reduction in such taxation was necessary if the housing industry was to be revived and unemployment insurance was the means to this end. The CMA, using the familiar forced-savings argument, called, as it had in the past, for a universal contributory pension plan to replace the selective deserving-poor program.[35]

The major attempt to place a program of social insurance in the context of an overall program for economic stability was that of the National Employment Commission, which reported in 1938. Its chairman, Arthur Purvis, was one of Canada's most influential businessmen. He was president of the Canadian branches of CIL and Dupont Rubber and a director of a large number of firms. Purvis, like Bennett, advocated a conservative form of state planning to ensure the existing property and power relations among the various social classes in Canada. His vice-chairman on the commission was the veteran Trades and Labour Congress president Tom Moore and the general concurrence of the two men on the best means to attack unemployment reflected the conservative ideology of the American-dominated crafts unions which predominated in the TLC.[36] Purvis believed that insurance and other spending programs could serve the purpose of lifting the economy when it began to sag and could also provide other benefits for industry. His report called for a "coordinated attack" on unemployment. This would include unemployment insurance and perhaps other insurance programs, a national network of labour exchanges, expanded federal vocational education programs, and a comprehensive housing policy including subsidized rental housing for the poor and state loans to persons seeking home improvements. The emphasis was on a strengthening of the role of the central government in dealing with unemployment. For reasons of efficiency, the wasteful and unco-ordinated municipal relief programs had to be eliminated and replaced by a program of federal planning that would make the central government a major source of investment in the marketplace when the private investors, for whatever reasons, were not sufficiently carrying on the process of capital accumulation to maintain employment and hence demand at reasonable levels.

The Purvis report was rejected as "Tory" by Mackenzie King. He was horrified by the commission's disregard for provincial rights and described Purvis's report contradictorily as an "academic treatise" and a Tory big business report.[37] Purvis had been suggested as chairman to King by Charles Dunning, minister of finance. King had appointed Dunning minister of finance because of his direct connections with Montreal capital and yet distrusted him and his appointees for these connections. Ironically, King, who always felt business exercised too great an influence over governments, both Liberal and Conservative, was to the right of many of the businessmen and rejected as "Tory" certain social measures they proposed despite the fact that they went no further than his prescriptions twenty years earlier in *Industry and Humanity*.

The Purvis report reflected the attitudes of those businessmen who were most keen to use the state to prevent the repeated crises from which capitalism, through the marketplace alone, could find no protection. The "national" business community, led by the Canadian Chamber of Commerce, gave support to the Purvis proposals and urged the federal government to alter the constitution so as to make possible its implementation. The Montreal Board of Trade told the Royal Commission on Dominion–Provincial Relations,

> taxation for the purpose of social services transfers purchasing power from the richer to the poorer classes, raises the standard of living of the poor, increases their demand for commodities and thereby tends towards industrial stability and prosperity. Furthermore, in a period of economic depression, heavier government expenditures, whether paid for by taxes or by loans, are justified and necessary in order to fill the gap resulting from the fear and inactivity which paralyze private enterprise."[38]

Indeed, the perspective of virtually all the business presentations before the Rowell-Sirois Commission was for increased federal government control over areas traditionally within the provincial sphere and for the weakening of the provincial governments. But the resource industries, who had fattened the most from provincial troughs, were as absent from the long roll call of companies and business organizations making their views known to the commission as they were from the similar list of industrialists praising R.B. Bennett's New Deal.[39]

The combined urgings of "Tory" businessmen and the depression militancy of farmers, workers, and the unemployed were insufficient to push cautious Mackenzie King to the point his Conservative predecessor had reached by 1935. But the onset of war strengthened the position of the working class and made it apparent that Bennett had been correct in his prognostication that capitalism was threatened by a working-class uprising if reforms were not forthcoming. During the 1930s, despite the general militancy of both workers and the unemployed, the state machinery had been used effectively to hold back attempts at unionization. The repression of Communists and the CIO, while it defeated neither group, held trade unionists in 1939 to a number not substantially greater than the 1930 figure. By the end of six years of war, however, the trade union movement had more than doubled in membership, the result largely of the successful organization of mass-production industries.[40] Government labour policies during the war were extremely repressive. But it proved impossible to prevent unionization under wartime conditions of full employment and even labour shortages. As a result, by war's end King had turned his attention not to the question of whether there would be unions but what kind of unions there would be.[41]

The militancy of the trade union movement had its counterpart in the rising popularity of left-wing political parties and especially the CCF.[42] The Conservative Party, in the face of working-class agitation and the CCF threat, began to reassert its New Deal programs. Arthur Meighen, briefly resuscitated as party leader in late 1941, lost to a CCF candidate in a by-election in February 1942 in York South, a supposedly safe working-class Tory seat in Toronto. Meighen had made conscription and the war effort the issue; the CCF had successfully argued that the real issue was reconstruction after the war and what working people should expect from governments after having sacrificed so much to defeat fascism.[43] Meighen, an admirer of the Roosevelt New Deal in the 1930s and a supporter of the Bennett reforms had moved far to the right by the 1940s.[44]

Indeed, the oscillations of Meighen, like those of Bennett and King, between the use of repression and the use of social programs to diminish class conflict, indicates the extent to which the latter was regarded as tactical. Meighen, after all, had sent in troops to break the Winnipeg General Strike and had, as minister of justice, composed the infamous Section 98 which outlawed all activities that might be construed as falling within the rubric of a vaguely defined "sedition." Yet, faced in the 1930s with a widening gulf between the workers and capitalists, he had decided it was tactically correct to introduce social programs to pacify the workers and became the Tory spokesman in the Senate for the Bennett New Deal programs. Later he turned against such programs, believing that the war effort might be used to unite the "nation" and obscure class conflicts.

But other Conservative Party leaders, and especially J.M. Macdonnell, recognized that more than ever it was tactically necessary to use the state machinery to initiate reforms that would blunt the working-class offensive of the war years. Macdonnell, president of National Trust, had thought even before the war years that it was dangerous to wait for private economic forces to correct the depression. He told a Conservative Party conference in 1933 that government had a role to play in stimulating demand during recessions. In an earlier address in the same year, Macdonnell had made his position clear: what was necessary was to "remove the grit from the individualist machine and make it run smoothly—meanwhile allowing the process of the last century to continue viz. the gradual socialization of those things which the sense of the community agrees should be socialized." In September 1942 Macdonnell organized an unofficial conference of Conservatives in Port Hope, Ontario, to draw up a possible program for the party to deal with "modern needs" and to prevent Canada from being engulfed by "totalitarianism" of either left or right. The full range of reforms in the New Deal were reasserted and, reflecting the new political realities, other reforms were added. Not only would the workers have a variety of social insurance programs for home-buying to protect them from the hazards of the marketplace, but they would have guaranteed rights to trade unions and collective bargaining.[45] Bennett, in 1935, had angrily rejected a CCF suggestion that blacklisting of trade unionists by employers be made illegal.[46] But, in 1942, with the trade union movement having established itself in many mass-production industries despite repressive state policies, the Conservatives accepted the inevitable.

Though the Montreal *Gazette* and other elements in the Conservative Party were still unconvinced that their party should commit itself to the welfare state, the party convention in December 1942 chose Macdonnell's candidate, John Bracken, the premier of Manitoba, as its new leader, and adopted substantially the Port Hope policies as the party platform.[47] The "duty of the state," said the platform, was to maintain both a "high level" of income for the individual and "the principle of private initiative and enterprise."[48]

Mackenzie King was finally being forced to act in this period. His earlier objections to the Purvis report's disregard for provincial rights were lessened by the report of the Rowell-Sirois Commission in 1940 that a strengthened federal government and correspondingly weaker provincial governments were necessary to equalize living standards across the country and to revive investor confidence shaken by the bankruptcies of many junior levels of government. Social insurance programs, for example, it recommended, should be under federal jurisdiction. Shortly after the report was tabled, King, taking advantage of Maurice Duplessis' defeat by Adelard Godbout's Liberals in Quebec (largely thanks to the aid of federal ministers) and Ontario premier Mitch Hepburn's temporary willingness to make concessions for the war effort, was able to secure a constitutional amendment allowing the federal government to reintroduce the unemployment insurance bill.[49]

The unemployment insurance bill, however, was not followed by further reform legislation until 1944. In the interim, the King government had actually considered discontinuing the programs of government mortgage-lending begun by Bennett in 1935 with the Dominion Housing Act and extended slightly by the Liberals in 1937 in the National Housing Act. The life insurance companies, mortgage companies, construction industry, and timber industry had all been active in convincing Bennett to include this legislation in the New Deal.[50] Now these business sectors all joined labour in opposing its removal; the legislation was left in place.[51]

But King, who had bowed to the most conservative elements of the business community before the war, was now faced with the certainty of political defeat if he did not act to create some or all of the programs that the other two major parties were advocating and which King had also supposedly supported since the First World War. The Liberal administration in Ontario had been badly defeated in the provincial election of 1943 and several federal Liberal seats had been lost in by-elections. A poll in September 1943 gave the CCF the support of 29 percent of the electorate; the Liberals and Tories each had 28 percent.[52] King had made, in a sense, his life's work the harmonizing of class relations in Canada and, during his years of employment with the Rockefellers, in the United States. As deputy minister of labour, minister of labour, and finally prime minister, he had sought to devise means of ensuring labour peace and the unity of labour and capital "under the ideal of social service." In his 1918 book, *Industry and Humanity*, to which he would make endless references in the future, King, with the aid of confusing and semi-mystical charts, argued that public opinion was the major means of forcing the parties within industry to co-operate.[53] In practice, King's labour policies had been designed to maintain the status quo of social relations.[54] *Industry and Humanity* also spoke favourably of the British Labour Party's idea of a National Minimum standard of living, which would be collectively guaranteed by society as a whole through state action. Minimum wages, maximum hours, and programs of social insurance were to be part of the state program to achieve the National Minimum. But again, in practice, King had been in office for many years without introducing such programs. Now, however, he was finally acting in order to introduce "a wholly new conception of industry as being in the nature of social service for the benefit of all, not as something existing only for the benefit of a favoured few."[55] A shift in class forces had occurred and made impossible the continuation of a do-nothing approach. King could at last dare to defy the more reactionary wing of the bourgeoisie and his party.

King, it might be emphasized, was not a businessman and did not pretend to act as a spokesman for business. His general views were compatible with business views but he always felt that businessmen were, at heart, Tories. He feared both the political and the economic consequences of offending the business community. Thus it is not surprising that programs to which King was committed twenty-five years earlier were not introduced until the mid-1940s. Given the Liberal Party's need of business support and King's commitment to keeping the business community happy enough that new private investment in the Canadian economy would not be reduced, it is hardly surprising that little social legislation was introduced in the 1920s, a period when the trade union movement was in retreat after its victories of the war period. Industry was hostile to social legislation at that time and there seemed to be no pressing need to act. While a shift in business thinking occurred in the 1930s as a result of the militancy of workers and the unemployed, such a shift was, as observed, less pronounced among Liberal businessmen than among traditionally Tory sectors of business. King could still not afford to go too far without committing political suicide. By 1944, however, he could argue that class conflict had reached such a point that social legislation was the only alternative to socialism. While some members of the ruling class remained unconvinced, and even actively opposed such legislation, the class as a whole was won over.

Jack Granatstein, in an excellent account of the wartime debate within government on the question of social security legislation, argues correctly that at the root of the social reform programs of 1944 and 1945—family allowances, mortgage-lending programs, spending programs for reconversion of the wartime economy to a peacetime economy—"was the fear of postwar unemployment, depression and possible disorder." He notes that these programs were balanced by various programs of assistance to industry as part of "an attractive—and expensive—package" to pacify the business community.[56] The "package" approach to various state programs meant to produce stability of class relations was not new. The Bennett New Deal, the Purvis report, the Montreal Board of Trade report to the Rowell-Sirois Commission, the Conservative Port Hope platform, all similarly integrated programs such as housing construction, social insurance, marketing boards, bonuses to business, etc., in an attempt to devise a system that would use the state to smooth out certain contradictions within capitalism and thereby calm the restiveness of the working people. Interestingly, while the *Report on Social Security for Canada*,[57] prepared by Professor Leonard Marsh for the Committee on Reconstruction set up by the Cabinet, received a great deal of government attention, the actual legislation fell far short of its recommendations, particularly in the ignoring of the recommendation for health insurance. Clearly, "welfare state" measures in Canada were not to be introduced all at once.

o

The government *White Paper on Employment and Income* of 12 April 1945 was a further attempt to make clear that the state was to play a large role in stabilizing the economy in order to legitimize the private-enterprise system. So as to maintain a "high and stable level of employment and income," the government would seek to keep its revenues and expenditures in balance not one year at a time but over longer—though unspecified—periods. This would allow the government to budget for surpluses when the economy was in a buoyant stage of the business cycle. When the cycle turned downward and unemployment threatened, the government would "incur deficits and increases in the national debt resulting from its employment and income policy, whether that policy in the circumstances is best applied through increased expenditures or reduced taxation."

While such crypto-Keynesianism was not a common demand of the business community, Granatstein exaggerates in commenting that "before the war, budget deficits had been akin to sin; in 1945 they were simply an economic tool."[58] It would be fairer to say that before the war proponents of greater government expenditure largely evaded the question of where the money for increased spending would be found. The Montreal Board of Trade, quoted above, seemed to regard financing by debt or taxation as equally acceptable measures, providing in both cases that the levels discussed were within reason.

The "welfare state" from the beginning was regarded as a contradictory blessing by the governments and businessmen who felt obliged to support it. Michal Kalecki, arguing in 1943 that businessmen still largely opposed government measures for stimulating employment and particularly measures which would subsidize consumption, believed that even if mass pressure converted them to the opposite view they would soon be in the opposition camp once again. The "maintenance of full employment," he argued, would remove from the bosses the threat of unemployment as a disciplinary measure. Working-class militancy would be increased and demands for wage increases and better working conditions would result in large numbers of strikes. This proved to be the case in the war years. And, as Kalecki noted, even the fact of increasing profits does not compensate capitalists for what appears to be a threat to their control over their factories. In this context, the attack against social insurance and government spending by the business community in recent years is a call for a return to the "individualism" of a former day when a job or relief from the state was a privilege and not perceived as a right.[59]

How far, then, will the capitalist class go to undo the measures that they were willing to concede in an earlier day in order to pacify working-class militancy and stabilize the economic system? No easy answer can be given to this question. What has been suggested is that the radicalism of the depression years and the fears that such radicalism engendered brought the first abortive attempt in 1935 to introduce state policies for stabilization. The even greater working-class militancy of the war years forced even the cautious members of the ruling class to give way at the war's end. It can be assumed that the curbing of working-class militancy remains an aim of Canadian businessmen and, to some degree, the welfare state that was meant to pacify workers now appears, as Kalecki argued, to encourage their militancy. On the other hand, from the beginning, capitalists who supported "welfare state" measures recognized the compensatory stimulus to consumption that these spending programs provided and their role in smoothing out the business cycle. It may be true, nevertheless, that the capitalist class as a whole would be willing to endure a steeper business cycle *if* this is the price of forcing the working class to be more insecure and less demanding. In this context, the extent to which workers resist cuts in state spending will play a crucial role, just as, at the present time, the future of wage controls appears dim because of the non-support of the working class.

The capitalist state's continued willingness and ability to maintain a high level of social expenditures is affected by still another factor—although more than a cursory discussion of this is beyond the scope of this essay— and that is the growth of the economy. From the beginning, ruling-class supporters of the welfare state believed that continuous economic growth was inevitable and that with the growth of the economic pie an analogous growth in social benefits could be allowed. Questions of what was produced and the question of relative distribution of wealth could be ignored as long as overall wealth increased and the share of income of various classes increased proportionately owing to state measures that put a floor on the income of the working class. But economic growth has slowed down, and state spending, involving spheres of activity that have little tendency to show increasing rates of productivity, has tended to increase at rates faster than the rates of economic growth.[60] It is clear that capitalists cannot continue to expect to get away with an availability of cheap resources, a continued neglect of environmental factors and the safety of workers, and the continued availability of an exploitable Third World from which super-profits can be extracted.

In these conditions, bourgeois politicians find themselves in the unpalatable role of having not only to justify temporary cutbacks in minimal social service programs, but more generally to "resocialize" a populace weaned on the ideology of permanent capitalist affluence. As Pierre Trudeau himself recently put it, "a large part of my message as a politician is to say: we have to put an end to rising expectations. We have to explain to people that we may even have to put an end to our love for our parents or old people in society, even our desire to give more for education and medical research."[61]

Of course the capitalist state, acting on behalf of the interests of the capitalist class as a whole, can afford to ignore reactionary demands from particular individuals or even particular sectors of the ruling class. Trudeau's recently acquired illiberalism with respect to social legislation reflects the growing sense of crisis amongst the capitalist class as a whole. It is not that Trudeau opposes in principle social legislation or even that he is a direct representative of the big bourgeoisie. Rather it is simply that, like Mackenzie King, Trudeau takes existing class relations as a given and determines policies within limits set by these class relations. In part, these limits can be understood in terms of the class origins of these politicians and the class composition of the bourgeois parties. But there are other, more directly economic, limits that the politicians dedicated to the existing class relations must labour under. These are perhaps best outlined in a speech by Liberal finance minister, Charles Dunning, in 1938:

> We must follow policies which will enable it [private enterprise] to work in accordance with its essential principles. The most important of these principles is that decisions as to whether the individual shall spend and consume or shall save and invest or shall save and hoard are left to the individual's own initiative. If therefore the answers to the questions as to whether plants are to be built or extended, new houses are to be created and industry is going to expand or to stagnate, depend upon the decisions of tens of thousands of individuals who are free agents and not regimented sheep, it follows that governments must pursue policies which cre-

ate confidence rather than fear and uncertainty, which give leadership and guidance and encouragement rather than stifle initiative and paralyze new enterprise.[62]

In short, then, the "welfare state" changes nothing that is fundamental about capitalism. While it places a floor on workers' incomes, it leaves unaltered the control of means of production. Production for profit and not for use and the reduction of labour to an extension of the machines it operates for the benefit of capital remain the goals of the economic system. Indeed, the oscillations in support for state social spending among the ruling class result from disagreements in particular circumstances as to how useful that expenditure is toward these goals. It is clear that the working class must defend every "welfare state" gain that it has won. On the other hand, there can be little doubt that government social programs do serve the function of legitimizing the system by making it appear that the worst aspects of laissez faire have been compensated. At the present time, though, the ruling-class pendulum seems to have swung away from these programs and back toward the idea of a large dose of unemployment as a means of teaching the working class respect for its betters. It is dangerous to hazard a guess as to how serious the current *economic* crisis of capitalism really is—it has recovered from crises before—but there can be little doubt that the *legitimization* crisis of capitalism will increase as it attempts to force workers to accept both lower wages and fewer state benefits. But one should be careful not to assume the stupidity of one's enemy: the class struggle has forced the ruling class to concede various reforms in the past and, in the Canadian case, part of the ruling class was willing to make these concessions before it was absolutely necessary. It would be wrong to assume blithely that, given a strong working-class reaction against government cut-backs, the capitalist class will not relent again. While cut-backs must be opposed, such opposition must be placed within the context of an attack on the capitalist system as a whole or, like wage struggles, it may prove episodic and leave unchanged the relative force of bourgeois ideology in the working class.

NOTES

1. Research Committee of the League for Social Reconstruction, *Social Planning for Canada* (1935; Toronto, 1975), xix.

2. Hugh G.J. Aitken, for example, says that the theory that the state acted merely as an agent for private economic interests in the nation-building period "could probably be supported" and that the distinction between "the state" and "private enterprise" in Canada "often seems artificial." "Defensive Expansionism: The State and Economic Growth in Canada" in *The State and Economic Growth* (New York, 1959), 79–114. From a more radical perspective, H. Viv Nelles details the virtually complete power that resource companies had in dictating provincial "regulatory" policies dealing with the resource industries. *The Politics of Development: Forests, Mines and Hydro-Electric Power in Ontario, 1849–1941* (Toronto, 1974).

3. *Canada Year Book* (1972), 1218–19.

4. Allan M. Maslove, *The Pattern of Taxation in Canada* (Ottawa, 1972), 64.

5. See R.B. Splane, *Social Welfare in Ontario, 1791–1893: A Study of Public Welfare Administration* (Toronto, 1965); Dennis Trevor Guest, "The Development of Income Maintenance Programmes in Canada, 1945–1967" (PhD diss., University of London, 1968); Elisabeth Wallace, "The Origin of the Social Welfare State in Canada, 1867–1900," in this text. On Montreal, see Terry Copp, *The Anatomy of Poverty: The Condition of the Working Class in Montreal, 1897–1929* (Toronto, 1974). On the education question, see Greg Kealey, ed., *Canada Investigates Industrialism: The Royal Commission on the Relations of Labor and Capital, 1889* (Toronto, 1973), xix, 15–16, 22, 39–40.

6. James Weinstein, *The Corporate Ideal in the Liberal State, 1900–1918* (Boston, 1969); Michael Bliss, *A Living Profit* (Toronto, 1974), 142; Michael Piva, "Workmen's Compensation Movement in Ontario," *Ontario History* (March 1975): 39–56.

7. Public Archives of Ontario, *Report of the Ontario Commission on Unemployment* (1916), 82–83.

8. Kenneth McNaught, *A Prophet in Politics: A Biography of J.S. Woodsworth* (Toronto, 1959), 218–20.

9. A complete list of Bennett holdings is found in Public Archives of Canada (hereafter PAC), R.B. Bennett Papers, vol. 901, pp. 563867–3900; Bennett's partnership with Beaverbrook is discussed in A.J.P. Taylor, *Beaverbrook* (London, 1972), 15, 34, 36–37, 86; Bennett's involvement with Eddy is detailed in Bennett Papers, vol. 915, 916, and 917; the labelling of Canada Packers and Imperial Tobacco as oligopolies appears in *Report of the Royal Commission on Price Spreads and Mass Buying* (Ottawa, 1935), 53, 59.

10. For example, C.H. Cahan, Bennett's only secretary of state, was a leading Montreal corporation attorney and industrialist and, like Bennett, a past Beaverbrook protégé. Cahan had been, on behalf of the Bank of Montreal, legal advisor and executive head of a vast array of tramway, electric light, and hydro-electric enterprises in South America, Trinidad, and Mexico. National Revenue Minister E.B. Ryckman was past president of Dunlop Tire and director of Gurney Foundry, IBM, Addressograph Company, Russell Motor Company, and others. When illness forced his retirement, he was replaced by millionaire investment banker, R.C. Matthews, later a president of the Canadian Chamber of Commerce. Finance Minister E.N. Rhodes was past president of the British America Nickel Corporation, later purchased by International Nickel. See *Canadian Parliamentary Guide* (1930–35). Links between politicians as well as leading civil servants and the corporations are traced in Libby C. Park and Frank W. Park, *Anatomy of Big Business* (Toronto, 1962); John Porter, *The Vertical Mosaic* (Toronto, 1965); Wallace Clement, *The Canadian Corporate Elite* (Toronto, 1975).

11. See Ronald Liversedge, *Recollections of the On-to-Ottawa Trek*, ed. Victor Hoar (Toronto, 1973).

12. *Labour Legislation: A Study Prepared for the Royal Commission on Dominion–Provincial Relations* (Ottawa, 1939), 5–6.

13. *Report of the Annual Meeting of the Bank of Montreal* (3 Dec. 1934).

14. Gordon to Bennett, 6 Jan. 1934, Bennett Papers, vol. 811, p. 503059 (emphasis added).

15. *Monthly Review of the Bank of Nova Scotia* (Aug. 1934), 4.

16. See Oscar Ryan, *Tim Buck: A Conscience for Canada* (Toronto, 1975), 128–29; A.B. McKillop, "The Communist as Conscience: Jacob Penner and Winnipeg Civic Politics, 1934–1935" in *Cities in the West*, ed. A.R. McCormack and Ian Macpherson (Ottawa, 1974), 181–209; Liversedge, *Recollections*, 15–34; "Some General Observations on the Administration of Unemployment Relief in Western Canada: Report for the Prime Minister's Office, 1932" in *The Dirty Thirties*, ed. Michiel Horn (Toronto, 1972), 272–76.

17. *Financial Times*, 21 Sept. 1934; Dorothy Kidd, "Women's Organization: Learning from Yesterday" in *Women at Work: Ontario, 1850–1930* (Toronto, 1974), 351–57.

18. *Pulp and Paper of Canada* (June 1935), 302.

19. *Winnipeg Free Press*, 10 and 19 Sept. 1935. There were, of course, businessmen who opposed unemployment insurance and indeed businessmen who opposed all of the Bennett reforms. Business opponents of unemployment insurance argued that it would add to the cost of doing business and hurt Canada's export position. It would encourage sloth and remove the insecurity of employees, which allowed employers to impose labour discipline. Further, it would hit all industries equally regardless of the incidence of unemployment in a given industry. Prominent opponents of unemployment insurance included CPR president Edward Beatty, Canadian Bank of Commerce vice-president Sir Thomas White, and the Montreal *Gazette*, among others.

20. Bennett to Howard Robinson, 11 June 1935, Bennett Papers, vol. 715.

21. The philosophy and programs of the "New Deal" were introduced in a series of radio speeches, which are reprinted in large part in Ernest Watkins, *R.B. Bennett: A Biography* (Toronto, 1963), 253–63.

22. J.R.H. Wilbur, *The Bennett Administration, 1930–1935*, CHA booklet no. 24 (Ottawa, 1969), 14.

23. The party's poor financial position in the period before the New Deal is discussed in J.R.H. Wilbur, "H.H. Stevens and the Reconstruction Party," *Canadian Historical Review* 45, 1 (March 1964): 6.

24. Bennett Papers, vols. 713, 714, 715, 718, 949.

25. On Flavelle, see Michael Bliss, "A Canadian Businessman and War: The Case of Joseph Flavelle" in *War and Society in North America*, ed. J.L. Granatstein and Robert Cuff (Toronto, 1971), 20–36; on Beatty, see D.H.

Miller-Barstow, *Beatty of the CPR* (Toronto, 1950).

26. The *Gazette's* defection must be balanced against the continued support in Montreal of the *Montreal Star*, presided over by financier Lord Atholstan and St Lawrence Sugar president J.W. McConnell. The Toronto *Evening Telegram* and the *Mail and Empire* gave enthusiastic support. Most importantly, F.N. Southam told Senator C.J. Ballantyne that he had directed his usually Liberal chain of newspapers to give positive support to Bennett and the New Deal. See Bennett Papers, vol. 715 and 949. A detailed discussion of reaction to the New Deal is found in Alvin Finkel, "Canadian Business and the 'Reform' Process in Canada in the 1930s" (PhD diss., University of Toronto, 1976), 125–28; and in Wilbur, *The Bennett Administration*, 20.

27. Canada, House of Commons, *Debates*, 28 April 1931, 1077; 29 April 1931, 1104.

28. Ibid., 6 May 1930, 1831.

29. See Leo Johnson, *Poverty in Wealth* (Toronto, 1974), 24–26.

30. *Financial Post*, 1 June 1935.

31. Mitch Hepburn, the premier of Ontario, for example, was seen by King as "in the hands of McCullagh of the *Globe* and the *Globe* and McCullagh in the hands of financial mining interests." PAC, King Diary, 13 April 1937. In general, King, in his diaries, regarded many Canadian politicians, both Liberal and Conservative, as "in the hands" of various business interest groups.

32. See Richard M.H. Alway, "Hepburn, King, and the Rowell-Sirois Commission," *Canadian Historical Review* 48, 2 (June 1967): 113–41.

33. King's desire to maintain the support of the mining companies is indicated, for example, by his opposition in 1934 to the Conservative government's 10 percent tax on the windfall profits gained by gold-mining companies when the price of gold

increased from $21 to $35. He wrote to an opponent of the tax: "The present Government has made many blunders, but I think this one with respect to the ten percent tax on the production of gold is perhaps the worst of the lot, considering, as you say, that it formed the major feature of this year's budget. . . . I hope that some of those who have suffered as a result of the Government's policies will lend us a hand when the time comes to put the present Administration out of office." King to James E. Day, barrister, 5 May 1934, PAC, King Papers, vol. 199, pp. 170306–7.

34. 12 Nov. 1937, ibid., vol. 238, p. 204650.

35. Royal Commission on Dominion– Provincial Relations, *Report of Hearings*, 31 May, p. 9691 (merchants); 19 Jan., p. 2739 (real estate); 17 Jan. 1938, p. 2375 (CMA).

36. The Canadian sections of CIO unions were, until 1939, still in the TLC. But they were clearly a minority within the organization and indeed only began to rival the crafts unions in their membership during the war period after their ouster from the TLC and the formation of their own federation, the Canadian Congress of Labour. See Irving M. Abella, *Nationalism, Communism, and Canadian Labour* (Toronto, 1973).

37. King Diary, 4 April 1938. After calling the report an "academic treatise," King said: "It was a mistake having Purvis as chairman, he being a big businessman and a Tory at heart, not understanding methods of politics."

38. Royal Commission on Dominion– Provincial Relations, *Report of Hearings*, pp. 524–25 (Chamber of Commerce); p. 8153 (Board of Trade).

39. See Finkel, "Canadian Business," 352–89.

40. Estimated trade union membership in Canada, according to the Dominion Department of Labour annual reports, was 310 534 in 1931 and 315 073 in 1939. Grauer, *Labour*

Legislation, 68. There were 711 117 trade unionists in 1945. Canada, Department of Labour, *Labour Organizations in Canada* (1963).

41. "Orders-in-council were passed freezing wage levels, facilitating the use of troops in labour disputes, and limiting the right to strike. The government also refused to force employers to negotiate with their workers and continued to appoint men whom the Congress [of Canadian Labour] considered 'anti-labour' to government boards." See Abella, *Nationalism, Communism*, 72; see also Stuart Jamieson, *Times of Trouble: Labour Unrest and Industrial Conflict in Canada, 1900–66* (Ottawa, 1968).

42. See J.L. Granatstein, *Canada's War: The Politics of the Mackenzie King Government, 1939–1945* (Toronto, 1975), 264–65.

43. J.L. Granatstein, *The Politics of Survival: The Conservative Party of Canada, 1939–1945* (Toronto, 1967), 110.

44. Roger Graham, *Arthur Meighen: No Surrender* (Toronto, 1965), 3: 67, 117.

45. Queen's University Archives, Macdonnell Papers, vol. 52, "Remarks on the History of Inflation: An Address Given to the Liberal–Conservative Summer School at Newmarket, September, 1933," and "The Canadian Institute on Economics and Politics: Reports of Two of the Addresses." The Port Hope conference is discussed in Granatstein, *Politics of Survival*, 125–50 and 207–10, and John R. Williams, *The Conservative Party of Canada, 1920–1949* (Durham, NC, 1956), 72.

46. Canada, House of Commons, *Debates*, 18 Feb. 1935, 949–52.

47. Williams, *Conservative Party*, 70. Bracken, like Macdonnell, was no recent convert to the Port Hope philosophies. In a statement to Canadian Press in 1933, he had praised the Roosevelt New Deal and concluded that "controlled inflation combined with new public works by the federal government would seem

to be inevitable if the problems of the unemployed and the debtors in all classes are to be met in a constructive way." *Winnipeg Free Press*, 10 Aug. 1933.

48. Granatstein, *Politics of Survival*, 213.

49. Canada, *Report of the Royal Commission on Dominion–Provincial Relations*, book 2, *Recommendations* (Ottawa, 1940), 151, 157, 270–74; J.W. Pickersgill, ed., *The Mackenzie King Record* (Toronto, 1960), 1: 60–61.

50. The Canadian Construction Association, in particular, took credit for the legislation. *Monetary Times*, 11 Jan. 1936. The position of the mortgage companies was outlined by T. Darcy Leonard, solicitor of the Dominion Mortgages and Investments Association, in *Journal of the Canadian Bankers' Association* (April 1936): 297–303. See also *Canadian Lumberman*, 1 July 1934; and Canada, House of Commons, *Debates*, 25 June 1935, 3948.

51. See PAC, Department of Finance Papers, 1942, vol. 704–6.

52. Granatstein, *Canada's War*, 264–65.

53. W.L.M. King, *Industry and Humanity: A Study in the Principles Underlying Industrial Construction* (1918; Toronto, 1973), 336.

54. An especially trenchant evaluation of King's labour policies is provided by Jamieson in *Times of Trouble*, 128–32, 276–94. Jamieson's conclusions are substantially the same as those of the stridently anti-King study, H.S. Ferns and B. Ostry, *The Age of Mackenzie King: The Rise of the Leader* (1955; Toronto, 1976).

55. Canada, House of Commons, *Debates*, 28 July 1944, 5535.

56. Granatstein, *Canada's War*, 276, 278.

57. (Ottawa, 1943; Toronto, 1975).

58. Granatstein, *Canada's War*, 277, 278.

59. "Political Aspects of Full Employment," reprinted in E.K. Hunt and Jesse Schwartz, *A Critique of Economic Theory* (Middlesex, 1972), 426–29. I would disagree with Kalecki that, by 1943, the pressure of the masses had yet to make itself felt in the viewpoints adopted by big business, at least in Canada.

60. The contradictions that confront the "welfare state" are discussed in James O'Connor, *The Fiscal Crisis of the State* (New York, 1973), and Rick Deaton, "The Fiscal Crisis of the State in Canada" in *The Political Economy of the State*, ed. Dimitrios Roussopoulos (Montreal, 1973), 18–56.

61. *Maclean's*, 10 Jan. 1977, 8.

62. Quoted in *Canadian Business* (July 1938), 12.

MACKENZIE KING AND THE
GENESIS OF FAMILY ALLOWANCES
IN CANADA, 1939–1944 ◇

RAYMOND B. BLAKE

o

In July 1945, the Canadian government introduced a system of universal family allowances providing monthly cash payments to all families with children under the age of sixteen. This was one of the most important events in Canada's evolving social security system. However, Canadian academics who have studied family allowances have rarely treated them primarily as a social security measure, perhaps because of the scepticism with which they view the enigmatic prime minister Mackenzie King, who introduced the measure. Whatever the reason, King's family allowances have been portrayed as a policy to appease labour and maintain the wartime price- and wage-stabilization program, as a political weapon to beat the surging socialist hordes in the Co-operative Commonwealth Federation, and as the triumph of macro-economic management and Keynesian economics.[1] In other words, Mackenzie King believed Canada should have family allowances if necessary, but not necessarily because of social security. This is only part of the story, however.

The Mackenzie King government adopted family allowances as part of its postwar social security program, but it realized that there were other benefits too. Mackenzie King had a life-long commitment to the ideals of social security. Academics have often commented derisively that he loved to point out that he had outlined the need for social security and many other things in 1918, when he wrote *Industry and Humanity: A Study in the Principles Underlying Industrial Reconstruction*. There is also general agree-

◇ This paper has not been previously published. It is used here with the permission of the author. He wishes to acknowledge the financial support of the Government of Canada through the Canadian Studies and Special Projects Directorate in preparation of this article.

ment that King was a cautious politician and acted only when he was convinced that policies would serve the interests of his country, his party, and his leadership. King believed that the conditions were right for the introduction of family allowances in 1945, as they had been in 1941 for his unemployment insurance scheme. Moreover, King was influenced by international discussions on social security and family allowances, and he believed that action on his part would re-establish his claim to be a pioneer in the field, a claim he made often to other allied leaders. Finally, King and many others in Canada recognized the importance of social security, together with increased government intervention to maintain full employment, as a way of preserving the liberal democratic state.

Mackenzie King and other world leaders were obviously worried about the postwar period. The memories of the turmoil and uncertainty in the aftermath of the First World War were fresh in their minds. So, too, was the prolonged economic crisis of the 1930s. Governments everywhere realized that the transition from war to peace had to be made without a return to the problems of unemployment and want that had characterized the prewar period. "When the war is won, there will be an immense task to repair the great physical destruction caused by the war," King told the American Federation of Labor at its 1942 convention in Toronto. "These tasks alone will provide work for millions of men and women for many years. But the work of repairing and restoring the ravages of war will not be enough," he warned. Governments everywhere had to work to eliminate the fear of unemployment and the sense of insecurity that workers faced when their capacity to meet the needs of their families was threatened. "Until these fears have been eliminated," he told Canada's labour leaders, "the war for freedom will not be won. The era of freedom will be achieved only as social security and human welfare become the main concern of men and nations." The specifics of social welfare, he admitted, would have to be spelled out in due course, but the "new order" he envisioned for Canada would include, as a "national minimum," full employment, adequate nutrition and housing, health insurance, and social security. "Men who have fought in this war, and others who have borne its privations and sufferings, will never be satisfied with a return to the conditions which prevailed before 1939," he acknowledge in closing. "The broader and deeper conception of victory will be found only in a new world order."[2]

Mackenzie King was not alone in recognizing the need for greater social security. Earlier, in January 1941, President Franklin D. Roosevelt had told the American Congress that international security rested upon four essential human freedoms. One of these was freedom from want. Only when each nation could provide an acceptable standard of living for its people would there truly be freedom. Anthony Eden, the British foreign secretary, had told his compatriots on 29 May 1941 that one of the postwar aims of the British government was to establish "social security abroad as well as at home, through co-ordinated efforts of Britain, the Dominions, the United States and South America to stabilize currencies, feed starving peoples, avert fluctuations of employment, prices and markets."[3] Roosevelt and British prime minister Winston Churchill reiterated these principles in the

Atlantic Charter on 14 August 1941: "[We] desire to bring about the fullest collaboration between all nations in the economic field with the object of securing, for all, improved labour standards, economic adjustment and social security." At a conference on social security in Chile in September 1942, over twenty countries from North and South America agreed that they should adopt policies promoting greater social security. The conference co-ordinator, Nelson Rockefeller, captured the outlook of the participants when he stated that "This is a war about social security; it is a war for social security."[4]

King's minister most interested in social security agreed. Ian Mackenzie, the minister of pensions and health, epitomized fears for the postwar period when he told an audience in June 1941 that, "if old dogmas and old doctrines—old philosophies of government—cannot solve that problem—then we must look to newer remedies and new faiths and newer solutions."[5] Speaking in September 1942, he said, "I want the working man in the factory, the soldier on the battle front, the young mother caring for her overseas husband's little children to know that the Government in whom they have reposed their confidence not only shares their aspirations for a brighter tomorrow, but is, in a direct and positive way, planning to that end."[6]

Reconstruction planning in Canada was a major concern almost from the onset of hostilities. Shortly after Canada declared war on Germany, the King Cabinet started to think about the postwar period and created a Cabinet Committee on Demobilization and Re-establishment on 8 December 1939, chaired by Ian Mackenzie. Initially, the committee was only interested in the demobilization and re-integration of the armed forces into civilian society. In 1941, Mackenzie convinced the Cabinet to create a Committee on Reconstruction "to examine and discuss the general question of post-war reconstruction, and to make recommendations as to what Government facilities should be established to deal with the question."[7] The committee was chaired by Dr Cyril James, principal of McGill University; Leonard C. Marsh was appointed research director.

In its first memorandum, prepared in May 1941, it suggested that the major aim of reconstruction policies must be to have adequate employment for veterans and displaced workers who had been engaged in war production. Like many other Canadians, members of the James Committee were worried about the preservation of democratic institutions. "If, for any reason, reconstruction should not proceed smoothly during the postwar recession the country would inevitably be confronted by rapidly mounting unemployment and widespread dissatisfaction."[8] Later, when the James Committee produced a series of recommendations, calling for, among other things, a minister of economic planning to administer the planning for the postwar period, it raised the ire of the Economic Advisory Council (EAC), a group of senior bureaucrats in Ottawa who were managing the war effort and who, perhaps, saw James as a threat. In an attempt to control postwar reconstruction themselves, they persuaded the Cabinet that the James Committee be made responsible to the privy council—to which the EAC ultimately reported. In January 1943, this was done, and the James Committee was renamed the Advisory Committee on Reconstruction.[9] The EAC also created its own committee on reconstruction. The decision to have the James Committee's recommendations overseen by the Advisory Committee on Economic Policy, whose mandate had been broadened to include post-war economic policy, has been interpreted as a failure of the James Committee and an attempt by the government to weaken its recommendations. Too much should not be read into the bureaucratic in-fighting, however. No one should have really expected the government and its senior bureaucrats to have surrendered their authority over postwar planning to a committee of outsiders. What is clear is that there was considerable public interest in, and pressure for, increased social security, as part of the postwar reconstruction process, and the bureaucracy was determined not to let the agenda be established by outsiders, no matter how well-intentioned these private citizens might have been.[10] Meanwhile, the House of Commons had established its own Special Committee on Reconstruction and Re-establishment in March 1942 and the Senate later followed with its own committee.

Prime Minister Mackenzie King considered social security an important aspect of the new world order he envisioned after the war, and he spoke of the great need for it early in the war. When he joined Roosevelt at the White House for dinner on 5 December 1942, the President discussed the British report on reconstruction, *Social Insurance and Allied Services*—popularly known as the Beveridge Report after its author, Sir William Beveridge—released a few days earlier in London. King was impressed when Roosevelt said that they should "work together on the lines of social reform in which we had always been deeply interested." Of course, King pointed out that much of the program Beveridge recommended could be found in his *Industry and Humanity*.[11] More important, King was relieved that he and Roosevelt could now turn to matters other than the war, and he thought that it was time for him to think more of reconstruction as the war seemed to be turning in the Allies' favour. "I would have something to say in that matter," he told his diary the next day.[12]

Over the coming weeks, King would continue to contemplate the issue of social security. When Ian Mackenzie accompanied him to a funeral in Brockville, Ontario, in January 1943, they discussed the need for social security, of which Mackenzie was already an advocate.[13] When Cyril James had presented him with a draft memorandum from the Committee on Reconstruction late in 1942, Mackenzie had told him that he was disappointed that there was no specific mention of social security, which "today, more than anything else, is occupying the attention of the peoples of the world."[14] In January, King also received a memorandum from Vincent Massey, the high commissioner in London, summarizing the Beveridge Report and a speech that Beveridge made after its release in which he credited Prime Ministers Lloyd George and Churchill for their creative social security measures earlier in their careers. King was determined not to be outdone, and he confided to his diary that "I should be happy indeed if I could round out my career with legislation in the nature of social security."[15]

King acted immediately. At a meeting of the Cabinet on 12 January, he pointed out the need to discuss social security during the upcoming session. He found a number of his powerful Cabinet colleagues, including the minister of finance, J.L. Ilsley, the minister of munitions and supply, C.D. Howe, and the minister of mines and resources, T.A. Crerar, opposed to the idea of greater social security. Such resistance prompted King to write, "The mind of the Cabinet, at any rate, does not grasp the significance of [the] Beveridge report."[16] He had encountered similar opposition in 1940 when he began discussions on the unemployment insurance bill, but he pressed forward and enacted legislation over the wishes of some of his ministers.[17] Again, despite the opposition of senior and influential ministers, King pushed ahead and outlined in the 1943 speech from the throne his government's objective to pursue a policy of social security.

Discussing his plans for social security seemed to rejuvenate the prime minister. In fact, King chose to write—with the aid of *Industry and Humanity*, of course—the sections on social security for the speech from the throne. He discussed those sections with both the Cabinet and the caucus so that "there could be no word said later that all was not fully understood."[18] In the speech from the throne on 28 January 1943, the governor general announced the government's commitment to social security and stated that a "comprehensive national scheme of social insurance should be worked out at once which will constitute a charter of social security for the whole of Canada." King did make it clear that the first and immediate objective of his government was to win the war. Only with victory within its grasp could the government concern itself with other matters. Moreover, he told his caucus that he would never allow an election on the matter of social security during the war, as this might be interpreted as a bribe from the public treasury. He said that his government was committed first to a policy of full employment and "it was wrong to think of increased outlays on anything that could be avoided until victory was won. Important, however, to keep everything in readiness for peace."[19] On 3 March 1943, King moved in the House of Commons the appointment of a special committee on national social insurance to study the matter further. King would later be criticized for not rushing forward to enact his plans for social security, but the British and the Americans, after showing considerable enthusiasm for the Beveridge Report and the report of the National Resources Planning Board, respectively, decided to do little.[20] In the end, King would go much further with social security than either his American or his British counterpart.

Shortly after the speech from the throne, Leonard Marsh released his *Report on Social Security for Canada*. The decision to have Marsh make his report came two weeks after the release of the Beveridge Report in England. Marsh presented his recommendations to the House of Commons Special Committee on Reconstruction in March 1943. It proposed a "comprehensive and integrated social security system for Canada, set our priorities for implementation of the different proposals, dealt with decisions respecting administration and constitutional jurisdiction, and with financial considerations."[21] It was a plan for freedom from want for every Canadian from the cradle to the grave. Marsh proposed maternity benefits and children's allowances to cover children until they could earn for themselves. For most of a person's adult life there were unemployment insurance and unemployment assistance, sickness benefits, free medical insurance, and pensions for permanent disability and surviving widows. For old age, Marsh proposed old age pensions and, finally, funeral benefits.

Interestingly, King seems to have largely ignored the report. Nonetheless, he continued to discuss and think about many of the issues that Marsh raised, and he must certainly have been aware of the interest in social security that Marsh had generated across the country. The Canadian Association of Social Workers, for instance, had written to King that it gave the Marsh Report its approval. He was certainly aware that both Britain and the United States had produced similar reports. Yet King might have believed that he really had no need for Marsh: King himself was the expert on social security and had seen years earlier the need for much of what Marsh and Beveridge were only now recommending. He did not record discussing the Marsh Report with either Anthony Eden or Beveridge when the two visited Ottawa late in March 1943.

Although the *Report on Social Security for Canada* was merely a position paper put forth by the James Committee on Reconstruction, and was not official government policy, it was clear to most inside and outside Ottawa that the King government was committed to the policy of social security. When R.B. Bryce, secretary of the EAC, produced a memorandum for W.C. Clark, the deputy minister of finance, suggesting items to be included in a statement of postwar economic policy, he reminded him that "the government will endeavour to develop and broaden the social security system of Canada."[22]

One proposal under consideration for broadening social security was family allowances. Indeed, when Ian Mackenzie appeared before the House of Commons Special Select Committee on Social Security on 16 March 1943 to discuss the government's health insurance plan, he talked briefly about the importance of family allowances.[23] Not long after, the bureaucracy started to discuss the possibility of family allowances as an alternative to wage increases. Norman Robertson, undersecretary of state for external affairs, wrote to King on 8 June 1943 that he had attended a small meeting with Judge C.P. McTague, who was investigating labour conditions in Canada. It was agreed that wage rates had to increase or some alternative be found to achieve the same end. Robertson thought that family allowances might meet the needs of workers. Moreover, he told King, family allowances were inevitable in the long run, and they would go a long way to meeting the demand for social justice.[24] Graham Towers, governor of the Bank of Canada, made a similar suggestion to W.C. Clark on 13 June 1943, that children's allowances be introduced to maintain the government's wage-stabilization policy, which had been implemented early in the war to control inflation. Towers noted that the government was determined to introduce a "reasonable minimum of [social] security after the war" and he would prefer to see family allowances introdued at that point. Yet family allowances would meet the "legitimate needs" of labour by placing more money in the hands of workers while allowing the government to keep the rate of inflation under control. The principle of children's allowances was not new, he reminded Clark: the government was already paying an allowance for each child in the form of an income tax credit to wage earners who made more than $1200 per year. Family allowances, he added, deserved a higher priority than old age pensions, for example, because "children are even more helpless than old people, and money spent to ensure children's minimum health and education needs are [sic] more likely to be a productive national investment." He also suggested that the introduction of family allowances would enhance Canada's prestige internationally as well as safeguard its economy. Canadian wartime controls had become an example to those in the United States who wanted to control inflation, and children's allowances "would be striking proof that Canada intended to push ahead with progressive policies after the war. It might have appreciable influence in strengthening the hand of like-minded administrations in other countries," Towers concluded.[25]

The Economic Advisory Council adopted Towers' suggestion in mid-July when it realized that it would be impossible to reconcile the wage-stabilization program with the demands of labour. It saw the introduction of children's allowances as a suitable alternative that would be popular with the general populace and with farmers and labour and, at the same time, would be an "important and well-timed step forward in social security." Hence, the EAC proposed in a draft memorandum on 16 July 1943 that a nation-wide system of family allowances be established to come into effect in January 1944. R.B. Bryce, who penned the EAC memorandum, noted that children's allowances were "widely recognized as an important element in modern systems of social security; they are in effect already in Australia and New Zealand and they have been recommended for Britain." Trying to convince the prime minister of the merits of family allowances, Bryce said that the introduction of such a policy as a wartime measure "would be the most convincing possible evidence of the government's intention to proceed with progressive measures." However, some EAC members argued that family allowances should be introduced only as a part of a postwar social security program.[26]

Throughout the summer, Cabinet was concerned with developing new labour policy and was discussing the issue of wages rates and cost of living. There was considerable debate on whether wage controls could be maintained by paying allowances to families, thus avoiding the need to raise wages. King took the opportunity to cast family allowances as a social security matter, not tied to wage rates: "I found the sentiment of Cabinet swinging towards that course [subsidies to large families], on which I think a real policy may be founded for dealing with social security measures."[27] Academics have often made a connection between family allowances and the retention of wage controls,[28] but one cannot simply ignore the fact that when King announced his labour policy of continuing wage controls in December 1943, the implementation of family allowances was still a full nineteen months away.[29] Indeed, the Cabinet had not even reached agreement on family allowances. Thus, such allowances could do little in the short term to make continued wage controls palatable to workers. Instead, to appease labour, the government promised to enact compulsory collective bargaining, to adjust wages where injustices and inequalities existed, to include cost-of-living bonuses in the basic wage rates, and to keep inflation under control.[30]

Meanwhile, Mackenzie King and the Liberal Party were obviously worried about the growing popularity of the opposition parties. Both seemed to be attracting popular support, and both threatened to outflank the Liberals with their emphasis on social security. This was especially true of the Co-operative Commonwealth Federation, which had slipped past the Liberals in 1943 public opinion polls and had won a number of federal by-elections. To reassert the progressive nature of King liberalism and to garner lost support, the National Liberal Federation convened in late September 1943 to outline its platform for the postwar period. It promised Canadians social security, noting that social security and national prosperity were indivisible. The party recommended children's allowances as one of the major planks in its social security program because they would contribute to "a healthy nation with good family life and adequate support of the raising of children."[31] In November 1943, King asked his ministers to make suggestions for postwar reconstruction. Of those who responded by the end of the year, only C.D. Howe wrote that he opposed family allowances, but Howe would garner considerable support from some of his colleagues. All the others who responded to King's query suggested that family allowances be pursued by the government, and Louis St Laurent, rapidly becoming one of King's favourites, told the prime minister that family allowances were the most important of all social security measures.[32]

Early in January 1944, the King government prepared its legislative agenda for the upcoming parliamentary session. One of the most important matters for King was the issue of family allowances, even though it created "great diversity" within the Cabinet.[33] Although in the previous year King had noted in his diary that to give family allowances to everyone was "sheer folly" that might create much resentment toward him and his party,[34] he remained committed to a program of social security and continued to believe that family allowances for larger families went "to the very root of social security in relation to the new order of things which places a responsibility on the State for conditions which the State itself is responsible for creating."[35]

In the Department of Finance, senior officials were preparing the final memorandum on family allowances for J.L. Ilsley. Even though King had divorced family allowances from the wage-stabilization plan, the department still hoped that he would introduce family allowances early in 1944 to ensure support among the general population for the government's economic policy. The bureaucrats agreed with the politicians that the "fundamental basis" for family allowances was that the wage system took no account of family size. Frequently workers with many children were not earning enough to support the whole family. Allowances paid to all children represented "the simplest, wisest, and cheapest way of providing the supplementary family income." Family allowances would also end discrimination against families in the lowest income groups who did not receive tax credits for dependent children. Moreover, allowances might help alleviate the problem many families were having with housing and help to improve the level of education in Canada. A program such as family allowances would bring the government of Canada closer to the people, help children live healthier and more productive lives, and might "allow even one Canadian Milton, Pasteur or Edison to realize possibilities that might otherwise have been frustrated by the accident of his father's income." Finally, the department argued that, although family allowances might be radical for Canada, they had been tried in over thirty-five countries. The memorandum also outlined possible criticisms of family allowances, but it was clear from the document that, no matter what views the bureaucrats held, family allowances were to be presented to the prime minister and his Cabinet as a social security measure.[36]

Interestingly, W.C. Clark made the presentation on family allowances for Ilsley to the Cabinet. King noted in his diary that Clark "touched upon the necessity of this measure [family allowances] if wage stabilization and price ceiling were to be maintained." King agreed with Clark that family allowances would serve an economic purpose, but he argued strenuously in the Cabinet that family allowances were an important social security measure that would create greater opportunity for all Canadian children. The Department of Finance wanted family allowances introduced immediately, but King refused to do so as victory in the war effort remained his most pressing concern. He stressed to Cabinet that modern society had changed and that "the present war was all a part of the struggle of the masses to get a chance to live their own lives." He also pointed out that social security measures, such as family allowances, might be the one thing necessary to save liberal democracies such as Canada.[37] Later, while alone at Laurier House, King thought he might have been too aggressive at the end of the discussion, and called Clark to apologize. Clark reassured him that in "dealing with this measure we had given real evidence of our zeal for social security and there could be no questioning of motives or sincerity of the government in its endeavour to do something practical in this way."[38] The Cabinet agreed to push ahead with family allowances despite the continued opposition from some of the most influential members. A few days later King told journalist Grant Dexter that he "was the only radical in the Cabinet. Some of his colleagues still think they can go out and shoot a bison for breakfast."[39] Later, in Toronto, Joseph Atkinson of the Star reassured King that family allowances were a "very absolutely necessary and right measure."[40]

King turned to drafting the section on social welfare policy and family allowances for the speech from the throne. This was an unusual role for the prime minister, although he had done the same a year earlier when he had drafted the section on social security. Again, he struggled to find the right words with which to introduce family allowances. He found some of them in his Industry and Humanity. Later, when he read the speech to the Cabinet, he was discouraged that several of his ministers, particularly Ilsley, Crerar, Gardiner, and Howe, persisted in their opposition to family allowances. King would have none of it, however, and reminded them that the Cabinet had already agreed upon family allowances.[41] The matter was no longer open for debate. Later, as the governor general read the speech from the

throne, King was pleased that he had used the phrase "the equality of opportunity in the battle of life" as the rationale for the introduction of family allowances, words he had written in 1918. When King stood in the House of Commons in June 1944 to introduce the legislation making family allowances law, he repeated much of the rationale for their introduction. He emphasized that while the "primary justification" for family allowances was on humanitarian and social grounds, it was also a great economic measure to stimulate the economy by increasing the purchasing power of the public; in other words, family allowances legislation was a wonderful piece of liberal ingenuity that would benefit the interest of all the people of Canada.[42] With the passage of the legislation a few weeks later, providing for family allowances to begin in July 1945, Prime Minister King was pleased that his government, which had earlier introduced old age pensions and unemployment insurance, had once again demonstrated to Canadians that it was the champion of social security.

NOTES

1. See Brigitte Kitchen, "Wartime Social Reform: The Introduction of Family Allowances," *Canadian Journal of Social Work* 7, 1 (1981); J.L. Granatstein, *Canada's War: The Politics of the Mackenzie King Government* (Toronto, 1975); Dennis Guest, *Emergence of Social Welfare in Canada* (Vancouver, 1986); and Doug Owram, *The Government Generation: Canadian Intellectuals and the State, 1900–1950* (Toronto, 1985).

2. National Archives of Canada (hereafter NAC), Ian A. Mackenzie Papers, vol. 41, file G-25-15, "The Rt. Hon. W.L. Mackenzie King, Prime Minister of Canada, Address to the American Federation of Labor 1942 Convention, 9 Oct. 1942."

3. Ibid., "Watchman—What of the Night," address delivered by Ian Mackenzie to the Canadian Club, Quebec City, 20 June 1941.

4. Ibid., vol. 4, file G-25-9, "Social Security Legislation of Other Countries," prepared by W.S. Woods, associate deputy minister in the Department of Pensions and Health, 18 Dec. 1942.

5. Ibid., "Watchman—What of the Night."

6. Ibid., "Target for Tomorrow," address by Ian Mackenzie to the Canadian Club, London, ON, 16 Sept. 1942.

7. PC 1218, 17 Feb. 1941.

8. Granatstein, *Canada's War*, 257.

9. Ibid., 257.

10. Ibid., 275.

11. King Diaries, 5 Dec. 1942.

12. Ibid., 6 Dec. 1942.

13. Ibid., 5 Jan. and 7 Jan. 1943.

14. NAC, Mackenzie Papers, vol. 62, f 527-64 (6), Mackenzie to Jame⁄ Dec. 1942.

15. King Diaries, 10 Jan. 1943.

16. Ibid., 12 Jan. 1943.

17. See Granatstein, *Canada's Wa*

18. King Diaries, 24 Jan., 26 Ja⁄ 1943.

19. Ibid., 24 March 1943. I⁄ was pretty much foll⁄ was happening elsewl⁄ met Churchill in Quebⁿ 1943, the British prir⁄ him that he had oⁿ mitment to social sⁿ necessary to devⁿ winning the waⁿ social program King Diaries, 1⁷

20. NAC, Canaⁿ Developmeⁿ 518, David⁷ 1943.

21. See Leonard Marsh, *Report of Social Security for Canada* (Ottawa, 1943).

22. NAC, Department of Finance, vol. 3976, file E-3-0, Bryce to Clark, 21 March 1943.

23. NAC, Mackenzie Papers, vol. 41, file G-25D, "Statement by the Honourable Ian Mackenzie, Minister of Pensions and National Health, before the Special Select Committee of the House of Commons on Social Security, March, 1943."

24. NAC, Mackenzie King Papers, C187885, Robertson to King, 8 June 1943.

25. NAC , Dept. of Finance, vol. 304, file 101-53-114, vol. 1, Towers to Clark, 13 June 1943, and the enclosed memorandum, "The Case for Children's Allowances."

26. Ibid., vol. 498, file 121-0-7, "Draft Report of the Economic Advisory Committee on the Price and Wage Stabilization Program," 16 July 1943.

27. King Diaries, 14 Sept. 1943.

28. See particularly, Kitchen, "Wartime Social Reform," 37–45.

29. Ibid.

30. J.W. Pickersgill, *The Mackenzie King Record* (Toronto, 1960), 599–601.

31. NAC, Dept. of Finance, vol. 3402, file 06301 to 06400, "Resolutions approved by Advisory Council," National Liberal Federation, 27–28 Sept. 1943.

32. NAC, King Papers, J4, vol. 371, file F3906, Pickersgill to King, 27 Dec. 1943 and file F3906, St Laurent to King, 18 Nov. 1943.

33. King Diaries, 6 Jan. 1944.

34. Ibid., 1 Oct. 1943.

35. Ibid., 13 Jan. 1944.

36. NAC, Dept. of Finance, vol. 304, file 101-53-114, vol. 1, "Children's Allowance," memorandum prepared for Ilsley, 12 Jan. 1944.

37. King Diaries, 13 Jan. 1944.

38. Ibid.

39. See Granatstein, *Canada's War*, 283.

40. King Diaries, 19 Jan. 1944.

41. Ibid., 24 Jan. 1944.

42. NAC, Dept. of Health and Welfare, vol. 1934, file R233-100-2, "Mr. Mackenzie King—July 25, 1944."

THE FLOWERING
OF STATE WELFARE

A lthough considerable acceptance of social welfare prevailed both within and outside of government at the end of World War II, by no means had concerns disappeared about its potential to jeopardize the country's social fabric or economic progress. Such is evident in Susan Prentice's article on the post-1945 fight in Toronto to retain the government-financed childcare centres that had enabled thousands of mothers to enter the war economy. Initially, the city's Day Nurseries and Day Care Parents Association convinced provincial and municipal politicians to provide funding for this service by arguing that it would reduce the number of neglected children and future juvenile delinquents. Yet by the late 1940s, financial support evaporated. The ongoing campaign to get women back home and make room in the workplace for the male breadwinner provided only part of the pressure to close daycare centres. In addition, ideologically conservative forces derived increased strength from an emerging Cold War atmosphere that permitted them to discredit Toronto's daycare advocates, because of the organizational support they received from the Communist Party of Canada, as leading a Red-inspired attack upon the traditional family by substituting the state for a mother's nurturing care.

Perhaps permanent government-supported childcare was an unrealistic legacy to anticipate from wartime welfare, for never during the conflict was the service cast as anything but a temporary measure. Federal committees, such as the one on reconstruction that began hearings in March 1941 under the chairmanship of McGill University president Cyril James, on the other hand, might well have legitimately raised expectations in many families about massive public housing ventures to end shortages of shelter stretching back to the end of the Great War. But John Bacher argues that, starting with the 1935 Dominion Housing Act, mandarins—especially the deputy minister of finance, W. Clifford Clark—enamoured with the "virtues of the free market," established an approach that had almost all Canadians obtaining accommodation from private developers whose interests were zealously protected as being synonymous with a healthy capitalist economy. Indeed, despite inadequate dwelling stock growing to crisis proportions both during and just after World War II, government reform was primarily restricted to collaborative efforts with mortgage companies to reduce down-payment requirements and increase amortization terms—measures that, Bacher insists, failed to provide decent shelter for multitudes of Canadians.

Countering the conservatism practised in some areas were spectacular postwar initiatives, arguably the most significant being universal state-run health care insurance. Yet, as Duane Mombourquette notes, its development was neither quick nor easy. Following World War II, profound disappointment was expressed by Canada's first CCF government in Saskatchewan over Ottawa's inability to reach a cost-sharing agreement with the provinces for a nationwide health care system and thus deliver upon a key recommendation made in the 1943 Marsh Report. Nevertheless, Premier Tommy Douglas pressed ahead. In spite of budget deficits and opposition from doctors, he established a provincially run scheme covering all costs associated with: hospital visits; the creation of regional health boards reaching isolated rural communities; an air ambulance service; more hospital beds, nursing homes, psychiatric services, and midwives; and a medical school at the University of Saskatchewan. This example, write Eugene Vayda and Raisa Deber, spawned government-run health care programs in British Columbia and Alberta, and, by the 1960s, after Saskatchewan implemented medicare, convinced Ottawa to create a national plan, in co-ordination with the provinces, covering most medical services.

The model used to finance medicare—which called upon the provinces to meet certain minimum standards to receive federal funds—was also employed during the 1960s to introduce or enlarge upon a number of other welfare measures that, as outlined in Rand Dyck's article, were placed under the aegis of the Canada Assistance Plan (CAP). Moreover, through its stages of conception, formulation, and implementation, as well as in dealing with problems arising over the years, the CAP, writes Dyck, demonstrated the potential of co-operative federalism to offer assistance beyond the financial or jurisdictional capability of any one level of government. Unfortunately, both he and Vayda and Deber suggest that the future may not be so bright. The financial power of Ottawa has made programs such as medicare workable, but it is now threatened by a mounting national debt. In other words, almost contiguous with the rise of the modern social service state have come ever more vocal questions concerning its financial feasibility, a dilemma which, it is sad to say, appears at present destined to grow more serious, rather than be resolved, with time.

WORKERS, MOTHERS, REDS: TORONTO'S POSTWAR DAYCARE FIGHT[*]

SUSAN PRENTICE

o

INTRODUCTION

The "common-sense" history of organized feminism in Canada assumes a black hole of inactivity in the long stretch of decades between the early suffragettes and the recent "second wave." Yet a closer reading of history reveals a continuous struggle by and for Canadian women to improve their economic, political, and social condition.

One example of such progressive and feminist organizing was the fight to ensure that postwar reconstruction addressed women's needs for childcare. There was a broadly based daycare movement in Toronto between 1946 and 1951. For six years after World War II, the Day Nurseries and Day Care Parents Association (in which women from the Canadian Communist Party played a key role) led a high-profile and largely effective fight to save the wartime day nurseries from closure. In a remarkable coalition, supported by Communist aldermen, school trustees, and their sympathizers, the association organized to defend and expand childcare service through struggles in and against the municipal and provincial governments. In the period immediately after the war, daycare organizing had a mass base: hundreds attended public events, scores attended City Council and Board of Education meetings and deputations, and over one thousand attended a public rally and demonstration. Through this militant organizing, the Association made a successful front-line defence of many wartime childcare services.

[*] *Studies in Political Economy* 30 (1899): 115–41. Reprinted with permission.

Despite the federal government's 1944 commitment that the primary object of postwar domestic policy would be "social and human welfare,"[1] it used a traditional economic rationale, the need for fiscal restraint, to justify cutting daycare. By late 1951, Toronto City Council and the provincial Ministry of Public Welfare had closed over half the nurseries and daycare centres. The once strong Day Nurseries and Day Care Parents Association had dissolved. Childcare, which had been defended as support to the family and a measure of prevention against juvenile delinquency was refashioned as a communist threat and evidence of mothers' neglect. Daycare and daycare organizing effectively "dried up" in Toronto, and didn't reappear again in any equally significant form for over two decades.

How was this remarkable rise and fall possible? And what does it mean? What is its relevance to current feminist struggles? This paper discusses these questions, using French regulation economic theory and the social reproduction literature to analyse the complicated interactions of the state and the old "new" social movement of women in the politics, history, and organization of daycare.

CHILDCARE AND WORLD WAR II: THE EARLIEST DAYS

On 8 May 1945, at the end of the war, there were thirteen day nurseries in operation in Toronto (part of Ontario's total of twenty-eight) and twenty-two daycare centres (part of the total of forty-two). Day nurseries cared for preschoolers under the age of five years, and daycare centres served children over the age of five. Together Ontario's day nurseries and daycare centres served a total of nearly 2500 children.[2] These childcare services were cost-shared between the provincial and federal governments under the 1942 Dominion–Provincial Day Nurseries Agreement, which was administered through the National Selective Services. Only Ontario and Quebec had taken advantage of available federal cost-sharing to establish wartime day nurseries to serve the needs of women employed in "essential war industry." Other provinces argued they were insufficiently industrialized and did not need childcare programs.[3]

The federal government moved to end its involvement with childcare at the end of the war. On 9 November 1945, Deputy Minister of Labour Robert MacNamara wrote to the Ontario minister of public welfare, William Goodfellow, to give notice of impending federal withdrawal from childcare funding: "You understand that the financing of these and similar plans by the Dominion Government has been done as a war measure and our Treasury Board naturally takes the position 'now that the war is over why do you need the money?'"[4] The federal government announced its intention to terminate cost-sharing on 1 April 1946. Despite the federal government's 1944 commitment that the primary object of postwar domestic policy would be "social security and human welfare," it invoked a traditional economic rationale—the need for fiscal restraint—to justify eliminating daycare expenditures.[5]

Beyond economic conservatism, state moves to revoke care were clearly based on sexist notions of the family and classist perceptions of why women worked. The *Globe and Mail* of 11 July 1946, reported that

> While the Provincial Government has expressed concern that any deserving cases should suffer from the cessation of the plan, welfare officials are agreed that whenever possible mothers shouldn't shirk their responsibility in caring for their children at home in order to boost what is already an equitable income by working daily. "We believe that a child should be brought up in the proper environment in its own home, when possible" said one official.

In Quebec, Duplessis's closing of day nurseries generated protests from the Montreal Council of Social Agencies, the Welfare Federation, the Federation of Catholic Charities, the Montreal Association of Protestant Women Teachers, and mothers of children in care.[6] Despite their efforts, all wartime services in Quebec were closed. The qualified success of Ontario and the defeat of Quebec in defending childcare services, needs further attention.

Childcare protests began immediately, with a 1 January 1946 deputation to City Council by the Toronto Welfare Council, the Women's Teachers Association, the Local Council of Women, the Toronto Trades and Labour Council, the YWCA, and the YMCA, which argued for more day nurseries.[7] One month later, on 30 January, sixty deputants to the Board of Control defended daycare services and demanded that civic government find a way to save them. They included representatives from welfare organizations, women's groups, cultural groups, teachers' organizations, and home and school associations.[8] On 9 February 1946 a large delegation, including Dr Gordon Jackson, medical officer of health for the City of Toronto, demanded City Council operate the nurseries "on a permanent basis."[9]

The Day Nurseries and Day Care Parents Association formed in Toronto on 14 February 1946, at a meeting sponsored by the United Welfare Chest.[10] It immediately took over the task of co-ordinating the broadly based lobby for continued government funding of childcare. Five weeks later, the association won its first, albeit double-edged, victory. On 22 March the Ontario government introduced the Day Nurseries Act. The act, which received royal assent on 5 April 1946 and became effective 30 June 1946, provided for joint cost-sharing between municipal and provincial governments, with the municipality assuming 50 percent of costs and taking responsibility for administration.[11] Municipalities, with their smaller tax base and different revenue structure, were thus asked to take over the responsibility for childcare formerly assumed by the federal government. Given the national commitment to postwar reconstruction and welfare state expansion, it is a significant contradiction that no federal funds were forthcoming for childcare until the Canada Assistance Plan of 1966.

The provincial government's involvement in this transfer of childcare responsibilities to municipal government was also significant. The Communist Party, which had small but important electoral representation on Toronto City Council and the Toronto Board of Education, quickly hailed it as part of a "Drew plot" to "prevent fulfillment" of the dominion government's program of limited social reform, a program to which the CP had committed its support.[12] The CP railed against the "setting of the province against the nation, the part against the whole" which had "the primary object of paralysing all efforts to achieve social legislation, and a reorganization of taxation to compel the rich to pay their share to meet the costs of the crisis."[13]

The Day Nurseries Act established minimum regulations and standards, as well as funding arrangements. The act's funding provisions had been essential to the continuation of wartime day nurseries. But the institution of relatively high standards of care, coupled with inadequate funds, resulted in the eventual closure of many centres. Schulz says that the standards and regulations of the act "proved to be a double-edged sword. Because the government was doing two contradictory things—setting good standards, but refusing to fund the service adequately—the net effect of the legislation was to close down a number of centres."[14] This was an early example of a contradiction deeply embedded within the state: simultaneous support and undermining of childcare.

Despite the Day Nurseries Act, and the province's apparent support for regulated childcare services, there was still strong resistance by and in the state to the idea of non-parental care. It was assumed that only those in "unfortunate circumstances" would need such services.[15] The province argued that nursery schools (which were primarily used by full-time homemakers, not mothers in the paid labour force) offered "the maximum benefit for the children" when compared to the full-time care of day nurseries or daycare centres.[16] Even Dorothy Millichamp, a trained early childhood educator who held a senior position with the Day Nurseries Branch, commented, "Professionally, we didn't want to see daycare bloom. . . . We never felt it was the right answer unless it was absolutely necessary. . . . [W]e felt daycare was for emergencies, not just for every child."[17]

THE DISCOURSE OF CHILDCARE

As important as the act, was the actual way childcare was talked about, organized around, defended, promoted, and fought over. In the postwar period, childcare was repeatedly defended and promoted, as a way of preventing juvenile delinquency. This language was widespread—Communists, welfare reformers, women's groups, and religious leaders all seized on the issue of juvenile delinquency. The discourse of juvenile delinquency imbued childcare activists with a sense of urgency and moral righteousness. This moral righteousness deflected conservative criticism that childcare provoked the breakdown of the family and an abandonment by women of their proper role. Indeed, by arguing that childcare, as a measure of prevention against juvenile delinquency, actually *strengthened* "the family," daycare activists manipulated a conservative idea without challenging it.

The media used the same discourse in its defence of childcare. The *Toronto Star*, in a 24 June 1946 editorial, entitled "Encouraging Juvenile Delinquency" asked

What is the use of professing concern about juvenile delinquency and at the same time turning 3000 [school-aged] children loose in the city streets with no parents, no teachers, nobody with authority or concern to look after them? . . . It would cost less to run them [daycare centres] than to reform a few of the children who become criminals or to repair them in hospitals if they develop chronic ailments through neglect!

Conservatives were equally adamant about the preventive value of child-care. On 30 May 1946, at a protest meeting that attracted hundreds of daycare supporters, the Rev. Tucker declared "Whatever day nurseries and day care cost us, it is small potatoes compared with keeping a lad in our penal system."[18] On 27 April 1946 the *Star* reported that the Ontario Educational Association and the Federation of Home and School Associations had issued a terse declaration: "Day nurseries provide a relatively inexpensive means of preventing ill-health and delinquency among growing children."

An editorial in the Communist *Canadian Tribune*, "Why Mothers Grow Grey," used the same argument about juvenile delinquency, but turned it around, noting that

Certain woolly-minded people, more interested in dollars than children, are spreading the idea that parental responsibility—or lack of it—is the main cause of delinquency. Rubbish. The major causes of delinquency are: bad housing, low pay, the lack of day nurseries and preschool care, poor recreational facilities and the medieval attitude that a mother must have no other interests in her life than minute-by-minute supervision of her children. . . . Day nurseries, preschool care, plenty of playgrounds, better houses, higher pay, maternal care, and a modern attitude to a mother as a citizen of Canada and the world—these would cut delinquency to the bone and bring happiness to thousands of families.[19]

The language of juvenile delinquency permitted a broad coalition to work together for expanded childcare services. The notion of defence against juvenile delinquency allowed widely differing organizations to align, compelled by a sense of moral urgency. The political credibility that it lent the Day Nurseries and Day Care Parents Association, with its broad membership, meant that City Council and the Toronto Board of Education—the targets of their lobbying—had to pay attention.

"Juvenile delinquency" has a particular relationship to class. However, its obliqueness hides its class content. May Birchard, one-time school board trustee and alderwoman sympathetic to the Communist Party, was one of the chief promoters of the daycare and juvenile delinquency connection. She argued that "daycare expansion should be on the basis of need," in the "industrial districts of the city."[20] Her indirect reference was probably carefully determined: it was a non-class specific way to refer to a service most needed by working-class mothers, without identifying them as such. This may explain why Communists used the juvenile delinquency argument to demand daycare for "working mothers" (another frequent, indirect reference to class), who were particularly disadvantaged through capitalist relations of work. Conservatives used the same terms, "juvenile delinquency" and "working mothers," in a very different and reactionary way.

THE DAY NURSERIES AND DAY CARE PARENTS ASSOCIATION

The Day Nurseries and Day Care Parents Association was founded on 14 February 1946.[21] The association was an umbrella group organized for the purpose of political action. Its aim and function was "specifically to provide an organizational machinery for the parents themselves to make known to the public and to the elected representatives of the people the extreme importance of maintaining the services which do exist and extending these."[22] It was "composed of parents whose children are in nursery school or daycare centres, have been in such centres, or are on the waiting list for such service."[23]

The Day Nurseries and Day Care Parents Association was the major coordinating vehicle of childcare organizing in Toronto between 1946 and 1951. It played a leadership role in the childcare struggle, conducted with other community and women's groups. The association undertook a wide and creative campaign to first defend, and later extend, childcare. The bulk of their organizing centred around lobbying, petitions, letter-writing, and deputations, although they also organized two mass rallies, and several public meetings. Many of their organizing efforts were particularly sensitive to the double day of working mothers. For example, they held a protest meeting simultaneously in four different locations in the City of Toronto to minimize the distances women and children would have to travel. Their public demonstrations at City Hall and Queen's Park were particularly radical in an era when women's prescribed role, paid labour, and domestic responsibilities strongly mitigated against participation in such activities.

A part of the association's work was the establishment of parent study groups at different childcare centres. These parent study groups undoubtedly differed greatly in both orientation and activity, between centres. Study groups undertook to educate parents about the "latest developments" in early childhood education. The University of Toronto's Institute for Child Study appears to have been involved in this educational work.[24] This "expert" advice was undoubtedly welcomed by some mothers, particularly isolated and first-time mothers; however, it was also an important vehicle for complex and subtle moral and gender regulation and was influential in the restructuring of "mothering." In addition to this conservative function, study groups also offered political education and an early form of "consciousness-raising" to parents. It is more than likely that parents were recruited to political action—and possibly to the Communist Party— through the study groups.

Perhaps the most intriguing fact about the Day Nurseries and Day Care Parents Association was that many of its members were also members of the Canadian Communist Party. Communist activity in women's organizations had been steady ever since their 1938 convention, at which the party had set up a program of work among women that included forming neighbour-hood groups, organizing women around the needs of their children, and forming and joining consumers' and housewives' associations.[25] The party was also clear about the "necessity of joining those organizations where the masses of women are to be found: church groups, Home and School Clubs, Women's Institutes, Cooperative Guilds, fraternal organizations, etc."[26]

Many of the Day Nurseries and Day Care Parents Association's public spokespeople were members of the Communist Party. By 1948, the group itself was considered by many municipal politicians to be a Communist organization. Certainly the involvement of party members in the associa-tion was a factor in the close co-ordination of the association with other mil-itant women's groups, like the Congress of Canadian Women and the Housewives' Consumers' Association. It is unclear whether these links between Communist women were organized formally through the party, or informally through private and personal networks. Whichever was the case, their working relations and shared political analysis were important factors in the strength and organization of the association.

Despite the strong presence of Communist women, women from the CCF also appear to have been members in, and supporters of, the associa-tion. This alignment of CCF and CP women (whose parties were otherwise most hostile) in defence of childcare, appears to have been unique to Toronto.[27] It is unclear what leadership role parents of children in day nurs-eries and daycare centres played. Leadership seems to have been provided by women with more extended political connections than direct involve-ment in childcare alone.

Communist women played an important role in the association in tying the issues of childcare, rising prices, housing, and the cost of living to a broader analysis. Their efforts to link these issues converged most dramati-cally on the issue of hot lunches and free milk for school children. Advocacy efforts around childcare and school feeding were co-ordinated, at the Board of Education and elsewhere, through their work. To a certain degree, childcare became linked with the issue of school feeding. This latter program linked the daycare fight to the "prices" campaign of the Communist Party, part of the party's attempt to appeal to women on the basis of their domestic role. Paradoxically, stretching the "prices" fight into the childcare struggle meant that policies designed to appeal to women based on assumptions about their role in the "private" realm were being combined with those designed to appeal to women who were clearly engaged in the realm of "public."

The Committee for a School Lunch, and the Day Nurseries and Day Care Parents Association regularly made joint deputations to the Board of Education. There were subtle distinctions, however, in their positions. The more strongly Communist-influenced association argued that families with "working mothers" (the standard reference to working-class families) needed assistance, whereas the committee (whose Communist membership was smaller) argued for charitable help to ensure the "success" (e.g. class transcendence) of the working-class child.

By late June 1946, it was clear that the existing thirteen day nurseries would continue to operate, but all twenty-two daycare centres were closed. Six daycare centres re-opened a few weeks later, on 1 August.[28] While the association had not accomplished all it had set out to do, all of the vital preschool spaces, and over a quarter of the school-age spaces, were secure. The next step for childcare activists was to extend services.

Childcare advocates besieged municipal politicians throughout 1946 and into 1947. On 12 November 1946, City Council finally agreed to appoint a Special Advisory Committee to investigate the childcare situation.[29] The Special Advisory Committee, established as a response to urgent need, took over eighteen months to report. Schulz says that although the committee "was ostensibly a response to the childcare community," the City's actions were characterized by "red tape, delay, and an unsympathetic attitude."[30]

Three months before the committee's report was finally released, City Council debated childcare for the 1948 budget year. During this meeting, Council heard deputations which supported twelve new daycare centres (estimated at $100 000) and a demonstration centre to integrate preschool and school-age children. In a debate over the cost of the new programs, Con. McKellar said, "the trouble is that the Daycare Association will not stop at 12, but will want more."[31] Con. Roelofsen, chair of the Special Advisory Committee, agreed saying, "these super socialists have it in their minds they are going to force this thing [daycare] down our throats," later warning that "the Communists will make an awful fight."[32] This heated exchange is evidence of both the rising identification of the childcare cause with communism, and a mounting Red-baiting.

Despite the efforts of its right-wing chair, the Special Committee did recommend twelve new daycare centres, as well as the integrated model childcare demonstration centre (later Jesse Ketchum Daycare Centre). However, at the same time, the report called for the doubling of daycare fees to "eliminate from care those children of mothers who work from choice rather than from economic necessity."[33] After a bureaucratic stalling of eighteen months, the final report of the committee was adopted by City Council on 23 June 1947, amidst massive public protest over the proposed fee increases.[34] The state's support of daycare (the twelve new school-age programs and the demonstration centre) was contradicted by its simultaneous undermining of childcare through the fee hike.

During the 1946–1947 period, a broad daycare advocacy coalition came together to defend childcare services. Their political analysis, while militant, was based on a limited understanding of the lives of working mothers, manifested in their argument about daycare as a measure of prevention against juvenile delinquency. The flexibility of their defence permitted a remarkable alliance of conservative and socialist women. Their successful struggle to preserve existing services against the very reluctant provincial government was based on this political strength and credibility. In municipal politics, the Day Nurseries and Day Care Parents Association's success at City Council and the Board of Education was due to collaboration with Communist (and sympathetic) aldermen and trustees and the party organization that supported them.

1948–1949: THE MIDDLE YEARS

The major fight undertaken by the association during the 1948–1949 period was the expansion of twelve new daycare centres and the establishment of the Jesse Ketchum Demonstration Project, an integrated day nursery and daycare centre for preschoolers and school-age children. Equally important was the work that the association undertook to defend the rights of families with working mothers to government-funded services.

This middle period saw the rise of Red-baiting, as well as a changing attitude toward working women. From a wartime acceptance of the legitimate right of working women to childcare, concern about "chisellers" and the "undeserving" family arose. Men like Alderman William Clifton, a Ward 6 conservative, argued against the right of two-parent families to care.[35] City Council reaffirmed its policy of "limiting Day Nursery care under Civic auspices to the children of mothers who must work in order to support their families and other special cases."[36]

> In November 1948, Mayor McCallum washed his hands of the day-care battle, and told the community to "go higher," to the province, for assistance.[37]

This marked a turn away from a minimally supportive civic administration to one that began to overtly organize to erode childcare; it also, not coincidentally, reflected (and helps to explain) the electoral defeat of progressive politicians. In recognition of this conservative municipal turn, Isabel Bevis, chair of the Day Nurseries and Day Care Parents Association gave the following dispirited summary:

> The result, after over two years, has been the stopping of parent study groups in the day nurseries, double and treble increases in the day nursery fees, and refusing to place children on the waiting lists of the day nurseries, very little improvement in the standards of daycare, no expansion of facilities, and finally the one concrete project passed and ordered at the beginning of this year, the alterations to the Jesse Ketchum Day Nursery building to provide a demonstration centre, has not even been started.[38]

By late 1947, Board of Education trustees were increasingly hostile to childcare and, although to a lesser extent, school feeding, which was linked to it. Trustee Borden, for example, argued that free milk would result in the "loss of initiative and entrepreneurship" on the part of children.[39] Free milk, he said, was "going to do far more harm than good" because "we want to teach our children to get what they want by themselves."[40] The agitation for free milk (i.e. paid for by the Board) by the "labour women" trustees appears to have contradicted the party's clear directives that social services should be centrally funded. Notwithstanding this, labour trustees (all women) carried out an effective milk fight. The strong opposition from right-wing trustees was insufficient to dissuade the Board from finally agreeing in late 1947 to CP trustee Elizabeth Morton's motion to distribute free milk to school children.[41]

The Board of Education, however, was stymied in the provision of milk because the provincial Education Act did not permit expenditures on non-education items. Communist school trustees actively organized for changes to the act. However, their campaign was heavily criticized. One *Globe and Mail* editorial, "A Communist Ramp," railed that

> The agitation for hot noon lunches has been one of the perennial policies of the communist trustee Mrs. Edna Ryerson and it was not surprising to find that a friend of hers, Mrs. May Birchard, was the chief spin in the delegation. . . . What is most surprising about the whole matter is the simple-minded manner in which leading women's groups will lend themselves to the malicious purposes of agitators.[42]

The *Globe* warned that attempts to change the Education Act were designed "to destroy the faith of democratic peoples in their government bodies." In stark contrast, the *Star's* editorial, "In Fairness to the Children," pointed out,

> Judging from some of the pronouncements, it may be inferred . . . that many community leaders who have identified themselves with the school lunch movement are the dupes of Communists. In fairness, the school lunch is not a Communist invention. It was initiated in England after the 1914–18 war. . . . Credit for it has been claimed by conservative regimes.[43]

The Board of Education's policy with respect to childcare also shifted as a result of the identification of childcare with communism. For instance the Board argued for the institution of junior and senior kindergarten programs. By routing four year olds into the education system, the Board attended to the question of care for a large group of children of working mothers, yet did so by organizing their care out of the realm of "Red" day nurseries. This also marked a shift away from the earlier stress on the prevention of juvenile delinquency.

The shifting of the childcare issue out of the realm of contested politics, and into the discourse of education offered certain political advantages. One *Toronto Star* editorial, "Gratifying Progress," went so far as to comment approvingly on a report about British kindergartens, pointing out that "the good nursery school is the maker of young democrats."[44] A belief in education's potential for combating communism—a manifestation of Cold War anticommunism—underpinned this shift in discourse.

Yet even this conservative education strategy met with opposition. The *Globe and Mail* editorialized that the need for junior kindergartens was "limited." While they agreed that many "mothers favour the idea," they noted ominously that "there is more at stake than freedom from the burdens of parenthood for a few hours. What is ultimately to be determined is the degree to which the state will be allowed to usurp the functions of the home."[45]

The 1948–1949 period saw a sharp increase in Red-baiting, and the linking of both childcare organizing and childcare service itself with communism. Through this process, the broad alliances that had formed during the crisis of the immediate postwar period weakened. The City of Toronto moved away from its earlier reluctant support for childcare. The municipal government doubled fees and began to restrict access to the day nurseries, as part of an ideological campaign to eliminate "undeserving" parents. At the Board of Education, anti-Red campaigns played an important role in defeating Communist trustees in elections and in handicapping their work. As the numbers of elected Communist representatives decreased, the Day Nurseries and Day Care Parents Association had increasingly less influence on civic politics, contributing further to its internal demoralization and to public perception of it as a marginal left-wing group. As the anticommunist campaign heated up, the childcare movement suffered losses of both reduced membership, and decreased political legitimacy and strength in the eyes of the state and the media.

Simultaneously, and partly in response, the Communist Party retreated from the remnants of its Popular Front strategy to focus its energies on defending the Soviet Union through advocacy of the policy of mutual co-existence. In 1949, the Communist Party dramatically reorganized itself. Women's work was reoriented away from involvement in women's coalitions, a policy adopted in 1938, and toward an all-out party effort to defeat the Mackenzie King government. This change was most dramatically seen in the Resolution on Women's Work passed at the February 1949 LPP convention, which read:

> Although our work among women is many-sided, including the real gains among the women engaged in gainful employment, concrete aids to housewives and mothers in care of children and services relating to the home; social services, etc., *all our work from now on must be centred around the federal election programs.*[46]

In response to Cold War anticommunism and as part of the party's strategy for the federal election of 1949, women were directed into peace work. Communist women were organized away from childcare advocacy, leaving only a small core of committed activists to carry on the childcare struggle. This strategy deflected the energies of some of the most skilled and committed organizers.

1950–1951: THE END

By the end of 1950, Edna Ryerson was the only Communist to retain her seat on the Board of Education. Communist aldermen were entirely absent from City Council. A fiercely anticommunist climate prevailed.

On 8 January 1950, the Board of Education announced its plans to open eight more junior kindergartens, to bring its total up to twenty-seven by September.[47] The Board had successfully taken childcare for four and five year olds out of the day nurseries and placed it in the education system, as part of a political (although unarticulated) response to the "threat" of communism. The Board of Education was increasingly reluctant to support childcare centres—the only exception was Trustee Ryerson.

In 1950, as City Council debated measures which might have prevented the imminent closure of three childcare centres, the *Star* wrote:

> It is known certain of the Board of Control's members, along with others on the City's Welfare Council, fear children's centres are the "camel's head" for what Alderman Belyea calls "statism." Since it is deemed politically unwise to attack progress with such a wide, logical and sentimental appeal, they fall back on the claim that care of the City's children is not the City's business.[48]

The *Star's* defence of "logical" childcare deflected rather than challenged the accusation of "statism."

The early 1950s saw the worst of Canadian Cold War anticommunism. Accusations flew thick and fast. One example of this hysteria is found in an article entitled "The Red's Pink Tea Circuit: This Communist Front Fools a Lot of Women," which ran in the *Financial Post* on 9 June 1951. It linked, by association, the Day Nursery and Day Care Parents Association to the Korean War, the Kremlin, and international communism, mainly by identifying the husbands of women active in the association as communists. Its author concluded that, "without the party liners and sympathizers there are enough outright party members of this organization to ensure that it stays on the rails to Moscow. All the evidence indicates that this organization's lines lead right to the Kremlin." While many members of the Day Nursery and Day Care Parents Association were Communists, or Communist sympathizers, it is interesting to note how Red-baiting functions to discredit and silence political opposition.[49]

At the level of municipal government, the commissioner of public welfare for the City of Toronto, with the support of the mayor and members of the Board of Control, was determined to undermine childcare services. Through close collaboration with the Ministry of Public Welfare of the province, he developed a series of bureaucratic mechanisms designed to decimate childcare services in the City.

On 15 January 1951, the City of Toronto asked for "frank and confidential" advice from the Ministry of Public Welfare on how to restrict admission.[50] On 8 February 1951, an inter-office memo from the Ministry of Public Welfare to the City, cautioned that, "mothers desiring to go to work should be very carefully investigated. . . . [T]housands of families have debts to pay off and eligibility for nursery care at public expense for this reason alone was questionable."[51] Senior bureaucrats emphasized the need for "careful screenings and meticulous follow-ups to make sure continued care is justified under public auspices."[52] In early February, representatives from the City and the province met to determine priorities for admission. As a result of a series of consultations with provincial bureaucrats in early 1951, the city commissioner of public welfare established a four-point priority scale for admission to care. The new criteria could be put into effect with reasonable ease, because in May 1950 the City had instituted a Central Registry for admissions to ensure "uniformity in investigational procedures."[53]

Under the new scheme, families were means-tested to determine eligibility, and were admitted accordingly. The first priority for admission were children from homes "which were being kept together and maintained chiefly through the personal efforts of the mothers, the fathers being out of the homes for various reasons, viz. death, illness, separation, desertion, etc." Second, were children having "individual and urgent needs for health or social reasons." Third were "children from homes in which both mothers and fathers were present, but where fathers' incomes were either insufficient or too insecure" to meet living expenses without the mothers also working. Fourth were children from homes in which both mothers and fathers worked, but in which there were "special and urgent situations which could only be met by the mothers employment in addition to that of the fathers and which in turn is contingent upon the securing of Nursery or Day Care Centre care for their children."[54] In his report to Council, Commissioner Rupert demurely noted that the priority scale had been "discussed" with Mr Heise, deputy minister of public welfare, who was "in agreement with the general principles expressed."[55]

These astonishingly strict eligibility requirements were deemed necessary by the province, based on the results of a January 1951 survey of family and children's services in Toronto. This study had determined that "the emphasis on care for children of working mothers has the effect of creating a large demand for such care where this may not be the most appropriate solution to the family problem."[56] In a press release discussing these findings, the provincial minister of public welfare further pointed out that "the practice of waiving the [daycare] fee or arbitrarily setting it at a low figure can discourage parental responsibility." In a breathtaking display of class privilege, the minister breezed, "It seems inequitable that, simply because the parents in the family *wished* to work for some purpose, public funds should provide a means of caring for their children if there is no real economic or social need for them both working."[57]

This regulation had both a moral and an economic quality. Its economic functions were contradictory: productive labour that didn't challenge women's reproductive role was eligible for state support through provision of childcare. Yet at the same time, state protection of woman-as-mother, firmly domesticated, was the chief way women were organized through state policy. This gender regulation establishes and legitimates particular sex and sexuality roles. State policy on childcare is located at the contradictory intersection of class, gender, and "family" issues. "Sex/gender systems" as Rubin reminds us, "are the products of historical human activity."[58] This state activity built on and intensified this historical regulation, paving the way for the "feminine mystique" of the 1960s.

While state-funded childcare is often considered the "gatekeeper" to women's labour force participation, it is clear that more than simple participation in productive labour was at stake for the City. Not just women's paid labour, but the *particular family form*, was the deciding factor. Two-parent families in which the mother worked for "frivolous" reasons such as debt repayment or economic need, were the last category to be eligible for admis-

sion. If the state were only concerned about ensuring that economically productive mothers received publicly funded care, then the four-point priority
scale based on family form would be inexplicable. The reserve army of
labour theory which posits a linear relationship between capital's need for
(female/cheap) labour and state provision of service is incomplete. The
City's admission policies are intelligible only when the regulatory and ideological function of childcare is theorized alongside an economic analysis.

The Day Nurseries and Day Care Parents Association responded to the
new admission policy with fury, in part to the moral regulation implicit in
the priority scale. On 30 May 1951, Mrs Isabel Bevis, association president,
addressed the Committee on Public Welfare on behalf of a large deputation
of working mothers and expressed strong opposition to the new regulations, fees, and administrative procedures. The association demanded the
City "withdraw all increases; dispense with the screening depot; discard the
means test and the investigators; and re-establish the waiting list method of
admission under the direction of the supervisors."[59] The demand that the
waiting list be re-established under the direction of the supervisors was a
tactic designed to limit the centralized power of the state to determine
which families were "most deserving." The association was adamant that
all working mothers, by right, were equally deserving and should be considered equally eligible for care. The deputation of over one hundred people was composed of members of the Congress of Canadian Women, the
Toronto Council of Women's International Union Auxiliaries AFL, the
Housewives' Consumers' Association, the United Electrical Radio and
Machine Workers Ladies Auxiliary, and "several mothers."[60]

The commissioner of welfare implacably defended the registry for the
"centralized and overall control of placement of children" it offered, and
explained the 200 percent fee increases, and admission scale, thus:

> It is a well known fact that in public welfare programs . . . eco-
> nomic need has been the governing factor in determining eligibil-
> ity. While many programs have broadened in scope during recent
> years in accordance with recognized standards in public welfare
> work, this basic principle has obtained. . . . There is a definite two-
> way responsibility which must be respected. It is therefore sound,
> both socially and economically that parents who are financially
> able to pay increased fees for Nursery and Day Care services
> should be expected to do so.[61]

Notwithstanding the strong protests of the association, the new regulations
were approved for 1 September 1951.

The flurry of organizing undertaken by the association in the spring
and summer of 1951 around the fee-increase proposals were its last activities. The association never again addressed any of the Committees of
Council or the Board of Education. One can only speculate that this last
ditch effort, undertaken in the fiercely anticommunist and anti-daycare climate, completely demoralized the already disorganized association. The

weakened daycare movement could no longer sustain itself. The demise of the daycare movement had been accomplished, and the state's cutbacks proceeded apace with only minimal opposition.

In early 1951, twelve day nurseries and three daycare centres were directly operated by the City of Toronto.[62] Childcare had dropped from a 1946 city-run high of thirteen day nurseries and six daycare centres. Accelerating cutbacks were publicly attributed to low rates of enrollment, which were interpreted to indicate that parents were not interested in childcare. For example, the commissioner of public welfare told the press in 1951, that falling attendance "proves that the actual need of the day nursery service was not as great as they [the Association] represented."[63]

Privately, the state told a different story. The City commissioner acknowledged that his regressive fee and admission policy had the intended effect of eliminating service. On 16 March 1954, Commissioner Rupert wrote James Band, deputy minister of public welfare, to say "I am of the opinion that the prime political reason for the decline in the number of children requiring care in recent years has been due to our admission and fee policies." He further noted with satisfaction that "in recognition of the decline in demand for care of children, there has been, as you know, a progressive closing of nurseries. We shall continue to watch the situation closely and will not hesitate to recommend the closing of additional nursery units if deemed necessary."[64]

In her evaluation of the role of the state after the war, Schulz says that while all three levels of government expressed their support for daycare during this period, their actions belied their words:

> The tactics used to limit the service included: passing responsibility for daycare to another level of government; allowing quality of care legislation to close centres rather than up-grade the service; implementing stated policy very slowly or not at all; making "fraudulent use" rather than extent of need the focus of attention; and rendering the service so costly and demeaning that parents were reluctant to use it.[65]

By late 1951, the daycare movement was effectively demolished. Turner argues that the 1950s and 1960s were the "doldrum years" of childcare organizing.[66] Another history of the daycare movement sadly concludes that "by 1962, the gains of the Second World War had almost entirely disappeared."[67]

CONCLUSIONS

Denise Riley persuasively argues that one of the most pernicious effects of state and social emphasis on "The Mother," has been to create two "irreconcilable parties: the house-wife/mother and the woman worker."[68] The Day Nurseries and Day Care Parents Association (including its Communist members) did not challenge the contradictions between women-as-mothers and women-as-workers. Their attempts to work with the experiential reality of this split (even as it was untheorized in their politics) led them to defend childcare with the weak arguments of "prevention of juvenile delinquency" and "service to families." These defences, because of their partial and contingent nature, were vulnerable—especially so during a period of intense hostility to communism, state cutbacks, and a fiercely ideological imposition of a particular family form. When daycare was no longer seen as a measure that might prevent juvenile delinquency, and instead was equated with an anti-family communism, the daycare movement collapsed.

The Communist Party and the Day Nurseries and Day Care Parents Association argued that "mothers are workers too." Yet, as Riley also warns, this defence is prone to deeply conservative uses, "especially at points when pro-natalist alarm seeks to 'preserve the family' and 'protect motherhood' in a way that marks off 'the mother' as a separate species-being."[69] Despite this, "mothers are workers too" was the fundamental argument that sustained the Day Nurseries and Day Care Parents Association. Because the association did not challenge the great division of women into "public" or "private" roles, its understanding of childcare was politically contradictory. The association was unable to notice the policy schizophrenia that Riley identifies when she says

> The lot of working mothers in war time and after points up the incoherence built into social policy addresses to "the family," which speak as if the interests and needs of women, men and children were always harmoniously unified. Mothers who work strain these assumptions of unity.[70]

To some degree, there was a division of labour: the Day Nurseries and Day Care Parents Association fought for "mothers," and the party fought for "workers." Neither the association nor the party could adequately advance a notion of social struggle that integrated the deeply complex intertwinings of class and gender at the levels of social policy, political practice, and personal lived experience. Nor could either organization address the real contradictions between women and men in their productive and reproductive roles; hence their appeals to a unified family. This highlights the need for socialist and feminist theory that can address both the complex intersections and alignments of class and gender, as well as their conflicts.

The demand made by the association was for a reconstruction of the relations between family and work—public and private—that no longer relied on the privatized work of women. In their insistence that working families—and more particularly, "working mothers"—required assistance, the association made a radical critique. This challenge was not always clear, and indeed (for tactical reasons) was occasionally inverted. Nonetheless, against a liberal notion of class transcendence, the daycare movement demanded service as a right, breaking a long association of childcare with charity and the "deserving" poor. In a preliminary way, the association's demand for the socialization of childcare was a demand for redistribution of the labour of social reproduction. It was a forerunner of contemporary feminist organizing with and against the state that forces us to question why social reproduction has been so undertheorized.

It also takes us to the strategy of using the state to redistribute women's work. This case study reveals that the state's decision to provide childcare services only to particular types of families had both an economic gatekeeping function (in terms of controlling women's labour force participation) and, equally importantly, an ideological and moral function—the regulation of mothering, and family. Welfare policies invariably (although with differing weights) address both these aspects of social reproduction. At the level of theoretical explanation, we must move beyond understanding the functions of the capitalist state as simple accumulation and legitimation, in order to account for the complexity of social and ideological regulation. This unravelling will be especially significant for contemporary feminist engagements with the state.

Perhaps most importantly, this case study has implications for Marxist social theory. Marxist economic theory (like the reserve army of labour theory) has a powerful explanatory value, yet it cannot address, for example, the gendered aspect of state policy. The long-standing and most basic assumptions of socialist theory are incomplete when they do not address the gendered nature of social organization. It is, of course, by now a truism to point out that this weakness in Marxist theory is crucially important and must be addressed by all political economists—not merely those who "do women." All adequate theory must address the mutual interdependencies, as well as the contradictions and outright conflicts, of gender, economics, class, and politics, without underestimating the full significance of each.

Despite the Day Nurseries and Day Care Parents Association's ultimate failure to prevent state closures of childcare centres, this moment in the history of childcare organizing is more than a story of defeat and political error. The childcare movement was, and is, more complex than that. In addition to their five-year defence of childcare, the Day Nurseries and Day Care Parents Association put forward a transformative demand. In their insistence, however articulated, that all working mothers and children needed and deserved care, they undermined a conservative notion of family and increased the possibilities of choice in women's (as well as men's and children's) lives.

One of the clearest lessons to be gained from an historical analysis of childcare is that we need better theory before we can predict the results of political practice with any certainty. Sophisticated and conjuncturally perceptive theory about the enormous power of the state to blunt, incorporate, and absorb political challenge is particularly necessary—but this must be complemented with theory that recognizes the existence of real moments of possibility and can shed light on strategy for those moments. This theorization can only be made with historically specific experiences. This history of daycare organizing is a small contribution to the long task of painstaking analysis and historical discovery. We need to recover, learn from, and move beyond the history of women's organizing with and against the state.

NOTES

In the preparation of this paper, material from the following collections was consulted: Public Archives of Ontario (PAO), James Band Papers; City of Toronto Archives, City Council Minutes; Toronto Board of Education, Newspaper Clipping File, 1946–51; the Kenney Collection, Thomas Fisher Rare Book Library, University of Toronto; and the Schulz Collection, Baldwin Room, Metro Library.

1. D. Wolfe, "The Rise and Demise of the Keynesian Era in Canada: Economic Policy 1930–1982" in *Modern Canada: 1930–1980*, ed. G. Kealey and M. Cross (Toronto: McClelland & Stewart, 1984), 54–55.

2. R. Pierson, "Women's Emancipation and the Recruitment of Women into the Labour Force in World War II" in *The Neglected Majority: Essays in Canadian Women's History*, ed. S. Mann Trofimenkoff and A. Prentice (Toronto: McClelland & Stewart, 1977), 138.

3. P. Schulz, "Daycare in Canada: 1860–1962" in *Good Daycare*, ed. K. Gallagher-Ross (Toronto: Women's Educational Press, 1978), 150.

4. Pierson, "Women's Emancipation," 142.

5. Wolfe, "The Rise and Demise of the Keynesian Era," 54–55.

6. Pierson, "Women's Emancipation," 141; *Canadian Tribune*, 6 Oct. 1945.

7. *Globe and Mail*, 1 Jan. 1946.

8. *Toronto Star*, 30 Jan. 1946.

9. *Toronto Telegram*, 9 Feb. 1946.

10. *Toronto Star*, 14 Feb. 1946.

11. Turnbull, May 1949, p. 2, "Day Nurseries, Correspondence with the City of Toronto, 1944–1945," PAO, RG29-01-840, ser. 74.

12. *Canadian Tribune*, 19 Jan. 1946.

13. Communist Party of Canada, "Brief on Dominion–Provincial Relations," Introduction, 3, Kenney Collection, box 7, Thomas Fisher Rare Book Library, University of Toronto.

14. Schulz, "Daycare in Canada," 153–54.

15. Letter, City of Toronto's Commissioner of Welfare to the Deputy Minister of Public Welfare, 18 Nov. 1949, PAO, RG29-01-840.

16. Deputy Minister of Public Welfare, Supplementary Memorandum on Day Nurseries, 3 July 1948, PAO, RG29-01-840.

17. Taped interview with Dorothy Millichamp, conducted by Pat Schulz, 20 April 1977, Schulz Collection, Baldwin Room, Metro Toronto Library.

18. *Toronto Star*, 30 May 1946.

19. *Canadian Tribune*, 7 June 1947.

20. *Toronto Star*, 22 Nov. 1946.

21. Ibid., 14 Feb. 1946.

22. Helen Muller, letter to editor, ibid., May 1947.

23. Ibid.

24. Taped interview with Millichamp, 1977.

25. Resolution on Work Among Women, *Proceedings of the Second Ontario Convention of the Communist Party*, 1938, 45, Kenney Collection, Thomas Fisher Rare Book Library.

26. Ibid., 55.

27. Interview with Joan Sangster, May 1988.

28. *Globe and Mail*, 1 Aug. 1946; *Toronto Star*, 31 July 1946.

29. Toronto City Council, *Minutes*, 12 Nov. 1946, 179.

30. Schulz, "Daycare in Canada," 154.

31. *Toronto Star*, 12 March 1948.

32. Ibid.

33. Toronto City Council, *Minutes*, Committee on Public Welfare, Report no. 5, 1946.

34. *Toronto Star*, 23 June 1947.

35. Ibid., Jan. 1947.

36. Toronto City Council, *Minutes,* Committee on Public Welfare, Report no. 5, 1947.

37. *Toronto Star,* 3 Nov. 1948.

38. Ibid.

39. *Globe and Mail,* 3 March 1947.

40. *Toronto Star,* 3 March 1947.

41. *Globe and Mail,* 5 Dec. 1947.

42. Ibid., 3 March 1950.

43. *Toronto Star,* 7 March 1950.

44. Ibid., 30 Sept. 1949.

45. *Globe and Mail,* 1 March 1949.

46. L.P.P. National Convention, Proceedings, Feb. 1949, Kenney Collection, box 3, Thomas Fisher Rare Book Library. Italics in the original.

47. *Globe and Mail,* 8 Jan. 1950.

48. *Toronto Star,* 8 June 1950.

49. Of even more interest is the astonishing regularity with which collective childcare is equated with communism. Attitudes toward childcare have careened wildly. One American report argued that nurseries were designed "to begin proper education and to Americanize foreign children." See D. Kerr in *Childcare: Who Cares?* ed. P. Roby (New York: Basic Books, 1973), 159. Later, critics argued that childcare would "sovietize" children. See E.T. Zeigler in *Daycare: Scientific and Social Policy Issues,* ed. E.T. Zeigler and T.W. Gordon (Boston: Auburn House, 1982). Childcare advocates have often tried to avoid the conflicts by avoiding the ideological debates and concentrating on simple service discourse.

50. Inter-Office Memo, 15 Jan. 1951, PAO, RG29-01-840.

51. Ministry of Public Welfare, Inter-office Memo, PAO, RG29-01-841.

52. Ibid.

53. Toronto City Council, *Minutes,* Committee on Public Welfare, Report no. 4, 14 Feb. 1951, 619.

54. Ibid., 619–20.

55. Ibid.

56. Goodfellow, Ministry of Public Welfare, News Release, 28 May 1951, p. 2, PAO, RG29-01-841.

57. Ibid.

58. G. Rubin, "The Traffic in Women: Notes on the 'Political Economy' of Sex" in *Towards an Anthropology of Women,* ed. R. Reiter (New York: Monthly Review Press, 1975), 204.

59. Toronto City Council, *Minutes,* Committee on Public Welfare, Report no. 145, 14 June 1951, 1546.

60. Undated newspaper clipping, Schulz Collection, Baldwin Room, Metro Library.

61. Toronto City Council, *Minutes,* Committee on Public Welfare, Report no. 147, 14 June 1951, 1546; *Toronto Star,* 30 May 1951.

62. *Toronto Star,* 30 May 1951.

63. Toronto City Council, *Minutes,* Committee on Public Welfare, Report no. 11, 14 June 1951, 1551.

64. Box 21, file 876, PAO, RG29, ser. 01.

65. Schulz, "Daycare in Canada," 155.

66. J. Turner, "Daycare and Women's Labour Force Participation: An Historical Study" (MA thesis, University of Regina, 1981).

67. Schulz, "Daycare in Canada," 157.

68. D. Riley, *War in the Nursery: Theories of the Child and the Mother* (London: Virago Press, 1983), 191.

69. Ibid., 185.

70. Ibid., 151.

W. C. CLARK AND THE
POLITICS OF CANADIAN
HOUSING POLICY, 1935–1952 ✧

JOHN BACHER

○

Lawrence B. Smith's neo-conservative assessment of Canadian housing policy praised the formative years, 1935 to 1954, as a sort of golden era, from
which successive governments have deviated along a socialist course that
has jeopardized national housing standards.[1] Federal housing policy did
flow along lines that would today win applause from neo-conservative
thinkers, largely because the designers of these policies in Ottawa held similar views. This was especially true in the case of William Clifford Clark, the
deputy minister of finance, who was the foremost shaper of Canadian housing policy from the first permanent program in 1935 until his death in 1952.
He would draft the critical Dominion Housing Act of 1935 in close association with the mortgage companies, fight a successful battle to curtail and
wind down socialized housing initiatives created during World War II, and
confuse social reformers with a dazzling array of legislative complexities
that disguised the intent of his policies. Clark, in co-operation with his close
associate, David Mansur, also created a federal housing agency, the Central
Mortgage and Housing Corporation, with an explicit mandate to encourage
private enterprise in the housing field.

In many ways Clark carried out the tradition of free-market liberalism
so favoured by Oscar Douglas Skelton (1878–1941), his mentor and one of
the founders of the modern Canadian civil service. Clark's earliest work in
opposition to government regulations, in 1917, in the grain trade, was
clearly along these lines and was not fundamentally altered either by his
remarkable experience as a pioneering Canadian labour statistician or by

✧ From *Urban History Review* 17, 1 (1988): 5–14. Reprinted with the permission of the
journal.

his association with labour educator Edmund Bradwin,[2] during years of labour turmoil from 1918 to 1923. Clark's sojourn in the United States as an investment consultant and executive for the real estate firm of L.W. Strauss and Company from 1923 to 1932 appears to have reinforced his free-market thinking. In a book co-authored with J.L. Kingston for the American Institute of Steel Construction, he gave an academic sanctification to the tendency of the real-estate market to intensify the capitalization of land and to make this the basis for skyscraper construction. They wrote that the optimal height of a building was the level at which the owner's returns were maximized, which he calculated to be sixty-three storeys given the state of existing technology, although the level would rise as land values increased. Clark warned that restrictions on the height of skyscrapers would invite disaster. He viewed "the whole economic fabric of society" as being "built to an important degree upon current property values." Looking forward to the days when such trends would place an entire city in one skyscraper, he believed it would be "the most profoundly efficient concept of gigantic size ever created by man." With land development being undertaken by large capitalists, the city's future would "be in more responsible hands," ensuring also "more scientific determination of supply and demand conditions."[3]

Clark's beliefs in the value of big business in land development and his firm conviction in the virtues of the free market in land and housing finance, which would characterize his housing policies, were firmly shaped when he was appointed to the post of deputy minister of finance by Prime Minister R.B. Bennett, on the advice of Skelton.[4] Clark did not recommend heavy expenditures for public works, such as subsidized housing, as an answer to depression-era unemployment. Although he has gained a reputation as the founder of Canadian Keynesianism, Clark advocated only that governments plan public works to counter recessions by not blindly cutting back in hard times and thus aggravating employment difficulties. He stressed that he did not "wish to be quoted as advocating the expenditure of large sums of money in construction of public works for the relief of unemployment." Instead he simply advocated "the expenditure of forethought." In 1931 he told a civil service gathering, "As citizens of local municipalities let us take to heart the warnings and good advice recently tendered by the Canadian Bankers Association to exorcise administrative waste and reduce borrowings to a minimum."[5]

Under conditions of prosperity such as those that existed in the short-lived boom in home construction from 1923 to 1929, Clark would never have encouraged any housing legislation. But with the Depression's creation of a widespread social housing movement, he was motivated to draft legislation that actually strengthened his market-oriented objectives and did nothing for the original concerns of reformers.

With mortgage institutions directly threatened by increasing public calls for social housing, Clark was able to defuse a growing public movement through his ingenuity in drafting the Dominion Housing Act of 1935. The movement for social housing had begun with the 1932 housing survey of Halifax and culminated in the 1935 report of the House of Commons housing committee. It was nurtured by a diverse coalition of groups around the National Construction Council [NCC], which included contractors and related building industries, both craft and industrial unions, architects, many municipal leaders, urban planners, and social workers. The NCC emerged out of a three-day conference in February 1933 sponsored by the building contractors' organization, the Canadian Construction Association [CCA]. Since its inception in 1919, the CCA had welcomed government stimulation of the housing industry and had held pro-labour views that were unusually enlightened for an employers' organization. One of the NCC's first tasks was to send out a questionnaire to its members, to boards of trade, and to larger municipalities regarding the benefits of certain public construction projects. Although not on the NCC's initial list, public housing soon appeared on many replies.[6]

The most important results of the NCC's concerns were the Montreal and Toronto housing surveys of 1934 and 1935 respectively. The reports of these surveys argued that subsidized housing for low-income families should become a government responsibility. The Montreal report concluded that "the provision of low rental housing" would tend "to reduce under-nourishment, tuberculosis, hospitalization, destitution, with their attendant social costs, and to release working class purchasing power for other necessities, comforts, and conveniences of life."[7] The Toronto survey's report, named in honour of Lieutenant Governor Sir Herbert Bruce, who encouraged social housing, reached similar conclusions. It "urged on the Dominion Government," that "no public work grants" were as "urgently needed" as those "for the rehousing of the poorest members of the community." Largely written by Toronto architect Eric Arthur and professor of social work Harry Cassidy, the report recommended the creation of a national housing commission to provide grants to municipalities and provinces for low-rental housing.[8]

Although it was not originally part of the agenda of his "New Deal," Bennett was forced to agree to a parliamentary housing commission in February 1935 because of a revolt by Conservative back-benchers, led by former Toronto mayor T.L. Church. Church quoted the Bruce Report extensively in a parliamentary motion and observed that "a wave of emotion seems to be sweeping the nation on the subject of slums."[9]

Reflecting the consensus of expert opinion in the areas of planning, social work, and architecture, the parliamentary committee made a unanimous recommendation in favour of a national housing authority, which would build its own projects and lend at favourable terms to municipalities for low-rental projects. From the time of the release of its report on 16 April 1935 to the introduction in the Commons of the Dominion Housing Act on 24 June 1935, Clark would, with his usual intensity, work to produce national housing legislation that would strengthen the private market.

Clark approached the drafting of national housing legislation in terms of the best deal that could be struck between himself and the Dominion Mortgage and Investment Association [DMIA], which represented most institutional mortgage lenders. He took the attitude that the government should "make use of private lending agencies instead of driving them out of business."[10] The association's president, D'Arcy Leonard, saw dangers inherent in public housing. He feared the threat it posed "of bringing down the rental values" of working-class housing. Clark and Leonard shared the belief that federal housing legislation should encourage the maximum use of both public and private investment to stimulate new residential construction. Leonard believed that although the DMIA companies had at least $25 million "which they would like to get out on new construction in Canada," this money was not being made available because mortgage companies could not legally provide a mortgage worth more than 60 percent of a home's value and "not many people" could afford a 40 percent down payment on a home.[11]

The Dominion Housing Act [DHA] of 1935 was drafted by Clark and Leonard to meet the problem of stimulating the mortgage market by allowing lower down payments and by providing a system of equal monthly installments of blended principal and interest. This was of assistance only to the relatively high income groups of Canadians in enabling them to become homeowners. The government decreased the required down payment from 40 to 20 percent by providing a 20 percent second mortgage at 3 percent, lower than the 3.5 percent rate at which it borrowed money. Lending institutions would set the rate for first mortgages at 6.6 percent so that the combined rate of interest to the borrower would be 5.5 percent. It was a scheme that in Leonard's words to Clark was "very practical and fairly simple." The negotiations between the two men took place between the 2nd and 6th of June, shortly before it was introduced in the Commons on 23 June 1935. A last minute change obtained by Leonard allowed companies to grant first mortgages for less than 60 percent of a home's value, thus reflecting regional customs of the lending institutions, especially in the Montreal district, to require larger down payments. Leonard also warned Clark that there would be many localities where DMIA "institutions do not operate and others where they would not recommend operating." Because of his pleasure with the final act, Leonard sent Clark a supportive telegram to be read during debate of the bill in the House of Commons.[12]

The difficulty in providing the joint government-lending institution loans became evident during discussions over DHA interest rates. Since in some areas lending institutions obtained 7 to 9 percent interest on their mortgages, the application of the DHA would cause their rates of return in these regions to be reduced. Clark told assembled DMIA representatives that the regional differential interest rate they wanted "was politically impossible." In response, Mansur, now inspector of mortgages for Sun Life, said that "very few loans would be made in areas which are residentially as hazardous as northern Ontario." Indeed in its first year of operation the DHA was confined largely to exclusive upper-class suburban areas of the major metropolitan centres of Ontario and Quebec. Even by the end of World War II, joint loans would remain largely absent from northern Ontario, the interior of British Columbia, the rural prairies, and small towns throughout the nation. From 1935 to 1945, not a single joint loan would be made in the entire province of Alberta because of lending institutions' hostility to the provincial Social Credit government.[13]

The only provision for social housing in the new DHA was the promise that Bennett's newly created Economic Council of Canada [ECC] would further study appropriate action for low-rental accommodation. Although an Economic Council of Canada Act was passed as part of Bennett's "New Deal," in the 1935 parliamentary session, the prime minister did not get around to making appointments. If he had, Clark's influence in housing matters would have been considerably curtailed. The ECC's proposed housing sub-committee, as suggested by Bennett's executive assistant, R.K. Finlayson, read like a roster of the nation's leading advocates of public housing: the president of the All Canadian Labour Congress, A.R. Mosher; leading urban planner Noulan Cauchon: Ontario farm and co-op leader W.C. Good; architect Percy Nobbs; J.C. Reilly of the Canadian Construction Association; and professional leaders in engineering and architecture.[14]

In defeating proposals for low-rental housing, Clark had acted in accordance with his desire to work with lending institutions; his opposition to a solution to unemployment based on an increase in public expenditure; and a desire to maintain the housing market as an area for private investment. He saw the legislation as allowing "the federal dollar" to "do as much as possible." He told Mansur that this would be accomplished "most effectively" by "the building of high cost houses" rather than by "the building of low cost houses."[15] Clark's tendency to encourage government aid to home building for the wealthy shows how strong his opposition continued to be regarding acceptance of the principle of low-cost, subsidized rental housing.

Clark would continue to set housing policy during the remainder of the depression under Prime Minister Mackenzie King. The threat of alternative advice was eliminated when King repealed the Economic Council of Canada Act early in the 1936 session, before any members were appointed. Clark's major political battle on housing matters would be with King's answer to unemployment, the National Employment Commission. Reflecting King's corporatist outlook, the commission was chaired by an enlightened corporate magnate, Alfred Purvis, and had as vice-chairman conservative construction trades union leader, Tom Moore.

Clark supported the NEC's only adopted recommendation, the Home Improvement Plan, instituted in 1936. This scheme involved no direct government expenditure, only loan guarantees. Even its advertising budget was paid for by Purvis's soliciting from his colleagues in the business community. In the area of low-rental housing the conflict reached the level of political crisis when Purvis was reported to be on the verge of resigning over the government's refusal to adopt his public-housing proposals. Favourably impressed by the recommendations of the Bruce Report, Purvis even arranged a tour of Great Britain for one of its authors, David Shepherd, to assist the NEC in formulating its low-rental housing recommendations to the government.[16]

Clark succeeded in blocking the NEC's proposals for legislation on low-rental housing for a year, until the publication of the commission's final report made further delay politically inexpedient. After wily delays by Mackenzie King, the report was released on 5 April 1938. Clark told Finance Minister Charles Dunning that the direct subsidies proposed for public housing by the NEC represented a dangerous "radical innovation in government programs in Canada." He rejected the commission's assumptions that Canadian families had incomes too low to "enable them to pay the ordinary economic cost of necessary family shelter" Clark also downplayed the severity of the unemployment crisis. He told Dunning that "many on relief do not want jobs now."[17]

In order to show that alternatives to public housing were possible, Clark encouraged a limited-dividend project in Winnipeg, in 1937. Limited-dividend housing is an approach that attempts to avoid the need for subsidized housing through government assistance to private housing companies whose returns are limited to a modest return on capital. Mansur attempted to sway Winnipeg mortgage and realty interests who viewed the project as a dangerous socialist experiment. He told the Sun Life inspector in Winnipeg, John Flanders, that Clark was "particularly anxious to arrange some such scheme" aimed at avoiding "the necessity of bringing in further legislation to provide for real low cost housing and slum clearance." Clark, Mansur, and Winnipeg alderman R.A. Sara met in Ottawa during August of 1937 to devise a limited-dividend scheme that would be acceptable to Winnipeg's property industry. Nothing came of the proposal, in part because real estate interests felt that no publicly assisted houses should "be built in Winnipeg until every house in that city for sale," had been "sold to a satisfactory purchase."[18]

Legislation for low-rental housing was included in the National Housing Act of 1938, which was part of the public works program stimulated by the release of the NEC's final report. Clark's drafting of this legislation, however, made its provisions for low-rental housing unworkable. Consequently, no housing was actually built under the NHA's provisions for low-income shelter.[19]

Clark had been able to make legislative provisions for low-income housing inoperative in the 1938 act by making major revisions to the program that had been suggested by the NEC. These placed heavier burdens on the provinces and municipalities, maximized red tape, and set standards that Clark was fully aware could not be met. He set maximum cost ceilings per unit below the level he estimated would be required for new housing units. He added provisions that required provincial guarantees of municipal efforts and limited municipal taxation of housing projects to 1 percent of their construction costs, which greatly discouraged the use of the legislation.[20] He gave little assistance to municipalities attempting to build public housing under the 1938 bill. At one point F.W. Nicolls, whom Clark had placed in charge of the Department of Finance's National Housing Administration, reported how he had accomplished a great deal of "stalling" of Winnipeg public-housing proposals.[21] The proposals had been rejected because their costs per unit violated the Department of Finance's limits.[22] In 1940 Clark presented an impossible list of tasks to be finished in eleven days to Nova Scotia Housing Commission chairman S.H. Prince for Halifax to meet the

31 March deadline for a low-rental housing agreement with the federal government.[23]

Clark's initial response to World War II on housing matters was to disband all existing programs. In advocating this course he took the view that these programs should be eliminated because the goal for which they existed, the reduction of unemployment, had been achieved. Any further stimulation of the housing market would be a wasteful drain on the war effort. New residential construction, his memorandums invariably stressed, should be delayed until after the war. Then the housing shortage encouraged by the cessation of residential building during the war years would prove to be an excellent contribution to postwar employment.[24]

Clark was placed in an excellent position to influence wartime housing policy by his chairmanship of the Economic Advisory Committee [EAC] at its critical meeting on 15 October 1940. After only a "brief discussion," the committee accepted Clark's arguments that the continuation of the Home Improvement Plan would be harmful since it simply encouraged "much unessential repair and improvement work." At this meeting the EAC also accepted Clark's advice for the termination of the NHA joint-loan scheme. This was later reversed, however, after the decision caused a storm of protest from mortgage and building supply companies, particularly retail lumber dealers, who benefited from the program.[25]

Clark was fully aware of the hardship his policies would cause. He was, however, convinced that "Canada must accept an increasing amount of 'doubling up' and overcrowding in existing housing units with all the social disadvantages which are thereby involved." Such "lowering [of] housing standards" were part of "the price of war." The Cabinet was duly warned by Clark that it "should not gloss over" the evils (i.e. hardships) and public criticism that would inevitably follow a cessation of home construction.[26]

In February 1941 he accepted the creation of a crown corporation for home construction, Wartime Housing Limited, after he became suspicious of the construction of houses for workers at government war plants. He complained to Angus L. Macdonald, acting minister of munitions and supply, that "the present national war interest" had suffered "by too much architectural refinement" and "too expensive a type of construction." He distrusted the influence of architects who sought "to plan garden villages, introduce special trim, special doors, special roofs, special porches, all of which increases expense."[27]

Clark suggested a number of alternatives to government-constructed housing for munitions workers. He suggested the use of "bunk houses . . . in mining, paper and other industrial towns." The families of workers could "easily remain in their home localities" and "thus facilitate the post-war return of population to its pre-war domicile." He advocated "filling up existing vacancies, such as they are, by encouraging the taking in of lodgers and by conversion of older houses to give more dwelling units."[28] He also envisioned a system of subsidized transit to move workers to homes in areas that had higher vacancy rates. After Clark's own National Housing Administration began to press for a crown corporation because the housing shortage was hurting the war effort, the federal Cabinet created Wartime Housing Limited on 24 February 1941.[29]

Although the placing of Wartime Housing Limited under the Ministry of Munitions and Supply freed it from Clark's rigid ideological supervision, the move set the stage for conflict over housing policy for the remainder of the war years. Basically, conflict over housing policy would take place along lines similar to those of the disputes of the Depression. Clark's principal adversaries on housing policy in the Depression, the Canadian Construction Association, now had many of their leaders well placed in government positions, including the president of Wartime Housing, Joseph Pigott, and the vice-president, William Summerville. Pigott attempted to push for a permanent program of public housing to serve as a stabilizer of the residential construction industry. Such a program he hoped, would both ease the housing shortage and lower construction costs by moderating labour's wage demands through the promise of secure employment opportunities.[30]

Clark and Pigott were clearly headed on a collision course over housing policy. A major dispute broke out when Pigott tried to negotiate an agreement with the city of Hamilton for a wartime housing project geared to meeting the needs of low-income families. Pigott had chosen Hamilton carefully as a beginning point for his plans; it had a severe emergency shelter problem, with 130 children and their families living in an old shirt factory. A draft agreement between Wartime Housing and the city had the corporation lending money to Hamilton at 3 percent interest for the construction of three hundred permanent homes. These would be rented at $24 a month to families with a severe need of shelter.[31]

The Hamilton agreement quickly created an uproar among Ontario lumber dealers, real estate agents, small residential builders, mortgage companies, and their allies in government. On 2 November 1942, federal rentals administrator Cyril DeMara warned that Pigott's plan would encourage "the socialization of all our housing." The agreement was, he cautioned, "in a nutshell," the dangerous "New Zealand plan of wide scale state-owned housing for low income groups."[32] On 9 November 1942 Clark hastily informed Wartime Prices and Trade Board chairman Donald Gordon that he feared DeMara's alarming memo reflected "pretty accurately" the views held by Pigott. After a critical meeting between the minister of munitions and supply (C.D. Howe), the minister of finance (J.L. Ilsley), Gordon, Clark, Pigott, and Wartime Housing's general manager (Victor Goggin), severe controls were placed on Wartime Housing to keep it out of competition with private enterprise. A Housing Co-ordinating Committee, established in early December 1942 and composed of representatives from several federal departments, was established to screen new Wartime Housing projects. To prevent a repeat of the Hamilton project's subsidies, all proposals would include "a budget for the financing of the project." Wartime Housing's task of initiating housing studies of community shelter problems was transferred to a newly created office of the real property controller created at the same time. Placed in the Wartime Prices and Trade Board, this controller was also to survey the existing housing stock and institute campaigns to persuade home owners to take in more lodgers and rent more rooms.[33]

In late December 1942 Pigott told Wartime Housing's board of directors how Clark had effectively opposed his housing plans. He informed his board that their suggestion had been rejected "because of the attitude of Dr. Clark." He felt there "was nothing we could do" in the face of the attitude of the Department of Finance.[34]

With the creation of the office of real property controller and the Housing Co-ordinating Committee, Clark had effectively secured the influence of his views on housing policy, which had been diminished by the creation and activities of Wartime Housing. His disputes with Wartime Housing had clarified his sense of the proper direction for government policy. He told the deputy minister of munitions and supply, A.K. Shields, that "doubling-up was a way of making the necessary savings to prevent civilians from sabotaging the war effort." He also stressed that "the deferment of this construction of permanent housing until after the war" would "make a fine contribution to the support of the business structure and improvement in the post-war years."[35]

Clark's vision of using a curtailment of wartime housing production as a boon to postwar prosperity, however, began to become seriously challenged when in September 1943 the man appointed to carry out this policy, real property controller Russell Smart, himself began advocating politics that were essentially the same as the heretical views of Pigott. Although a man of socialist sympathies, as witnessed by his prewar support for the League for Social Reconstruction, Smart had attempted to promote Clark's policies vigorously. As Pigott had warned, Clark's surveys and campaigns had provided little additional housing. Instead they served to demonstrate the severity of shortages and to arouse public opinion further on the issue. The registries set up to find the homeless shelter, established early in 1943, began to press for more housing construction as their waiting lists mounted. In Ottawa they reported that large numbers of families had to be divided because of the inability to find shelter for them. Shelters in Halifax and Quebec City stopped publicizing their efforts after they became swamped trying to find homes for families who had already applied for shelter. In Montreal considerable embarrassment was caused by the delay in opening the housing registry because the city's housing shortage made it difficult to obtain the needed stenographers.[36] On 24 September 1943 Smart told Donald Gordon that the housing shortage had developed to "the point where it will seriously interfere with the war effort and be likely to produce a social or political disturbance." As a first step to reversing this situation he urged Gordon to press for a major Wartime Housing project for Montreal, which he hoped would serve as a model for other cities. Gordon fully backed Smart's recommendations and they would not be as easily dismissed as Pigott's proposed Hamilton agreement. Consequently, in November 1943 Clark cagily used a limited-dividend proposal to put calls for public housing in a dead-end direction, as he had done successfully in Winnipeg with the NEC's recommendations in 1938.[37]

Clark put the directors of the Montreal Limited Dividend Company in an impossible position. They would either build housing below the standards that the city's business and professional communities accepted as minimal-quality accommodation, or they would end up building for a restricted upper-income group. This made it difficult to obtain directors for the project. The Liberal publisher of the *Montreal Star*, J.M. McConnell, took the view that the scheme was a dishonest "gesture towards placating those who are clamouring for immediate housing relief." He also did not want "any committee of private citizens" to assume responsibility for building homes along Clark's preferred lines with their "out-dated method of heating by stoves," which he believed posed an "ever present fire hazard."[38] Clark did succeed in persuading the president of the Bank of Montreal, G.W. Spinney, to assume responsibility for the project. Spinney's directors also concluded that stoves for heating were a "retrograde step." However, after they agreed to install central heating, estimates of cost had to be increased by 10 percent. Spinney told Clark that this caused their plan to become "completely outside the original orbit of low rental housing." Consequently, in September 1944 the directors agreed to terminate the project.[39]

When Spinney told Clark on 9 September of his directors' decision, King's government was placed in an awkward situation. Spinney's efforts during 1944 delayed what Smart had kept quiet during 1943, a government commitment to a long-term public-housing program. Spinney's failure took place less than a month after the passage of the National Housing Act of 1944, in which Clark placed a limited-dividend clause, demonstrated to be unworkable, as the sole housing program for two-thirds of the nation's population. Consequently, he waited for almost a month to give Finance Minister Ilsley a copy of Spinney's decision. When this was done, he urged Ilsley to take special pains in thanking Spinney to "avoid giving a formal reply in case production of correspondence is later asked for in the House."[40]

Clark wrote the National Housing Act of 1944 in a manner similar to his drafting of the Dominion Housing Act of 1935. Both were written through negotiations with representatives of the Dominion Mortgage and Investments Association in 1944. The result essentially liberalized the existing joint-loan program. Clark adopted their recommendations for reductions in down payments, an extension of the amortization period, and a reduction from 5.5 to 4.5 percent in the interest rate charged to the borrower of NHA joint loans. Although the DMIA itself no longer opposed public housing, recognizing it had been demonstrated as necessary "to provide proper housing for many families" in Europe, Great Britain, and the United States, Clark's opposition remained.[41]

In response to the 1942–1943 work of the sub-committee (which dealt with housing and community planning) of the James Committee on postwar reconstruction, Clark instituted the family allowance program. The sub-committee had shown that housing subsidies were required so that the lower two-thirds of Canadian families who were renting could afford adequate shelter. Clark attempted to solve this problem by providing direct subsidies in the form of family allowances. The James Committee saw both shelter subsidies and family allowances as integral to its comprehensive program of income security. Clark seized upon family allowances as the critical remedy to postwar reconstruction. He told the Cabinet that with "children's allowances on anything like an adequate scale" the federal government could avoid the need to finance "municipally constructed and municipally managed low rental projects."[42]

Toward the end of World War II the rigid dominance of Clark's views on housing policy came in for increasing criticism as housing shortages mounted with the return of veterans. Concern was widespread in the Department of Veterans' Affairs, the Wartime Information Board, and the demobilization branches of the armed services. Housing shortages were playing havoc with the government's efforts to rehabilitate returned servicemen.[43] The NHA's plans for limited-dividend housing continued to be fruitless.

This led C.D. Howe to conclude that their "workability" was "doubtful."[44] Likewise, John Baldwin, secretary of the Cabinet committee on reconstruction, complained that despite the fact the "only solution" to the housing of low-income groups was "some form of limited subsidization," the Department of Finance still refused "to accept the principle of government subsidy, or, of any government aid to municipalities in this connection."[45] Such concerns led to the replacement of the purely regulatory Housing Co-ordinating Committee with the Interdepartment Housing Committee. Unlike its predecessor, it had the ability to initiate new housing policy proposals. It was chaired by W.C. Clark, who began the IHC's first meeting, on 23 May 1945, with the observation that Canada was faced by "a grave national emergency" from the housing shortage. In these extreme circumstances he agreed that Wartime Housing should be "employed for a considerable extent during the next few months building houses for veterans."[46]

Clark used his chairmanship of the IHC to put forward one of his most cherished goals, the encouragement of large residential developers who could build entire communities. This scheme, known as Integrated Housing, provided bank loans to housing corporations at 1 percent below interest rates. If the dwellings built under the scheme could not be sold, the government would purchase them on a cost-plus basis. Builders operating under Integrated Housing would also be given priorities for scarce construction materials. Clark felt large land developers encouraged under his proposal would end the "higgledy-piggledy, piecemeal and ugly development of our communities."[47] On 1 May 1945, the Canadian Bankers' Association and Clark had reviewed this proposal. Their acceptance came soon after Clark assured the bankers that the government would only select companies for the Integrated Housing scheme that had been approved by the banks through "a thorough review of their clientele." The banks would in turn encourage their favourite builders to purchase "well-located" tracts of land for subdivisions.[48]

A serious illness prevented Clark from participating in the dramatic events that engulfed the government in controversy in the summer of 1945. As a result of widespread protests against evictions in July 1945, a freeze on evictions of well-behaved tenants was imposed and Wartime Housing's program of rental construction for veterans was greatly expanded. These moves led to an important meeting in the Department of Finance on 24 July.

That day the decisions on rent control and expanded direct federal rental housing were being made. At the meeting Mansur, Gordon, Mitchell Sharp (acting minister of finance), W.A. Mackintosh (associate deputy minister of finance), and William Anderson (National Housing Act administrator) revived Clark's prewar concept of a Central Mortgage Bank. This would eventually take the form of what would become the sole federal housing agency, the Central Mortgage and Housing Corporation [CMHC].[49]

CMHC took its shape from Clark's stillborn creation of the late depression years, the Central Mortgage Bank of Canada. This was originally conceived as a mechanism by which a mortgage on a residential property that was worth more than the home's market value could be adjusted downwards in value. Although lending institutions could accept such decreases in their assets for similarly inflated farm mortgages, they refused to consider home owners as deserving of the same treatment. Consequently, the Central Mortgage Bank closed in 1940 a year after the legislation was forced through a reluctant Senate by King's government. A participant with Clark in the drafting of the legislation and the bank's only president was Clark's close associate Mansur, who then left Sun Life for a career in public service that would culminate in his drafting of the NHA of 1954.[50]

Although Mansur and Clark saw a need to revive the Central Mortgage Bank toward the end of World War II, to stimulate the mortgage market, they originally did not conceive the institution as necessary during the immediate postwar period. This rapidly changed as a result of the unrest over housing issues in July 1945. Mansur took much of the wording of the legislation for the new CMHC from the old Central Mortgage Bank Act. He told his Department of Finance colleagues that the "primary duty" of the new corporation would be "finding ways and means for private enterprise to look after needs in the economic (ie. unsubsidized) housing field." The corporation would even measure its success "by the amount of activity not undertaken" by government agencies "in the public housing field."[51]

After Clark's recovery from illness he ceased to play the detailed supervisory role over housing matters characteristic of the decade after the DHA of 1935. This task was assumed by his subordinates in the Department of Finance. They effectively controlled CMHC's board of directors, with the watchdog role falling primarily to Mitchell Sharp. Sharp's advice to Clark included an assessment of the possible political impact of changes in housing policy on the Liberal government. In 1948 he warned Clark against Mansur's plans for a rental insurance scheme since he believed it "would not react favourably on the government" if the plan, as predicted, would prove to be "comparatively ineffective."[52] Similarly Mackintosh wished to spare C.D. Howe political embarrassment over the "relatively minor matter" of NHA amendments dealing with limited-dividend housing.[53] With his subordinates in firm command of housing policy after Wartime Housing's integration into CMHC in 1946, Clark left the details of housing policy to those who had demonstrated a similar outlook during many years of close association.

Clark's final victory in an important civil service dispute came when he defeated Bank of Canada official James Coyne when he attempted to terminate the joint-loan scheme during the Korean War. Coyne argued that the scheme was an unnecessary drain on the war effort doing nothing to encourage the building of homes where they were needed to house munitions workers. He also believed joint loans undermined federal fiscal and monetary policy. Coyne argued that government funds for housing should be restricted to assist the construction of rental accommodation which could "facilitate an expansion of employment in defence industries."[54] Clark emerged triumphant after he, Mansur, and Coyne met to discuss this issue in January 1951. He had successfully argued that NHA joint loans raised standards in home construction and that termination of the program would leave the government "open to the charge of disregarding the small man if things were left entirely to private enterprise."[55]

Clark's influence on federal housing legislation and administration made him the foremost shaper of what economist James Lorimer has characterized as the "corporate city," marked by the importance of large land development companies in shaping new urban construction.[56] Clark's vision of the future was complimentary to the balance sheets of important real estate and financial interests, who recognized, as Clark did, that the corporate city would favour obtaining maximum returns from the capitalization of urban land. His success in marshalling the powers of government to his urban vision was embodied not only in the private market mission of the CMHC but also in the design of its head office. It was built, as Humphrey Carver, a civil servant critical of the CMHC, recalled, "in a redbrick American colonial style, looking not unlike a glorified Howard Johnson's highway restaurant." This was done to meet Mansur's desire that the building "look like the head office of an insurance company."[57] Carver's dislike of the architectural style of CMHC's head office reflected his disagreement with the business-oriented thrust of its policies. However, he never became aware of the extent to which Clark had shaped these policies. While a leader of the movement for social housing in Canada, he actually wrote to Clark to seek advice in how to move Canadian housing policy in a more socially sensitive direction, oblivious to the fact that Clark was the very architect of what he opposed.[58]

The views of Clark and Carver on architecture reveal their conflicting ideals for the Canadian city. The former's emerged triumphant, in part, because of his more profound knowledge of social reality. Carver dreamed of public-housing projects with high levels of amenities and beautifully landscaped grounds, but he failed to understand the major changes in Canadian society required to bring about such urban development. Clark, in contrast, shaped his visions of the urban future to the profit motives of private investors, which required no social change. He was able to push this vision through the federal government, not only because of his prominent position in the federal civil service but also because of his ability to incorporate, at least on paper, the views of his more progressive critics.

NOTES

1. L.B. Smith, *Anatomy of a Crisis* (Vancouver: Fraser Institute, 1977), 9–10. Smith's affinity to Clark is even more apparent by what he omits from his glowing praise of "Pre-1954 Demand Policies." No mention is made of the programs that Clark opposed, such as the munitions' workers and veterans' housing programs of Wartime Housing.

2. John Porter, *The Vertical Mosaic* (Toronto: University of Toronto Press, 1965), 452–58; Edmund Bradwin, *The Bunkhouse Men: A Study of Work and Pay in the Camps of Canada 1903–14* (Toronto: University of Toronto Press, 1972), 12; James Struthers, *No Fault of Their Own: Unemployment and the Canadian Welfare State, 1914–1941* (Toronto: University of Toronto Press, 1983), 20, 21, 41.

3. W.C. Clark and J.L. Kingston, *The Skyscraper: A Study in the Economic Heights of Modern Office Buildings* (New York: American Institute of Steel Construction, 1930), 4–74, 81, 82, 127, 150, 151.

4. Porter, *Vertical Mosaic*, 452–58.

5. W.C. Clark, "What's Work with Us," address to the Professional Institute of the Civil Service of Canada, Dec. 1931, and W.C. Clark, "Regularization of National Demand for Labour by Government Employment," paper given to the International Association of Public Employment Services, both in Public Archives of Canada (hereafter PAC), RG19, vol. 3993.

6. "Plan to Revive the Construction Industry," *Journal of the Royal Architectural Institute of Canada* (hereafter *JRAIC*) 9 (1932): 256; "Component Parts of Construction Council Organize Permanent Council," *JRAIC* 10 (1933): 96; J.H. Craig, "What Can Be Learned from State Housing in Great Britain and the United States?" *JRAIC* 11 (1935): 79–81; "National Survey of Housing Needs Planned," *Canadian Engineer* (1935): 13; "A Plan to Revive the Construction Industry," *JRAIC* 10 (1933): 25–32; Walter Van

Nus, "The Plan Makers and the City: Architects, Engineers, Surveyors and Urban Planning in Canada, 1890–1939" (PhD diss., University of Toronto, 1975), 125–26.

7. Montreal Board of Trade, Civic Improvement League, *A Report on Housing and Slum Clearance for Montreal* (Montreal: Montreal Board of Trade, 1935), PAC, RG19, vol. 706, file 203-1A, 5, 21, 22.

8. *Report of Lieutenant-Governor's Committee on Housing Conditions in Toronto* (Toronto: Board of Control 1934), 44–112.

9. Canada, House of Commons, *Debates*, 1935, 1: 153–62.

10. Canada, Parliamentary Committee on Housing, *Minutes of Proceedings and Evidence of Special Committee on Housing* (Ottawa: King's Printer, 1935), 354–57.

11. Ibid, 334–51.

12. Letter from T.D. Leonard to W.C. Clark, 2 June 1935, and cable from Leonard to Clark, 25 June 1935, both in PAC, RG19, vol. 705, file 203-1A; Canada, House of Commons, *Debates*, 1935, 4: 3771–73.

13. Letter from D.B. Mansur to W.C. Clark, 6 July 1937, in PAC, RG19, vol. 710, file 203-1A, 51-10C-4. "Memorandum to Mr. W.C. Clark from F.W. Nicolls—The Lending Institutions' reaction to the Dominion Housing Act, 1935," PAC, RG19, vol. 706, file 203-1A.

14. "Committee on Housing," PAC, R.B. Bennett Papers, MG26 K.F.A. 434, 525484.

15. "Memorandum from David B. Mansur to Arthur Purvis re: Dominion Housing Act—1935," and Letter from W.C. Clark to D.B. Mansur, 10 Aug. 1936, both in PAC, RG19, vol. 711, file 203-22.

16. Low Cost Housing Diary, D. Shepherd, Housing Consultant, PAC, RG27, vol. 3356, file 12.

17. "Memorandum to Mr. Dunning, re: Low Rental Housing Program, March 7, 1937" and attached "Low Rental Housing Program Summary of Criticisms," PAC, RG19, vol. 3886.

18. Copy of letter from D.B. Mansur to J.A. Flanders, 14 June 1937, and letter from R.A. Ford to W.C. Clark, 31 Aug. 1937, both in PAC, RG19, vol. 3435.

19. "Act to promote Slum Clearance and Assist the Construction of Low Rental Housing," and "National Employment Commission Low Rental Housing Proposal, February 3, 1937," both PAC, RG19, vol. 3388, file 1; W.C. Clark, "A Low Rental Housing Program Summary of Criticisms," PAC, RG19, vol. 3435; Canada, *Statutes*, 1939, 358–64.

20. Ibid.

21. "Memorandum to Mr. Ralston from W.C. Clark," PAC, RG19, vol. 2679.

22. Winnipeg Housing Survey, PAC, RG19, vol. 716, file 203, 1–15.

23. Letter from W.C. Clark to H. Prince, 20 March 1940, and letter from Prince to Clark, 26 April 1940, both in PAC, RG19, vol. 706, file 203-1A.

24. See especially W.C. Clark, Report of the Economic Advisory Committee on Housing Policy, 13 Nov. 1940, PAC, RG19, vol. 3890.

25. See for example, W.C. Clark to A.K. Shields, 30 Aug. 1941, PAC, RG19, vol. 715, file 203C-11, and Minutes of Wartime Housing Executive Board, PAC, RG83, vol. 70, book 1.

26. W.C. Clark. "Report of the Economic Advisory Committee on Housing Policy," 4, 5, PAC, RG19, vol. 3890.

27. "Memorandum for the Economic Advisory Committee of Wartime Housing Policy," PAC, RG19, vol. 3890.

28. Ibid.

29. Letter from F.W. Nichol to J.L. Ilsley, 8 May 1942, and "Memorandum to the Honourable J.L. Ilsley and Dr.

W.C. Clark from F.W. Nichol," both in PAC, RG19, vol. 704, file 203-1A.

30. Pigott's views are neatly summarized by a civil servant from the real estate industry who found them to be "far reaching and rather startling." See "Inter-office correspondence from Rentals Administrator, Cyril R. DeMara to Assistant Secretary of Wartime Prices and Trade Board, R.C. Carr," PAC, RG19, vol. 3890, file H-1.

31. Minutes of Wartime Housing National Executive Committee, PAC, RG83, vol. 70, book 1.

32. DeMara to Carr, PAC, RG19, vol. 3890, file H-1.

33. Letter from W.C. Clark to Donald Gordon, 9 Nov. 1942, PAC, RG19, vol. 3990. Letter from C.D. Howe to J.L. Ilsley, 2 Nov. 1942. The ban on new Wartime Housing projects was so severe that it even extended to the heavily congested city of Halifax. See C.D. Howe to J.L. Ilsley, 7 Dec. 1942 , PAC, RG19, vol. 845.

34. Minutes of Wartime Housing National Executive Committee, PAC, RG83, vol. 70, book 1.

35. Letter from W.C. Clark to A.K. Sheilds, 30 Aug. 1941, PAC, RG19, vol. 6425.

36. Monthly Reports of Housing Registries, March to Aug. 1943, PAC, RG64, vol. 699.

37. "Memorandum on the Housing Situation in Canada as of May 24, 1943, from Russell Smart to Donald Gordon," PAC, RG64, vol. 699; "Memorandum November 19, 1943, Smart to Gordon re: Housing Policy," PAC, RG19, vol. 704, file 203-C, vol. 1; letter from Donald Gordon to J.L. Ilsley, 25 Feb. 1944, PAC, RG19, vol. 3980.

38. Letter from J.W. McConnell to J.L. Ilsley, 20 Nov. 1943, letter from Ilsley to McConnell, 25 Nov. 1943, PAC, RG19, vol. 3980.

39. G.W. Spinney, "Private and Confidential memorandum for the Honourable J.L. Ilsley," 9 Sept. 1944, PAC, RG19, vol. 3980.

40. "Memorandum to Mr. Ilsley, Re: Montreal Housing Project," from W.C. Clark, PAC, RG19, vol. 3980.

41. Dominion Mortgage and Investment Association Brief, "Housing in Relation to Post-War Reconstruction," 24 Feb. 1944, PAC, RG19, vol. 3980, File "Housing."

42. W.C. Clark, Memorandum on Family Allowances, Ian Mackenzie Papers, cited in J.L. Granatstein, *Canada's War* (Toronto: Oxford University Press, 1975), 281.

43. Minutes of the Twelfth Meeting of the Inter-Departmental Committee on Rehabilitation, 21 May 1945, PAC, RG19, E3(1), vol. 3586.

44. Letter from C.D. Howe to J.L. Ilsley, 24 Feb. 1945, PAC, RG19, vol. 709.

45. Letter from J.R. Baldwin to M.W. Sharp, 11 May 1945, PAC, RG19, vol. 359; Housing Statement of Government Policy, PAC, RG2, ser. 18, vol. 9.

46. Minutes of the First Meeting of the Inter-Departmental Housing Committee, 21 May 1945, PAC, RG19, vol. 699.

47. W.C. Clark, "Proposal to Promote Integrated Housing Projects Through the Medium of Private Housing Corporations," PAC, RG19, vol. 710, file 203-1A-12.

48. W.C. Clark, "Memorandum No. 2, Re: Integrated Housing Developments," PAC, RG19, vol. 4017; "Housing: Extracts From Replies of the Banks," PAC, RG19, vol. 3539.

49. Letter from David Mansur to W.A. Mackintosh, 30 July 1945, PAC, RG64, vol. 700.

50. Alvin Finkel, *Business and Social Reform in the Thirties* (Toronto: Lorimer, 1979), 108–12; the lending institutions' views were well expressed by the Conservative members of the Senate. See Canada, Senate, *Debates*, 1939, 1: 577–85.

51. Mansur to Mackintosh, 30 July 1945, PAC, RG84, vol. 700.

52. "Memorandum to Dr. Clark Re: Housing Proposals, November 26, 1947," PAC, RG19, vol. 727, "Memorandum to Dr. Clark, January 16, 1948," PAC, RG19, vol. 3980.

53. "Memorandum to Dr. Clark, January 16, 1948," PAC, RG19, vol. 3980.

54. Letter from R.H. Winters to Louis St Laurent, 12 Jan. 1951, and "Memorandum for Mr. N.A. Robertson, January 13, 1951," both in PAC, RG2, ser. 1, vol. 163; J.E. Coyne, "Mortgage Lending by CMHC," PAC, RG19, vol. 3439.

55. "Memorandum for Mr. N.A. Robertson, January 13, 1954," PAC, RG2, ser. 11, vol. 163.

56. James Lorimer, *The Developers* (Toronto: Lorimer, 1978), 77–79.

57. Humphrey Carver, *Compassionate Landscape* (Toronto: University of Toronto Press, 1975), 112.

58. Letter from H.M. Carver to W.C. Clark, 17 Aug. 1939, PAC, RG19, vol. 709.

"AN INALIENABLE RIGHT":
THE CCF AND RAPID HEALTH
CARE REFORM, 1944–1948 ⬦

DUANE MOMBOURQUETTE

O

In 1944 the Co-operative Commonwealth Federation (CCF) came to power in Saskatchewan with the intention of overhauling the province's health care system. The party had consistently advocated the introduction of "socialized medicine," it had studied the question in party committees, and it had contributed to the popular demand for improvements in health care. Ultimately it was the new government's intention to build and improve on the existing structure to provide unrestricted access to health care for all Saskatchewan residents. With an apparent ardour for reform, the CCF realized much of this goal in its first term of office, 1944–1948.

The CCF, led by Thomas Clement Douglas, formed the government in a province already accustomed to innovations in health care. Bit by bit, preceding administrations had done much to advance the state of health care. In 1909 the Public Health Act created a Bureau of Public Health responsible to the minister of municipal affairs. The Bureau played a largely supervisory role and was replaced by a more powerful Department of Public Health in 1923. The Department had responsibilities for control of sanitation, child welfare, communicable diseases, and the collection and tabulation of vital statistics. The government provided financial assistance to hospitals. Saskatchewan was also home to innovative methods of health care delivery such as the municipal doctor and union hospital schemes, which collectively allowed a large number of people access to pre-paid hospital and medical care. By 1930 Saskatchewan residents could expect free

⬦ Adapted from chapter 2 of the author's unpublished MA thesis, "A Government and Health Care: The Co-operative Commonwealth Federation in Saskatchewan, 1944–1964" (University of Regina, 1990). It originally appeared in *Saskatchewan History* 43, 3 (1991): 101–16. Reprinted with the permission of the author.

treatment for venereal disease and tuberculosis, and government-assisted treatment for cancer.[1] (In 1944 the Liberal government passed a new Cancer Control Act which provided "care and treatment at the expense of the province."[2]) Most of these advances were the result of the government reacting to pressures from farm organizations, local governments, professional associations, and political parties. There was no preconceived government plan of development for health care.

In 1944 there were still many gaps in the health care system. For the majority of the population, access to hospital and medical care was still dependent upon one's ability to pay or on "charity,"[3] many health care professionals struggled on irregular earnings, areas of the province were underserved, and programs were incomplete. The CCF intended to change this.

The CCF's rise to power in Saskatchewan coincided with, and contributed to, a growing public and political interest in social reform. The severity of the depression had heightened interest in government participation in the payment of medical services. Throughout the western world, the war effort had given rise to the demand for something better after the war ended and governments were attempting to deal with this. Both the federal and provincial governments had made promises regarding prepaid health insurance. The federal Liberal government of William Lyon Mackenzie King had begun studying the idea of health insurance as early as 1941. Two years later it created the Special Committee on Social Security, which considered recommendations of the Advisory Committee on Health Insurance, set up in 1942.[4] In Saskatchewan, health care and other matters of social reform were considered by both the Select Special Committee on Social Security and Health Services and by the Saskatchewan Reconstruction Council.[5] But the province, still recovering from the financial impact of depression and war, could not act entirely on its own—it needed federal aid. Finally, in its dying days in office, William J. Patterson's Liberal government passed the Saskatchewan Health Insurance Act, legislation designed to take advantage of any federal initiatives that might arise.[6]

So, when Douglas led his party to power as the first socialist government in North America, it was amidst great expectation and hope. This was not lost on the new government. As Dr Henry E. Sigerist, a well-known professor of medical history and head of the CCF's first survey of health conditions, noted at the time, "The CCF is determined to make a demonstration of what a socialist government can do for the people. They find that the health field is best suited because the people are aware of the problem and ready for a plan."[7]

Perhaps one of the strongest motivational factors behind the CCF's drive for reform was T.C. Douglas's personal commitment to it. He later recalled that he had been dedicated to the ideal of providing free health care "as an inalienable right of being a citizen of a Christian country."[8] The new premier emphasized this commitment by assuming the portfolio of minister of public health.

Douglas wasted no time in acting on his election promise for socialized medicine. It was decided that the first step in the program would be to conduct a survey of health conditions. The recommendations from such a survey could provide the CCF with an outline from which to work. In addition a public survey would heighten interest and participation in reforms. Perhaps most importantly, Douglas was aware that if the survey was properly conducted by a respected expert, it would lend credibility to the government's intentions in the eyes of the medical profession.[9]

A Health Services Survey Commission (HSSC) was appointed in September 1944. It was headed by Dr Henry E. Sigerist, Professor of Medical History at Johns Hopkins University, Baltimore, Maryland. Sigerist was a recognized expert in both public health and, more importantly for Douglas, in "socialized medicine."[10] Dr Hugh MacLean, a long-time Saskatchewan doctor to whom Douglas often turned for advice, assured the premier that Sigerist would be "accepted by medical and lay people alike."[11]

Sigerist arrived in Regina on 8 September 1944 and for the next three weeks the HSSC toured the province visiting health facilities and holding public meetings. The commission received briefs from many private and professional groups and it reviewed many previous provincial, federal, and foreign government reports.[12] When the final report was presented to Douglas on 4 October 1944, Sigerist commented in his diary that he believed the report was good. He wrote: "It is realistic and foresees a gradual socialization of service. It is by no means complete, but is the best I could do in less than four weeks."[13] Sigerist indicated that the goal of improving health services was clear:

It must be to provide complete medical services to all the people of the Province, irrespective of whether they live in town or country. A promising beginning has already been made. Further steps can be taken without delay by using and extending existing facilities. The final steps may have to wait until the Province can count on subsidies from the Dominion or on other sources of revenue.[14]

Most importantly, the report outlined improvements for rural health services. Emphasis was placed on developing a system of health regions within which the municipal doctor schemes would be expanded, with a new emphasis on group practice among physicians. Sigerist dealt extensively with the need for several large hospitals as well as many small rural hospitals. He referred more briefly to specific health needs relating to tuberculosis, mental diseases, cancer treatment, venereal disease, rehabilitation, children's dental health, and Native persons. A section was devoted to traditional public health, services. Finally, Sigerist reviewed the need for physicians, dentists, nurses, medical social workers, and other health professionals.

Not all of the ideas presented in the report were original to the commission. In fact many had been suggested over the years by public organizations, farm groups, the medical community, special interest lobbies (such as the State Hospital and Medical League), government studies, and by members of the general public.[15] What was unique about the report was that this was the first time the ideas were presented in a comprehensive package to a government that had the political will to put the reforms into effect.

In the speech from the throne in October 1944, the Saskatchewan government announced that as the "conditions of the wartime emergency
[became] less stringent, legislation [would] be introduced to fulfil the spirit
of [the Sigerist] report."[16] However, even though Douglas was outwardly
cautious, the party could not simply adopt a wait-and-see attitude—the
people and the party itself were eager for reform. Fortunately there was a
great deal that could be accomplished without large capital outlay or substantial tax increases.

One of the first steps, and one of the most significant in terms of subsequent government policy, was the creation of the Health Services Planning
Commission (HSPC). The creation of this commission on 14 November 1944
provided the Douglas government with several immediate advantages. In
the beginning, the group was small and efficient, and so there could be a
rapid exchange of ideas without concern for departmental hierarchies. To
this group Douglas was able to appoint persons who held similar socialist
goals and aspirations, thereby bypassing the need to immediately restaff
senior positions within the Department of Public Health. The Department,
of course, had been built up under successive Liberal and Conservative governments and was not necessarily disposed to rapid and broad changes.[17] By
setting up the HSPC so quickly on the heels of the Sigerist Report, Douglas
was able to take advantage of the momentum that Sigerist had generated, a
momentum the premier augmented by appointing members of the recently
defunct HSSC to the newly formed HSPC. The three initial members, C.C.
Gibson, superintendent of the Regina General Hospital, later director of
Hospitals Division, Department of Public Health, T.H. McLeod, economic
advisor to the government, and Dr M.C. Sheps, a CCF supporter from
Manitoba, as member and secretary, had served in some capacity with the
survey. The HSPC became the nucleus of health care planning activity,
bypassing the older, more established, Department of Public Health,
although as the HSPC evolved beyond that of a planning board the roles of
the two bodies became convoluted.[18]

The HSPC was careful to study health needs and solutions, and to
apply reform in co-ordinated fashion. The HSPC worked to develop new
programs which would complement existing activities and which would
result in a complete and comprehensive health care package. The HSPC
began meetings in November 1944 and by December it was able to submit
an impressive progress report to the government.

The report noted that a health care plan for pensioners and mothers'
allowance recipients was basically set to go. The HSPC wanted to begin
drawing up plans for hospitals and health centres, and for health regions
based on proposed larger municipal units. The HSPC also reported that a
health plan for maternity patients would be ready by January 1945 (this
idea was later abandoned due to the cost and because the HSPC did not
wish to develop programs in such a "piecemeal way"[19]), that regional
health services were being studied in detail, and that work had been done
on a host of other projects including a free hospitalization plan for the
province, prepaid medical services for the cities, a central purchasing plan

for hospitals, the recruitment of personnel, dental services for school children, and a dental program within the Department of Public Health.[20]

Such an impressive progress report was possible only a month after the commission was formed because work on the CCF reforms was actually begun before Sigerist's arrival in Saskatchewan. In August, Premier Douglas met with members of the College of Physicians and Surgeons to discuss the provision of health care for persons receiving old age pensions, blind pensions, and mothers' allowances. Over the ensuing months, details of an agreement were worked out between a College negotiating committee and Dr M.C. Sheps. At the same time the government carried on discussions with various other health professions and with the Saskatchewan Hospital Association to ensure that a complete line of health services was available to this group of needy persons.[21]

The plan was announced as "a practical Christmas message from the people of Saskatchewan to their old folks, lonely mothers, dependent children, and a number of blind persons."[22] It went into effect on 1 January 1945. The benefits included medical care, hospital care, and in-hospital drugs for approximately 25 000 people. Over the next few years, the government worked to add additional benefits and by 1950 there were 30 680 beneficiaries who were eligible for medical and surgical care, hospitalization, dental services, appliances, optical services, nursing, physiotherapy, and chiropody.[23]

As both Sigerist and the HSPC stressed, the provision of proper health care in rural Saskatchewan was one of the new government's most pressing concerns. In early 1945 the HSPC presented to the government proposals for rural health care. The HSPC suggested a co-ordinated system of rural health care based on the division of the province into health regions. Each doctor's practice would become a fully equipped Local Health Centre. General practitioners would be paid on a salary basis, and would be eligible for a pension, paid holidays, and periodic paid leave for postgraduate work. In the larger population centres, regional health centres would be formed where specialists could perform more intense treatment and diagnosis, and major surgery.[24]

In November 1945, after much discussion and revision, fourteen proposed health regions were created. Each region was to contain approximately 50 000 people, the region in turn being divided into health districts encompassing about 15 000 persons. Each district would be served by a local health council and these councils, in turn, would elect one or more representatives to serve on a regional board. The government wanted the voluntary co-operation of local communities and so at least ten municipalities had to petition the minister of public health, after which the people had to approve of the plan in a referendum.[25]

The HSPC promoted the idea through the distribution of printed material. In addition, as early as June 1945, McLeod and Sheps held meetings in areas that had expressed some interest in health regions. At these meetings and in literature made available to the local committees, the HSPC suggested that regions could be formed for three basic purposes: to provide public health services, to plan and encourage development of hospital and diagnostic facilities, and to "pay for medical and hospital care for its residents." Emphasis was placed first on public health, second on hospital planning, and, finally, on prepaid treatment services.[26] In September the HSPC appointed Dr O.K. Hjertaas as regional organizer, with full-time responsibilities for promoting the scheme. However, while at least ten of the fourteen regions expressed interest in the first year, only six had been formed by 1950.[27] This was probably more the result of a shortage of health personnel than a lack of local interest.[28]

The HSPC's proposal for salaried doctors working in rural health centres met with strong condemnation from the medical profession. The Health Services Committee of the College of Physicians and Surgeons passed a resolution in March 1945 which stated that the plan proposed by the HSPC did not offer "a system of health services which will meet the needs of the people of the province, nor prove satisfactory to those rendering the service."[29] The College wanted medical practice based on a fee-for-service method of payment, not Local Health Centres with salaried positions; it demanded the appointment of an "independent commission" to replace the HSPC; and it argued that health regions would lead to fractionalization, more control at local levels, and a less influential position for the College. Faced with this strong opposition, and in light of College suggestions that the government's proposals would lead to a decrease and not an increase in the number of physicians, the government shifted the thrust of its efforts to improving the municipal doctor system. This had been advocated as an appropriate first step by Sigerist and also had the approval of the College of Physicians and Surgeons and the old Health Services Board.[30]

Municipal doctor plans originated with the residents of the rural municipality of Sarnia in the 1910s. The basic intent of this and subsequent plans was to offer a salary as an inducement for a doctor to settle in an area where he or she might not otherwise be willing to stay. Because the plans were tax-supported, they also provided the residents of an area with pre-paid medical services. The CCF intended to improve these schemes through the adoption of a model contract drawn up by a sub-committee of the Advisory Committee to the HSPC. In addition the government hoped to make the model contract attractive by offering financial assistance to those municipalities that chose to use it. The grants, available as of June 1945, were provided to municipalities, or parts thereof, that had a municipal doctor contract approved by the HSPC, and that included preventive services, immunization, child and mental health, and prenatal care. The doctor could not charge fees, except a deterrent fee for house calls, for service after 6 p.m., and for service on Sundays. The physician had a minimum salary of $5000, three weeks' holidays, and three weeks' postgraduate leave on alternate years. After discussions with the College it was also agreed that a fee-for-service contract would be acceptable. As a result of these efforts the number of municipal doctor plans rose from 50 in 1943 to 58 government-approved plans in 1946, 98 in 1947, and 117 in 1950. (There were actually 173 contracts in effect in 1950 but the remainder were not government approved.)[31]

Sigerist had recommended in his report that the HSPC experiment with a compulsory health insurance plan in one or more of the cities. In 1945 the government arranged for Dr Paul Dodd, an economist with the University of California, to conduct a study and make recommendations regarding compulsory health insurance in cities. However, by the time his report was completed the focus for development had shifted to health units.[32] Regional health boards were given the power, subject to the approval of the minister, to provide medical, dental, nursing, and health services. Two regions were quick to take advantage of this. As of 1 July 1946, Weyburn, Health Region No. 3, offered a full hospitalization scheme and Swift Current, Health Region No. 1, initiated complete medical as well as hospital care.[33]

The primary reason for establishing a health region was to develop public health services; however, local organizers of the Swift Current Health Region were particularly interested in prepaid hospital and medical care. These features were highlighted in local campaigning prior to the November 1945 referendum on the establishment of the region.[34] Benefits under the resulting Swift Current plan included access to the services of a general practitioner, specialists, diagnostic and out-patient service, a reasonably complete dental service for children under sixteen years of age, and the services of a full-time public health staff. Doctors were paid on a fee-for-service basis. Initially the College of Physicians and Surgeons was opposed to the inclusion of medical benefits in the scheme and advised doctors not to participate; however, the Swift Current District Medical Society, representing doctors in the region, continued negotiating with the regional health board. The College was also unsuccessful in attempts to convince Douglas not to allow the region to proceed with its plans and eventually it had to take consolation in the thought that the scheme would prove a useful experiment. Certainly the doctors in the Swift Current District Medical Society seemed relatively pleased with the scheme; in fact, between July 1946 and December 1947 the number of doctors there increased from twenty-one to thirty-four.[35]

Sigerist's third major concern for long-term development had been a plan of free hospitalization for the entire province. This was something the CCF favoured; however both Sigerist and the CCF were aware of the fact that a universal hospitalization scheme would not be universal if large areas of the province had limited access to hospitals. It was clear that more hospitals were needed. Sigerist suggested the need for a thousand new hospital beds made up of fifty "Rural Health Centres" of ten beds each and a five-hundred-bed University Hospital. In addition, he suggested the construction of many small nursing homes for old age persons, thereby removing them from needed hospital beds.[36]

In March 1945 the government set up a system of grants for hospital construction, subject to the approval of the HSPC. These grants resulted in considerable hospital construction. Between 16 March 1945 and 1 March 1949 the government had approved $653 713.86 in grants and $173 500.00 in loans, and the number of union hospitals grew from twenty-six in 1944 to seventy-eight in 1948.[37]

In June 1945 the HSPC submitted a "Report on Free Hospitalization" which indicated that "present planned construction" of hospital facilities "should be adequate" for the inception of hospitalization.[38] The government also expected that with the end of the war in Europe, equipment and health care personnel would become more readily available. It is also significant that at the Dominion–Provincial Conference of 1945, the federal government had promoted federally supported national health insurance and had proposed a series of public health grants to the provinces.[39] In light of these events the government granted approval for the HSPC to study the question of free hospitalization and prepare, for Cabinet's consideration, a plan which could be put into effect in the fiscal year, 1945–1946. A permanent "Committee on Free Hospitalization" was set up. The committee included Dr C.G. Sheps, Dr C.J. Kirk, C.C. Gibson, and T.H. McLeod. They began meetings in late October 1945.[40]

In the summer of 1946, Dr F.D. Mott, former assistant surgeon-general of the United States (and highly respected in the medical community in both Canada and the U.S.), arrived to assume the chairmanship of the HSPC and, it was hoped by Douglas, shortly thereafter to become chairman of a proposed Health Insurance Commission. Douglas had indicated to Mott that this commission would be set up soon because he felt "the time [was] ripe when with some progressive leadership [they could] make giant strides in the field of socialized health services."[41] Dr Mott had given up several attractive offers in order to come to Saskatchewan to work with "such a forward-looking and progressive group."[42] Dr Mott and Dr Leonard S. Rosenfeld, also from the U.S. Public Health service (and whom Mott had appointed), brought with them a level of enthusiasm and technical expertise that did much to help complete the hospitalization plan.[43]

On 12 March 1946 the Saskatchewan Hospitalization Act was introduced in the legislature and received assent on 4 April 1946. The Saskatchewan Hospital Services Plan (SHSP), which went into effect on 1 January 1947, offered hospitalization at any hospital in the province (and out of province to a limited extent), to all residents of Saskatchewan who were not already covered by some other provincial or federal program. The benefits included all hospital costs with the exception of preferred-ward care, patients admitted when in-patient service was not necessary, private duty nursing, whole blood derivatives (included as of January 1949), and several new expensive drugs.[44] The plan was to be administered by the HSPC, not the Department of Public Health or an independent non-political commission.

Doctors in the province seemed to generally favour the plan. After examining the draft legislation in February 1946, Dr J.L. Brown, of the College's Health Services Committee. commented that "the authors of the draft legislation are to be complimented on the approach to the problem as outlined in this draft. The provision of free hospitalization to all the citizens of the province is a principle which is most commendable."[45]

The group that was most closely affected by the legislation were the hospital administrators themselves. A short three weeks before the plan was to take effect Douglas recalled that the entire executive of the Saskatchewan Hospital Association marched into my office and said they were not prepared to co-operate with our legislation. . . . Their objections were on the grounds that the government would virtually take over the hospitals. . . . I explained that our intention was to centralize finance and de-centralize administration. We would collect money and then pay the hospitals for the care given to the people protected under the plan. As far as we were concerned, the running of the hospital would continue to be in the hands of hospital administrators. But I told them that if they couldn't run the hospitals under this plan then on 1 January, we would take over the hospitals. . . . They decided to go along but they were most reluctant. . . . It's rather significant that today the hospitals are the strongest advocates of the plan.[46]

Hospitalization Card No. 1 Given to Premier

In a short public ceremony at the city hall Thursday, City Assessor Arthur Robins presented Premier T.C. Douglas with hospital services card no. 1 which entitles Mr. Douglas to receive hospitalization benefits after Jan. 1.

"I consider this to be one of the most memorable occasions in the history of the province," said Mr. Robins, "representing as it does the official inauguration of a social hospitalization scheme never before attempted in any part of the Dominion. . . . " Mr. Robins said he hoped the premier would have many more years of health and happiness and never be required to use the card.

Replying, briefly, Mr. Douglas said he also hoped that he would never be required to use the card.

"I see some of our hospital people present and they too, no doubt, will be hoping that not too many people require hospitalization," he said smiling. "But services will be available for those who need it."

. . . "The eyes of Canada are on this province," he said. "We are establishing a pattern for socially-minded people everywhere to follow."

—*Leader-Post* (Regina), 20 December 1946

The program was financed from general revenues and from the collection of a flat-tax or premium of $5 per person with a family maximum of $20. In fact this was not the government's first choice for a method of payment. Douglas admitted that the CCF would have preferred "a graduated tax or some other tax based on ability to pay. . . . "[47] The flat payment was chosen because it complied with the federal government's proposals for health insurance which required a registration fee to be paid by or on behalf of each registrant. The province wanted to ensure compatibility with any federal plan so that the cost to the province could be reduced. In spite of pressure from the public and from the HSPC, Cabinet would not agree to a change (probably in the eternal hope that the federal government would soon step in to assume a share of the cost).[48] Overall, the plan was extremely successful for several reasons. First, the medical community supported the idea. Second, the combined operating deficit of all the hospitals in the province was made almost negligible; in 1956, the aggregate deficit was less than one-quarter of 1 percent of the total operating budget. Third, municipalities no longer had to worry about paying for hospital care for indigents. Fourth, patients were not restricted to one hospital but had the choice of any in the province. Finally, because of the centralization of financing and technical advice offered by the HSPC, the standards of hospital care were equalized and greatly increased in many cases.[49]

Another major accomplishment of the CCF which had its beginnings in this period was the establishment of a medical school and hospital at the University of Saskatchewan. Agitation for a project of this nature had actually begun before the CCF came to power. Dr W.S. Lindsay, dean of medical science at the university, had begun to petition the provincial government in 1943. Additional support for the idea was received from the Saskatchewan Medical Association which, in 1943, passed a resolution calling for a complete medical course to be offered at the University of Saskatchewan. Finally Sigerist stressed the importance of such an institution in his 1944 report.[50]

Steps were taken to begin construction of a new medical school in 1946 and the school was opened in 1950. However, there was some uncertainty about constructing the University Hospital. Douglas, Mott, and others strongly supported the idea, but there were members of the government who would have preferred to expand the two existing hospitals in Saskatoon. To help settle the dispute a survey committee was formed in the fall of 1945 to consider the "integration of the medical school with the university [sic] hospital."[51] This was followed in December by a committee set up to engage an architect and prepare plans for a hospital. By September 1946 a University Hospital Board was constituted and the project was underway.[52]

A final area in which the government expended tremendous energy and which, over the next two decades, would become increasingly important was that of mental health. In November 1944 the Mental Hygiene Act was amended to provide free treatment for mental patients when admitted to an institution.[53] Following a survey by Dr C.M. Hincks of the National Committee for Mental Hygiene the government converted the former air training centre at the Weyburn Airport into the Saskatchewan School for Mental Defectives. In November 1946, Douglas appointed Dr D.G. McKerracher as commissioner of mental services and chief psychiatrist for Saskatchewan. McKerracher had formerly been with the Ontario Health Department, the Toronto Psychiatric Hospital, and the Toronto Academy of Medicine.[54]

Under McKerracher's direction the mental health program of Saskatchewan was revamped. In the 1947 session of the legislature the Mental Hygiene Act was amended to allow for several changes. Names of institutions were officially changed to remove any stigma associated with them, every aspect of operating the institutions was consolidated within the Department of Public Health (formerly the Department of Public Works had been responsible for running the institutions and until 1930 had even been responsible for patient care), admissions were made quicker while at the same time guaranteeing the patient's protection, admissions to the psychiatric ward at the Regina General Hospital were changed to imitate admissions to a general hospital, and provision was made for the appointment of an impartial committee to visit any institution and report to the minister.[55] In 1950 a new Mental Hygiene Act was passed that finally placed the power to institutionalize patients entirely in the hands of the medical community. "Insanity had finally become a mental illness."[56]

One of McKerracher's most significant accomplishments was the development of a "Community Program" for mental hygiene. This program included full-time mental health clinics in Regina and Saskatoon as well as part-time clinics in Weyburn, Moose Jaw, Swift Current, and North Battleford. Also, increased attention was given to mental health education through the training of teacher-psychologists for work in the school system. The standard of care was greatly enhanced by the establishment of a new three-year training course for psychiatric aides (which attracted two hundred students in its first year) and by the introduction of an eight-hour shift for the nursing and custodial staff of the mental hospitals.[57]

Both the Sigerist Report and the Hincks Report made the controversial suggestion of sterilizing mental defectives. Douglas had begun considering the idea as early as August 1944 and in fact had advocated eugenics in his 1932 master's thesis for McMaster University,[58] but by late 1949 the government had gone no further. Neither Mott nor Douglas appeared to have placed sterilization in a priority list. And following the release of the Hincks Report the government received many letters protesting such a move.[59]

One of the major shortcomings of Saskatchewan's health care system in 1944 was the general lack of qualified health care professionals. This frequently resulted in an inequitable distribution of health care. The government took immediate steps to alleviate these shortages.

One of the first areas into which the government ventured was midwifery. The government wished to train midwives for service in remote areas of the province which did not have the services of a physician. On 11 October 1944, just seven days after Sigerist released his report, Douglas wrote to Dr A.W. Argue, registrar of the College, about midwives. Douglas noted that Alberta had such a system and that the government was "considering developing something similar here, and [would] be interested in learning the reaction of the medical profession to such a proposal." Douglas emphasized that it "would be necessary . . . to have the co-operation of the profession in organizing a course. . . . "[60] The government had already received assurances from the university that it would provide a course in midwifery for public health nurses provided the College of Physicians and Surgeons approved.[61] The College, however, did not approve. It suggested the move was regressive and that pregnant women would not seek the help of a physician if a midwife were present. It also declared that the problem of poorly served areas would ease up after the war.[62] The HSPC advised Douglas to press ahead with the idea even without the support of the doctors. It suggested that the

> stand of the College ignores the realities of the Saskatchewan situation, in favour of a perfectionist standard which will be impossible of attainment for some time to come. They ignore the fact that a

number of nurses without training in obstetrics are now doing this work fairly successfully, and that many women are being delivered without attendance.[63]

The decision was made to proceed without the doctors' approval and in the fall of 1945 the first two public health nurses were sent to the School of Nurse Midwifery in New York. The cost of the program was initially shared by the Department of Public Health and the Rockefeller Foundation. Upon their return they took up duties at Cumberland House and Buffalo Narrows.[64]

Efforts were also made to increase the numbers of traditional health care workers in Saskatchewan. Partially in response to suggestions that the College was using its powers to restrict immigrant doctors from settling in Saskatchewan, the government investigated and considered removing the licensing powers of professional groups in the province. However, when this suggestion met with widespread protest the government settled on a compromise. It left the licensing powers of the College intact but asked for a full report of any incident where a person was refused a licence.[65] Despite objections from the College of Physicians and Surgeons, the government also passed amendments to the Medical Profession Act allowing easier movement of doctors to Saskatchewan from the United Kingdom and all dominions within the Commonwealth.[66] The HSPC, and later the Department of Public Health, co-operated with the College of Physicians and Surgeons in placing physicians in underserviced areas.[67] The government also instituted a system of grants for postgraduate studies administered by the HSPC.[68] In 1945 the government began offering grants to hospitals that maintained schools of nursing. In 1946, in co-operation with the Department of Education and the federal Department of Vocational Training, the HSPC set up a training course for laboratory and x-ray technicians destined for smaller hospitals. At the same time the HSPC worked with the Saskatchewan Registered Nurses' Association to establish a course for nurses' aides. Perhaps the most important initiatives were the new University Medical School and the University Hospital, which the CCF believed would benefit more than just medical students.[69]

One of the most serious deficiencies in health care in Saskatchewan in 1944 was dental care. Sigerist reported:

> Dental conditions [were] appalling in [the] province. A large percentage of the population [had] no dental care whatsoever, and the overwhelming majority of the people [had] not sufficient dental care. It [was] no exaggeration to say that dentistry . . . [had] failed to serve the population, whatever the causes may be. Before the war, in 1938, the province had 210 dentists or 1 per 4481 population. In 1943 the province had 147 dentists or 1 per 6095 population.[70]

The government found, however, that this was not a problem which could be easily solved. The HSPC tried unsuccessfully to obtain war surplus mobile dental clinics to service rural Saskatchewan. There had been suggestions that the province needed a dental school; however the government was quick to state that a dental school would not be considered until the new medical school was "properly rolling." There was some success with a government offer to pay 50 percent of the cost of a children's dental program operated by a health region. This helped support dental programs in Health Regions Numbers 1 and 3.[71] In 1948 the government confirmed its commitment to improve the state of dental health in the province by setting up a Division of Dental Health in the Department of Public Health.

One of the most dramatic innovations of the period occurred in the area of ambulance service. There were road ambulance companies in Saskatchewan and the CCF sought to improve the standard of service by updating regulations for ambulances and drivers; however these were only implemented in July 1947 after much vocal opposition from several operators in the province.[72] Even with these improvements the government was still concerned with the lack of service in many remote areas. To access these areas the HSPC studied the feasibility of using snowmobiles, cars converted for use on railroad tracks, and a government-operated car ambulance fleet. None of these proved entirely satisfactory. The HSPC chose instead to establish a flying ambulance service.

The Air Ambulance Service (AAS) was inaugurated on 3 February 1946 with a single aircraft operating out of Regina. The service was operated by the HSPC, and serviced the southern half of the province. North of Prince Albert, arrangements were made to use planes of the Department of Natural Resources. A nominal fee of $25 was charged for each trip, regardless of the distance travelled. The service expanded rapidly and soon included out-of-province flights and parachute drops of medical supplies to isolated areas. In late 1946 the HSPC began a campaign to encourage towns, villages, hamlets, and rural municipalities throughout the province to construct small airfields for the use of the service. By 1948 the Air Ambulance Service had grown to include four aircraft and a staff of sixteen.[73]

The CCF also carried out reforms that were less dramatic, many of which could be viewed as departmental housekeeping. The cancer and venereal disease programs were continually improved. A physical fitness program, initiated by the departing Liberals and the federal government, was promoted by the CCF. Through agreements with the federal Department of Veterans' Affairs (DVA) and the Canadian Paraplegic Association the government began to provide assistance for treatment of paraplegic patients. The government added a Division of Health Education to co-ordinate the educational activities of the Department, a Division of Nutrition, which began by encouraging hot lunch programs in schools, and a Division of Industrial Hygiene to deal with urban and agricultural industrial health matters. The Division of Sanitation, among other things, offered engineering services to municipalities to encourage construction of waterworks and sewage systems and it improved inspection of milk pasteurizing plants.[74]

The government also sought to include Treaty Indians in the SHSP. However, while this topic was discussed as early as 1947 it was decided that Treaty Indians would not be included until the federal government decided to pay for the full cost of treating Native people under the plan.

The HSPC pursued the possibility of manufacturing optical supplies such as lenses and frames for glasses. In addition the government investigated the possibility of providing institutions for treatment of arthritis and multiple sclerosis, although both ideas were rejected for the time being.[75]

There were restrictions on what the government could do in these first few years after the war. First, there was a lack of facilities and personnel needed for the implementation of a comprehensive health program. Second (and this relates to the first problem), the government was constrained by the condition of the province's finances. Saskatchewan had just emerged from fourteen years of depression and war and this limited the degree to which the provincial government could both raise revenues through taxes and spend on costly new health programs. Despite this, health care expenditures rose from $1 852 079 (6 percent of the provincial budget) in 1943–1944 to $10 246 194 (20 percent) in 1947–1948.[76] The CCF had hoped the federal government would assist by enacting national health insurance but at the same time Douglas and his colleagues were prepared and willing to go it on their own. They did, however, continue to press the federal government to make health grants to the provinces?[77]

One of the major disappointments of this first term in office was the failure of the federal government to enact its promised national health insurance plan, although there were some moments of optimism. Following Douglas's first Dominion–Provincial Conference in 1945 he was so optimistic regarding health insurance that he made the following statement: "there is a distinct likelihood that we, in Saskatchewan, may be in the position shortly to initiate the provision of health services on a province-wide basis." In fact Douglas was so confident about this that he began talks with different provincial groups with the object of establishing a representative board to administer a health insurance scheme; that body would be "directly responsible to the people of this province."[78] Douglas was soon disappointed as health insurance became entangled in attempts to work out new tax agreements between the provinces and the federal government. By the spring of 1947 Douglas reported that while there was considerable pressure on the federal government to hold a conference to deal solely with health matters, the federal government "feels, however, that they should not proceed until all tax matters are settled, as they are inextricably bound together . . . so I think we should plan our campaign on the basis planned before, namely, that of carrying on ourselves."[79]

The government and the HSPC had chosen to undertake careful studies of health needs and use the information gathered to reform health care in Saskatchewan. This was a considerate and intelligent approach, yet it did not meet with the whole-hearted support of all interested groups. The most influential and vocal opposition came from the College of Physicians and Surgeons. While both the government and the College of Physicians and Surgeons were interested in improving the delivery and quality of health care, they differed sharply over how this should take place. The executive of the College seemed to be opposed not only to any changes in the status quo but to the idea of a small group of government-employed experts determining what future priorities should be in the field of health care. This had tra-ditionally been an area in which the College held a leadership role and it was anxious to maintain this degree of influence. The College bypassed the HSPC, choosing instead to meet directly with Douglas. Furthermore, mem-bers of the College repeatedly criticized the direction and leadership of the commission, and at times were at odds with the premier himself.[80]

As the CCF government and its programs matured there was a growing concern for administration matters and fiscal constraint. On 1 April 1950 the operative programs of the Department of Public Health and the Health Services Planning Commission [HSPC] were combined into a newly reorgan-ized Department of Public Health.[81] The HSPC continued to exist, but as a little-used advisory and planning body.[82] The change in attitude is perhaps most succinctly illustrated by T.C. Douglas passing on the Public Health portfolio to T.J. Bentley in November 1949 (Douglas took over the Depart-ment of Co-operation and Co-operative Development).[83] Increasingly Cabinet came to rely on its civil servants and not on itself for direction in matters of health care policy. Not until the introduction of the Medical Care Insurance Act in the early 1960s would Cabinet again become so involved in health care.

Upon coming to power, the CCF had quickly begun the process of reform. The Sigerist Report came only months after the formation of the new government. In the first session of the legislature the CCF passed three health-related pieces of legislation including a new Health Services Act which created the HSPC. Under the HSPC's and Douglas's guidance the province ventured into areas traditionally outside the realm of government. A comprehensive program was established for old age pensioners, mothers' allowance recipients, and blind pensioners—some of the most needy groups in the province. An Air Ambulance Service was set up, new divisions of public health were created, and rural areas received assistance with the cre-ation of health regions and funding for municipal doctor schemes. There were grants and loans for hospital construction and provision was made for the establishment of regionally based, prepaid medical, hospital, and dental schemes. The CCF government also turned its attention to mental health, the needs of disabled persons, communicable diseases, health personnel, and a wide variety of other areas. Of course the most immediately impor-tant initiative was undoubtedly the introduction of the Saskatchewan Hospital Services Plan.

Encouraged by Premier Douglas and by an enthusiastic population, the CCF had accomplished much of what it had promised in 1944. The HSPC was created independent from the older Department of Public Health and was able to concentrate on planning and review rather than administration. The HSPC demonstrated a remarkable ability to pursue the reforms set out by Sigerist, by CCF planners, and by the commission itself. Yet there was also a good deal of pragmatism evident in the HSPC and in the govern-ment. When the medical profession was opposed to suggestions for salaried positions in rural areas, the government pursued the more acceptable option of supporting municipal doctor plans. Compulsory health insurance for cities and maternity hospitalization were abandoned as unworkable. The CCF and HSPC also demonstrated the ability to succeed in the face of challenge. Without waiting for financial support from the federal government, Saskatchewan pushed ahead with Canada's first province-wide, prepaid hospitalization plan. The next major advance in socialized health care—medical care insurance—would not happen for more than a decade. However, by 1948 the CCF had helped to alleviate many of the hardships of the preceding decades and had set the framework for future reform.

NOTES

1. For more information regarding the early history of government involvement in health care, see Duane Mombourquette, "A Government and Health Care: The Co-operative Commonwealth Federation in Saskatchewan, 1944–1964" (MA thesis, University of Regina, 1990).

2. Saskatchewan, *Statutes of the Province of Saskatchewan*, 1944, c. 78, s. 3.

3. Charity was often received from doctors who would reduce charges, accept goods in trade, or even request no payment. Officially, municipalities were responsible to provide financial support to medical indigents. However, this was often looked upon as charity by the individuals in need. In 1922 the Anti-Tuberculosis Commission found that the stigma associated with municipal aid was significant. The commission reported that the "greatest obstacle to early treatment is the difficulty the majority of patients have in providing for the cost of their care. Unfortunately a large number of our citizens ... refuse to apply for charity until compelled to discontinue work of any kind and to remain in bed. . . . It is easy to imagine the agony of mind that must be expressed when a person first confronted with the seriousness of tuberculosis, is compelled to decide whether he will apply to his municipality for charity, such charity being usually delayed as long as possible, and often secured by mortgages on personal belongings, assignments of life insurance, and other forms of security." Saskatchewan, *Report of the Saskatchewan Anti-Tuberculosis Commission* (Regina: King's Printer, 1922), 50.

4. M.G. Taylor, "The Saskatchewan Hospital Services Plan: A Study in Compulsory Health Insurance" (PhD diss., University of California, 1949), 65, 68–69, 70–71.

5. Joan Feather, "Horse-Trading and Health Insurance: Saskatchewan and Dominion–Provincial Relations, 1937–1947," *Saskatchewan History* 39, 3 (1986): 98–99.

6. Saskatchewan, *Statutes*, 1944, c. 76.

7. Henry E. Sigerist, *Autobiographical Writings*, selected and trans. by Nora Sigerist Beeson (Montreal: McGill University Press, 1966), 189.

8. Regina *Leader-Post*, 2 April 1954.

9. Saskatchewan Archives Board (hereafter SAB), Dr Hugh MacLean Papers, file 12, T.C. Douglas to MacLean, 7 Aug. 1944.

10. SAB, Records of the Health Services Survey Commission (hereafter HSSC), file 15, Order-in-Council 1013/44, 8 Sept. 1944; file 12, "Dr. Sigerist and members of the Commission."

11. SAB, MacLean Papers, file 12, MacLean to Douglas, 11 Aug. 1944.

12. SAB, HSSC, files 1–27.

13. Sigerist, *Autobiographical Writings*, 190.

14. SAB, HSSC, file 20, Miscellaneous, Henry E. Sigerist, *Saskatchewan Health Services Survey Commission: Report of the Commissioner* (Regina: King's Printer, 1947), 4.

15. SAB, HSSC, file 8, brief 75, The State Hospital and Medical League of the Province of Saskatchewan; file 2, Brief of the Saskatchewan Association of Rural Municipalities; Harry M. Cassidy, *Public Health and Welfare Reorganization: The Postwar Problems in the Canadian Provinces* (Toronto: Ryerson Press, 1945), 17.

16. SAB, Thomas Clement Douglas Papers, file 818(35-4)a, "Speech from the Throne," Oct. 1944.

17. C.A. Meilicke argues that the department was not "organizationally structured for effective operation in highly specialized fields—there was no tradition or structure for, or strong commitment to, the type of broad-gauge and innovative administrative planning, control, and coordination which was necessary." Carl A. Meilicke, "The Saskatchewan Medical Care Dispute of 1962: An Analytic Social History" (PhD diss., University of Minnesota, 1967), 41.

18. SAB, Records of the Health Services Planning Commission (hereafter HSPC), file 5b(1-1), Dr F.D. Mott's address to the Advisory Committee to the HSPC, 9 May 1947; Douglas Papers, file III, 133(14-24)b, Dr C.F.W. Hames to Douglas, 3 May 1947.

19. SAB, Douglas Papers, file III 120(14-6-6), "Free Hospitalization of Maternity Patients"; HSPC, file 67a(4-2-3), Memorandum Re: Meeting of HSPC with the Executive of the Saskatchewan Hospital Association, 19 Jan. 1945; Hames to M.C. Sheps, 10 July 1945; M.C. Sheps to Dr O.K. Hjertaas, 24 Jan. 1946.

20. SAB, HSPC, file 4a(1-0-3), "Health Services Planning Commission: Progress Report," 30 Dec. 1944.

21. SAB, HSPC, file 21a(1-7), Memorandum for Douglas from Sheps, 23 Aug. 1944; M.G. Taylor, *Health Insurance and Canadian Public Policy: The Seven Decisions that Created the Canadian Health Insurance System* (Montreal: McGill-Queen's University Press, 1978), 87.

22. SAB, HSPC, file 21a(1-7), News release by the Division of Health Education, 22 Dec. 1944.

23. Saskatchewan, *Annual Report of the Department of Public Health* (hereafter *AR Health*), 1950–51 (Regina: Queen's Printer, 1952), 84–86.

24. SAB, McLeod Papers, file 19, "Memorandum IV, Re: Local Health Services"; file 46, "Report on Regional Health Services: A Proposed Plan," 15 Feb. 1945.

25. SAB, HSPC, "Health Services Planning Commission: Progress Report"; Taylor, "Saskatchewan Hospital Services Plan," 125–26.

26. SAB, McLeod Papers, file 2, Circular No. II, M.C. Sheps to Councillors in Proposed Health Region No. 2, n.d.

27. SAB, HSPC, file 4(1-0-3), "Annual Report, 1945," 5; McLeod Papers, file 2, "Memorandum Re: Meeting at Assiniboia, 20 June 1945"; *AR Health*, 1945, 13. The six Health Regions were: Swift Current (31 Dec. 1945); Weyburn-Estevan (31 Dec. 1945); Moose Jaw (15 June 1946); Meadow Lake (15 Aug. 1946); Assiniboia-Gravelbourg (31 May 1947); and North Battleford (15 Aug. 1947). *AR Health*, 1950–51, 18; 1953–54, 20.

28. Taylor, "Saskatchewan Hospital Services Plan," 125–26.

29. *Saskatchewan Medical Quarterly* (hereafter *SMQ*), 1945, 360, quoted in Meilicke, "Saskatchewan Medical Care Dispute," 142.

30. SAB, HSPC, file 5b(1-1), "Proceedings: Plenary Session, May 1947," 13, 18; HSB, file 2, "Municipal Medical Services in Saskatchewan, May 1941"; file 14, "Submission to the Select Committee of the Legislature by the College of Physicians and Surgeons, March 1943"; Taylor, *Seven Decisions*, 245–46.

31. SAB, Douglas Papers, file III, 118(16-6-4), M.C. Sheps to Hames, 6 Nov. 1945; file III, 114(14-4-1)a, Order-in-Council, 11 June 1945; Milton I. Roemer, "Prepaid Medical Care and Changing Needs in Saskatchewan," *American Journal of Public Health* 46, 9 (Sept. 1956): 1083.

32. *AR Health*, 1945, 12; Taylor, "Saskatchewan Hospital Services Plan," 127.

33. Taylor, "Saskatchewan Hospital Services Plan," 127–28; A.D. Kelly, "The Swift Current Experiment," *Canadian Medical Association Journal* 58 (May 1948): 506.

34. Joan Feather, "From Concept to Reality: Formation of the Swift Current Health Region," *Prairie Forum* 16, 1 (1991): 74–75.

35. *SMQ*, 1946, 577, quoted in Meilicke, "Saskatchewan Medical Care Dispute," 180; Kelly, "The Swift Current Experiment," 507, 511.

36. Sigerist, *Report*, 6.

37. SAB, Douglas Papers, file III, 114(14-4-1)a, Order-in-Council, 16 March 1945; file III, 91(13-1-3), "Hospital Planning and Administration." Hospital construction was ultimately a local decision, and although enthusiasm for the plan was great in the first year, the HSPC reported that this quickly died off as groups realized the costs involved. Also, in several instances local rivalries over the location of a hospital became problem points in developing a province-wide plan. See also SAB, HSPC, file 4(1-0-3), Annual Report, "Division of Hospital Planning and Administration: Preliminary 1947 Annual Report," n.p.

38. SAB, McLeod Papers, file 10, "Report on Free Hospitalization," n.d.

39. Feather, "Horse Trading and Health Insurance," 100.

40. SAB, HSPC, file 67a(4-2-3), Minutes of meeting of HSPC, 31 Aug. 1945; McLeod Papers, file 10, "Report #1: Committee on Free Hospitalization." The committee later came to be known as the Planning Committee for Hospitalization. Douglas Papers, file III, 123 (14-6-33)b, Dr C.G. Sheps to Douglas, 27 March 1946.

41. SAB, T.J. Bentley Papers, file 14-4, Dr F.D. Mott to Douglas, 14 Feb. 1946; Douglas to Mott, 11 April 1946.

42. SAB, T.J. Bentley Papers, File 14-4, Mott to Douglas, 16 March 1946.

43. A.W. Johnson, "Biography of a Government: Policy Formation in Saskatchewan, 1944–61" (PhD diss., Harvard University, 1959), 340.

44. SAB, HSPC, file 179(8-1-4), Mott to Douglas, 8 Jan. 1949; Taylor, "Saskatchewan Hospital Services Plan," 136–37, 161–69. Whole blood derivatives can include plasma, platelets, and cryoprecipitate, among other things (Canadian Red Cross Society pamphlet).

45. SAB, Douglas Papers, file III, 124(14-6-46), Dr J.L. Brown, Chairman of the Medical Advisory Committee, College of Physicians and Surgeons, to Douglas, 17 Feb. 1946.

46. Lewis H. Thomas, ed., *The Making of a Socialist: The Recollections of T.C. Douglas* (Edmonton: University of Alberta Press, 1982), 229.

47. SAB, Douglas Papers, file III, 123(14-6-33)a, Douglas to C. Evans Sargent, Secretary-Treasurer, R.M. of Mantario, 22 Oct. 1946.

48. Ibid., Mott to Douglas, 16 Nov. 1946. The federal government did not begin to contribute to hospitalization until 1957, and it was shortly after that that Saskatchewan actively began to plan for medical care insurance.

49. Milton I. Roemer, "'Socialized' Health Services in Saskatchewan," *Social Research* 25, 1 (Spring 1958): 92; Taylor, "Saskatchewan Hospital Services Plan," 315.

50. SAB, Douglas Papers, file XIV, 564(14-18), "Progress Report, University Hospital, Saskatoon, 1943–57," 1–2; HSSC, file 8, brief 75, State Hospital and Medical League, p. 8; Sigerist, *Report*, 10–12.

51. SAB, Douglas Papers, file XIV, 564(14-18), "Progress Report, University Hospital, Saskatoon, 1943–1957," 24 Aug. 1957, by A.L. Swanson, MD, 5.

52. Ibid., 6.

53. Saskatchewan, *Statutes* 1944 (Second Session), c. 47.

54. SAB, Douglas Papers, file III, 114(14-4-1)b, Order-in-Council, 14 Nov. 1945; *AR Health*, 1946, 70, 93; SAB, HSPC, file 28(2-11), Clipping from Regina *Leader-Post*, 25 Nov. 1946.

55. *AR Health*, 1947, 7.

56. Harley D. Dickinson, *The Two Psychiatries: The Transformation of Psychiatric Work in Saskatchewan, 1905–1984* (Regina: Canadian Plains Research Center, 1989), 108.

57. *AR Health*, 1947, 80; Johnson, "Biography of a Government," 337.

58. Thomas H. McLeod and Ian McLeod, *Tommy Douglas: The Road to Jerusalem* (Edmonton: Hurtig Publishers, 1987), 39.

59. SAB, Douglas Papers, file III, 134(14-25), A. Somerville, MC, Director of the Division of Communicable Diseases, Department of Health, Alberta, to Douglas, 30 Aug. 1944; HSPC, file 73, Mott to McKerracher, 21 Nov. 1949.

60. SAB, Douglas Papers, file III, 133(14-24)b, Douglas to Argue, 11 Oct. 1944.

61. SAB, HSPC, file 67a(4-2-3), "Memorandum re: Advanced Course in Obstetrics for Public Health Nurses."

62. SAB, Douglas Papers, file 3, 133(14-24)6, Argue to Douglas, 9 Nov. 1944.

63. SAB, HSPC, file 67a(4-2-3), "Memorandum re: Advanced Course in Obstetrics for Public Health Nurses."

64. *AR Health*, 1946, 11; 1947, 9–10.

65. S.M. Lipset, *Agrarian Socialism: The Cooperative Commonwealth Federation in Saskatchewan—A Study in Political Sociology* (Garden City, NY: Doubleday, 1968), 294.

66. SAB, Douglas Papers, file III, 133(14-24)a, Dr C.J. Houston to Douglas, 6 Aug. 1947; Hames to Dr G. Gordon Ferguson, Registrar of the College of Physicians and Surgeons, 3 Nov. 1947; Douglas to Dr O.K. Hjertaas, 7 May 1948; Meilicke, "Saskatchewan Medical Care Dispute," 186–87.

67. SAB, HSPC, file 4(1-0-3), "Report of the Health Services Planning Commission for the Period January 1 to December 31, 1946," 4; Douglas Papers, file III, 113(14-4)d, Bentley to Douglas, 24 Nov. 1950.

68. SAB, HSPC, file 69, Dr G.W. Fitzgerald to Dr R.O. Davison, 23 Nov. 1945.

69. SAB, Douglas Papers, file III, 114(14-4-1)a, Order-in-Council, 16 Oct. 1945 and Order-in-Council, 29 Oct. 1945; HSPC, file 4(1-0-3), "Report of the Health Services Planning Commission for the Period January 1 to December 31, 1946; HSPC, file 71, Keith S. Armstrong to F. D. Mott, 14 Nov. 1949; HSPC, file 5b(1-1), Mott's address to the Advisory Committee to the HSPC, 7 May 1947.

70. Sigerist, *Report*, 8.

71. SAB, HSPC, file 125(6-2-1-1), Dr G.B. Chisholm, Deputy Minister of National Health, to Hames, 2 Aug. 1945; HSPC, file 125(6-2-1-1), Sheps to Hames, 8 Aug. 1945; HSPC, Dr C.G. Sheps to A.M. Nicholson, MP, 15 May 1946; HSPC, file 66(4-2), "Saskatchewan's Health Program," 8 Aug. 1946; file 14(2-1), Mott to S. Robertson, Sec. Treas., Health Region No. 1, 11 April 1949; *AR Health*, 1949, 24.

72. SAB, Douglas Papers, file III, 114(14-4-1)b, Order-in-Council, 17 Jan. 1946; Hames to Dr W.A. Thomson, 3 April 1947; Hames to J.C. Svare, 14 Feb. 1947.

73. SAB, HSPC, file 43, all file; file 14 (2-0), "Saskatchewan Government Air Ambulance Service," 19 Oct. 1945; file 14(2-0), clipping from the *Saskatchewan Commonwealth*, 22 May 1946, clipping from *Leader-Post*, 4 July 1946, Memo from D.K. Malcolm, Supervisor, Air Ambulance Service, 22 Nov. 1946; *AR Health*, 1948, 11.

74. *AR Health*, 1944, 44, 56, 60–61; 1945, 46, 51, 79; 1954–55, 150; SAB, HSPC, file 63b(4-1-8), note to file by Dr M.S. Acker, 27 Jan. 1948.

75. SAB, HSPC, file 14(2-0), Mott to Douglas, 4 Dec. 1947; file 67b(4-1-9), C.G. Sheps, Acting Chairman, HSPC to S. Robertson, Secretary-Treasurer, Health Region No. 1, 9 April 1946; Mott to Douglas, 26 Jan. 1949; file 866(4-2), Mott to M.G. Taylor, 29 Nov. 1948.

76. Saskatchewan, *Public Accounts of the Province of Saskatchewan* (Regina: King's Printer, 1949), xlv.

77. SAB, HSPC, Advisory Committee, file 5b(1-), Douglas's address to the committee, 9 May 1947.

78. SAB, Douglas Papers, file III, 125(14-6-47), Douglas to Frank Eliason, Secretary, United Farmers of Canada, Saskatchewan Section, 24 Nov. 1945.

79. SAB, Douglas Papers, file III, 133(14-24)b, Dr J.L. Brown, Chairman, Central Health Services Committee, College of Physicians and Surgeons, to Douglas, 26 Jan. 1946; Dr C.J. Houston to Douglas, 27 Dec. 1945; Dr G. Gordon Ferguson, Registrar of the College of Physicians and Surgeons, 10 Sept. 1947.

80. *AR Health*, 1950–51, 9–10.

81. SAB, Department of Public Health Records, see all of file VI, 1a for problems of the commission.

82. SAB, Douglas Papers, file III, 128(14-9)a, Douglas to Mrs J.E. Powell, 10 March 1950.

THE CANADIAN
HEALTH CARE SYSTEM:
A DEVELOPMENTAL OVERVIEW*

EUGENE VAYDA
RAISA B. DEBER

o

Canada's health care system, although distinctive, contains elements recognizable to students of health care in the United States and the United Kingdom. At its core is a government-run insurance plan that uses public funds to pay for a private system. Medical care services are provided primarily by physicians trained in the North American style; indeed, Canadian and American medical schools are accredited by a common body. Patients have free choice of physicians, who in turn are paid by the provincial plans on a fee-for-service basis. Public hospitals receive most of their budgets directly from government. Although national health insurance is among the most popular government programs, in recent years the declining economy and increasing health care costs have produced pressure for cost containment similar to that which has occurred in virtually every other developed country. Since nearly three-quarters of the public expenditures for health care in Canada are for institutional and physician services, these sectors of the health care system have come under increasing government scrutiny. The institutional sector is particularly vulnerable because it alone accounts for about half of the government-paid health care expenditures, with an annual rate of increase above inflation.

To understand the genesis of the current system, one must first consider its constitutional matrix. Under the British North America (BNA) Act of 1867 (now known as the Constitution Act 1982), all matters of national concern, plus those activities likely to be costly, were assigned to the federal

* From David C. Naylor, ed., *Canadian Health Care and the State: A Century of Evolution* (Montreal: McGill-Queen's University Press, 1992), 125–40. Reprinted with the permission of the publisher.

government, which had, obviously, the broadest tax base. In the health field Ottawa was given jurisdiction over quarantine, marine hospitals, and health services for Native peoples and the armed forces. The provinces were given authority for those local concerns that were, at the time, thought unlikely to be costly—including roads, education, and "the Establishment, Maintenance and Management of Hospitals, Asylums, Charities, and Eleemosynary Institutions in and for the Province other than Marine Hospitals." Municipal governments have only such powers as are delegated to them by the provinces.

Health care was seen as a natural extension of hospitals and as such a provincial responsibility. Thus it must be recognized that Canada has never had a national health care system; it has ten provincial health care systems plus two in the northern territories (where the federal government played a more direct role). However, the escalation in health care costs and disparities in provincial wealth soon involved the federal government in financing health services. Ottawa could therefore use fiscal levers to exert an influence on health policy despite its lack of constitutional authority; as discussed below, this has occurred repeatedly during the development of the Canadian health insurance system.[1]

HEALTH INSURANCE IN CANADA

Although universal health insurance was first proposed in 1919, it was not enacted until much later. Local governments, industries, and voluntary agencies instead developed a variety of prepayment plans in the 1920s and 1930s that inevitably left some services not covered and some people not insured.

Following the Depression of the 1930s and the Second World War, the federal and provincial governments turned their attention toward domestic matters. A federal–provincial conference, convened in 1945 to consider programs of social reform, proposed universal health insurance with federal–provincial cost-sharing. The conference also produced a draft health care bill for the provinces, partly modelled on the United Kingdom National Health System proposal. The bill provided for patient registration with family physicians in health regions; these physicians would be responsible for their patient "lists" and paid on a capitation basis. They would also be paid additional sums to provide prevention services as medical health officers. Services would be provided, wherever possible, in health centres. The plan would have been administered in each province under the direction of a commission representing both consumers and the professions. Although the 1945 proposals were viewed favourably by the public and key professional groups, including the Canadian Medical Association, they failed to be enacted because they were viewed as federal incursions into provincial jurisdiction.[2]

Nonetheless, hospital facilities were perceived to be insufficient in number, inadequate, and outdated, and government action was seen to be necessary. In lieu of a full health insurance program, the federal government made grants for planning and hospital construction available to the provinces. This marked the first acceptance of the concept of federal–provincial cost-sharing for health services, a principle that has been the foundation of all subsequent health policy in Canada.[3]

Hospitals and hospital care in Canada had previously been financed by municipal governments, religious groups, voluntary insurance programs, and patient payments. As facilities were built and modernized with government help, this funding base became increasingly inadequate, particularly in the hospital sector. By 1955 five provinces had enacted universal hospital insurance plans to stabilize their hospital funding. These plans, though politically popular, proved expensive. The five provinces soon pressed the federal government to honour its 1945 hospital insurance cost-sharing offer by enacting nation-wide universal hospital insurance. Financial incentives in the ensuing Hospital Insurance and Diagnostic Services Act (HIDS) induced all provinces to adopt universal hospital insurance by 1961. Under the act, services were insured and eligible for 50 percent federal cost-sharing only when provided in hospitals; there were no incentives to use less expensive sites. (Proposals to cover home care, for example, were not adopted.) Moreover, although universal hospital insurance in Canada provided payment to hospitals, it did not mandate an organizational framework to increase efficiency or prevent duplication of services. As a result, hospital-based patterns of practice, paid for by the provinces with "fifty-cent dollars," were solidified, leading to some of the current financial problems.

Hospital construction continued; between 1961 and 1971 the number of hospital beds in Canada increased twice as rapidly as the population (33 percent, as compared to 18 percent). Bed occupancy, which tends to correlate with bed availability, remained at about 80 percent.[4] Thus, per capita utilization was also increasing. More recently, in response both to budgetary restraints and technological advances that permit greater use of out-patient care, hospitals have been pressured to reduce their bed numbers.[5]

With hospital expenditures covered, public pressure grew to insure medical care costs. By this time, however, the concept of state-administered medical care insurance was opposed by powerful providers, including the Canadian Medical Association and the private insurance companies. In 1961 the federal government set up a royal commission headed by a Supreme Court judge (the Hall Commission) to study health services in Canada.[6] While it was deliberating, the Province of Saskatchewan enacted universal medical care insurance. That program survived a twenty-one-day doctors' strike to become both popular and successful. In 1964 the Hall Commission delivered its lengthy report. Among its many recommendations was one that the federal government cost-share a universal medical insurance program based on the Saskatchewan model. The resulting Medical Care Act of 1968 incorporated some of Hall's recommendations; however, it did not include his suggested reorganization of medical services delivery. A decade later Hall was again asked to study (in less depth) the existing health care system. As will be noted, he used the opportunity to repeat many of his previous recommendations.

The Medical Care Act, like the previous Hospital Insurance and Diagnostic Services Act, removed financial barriers but entrenched the most expensive means of delivering services; this time federal–provincial cost-sharing was allowed for those services provided by physicians. Although other health professionals may be allowed to bill the provincial insurance plans in some provinces, for the most part such services are not required under the terms of the federal program.

Because the federal government had no direct jurisdiction in health care, both the hospital and medical care insurance programs were co-operative and voluntary. To qualify for federal–provincial cost-sharing, the provincial program had only to meet certain terms of reference:

1. Universal coverage, on uniform terms and conditions, "that does not impede, or preclude, either directly or indirectly whether by charges made to insured persons or otherwise, reasonable access to insured services by insured persons" (95 percent of the population, without exclusion, had to be covered within two years of provincial adoption of the plan);

2. Portability of benefits from province to province;

3. Comprehensive insurance for all medically necessary services;

4. A publicly administered non-profit program.

Not only did federal–provincial cost-sharing stimulate the provinces to adopt health insurance programs; it also served as a means of income redistribution between the wealthier and poorer provinces. The 50 percent federal share was distributed as follows: each province was paid 25 percent of the per capita costs it incurred for hospital in-patient services plus 25 percent of the national average per capita cost; this sum was then multiplied by the province's population. For medical insurance, each province received 50 percent of the average national per capita medical care expenditure multiplied by its population. As a result, the wealthier provinces that spent more received less than 50 percent of their costs. The differentials were especially apparent for medical care cost-sharing, which was entirely based on national rates. In 1973–1974, for example, Ontario received 49.4 percent of its hospital costs and 44.8 percent of its medical care costs from federal contributions; at the other end of the spectrum, Newfoundland received 57.6 percent of its hospital and 81.5 percent of its medical care costs from the federal government.[7]

It was soon evident that the federal government had no control over the total amounts expended by the provinces and received no political credit for its contributions. After initial unilateral attempts by the federal government to limit its contributions without otherwise altering the program, the federal and provincial governments settled on a new fiscal formula in 1977. Bill C-37 (Federal–Provincial Fiscal Arrangements and Established Programs Financing Act, commonly known as EPF) reduced the direct federal contribution for health care to 25 percent of total 1975–1976 expenditures and tied any subsequent increases in federal payments to the growth of the gross national product (GNP) after 1975. To compensate, federal income and corporate taxes were decreased in order to create "tax room" for the provinces, which could (and did) increase their tax rates to balance the federal reductions without increasing total taxation levels.[8] Additional revenues required to meet any cost increases in excess of growth in the GNP would be primarily the responsibility of the provinces rather than, as in previous years, a responsibility shared with the federal government. Cost control was thereby shifted to the provinces, where both the constitutional authority for health care and the management of health care services rest. Similar treatment was given to postsecondary education, another expensive and formerly open-ended cost-shared program under provincial jurisdiction.

EPF did not alter the four requirements for provincial health insurance programs. However, the federal contributions for health care and postsecondary education were no longer earmarked but became part of general provincial revenues. Both health and postsecondary education now had to compete for dollars with other provincially funded programs. Some federal ability to "steer" provincial programs continued because the original terms of reference were retained and a series of additional per capita grants tied to specific programs were adopted (for example, grants to try to reduce the hospital focus by developing potentially less costly services like home care and extended care). Nonetheless the overall federal capacity to steer programs was reduced. Since reporting requirements were eased, it was also difficult for the federal government to monitor compliance with its terms of reference. The federal government was thus pursuing two policies that might be seen as contradictory; it wished to alter the EPF fiscal agreements to reduce its financial commitments further, while increasing its control over health policy. In recent years limiting federal transfers have had a higher policy priority with the national government; the resulting erosion in the cash portion of federal transfers has sparked concern over whether the continuation of these trends would mean loss of any ability to enforce national standards.[9]

Among the most controversial issues was the question of direct charges to patients beyond the level paid by the provincial health insurance plan, whether these be levied by institutions ("user charges") or physicians ("extra billing"). To many, such charges threatened to erode medicare. In 1984, after considerable discussion and despite widespread opposition from organized medicine and the provincial governments, the federal government moved to eliminate such charges through passage of the Canada Health Act (Bill C-3). This act stipulated that federal payments to the provinces would be reduced, on a dollar-for-dollar basis, by the amount of user charges by hospitals and extra billings by physicians. Direct federal prohibition was impossible because, constitutionally, health care is a provincial responsibility. However, Quebec had already in essence banned such charges, and all other provinces eliminated them before the expiration of the three-year grace period.[10] Such charges did not always go quietly; in Ontario the passage of legislation (Bill 94) to eliminate extra charges led to a month-long, unsuccessful doctors' strike. A court challenge by organized medicine to the Ontario and federal legislation also resulted, but was eventually withdrawn. By 1987 the Canada Health Act's formal goal of universal comprehensive first-dollar coverage across Canada had been met. However, as the federal cash payment has declined, provinces have again expressed an interest in user fees. For example, Quebec's recent *Reform Centred on the Citizen* has proposed a $5 user fee for "unnecessary" emergency room visits,[11] while Alberta's Rainbow Report proposed using a "smart card" with a per capita limitation on health spending.[12] The user-fee issue is evidently not yet dead.

Although EPF accentuated differences among provinces as the federal role decreased, essential similarities across the provincial plans remain. Virtually every Canadian has comprehensive medical and hospital insurance, with no co-payments permitted for insured services delivered within the province. Most hospitals are paid by provincial governments on the basis of negotiated budgets. Most physicians are paid fee-for-service on the basis of provincially negotiated fee schedules.

Taxes and premiums collected by federal and provincial governments finance the publicly funded health care system. Although public administration was mandated from the outset of universal hospital insurance, the medical insurance plans allowed for a brief transition period during which private health insurance companies continued to operate. However, private health insurance now plays almost no part in the universal plan, covering only supplemental benefits (such as semi-private accommodation and other amenities) and, in some provinces, service out of country (service in other provinces is covered, in theory, under the portability arrangements). Services by other professional groups are financed in a number of ways. Hospital-based workers are usually paid through the government-funded hospital budgets. The decision about which other kinds of health practitioners can bill the provincial insurance plans varies across Canada; in some provinces, for example, chiropractors can bill directly with dollar limitations. Most usually, out-patient non-physician professional services are covered to some extent if ordered by a physician (for example, physiotherapy), while other services are excluded from the plan altogether (for example, dentistry).

Initially, most provinces administered the programs with quasi-public medical care and/or hospital commissions. In recent years most of these provincial hospital and medical care commissions have been eliminated and their functions assumed by the provincial ministries of health. Outside of the formal health care plans, patient self-help groups are becoming increasingly active, while other health-related activities fall under the jurisdiction of other ministries such as community services, social services, labour, or housing.

HEALTH CARE UNDER UNIVERSAL INSURANCE

In 1965 the total cost of all health care services in Canada was $3.3 billion, in 1970 $6 billion, in 1975 more than $11 billion, and in 1985 almost $40 billion. Of the total health care expenditures in 1985, approximately 52 percent went to institutional care and 22 percent to physician services. Health care costs now make up over 30 percent of Ontario spending, sums that must be raised by taxes or premiums. The magnitude of these expenditures and the rate of their increase (which has continued) have captured the attention of politicians.

Following the introduction of hospital insurance, health expenditures in Canada rose, both in absolute terms and as a percentage of GNP. The proportion of GNP devoted to health care rose from 5.5 percent in 1960 to 7.3 percent in 1971, and actual expenditures increased from $2 billion to $7 billion (a 250 percent increase).[13] The introduction of medical care insurance has had less of an effect. Between 1971 and 1976 expenditures rose again (from $7 billion to almost $12 billion), but the percent of GNP spent on health care remained constant at about 7 percent until the late 1970s. As a result of low economic growth, it subsequently rose to its current level near 9 percent.[14] However, because of government insurance, public-sector funding of health care rose from 43 percent to 75 percent of costs; actual government spending thus increased from about $1 billion in 1960 to $5 billion in 1971, $9 billion in 1975, $13 billion in 1978–1979, and over $30 billion in 1985. The size of total health care expenditures became more visible once governments started paying almost all the bills.

In the period before universal hospital and medical care insurance the private sector had covered some hospital and physician care. At present over 90 percent of the cost of hospital and physician services are paid by the public sector. Private payments are now limited primarily to nursing homes (40 percent of costs), dental care (90 percent), and drugs and prostheses (75 percent).[15]

Hospital use and its attendant costs were particularly vulnerable to examination in Canada because, compared to many countries, particularly to the United States, Canada had high bed-to-population and bed-use-to-population ratios. For example, in Ontario 8.9 percent of the population aged sixty-five and over were in an institution on any one day, a higher utilization rate than in the United States or the United Kingdom.[16] While a small portion of the higher Canadian bed use could be explained by its remote and isolated North, which was served by many small hospitals, some was a reflection of increased bed supply. By 1971 Canada had 23 percent more hospital beds per capita than the United States and used 30 percent more hospital days per capita.[17]

FEDERAL AND PROVINCIAL PLANNING REPORTS

Beginning in the late 1960s, concern regarding the above-inflation increases in health care expenditures was reflected in a number of government planning reports that identified rising expenditures and stressed the need for greater efficiency and the provision of less expensive forms of health service delivery. Their goal was not necessarily to cut costs but rather to contain the rate of increase. They were influenced by a strong body of expert opinion calling for improving the efficiency and containing the costs of the health care system through such measures as shifting from in-patient to out-patient care, reducing the number of hospital beds, and promoting paramedical workers and community health (and social service) centres. This emphasis was further justified by the work of Illich, Fuchs, and McKeown, which challenged both the efficacy and the marginal benefits of further increases in health care expenditures in developed countries.[18] At the national level a

1969 task force on the costs of health services concluded that increased costs could only be dealt with by reduced standards of care, increased taxes, premiums and/or deterrent fees, or more efficient operation of the system.[19] The 1973 report of the Community Health Centre Project, commonly known as the Hastings Report,[20] recommended the large-scale development of community health centres by the provinces as well as reorganization and integration of all health services and reduction in the number of hospital beds. The Lalonde Report of the federal Department of National Health and Welfare, in what some have termed primarily a government justification for reduced spending for personal health care services, stressed the importance of health promotion, lifestyle modification, and greater individual responsibility for health instead of increased provision of medical services.[21]

Many provincial governments conducted or commissioned their own studies, all of which reached similar conclusions. The 1972 Manitoba white paper on health suggested regionalization of health services and the establishment of community health and social services centres in order to shift from hospital to ambulatory care services.[22] In Quebec a 1970 four-volume health section of the report of the Commission of Inquiry on Health and Social Welfare, known as the Castonguay Report, also suggested decentralization, community clinics, and greater consumer input into the organization of health care services.[23] A 1973 report commissioned by the recently elected New Democratic Party government of British Columbia recommended complete reorganization of the British Columbia health care system with regionalization and rationalization based on community health resource and health centres and a de-emphasis on hospital use.[24] In Ontario the 1970 report of the Committee on the Healing Arts, the 1976 Health Report of the Ontario Economic Council, and the 1974 report of the Health Planning Task Force, known as the Mustard Report, all identified increased cost, excessive use of hospital services, and the control and deployment of medical and health manpower as key issues, and included rationalization, regionalization, and deinstitutionalization among their remedies.[25]

Although most of these recommendations were never implemented, the concepts contained within the reports are now being more actively debated and have given rise to a new slew of provincial reports.[26] This largely ideological debate about the roles and responsibilities of physicians, other providers, government, and the public has been forced on the system because of the worsening economic climate in Canada and the perceived need to control cost escalation in health care and other publicly funded programs.

THE HALL REVIEW OF HEALTH SERVICES

Canadian health insurance was a mix of public funding and private practice. The universal system initially paid the bills but did not attempt to manage the programs. Providers, particularly physicians, were (and still are) treated as private entrepreneurs who happen to operate in a publicly funded system. Hospitals have continued under community control with independent boards of trustees. However, virtually all of their budgets are now determined and paid by provincial governments; some cost containment in the hospital sector has thus been possible, although changes in hospital governance had not yet become an issue.

During the 1970s the percentage of GNP spent on health care remained constant at about 7 percent. Although health economists hailed this as an example of successful containment, providers (both physicians and hospitals) charged that the system was underfunded and demanded that more money be devoted to health care. If public funds were not available, physicians and hospital administrators favoured the injection of private money through user charges and private insurance. Opting out and extra billing by physicians increased, and negotiations between provincial governments and their doctors became more acrimonious. Confrontations resulted, and in many provinces work stoppages and rotating strikes took place. Hospital budgets that had been calculated on a line-by-line basis were converted in most provinces to global budgets, and the annual rates of increase were frequently less than the rate of inflation. Hospitals protested these "inadequate" increases both privately and publicly and were not infrequently successful in obtaining additional money to cover their budgetary deficits.

It was in the context of confrontation and charges of underfunding of the health care system that the federal government in 1979 asked Justice Emmet Hall to examine the universal health insurance program his 1964 royal commission report had recommended. Specifically, he was asked to examine two charges: that the total federal contribution plus the "tax room" was resulting in fewer health care dollars for the provinces; and that, since these monies were no longer earmarked for health care, the provinces were diverting them to other programs. He was also asked to examine extra billing and the adversarial relationship that had developed between provincial governments and their physicians.

Hall concluded that both of the charges were false: the federal contributions plus "tax room" were actually producing more money than the earlier cost-sharing formula would have, and the provinces were not diverting these dollars from health care. Both federal and provincial health care spending was actually increasing.[27]

In his review of extra billing, Hall concluded that physicians should not be allowed to opt out or extra bill. Instead he recommended that they should be "adequately paid" and that differences between provincial governments and physicians should be settled by compulsory binding arbitration. His recommendations regarding physicians were weakened because Hall did not suggest a mechanism for determining "adequate" compensation, and provincial governments have been unwilling to accept the constraints on their spending authority implied by compliance with arbitration reports. In 1981 a federal parliamentary task force was set up on federal–provincial fiscal arrangements; it took an even stronger stand against user charges and opting out than Hall had done.[28] Although the subsequent elimination of extra billing following passage of the Canada Health Act was accompanied in some provinces with commitments to a system of binding arbitration, most provincial governments have proved unwilling to accept judgments that run contrary to their own priorities. As a result, relationships between physicians and government remain strained.[29]

CURRENT PROBLEMS

Not surprisingly, the universal health plan has encountered both difficulty and conflict. Government began by paying bills. With rising costs, government paymasters took on an increased role. They chose to use the blunt instrument of cost containment rather than the more difficult step of modifying the organization and management of the system. As a result, providers now complain that the system is underfunded, while governments see only what they perceive as the insatiable financial appetite of the health care system. Both charge that the system is in crisis.

When charges of crisis are carefully examined, they have proved to be unfounded. However, there are justifiable concerns that the system is rigid and inflexible and may soon be faced with a rapid increase in costs. Preservation of the autonomy of local institutions has been valued, but there has been a resulting weakness in control over the acquisition of new technology and fears that the system is inefficient. As a result, concerns are increasingly voiced that a focus on technology coupled with an oversupply of physicians and services may have produced a system that will be unable to adapt to the problems of an aging population, a postindustrial society, and changing human service needs. One consequence was a reorganization of the Ontario Ministry of Health, including the introduction of program management, in an attempt to focus more on health outcomes in making allocation decisions. There has also been a new flurry of planning reports from provincial governments, including the Rochon Commission in Quebec and Ontario's triumvirate of Spassoff, Evans, and Podborski; these have been reviewed by Angus and Mhatre and Deber.[30] The perception that Canada's health system may be heading for trouble appears to be widespread, and cries for reform are becoming louder.

A second problem arises from Canada's current constitutional ferment. Health care, as a national program within provincial jurisdiction, may therefore be affected by efforts to restructure the federal system.[31]

A third problem arises from a trend we term "deprivatization"—the systematic tendency of government services to expand into new areas that formerly were considered private concerns. For example, there has been pressure for government to increase provision of services in areas not included under medicare, such as long-term care, assistive devices, dentistry, and even housing and provision of homemaking services.[32] The burden on government has thus continued to grow, and health expenditures to increase at well above the rate of inflation.

The federal government wishes to reduce its contributions for health care, placing more financial responsibility on the provinces. Providers are demanding more money, which they will accept from provincial governments or from the private sector. Supplemental private insurance for insured benefits continues to be prohibited. When coupled with growing provincial deficits, the provincial publicly funded health care programs are moving toward potentially untenable financial positions.

At least two scenarios are possible. One would place the health sector under greater government control; the government would then take a major role in the management of the system, the control of resources, and the employment of physicians. The second scenario would shift responsibility for health care away from government into the private sector. The first scenario, greater government control, implies increasing confrontation with providers and the need for tough and consistent stances by the provinces. It is also more likely to maintain the integrity of the publicly funded universal system.

The second scenario, shifting control, may be superficially more attractive. It implies a diminished provincial role (and budgetary responsibility) as private funding increases. However, this policy will lead to greater total costs for health care and possibly to a two-class hospital and medical care system. It would also be in violation of the Canada Health Act—which requires government to fund all medically necessary services—and would be enormously unpopular with the public. Accordingly, most provincial governments appear to be moving toward greater attempts to control the system, including the threat of controls over the number of physicians allowed to bill the health care system.

The issues are basically ideological, and after twenty-two years they can no longer be avoided, particularly when poor economic performance is coupled with a rising proportion of GNP devoted to health care.[33] The alternatives have been defined at one extreme by the system in the United Kingdom. There, costs were controlled, but physicians were essentially government employees, paid by salary or capitation rather than on a fee-for-service basis, and groups of hospitals were directed by regional authorities rather than community boards. At the other extreme is the more costly, essentially free-enterprise system in the United States, with means testing, accessibility limited by patients' finances, and government funding only for the needy.

Until now Canada has used public funds to pay for a private system. It has avoided key issues of reorganization and management of the system as a whole. Australia, in confronting similar issues, moved temporarily to a more private system,[34] but the popularity of Canada's present universal system—particularly in contrast to the American model—makes a private solution less likely here. The Canadian solution to most problems has typically been moderation and compromise. Extreme moves in either direction would thus represent an unlikely break with tradition. Contemplating those alternatives, however, will be healthy if it helps to produce the changes necessary to ensure the survival of Canada's medicare program.

NOTES

1. R.G. Evans, "'We'll Take Care of It for You': Health Care in the Canadian Community," *Daedalus* 117 (1988): 155–89; R.B. Deber, "Philosophical Underpinnings of Canada's Health Care System," *Canada U.S. Outlook* 2 (1991): 20–45; R. Van Loon and M.S. Whittington, *The Canadian Political System: Environment, Structure and Process*, 4th ed. (Toronto: McGraw-Hill Ryerson, 1987).

2. M. Taylor, *Health Insurance and Canadian Public Policy*, 2nd ed. (Montreal: McGill-Queen's University Press, 1987).

3. Ibid.

4. E. Vayda, R.G. Evans, and W. Mindell, "Universal Health Insurance in Canada: History, Problems, Trends," *Journal of Community Health* 4 (1979): 217–31.

5. P. Gamble, "Hospital Resources in Metropolitan Toronto: The Reality versus the Myth" in *Restructuring Canada's Health Services System: How Do We Get There from Here?* ed. R.B. Deber and G.G. Thompson (Toronto: University of Toronto Press, 1992).

6. Canada, *Royal Commission on Health Services* (Hall Report), summary, vols. 1 and 2 (Ottawa: Queen's Printer, 1964, 1965).

7. S. Andreopoulos, ed., *National Health Insurance: Can We Learn from Canada?* (Toronto: Wiley, 1975).

8. L. Soderstrom, *The Canadian Health Care System* (London: Croom Helm, 1978); R.J. Van Loon, "From Shared Cost to Block Funding and Beyond: The Politics of Health Insurance in Canada," *Journal of Health Politics, Policy and Law* 2 (1978): 454–78.

9. A. Thompson, *Federal Support for Health Care* (Ottawa: HEAL, the Health Action Lobby, 1991).

10. S. Heiber and R. Deber, "Banning Extra Billing in Canada: Just What the Doctor Didn't Order," *Canadian Public Policy* 13, 1 (March 1987): 62–74, and "Freedom, Equality, and the Charter of Rights: Regulating Physician Reimbursement," *Canadian Public Administration* 31, 4 (Winter 1988): 566–89.

11. Quebec, *A Reform Centred on the Citizen* (Quebec: Ministère de la Santé et des Services sociaux, 1989).

12. L. Hyndman, chair, *The Rainbow Report: Our Vision For Health*, Premier's Commission on Future Health Care for Albertans, 3 vols. (Edmonton, 1989).

13. M.L. Barer and R.G. Evans, "Riding North on a South-bound Horse? Expenditures, Prices, Utilization and Income in the Canadian Health Care System" in *Medicare at Maturity*, ed. R.G. Evans and G.L. Stoddart (Calgary: University of Calgary Press, 1984), 53–73; R.G. Evans,

"Health Care in Canada: Patterns in Funding and Regulation" in *The Public/Private Mix for Health*, ed. G. McLachlan and A. Maynard (London: Nuffield Provincial Hospitals Trust, 1982); G.H. Hatcher, *Universal Free Health Care in Canada, 1947–1977*, NIH pub. no. 81-2052 (Washington: U.S. Department of Health and Human Services, 1981).

14. G.J. Schieber and J.-P. Poullier, "International Health Care Expenditure Trends: 1987," *Health Affairs* 8, 3 (Fall 1989): 169–77.

15. Barer and Evans, "Riding North."

16. M.J. Gross and C. Schwenger, *Health Care Costs for the Elderly in Ontario: 1976–2026* (Toronto: Ontario Economic Council, 1981).

17. Vayda, Evans, and Mindell, "Universal Health Insurance."

18. E. Illich, *Limits to Medicine: Medical Nemesis, the Expropriation of Health* (Toronto: McClelland & Stewart, 1975); V.R. Fuchs, *Who Shall Live: Health, Economics and Social Policy* (New York: Basic Books, 1974); T. McKeown, *The Role of Medicine* (Oxford: Blackwell, 1979).

19. Canada, *Task Force Reports on the Cost of Health Services in Canada*, 3 vols. (Ottawa: Queen's Printer, 1969).

20. J.E.F. Hastings, chair, *The Community Health Centre in Canada*, vol. 1 (Ottawa: Information Canada 1973).

21. M. Lalonde, *A New Perspective on the Health of Canadians* (Ottawa: Information Canada, 1974); R. Evans, "A Retrospective on the 'New Perspective,'" *Journal of Health Politics, Policy and Law* 7 (1982): 325–44; E. Vayda, "Preventive Programs and the Political Process," *Modern Medicine in Canada* 32 (1977): 260–64.

22. Manitoba, *White Paper on Health Policy* (Winnipeg: Department of Health and Social Development, 1972).

23. Quebec, *Report of the Commission of Inquiry on Health and Social Service*, part 2, tome 2, *The Health Plan* (Castonguay Report) (Quebec, 1970).

24. R. Foulkes, *Health Security for British Columbians*, vol. 1 (Vancouver: Province of British Columbia, 1973).

25. Ontario, *Report of the Committee on the Healing Arts*, vol. 1 (Toronto: Queen's Printer, 1970); Ontario Economic Council, *Issues and Alternatives 1976: Health* (Toronto: Ontario Economic Council, 1976); Ontario, *Report on the Health Planning Task Force* (Mustard Report) (Toronto: Ontario Ministry of Health, 1974).

26. R.B. Deber and E. Vayda, "The Environment of Health Policy Implementation: The Ontario, Canada, Example," in *Investigative Methods in Public Health*, ed. George Knox, vol. 3 of *Oxford Textbook of Public Health*, ed. Walter Holland (Oxford: Oxford University Press, 1985); D.E. Angus, *Review of Significant Health Care Commissions and Task Forces in Canada since 1983–84* (Ottawa: Canadian Hospital Association Press, 1991).

27. E.M. Hall, *Canada's National–Provincial Health Program of the 1980s*, Health Services Review 1979 (Saskatoon: Craft Litho, 1980).

28. Canada, *Fiscal Federalism in Canada*, Report of the Parliamentary Task Force on Federal–Provincial Arrangements (Ottawa: Minister of Supply and Services, 1981).

29. C.J. Tuohy, "Medicine and the State in Canada: The Extra-Billing Issue in Perspective," *Canadian Journal of Political Science* 21, 2 (June 1988): 267–96.

30. Angus, *Review of Significant Commissions and Task Forces*, and S.L. Mhatre and R. Deber, "From Equal Access to Health Care to Equitable Access to Health: Review of Canadian Provincial Health Commissions and Reports," *International Journal of Health Services*, forthcoming.

31. R.B. Deber, "Regulatory and Administrative Options for Canada's Health Care System" (background paper prepared for HEAL, the Health Action Lobby, 8 Oct. 1991).

32. B.J. Fried, R.B. Deber, and P. Leatt, "Corporatization and Deprivatization of Health Services in Canada," *International Journal of Health Services* 17, 4 (1987): 567–83, reprinted in *The Corporate Transformation of Health Care*, ed. J. Warren Salmon (Amityville, NY: Baywood Publishing, 1990), 167–86.

33. A.J. Culyer, *Health Expenditures in Canada: Myth and Reality, Past and Future* (Toronto: Canadian Tax Foundation, 1988); R.G. Evans, J. Lomas, M.L. Barer, et al., "Controlling Health Expenditures—The Canadian Reality," *New England Journal of Medicine* 320, 9 (1989): 571–77.

34. J.S. Deeble, "Unscrambling the Omelet: Public and Private Health Care Financing in Australia" in *The Public/Private Mix for Health*.

THE CANADA ASSISTANCE PLAN: THE ULTIMATE IN CO-OPERATIVE FEDERALISM◇

RAND DYCK

○

"Co-operative federalism" is the term that has generally been used to catego-rize Canadian federal–provincial relations in the 1960s. Although it has been given many definitions by academics and politicians alike,[1] the concept is commonly accepted to refer to an intense degree of intergovernmental con-sultation, to the basic equality of the relationship, and to the decentralizing nature of the results in this period. In these respects federal–provincial rela-tions in the 1960s were distinct from the federal dominance, the centraliza-tion, and the lesser degree of interaction that characterized Canadian federalism up to that time.

While co-operative federalism implies a spirit of co-operation, we know that federal–provincial relations in the 1960s were not entirely free of con-flict. In fact, two basic models of Canadian federalism in the period could be suggested. The first, which emerges from analyses of the Canada Pension Plan, medicare, financial relations, and vocational training,[2] emphasizes the conflict and bargaining involved. The other, first noted and most thor-oughly documented by Smiley, stresses harmonious executive relation-ships—genuine co-operation.[3] Yet to be discussed in any detail in this context is the Canada Assistance Plan, another significant product of this period and the one which probably best exemplifies the genuine co-operative federalism process.

The Canada Assistance Plan began as a means of improving existing federal–provincial public assistance programs. It was developed over a three-year period beginning in 1963 and was designed to consolidate,

◇ *Canadian Public Administration* 19, 4 (1979): 587–602. Reprinted with the permission of the Institute of Public Administration of Canada.

extend, and replace the Unemployment Assistance Act, and the three existing "categorical" programs—the Old Age Assistance and Blind and Disabled Persons Allowances Acts. It provided for federal contributions for the first time to provincial mothers' allowance schemes, to provincial costs in providing health services to public assistance recipients, to rehabilitative and preventive welfare services, and to the administrative costs of such programs. The Canada Assistance plan also shared in provincial child welfare expenditures, and, where the provinces so used it, in work activity projects and Indian welfare programs. At the option of the provinces, it could also be used to assist those working part- or full-time, if such persons continued to be in need. In return, the plan required that provincial assistance programs be based on a needs or budget deficit test, that they incorporate an appeals procedure for recipients, and that any residence requirements for eligibility be removed.

In this article it will be seen that five aspects of the Canada Assistance Plan combined to distinguish it as perhaps the most harmonious product of the co-operative federalism period.[4] Two of these aspects concern the conception stage of the plan; two, the formulation stage; and one has to do with its implementation. In each case brief contrasts will be drawn between CAP and other measures developed in the 1960s. Some attention will then be devoted to the conflictual aspects of the plan, as insignificant as these were, in order to ascertain the relevance of the Simeon bargaining model to this case.

CONCEPTION

The first distinctive aspect of the Canada Assistance Plan was the nearly simultaneous recognition by both levels of government that it was a desirable move. This realization struck many of the provinces first, but their sporadic, isolated early demands produced no effect. Almost as soon as they began to demand such a measure in a concerted, forceful manner, however, the federal level indicated its willingness to take action.[5]

It is not difficult to account for the provincial demands. They were primarily based on the desire for greater federal financial assistance. To them it seemed that obvious gaps remained in federal cost-sharing under the Unemployment Assistance Act: mothers' allowance payments, the cost of medical care of persons on social assistance, and the administrative costs of welfare programs were all borne entirely by the provinces. They were generally anxious to have this financial burden shared by Ottawa.

That the federal response to these demands was so prompt and generous can be attributed to a variety of political and bureaucratic factors. At the official level, health and welfare administrators were first anxious to help develop more effective provincial welfare programs, which could be achieved with more federal money combined with high federal standards. Secondly, they recognized the need for a unification of the administration of unemployment assistance and categorial assistance programs which could result from a new initiative of this kind. In the third place, they looked forward to experimenting with new concepts in dealing with the chronically unemployed and to modernizing other aspects of welfare administration. Finally, Indian Affairs officials hoped to develop improved welfare services for the Native population through a new co-operative effort with the provinces.

The federal political response also involved several different factors. One was the realization that after the adoption of the Canada Pension Plan there would need to be certain changes made to related welfare measures. In its initial stages, CAP was not seen as a major innovation, but merely as a "tidying up" exercise in the wake of the CPP. Subsidiary to this motive was the Pearson government's general willingness to proceed with new ventures in the welfare field—"to complete the welfare state" as the prime minister sometimes put it. Thirdly, the Pearson Cabinet, especially in its first few years, was particularly sensitive to provincial demands and could hardly bring itself to reject one which was expressed with such force and unanimity and which at first did not appear to be costly. Later, as the scope of CAP expanded, so did the federal Cabinet's appetite for reform in this area. The Canada Assistance Plan fell neatly within the Pearson–Kent conception of a Canadian "War on Poverty," under which guise the Cabinet was persuaded to accept a measure of considerable breadth.

The second distinctive aspect about the conception of CAP was the degree to which both levels of government were involved in establishing the basic outline of the plan. Once the decision had been made to go ahead, the plan was deliberately developed on a joint basis and a consensus on its main components was easily and almost spontaneously achieved.

What the plan should contain was first discussed by federal and provincial welfare officials, chiefly deputy ministers, in February 1964. The participants at this initial meeting were unanimous in the belief that the federal government should begin to cost-share provincial mothers' allowance payments. On most other issues there was widespread agreement, coupled with a certain amount of indecision.[6] Being left to such officials to discuss the basic content of the plan in the first instance, it is not surprising, perhaps, that a large degree of harmony prevailed. As Smiley has convincingly established,

> federal–provincial administrative relationships have been harmonious and constructive to the extent that they have been dominated by program specialists . . . the attitudes, procedures and values common to particular groups of program specialists . . . provide common standards to which officials from federal and provincial levels defer.[7]

Such was clearly the situation here, as welfare officials from both levels of government together discussed the form of a joint program that would improve the entire welfare system and which, in the process, would reflect their professional norms.

To a large extent, the norms to which they were all deferring had been set down clearly by the Canadian Welfare Council in its 1958 document, "Social Security for Canada." In that statement, to which many of the officials at the 1964 meeting had contributed, the CWC laid down a blueprint for welfare reform which the eventual Canada Assistance Plan reflected almost word for word.

Federal–provincial co-operation was also facilitated by the mutual acquaintance, often friendship, of many of the participants at the meeting. In addition to their participation in CWC activities, prior intergovernmental interaction and old social work "school ties" put most of the deputy ministers and other officials on a first-name basis.

A final aspect of the joint conception of the plan, and another measure of the influence of the "bureaucratic elite" in the welfare field, was the rapidity with which welfare *ministers* absorbed the norms and attitudes of their departments. After the deputy ministers returned home to further consider the issues raised and to discuss them with their political "lords and masters,"[8] the welfare ministers met and readily approved the basic features of the plan at meetings in May 1964 and April 1965.

To reinforce the distinctiveness of the conception of the Canada Assistance Plan in terms of both timing and design, reference can be made to some of the other federal–provincial measures developed in the same period. In the case of adult occupational training, for example, Dupré demonstrates that the new plan was sprung on the provinces by the federal government when the former were not conscious that any significant change was needed. He also documents a clash of two very different "grand designs," an economists' design developed in Ottawa in isolation from an educationists' design formulated in Toronto. Somewhat similarly, the Canada Pension Plan and medicare were precipitated upon the provinces by the federal government at a time and in a form that some provinces at least found unacceptable. That this process of joint conception was distinctive can also be seen in contrasting CAP with the Unemployment Assistance Act, predecessor to CAP, which evolved ten years previously. At that time, in a period of "federal dominance" prior to co-operative federalism, the federal government was responding to provincial demands but then designed the measure unilaterally and presented it to provinces almost as a fait accompli.[9]

FORMULATION

In the formulation stage of the Canada Assistance Plan, there were also two striking features which reveal a particularly congenial process of co-operative federalism at work. The first of these was the hypersensitivity of federal officials to provincial demands for flexibility. It must be remembered that CAP was a shared-cost program developed at precisely the time that both the Quebec administration and the federal Liberal government had declared themselves opposed to any additional measures of this kind. It was only to be expected, therefore, that certain federal officials would be highly sensitive to Quebec's reaction to the proposal and anxious to avoid the strict federal standards and controls that were the marks of most earlier joint programs.

Quebec raised the issue of contracting out of CAP as soon as serious discussion of the measure began, and continued to voice its intention to do so throughout the formulation process. Similarly, but in a less extreme way, other provinces demanded more flexibility than under predecessor programs. Federal welfare officials were not particularly forthcoming in reaction to these provincial attitudes. They believed that to achieve maximum effectiveness, fairly stringent federal standards and controls would have to be incorporated. Instead, it was officials of the Department of Finance, the Treasury Board, and the Privy Council Office who were most concerned about this problem. A.W. Johnson, assistant deputy minister of finance, and R.B. Bryce, the deputy minister, were the main protagonists of this point of view.

The prevailing philosophy of the Finance Department was that such measures should be as flexible as possible and contain as few conditions as necessary—only enough to satisfy Parliament and to maintain an element of federal financial control. This attitude resulted partly from a new recognition at the federal level that the provinces were getting stronger and better staffed and managed all the time, and partly from the increasing resentment expressed by the provinces about inflexibility in joint programs. Johnson, an ex-deputy minister at the provincial level, did not feel it was up to the federal government to force reform on the provinces. These sentiments were reiterated by officials of the Federal–Provincial Relations section of the Privy Council Office. The prime minister's policy secretary, Tom Kent, also urged the strongest supporters of CAP and welfare reform among the federal bureaucratic and political elites to adopt a more flexible attitude toward the provinces.

While most provincial officials responded appreciatively to the maximum flexibility which Johnson, Bryce, and Kent were offering them, others at the provincial level valued high federal standards. Such standards were regarded by some provincial deputy ministers as a device to achieve progress within the province, progress normally retarded by conservative Cabinet ministers. In the end, however, flexibility carried the day.

The second aspect of the formulation stage that marks the Canada Assistance Plan as perhaps the ultimate in co-operative federalism concerned the extensive consultation that took place among the federal and provincial officials on the details of the plan. Judy LaMarsh, the federal welfare minister at the time, accurately predicted that "detailed technical consideration will be the key to success in developing this program."[10]

Federal officials were initially concerned about how far they could go in revealing their intentions to the provinces, Later, they decided to discuss the measure on the basis of the instructions they had drawn up for the use of the Department of Justice in the eventual drafting of the new legislation. Federal political authorization of these drafting instructions was apparently considered unnecessary.

A closely knit three-man team was formed in the new Canada Assistance Plan Division of the federal Welfare Department to visit each province. This group usually spent two or three days in the provincial capital, engaged in fairly intensive discussions in a "semi-informal" atmosphere. The sessions lasted all day long with the provincial deputy minister of welfare and a varying number of other officials present. In some cases the provincial minister was visited briefly, but this was only in the nature of a courtesy call or as part of generous provincial hospitality. The officials went through the drafting instructions in each province, point by point, acquainting provincial authorities with federal thinking and plans, getting feedback from the provinces on their thoughts, and then working this into the consensus of the overall plan. They would ask for example: "If CAP were written in this way, what would be your province's reaction to it?" "Do you feel that this provision would adequately cover your situation?" "If you foresee problems, what are they?"

There were basically three kinds of consultation involved in this process. The first area was where federal officials willingly enlarged their original proposals in order to accommodate under the plan unanticipated worthwhile provincial programs and practices. For example, on the question of health care for welfare recipients, the new measure was expanded to cover practices and agencies already involved in this area in the provinces, even if administered by a health rather than a welfare department.

A second area was where federal officials reluctantly conceded to provincial objections or demands. While the hope had been, for example, to avoid identifying specific causes in defining a "person in need," provincial resistance to this open-endedness led to a compromise on this definition, as follows: "a person who, by reason of inability to obtain employment, loss of the principal family provider, illness, disability, age or other cause of any kind acceptable to the provincial authority, is found to be unable . . . to provide adequately for himself. . . . " On this set of issues, then, federal officials were conciliatory, but did not entirely abandon their original objectives.

A third kind of consultation consisted of a simple exchange of information. To illustrate, federal officials told their provincial counterparts what they meant by a "work activity project"; the latter agreed to supply a list of all welfare institutions in the province to the federal department.

The extent of such intimate federal–provincial consultation prior to the final drafting of the measure was highly unusual. Also extraordinary was a supplementary special trip which federal officials made to Nova Scotia in order to study a typical welfare system in detail and to determine exactly how federal proposals would work in practice. Less surprising, but equally conducive to the success of the plan, a process identical to that described was followed on the drafting of the regulations and the agreements under the plan. The same three-man team criss-crossed the country on these two other occasions before the regulations were issued and before the federal–provincial agreements were signed.

It is not surprising, in the light of all this consultation, to find that the reaction of provincial officials was highly laudatory. It was said that the plan was developed in the "very best of co-operation and assistance"; the federal officials involved were called "princes of men of great personal integrity and ability"; and the plan was termed the result of the "best arrangements of any federal–provincial program that ever came into being."[11]

It may be wondered, however, why the federal government was willing to invest so much time and effort in this consultative process with the provinces. To this question there appear to be three main answers: jurisdictional, informational, and personal.

The federal level trod lightly in dealing with the provinces over CAP for several jurisdictional reasons. As mentioned above, Quebec was feeling highly sensitive about its own jurisdiction in the welfare field, and was at the same time arousing the consciousness of other provinces. Both the Quebec and federal governments had declared their opposition to new shared-cost programs. Furthermore, there had been general provincial criticism expressed about the rigidity of predecessor measures. Extensive provincial consultation was therefore considered essential because the federal government was expanding its role in an area of provincial jurisdiction.

A second reason had to do with the limited experience and information available at the federal level. To design a measure that would intimately affect ten distinctive provincial welfare systems obviously necessitated close consultation with the directors of those systems. Moreover, in the attempt to introduce entirely new concepts into welfare programs, the advice of provincial administrators was highly advantageous. Such interaction became all the more essential given the lack of practical experience in the delivery aspect of welfare programs on the part of the federal officials who sometimes referred to themselves as "babes in the woods."[12]

On a personal level, federal officials were already well acquainted with their provincial counterparts and realized that the success of the new plan would depend upon future congenial relations between them. Besides hoping to influence provincial actions in certain directions, they wanted to help the provinces gear up to the plan and generally to provide a means for the fullest mutual reaction before either side was cemented into position. For these reasons, then, extensive consultation in the formulation stage was considered the appropriate, advisable, and courteous course to follow.

What has been said about the formulation of the Canada Assistance Plan shows it to be a classic example of Smiley's description of "executive federalism." It probably goes a step further, however, than even he has documented previously. Again, the distinctiveness of CAP when contrasted with the other prominent federal–provincial measures of the day, is quite striking.

Dupré demonstrates, for example, that in the adult training program it was only after the clash of the Ottawa and Ontario "grand designs" that federal concessions were made. Similarly, the Canada Pension Plan was salvaged by last-minute secret summit diplomacy with Quebec only after repeated clashes of grand designs in this field. The federal level showed no reluctance to reform provincial medicare programs which did not comply with Ottawa's conditions. In that case, provincial objections were simply ignored, for the most part, until the financial incentives involved forced the provinces into submission.

IMPLEMENTATION

The extensive federal–provincial interaction out of which the plan emerged provided a model and a disposition for a continuation of such intimate intergovernmental consultation once CAP was adopted and implemented.

This consultation took the form of daily contact between provincial officials and federal consultants and field representatives, less frequent referral of problems to federal head office personnel, and periodic meetings of ministers and deputy ministers of welfare. In this respect, too—in the harmony of such contacts—CAP was distinctive among the federal–provincial measures of the period.

Under the Canada Assistance Plan one or more federal field representatives were appointed to be located in each provincial capital. These officials usually occupied an office in the midst of the provincial welfare department and were in constant communication with provincial welfare administrators. They had two main functions. One was to control the operation of the plan to ensure that the province carried out its responsibilities, met federal conditions, and made valid claims on the federal treasury. The other was a liaison function between the federal and provincial departments, to advise both levels on issues raised, to report on current or expected developments in both directions, and to solve or minimize potential problems. These field officers were more than financial auditors, and were not necessarily concerned to minimize federal contributions. In many instances they showed a province where cost-sharing was available but was not being claimed. The good relations they developed with the provinces often led to invitations to attend provincial welfare meetings.

At the same time, the federal department appointed consultants in some fifteen welfare fields such as child welfare and community development. They were available to travel to any province to offer advice on problems in their area of expertise. Without exception, the provinces found their services very useful.

While small problems could generally be solved through the use of consultants and field representatives, however, some issues required the attention of more senior personnel. Here, too, the contract was frequent, immediate, and friendly. Finally, the issues that still remained unresolved were brought to the attention of the federal minister or deputy minister who discussed them at federal–provincial meetings at those levels. Ministers of welfare met five times between 1968 and 1971, and deputy ministers an additional four times, to deal primarily with matters relating to CAP. By 1971 the program was operating with virtually no significant problems.

This congeniality of the implementation process contrasts sharply with Dupré's account of adult occupational training. In that case, the federal level had a much larger staff in the field—primarily the Canada Manpower Centre managers and economists. While the total number of federal–provincial contacts may thus have been greater than in the case of CAP, they were invariably indifferent to antagonistic in tone. Much of the contrast between the two sets of relationships can be explained by the Smiley conception of shared norms among officials. Federal and provincial social workers and other welfare administrators—even financial auditors connected with welfare—were able to work harmoniously with each other; on the other hand, federal economists and manpower officials shared few norms with provincial educators and educational administrators, whether located in provincial ministries or in institutions in the field. It is also important to note, however, that the basic orientation of federal and provincial programs in adult training was very different, while in welfare the orientation was essentially identical.

AREAS OF CONFLICT

This somewhat idyllic account of spontaneous unanimity on most aspects of the Canada Assistance Plan should not obscure the fact that certain areas of federal–provincial conflict did arise from time to time. These can be found in one basic feature of its conception, in two main facets of its formulation, and in two principal issues in its implementation.

As far as the general conception of CAP was concerned, the only conflict of any magnitude developed with respect to Quebec's desire to contract out. Even this presented no major problem once the federal government clarified its thinking on what "contracting out" meant, in the form of the Established Programs (Interim Arrangements) Act of 1965. Under that act a province could contract out of the four predecessor measures to CAP and ultimately the same provisions applied to CAP itself. If this issue was not long one of substance, however, it did provide the Quebec delegation at many welfare conferences with an opportunity to emphasize its sovereignty in the welfare field, to denounce new federal initiatives, and to insist on alternative financing arrangements being written into the plan. The federal decision to accede to the contracting out demand rendered most of this rhetoric unnecessary.

Two more substantive issues arose in the formulation stage of the plan: child welfare services and the cost-sharing formula, although even these were not clear-cut federal–provincial disputes. Throughout the formulation stage, the extent of federal cost-sharing envisaged in the child welfare field had been ambiguous. Once it became clear that federal contributions would be limited, a number of provinces demanded more. Ontario, acting on its own, and British Columbia, trying to construct a provincial alliance on the issue, managed to get the federal level to review the extent of shareability in this field and eventually to expand federal contributions considerably. Here was a logical request, unopposed at the provincial level,[13] and not meeting any particular resistance at the federal level, once the demand was clearly made.

On the cost-sharing formula, the initial assumption among all participants was that a straight 50–50 federal–provincial division of costs would be adopted. As time went on, however, the Atlantic provinces began to see that such a cost division would leave all provinces in their existing relative condition. Led by Nova Scotia, and particularly by its deputy minister of welfare, the Atlantic provinces began to demand a differential sharing formula based on provincial need. This demand was put most forcefully at the Welfare Ministers' Conference of January 1966. The federal level did not respond so readily in this case, however, as there were two strong opponents of the request. On the one hand, the richer provinces were opposed to any distinction in the cost-sharing formula from one province to another. On the other hand, the federal Department of Finance was adamant that regional disparities would be dealt with through general equalization payments rather than by differential formulas in specific joint programs. The federal Welfare Department's intervention on behalf of the Atlantic provinces was to no avail, as the Finance Department insisted on the 50–50 division of costs across the board.

The two main disputes that developed in the first few years of implementation of the plan were more genuinely federal–provincial ones. These conflicts centred on appeal procedures and on paying social assistance to persons on strike. The act required each province to establish an appeals procedure for dissatisfied welfare recipients within one year of signing a CAP agreement. Although most provinces had some kind of appeal system even prior to CAP, federal officials did not regard these as adequate in most cases. They soon became impatient with provincial inaction in improving them and made known their unhappiness to provincial officials and ministers on several occasions. Later, they issued guidelines on the kind of appeal system they considered adequate. It was only after a good deal of further prodding that all provinces adopted satisfactory appeal procedures.

In the case of persons on strike, the federal viewpoint was that everyone in need was entitled to assistance, regardless of the cause of need. In several provinces or municipalities, however, authorities refused to give assistance to those in need on account of strike action. This refusal was based on a reluctance "to interfere in labour–management disputes" as well, of course, as on a desire to save money. After pressure from federal officials and upon the personal intervention of the minister on occasion, provincial and municipal authorities have usually softened their stand, at least when the issue obtained real prominence.

RELEVANCE OF THE BARGAINING MODEL

Up to this point it has been suggested that the policy development involved in the Canada Assistance Plan can best be understood in terms of Smiley's discussion of shared norms among program administrators. The main alternative—the bargaining model—appears to be less relevant because of the small degree of conflict involved in this case. Nevertheless, it is instructive to apply a bargaining model to the areas of dispute involved, however small their proportions. Such a model, as outlined by Simeon in his *Federal–Provincial Diplomacy*, for example, characteristically emphasizes the issues, resources, and strategies that make up the bargaining process. Having dealt with the few significant issues of conflict that arose under CAP, we may turn directly to resources and strategies.

The main political resources involved in the Canada Assistance Plan were legal authority, money, and expertise. Because it was agreed that public assistance was primarily a provincial responsibility, few federal controls on the provinces were ever proposed. Moreover, most of the remainder gave way under the combined resistance of Quebec, some other provinces, and federal finance officials. The very significant role of Quebec in this regard hardly requires further comment. Depending heavily on that province for its support, and being deeply committed to keeping Quebec within Confederation, the Pearson government was quick to respond to the demands of the Quebec provincial government, especially on issues it could claim were within provincial jurisdiction. It thus readily acceded to Quebec's demand to opt out.

Against the provincial resource of jurisdiction, the federal government held the power of the purse. Federal fiscal capacity, based on its unlimited powers of taxation and its domination of joint tax fields, was an important resource in dealing with what were, in most cases, impecunious provinces. The federal Cabinet had the last word on which new services or programs it would help to finance, though provincial demands were rather restrained and it hardly had to exercise this ultimate power.

As far as provincial size and wealth are concerned, in this connection, two points of view have been expressed. Is it the larger, wealthier provinces or the smaller, poorer ones that carry more weight in federal–provincial negotiations? Simeon suggests that the latter is often the case; that "wealth in some circumstances may be a positive disadvantage in . . . negotiations."

> One of the strongest arguments the provinces can make in financial discussions is their great need for funds. For the Maritimes the need is obvious, and . . . Ottawa is strongly committed to help alleviate the need.[14]

As far as CAP is concerned, however, it was the other point of view that held sway. Repeated pleas from the Atlantic provinces, supported by federal welfare officials, for a differential sharing formula based on provincial need were over-ridden by an intransigent federal Finance Department supported by some of the larger provinces.

A third political resource is information, skill, or expertise. It has now been widely accepted in Canada that one of the reasons for federal dominance in the 1945–1960 period was the skill of the Ottawa bureaucracy (and to some extent, politicians) compared to that of the provinces. By the early 1960s the average provincial civil service was of increasing competence and in the welfare field almost every province had at least a deputy minister and a few officials with considerable training and experience. At the same time, the federal officials immediately involved were, despite impressive credentials, operating somewhat outside their area of expertise. None was familiar with the nuts and bolts of an operating welfare program. In this situation, with experience heavily on the provincial side, it is not surprising that a large number of original federal ideas were modified in the process of consulting the provinces as to their practicality.

It is sometimes suggested that solidarity is another political resource of some importance. In the case of the Canada Assistance Plan, however, beyond the original consensus on the part of all those involved to go ahead with the measure, this factor was of little account. There were divisions both within the federal side and among the provinces on the questions of the conditions to be required of the provinces and of the sharing formula. The eventual unanimity of the provinces on the child welfare matter, however, did provoke federal acquiescence, even though the expenditure of additional federal funds was involved.

On the question of strategies and tactics, Simeon suggests that these are used covertly, that participants in federal–provincial negotiations claim to engage in "discussion" rather than "bargaining."[15] Few if any of those involved in the development of CAP regarded it as a bargaining process, but certain strategies and tactics can be detected, at least at the provincial level.

First of all, there was the provincial alliance. This strategy was used on two occasions in particular. One was the widespread interaction of Atlantic welfare ministers and deputy ministers out of which came the united front against the 50–50 sharing formula. On the child welfare issue, British Columbia tried to develop a common provincial point of view before going into the January 1966 Ministers' Conference. Otherwise, provinces were content to put forward their views on an individual basis to federal–provincial conferences or in discussions with the federal team of officials.

A second provincial tactic that can be identified is therefore simple preparedness, having information at hand, or at least giving the appearance of being prepared. Quebec's formal written briefs at federal–provincial conferences, for example, were first admired and then imitated by certain other provinces which had previously made only an informal, verbal presentation.

This is closely related to a third provincial tactic used with great effect in this development: taking a parochial point of view. More accurately, it was to ensure that the other side was fully aware of the province's local policies, practices, and concerns. It was precisely this knowledge of local problems and procedures that the cross-country tours of federal officials were designed to achieve. Given their flexible attitude in most cases, the more local peculiarities they were informed of, the more general and encompassing the final proposal became.

A final strategy involved in the federal–provincial aspects of the measure was the threat. Though it could not be used as effectively in this situation as in the three cases Simeon deals with, Quebec could and did threaten to have no part of the plan unless an opting out provision was included and federal conditions were left virtually impotent.

Alliances, preparedness, parochialism, and threats can therefore be identified as provincial strategies and tactics used in the development of the plan. While the first and third of these are somewhat at odds with Simeon, it must always be recalled within what a restricted scope they were used.

Once the act was passed and federal–provincial agreements signed, there were minor modifications in this pattern of resources and strategies. The act, regulations, and agreements were themselves resources on the part of the federal government since the provinces were now committed to meeting the federal conditions established. The power to contribute or withhold funds continued to be a significant federal political resource and this was now complemented by the vast amount of expertise amassed at the federal level in the process of formulating and implementing the plan.

The provinces' chief resource remained their legal authority in the welfare field. In spite of the agreements they had signed, they could continue to complain, where it suited their purposes to do so, of federal interference in an area of provincial jurisdiction. As at the federal level, most provinces were also continually increasing their stock of bureaucratic skill.

In respect to strategies and tactics in the implementation process, these were for the most part very civilized and unspectacular. Both federal and provincial officials made use of persuasion as they engaged in courteous negotiation. On rare occasions the federal minister threatened to cut off contributions, but no one took such threats very seriously.

CONCLUSION

While it was not without elements of conflict and bargaining in several minor respects, the development of the Canada Assistance Plan was undoubtedly the most harmonious major product of federal–provincial relations in the 1960s. CAP stands in sharp contrast in this respect to the other significant federal–provincial initiatives of the period: the Canada Pension Plan, medicare, financial relations, constitutional review, and vocational training. Three main reasons for this contrast can be advanced.

The first relates to the dominant place that the norms of program administrators occupied in its development. Federal and provincial deputy ministers of welfare essentially determined the scope of the measure in the first instance and they and their leading officials went on to play the major role in formulating its details. A measure of this magnitude naturally requires a large degree of political input as well, but this is a case in which ministers of welfare and cabinets in general were usually willing to go along with the recommendations of their advisors.

A second reason for the harmonious nature of CAP's development is that the initiative came largely from the provinces, rather than from the federal government. While the federal level almost simultaneously arrived at the same realization of its need, there was no "grand design" unilaterally created in Ottawa. Instead, the federal government was prepared to provide what the provinces demanded in the wake of the Canada Pension Plan and even anxious to take action along these lines as part of the "War on Poverty."

The attitude of federal officials toward the provinces is the third major distinguishing feature of the Canada Assistance Plan's development. Partly because of friendship ties, partly because of previous provincial experience, and partly because of provincial objections (Quebec's in particular) to the old-style shared-cost programs, federal officials dealt with their provincial counterparts in a most conciliatory way. While welfare officials wished to impose certain standards on the provinces, they were also anxious to develop a flexible, workable program. Finance and Privy Council officials were even more conciliatory and insisted on keeping federal conditions to a minimum.

These three factors were embodied in the doctrine of co-operative federalism as espoused by the Liberal Party of the period. The Canada Assistance Plan therefore stands as a product of the co-operative federalism process as it was officially enunciated. The surprise is perhaps not so much that it reflected such genuine co-operation as that so few other major federal–provincial programs developed in the 1960s were consistent with stated political objectives.

NOTES

1. See, for example, "The Liberal Program (1962)" reproduced in *Canadian Party Platforms 1867–1968*, comp. D.O. Carrigan (Toronto, 1968), 262; Jean-Luc Pepin, "Cooperative Federalism," *Canadian Forum* (Dec. 1964); and D.V. Smiley, "Public Administration and Canadian Federalism," *Canadian Public Administration* 7, 3 (Sept. 1964).

2. The analytical model as well as much documentation is provided by Richard Simeon, *Federal–Provincial Diplomacy* (Toronto, 1971). J. Stefan Dupré, et al., have furnished a case study teeming with conflict in their study of adult occupational training, *Federalism and Policy Development* (Toronto, 1973).

3. Among his voluminous work on the subject, see in particular, D.V. Smiley, "Public Administration and Canadian Federalism" and *Constitutional Adaptation and Canadian Federalism Since 1945* (Ottawa, 1970).

4. Parts of this article are extracted from my PhD thesis, "Poverty and Policy-making in the 1960s: The Canada Assistance Plan" (Queen's University, 1973). The material on which it is based includes interviews with a large number of federal and provincial policy makers and most of the confidential documentation involved, courtesy of certain broad-minded public servants.

5. The early, sporadic provincial demands addressed to the Diefenbaker government were not given much response. The more forceful demands made upon the Pearson government led to federal action for reasons noted below.

6. *Meeting of the Federal–Provincial Working Group on Welfare Programs*, Ottawa, 14 and 15 Feb. 1964.

7. Smiley, "Public Administration and Canadian Federalism," 378.

8. An expression used frequently by the deputy ministers at their meeting.

9. Dyck, "Poverty and Policy-making in the 1960s."

10. Position Statements of the Minister of National Health and Welfare on the Agenda Items of the Conference of Ministers of Welfare, 8 and 9 April 1965.

11. Expression used in interviews with provincial welfare officials.

12. Interviews with federal welfare officials.

13. Except by a few provinces that, while anxious for additional funds, were reluctant to press for them in the fear that this would jeopardize some of the gains already made.

14. Simeon, *Federal–Provincial Diplomacy*, 219.

15. Ibid., 229.

5

CONTEMPORARY TRENDS

I n recent years, Canada's social safety net has had to contend with mounting demands and tighter budgets. On the one hand, governments have been compelled to create programs to deal with new problems such as rising teenage pregnancy rates or the ravages of the AIDS epidemic. Hampering the expansion of state-sponsored assistance has been a national debt growing at a near-exponential rate that, if not reversed, will, according to countless economists, bring economic disaster. From some provincial governments have come accusations about a general trend developing in Ottawa that will soon undermine the ability of shared-cost programs to cope with social problems. Such complaints often ring hollow, because many provinces have also recently instituted austerity measures. Nevertheless, intergovernmental disputes over funding continue to occur in areas such as medicare where, despite Ottawa's ban against extra billing, federal monetary support sank to levels that forced several provinces to consider user fees or the coverage of fewer services. To what extent voters will permit the cost-cutting pattern to persist, and possibly to undermine a social welfare system that, since World War II, many have come to regard as a birthright, remains unclear. Offsetting those who condemn universality as frivolous and speak contemptuously of indolent citizens taking advantage of the dole are those who worry about the return of humiliating means tests and the socio-economic consequences of cutting assistance.

Bruce Smardon's article suggests that there are powerful countervailing forces to the extensive application of neo-conservative ideology in Canada. Federal politicians have come to realize that welfare, because of its role in alleviating regional imbalances, has become one of the principal means by which they can prove their worth to poorer parts of the country. Supposedly, because Washington and London are not saddled with the responsibility of redistributing national wealth in such a manner, Presidents Reagan and Bush as well as Prime Minister Thatcher enjoyed greater leeway than Prime Minister Brian Mulroney to slash social service expenditures. Indeed, Mulroney toned down a number of cost-cutting proposals to avoid a concentrated and electorally significant backlash.

Nonetheless, during the 1980s, the central government clawed back old age pensions from well-off recipients, extended the qualifying period one had to work before receiving unemployment insurance, and, as Andrew Johnson's article notes, ended universality in family allowances. Perhaps the so-called collectivist nature of Canadian society or Ottawa's role in equalizing wealth between regions will act to minimize attacks upon social services. Still, it appears that heated debates and tough choices lie ahead. This is clear from changes in government policy toward Canada's Aboriginal people. John MacDonald's article reveals a strong desire on the part of Ottawa and the provinces to devolve responsibility for social welfare measure, such as childcare, back to Native communities which, with good reason, believe themselves capable of doing a better job than the government.

Still, in most circumstances involving social welfare, large-scale government assistance, whether administered by the federal, provincial, or municipal level, will no doubt be sought as the most appropriate option. While many focus upon Canada's homeless, hungry, jobless, and poverty stricken and claim that government programs are inadequate, others emphasize that state-sponsored aid has spiralled out of control and may well, if not constrained, soon bankrupt the country. Ideally, over the coming years, in the process of breaching the gap that supposedly exists between what people need as opposed to what they want, Canadians will not permit too many of their fellow citizens to fall between the cracks and will ensure that any cutbacks (or constitutional changes) not imperil national unity by reducing Ottawa's role in the social welfare field to that of a bit player.

THE FEDERAL WELFARE STATE AND THE POLITICS OF RETRENCHMENT IN CANADA [*]

BRUCE SMARDON

○

INTRODUCTION

In recent comparative theories, the Canadian welfare state is seen as an example of a "liberal-residualist" type of regime.[1] It is argued that Canadian social programs share with their Anglo-American counterparts a common situation in which "means-tested assistance, modest universal transfers, or modest social insurance plans predominate. These cater mainly to a clientele of low income, usually working class, state dependents."[2] As a result, it is claimed that the Canadian welfare state also shares with its Anglo-American counterparts a common weakness in terms of its political support and a common susceptibility to welfare state cutbacks in the current period. The residual and limited nature of Canadian social programs means that, in contrast to social democratic welfare state regimes, they are not supported to the same extent by a wide cross-section of the population, particularly the middle class, and thus are prone to welfare state "back-lash."[3]

This "liberal-residualist" characterization of the Canadian welfare state misses, however, some crucially important redistributive and solidaristic dimensions of its operations at the federal level which greatly increase the basis of support for federal social programs. While it is true that Canadian social programs have been shaped by a "liberal-residualist" logic which has been concerned to minimize the extent to which social benefits interfere with market operations (for example, the concern with less eligibility in the development of unemployment insurance), it is also true that there has

[*] *Journal of Canadian Studies* 26, 2 (Summer 1991): 122–41. Reprinted with the permission of the journal.

been a competing and contradictory logic in the design and implementation of the Canadian welfare state.[4] Canadian social programs are also greatly concerned with forms of redistribution and inter-regional solidarity that are not consistent with the market-based approach of the "liberal-residualist" model.

The various dimensions of this redistribution process include the following: (1) the provision of flat-rate, non-contributory pensions and family benefits so that these benefits are available regardless of the region of the country in which one lives; (2) the provision of federal funding through equalization payments and through transfer payments for medicare, social assistance, and postsecondary education, so that regionally equivalent welfare state programs can be provided by the provinces; and (3) the development of regionally concentrated social benefits, particularly in the unemployment insurance program, which compensate for regional inequalities of employment and income.

These dimensions of the federal welfare state are explicitly based on using the federal state apparatus as a means either of redistributing wealth from the richer to the poorer areas of the country or of compensating particular areas of the country for their higher unemployment rates. In this manner, the federal welfare state has been developed as a means of working against the inequalities that derive from the lower level of market-based production and income in certain provinces and regions. Various commitments have thus been established at the heart of the federal welfare state which are not consistent with the market-based logic of neo-conservatism.

This resistance occurs in several ways. First, federal social programs, and the redistributive processes of which they are a part, represent one of the few sets of federal policies that continue to receive a high level of popular support in *both* Central Canada and the peripheral regions. As has been pointed out by several observers, the welfare state and its associated redistributive commitments represent a crucial source of national legitimacy for the federal state.[5] In contrast to other initiatives undertaken by the federal government, such as the National Energy Program of Pierre Trudeau, federal welfare state programs have provided an effective and enduring means of generating national political support both for federal political parties and for the central institutions of government.

Secondly, the federal welfare state has developed as a means of supporting and sustaining the constitutional division of responsibilities between the federal government and the provinces. In particular, federal transfer payments to the provinces for social programs have grown spectacularly over the last thirty years and represent a major means by which the gap between provincial constitutional responsibilities and provincial revenue sources has been reduced.

Thirdly, the federal welfare state, especially in the case of unemployment insurance, has developed as a form of compensation for the inequalities of Confederation. In the Atlantic region, federal social benefits are seen as a crucial means of sustaining the economic existence of various communities which, it is felt, continue to be largely excluded from the benefits of federal policies that primarily assist Central Canada. In this context, any cutbacks to federal social programs are viewed as an attack on the economic foundation of Atlantic Canada as well as a betrayal of a central commitment of the Confederation arrangement.

Finally, in part for the reasons stated above, none of the three major parties has decisively broken with the consensus on the federal welfare state that developed during the Second World War. There have been substantial cumulative cutbacks to certain programs, such as Unemployment Insurance and Family Allowances, but there has been no attempt by a party, such as the Tories, to articulate systematically a neo-conservative critique of federal social programs. The absence of this critique has reinforced the high level of popularity across the country for federal social benefits and removed the main source of opposition to the welfare state at the federal level.

For all of these reasons, the class-based political agenda of the new right has not been applied to federal social programs in either a consistent or wide-ranging fashion. As Allan Moscovitch points out:

> The role of social welfare in Canadian public ideology has been and remains less disturbed by currents of counter reform than in either the U.S. or Britain, where we find the more extreme examples of the attempt by the new right to assert its ideology of nineteenth-century individualism, markets, and law and order. Consequently, while institutions of social welfare have, to varying degrees, been eroded, there are few examples of attempts at the wholesale dismantling of social programmes.[6]

The differences between Canada on the one hand and Britain and the United States on the other are particularly apparent at the central government level. In both America and Britain there has been a much more concerted effort by central governments to reduce the size and importance of welfare state programs.

In the United States during the period 1980–1984 the Reagan government reduced in real terms, and in some cases nominal terms, the amount of expenditure on income security, education, training, employment, and social services, as well as on community and regional development.[7] Entire programs, such as the job-training schemes under the Comprehensive Employment and Training Act, were eliminated. The result was a major erosion of the "Great Society" programs established in the 1960s.

The Thatcher government also mounted a sustained assault on the British welfare state through administrative changes, privatization, and spending cuts. The assault was particularly pronounced in the third term of the Thatcher government. In 1988 a series of market-oriented changes were made to various aspects of the British welfare state in the areas of housing, education, and health care.[8] In addition, the Supplementary Benefits system was converted into a Social Fund with strict limitations on the amount that can be paid to any given individual; the aid is now composed primarily of loans rather than grants.[9]

Childcare spending was also reduced through various funding limitations imposed on the local governments. This change was particularly severe in that the unemployment insurance regulations were also changed so that a woman can be denied benefits if she cannot show that she has sufficient childcare arrangements.[10] This was in addition to the new stipulation that a person could be disqualified from receiving UI benefits for up to twenty-six weeks for voluntarily leaving a job.[11] The Thatcher government also continued its campaign to privatize elements of the National Health Service.

The differences between Canada and Britain concerning welfare state programs were starkly illustrated by the 1988 Tory budget in Britain and the 1989 Tory budget in Canada. While the Tories in Britain *cut* taxes by greatly reducing the progressivity of the income tax system and refused to use a hefty budgetary surplus to provide a much-needed boost in the level of funding for social programs, the Tories in Canada continued to run a large budgetary deficit and *raised* taxes in order to continue to fund federal social expenditures.[12]

In general, the Canadian federal welfare state has not been subjected to the same permanent changes as in the U.S. and Britain. Certain areas of the federal welfare state have been cut back and transfer payments to the provinces have been eroded. But there has not been the same attempt to cut social spending through the privatization of major social programs or the implementation of wholesale market-oriented changes to existing programs.

The more muted approach to reducing social expenditures in Canada is particularly striking, given their importance as the largest component of overall spending (in 1988 the Social Envelope, primarily composed of social programs, accounted for 45 percent of total spending)[13] and the concern on the part of the Mulroney Conservatives with deficit reduction. It is also striking given the willingness of the Tories to pursue a neo-conservative agenda in other areas, such as the privatization of crown corporations, the development of free trade with the United States, the restriction of collective bargaining in the public sector, and the reduction of subsidies of rail transportation and for women's programs. Even with rising expenditures on the public debt, the federal government has not been willing to undertake the kinds of dramatic welfare state changes that have been implemented in the United States and Britain.

Because of the tendency to treat the Canadian welfare state in the same terms as its Anglo-American counterparts, this aspect of Canadian welfare state politics has not received the attention that it deserves. There has been no adequate explanation provided for the relatively low and more inconsistent attack on the federal welfare state in Canada. As a result, a major contradictory feature of the current politics of retrenchment has not been adequately addressed.

This paper is an attempt to examine the reasons for the lower level of attack on the welfare state at the federal level in Canada. It does not deal with the various attempts on the part of the provinces to cut back on their social programs. There is not sufficient space available here to consider adequately the diverse situations both at the federal level and in the different provinces. The paper thus discusses the provincial situation with respect to the welfare state only insofar as it pertains to the federal welfare state and the attempt by the federal government to diminish and control social expenditures.

THE WELFARE STATE AND POLITICAL LEGITIMACY

The development of the federal welfare state cannot be understood in isolation from the overall patterns of Canadian politics that have developed from the time of Confederation. A central aspect of those patterns has been the extreme importance placed upon economic initiatives as the foundation for both the role and significance of the federal government in national political life and the connection of the peripheral regions to the federal government.[14]

Economic ties have been crucial in the development of political legitimacy for the Canadian federal state. The pattern can be seen in a succession of federal government policies that have been concerned with the development of legitimacy through the construction of economic linkages: the initial "Macdonald–Laurier national policy"; the "surrogates" for a national policy represented by Keynesian economic measures, various welfare state initiatives and regional economic incentive programs; and, finally, the abortive attempt on the part of the Trudeau Liberals to construct a new national policy on the basis of the National Energy Program.[15]

However, these economic ties have not been equally successful in terms of their legitimizing impact. In contrast to the regional divisions created by federal economic management measures, such as the National Policy tariffs or the National Energy Program, the federal welfare state has increased the level of inter-regional support for federal institutions.[16]

The legitimizing impact of the federal welfare state can be seen from its inception during the Second World War. The ruling Liberal Party was able to rebuild both the level of its national support and its extra-parliamentary organization by means of a reform strategy that was heavily oriented toward new welfare state initiatives.[17] By moving toward welfare state reforms, the Liberal Party was able to out-manoeuvre both of the other major parties at the federal level, particularly the socialist CCF party which had risen to unprecedented heights of popularity during the war years.[18]

There were several additional reasons for the appealing character of new social programs at the federal level. First, the benefits of new programs were spread across the country and were not regionally concentrated as in the case of Keynesian stimulative measures—which mainly benefited the industrialized area of Central Canada.[19] Social programs also provided directly tangible benefits that were more appealing than the remote and less easily understood benefits of Keynesian counter-cyclical policies.

Secondly, federal government initiatives in the area of social programs provided important forms of financial assistance to all of the provinces— particularly the Prairie provinces. As was pointed out by the influential and widely respected Rowell-Sirois Commission, all of the provinces experienced great difficulty in financing their welfare state responsibilities during the Depression of the 1930s; several western provinces were in fact driven to the brink of bankruptcy because of unsustainable unemployment relief payments.[20] The development of federal unemployment insurance in 1940 and the various welfare state initiatives of the federal government during the period of the Second World War thus represented an important means of avoiding a serious source of financial instability on the part of provincial governments in future recessions or depressions.

Thirdly, federal social programs provided an important form of compensation for the perceived inequalities of the Confederation arrangement. The limited financial resources of the Maritime and Western regions were seen as a direct outgrowth of the development policies pursued by the federal government in which the Northwest Territories were developed as a hinterland market for central Canadian industrial/commercial capital, and by which the Maritime provinces were largely excluded from the economic benefits of central government policies.[21] As such, federally funded social programs financed disproportionately by taxes raised in Central Canada and federal subsidies to the provinces designed to provide an equal level of social services to the populations within their boundaries represented an important form of compensation for the regional inequalities that had been created in Canada. As the Rowell-Sirois Commission stated,

> There is a second aspect of the distribution of the national income which is of great importance in a federal system, and of particular importance in Canada. The unequal distribution of the national income as between the people of different regions may excite feelings quite as dangerous to national unity as those aroused between different income groups. The provision of a national minimum standard of social services in Canada cannot (without complete centralization of all social services) be divorced from the assurance to every government of Canada of the revenues necessary for the adequate performance of its recognized functions.[22]

The redistributive proposals contained in the Rowell-Sirois Report provided the basis for an entirely new role for the federal state in which federal spending and taxation powers could be used as a means of reducing regional tensions and ensuring common standards of social services across the country. In a political context that was highly divided along regional and linguistic lines, the legitimizing and unifying characteristics of this new role were highly attractive to the federal government and there was prompt action in response to the Rowell-Sirois recommendations.[23]

In 1941 the federal government "raised its own taxes to a level which forced the provinces out of the fields of personal and corporate income tax and succession duties. In return, they received annual payments set at levels suggested by the Rowell-Sirois report."[24] The government also convened the 1945 Conference on Reconstruction. At that conference, it proposed to provide increased assistance for various welfare state programs in exchange for complete jurisdiction over the fields of personal and corporate taxes. The provinces were not willing to accept federal assistance on that basis and the federal proposals in the areas of health insurance and income security were withdrawn.[25] However, the extent to which the federal government had embraced the new redistributive role suggested by Rowell-Sirois was clearly in evidence.

REGIONAL CHARACTERISTICS OF WELFARE STATE PROGRAMS

Federal government use of social programs as a means of dealing with regional disparities and of promoting national unity has not declined since the Second World War. In fact, these uses have become more entrenched in the federal welfare state.

This point is readily apparent when one looks at the development of unemployment insurance in Canada. Over time, the program has become increasingly defined as a regional support mechanism. The unemployment insurance fund was extended in 1950 to cover seasonal workers and in 1955 to cover "self-employed fishermen."[26] These extensions were intended to assist certain categories of workers in regions of high unemployment—particularly in the Atlantic region—systematically excluded from the unemployment insurance program. Unemployment insurance became a means of supplementing the incomes of persons living in areas where it was difficult to find full-time, year-round forms of employment. While understandable in terms of the regional distribution of unemployment, these extensions were striking given the concern, in the development of Canadian unemployment insurance, with maintaining actuarial purity and with providing support only to full-time, permanent workers who were cyclically unemployed.[27]

The use of unemployment insurance for this purpose was extended and more clearly articulated in terms of regional inequities in the 1971 reforms. Persons living in regions with higher unemployment could receive benefits for longer periods of time. The length of the regionally extended benefit was tied to the number of percentage points by which the regional unemployment rate exceeded the national rate.[28] With these changes, the unemployment insurance program was firmly established as a mechanism for compensating different regions according to the extent to which they experienced higher than average unemployment rates.

The series of cutbacks to unemployment insurance that have occurred since the latter part of the 1970s have only reinforced this aspect of the program. As is pointed out by Leslie Pal, unemployment insurance restrictions in the latter part of the 1970s and the beginning of the 1980s were explicitly structured so that regions with the highest unemployment rates, such as the Atlantic region, would not experience the full impact of the cutbacks.[29] For example, in 1977 the eight-week minimum period to qualify for benefits was replaced with a "Variable Entrance Requirement" of from ten to fourteen weeks, depending on the regional unemployment rate. Because of the higher unemployment rates in the Atlantic provinces, workers in that area experienced an increase of only two weeks in their qualifying period as compared with the six-week increase experienced by workers in areas of Central Canada.

This pattern of reducing the extent of cutbacks by region was greatly reinforced by the unemployment insurance restrictions that were announced in April 1989. Even though the 1986 Forget Report explicitly criticized regionally based uses of the Unemployment Insurance fund, the Mulroney government decided to entrench further this aspect of its operations.[30]

As can be seen from Table 1, the regional differences in terms of both the benefit period and the qualifying period were dramatically increased. When the reforms were announced, unemployment in the Toronto area was less than 6 percent. The maximum benefit period would have been thirty-five weeks and the minimum qualifying period would have been twenty weeks. In St John's unemployment was over 16 percent. The maximum benefit period would have been fifty weeks and the minimum qualifying period would have been ten weeks. In effect, workers in the St John's area would have experienced little change in the availability of unemployment insurance, while workers in the Toronto area would have been faced with serious restrictions in terms of both the benefit period and the qualifying period.

As a result of the current recession, regional differences have been reduced somewhat but they are still substantial. At 10 percent unemployment, Toronto workers still must have sixteen weeks of employment before they can qualify for unemployment insurance benefits and with only that level of employment can receive UI for a maximum of twenty-seven weeks. In St John's, a worker with sixteen weeks employment can collect for forty-five weeks. These differences will only widen as the Ontario economy recovers from its most serious recession in the postwar period.

In 1984 the ratio of UI benefits to contributions in the Atlantic provinces was the highest in the country—ranging from 3.38 in Newfoundland to 1.40 in Nova Scotia. This contrasted with a ratio of 0.67 in Ontario.[31] The effect of the recent changes has been to reinforce this aspect of the UI program, which has moved even further away from its original purpose to provide insurance for cyclically unemployed workers. From a neo-conservative "free-market" standpoint, this pattern is the exact opposite of what is desirable. UI benefits are collected most easily in the areas of the country with the lowest labour demand, thereby reducing the movement of workers to areas of higher labour demand.

This pattern of development is only part of a more general trend that has seen a greater and greater concentration of benefits in the Atlantic region. In Newfoundland and Prince Edward Island, to take the two most extreme examples, the federal welfare state is accounting for a higher proportion of personal income than ever before. In those areas, federal transfers in the form of unemployment insurance, old age security, family allowances, etc., accounted for 22.9 and 22.3 percent respectively of total and net domestic income at factor cost in 1986.[32] This represented a substantial increase over the 1961 levels of 17 and 12.7 percent respectively.[33]

As a result of the heavy concentration of federal transfer payments in Atlantic Canada, the federal welfare state has become an integral part of the seasonally based, part-time nature of the Atlantic regional economy and is regarded as a central support mechanism, a "second wage," for persons living in that area.[34] In combination with the large proportion of provincial government revenues in the Atlantic provinces in the form of federal transfer payments (between 39 and 48 percent of total government revenues in the four provinces in 1986),[35] the importance of federal social benefits as a crucial means of underpinning the Atlantic society and economy is greatly magnified.

TABLE 1   AMENDMENT TO UI BENEFIT SCHEDULE

Number of weeks claimant can receive benefits
• Unemployment rate in claimant's region •

	6% and under	over 6% to 7%	over 7% to 8%	over 8% to 9%	over 9% to 10%	over 10% to 11%	over 11% to 12%	over 12% to 13%	over 13% to 14%	over 14% to 15%	over 15% to 16%	over 16%
10											37	39
11										36	38	40
12									35	37	39	41
13								34	36	38	40	42
14							33	35	37	39	41	43
15						30	34	36	38	40	42	44
16					27	31	35	37	39	41	43	45
17				24	28	32	36	38	40	42	44	46
18			21	25	29	33	37	39	41	43	45	47
19		19	22	26	30	34	38	40	42	44	46	48
20	17	20	23	27	31	35	39	41	43	45	47	49
21	18	21	24	28	32	36	40	42	44	46	48	50
22	19	22	25	29	33	37	41	43	45	47	49	
23	20	23	26	30	34	38	42	44	46	48	50	
24	21	24	27	31	35	39	43	45	47	49		
25	22	25	28	32	36	40	44	46	48	50		
26	22	25	28	32	36	40	44	46	48			
27	23	26	29	33	37	41	45	47	49			
28	23	26	29	33	37	41	45	47	49			
29	24	27	30	34	38	42	46	48	50			
30	24	27	30	34	38	42	46	48				
31	25	28	31	35	39	43	47	49				
32	25	28	31	35	39	43	47	49				
33	26	29	32	36	40	44	48	50				
34	26	29	32	36	40	44	48					
35	27	30	33	37	41	45	49					
36	27	30	33	37	41	45	49					
37	28	31	34	38	42	46	50					
38	28	31	34	38	42	46						
39	29	32	35	39	43	47						
40	29	32	35	39	43	47						
41	30	33	36	40	44	48						
42	30	33	36	40	44	48						
43	31	34	37	41	45	49						
44	31	34	37	41	45	49						
45	32	35	38	42	46	50						
46	32	35	38	42	46							
47	33	36	39	43	47							
48	33	36	39	43	47							
49	34	37	40	44	48							
50	34	37	40	44	48							
51	35	38	41	45	49							
52	35	38	41	45	49	50	50	50	50	50	50	50

Source: Employment and Immigration Canada, "Success in the Works" (Ottawa, 1989), April, 1989, 17.

The entrenched status of this dimension of the federal welfare state has been reflected not only in the structuring of cutbacks to unemployment insurance, but also in the greater support provided to the Atlantic provinces in the Tories' proposed Canada Child Care Act of 1988. In that proposal the Atlantic provinces received various additional amounts of federal funding to assist with capital expenditures on childcare so that they could catch up with the wealthier provinces.[36] Similarly, in the 1990 federal budget the Atlantic provinces, along with other provinces receiving equalization payments, were exempted from the 5 percent limitation on growth in Canada Assistance Plan spending.[37]

The federal welfare state thus continues to be heavily influenced by a redistributive logic that provides an important means through which the Atlantic region is bound to the central government—a logic that was entrenched in the Constitution Act of 1982.[38] Article 36 of the Constitution now explicitly commits the federal government to equalization payments and to the provision, along with the provinces, of "essential public services of reasonable quality to all Canadians."[39]

All of this greatly increases the contradictions that are involved in a systematic, across-the-board attack on the federal welfare state. Any such attack would be viewed as an unconstitutional violation of a central commitment of the Confederation arrangement as well an abandonment of the "have-not" region of Atlantic Canada. Major cutbacks to social programs, while leaving intact the chronically depressed levels of economic activity in that area, would compound an already unacceptable situation in which, from the point of view of the people living in the Maritimes, there has been systematic discrimination against their regional economy to the benefit of the industrial heartland in Central Canada.[40]

STABILIZATION OF FEDERAL-PROVINCIAL FINANCES

The same process of further entrenchment can be seen in the case of federal transfer payments to the provinces for social programs. As was pointed out above, a significant element of welfare state development at the federal level during the Second World War was its contribution to the reallocation of federal–provincial revenues so that they were more in line with the constitutional responsibilities of the two levels of government. This aspect of the federal welfare state has grown with the passage of time. Table 2 reveals that federal transfers to the provinces for various purposes grew from a level of $1.095 billion in 1961 to $21.240 billion in 1985. The major areas of expansion were in health care, postsecondary education, the Canada Assistance Plan, and Tax Agreements—accounting for 90 percent of the increase in transfer payments.

The rate of growth was particularly rapid in the first half of the 1980s. Health care transfer payments increased by 63.1 percent in the period 1981–1985. While far lower in percentage terms than the tremendous increase between 1971 and 1981, in absolute terms the growth in this four-year period almost equals that achieved over the entire previous ten-year period. Transfer payments for postsecondary education and for the Canada Assistance plan also increased substantially—by 53.6 and 72.3 percent respectively.

In the latter part of the 1980s, the Tories reacted by gradually reducing the rate of growth of transfer payments to the provinces.[41] And, as of the 1990 and 1991 budgets, transfer payments for health care and postsecondary education have been frozen for a period of five years while increases in Canada Assistance Plan spending have been capped at 5 percent for the three richest provinces. It is clear that these changes represent serious cumulative reductions in the level of transfer payments, but the reduction is rather like closing the barn door after the animals have left.[42] The increases in per capita transfers built up over the period 1961–1985, especially in the early 1980s, remain in place and have not been reversed by the Tories' decision to freeze expenditures or to limit increases in CAP spending for the three richest provinces. In addition, the Tories have not permanently altered the structure of spending on transfer payments but have limited the changes to a period of five years.

The decision to temporarily freeze rather than permanently reduce nominal per capita transfer payments and to restrict the rate of growth in CAP spending for only three provinces reflects a recognition on the part of the Mulroney government that there are limits to what can be done in this area. The rapid increase in transfer payments up to 1985 established them as a key means of reducing the imbalance between provincial constitutional responsibilities and provincial revenue sources. Any attempt to cut back substantially on existing levels of nominal per capita transfers would lead to massive federal–provincial conflict over the funding of existing welfare state programs, and a return to the wrangling that characterized the Depression years over how the welfare state should be financed. This conflict would place further stress on Canadian national unity and would be particularly harmful to the Mulroney government in the wake of the failure of the Meech Lake accord.

While Canadian federalism has placed major obstacles in the path of certain welfare state improvements, such as the proposals arising out of the

TABLE 2   TRANSFER PAYMENTS TO THE PROVINCES BY MAJOR AREA OF EXPENDITURE, 1961–1985

| | Billions of dollars | | | |
	1961	1971	1981	1985
Canada Assistance Plan	0	.466	2.223	3.831
Postsecondary education	0	.463	1.652	2.538
Health sector	.317	1.421	4.250	6.933
Tax agreements	.510	1.089	4.154	5.709
Total transfer payments	1.095	4.230	13.770	21.240

Source: Canada, Statistics Canada, *Provincial Economic Accounts, Historical Issue, 1961–1986*, cat. 13-213S, June 1988, table 15, 376–79.

Social Security Review in the 1970s and the proposed pension plan improvements in the early 1980s, it is clear that the structure of Canadian federalism remains as a major bulwark against large-scale cutbacks to federal spending on existing programs.[43] Even when provincial governments are interested in cutting back on social expenditures, they still vehemently oppose federal reductions in spending. Particularly with the advent of block funding for the federal share of social programs, there is every incentive on the part of provincial governments to maintain federal transfer payments at as high a level as possible. By so doing they also maintain maximum leeway in their ability to control the level of their own spending and avoid politically unpopular tax increases.[44]

The dependence of provincial governments on transfer payments also means that they do not attempt to mobilize opposition to the federal welfare state. Indeed, by arguing for the maintenance of federal social programs, the provinces also reinforce the overall level of political legitimacy that is attached to them.

INTER-PARTY CONSENSUS

In one very important respect, the inter-party consensus around the welfare state that was established during the Second World War has also continued into the present. None of the three major federal parties is committed to extensive privatization or market-oriented restructuring of social programs.[45] Instead, the focus has been on introducing greater selectivity into existing programs while avoiding across-the-board cutbacks or on implementing temporary changes that do not permanently alter the structure of federal spending.

This pattern was evident in the 1989 and 1990 Tory budgets, which made the greatest reductions in social spending. In the 1989 budget, the universality of old age pensions and Family Allowances was reduced through taxing the benefits back at the rate of 15 percent of individual net income over $50 000.[46] These changes continued a well-established trend in which the relative size of child tax credits, the value of which decline as income rises, has increased at the expense of Family Allowances in the provision of federal family benefits; and the relative size of Old Age Security payments has fallen when compared with the means-tested Guaranteed Income Supplement.[47]

This pattern of changes has avoided any across-the-board cutbacks while implementing substantial cumulative reductions for certain groups. Those pensioners with net incomes over $50 000 do not receive the Guaranteed Income Supplement and will be subject to the clawback of the 1989 budget. They will therefore experience the full cumulative impact of the slower relative growth rate of Old Age Security payments as well as the 1989 budget changes. Similarly, persons in this category will experience the combined impact of the clawback provision as well as the partial de-indexation of Family Allowances that occurred prior to the 1989 budget. However, by focussing the cumulative impact of these changes on a particular group of people, the Tories have avoided a full-scale attack on these universal programs.

In the 1990 and 1991 budgets the Tories followed a strategy of temporary, as opposed to selective, changes. As was discussed above, transfer payments for health care and postsecondary education were frozen and the growth in Canada Assistance Plan expenditures was capped for the three richest provinces. However, in a manner consistent with their overall approach to welfare state cutbacks, the Tories softened the impact of the changes by making them temporary and by leaving untouched the substantial accumulation of transfer payments that preceded the period of restraint.

In this regard, the 1985 Tory budget, which included a proposal to de-index old age pensions, represented a turning point.[48] If the proposal had succeeded, the change would have meant a substantial, permanent erosion in the level of benefits for all recipients of Old Age Security payments. However, the outcry that was created by that proposal and the refusal of the Tory party to back a change of that magnitude led to the restoration of full idexation. The unwillingness of the Tories to continue with the proposed change provided a clear indication of the extent to which they were not prepared to argue for, and stand behind, permanent across-the-board reductions in the level of social benefits for a major universal program.

The Liberal Party has also not articulated or implemented a decisive anti-welfare state agenda. The Liberal Party was responsible for many of the federal social programs that were put into place during the Second World War and the 1960s.[49] This historical connection to the federal welfare state has not been rejected by the Liberal Party even with the onset of fiscal crisis and the need to reduce federal expenditures. While it was the Liberals who initiated the policy of retrenchment in federal state expenditures in the latter part of the 1970s and who implemented a series of cutbacks to unemployment insurance during the same period, those restrictions were not effective in decreasing the overall size of the welfare state. Social expenditures increased by 48.7 percent in constant dollars in the period 1974–1975 to 1982–1983.[50]

The Liberals also promoted forms of expansion or consolidation in several areas of the welfare state. They were a major force behind the Social Security Review in the 1970s and the proposed pension plan reforms in the early 1980s.[51] They also passed the Canada Health Act in 1984. The legislation was approved near the end of the Trudeau period of government despite the strenuous objections of several provincial governments. Banning extra-billing and limiting the scope of user fees in the medicare system, it was clearly intended as a means of eliminating market-based aspects of the health care system in Canada.[52] As such, it was obviously not a piece of legislation that was inspired by neo-conservative principles. While in opposition the Liberal Party has also continued to criticize the Tories for any reductions in federal social programs.

The CCF's successor at the federal level, the NDP, has also maintained a strong attachment to the federal welfare state and indeed regards its development as a central achievement of the party.[53] The NDP views the federal welfare state as a key component of the social democratic legacy in Canada and has no intention of changing its support for the maintenance of Canada's social programs.

The three major parties at the federal level have thus avoided a systematic attack on the federal welfare state. There has been no clear attempt by parties on either the right or the left to provide a definition of politics in which the welfare state is systematically attacked or criticized. In particular, there has been no clear or coherent attempt by the leadership of the Tory party to characterize welfare state programs in terms of the rhetoric of the new right. There has been no counterpart at the federal level to Thatcher's welfare state "scroungers" or Reagan's claim that social programs are directed "towards the greedy, rather than the needy."[54]

POLITICAL POPULARITY

The various forces explained above strongly reinforce the high level of popular support that continues to exist for federal social programs across the country. A review of the regional support for welfare state programs finds that

> A broad consensus on the basic elements of the existing income security system exists in all regions, and the distribution of opinion on the specific questions concerning the scope and generosity of the system does not differ dramatically among regions. Further, the regional differences in attitudes that do exist are not particularly surprising since, with a few exceptions, the greatest approval of existing programs and the strongest support for their expansion are to be found in Quebec and Atlantic Canada, the regions with the greatest income security needs.[55]

The existence of this support signifies the importance of the federal welfare state in terms of its national political legitimacy and of the adverse electoral consequences that would flow from a sweeping attack on federal social expenditures. In a political context dominated by linguistic and regional divisions, welfare state programs represent one of the few forms of appeal to the nation at large that do not contribute to regional or provincial alienation. Indeed, they are supported to the greatest extent in an area of the country, Quebec, which is currently exhibiting the greatest level of alienation from the federal arrangement.

This situation greatly complicates the process of applying the nostrums of the neo-conservative right to the federal welfare state even as it increases the contradictions involved in reducing federal social expenditures. Each time a governing party cuts back on federal social programs, it risks weakening not only its electoral support but also one of the most successful and enduring bases of national political appeal for the federal state apparatus.

WELFARE STATE DEVELOPMENT IN THE U.S. AND BRITAIN

The entrenched position of the welfare state in Canadian politics can be further seen through comparing its situation with that in both the United States and Britain. While it is not possible here to provide a detailed comparison, a brief outline of the major differences can be provided.

A key difference between the Canadian and American welfare states grows out of the fact that there was no coalition of political forces in the United States capable of pushing for a welfare state with more redistributive dimensions in the crucial period after the Second World War. If anything, there was a decline in the support for welfare state development in the post–Second World War period. Andrew Martin points out that

> the components of the New Deal coalition that had given it whatever social democratic thrust it possessed lacked sufficient strength to be combined into a sustainable political basis for full employment and an expanded welfare state after the end of World War II. Instead, Congress came to be dominated by a conservative coalition of Republicans and Southern Democrats, and the management of the war economy was in the hands of business leaders. This shift in the distribution of power continued with the Republican capture of Congress in 1946, and while Truman retained the presidency for the Democrats, this served mainly to retard the drift of domestic policy to the right.[56]

In addition, American politics was not nearly as influenced by the need to "reach out" to alienated regions through welfare state programs. There was no counterpart to the Rowell-Sirois Report and its emphasis on constructing greater national unity through redistributive welfare state reforms. Moreover, as part of a trend that has continued until the present time, the American government was not perceived as the representative of a particular area of the country.[57] Neither was there in the United States a pattern whereby a particular region was clearly favoured over others in the design and implementation of central government economic management policies—as occurred in Canada with the National Policy and its systematic development of Central Canada as an industrial heartland. As a result, there was not the same impetus in the United States to develop welfare state programs as a means of compensating for regional inequalities or for reducing regional alienation.

Thus, while in Canada the federal welfare state and its associated redistributive commitments were used as a means of reconstructing the governing Liberal Party and of generating greater support for central government institutions both during and after the Second World War, there was little further development of the American welfare state during this period. Instead, American social programs remained tied to the more limited purposes of the New Deal reforms of the 1930s,[58] whereby the two contributory programs of Social Security and Unemployment Insurance were intended to provide coverage for the majority of Americans through their own individual contributions. This original intention was strengthened over time by the actions of Social Security administrators who used every opportunity to reinforce the desirability of Social Security, and contributory pensions, as against the demeaning consequences of dependence on public assistance.[59] A strong bifurcation was thus established in the United States between "earned" social insurance and "unearned" public assistance or welfare—a bifurcation that was further reinforced by the focus on poverty of the "Great Society" welfare state reforms in the 1960s.[60]

There was thus little development within the American welfare state of the redistributive arrangements and purposes that play such a major role in the Canadian welfare state. There was no development of a counterpart to the extensive redistributive apparatus that has been established in Canada between the federal government and the provinces to fund social programs such as medicare, postsecondary education and the Canada Assistance Plan. Neither was there the same concern with using social programs as a means of compensating for regional disparities or for redistributing wealth between the richer and poorer areas of the country. Indeed, those purposes went against the grain of the New Deal reforms and of later developments in the American welfare state which were concerned with maintaining as close a connection as possible between welfare state contributions and benefits. This is particularly clear in the case of American unemployment insurance which never developed as a means of compensating specific regions for higher than average unemployment rates, or of supplementing the seasonal incomes of various categories of workers regardless of the level of contributions they made to the plan.[61]

The British welfare state also developed on the basis of principles different from those in Canada. The recommendations of William Beveridge which formed the basis for the British welfare state were heavily oriented toward flat-rate contributions and subsistence-level benefits as the means of ensuring that the link between work and social benefits would not be lost. This approach also minimized the extent to which social benefits redistributed wealth.[62] As a result, the notion that social programs should be systematically used as a means of redistributing wealth between richer and poorer areas of the country, regardless of the welfare state contributions of the people living in the poorer areas, did not play a role in the development of the British welfare state.

In addition, the British welfare state was constructed on the basis of universalist or "one-nation" themes in which it was seen as a common system of protection for all British citizens after the deprivations of the Second World War.[63] It was thus not developed in response to regional divisions or inequalities and was not defined by an attempt to reduce those inequalities through redistributive arrangements. Rather, the focus was on "the British people" as a whole and their protection through a comprehensive system of social programs.

The result of these different patterns of development in both the U.S. and Britain is that when the Reagan and Thatcher governments launched their attacks on the welfare state they were not confronted to the same extent by an opposition that viewed the changes as a divisive and insensitive attack on the "have-not" regions of their countries. Neither were they forced to reduce programs that had grown to include a wide variety of other purposes besides simply the provision of welfare state benefits to a narrowly defined group of recipients. And, most importantly in terms of the strength of opposition to welfare state cutbacks, they were not forced to deal with any counterpart to the powerful provincial governments in Canada and the reliance of those governments on federal transfer payments.

All of these differences were magnified by the fact that there has not been the same reliance in the U.S. and in Britain on the development of economic ties as a singular source of political legitimacy for central government institutions and political parties. This is particularly the case with regard to the welfare state. In both countries there were major forms of political appeal which were quite separate from welfare state programs and which operated as a means of building national support even while welfare state programs were being reduced.

In Britain, the Falklands/Malvinas War and its associated myths of Empire provided a dramatic illustration of the ability of the Thatcher government to deflect attention from its social policies and the sorry state of the British economy, and to build an alternative basis of appeal for both the Conservative Party and the institutions of the British state. In the United States, the status of the American government as the defender of the "free world" and the mythology surrounding the American Constitution provided strong alternative bases of national support for central government institutions and for the Republican Party, even in the face of substantial welfare state cutbacks.

CONCLUSION

Historically, Canadian federal parties have relied on economic initiatives and/or forms of economic benefits as a crucial means of developing support for both themselves and central government institutions. Of these initiatives and forms of economic benefits, the federal welfare state stands out as a set of policies and programs that have a solid basis of inter-regional and inter-provincial support. The social programs developed during the Second World War served as a key source of national political legitimacy for both the federal state and federal parties. Over time, they have become more entrenched because of the continued inter-party consensus around the welfare state, the growth of federal transfer payments as a key source of provincial government revenues, and the further development of federal social benefits as an important form of compensation for regional inequalities of employment and income. In a federal arrangement that does not possess very many national bases of appeal (particularly in the constitutional area as is shown by the serious divisions arising over the failure of the Meech Lake accord), the legitimizing qualities of federal social programs are highly attractive indeed.[64]

A significant neo-conservative assault on the federal welfare state thus means much more than an attack on various social programs which "distort" market incentives. It also involves an attack on a set of redistributive policies and programs that are deeply implicated in the process by which political order and legitimacy are constructed in Canada. The existence of this aspect of the Canadian welfare state greatly complicates any systematic attempt to implement a neo-conservative agenda with respect to federal social programs. The complications surrounding systematic cutbacks point to a wider tension that has always existed in the federal welfare state between the "liberal-residualist" concern to minimize the impact of social programs on market operations, and the use of federal social programs as a key means of establishing national political legitimacy through various forms of inter-regional redistribution.

The contradictory dimensions of the Canadian welfare state also represent a major point of departure from the situation in both the U.S. and Britain. In both countries the welfare state is not as crucially important as a source of national political legitimacy, is not backed by any counterpart to the provincial governments in Canada, and is not as clearly involved in the moderation of regional disparities through regionally concentrated social benefits. As a result, the governments of Thatcher and Reagan displayed a much greater willingness to systematically articulate a neo-conservative vision concerning social programs, and had a freer hand with which to pursue an agenda that included wide-ranging changes to the welfare state through both expenditure reductions and market-oriented restructuring.

While there are no guarantees that a systematic attack on the federal welfare state in Canada will be prevented in the future, particularly in the event of an all-out attempt to reduce the federal deficit, it is clear at the present time that the entrenched status of the welfare state in Canadian politics has greatly reduced the willingness of neo-conservative forces in the country to articulate and implement wide-ranging changes. Because of the tendency to focus on the "liberal-residualist" aspects of federal social programs and thus to treat the Canadian welfare state in the same terms as its Anglo-American counterparts, the very different position of social programs in Canadian politics has not been sufficiently appreciated.

NOTES

1. See Gosta Esping-Andersen, "Power and Distributional Regimes," *Politics and Society* 14, 2 (1985): 232; John Myles, "Introduction—Understanding Canada: Comparative Political Economy Perspectives," *Canadian Review of Sociology and Anthropology* 26, 1 (1989): 3; Gosta Esping-Andersen, "The Three Political Economies of the Welfare State," ibid., 25; and David Wolfe, "The Canadian State in Comparative Perspective," ibid., 113–14.

2. Esping-Andersen, "Political Economies of the Welfare State," 25.

3. Ibid., 31.

4. For a discussion of the pervasive influence of the concept of "less eligibility" in the development of unemployment insurance, see James Struthers, *No Fault of Their Own* (Toronto: University of Toronto Press, 1983).

5. Donald Smiley, *The Canadian Political Nationality* (Toronto: Methuen, 1967); Keith Banting, *The Welfare State and Canadian Federalism* (Montreal: McGill-Queen's University Press, 1987); Garth Stevenson, *Unfulfilled Union* (Toronto: Gage, 1982).

6. Allan Moscovitch, "The Welfare State Since 1975," *Journal of Canadian Studies* 21, 2 (Summer 1986): 78. The more muted neo-conservative response in Canada has also been pointed to by Keith Banting, "The Welfare State and Inequality in the 1980s," *Canadian Review of Sociology and Anthropology* 24, 3 (1987): 319–23.

7. Executive Office of the President, Office of Management and Budget, *Budget of the United States Government,*

Supplement 1988 (Washington, 1987), table 18, 6C-38. For a discussion of the cutbacks implemented during this period, see D. Lee Bawden and John L. Palmer, "Social Policy: Challenging the Welfare State" in *The Reagan Record*, ed. John Palmer and Isabel V. Sawhill (Cambridge, MA: Ballinger Publishing, 1984), and Joel Krieger, "Social Policy in the Age of Reagan and Thatcher" in *Socialist Register 1987*, ed. Ralph Miliband, Leo Panitch, and John Saville (London: Merlin Press, 1987), 188–93.

8. Concerning the attempt on the part of the Thatcher government to undermine the NHS through privatization and underfunding, see Angela Coyle, "Going Private" in *Waged Work: A Reader*, ed. Feminist Review (London: Virago, 1986), and Elim Papadakis and Peter Taylor-Gooby, *The Private Provision of Public Welfare* (Sussex: Wheatsheaf Books, 1987), 40–70. For a general summary of the many changes implemented by the Thatcher government in its second and third terms in office, see Anne Digby, *British Welfare Policy* (London: Faber and Faber, 1989), 100–31; Krieger, "Social Policy in the Age of Reagan and Thatcher," 181–87; and Jill Walker, "Women, the State and the Family in Britain: Thatcher Economics and the Experience of Women" in *Women and Recession*, ed. Jill Rubery (London: Routledge & Kegan Paul, 1988), 218–50.

9. Digby, *British Welfare Policy*, 111.

10. Walker, "Women, the State and the Family," 236.

11. *London Times*, 2 March 1988, 4.

12. For a summary of the tax changes in the 1988 British budget, see United Kingdom, The Treasury, "The Budget in Brief," 15 March 1988. Concerning the tax changes in the Canadian budget, see Canada, Department of Finance, "The Budget Speech," 27 April 1989, 10–11.

13. "Fiscal Facts and Trends" in *How Ottawa Spends 1989–90*, ed. Katherine Graham (Ottawa: Carleton University Press, 1989), 293.

14. Reg Whitaker, "Federalism, Democracy and the Political Community" in *The Integration Question*, ed. Jon H. Pammett and Brian W. Tomlin (Don Mills, ON: Addison-Wesley, 1984), and Donald Smiley, "Canada and the Quest for a National Policy," *Canadian Journal of Political Science* (March 1975): 40.

15. The term *surrogates* as a designation for the various Keynesian welfare state initiatives that were followed is taken from Smiley, "Canada and the Quest for a National Policy," 46. For a discussion of the attempt of the Trudeau liberals to use the National Energy Program as a means of increasing the role and importance of the federal government in national politics, see G. Bruce Doern and Glen Toner, *The Politics of Energy* (Toronto: Methuen, 1985), 30–34.

16. Concerning the tensions that were created by the National Energy Program, see Doern and Toner, ibid., 106, 266–75, 281–83.

17. Reg Whitaker, *The Government Party: Organizing and Financing the Liberal Party of Canada 1930–58* (Toronto: University of Toronto Press, 1977), 132–64.

18. For a discussion of the stronger position of the CCF and of labour in general and the impact of those forces on the welfare state, see Whitaker, *The Government Party*, 137–43; David Wolfe, "The Delicate Balance: The Changing Economic Role of the State in Canada, 1939–1957," (PhD diss., University of Toronto, 1980), 8–9, ch. 5; Robert Campbell, *Grand Illusions: The Politics of the Keynesian Experience in Canada, 1945–1975* (Peterborough, ON: Broadview Press, 1987), 2–23; and Dennis Guest, "World War II and the Welfare State in Canada" in *The Benevolent State: The Growth of Welfare in Canada*, ed. Allan Moscovitch and Jim Albert (Toronto: Garamond Press, 1987).

19. For an example of the federal government's awareness of this limita-

tion, see Campbell, *Grand Illusions*, 94–96.

20. Canada, *Royal Commission on Dominion–Provincial Relations*, book 1 (Ottawa, 1940), 162–63.

21. For a discussion of the role of federal government policies in encouraging a dominant economic relationship between Central Canada and the western and eastern regions, see Donald Smiley, *Canada in Question: Federalism in the Eighties*, 3rd ed. (Toronto: McGraw-Hill Ryerson, 1980), 261–69, and Paul Phillips, *Regional Disparities* (Toronto: Lorimer, 1982), 54–79.

22. Canada, *Royal Commission on Dominion–Provincial Relations*, book 2, 10.

23. On Maritime alienation, see E.R. Forbes, *The Maritime Rights Movement* (Montreal: McGill-Queen's University Press, 1979). On the role of regional alienation in the success of western-based protest parties, see Janine Brodie and Jane Jenson, *Crisis, Challenge and Change* (Ottawa: Carleton University Press, 1988), 107–11. On the divisiveness of the Conscription Crisis, see J.L. Granatstein, *Canada's War* (Toronto: University of Toronto Press, 1990).

24. Struthers, *No Fault of Their Own*, 206.

25. Guest, "World War II and the Welfare State," 217.

26. Robert Kudrle and Theodore Marmor, "The Development of Welfare States in North America" in *The Development of Welfare States in Europe and America*, ed. Peter Flora and Arnold Heidenheimer (New Brunswick, NJ: Transaction Books, 1981), 96.

27. Leslie Pal, *State, Class and Bureaucracy: Canadian Unemployment Insurance and Public Policy* (Montreal: McGill-Queen's University Press, 1988), 104–12.

28. Canada, Statistics Canada, "Chronological Overview," *Unemployment Insurance Statistics*, cat. 73-202S, 1988, 14.

29. Leslie Pal, "Revision and Retreat: Canadian Unemployment Insurance

1971–1981" in *Canadian Social Welfare Policy*, ed. J. Ismael (Montreal: McGill-Queen's University Press, 1985), 92–94.

30. Canada, Commission of Inquiry on Unemployment Insurance, *Report* (Ottawa: Minister of Supply and Services, 1986), 108–15.

31. Ibid., appendix G, fig. G.12, 388.

32. Canada, Statistics Canada, *Provincial Economic Accounts, 1961–1986*, table 13, 329 and table 1, 8; table 13, 33 and table 1, 13.

33. Ibid., table 13, 326, and table 1, 6; table 13, 330 and table 1, 10.

34. For a discussion of the importance of unemployment insurance in the seasonally based Atlantic economy, see M. Patricia Connelly and Martha MacDonald, "Women's Work: Domestic and Wage Labour in a Nova Scotia Community," *Studies in Political Economy* 10 (Winter 1983): 45–72.

35. Statistics Canada, *Provincial Economic Accounts*, table 5, 117, 121, 125, 129.

36. Susan Phillips, "Rock-A-Bye, Brian: The National Strategy on Child Care" in *How Ottawa Spends 1989–90*, ed. Graham, 191.

37. Canada, Minister of Finance, *The Budget*, 20 Feb. 1990, 76.

38. For federal government statements that recognize this importance, see Banting, *The Welfare State and Canadian Federalism*, 118–19, and Smiley, *Canada in Question*, 171.

39. Canada, Department of Justice, Constitution Act, 1982, s. 36 (1) and (2).

40. Clear examples of this perception on the part of individuals and organizations in the East are provided in the Pépin-Roberts Report on national unity: Canada, The Task Force on Canadian Unity, *A Time to Speak: Views of the Public* (Ottawa: Minister of Supply and Services, 1979), 79–89, 200–4.

41. Transfer payments from the federal government to the provinces increased by only 13.2 percent in the

period 1985–88. Statistics Canada, *Provincial Economic Accounts, 1984–1988*, March 1990, table 5, 29.

42. Concerning the decrease in transfer payments prior to the 1990 budget, see National Council of Welfare, *The 1989 Budget and Social Policy*, Sept. 1989 (Ottawa: Minister of Supply and Services, 1989), 32.

43. The inhibiting impact of Canadian federalism in the areas of pension plan and social security reform is discussed in Banting, *The Welfare State and Canadian Federalism*, 69–73, 75–76, 207–8.

44. This logic also extends to programs administered by the federal government. Federal cutbacks to unemployment insurance increase the demands on provincial governments for social assistance—programs that are only cost-shared on a 50–50 basis.

45. The use of privatization has been particularly pronounced in Britain with the Thatcher government and its attempt to privatize education, health services, and housing.

46. Canada, Department of Finance, "The Budget Speech," 27 April 1989, 10.

47. James Rice, "Restitching the Safety Net" in *How Ottawa Spends 1987–88*, ed. Michael Prince (Agincourt, ON: Methuen, 1987), 220–23, and Moscovitch, "The Welfare State Since 1975," 84–85.

48. Concerning this proposed change, see Rice, "Restitching the Safety Net," 218–20.

49. On the important relationship between the Liberal Party and the development of the federal welfare state, see Tom Kent, *A Public Purpose: An Experience of Liberal Opposition and Canadian Government* (Montreal: McGill-Queen's University Press, 1988).

50. Concerning the policy of fiscal restraint implemented by the Liberals and the cutbacks to unemployment insurance imposed in the

latter part of the 1970s, see Pal, "Revision and Retreat," 84–91. The growth figure for federal social spending is taken from Moscovitch, "The Welfare State Since 1975," 79.

51. Concerning these proposed changes, see Banting, "Institutional Conservatism: Federalism and Pension Reform," 48–74, and Derek Hum, "Social Security Reform in the 1970s" in *Canadian Social Welfare Policy*, ed. Ismael, 29–47.

52. On the development of the Canada Health Act, and the thinking that lay behind it, see Monique Bégin, *Medicare: Canada's Right to Health* (Montreal: Optimum Publishing, 1988).

53. For a clear statement of this position from a central figure in the CCF/NDP, see David Lewis, *The Good Fight* (Toronto: Macmillan, 1981), 293–94, 504.

54. The Reagan quotation is taken from his 1982 State of the Union address as cited in Bawden and Palmer, "Social Policy: Challenging the Welfare State," 177.

55. Banting, *The Welfare State and Canadian Federalism*, 129.

56. Andrew Martin, "The Politics of Employment and Welfare: National Policies and International Interdependence" in *The State and Economic Interests*, ed. K. Banting (Toronto: University of Toronto Press, 1986), 182–83.

57. Concerning the less regionally defined nature of the American central government, see Richard Simeon, *Federal–Provincial Diplomacy* (Toronto: University of Toronto Press, 1972), 20–39; Roger Gibbins, *Regionalism: Territorial Politics in Canada and the United States* (Toronto: Butterworth, 1982); Donald Smiley and Ronald Watts, *Intrastate Federalism in Canada* (Toronto: University of Toronto Press, 1985).

58. For a discussion of the failure of the American welfare state to move beyond its origins in the New Deal

reforms of the 1930s, see Theda Skocpol, "America's Incomplete Welfare State: The Limits of New Deal Reforms and the Origins of the Present Crisis" in *Stagnation and Renewal in Social Policy*, ed. M. Rein, G. Esping-Andersen, and L. Rainwater (New York: M.E. Sharpe, 1987).

59. Theda Skocpol and John Ikenberry, "The Political Formation of the American Welfare State," *Comparative Social Research* 6 (1983): 133–39.

60. Skocpol, "America's Incomplete Welfare State," 48–49.

61. Concerning the emphasis placed on flat-rate contributions and subsistence-level benefits in Beveridge's recommendations, see Pete Alcock, *Poverty and State Support* (London: Longman, 1987), 48–54, and Karel Williams and John Williams, *A Beveridge Reader* (London: Allen & Unwin, 1987), 18–20, 43–48.

63. Peter Flora and Arnold Heidenheimer, "The Historical Core and Changing Boundaries of the Welfare State" in *The Development of Welfare States in Europe and America*, ed. Flora and Heidenheimer, 19–21.

64. The failure of Meech Lake to provide a basis of unity is consistent with previous efforts at constitutional reform. A summary of the failure of constitutional negotiations up to 1980 is provided in Smiley, *Canada in Question*, 66–88. Concerning the tensions created by the constitutional agreement of 1982 and its failure to create a new basis of national political legitimacy for the institutions of the federal state, see: Gerard Bergeron, "Quebec in Isolation" in *And No One Cheered: Federalism, Democracy and the Constitution Act*, ed. Keith Banting and Richard Simeon (Toronto: Methuen, 1983), 59–73; Donald Smiley, "A Dangerous Deed: The Constitution Act, 1982," ibid., 74–92; Roger Gibbins, "Constitutional Politics and the West," ibid., 119–32; and Reg Whitaker, "Democracy and the Canadian Constitution," ibid., 240–60.

RESTRUCTURING FAMILY ALLOWANCES: "GOOD POLITICS AT NO COST?"◊

ANDREW F. JOHNSON

○

Few contemporary observers of Canadian federalism would dispute J.R. Mallory's claim that "governments find themselves making decisions all the time which can be effective only if taken in concert with other governments."[1] Mallory's remark is especially applicable to decision making in the realm of income security policy. Canada's myriad of income security programs are so closely related that a program change initiated by one level of government will most certainly trigger changes in programs administered by other levels. The task force report prepared for the provincial ministers of social services comments that by the early 1970s "as income security programs . . . increased in scope, complexity, and number it became more apparent that no single program could be considered in isolation from another."[2] And yet, the same report laments the federal government's apparent unwillingness "to maintain serious consultations with provincial governments."[3]

In 1978 the minister of finance, Jean Chrétien, hailed major changes to the federal family allowances program as "one of the most significant policy reforms of the decade."[4] The changes were a milestone in the sense that they represented a shift from a universal to a selective program. Moreover, they served as a basis for subsequent modifications to the program in 1982. Despite the significance of the alterations to the family allowances program since 1978, available evidence clearly demonstrates that the provinces were not involved in the decision-making process. Thus the purpose of this paper

◊ From Jacqueline S. Ismael, ed., *Canadian Social Welfare Policy: Federal and Provincial Dimensions* (Montreal: McGill-Queen's University Press, 1985), 105–19. Reprinted with the permission of the publisher.

is to explain why the provinces were not involved and, more importantly, to determine how effective the federal government has been in attaining its purported goal of a more redistributive system in the absence of concerted decision making.

TOWARD A CHILD BENEFITS SYSTEM

Constraining expenditures and helping those most in need were the two objectives that the federal government set for itself as the post-controls period began in 1976.[5] A strategy to fulfil these objectives was also provided; income transfers were to be integrated with the income tax system. Such was the recipe that was used to restructure the family allowances program in 1978 and in 1982 since it has become apparent that the program was costly and not particularly redistributive.

By 1977 family allowance payments amounted to over $1.9 billion, three times as much as they had been prior to the previous program reform which had been approved four years earlier.[6] Costs were expected to continue to climb because benefits were indexed to the cost of living. Allen Lambert, the chairman of the Royal Commission on Financial Management and Accountability, was quick to recognize that if income security programs such as family allowances continued to increase at previous rates, the income tax burden would become intolerable.[7] Significantly, he singled out family allowances as a case in point by recommending a means test for that program as a way to cut spending. A means test would have curbed expenditures by directing payments to those most in need.

The family allowances program held the dubious distinction of being the least redistributive of the federal government's five most expensive income security programs.[8] While net benefit payments were moderately progressive, the costs of the program were borne unequally among family income groups. In other words, the income tax system was perceived as a major obstacle to forging a more redistributive system of family allowances. Thus, the Economic Council of Canada commented that "if the personal income tax exemption for young dependents is considered in conjunction with the program itself, the effect on income redistribution is regressive, with the highest income quintile receiving the largest proportion of net benefits."[9]

The federal government had already identified a strategy to make income security programs more redistributive. Thus it appeared to be more or less consistent with its rather vague intentions of the immediate post-controls period when it used the income tax system to redress regressivity in the family allowances program. In 1977, a $50 child tax credit was provided to families earning incomes of less than $26 000. However, within a year, the minister of finance admitted that the redistributive intent of child tax credits had not been realized;[10] it was of little value to the majority of low income earners who did not pay income taxes. Nevertheless, the existence of a child benefits system had been recognized. Furthermore, it had been recognized that the redistributive thrust of the family allowances program could not be altered without simultaneous modifications to related child benefits included in the income tax system."[11] Moreover, the child benefits system was ripe for reform because its three elements worked at cross purposes.[12] The family allowances program provided substantial benefits for low income families; child tax credits largely benefited middle income families; and the child tax exemption continued to be of greatest value to high income families because it reduced the amount of income which was taxed at the highest rate and in some instances moved the taxpayer into a lower tax bracket with a lower marginal rate.

The 1978 reform of family allowances was fully compatible with the government's objectives for income security programs in the post-controls period and was fully aligned with its strategy for redistribution. First, family allowance payments were reduced by 23 percent, from $312 per annum to $240. Second, the $50 child tax credit was replaced with a $200 refundable child tax credit payable to families earning less than $18 000 per annum; its value was to be reduced by 50 percent of family income in excess of $18 000.[13] However, the most regressive element of the child benefits system, the child tax exemption, was not altered substantially.[14] In other words, savings accrued by the reduction in family allowance payments were to be funnelled into the pockets of lower-income families via the refundable child tax credit. The new package of benefits was to cost an additional $35 million which was, from the minister of finance's perspective, a scheme that would be virtually self-financing.[15] It was thought that a major step toward a more progressive system of child benefits had been accomplished with meagre cost implications.

However, costs continued to rise. By 1982 overall family allowances payments surpassed 1977 levels by about $3 million. Costs were expected to continue to rise due to the indexation of benefits. In addition, revenues lost through the refundable child tax credit had exceeded expectations.[16] More families than initially expected had applied for and received the credit. Forgone revenues were estimated to be approximately $1 billion, slightly less than half of the total disbursements on family allowances. Clearly, the child benefits system was a primary candidate for the program of expenditure restraint announced in the June budget. Thus family allowances was one of the first programs to be cut by the government's "six and five" program. Full indexation of family allowances was to be suspended by January 1983. Benefits would be limited to a 6 percent cost of living adjustment in 1983 and to a 5 percent adjustment in 1984. The refundable child tax credit was to remain fully indexed to the cost of living and a "one shot" $50 increase was to be added for 1983 in order to compensate lower-income families for the capping of their family allowances.[17] Although the minister of health and welfare had long advocated the elimination of the child tax exemption, that element of the child benefits system had been left untouched.

Hence the 1978 formula was resurrected in 1982 with similar results. Costs were cut. Total savings were expected to amount to $70 million; approximately $320 million were expected to be shaved from the family allowances program but $250 million were to be channelled into the refundable child tax credit. In theory, a small measure of redistribution was achieved by using the income tax system to transfer funds to lower-income families. However, in practice, the full value of the tax credit has not been passed on to low-income families who are most in need of financial assistance. It appears that many provinces have quietly prevented their welfare recipients from receiving the tax credit benefit.

THE QUIET SUBVERSION OF THE PROVINCES

The 1978 and 1982 changes to the child benefits system indirectly affected the financing of provincial income security schemes. Provincial social assistance plans are income tested; that is, all sources of income, including provincial and federal transfers, may be considered in establishing social assistance benefit levels. Thus reductions in child benefits may force the provinces to pour more monies into social assistance payments in order to maintain desired benefit rates. Most provinces claim to maintain a "summing interaction" with family allowances; that is, the amount of social assistance a claimant receives does not take into account the amount of family allowances the claimant may also receive.[18] However, the interaction is difficult to monitor. In 1978, only three provinces had statutory increases in social assistance; currently, only two, Quebec and Nova Scotia, have statutory increases.[19] The remaining provinces increase social assistance levels at ministerial discretion. While some provinces formulate rate increases on the basis of detailed information pertaining to income and other types of assistance available, officials concede that others, especially the smaller provinces, make increases on "a purely ad hoc basis."[20] The point is that the procedures used for determining social assistance benefit increases do not guarantee that federal attempts to target child benefits to the lowest-income families will succeed. After all, even statutes can be amended. The provinces can accept federal initiatives. Alternatively, they can openly reject or quietly subvert federal measures.

Initially, the provinces did not choose any of these alternatives. They simply did not react to the proposals. Clearly, this was of considerable concern to the minister of health and welfare, Monique Bégin, because the opposition threatened to filibuster the bill unless provincial acceptance was secured. Hence, Bégin told the House of Commons that she had sent letters to her provincial counterparts in late October of 1978 urging them to pass on the full benefits of the tax credit to social assistance recipients.[21] Further representations were made, including discussions with her provincial counterparts at the meeting of welfare ministers held in late November. Only five provinces had officially indicated that their cabinets were about to accept the new scheme. In view of the delay, Bégin urged pressure groups and MPs to do what the federal government would not—to lobby with the provinces in order to gain their acceptance. Thus, during debate, Bégin presented her position vis-à-vis the provinces:

> It is good politics at no cost to the provinces. It is federal tax payers'
> money which will be transferred to individual Canadian families by

a program similar to family allowances. We do not think it should become an additional transfer payment to the provinces . . . I invite voluntary associations interested in the development of social policies or my colleagues in Parliament to make their views known to their provincial governments."[22]

It has been claimed that subsequently "scarcely a provincial voice was raised in dissent" as the bill was transformed into law.[23] However, once the bill became law, Quebec raised its voice. Quebec refused to transfer the full benefits of the refundable child tax credit to welfare recipients with children by reducing their welfare payments by an almost equal amount. Instead of receiving the statutory increase of 9 percent for social assistance payments in 1979, mothers with children were to receive a 4.5 percent increase. At the same time, Quebec's minister of social affairs, Denis Lazure, tabled legislation to reduce Quebec's family allowance payments by 23 percent. In effect, Quebec's actions erased the benefit of the tax credit for the lowest-income families and transformed it into a transfer to the province.

Lazure used familiar arguments to defend his government's actions: Quebec has an integrated income security system and, therefore, cannot tolerate federal intrusions, however indirect.[24] According to Lazure, twenty years of unilateral federal policy making in the field of income security was tantamount to "guerilla tactics" designed to "frustrate and humiliate" Quebec in exercising its de jure, if not de facto, jurisdiction over income security policy.[25] However, the specific logic of Lazure and his government's initial rejection of the refundable child tax credit was made clearer in a document prepared for the Quebec minister of state for economic development:

> Les taux de l'aide sociale au Québec sont établis de façon à ce que, combinés aux allocation familiales, il se situent à un niveau inferieur au salaire minimum; ceci afin de ne pas desinciter au travail les bénéficiaires. Lorsque le nouveau programme de crédit d'impôt fédéral a été introduit, il a fallu obligatoirement ne pas indexer au même rythme les barèmes d'aide sociale pour les familles avec enfants, afin de ne conserver l'écart avec le salaire minimum. C'est un exemple supplementaire pour signaler la nécessité de repenser les deux programmes en même temps.[26]

Lazure also objected to the revisions in principle because the federal government was perceived to have unilaterally breached an agreement reached in 1973 whereby the provinces could vary family allowance payments.[27] The federal government's reduction in payments was seen as an imposition on Quebec to lower its payments or to make up the shortfall with its own revenues. Quebec was apparently hard pressed to raise its family allowance payments because its statutory indexation of social assistance payments for 1979 was expected to cost $67 million, a price that it could ill afford. Finally, Lazure was disturbed by the administrative problems that he foresaw in implementing the refundable child tax credit.

Manitoba followed Quebec's lead by refusing to pass on the full value of the refundable child tax credit to its social assistance recipients. However, by April 1979 Manitoba had joined with the other provincial governments in assuring Ottawa that it would not absorb the value of the tax credit. The governments of Quebec and Manitoba appear to have recognized the common sense in Bégin's claim that it was "good politics." While Manitoba's Conservative government might have had little difficulty in justifying its rejection, the social democratic Parti Québécois government would have been strained to defend its alleged position of "playing politics on the backs of the poor."[28] More to the point, both governments began to realize that continued opposition could backfire. Provincial opposition was based on rather complex arguments and statements of principle, hardly the right stuff to stir voter antipathy to the federal government. Moreover, the family allowances program is a "sacred cow," to borrow one provincial official's choice description.[29] Opposition to the scheme could have been easily construed or misconstrued by the federal government into a clear and simple issue, an affront to motherhood. In short, the federal government had the political advantage, especially since the new scheme had all-party support. Finally, Van Loon claims that the provinces had become sympathetic to tax credits during the federal–provincial negotiations conducted in relation to the social security review. According to Van Loon, "the Review had accustomed people to the idea of income supplementation and refundable tax credits."[30] That may explain the increased use of these devices by both levels of government but it does not entirely explain provincial willingness to accept a federal initiative, especially one that is not fully compatible with provincial income security policies. It seems likely that the provinces were quick to see that cost implications of the federal plan would not significantly affect them. In the long term, the provinces could simply appropriate the tax credit, if necessary.

The provinces did not rush to appropriate the tax credit. Quite the contrary. New Brunswick and Nova Scotia allowed welfare recipients to keep their tax credits and to receive their statutory increases in social assistance. British Columbia, Saskatchewan, and Prince Edward Island raised their social assistance payments per child to match the drop in family allowances. Ontario, on the other hand, raised its social assistance payments by only 6 percent, which was well below the rate of inflation in 1979.[31] Although the outcome may not have been intentional, Ontario's decision amounted to a quiet subversion of federal intentions to allocate more funds to a large segment of low-income families. Other provinces could do the same because the timing and size of social assistance increases are not prescribed by law in most of the provinces. Leonard Shifrin put the case another way: "If, for example, a province planning a $30 rate hike decides to appropriate a $20 benefit coming from Ottawa, all it has to do is cut back the intended increase to $10, and no one will be the wiser."[32] Shifrin, writing in 1979, added: "the fate of indirect interception may yet befall the child tax credit in some provinces, but the rumour mill hasn't come up with any evidence thus far." However, the rumour mill of 1983 suggests that most of the provinces have deducted the value of the tax credit by 100 percent in the last four years.[33] In December 1982, Bégin admitted that there is a close relationship between the child benefits system and social assistance benefits but that "none of that has been explored."[34] Officials of Health and Welfare confirm that no study has been undertaken to assess the relationship in this "grey area."

Not a single voice of dissent was raised when the federal government revised the child benefits system again in 1982. The provinces had long since recognized that they could either quietly accept or quietly subvert federal intentions to redistribute income without the political risks that might accompany a public rejection. Quebec, for instance, appears to have caught on quickly. This time Quebec agreed to pass on the full value of the increased tax credit. But Quebec had quietly reduced its social assistance payments for mothers with children in January 1982 and intended to raise payments by only 2 percent in 1983. However, in 1978 and in 1982, there was another factor related to costs that obviated the need for provincial protests: the dollar amounts involved in the restructuring of family allowances were not great. The 1978 changes were to cost the federal government $35 million; the tax revenues lost by the provinces due to the lowering of family allowance payments were negligible. The $70 million to be saved from the second round of changes were hardly going to break the provinces either. In both instances, the poorer provinces stood to gain because funds were to be reallocated to lower-income families. At the same time, the richer provinces had no need to be overly concerned about costs. An official from the Ontario Ministry of Community and Social Services succinctly summarized his government's view of the matter: family allowances tend to be more costly to Ontario residents as a whole than to residents of other provinces because benefits are taxable and because Ontario has higher marginal taxation than other provinces.[35] In any event, the cost of the changes was small by comparison to the other financial matters that the provinces had to worry about.

In 1978 the provincial treasurers and ministers of finance were still trying to assess the impact of the Established Programs Financing arrangements on their treasuries. In April 1977 the federal government had given notice of its intention to reduce spending on transfers for the established programs (medicare, hospital insurance, and postsecondary education). Under the new arrangements, cost-sharing for these programs was replaced by a "block fund," which, unlike the former, is not related to actual program costs. Block funding was expected to reduce provincial revenues. The restructuring of family allowances coupled with legislation designed to generate massive cutbacks in the unemployment insurance program were announced against this backdrop. The federal government proposed to save an estimated $655 million in 1979–1980 by amending the Unemployment Insurance Act and a further $935 million in 1980–1981.[36] While most of the savings were to be offset by additional disbursements for job creation, it was estimated that the cutbacks would cost the provinces additional welfare payments of $25.5 million in 1979–1980 and $43.4 million in 1980–1981. In addition, in September 1978, the prime minister had announced that $370 million would be shaved from the Canada Assistance Plan and related expenditures.[37] The provinces jointly reacted to these cutbacks by denouncing the federal government's "cavalier attitude" which had "denied provincial governments the opportunity to examine the far-reaching implications of these changes on provincial taxpayers."[38] However, their statement was addressed to federal intentions to effect cutbacks of considerable magnitude. The restructuring of family allowances was brushed aside while the provinces attempted to persuade the federal government to delay the implementation of other and more costly measures.

In 1982, once again the provinces were not in a suitable position to harangue the federal government about the cost implications resulting from the revisions to the child benefits system. The provinces were also faced with mounting deficits and declining revenues. Supported by a rising tide of social conservatism, the provinces were enacting legislation to restrain expenditures in general and to trim social security costs in particular. They could not criticize the federal government for doing what they were doing. Indeed, "no cost" added to "good politics" made the revisions palatable to the provinces.

However, both sets of changes also made good political sense and involved insignificant costs for the federal government. Why didn't the federal government therefore use these opportunities to consult with the provinces as a modest gesture of good will and to ensure that its redistributive intentions were fully realized?

First and foremost, federal officials insist that there has been no good reason to do so because family allowances and related programs lie clearly within the federal government's authority to make direct payments to Canadian citizens.[39] In his study of Canadian social security policy, Banting recognizes the federal government's growing predisposition to steadfastly safeguard its authority to legislate in the field of income security.[40] According to Banting, income security programs are "instruments of statecraft" which provide the federal government with handsome opportunities to forge patron–client relationships with millions of Canadians. Income security programs therefore enhance the federal government's political legitimacy in the eyes of Canadians. What better way to reach out to Canadians than through the family allowances program which benefits 3.6 million mothers and through the refundable child tax credit which benefits 2.5 million mothers? What better way to erode political legitimacy than to consult with the provinces over this vital instrument of statecraft?

Second, federal officials claim that the child benefits system has never been a "priority matter." The restructuring of family allowances has been but a small part of the government's overall imperative to reduce expenditures and thereby to curb inflation. The 1978 speech from the throne described the introduction of the new child benefits system as one of several measures to reduce inflation.[41] In 1982, Bégin repeatedly stressed that cutbacks in family allowances and in old age security payments had a much broader purpose than simply to trim expenditures and to set an example of fiscal restraint; they were part of a general strategy for economic recovery launched in the June budget.[42] The federal government has been unwilling to brook provincial interference in the development of parts of an overall package to regenerate the economy. Moreover, the Department of Finance has been the conduit of the federal government's imperative of restraint since the mid-1970s. Senior officials of departments within the Social Affairs envelope take pains to point out that "Finance changed the rules of the game so that departments would be more cost conscious."[43] One new rule has been to prevent departments from initiating proposals without the benefit of very close scrutiny by interdepartmental structures and by central agencies. In the realm of income security this rule has been superseded by another: the Department of Finance has been charged with initiating revisions to programs. The details of the initial restructuring of family allowances were first announced in the August 1978 minibudget and the details of the subsequent revisions were announced in the June 1982 budget. In other words, while the 1973 amendment to the Family Allowances Act was largely an expenditure change, recent revisions have been largely income tax changes. The generic differences of the changes have led to differences in federal–provincial interaction in the policy-making process. Officials from Health and Welfare point out the obvious: the budgetary process is secretive and thus prohibits the inclusion of the provinces in specific policy-making processes.

Finally, there appears to be a consensus among officials of Health and Welfare that there is a reluctance to consult with the provinces because their positions are predictable; the federal government can only expect disagreement. Bud Cullen, a former minister of employment and immigration, adequately expressed this view while referring to amendments to the unemployment insurance program that were tabled in conjunction with the restructuring of family allowances in 1978:

> At the federal level, we initiate changes in federal legislation and discuss it with them [the provinces]. They thought that before we'd done anything or got cabinet approval, we should talk to them. If I can't get it through my caucus and cabinet, then there is no point of going through the headache of going and having the provinces unload on us. Once your cabinet and caucus are prepared to back you, then you can take it to the provinces and then have a discussion. Now whether you call that "consultation," I don't know.[44]

In 1978, it took three weeks for Cabinet to agree to the restructuring of family allowances. In 1982, it took three months, punctuated by contradictory statements of Cabinet ministers and public opposition by groups of Liberal backbenchers, for Cabinet and the Liberal caucus to agree to the changes. Under these circumstances, the federal government could hardly afford the luxury of inviting the provinces to participate in the policy-making process. However, if the federal government continues to deny itself this luxury, over half a million families at the lowest end of the income scale may well be denied the full benefits of the child benefits system.

REFORMING THE CHILD BENEFITS SYSTEM

The child benefits system is likely to be subjected to changes in the near future. In 1982, Flora MacDonald, then the Progressive Conservative social affairs critic, called for a comprehensive review of the system.[45] The

Liberals acknowledged the need for a "rational discussion and careful examination of the issues" related to the system.[46] Furthermore, the major political parties are promoting two common objectives for change: first, costs must be restrained and, second, regressive features must be removed.

The total cost of the child benefits system amounts to $4 billion: $2.2 billion is paid out through the family allowances program; $1 billion is disbursed through the refundable child tax credit program; and forgone revenues from the child tax exemption amount to approximately $800 million. The Conservatives endorsed the objective of restraining costs in a rather oblique but, nevertheless, heavy-handed manner while enjoying their brief tenure of office. The Clark government proposed to terminate family allowances, the most expensive element of the system, by 1981. The record of Liberal governments also demonstrates sensitivity to costs. Thus Bégin commented in October 1982 that in the next few years it was highly unlikely that additional funds would be directed to the system, for the "hundreds of millions of dollars" that had been available "no longer exist."[47] She added that redistribution should be the basis for any future changes to the system but that redistribution would have to be generated from funds already within the system. Bégin and her Conservative counterpart designated the most regressive feature of the system, the child tax exemption, as the likely source of funds for redistribution. However, Bégin cautiously noted that her views did not necessarily correspond to government policy because tax measures were under the jurisdiction of the minister of finance, not the minister of health and welfare.

Advisory groups, community groups, and policy analysts appear to support the contention that the child tax exemption should be abolished. However, there are two competing proposals to make the system more progressively redistributive with savings derived from the child tax exemption. One recommends that the savings be directed into the refundable child tax credit program while another holds that family allowances be the vehicle for redistribution.

The National Council of Welfare favours abolishing the child tax exemption and applying the proceeds to the child tax credit program.[48] Its scheme for restructuring the system would include lowering the eligibility threshold from its current level of $26 330 to $21 000 so that the child tax credit could be raised by 68 percent, that is, from $343 to $575. The family allowance program would not be altered; payments decrease as income increases because benefits are taxable. The council claims that its proposal would not add one cent to government spending and would provide a boost for low and modest income earners. For instance, a family with two children, earning less than $21 000, would have received $1150 in 1983 as opposed to $686 under the existing program.

Economist Jonathan Kesselman, on the other hand, advocates abolishing the child tax exemption and the refundable child tax credit.[49] The savings would be used to increase family allowances by 145 percent. Thus in 1982 payments would have amounted to $65.93 a month or $791 per annum, per child. Kesselman proposes a special tax recovery device to recover increasing portions of family allowance payments at higher family income levels. The plan is unquestionably redistributive and, according to Kesselman, the government would have saved about half a billion dollars had his plan been implemented in 1982.

The proposal for a 145 percent increase in family allowance payments is not as outrageous as it may seem at first glance. After all, the Canadian Council on Social Development assesses the total value of family allowance payments to be about the same level as it was in 1976 and about half of what it was in constant dollars.[50] Moreover, the combined value of the child tax exemption and the refundable child tax credit is roughly equal to 100 percent of the value of total family allowance payments. In addition, a long list of administrative and social arguments have been advanced to support enriched family allowances over increased child tax credits.[51]

Several of the frequently cited arguments run as follows: universal family allowances are administratively simple and inexpensive. A parent merely files one application and a child receives benefits until the age of eighteen. However, a parent must file an income tax return annually in order to apply for the child tax credit. In 1978, it was estimated that the Department of National Revenue required an additional 350 person-years to process approximately 1.5 million income tax returns which would not have been filed otherwise.[52] Family allowances do not pose budgeting problems for families in need because payments are made monthly rather than in a yearly lump-sum as are child tax credits. Furthermore, child tax credits are slow to respond to changes in family income because an income test is applied before benefits are disbursed, not after. The National Council of Welfare's proposal to divide the credit into three installments would only provide a partial remedy to these problems. In the final analysis, the family allowance demo-grant is stigma-free whereas the selective system of child tax credits smacks of residual welfare; children are entitled to family allowances by right, not by social beneficence. There is still another advantage which is crucial in the absence of concerted federal–provincial decision making: enriched family allowances are likely to be more acceptable to the provinces.

The federal government has the right to pay child tax credits. However, Michael Mendelson perceptively notes that "matters become less clear as credits become further removed from the tax system" because "the right of the federal government to run a general income supplement or assistance program becomes unclear."[53] It is conceivable that child tax credits could be construed as charities under provincial jurisdiction. On the other hand, enriched family allowances are likely to be welcomed by provinces such as Manitoba, Saskatchewan, and Quebec. Increased payments would provide a much needed increment to their income supplementation programs which are designed to complement family allowances.[54]

In addition, a reliance on child tax credits is accompanied by the risk that the provinces will appropriate the benefits to those at the lowest rungs of the income ladder. This is not to exaggerate the problem. Indeed, about five times as many low and modest income families receive the full benefit as those who do not. However, it is still a major problem insofar as the raison d'être of the child benefits system remains to help those in need. The enriched family allowances proposal would largely avoid this problem for two reasons: first, the magnitude of the increases would present political difficulties for provinces intent on quietly subverting the redistributive thrust. Second, the provinces would have less incentive to do so. By Kesselman's accounting, the provinces would gain about $180 million from the joint abolition of the child tax exemption and family allowance taxability, if his scheme were adopted.

Despite the advantages, the federal government is unlikely to follow a course that vaguely resembles Kesselman's proposal. Conservatives and Liberals alike do not appear to favour a universal system of increased family allowances. Moreover, while the child tax credit option is good politics at no cost, the family allowances option is bad politics at no cost. The restructuring of family allowances plays a major part in the politics of restraint. However, the child tax credit option, unlike the family allowances option, provides what governing parties require in order to be successful at the politics of restraint, namely a fiscal illusion. A tax expenditure such as the refundable child tax credit provides redistribution without the political liability of increases in public spending. Thus the challenge of the 1980s will likely be to ensure that the continued erosion of family allowances, combined with the enrichment of child tax credits, benefits those most in need. That challenge will require concerted federal–provincial decision making in the restructuring of family allowances.

NOTES

1. J.R. Mallory, *The Structure of Canadian Government* (Toronto: Macmillan, 1971), 37.

2. Interprovincial Conference of Ministers Responsible for Social Services, *The Income Security System in Canada* (Ottawa: Canadian Intergovernmental Conference Secretariat, 1980), 27.

3. Ibid., 28.

4. House of Commons, *Debates*, 31 Oct. 1978, 652.

5. Canada, *The Way Ahead: A Framework for Discussion* (Ottawa: Minister of Supply and Services, Oct. 1976), 26.

6. In 1973 the Family Allowances Act was amended. Under the new act, benefits were increased substantially and indexed to increase annually with the Consumer Price Index. Benefits were also made taxable. For a detailed discussion of these and other changes that were proposed in the early 1970s, see Simon McInnes, "Federal–Provincial Negotiation: Family Allowances 1970–1976" (PhD diss., Carleton University, 1978).

7. *Toronto Star*, 17 Dec. 1977.

8. J.E. Cloutier, *The Distribution of Benefits and Costs of Social Security in Canada, 1971–1975*, Discussion Paper No. 108 (Ottawa: Economic Council of Canada, Feb. 1978). See pp. 24–31 for a detailed analysis of the redistributive impact of family and youth allowances.

9. Economic Council of Canada, *A Time for Reason* (Fifteenth Annual Review) (Ottawa: Minister of Supply and Services, 1978), 110.

10. House of Commons, *Debates*, 31 Oct. 1978, 652.

11. Canada, *Integration of Social Program Payments into the Income Tax System: A Discussion Paper* (Ottawa: Department of Finance, Nov. 1978), 33.

12. National Council of Welfare, *Bearing the Burden, Sharing the Benefits* (Ottawa, March 1978).

13. Brigitte Kitchen, "A Canadian Compromise: The Refundable Child Tax Credit," *Canadian Taxation* 1, 3 (Fall 1979): 44–51, provides a detailed analysis of the 1978 changes.

14. The differential exemption rate for children under sixteen and children over sixteen was abolished.

15. House of Commons, *Debates*, 31 Oct. 1978, 653.

16. Interviews. Interviews were conducted with officials from the Department of Health and Welfare and from provincial ministries of social services during September and October 1983.

17. The income threshold for eligibility was raised to $26 330 in 1982.

18. Interprovincial Conference, *Income Security System*, 104.

19. New Brunswick recently abolished statutory increases.

20. Interviews.

21. House of Commons, *Debates*, 29 Nov. 1978, 1625.

22. Ibid.

23. Rick Van Loon, "Reforming Welfare in Canada," *Public Policy* 27, 4 (Fall 1979): 499.

24. See the remarks of Mr Gauthier, MP (Roberval) in House of Commons, *Debates*, 7 Feb. 1979, 2994.

25. Denis Lazure, *Les contentieux Québec–Ottawa dans le champ des affaires sociales* (Montreal: Notes pour un discours de Monsieur Denis Lazure [Ministre des Affaires Sociales] prononcé devant la Société Saint-Jean-Baptiste, 16 janv. 1978), 30–31.

26. Québec, *L'impact des transferts sur la répartition des revenus du Québec 1967–1975* (Quebec: Office de planification et de développement du Québec, 1979), 76.

27. In 1973 an agreement was reached whereby a provincial government may request the federal government to vary the rates payable under the Family Allowances Act in that province on the basis of the age of the child or the number of children in the family, or both, provided the smallest monthly payment in that province is at least 60 percent of the federal rate and the average monthly amount paid for all children in that province is equal to the monthly federal rate. The provinces of Alberta and Quebec took this option. In addition, Quebec has its own family allowances program.

28. *Montreal Star*, 10 Feb. 1979.

29. Interviews.

30. Van Loon, "Reforming Welfare," 499.

31. Leonard Shifrin, "Federal Tax Credit Means Nothing in Quebec," *Montreal Star*, 16 Feb. 1979.

32. Ibid.

33. Interviews.

34. House of Commons, Standing Committee on Health, Welfare and Social Affairs, *Proceedings*, 9 Dec. 1982, 54.

35. Interviews.

36. Canada, *Detailed Impact of the 1978 Changes to the Unemployment Insurance Act* (Ottawa: Employment and Immigration Commission, November 1978), A–2.

37. *Montreal Gazette*, 9 Sept. 1978.

38. *Canadian News Facts*, 10 Sept. 1978, 2010.

39. Interviews.

40. Keith A. Banting, *The Welfare State and Canadian Federalism* (Montreal: McGill-Queen's University Press, 1982), 177.

41. House of Commons, *Debates*, 11 Oct. 1978, 2.

42. Ibid, 28 Oct. 1982, 21194.

43. Interview, July 1981.

44. Interview with Bud Cullen, Nov. 1980.

45. House of Commons, *Debates*, 28 Oct. 1982, 21180.

46. Ibid., 3 Nov. 1982, 20341. The remarks were made by the minister of finance, Marc Lalonde.

47. Ibid., 28 Oct. 1982, 21178.

48. National Council of Welfare, *Family Allowances for All?* (Ottawa, March 1983). Also see National Council of Welfare, *The June 1982 Budget and Social Policy* (Ottawa, July 1982).

49. Jonathan R. Kesselman, "Family Allowances: How to Save and Pay to All," *Financial Post*, 11 Dec. 1982.

50. House of Commons Standing Committee on Health, Welfare and Social Affairs, *Proceedings*, 13 Dec. 1982, 9–13 provides a statement by the CSSD.

51. Jonathan R. Kesselman, "Credits, Exemptions and Demogrants in Canadian Tax-Transfer Policy," *Canadian Tax Journal* 27, 6 (Nov.–Dec. 1979): 676–82, and Dennis Guest, "Canada's Universal Family Allowance System—the Keystone of a Guaranteed Annual Income" (paper delivered at the annual meeting of the Society for the Study of Social Problems, Detroit, Aug. 1983).

52. Kesselman, "Credits, Exemptions," 679–80.

53. Michael Mendelson, *Universal or Selective? The Debate on Reforming Income Security in Canada* (Toronto: Ontario Economic Council, 1981), 58.

54. See ch. 7 of *Canadian Social Welfare Policy: Federal and Provincial Dimensions*, ed. Jacqueline S. Ismael (Montreal: McGill-Queen's University Press, 1985).

THE PROGRAM OF THE SPALLUMCHEEN INDIAN BAND IN BRITISH COLUMBIA AS A MODEL OF INDIAN CHILD WELFARE*

JOHN A. MACDONALD

o

The plight of Native Indian children and youth in Canada has been a subject of grave public concern for the past two decades. During this time, public attention has been focussed on high rates of infant mortality, suicide rates among Native teenagers six times the national average, a secondary school drop-out rate of 80 percent, and widespread family breakdown contributing to disproportionate admissions of Indian children to the care of provincial child protection agencies.[1]

Readers will probably be very familiar with the shocking rates of child separation experienced by Indian families in Canada's western provinces since the early 1960s. In British Columbia, throughout most of this period, Native children have comprised between 35 and 40 percent of the children in the care of the provincial superintendent of child welfare.[2] A smaller but still significant number of Indian children have had substitute care in residential schools or with relatives and friends because of family problems.[3]

The causes of the widespread breakdown in Indian family life are complex, but they seem principally rooted in a lengthy Indian experience in this country of poverty, cultural deprivation, and enforced dependency. It is also the belief of this writer that the family problems of Native Indians have been exacerbated by the failure of provincial child welfare policies and pro-

* MacDonald, John A. "The Program of the Spallumcheen Indian Band in British Columbia as a Model of Indian Child Welfare," in *Perspectives on Social Services and Social Issues*. Edited by Jacqueline Ismael and Ray J. Thomlison. Ottawa: The Canadian Council on Social Development, 1987. Reprinted with permission.

grams to engage fully the capacity of Indian people to address family problems within their own communities.

In recent years, federal and provincial authorities have sought, by various means, to increase participation by Native Indians in the resolution of child welfare problems. A model which reflects a high degree of Native self-determination is the child welfare program of the British Columbia Spallumcheen Band. This paper examines the history of this program, its principal features, and its future prospects.

THE CHILD WELFARE EXPERIENCE OF THE SPALLUMCHEEN BAND DURING THE 1970s

The Spallumcheen Indian Band is located on a reserve which straddles both sides of the Shuswap River near Enderby at the northern end of British Columbia's beautiful Okanagan Valley. The Band is relatively small in number, consisting of approximately four hundred members, over a hundred of whom reside off the reserve, principally in adjoining communities.

Most Canadians look back on the 1970s with some nostalgia as a time of prosperity and promise when young people could look forward to a steady improvement in lifestyle and material attainment. For most B.C. Indian Bands, this same period was one of growing awareness of their disadvantaged status in Canadian society and of increasing concern to prevent the erosion of their Indian culture by pervading pressures from the outside society. The Spallumcheen Band shared with other B.C. Indian bands high rates of unemployment and welfare dependency among its members. It also experienced family discord and social disruption occasioned by alcoholism and petty crime. This decade was especially traumatic for the Band's families; during that time eighty children were apprehended and admitted to the care of the B.C. superintendent of child welfare.[4]

To appreciate fully the shocked reaction of Band leaders and members at the loss of their children, it is important to recognize several features of provincial child welfare policy that characterized this period. First, although provincial child protection services had been extended to Indian reserves since the mid-1950s, they did not include preventive family counselling services as in the case of non-Indian families. The typical pattern was for non-Indian social workers to apprehend children in severe crisis situations and seek court-ordered committals to care, followed by placement in substitute homes off the reserve. Second, given the absence of services for Indians on reserves to facilitate family re-unification, social workers tended to favour adoption or long-term foster care for the children who had been separated from their parents. Thus, children apprehended from families of the Spallumcheen Band, as in the case of other Indian children, often experienced much longer periods of foster care when compared to non-Indian children needing protection.[5]

While the widespread apprehensions of the children of Spallumcheen Band members caused trauma and heartache to the families concerned, they also posed a potential threat to the survival of the Band itself. Thus, at a time of rising political consciousness among Indians of their right to a better future in Canadian society, this future seemed jeopardized by the loss of their children to what were perceived as alien agents of assimilation. And, while many Indian bands gave priority in their political activities to negotiating improved economic arrangements for their people, the Spallumcheen Band combined such initiatives with a vigorous attempt to reclaim control over the decisions affecting the well-being of their children.

Late in 1978, the Band hired Earl Shipmaker, a non-Indian social worker, to assist Band members to develop childcare resources on the reserve. This resulted in increased utilization of the Band members' homes for voluntary placement of children requiring short or longer term care. Mr Shipmaker also developed close working relationships with social workers from the district offices of the provincial Ministry of Human Resources in an effort to avoid, where possible, the off-reserve placement of Band children. However, these attempts to address child welfare problems at the Band level proved insufficient to tap the full caring potential of Band members. The most critical decisions continued to be made by staff of the Ministry of Human Resources. Moreover, by the beginning of 1980, approximately twenty-five children of the Band remained in the care of the Ministry in off-reserve foster homes.

1980—A YEAR OF POLITICAL ACTION

In the early spring of 1980, the Spallumcheen Band began a series of decisive steps to achieve Band control over child welfare decision making. Following consultation with the staff and legal advisors of the B.C. Union of Indian Chiefs, the Band Council passed a bylaw entitled "A Bylaw for the Care of our Indian Children," which assigned to the Band exclusive jurisdiction over any custody proceeding involving a Band child, whether on or off the reserve. However, when the bylaw was forwarded to Ottawa for scrutiny by John Munro, the minister of Indian affairs, he was at first disposed to disallow it, based on legal advice that the bylaw was probably unconstitutional. Subsequently, however, following intensive lobbying and minor changes in content, the bylaw was again submitted to the minister, who this time chose not to exercise his powers of disallowance. Thus, the bylaw came into effect on 3 September 1980.

With this tacit, although far from enthusiastic, support from the federal government, the Band proceeded during the early fall of 1980 to mount a vigorous political campaign to persuade the provincial Ministry of Human Resources to respect the child welfare authority of the Band conferred in the bylaw. This culminated in a well-publicized protest march by some six hundred Indian men, women, and children which ended in a demonstration in front of the minister's home in the fashionable Shaughnessy district of Vancouver. The following day, after an extended discussion between Chief Wayne Christian and Grace McCarthy, B.C.'s minister of human resources, a short hand-written agreement was concluded. The agreement read as follows:

The Minister of Human Resources agrees to respect the authority of the Spallumcheen Band Council to assume responsibility and control over their children. The Minister of Human Resources agrees to the desirability of returning Indian children of the Spallumcheen Band presently in the care of the Minister . . . to the authority of the Spallumcheen Band and both parties agree to work out an appropriate plan in the best interests of each child presently in care, assuming that the Spallumcheen Band will develop necessary resources in negotiation with the federal government.

During the next six months, Chief Christian and other employees of the Band moved expeditiously to consolidate a Band child welfare program within the mandate provided by the new bylaw and within the accord reached with the minister of human resources. On 1 April 1981, a formal agreement was signed between the Band and regional officials of the Indian Affairs Branch whereby the branch undertook to contribute $263 000 to the Band's child welfare program for the 1981–1982 fiscal year.[6] The agreement was to cover a five-year period terminating in 1986, with the amounts of federal contributions to be negotiated annually. The Band agreed to provide regional officials of the Indian Affairs Branch with annual audited financial statements as well as monthly reports on program activities.

With the foregoing agreements in place, the Band social worker met in May 1981 with the minister of human resources and worked out arrangements for transferring the care and supervision of Band children then in the care of the Ministry of Human Resources to the Spallumcheen Band. This entailed the formulation of a written care plan for each child signed by the Band social worker, the Ministry social worker, the foster parents and, in some cases, the natural parents and children. These individual care plans were subsequently approved by the Band Council and incorporated in case records for each child. This process was completed within three months, entailing for the most part no transfer of children from their foster homes but rather the assumption of supervision of existing foster care arrangements by the Band social worker. Also, significant from a legal perspective was the fact that the written care plans, while transferring supervision of the children to the Band, contained a statement that the B.C. superintendent of child welfare would continue to serve as legal guardian of each child. It was, therefore, evident that the provincial child welfare authorities were not prepared to acknowledge legally the jurisdictional claims of the Band's child welfare bylaw. I turn now to an examination of the principal features of this bylaw.[7]

THE SPALLUMCHEEN BAND CHILD WELFARE BY-LAW

The preamble to the bylaw stresses the right of Native Indians to self-determination and emphasizes the right of the Spallumcheen Band to care for its children, who are considered its most vital resource in ensuring its integrity and future. The preamble also voices concern that, in the past, a high percentage of Indian families experienced breakdown as a result of the often unwarranted removal from the reserve of Indian children by non-Band agencies, thereby hurting "our children emotionally," fracturing "the strength of our community," and "contributing to social breakdown and disorder within our reserve."[8]

The main body of the bylaw assigns to the Band exclusive jurisdiction over any child custody proceeding involving a child (defined as an unmarried person under age 21) who is a member of the Band, regardless of residence. For purposes of child protection, the Chief and Band Council or any persons authorized by them are empowered to apprehend an Indian child and bring the child before a meeting of the Chief and Band Council within seven days in the following circumstances:

(a) when a parent, extended family member or Indian guardian asks the Band to care for a child;

(b) when the child is in a condition of abuse or neglect endangering his/her health or well-being;

(c) when the child is abandoned;

(d) when the child is deprived of necessary care because of death, imprisonment, or disability of his/her parents.[9]

Where a child has been apprehended, the Chief and Band Council are authorized to decide on placement, guided by Indian customs and preferences. In making this decision, they are required to consider the wishes of the child if he is old enough to appreciate his situation. When the child cannot be immediately returned to his family, placement is to be made according to the following order of preference:

(a) with a parent (presumably the parent not exercising custody at apprehension);

(b) with a member of the extended family living on the reserve;

(c) with a member of the extended family living on another reserve;

(d) with a member of the extended family living off the reserve;

(e) with an Indian living on a reserve;

(f) with an Indian living off a reserve;

(g) as a last resort, with a non-Indian living off the reserve.[10]

However, in reaching placement decisions, the Chief and Band Council are required to give paramount consideration to the best interests of the individual child.[11]

Further sections of the bylaw authorize a general Band meeting to review a decision on placement at the request of any Band member, including the child's parent. Review decisions are to be made by majority vote of those attending in accordance with Indian customs and the order of preferences. Upon review, the decision of the general meeting may be to return the child to his parent(s) or place him in another home.[12]

THE SPALLUMCHEEN BYLAW COMPARED TO CONVENTIONAL CHILD WELFARE LEGISLATION

This bylaw differs in a number of ways from conventional child protection statutes. Significantly, it assigns apprehending, fact-finding, and disposition powers to the same persons, namely the Chief and members of the Band Council. These persons, therefore, are given both protective intervention and judicial functions. Moreover, both placement and review decisions are made, not in the context of a formal judicial hearing, but rather by discussion at a Band Council or general Band meeting, followed by a vote of those present. An obvious danger exists that decisions affecting the future of children could be made without the safeguards of an impartial judicial hearing. However, Indian leaders tend to discount this potential problem, pointing to the protracted pattern of careful and consensual decision making typical of Band Council meetings. Moreover, to date this problem has not surfaced in the application of the Spallumcheen bylaw, since apprehension has been necessary only on four occasions during its first four years of operation and the parents of the children apprehended have subsequently supported the placement decisions of the Band Council. In all other cases, children admitted to the care of the Band since enactment of the bylaw have been admitted at the request of their parent or parents.

The Spallumcheen Child Welfare bylaw can also be distinguished from regular child welfare statutes in the priority assigned to Native Indian foster care placements, commencing with those on the home reserve. Here the Band is concerned equally with the well-being of its children and with its future as a collective Indian community. Whether, in these circumstances, the welfare of the Indian child could become subordinated to the collective concerns for future Band strength and continuity would seem to depend largely on the resources available for childcare on the reserve. Assuming the availability of such resources, the priority assigned in the bylaw to Native Indian placements goes a considerable way toward ensuring that most children admitted to care will have their personal needs met while retaining an affinity with the traditions and culture of the Spallumcheen Band.

Finally, the Spallumcheen bylaw can be contrasted with many provincial child protection statutes in Canada in that it requires the Band to consider the wishes of the Indian child, when he is old enough to appreciate his situation, before making a decision as to custodial or living arrangements.[13] This may be contrasted with the B.C. Family and Child Service Act, also enacted in 1980, which permits a judge of the Provincial Family Court to make a disposition in a child protection case without seeing the child or being apprised of his wishes.[14]

SOME KEY FEATURES OF THE SPALLUMCHEEN CHILD WELFARE PROGRAM

In our society, child welfare services tend to be regarded as residual services activated to sustain families in crisis or to provide substitute care for children whose health and well-being would be in serious jeopardy if they remained in their homes. Given this residual societal mandate, child welfare services have also evolved separately from other human services such as education, recreation, and health services. A key feature of the Spallumcheen Band child welfare program is the degree to which traditional child welfare functions are integrated with other services promoting the collective well-being of the Band community, its families, and its children.

Within the mandate of the child welfare bylaw, and under the general guidance of the Chief and Band Council, the program employs a director of child and youth services, who is responsible for the co-ordination and supervision of the work of direct service staff members. These include a family support worker, who is responsible for protective services and foster care services to the children admitted to the care of the Band. The child welfare staff also includes a preventive youth counsellor, who provides individual and group counselling services to school-age children, especially those experiencing difficulty in school or encountering stressful family situations. This counsellor works in close liaison with teachers in the local elementary and secondary schools. Since 1983, the Band has also employed a childcare worker to provide special therapeutic services to children of the Band with severe speech and hearing problems and related learning, behavioural, or emotional problems.

While these services are both preventive and remedial, the Band also employs within its child welfare program a group recreation worker whose functions include the organization of special cultural and recreational activities for older teenagers designed to foster healthy leisure-time pursuits and identification with the collective activities and traditions of the Band.

Since commencement of the program four years ago, the Band has been able to provide foster home or group home placements on the reserve for all children admitted to care. A group home capable of serving up to eight children in the age range of ten to fourteen years was opened in August 1982. This home provides full-time employment for two house parents and part-time employment for one relief worker.

Child welfare staff members work closely with a registered nurse who, in addition to providing basic nursing care and referral services for Band members, offers guidance to Band members in family planning and home-making skills. Child welfare staff also work in close liaison with the Band's alcohol counsellor.

Although the Spallumcheen Band child welfare program has much in common with progressive child welfare programs in other settings, the observer is struck by the level of commitment and energy displayed by the staff members, most of whom are women. One also senses a high degree of pride in the work accomplished over the past few years, especially in the area of preventive programming. In addition, the concern for the Band families extends beyond the boundaries of the reserve to families in crisis elsewhere in the province. Thus, an important service rendered by the Band consists of offering placement resources for the temporary or long-term care of Band children apprehended by provincial child welfare staff in off-reserve communities.

Any discussion of the Spallumcheen program would be incomplete without acknowledgment of the leadership and organizational skills of Chief Wayne Christian. As a result of his efforts, the Band has been able to negotiate annual renewals of the funding arrangements with the federal government, which have permitted consolidation and expansion of the program. Chief Christian has also been responsible for negotiating loans with the Central Mortgage and Housing Corporation, which have enlarged and modernized the housing stock on the reserve in recent years. This in turn has enabled the Band to develop necessary on-reserve placement resources for children. In addition, Chief Christian has facilitated an extensive program of in-service training for staff and Band members, focussing both on practical skills and cultural awareness. Finally, he has maintained positive contacts with social work professionals throughout the province, thereby contributing to continuing professional support for the Band's program.

The Spallumcheen child welfare program is not without its problems. Alcohol abuse and unplanned pregnancies among teenage Band members continue to place many children at risk. Moreover, young persons returning to reside on the reserve following lengthy foster care often display serious behaviour problems predictive of future instability in family relationships. The Band has also had difficulty attracting and retaining professionally qualified persons to serve as program director. The most serious problem, however, is the uncertain future of the program, in light of its vulnerability to legal attack on constitutional grounds and current federal policy toward tripartite arrangements in Indian child welfare. These subjects will now be addressed.

LEGAL VULNERABILITY OF THE SPALLUMCHEEN PROGRAM AND THE ALTERNATIVE TRIPARTITE MODEL

We noted earlier that the minister of Indian affairs in 1980 chose not to exercise his authority to disallow the Spallumcheen Band bylaw, in spite of advice that it lacked constitutional validity. This advice was probably based on the absence of clear authority in section 81 of the Indian Act for Indian Bands to legislate in the field of child protection. This being the case, any such bylaw would run the risk, in a court challenge, of being declared unconstitutional as infringing on the general legislative powers of the province in this field.[15] A clear indication that the federal government has adopted this view of the law is seen in a policy statement issued by the Department of Indian and Northern Affairs on 1 May 1982, part of which reads as follows:

> Indian people living on or apart from reserves are governed by provincial and territorial legislation pertaining to the protection and care of children. . . .
> Section 91(24) of the British North America Act empowers Canada to enact legislation in respect of Indians and Indian lands.

Canada has not exercised this discretionary power in respect of leg-islation to govern the protection and care of Indian children and, accordingly, Section 88 of the Indian Act makes Indian people residing on or apart from reserves subject to provincial child wel-fare laws.[16]

This interpretation of the law was reinforced in practice in October 1982, when the minister of Indian and northern affairs disallowed a child welfare bylaw of a small Indian Band in the East Kootenay area of British Columbia. The bylaw in question was almost an exact copy of the one estab-lishing the Spallumcheen child welfare program.[17]

Although it is clearly within the powers of the federal government to amend the Indian Act to grant Indian Bands legal authority to enact child welfare bylaws, it appears that the federal authorities have decided to pur-sue a different course of action without recourse to legislative change. Thus, the same policy statement which endorsed provincial legislative jurisdiction in child welfare gave official support for the negotiation of tripartite agree-ments among Indian child welfare organizations, the federal Indian Affairs ministry, and provincial child welfare authorities for Indian child care agen-cies' delivery of welfare services to Native families in designated areas.[18] The first such agreement came into effect on 1 February 1982, when the fed-eral and Manitoba governments and the Four Nations' Confederacy signed an agreement to delegate to the Confederacy major responsibilities for the development and delivery of child welfare services on Indian reserves in western Manitoba.[19] Since that time, agreements have been struck covering services to all Indians on reserves in that province.

The experience to date under the Manitoba arrangements will be of great interest to Native peoples and social workers throughout Canada. For the purposes of this paper, however, it is useful to comment briefly on the comparative strengths and weaknesses of the Manitoba model compared to that adopted in B.C. by the Spallumcheen Band.

From the beginning, the Spallumcheen Band program has been limited to Band members and has been delivered through the authority of the Band Council. Adjoining bands, which share a common historical and cultural her-itage, have not been the beneficiaries of similar or shared Native-administered child welfare services. In contrast, the Manitoba model has evolved in a man-ner that has facilitated the comprehensive delivery of child welfare services through Native agencies representing the larger organizations of tribal coun-cils or amalgamations of bands. This model draws together the childcaring energies and resources of tribal groups sharing the same linguistic and cul-tural heritage. Thus, provided adequate funding is made available by the fed-eral government, the Manitoba system seems capable of concerting the full potential of Native professional and volunteer resources to serve Native peo-ple residing in contiguous communities. This model, therefore, avoids the splintering of services organized around separate Band councils.

The Manitoba tripartite model appears to envision active support by provincial child welfare authorities, coupled with collaboration between social workers employed by the provincial and those from Native child welfare systems. Assuming the co-operation of provincial authorities, this collaboration could have positive potential for the co-ordinated delivery of services to status Indians off reserves. In British Columbia, the Spallumcheen Band program operates as a small island of Native child welfare surrounded by a provincial child welfare system perceived as threatening to the program's survival.

One potential shortcoming of the Manitoba model is that it incorporates the Manitoba Child Welfare Act in defining standards of child protection, modes of judicial decision making, and dispositional options available when a child is in need of protection. One of the strengths of the Spallumcheen model is that its bylaw expresses Indian standards of child care while ensuring decision making by Band members designed to foster in Indian children a strong and positive sense of Indian identity.

CHILD WELFARE AND URBAN INDIANS

From the foregoing discussion it is evident that both the Spallumcheen and Manitoba tripartite models focus essentially on the child welfare problems of Indians on reserves. Neither model is explicitly designed to address the problems of status and non-status Indians in cities. The present reality in British Columbia, however, is that most families of Indian descent currently reside in towns and large cities, and demographic forecasts indicate that the trend toward urban migration will continue in the coming years.[20] Given the serious problems of unemployment, racial prejudice, and culture shock experienced by most urban Indians, it seems clear that Native Indian childcare problems will become increasingly prevalent among urban Indian families. This is not meant as a criticism of either the Manitoba or Spallumcheen Indian child welfare models. It does emphasize, however, that policy makers should give priority to urban-based delivery systems that maximize Native Indian involvement in services, both to status and non-status Indians.

SOME CONCLUDING COMMENTS

I noted earlier that the policy stance of the Department of Indian Affairs for the past three years has been to support tripartite child welfare service delivery for Native Indians on reserves. This, of course, involves the active support and participation by provincial child welfare authorities as well as support by Native Indian bands and organizations. It is significant that as of 31 December 1985 no tripartite agreements have been entered into in the province of British Columbia. At the provincial government level, this in part reflects a lengthy conservative stance on social services, coupled with reduced priority attached to child welfare services for the past two years.

There is also an evident reluctance, on the part of Native Indian leaders in this province, to embrace tripartism. This seems to be in part based on the long-standing adversarial relationship between the B.C. government and Indian organizations stemming from the government's refusal to acknowledge the legitimacy of Native land claims. It could also reflect a belief on the part of many Indian leaders that tripartite arrangements in the field of child welfare could impede progress toward Indian self-government. In this connection it should be noted that the 1983 Report of the Special House of Commons Committee on Indian Self-Government in Canada specifically identified child welfare as an area over which a band, or group of bands, should have the option to exercise full legislative and policy-making powers.[21]

The current constitutional negotiations on Indian self-government between Native organizations and the federal and provincial governments are also relevant to Indian child welfare concerns from a broader vantage point. It seems that the goal of self-government, while partly a political and cultural concern to Native peoples, is also closely linked to legitimate and long-standing economic concerns. Native leaders recognize that viable self-governing structures will only be achieved when Indian people can gain access to self-sustaining economic resources. In the absence of such resources, child welfare services, no matter how enlightened and progressive, are unlikely to resolve the persistent problems of Indian poverty and government dependency.

This paper has attempted to shed light on the emergence, content, and present status of the Spallumcheen child welfare program. This program would not have come about were it not for the organizational skills and political activism of the leaders and members of the Spallumcheen Band. Moreover, the activism that helped shape the Spallumcheen program also closely linked Native-controlled child welfare services to self-determination in the economic, cultural, and political spheres. These goals are now being pursued by Indian people across Canada in protracted political and judicial engagements. As professional social workers committed to the well-being of children and young people everywhere, we should render the Indian people our full support in their struggle for a secure and promising future for their children.

NOTES

1. Canada, Department of Indian and Northern Affairs, *Indian Conditions: A Survey* (Ottawa: Department of Indian and Northern Affairs, 1980).

2. Statistics provided by the B.C. Ministry of Human Resources reveal that for the fiscal year 1980–81, Native children, status and non-status, constituted 36.7 percent of all children in care in British Columbia, a reduction of 2.5 percent from the fiscal year 1978–79. During 1980–81, Native children constituted 42.7 percent of all children in foster homes in the province. Patrick Johnson, *Native Children and the Child Welfare System*

(Ottawa: Canadian Council on Social Development, 1983), 27.

3. During the fiscal year 1980–81, an average of 1313 children with registered Indian status in BC were residing in the homes of relatives or friends because of family problems. *Report of the Child Care Task Force on B.C. Indian Child Care* (Ottawa: Department of Indian and Northern Affairs, 1982).

4. Louise Mandell, legal counsel for the Spallumcheen Band and B.C. Union of Indian Chiefs, letter to Hugh Millar, executive director, B.C.

Association of Social Workers, 11 June 1980.

5. In a report prepared for the B.C. Royal Commission on Family and Children's Law, W.T. Stanbury found, on the basis of 1972 statistics, that 53 percent of the status Indian children in the care of the superintendent of child welfare had been in care for longer than five years, compared to 23 percent of the non-Indian children in the superintendent's care. W.T. Stanbury, *The Social and Economic Conditions of Indian Families in British Columbia*, report prepared for the B.C. Royal Commission of Family and Children's Law (Vancouver, 1974).

6. Agreement between the Spallumcheen Band of Indians and Her Majesty the Queen in Right of Canada, 1 April 1981. This agreement has been renewed annually since 1981. The budget for 1984–85 is $404 000.

7. Spallumcheen Indian Bank, A Bylaw for the Care of Our Indian Children: Spallumcheen Indian Band Bylaw #3, 1980.

8. Ibid., preamble.

9. Ibid., s. 7.

10. Ibid., s. 10.

11. Ibid.

12. Ibid., ss. 12, 15, 18, 19, and 23.

13. Ibid., s. 10 (i).

14. Family and Child Service Act, *Statutes of British Columbia*, 1980, c. 11.

15. This view seems to be supported by the Supreme Court of Canada decision in the case of *Natural Parents v. Superintendent of Child Welfare* (1976), 60 DLR 148, which held that the B.C. Adoption Act, a child welfare statute, had full application to status Indian children. It remains to be seen, however, whether the recognition of "existing aboriginal rights" in the Canadian Charter of Rights and Freedoms will lead to a modified judicial interpretation of an Indian Band's jurisdiction to legislate in the field of child welfare.

16. Canada, Department of Indian and Northern Affairs, *Programme Circular on Child Welfare Policy* (Ottawa, 1 May 1982), 8, 11–12.

17. Declaration of Hon. John C. Munro, 19 Oct. 1982, disallowing bylaw no. 3-1982, a bylaw for the care of Indian children enacted by the Tobacco Plains Band of Indians, in the Province of British Columbia, at a meeting held 21 Sept. 1982.

18. *Programme Circular*, 13–19.

19. Canada, *Canadian Family Law Guide* (Toronto: CCH, 9 March 1982).

20. In 1980, researchers from the Department of Indian and Northern Affairs predicted that, by 1986, 42 percent of status Indians in B.C. would be residing off reserves. Andrew Siggner and Chantal Locatelli, *An Overview of Demographic Social and Economic Conditions Among B.C.'s Registered Indian Population* (Ottawa: Research Branch, Department of Indian and Northern Affairs, 1980), 11. It has also been estimated that the number of non-status Indians, most of whom reside in towns and cities, exceeds the population of registered Indians in B.C. by 20 percent. See Gene Elmore, et al., "Survey of Adoption and Child Welfare Services to Indians of B.C.," report to the B.C. Department of Human Resources, 1974).

21. Canada, *Report of the Special Committee of the House of Commons on Indian Self-Government in Canada* (Ottawa: Queen's Printer, 1983), 63–64.

FURTHER READINGS

○

This is not meant to be a comprehensive bibliography of the welfare state in Canada. It should be used only as guide to the growing literature on the history of social security in Canada.

BIBLIOGRAPHIES AND GENERAL WORKS

Armitage, Andrew. *Social Welfare in Canada*. Toronto, 1975.

Bacher, John C. *Keeping to the Marketplace: The Evolution of Canadian Housing Policy*. Montreal, 1993.

Banting, Keith. *The Welfare State and Canadian Federalism*. 2nd ed. Montreal, 1987.

Bryce, Robert G. *Maturing in Hard Times: Canada's Department of Finance Through the Great Depression*. Montreal, 1986.

Godfrey, Stuart R. *Human Rights and Social Policy in Newfoundland, 1832–1982*. St John's, 1985.

Gray, Gwendolyn. *Federalism and Health Policy: The Development of Health Systems in Canada and Australia*. Toronto, 1991.

Guest, Dennis. *The Emergence of Social Security in Canada*. 2nd ed. Vancouver, 1985.

Hulchanski, J. David. *Canadian Town Planning and Housing, 1940–1950: A Historical Bibliography*. Toronto, 1979.

Ismael, Jacqueline S., ed. *Canadian Social Welfare Policy: Federal and Provincial Dimensions*. Montreal, 1985.

Ismael, Jacqueline S., ed. *The Canadian Welfare State: Evolution and Transition*. Edmonton, 1987.

Mitchinson, Wendy and J.D. McGinnis, eds. *Essays in the History of Canadian Medicine*. Toronto, 1992.

Moscovitch, Allan. *The Welfare State in Canada: A Selected Bibliography, 1840–1978*. Waterloo, 1983.

Moscovitch, Allan, and Glenn Drover, eds. *Inequality: Essays on the Political Economy of Social Welfare*. Toronto, 1981.

Naylor, C. David. *Canadian Health Care and the State: A Century of Evolution*. Montreal, 1992.

Owram, Doug. *The Government Generation: Canadian Intellectuals and the State, 1900–45*. Toronto, 1986.

Owram, Doug. *Canadian History: A Reader's Guide*. Vol. 2. *Confederation to the Present*. Toronto, 1994.

Panitch, Leo, ed., *The Canadian State: Political Economy and Political Power*. Toronto, 1977.

Parr, Joy, ed. *Childhood and Family in Canadian History.* Toronto, 1982.

Patriqun, Larry. *Income, Income Security, and the Canadian Welfare State, 1981–87: A Selected Bibliography.* Ottawa, 1989.

Roland, C.G. *Secondary Sources in the History of Canadian Medicine.* Waterloo, 1985.

Rooke, P.T., and R.L. Schnell. *No Bleeding Heart. Charlotte Whitton: A Feminist on the Right.* Vancouver, 1987.

Ross, Kathleen Gallagher, ed. *Good Day Care: Fighting For It, Getting It, and Keeping It.* Toronto, 1978.

Shortt, S.E.D., ed. *Medicine in Canadian Society: Historical Perspectives.* Montreal, 1981.

Taylor, M. Brook. *Canadian History: A Reader's Guide.* Vol. 1. *Beginnings to Confederation.* Toronto, 1994.

Webb, Jeff A. "In Sickness and In Health." *Acadiensis* 22, 1 (Autumn 1992): 185–90.

Yelaja, Shankar, ed. *Canadian Social Policy.* Rev. ed. Waterloo, 1987.

PRE-CONFEDERATION DEVELOPMENTS

Eccles, W.J. "Social Welfare Measures and Policies in New France." In *Essays on New France.* Ed. W.J. Eccles. Toronto, 1987.

Fingard, Judith. "Attitudes Towards the Education of the Poor in Colonial Halifax." *Acadiensis* 2 (Spring 1973): 15–42.

Fingard, Judith. "The Relief of the Unemployed Poor in Saint John, Halifax and St. John's, 1815–60." *Acadiensis* 2 (Autumn 1972): 32–54.

Fingard, Judith. "The Winter's Tale: The Seasonal Contours of Pre-Industrial Poverty in British North America, 1815–1860." Canadian Historical Association *Historical Papers* (1974): 65–94.

Greenhous, Brereton. "Paupers and Poorhouses: The Development of Poor Relief in Early New Brunswick." *Histoire sociale/Social History* 1 (April 1968): 103–28.

Reed, Allana G. "The First Poor-Relief System of Canada." *Canadian Historical Review* 37, 4 (1947): 424–31.

Splane, Richard. *Social Welfare in Ontario, 1791–1893.* Toronto, 1965.

Whalen, J.M. "The Nineteenth Century Almshouse in St. John County." *Histoire sociale/Social History* 7 (April 1971): 527.

Whalen, J.M. "Social Welfare in New Brunswick, 1784–1900." *Acadiensis* 2 (Autumn 1972): 54–64.

CONFEDERATION TO 1914

Ames, Herbert Brown. *The City Below the Hill.* Toronto, 1972.

Copp, Terry. *The Anatomy of Poverty: The Conditions of the Working Class in Montreal, 1897–1929.* Toronto, 1974.

Gagan, David. *A Necessity Among Us: The Owen Sound General and Marine Hospital.* Toronto, 1990.

Graham, John R. "The Haven: A Toronto Charity's Transition from a Religious to a Professional Ethos." *Histoire sociale/Social History* 25, 50 (Nov. 1992): 283–306.

Kealey, Greg, ed. *Canada Investigates Industrialism: The Royal Commission on the Relations of Labour and Capital, 1889.* Toronto, 1973.

Noble, Joey. "Classifying the Poor: Toronto Charities, 1850–1880." *Studies in Political Economy* 2, 1 (Autumn 1979): 109–28.

Pitsula, James. "The Emergence of Social Work in Toronto." *Journal of Canadian Studies* 14, 1 (Spring 1979): 35–42.

Piva, Michael J. "The Workman's Compensation Movement in Ontario." *Ontario History* 67 (1975): 39–56.

Rutherford, Paul, ed. *Saving the Canadian City: The First Phase, 1880–1920.* Toronto, 1974.

1914–1945

Allen, Richard. *The Social Passion: Religion and Social Reform, 1914–28.* Toronto, 1971.

Bryden, Kenneth. *Old Age Pensions and Policy-Making in Canada.* Montreal, 1974.

Cassidy, Harry. *Social Security and Reconstruction in Canada.* Toronto, 1943.

Finkel, Alvin. *Business and Social Reform in the Thirties.* Toronto, 1979.

Granatstein, J.L. *Canada's War: The Politics of the Mackenzie King Government, 1939–1945.* Toronto, 1975.

Horn, Michiel. "Leonard Marsh and the Coming of the Welfare State to Canada." *Histoire sociale/Social History* 9 (May 1976): 197–204.

League for Social Reconstruction. *Social Planning for Canada.* Toronto, 1975.

Kitchen, Brigitte. "The Marsh Report Revisited." *Journal of Canadian Studies* 21, 2 (Summer 1986): 38–48.

Marsh, Leonard. *Report on Social Security for Canada* (1943). Toronto, 1975.

Morton, Desmond, and Glenn Wright. *Winning the Second Battle: Canadian Veterans and the Return to Civilian Life, 1915–30.* Toronto, 1987.

Naylor, James. *The New Democracy: Challenging the Social Order in Industrial Ontario, 1914–25.* Toronto, 1991.

Neatby, Blair. "The Saskatchewan Relief Commission." *Saskatchewan History* 2, 2 (1950): 41–56.

Neatby, Blair. *William Lyon Mackenzie King.* Vol. 3. Toronto 1963.

Richter, L. "The Employment and Social Insurance Bill." *Canadian Journal of Economic and Political Science* 1, 3 (1935): 436–48.

Pierson, Ruth Roach. "Gender and the Unemployment Insurance Debates in Canada, 1934–1940." *Labour/Le Travail* 25 (Spring 1990): 77–103.

Struthers, James. *No Fault of Their Own: Unemployment and the Canadian Welfare State, 1914–1941.* Toronto, 1983.

Struthers, James. "Regulating the Elderly: Old Age Pensions and the Formation of a Pension Bureaucracy in Ontario, 1929–1945." *Journal of the Canadian Historical Association* 3 (1992).

Vigod, B.L. "Ideology and Institutions in Quebec: The Public Charities Controversy, 1921–1926." *Histoire sociale/Social History* 11 (1978): 167–82.

Wade, Jill. *Houses for All: The Struggle for Social Housing in Vancouver, 1919–50.* Vancouver, 1994.

Whitton, Charlotte. *The Dawn of Ampler Life.* Ottawa, 1943.

POST-1945

Brown, Malcolm. "Health Care Financing and the Canadian Health Act." *Journal of Canadian Studies* 21, 2 (Summer 1986): 111–32.

Canada. Dominion–Provincial Conference on Reconstruction. *Proposals of the Government of Canada.* Ottawa, 1945.

Canada. Report of the Special Senate Committee on Poverty. *Poverty in Canada.* Ottawa, 1971.

Canada. *Royal Commission on Health Services.* Ottawa, 1964.

Canada. Department of National Health and Welfare. *Income Security for Canadians.* Ottawa, 1970.

Grove, Sarah Jane. *Who Cares? The Crisis in Canadian Nursing.* Toronto, 1991.

Haddow, Rodney S. *Poverty Reform in Canada, 1958–78: State and Class Influence on Policy Making.* Montreal, 1993.

Jean, Dominique. "Family Allowances and Family Autonomy: Quebec Families Encounter the Welfare State, 1945–55." In *Canadian Family History: Selected Readings.* Ed. Bettina Bradbury. Toronto, 1992.

Johnson, Andrew F., Stephen McBride, and Patrick J. Smith., eds. *Continuities and Discontinuities: The Political Economy of Social Welfare and Labour Market Policy in Canada.* Toronto, 1994.

Kent, Tom. *Social Policy for Canada.* Ottawa, 1962.

Lesemann, Frederic. *Services and Circuses: Community and the Welfare State.* Trans. Lorne Huston and Margaret Heap. Montreal, 1984.

McBride, Stephen. *Not Working: State, Unemployment and Neo-Conservatism in Canada.* Toronto, 1992.

McLeod, Thomas H., and Ian McLeod. *Tommy Douglas: The Road to Jerusalem.* Edmonton, 1987.

Mishra, Ramesh. *The Welfare State in Capitalist Society: Politics of Retrenchment and Maintenance in Europe, North America and Australia.* Toronto, 1990.

Moscovitch, Allan. "The Welfare State Since 1975." *Journal of Canadian Studies* 21, 2 (Summer 1986): 77–95.

Pal, L. *State, Class and Bureaucracy: Canadian Unemployment Insurance and Public Policy.* Montreal, 1987.

Pesando, J.E., and S.A. Rea. *Public and Private Pensions in Canada: An Economic Analysis.* Toronto, 1977.

Rose, Albert. *Canadian Housing Policies, 1935–1980.* Toronto, 1980.

Rose, Albert. *Regent Park: A Study in Slum Clearance.* Toronto, 1958.

Shillington, C. Howard. *The Road to Medicare in Canada.* Toronto, 1972.

Taylor, Malcolm G. *Health Insurance and Canadian Public Policy: The Seven Decisions that Created the Canadian Health Insurance System.* Montreal, 1978.

Weller, G.R. "The Delivery of Health Services in the Canadian North." *Journal of Canadian Studies* 16, 2 (1981): 69–79.